AMERICAN PRESIDENTIAL CAMPAIGNS

★ ★ ★ ★ ★ ★ *and* ★ ★ ★ ★ ★ ★

ELECTIONS

Volume Three

WILLIAM G. SHADE
BALLARD C. CAMPBELL
EDITORS

CRAIG R. COENEN
DOCUMENTS EDITOR

SHARPE REFERENCE
an imprint of M.E. Sharpe, Inc.

SHARPE REFERENCE

Sharpe Reference is an imprint of M.E. Sharpe INC.

M.E. Sharpe INC.
80 Business Park Drive
Armonk, NY 10504

© 2003 by M.E. Sharpe INC.

All rights reserved.

Library of Congress Cataloging-in-Publication Data

American presidential campaigns and elections / William G. Shade, Ballard C. Campbell, and Craig R. Coenen, editors
    p. cm.
    Includes bibliographical references and index.
    ISBN 0-7656-8042-4 (set: alk. paper)
  1. Elections—United States—History. 2. Political campaigns—United States—History. I. Campbell, Ballard C., 1940- II. Shade, William G. III. Coenen, Craig R.

JK1965 .A57 2002
324.973—dc21

2002021185

Printed and bound in the United States of America

The paper used in this publication meets the minimum requirements of American National Standard for Information Sciences--Permanence of Paper for Printed Library Materials, ANSI Z 39.48.1984.

BM (c) 10 9 8 7 6 5 4 3 2 1

Vice President and Editorial Director: Patricia Kolb
Vice President and Production Director: Carmen Chetti
Executive Editor: Andrew Gyory
Project Editor: Wendy E. Muto
Editorial Assistant: Cathleen Prisco

CONTENTS

APPENDIXES

LIST OF FEATURES

THE ELECTION OF 1944

In 1944, it must have seemed to many Americans as if Franklin D. Roosevelt (see fact box, p. 722) had been president forever. Indeed, for many younger people, Franklin Roosevelt had been president all their lives. During the 1930s he led them through the most severe economic downturn in the nation's history. More recently, as commander-in-chief, he was leading them in a world war against the forces of Nazi Germany and Japan. During this time he won three presidential elections, one more than anyone else in the nation's history. Perhaps no other president in United States history had ever dominated domestic, or even foreign, affairs as much as Franklin Roosevelt. Still, 1944 was an election year, and Americans had to decide once again whether they still wanted Roosevelt, or it was time for a change.

Roosevelt Selects a New Running Mate

In 1940, Roosevelt kept secret his intentions to run again for the presidency because of the controversy over breaking the up two-term tradition. But in 1944, there was never any doubt. Nor was there ever any doubt that the nomination was his if he wanted it. No one in the party would dare run against a popular president who had led the country through a depression and was successfully waging war against Nazi Germany and Japan. In July, just before the Democratic convention, chairman of the Democratic National Committee Robert Hannegan assured Roosevelt that more than a majority of the delegates were pledged to him. The real question in 1944 was: Who would be his running mate?

In 1940, Roosevelt insisted on Secretary of Agriculture Henry Wallace over the vehement objections of the party regulars, who were aghast that the president would select an ex-Republican with little political savvy and a reputation for being aloof, mystical, and impractical. When Harry Hopkins heard of the choice, he warned the president, "There's going to be a hell of a lot of opposition. So far there must be at least ten candidates who have more votes than Wallace."

Roosevelt stood firm on Wallace. He even instructed his chief speechwriter, Samuel Rosenman, to polish up a draft of a withdrawal message he wrote just in case the delegates refused to ratify Wallace. Although the reasons he wanted Wallace are not entirely clear, evidently FDR believed that he could strengthen the ticket in the farm belt, where disaffection with Roosevelt had grown noticeable. Furthermore, he was a dependable New Dealer and an ardent supporter of Roosevelt's foreign policy. With a convention fight brewing, Frances Perkins, the secretary of labor, suggested that First Lady Eleanor Roosevelt should fly to Chicago and make a speech in the interest of harmony. She agreed to come. In her book *This I Remember* (1949), Eleanor Roosevelt recounted that when she spoke to the convention, she asked the delegates to "sink all personal interests in the interests of the country." The speech worked, and Wallace was nominated on the first ballot.

Roosevelt had put his prestige on the line for Wallace in 1940—but would he do so again in 1944?

CHRONOLOGY

1941

DECEMBER 7   Japan attacks Pearl Harbor.

1944

JUNE 6   D-Day invasion of France by the Allies.

JUNE 26–28   Republican National Convention nominates Thomas E. Dewey for president.

JULY 11   President Roosevelt announces that he will run for a fourth term, if nominated.

JULY 19–21   Democratic National Convention nominates Franklin D. Roosevelt for president.

AUGUST 12   Roosevelt delivers speech at Bremerton Navy Yard.

SEPTEMBER 23   Roosevelt delivers the "Fala" speech at Teamsters Union dinner.

OCTOBER 8   Wendell Willkie dies in New York City.

NOVEMBER 7   Roosevelt reelected as president.

1945

JANUARY 20   Roosevelt inaugurated for a fourth term as president.

FEBRUARY 4–11   At Yalta conference, FDR confers with Churchill and Stalin.

APRIL 12   Franklin D. Roosevelt dies at Warm Springs, Georgia; Harry S Truman becomes president.

The answer was no. Although the president liked Wallace as a person, an outspoken liberal, and an internationalist, he was convinced that he would have to go through another "knock-down and drag-out" fight, as he had in 1940, to put him on the ticket. Faced with the prospect of a fight over his running mate, he confided in Samuel Rosenman: "I am just not going through a convention like 1940 again. It will split the party wide open, and it is already split enough between North and South; it may kill our chances for election this fall." Some took it as a sign that he no longer wanted Wallace when, in May 1944, he sent him on a two-month trip to Russia and China, just when Wallace should have been lining up support for the nomination.

On July 11, 1944, Roosevelt met with three prominent Democratic leaders, Robert Hannegan, Frank Walker, and Ed Flynn, to examine the full list of possible vice presidential candidates. All of them seemed to agree that Wallace was out, so they spent little time discussing him. James Byrnes, the current director of the Office of War Mobilization, was rejected because he was unacceptable to organized labor, Catholics, or blacks. Roosevelt raised the possibility of either John

Winant or Supreme Court Justice William O. Douglas, but the consensus was that they would not add any vote-getting strength to the ticket. But when the name of Harry Truman came up, no one could find any major disqualification against him. According to Flynn's recollections of the meeting, although no one was very impressed with Truman's first term as Senator from Missouri, they all agreed that his record as head of the Senate Committee to Investigate the National Defense Program was excellent. Also in his favor: Truman's labor votes were good, he came from a border state, and he never made any offensive racial remarks. By the end of the meeting, it was agreed that Truman was their man.

Even though the decision was made, true to form, Roosevelt still wanted to keep everyone guessing. When Byrnes confronted Roosevelt about the meeting, the president hedged and said he was "not favoring anybody," but had merely said that he would not object to Truman. Convinced that Roosevelt had given him the green light, Byrnes actually arranged for Truman to nominate him at the convention. Nor did Wallace know he had been ruled out. In fact, he had strong reasons to believe that Roosevelt wanted

The connection between President Franklin D. Roosevelt and World War II is plain in this campaign poster by James Montgomery Flagg. The artist's fame originated with his Uncle Sam posters during World War I. With a successful conclusion to the war in sight, the theme that the nation should not switch horses in mid-stream—or be concerned about Roosevelt's unprecedented bid for a fourth term—contributed to the president's reelection in 1944. *(Nanine Young Accession, National Museum of American History)*

him for vice president. Just before the convention, the president wrote to Samuel Jackson, the convention chairman, that "he personally would vote for [Wallace's] nomination if I were a delegate to the convention." And a few days later, Wallace would recall that Roosevelt told him, "Henry, I hope it's the same old ticket." Wallace went to the convention convinced he had the president's blessing.

When the Democrats met in Chicago that year, Samuel Rosenman would later recall in *Working with Roosevelt* (1952), the convention was in a state of confusion over who the vice presidential candidate would be. There were delegates lined up behind Wallace and behind Byrnes. Truman, who obviously was still in the dark, kept insisting he was for Byrnes. It was not until July 20, the day that Roosevelt was to be nominated, that Democratic bosses met with Truman in a room at the Blackstone Hotel to line

him up as a candidate. Although Truman was reluctant at first, he was a loyal party member and eventually gave in. When the voting started, Wallace pulled ahead on the first ballot with 429½ votes to 319 for Truman; but on the second ballot Edwin Pauley, treasurer of the Democratic National Committee (DNC), and DNC chairman Robert Hannegan lined up the city bosses and anti-Wallace southerners to push Truman over the top, 1,031 votes to 105. Both Brynes and Wallace were deeply disappointed by the results. Each man firmly believed he had the president's support when he went to the convention, and that the president had deceived him.

Searching for a Republican Opponent

No one early on gave the Republicans much of a chance of defeating Roosevelt in 1944. Whoever they picked would have the unenviable task of trying to create dissension against a popular president, just at the time when the nation was at war in Europe and Asia. The eventual nominee, Thomas E. Dewey, probably had his eyes set more on running in 1948. Even in his most optimistic moments, Senator Robert Taft of Ohio, who said he was less optimistic about predicting a Republican victory than at any time in his career, concentrated instead on getting himself reelected as senator. Harold Stassen of Minnesota, who usually could be counted on to have the presidential bug in election years, said that he would accept the nomination but he would not actively seek it. General Douglas MacArthur indicated that he was available—but only if the party drafted him. This left only two viable contenders for the nomination: 1940 standard-bearer Wendell Willkie, and New York governor Thomas E. Dewey.

From the start, the odds were stacked against Willkie winning another party nomination. In January 1944, a Gallup poll showed that only 23 percent of Republicans favored him compared with 42 percent for then non-candidate Dewey. Not only did he not have the support of the Republican rank and file, but the leadership was against him too. Most prominent Republicans, including former president Herbert Hoover, Robert Taft, former presidential candidate Alfred Landon, and Thomas Dewey all actively assisted in efforts to stop Willkie from getting the nomination. Willkie just had too many negatives. Few Republicans could feel comfortable with a candidate who had defended a communist in a landmark civil liberties case (*Schneiderman v. United States*), or who promised to appoint a black Supreme Court justice or cabinet member if he were elected president, or who promoted internationalism while urging the party to weed isolationist elements out of the GOP.

Willkie knew that his chances were slim, but

HARRY S TRUMAN

PARTY: Democrat

DATE OF BIRTH: May 8, 1884

PLACE OF BIRTH: Lamar, Missouri

PARENTS: John Anderson Truman and Martha Ellen (Young) Truman

EDUCATION: Kansas City School of Law, 1923–25

FAMILY: Married Bess Wallace, 1919; one child: Margaret (Mary)

MILITARY SERVICE: First lieutenant, later captain, U.S. Army (World War I)

CAREER: Opened men's haberdashery store in Kansas City (Mo.), 1919; judge, Jackson County Court, 1922–24 (presiding judge, 1926–34); U.S. Senate, 1935–45; U.S. vice president, 1945; U.S. president, 1945–53; returned to Independence, Mo., to write memoirs and participate in creation of Truman Library

DATE OF DEATH: December 26, 1972

PLACE OF DEATH: Kansas City, Missouri

CAUSE OF DEATH: Kidney failure

PLACE OF BURIAL: Independence, Missouri

decided to enter the Republican primaries in New Hampshire, Maryland, Wisconsin, Nebraska, and Oregon. After winning a small victory in the New Hampshire primary, he launched an intensive two-week campaign in Wisconsin. Despite an extensive schedule that took him to every corner of the state, Willkie failed to win a single delegate. Dewey won 17 of the 24 Wisconsin delegates, with the rest split between Stassen and MacArthur. Willkie was in Nebraska at the time, preparing for the primary there, when he received news of his defeat. Earlier, he had promised to drop out of the race if he did not do well in Wisconsin—which he did, after delivering a speech on American foreign policy in Omaha. On October 8, after suffering a series of heart attacks, Wendell Willkie died at the age of 52.

With Willkie out of the race, Dewey had a clear road to the nomination. As governor of the nation's most populous state, Dewey was a credible candidate. Early in his career, he made his reputation as special prosecutor in an investigation of organized crime in

New York. He obtained seventy-two convictions of key underworld figures including "Waxey" Gordon, "Legs" Diamond, and "Lucky" Luciano. After unsuccessful efforts to win the New York gubernatorial race in 1938 and the Republican presidential nomination in 1940, he was elected governor of New York in 1942, the first Republican to do so in two decades. As governor, he built an impressive record by modernizing the state's fiscal system, improving workers' compensation, providing subsidies for low-income housing, and restructuring legislative apportionment.

The Republican convention in 1944 was dull by anyone's standards. Before the delegates met in Chicago that July, most of the other major aspirants had dropped out of the race for the nomination, practically handing the nomination to Dewey. Governor Earl Warren of California gave the nominating speech, and the delegates selected Dewey on the first ballot with only one dissenting vote. He chose Governor John Bricker of Ohio as his running mate. In his acceptance speech, Dewey told the delegates that the war was outside the scope of partisan politics, and complimented General George C. Marshall and Admiral Ernest J. King for their roles in it. However, he cautioned that America needed to not only win the war, but also to assume its responsibilities on the world stage to insure that the war stayed won. At home, he declared that he was crusading against an administration filled with "tired old men," where "wrangling, bungling and confusion" were the accepted order of the day.

Although Dewey claimed, to the delight of the convention audience, that New Deal economic policies never worked, in reality he endorsed almost all of the reform programs, including Social Security, unemployment insurance, farm price supports, relief for the needy, and collective bargaining. What he promised to bring to the table was a fresh and vigorous administration that would administer the programs more efficiently than the "tired old men" who were then in office. Energy was a theme of his campaign. He liked to portray himself as an athletic and energetic man only forty-two years old, although by doing so he ran the risk of inviting comparisons between himself and a seemingly frail president. Dewey was careful not to make Roosevelt's health a campaign issue, because it could backfire by creating undue sympathy for the president.

The Campaign

Dewey's avoidance of making the president's health an issue did not stop some of his aides from circulating photographs that made the president appear frail, or spreading rumors that Roosevelt could be closer to death than anyone realized. A photo of the president delivering his acceptance speech from a train in San Diego made him appear haggard, tired, and old. In a speech at the Bremerton Navy Yard in August, his voice seemed halting and uncertain. The reason he

THOMAS EDMUND DEWEY

PARTY: Republican

DATE OF BIRTH: March 24, 1902

PLACE OF BIRTH: Owosso, Michigan

PARENTS: George Martin Dewey, Jr., and Annie Louise (Thomas) Dewey

EDUCATION: B.A., University of Michigan, 1928; Columbia University Law School, 1925

FAMILY: Married Frances Eileen Hutt, 1928; children: Thomas Jr., and John

CAREER: Admitted to New York bar, 1925; chief assistant U.S. attorney, Southern District of New York, 1931; U.S. attorney, 1933; special prosecutor to investigate organized crime, 1935; district attorney, New York County, 1937; unsuccessful candidate for New York governor, 1938; unsuccessful candidate for Republican presidential nomination, 1940; governor of New York, 1942–54; unsuccessful candidate for U.S. president, 1944, 1948; private law practice, after 1955

DATE OF DEATH: March 16, 1971

PLACE OF DEATH: Bal Harbour, Florida

CAUSE OF DEATH: Heart attack

PLACE OF BURIAL: Pawling, New York

sounded bad was that, for the first time in months, he wore his leg braces—and they were painful—but radio listeners could not have known. Also, while onboard the ship to give his speech, the wind made it difficult for him to turn pages. Samuel Rosenman, who heard the speech on the radio, would later remark in *Working with Roosevelt* that he, too, had the impression that the president's "voice and delivery seemed so different."

Harry Hopkins would later write that "the President told me he meant it when he said that this was the meanest campaign of his life." And yet by choosing not to campaign, Roosevelt unwittingly confirmed the rumors that he was physically unfit to do so. Actually, there were other reasons why he chose not to campaign. In his acceptance speech, Roosevelt had said: "I shall not campaign in the usual sense. . . . In these days of tragic sorrow, I do not consider it fitting." He considered himself too busy winning a war and being commander-in-chief to bother campaigning. But while Roosevelt stayed in Washington, and the rumors continued to spread about his health and apparent disinterest in the campaign, as the summer wore on, Dewey's prospects for victory seemed to brighten considerably. At every campaign stop, Dewey leveled his attacks on the "tired old men" who were running the government, and continued with the theme that the government should be turned over to fresh, younger, and more energetic hands. He seized on a remark by General Lewis W. Hershey of the Selective Service that soldiers would have to be kept in the armed forces after the war to prevent unemployment. Actually, the administration was gearing up for a postwar economy with full employment for all returning veterans; but the more Dewey kept repeating the charge, the more Americans started to believe him. Democratic leaders and friends began urging the president to start campaigning, to set the record straight about these and other misstatements and distortions about the Roosevelt record. He also needed to dispel rumors that he did not have the physical or mental strength to campaign. Roosevelt knew it, too. In August, he announced that he would launch his campaign at a September 23 dinner of the International Brotherhood of the Teamsters at the Statler Hotel in Wash-

Republican candidate Thomas Dewey visits with a crowd of supporters in Queens, New York. The dignified, low-keyed demeanor of the people in the photograph fits Dewey's uncharismatic personality. *(Brown Brothers)*

ington, D.C. Unlike Bremerton, where he decided to speak standing up to dispel rumors about his health, this time he sat down as he read his speech. For the rest of the campaign, FDR avoided giving speeches where he had to stand. Because he had lost considerable weight, his braces no longer fit him or gave him much support when he stood at a podium. As a result, he limited his speaking engagements to dinners such as this one, or from the rear seat of an automobile from which he could speak naturally.

According to observers, he was never in better form. He started by systematically ridiculing Dewey's contentions that he was a "tired old man," that the Republicans were pro-labor, that the country was not properly prepared for war, and that it was the Democrats (and not the Republicans) who were responsible for the Depression. To the last of these charges, Roosevelt responded, "If I were a Republican leader speaking to a mixed audience, the last word in the

whole dictionary that I think I would use is that word 'depression.'" Then came the climax of his speech when he recounted how his dog Fala resented a tale the Republicans concocted about how Roosevelt had left Fala behind on an Aleutian Island, and sent a destroyer back to find him at considerable taxpayer expense. Roosevelt explained that, although he does not resent malicious falsehoods about himself, Fala does resent them. (See "The Fala Speech," p. 782.) FDR went on to say,

> These Republican leaders have not been content with attacks on me, or my wife, or on my sons. No, not content with that, they now include my little dog Fala. Well, of course, I don't resent attacks, and my family doesn't resent attacks, but Fala does resent them. . . . He has not been the same dog since. I am accustomed to hearing malicious falsehoods about myself—such as that old, worm-eaten chestnut that I have represented myself as indispensable. But I think I have a right to resent, to object to, libelous statements about my dog.

In one speech, Roosevelt dispelled all the doubts raised about Bremerton, and infused new life into his campaign. Eleanor Roosevelt later recalled, in *This I Remember*, that she always felt that this story about Fala laid the foundations for Dewey's defeat in November. From that time on, Dewey would now be running not only against Roosevelt, but his dog as well.

Dewey's Charges

Dewey's reaction was predictable. Sounding the battle cry, he warned on the radio, "He asked for it, now we'll let him have it." He attacked the waste of the New Deal and blamed the president for the deaths of American servicemen because the country had not been adequately prepared for war. As evidence, he cited both General Henry H. "Hap" Arnold of the Air Force and Harry Truman himself, who in the past had been quoted as saying the nation was woefully unprepared prior to the Pearl Harbor attack. He even charged that the president was not providing General MacArthur with adequate amounts of supplies

In one of the most striking campaign photographs ever taken, supporters in Springfield, Massachusetts, turn out en masse to greet President Franklin D. Roosevelt, who headed the Democratic Party ticket for the fourth time in 1944. *(Brown Brothers)*

and forces to carry out the war. Roosevelt would put this last charge safely to rest in his Navy Day speech in Philadelphia on October 27, with a glowing account of the recent victories by General MacArthur and Admiral Chester Nimitz in the Philippines.

During the campaign, Dewey avoided the one foreign policy issue that had the potential to supercharge his campaign—and that was the American response to, and anticipation of, the attack on Pearl Harbor. According to Dewey's information, the government had broken the secret Japanese codes before Pearl Harbor. When General George C. Marshall caught wind that Dewey was thinking of using this information in his campaign, he sent a letter to Dewey cautioning that any disclosure about the codes would have a detrimental effect on the war

effort at a time when MacArthur was poised to invade the Philippines. While it was true that the machine capable of deciphering Japanese codes had in fact been built before December 7, 1941, Marshall claimed that the War Department did not receive any messages that singled out Hawaii as a target before it was too late.

Dewey was not the only one who was critical about the whole Pearl Harbor tragedy. The Army's own board of inquiry questioned whether Marshall had made sure Pearl Harbor was adequately defended before the attack. The group's most damaging finding was that decoded messages from as early as December 4 or 5, under the code-name "Magic," clearly forecast a Japanese attack within two or three days, and concluded that the War Department should have warned

THE FALA SPEECH

*F*ew presidential pets in United States history achieved the notoriety that Franklin Roosevelt's Scottish terrier Fala did during the 1944 election year. That year, the president decided to forego his usual campaigning until shortly before the election, so he could concentrate on his role as commander-in-chief. After delivering his acceptance speech over the radio to the Democratic convention in Chicago, FDR sailed from San Diego on an inspection tour of American bases in Alaska and Hawaii, and to discuss war strategy with General MacArthur and Admiral Nimitz. Fala, of course, came along, just like he did whenever the president went anywhere.

When Roosevelt returned, a rumor began to circulate that the president had accidentally left Fala behind on an Aleutian island, after which the president supposedly sent a destroyer back to retrieve the dog at considerable taxpayer expense. As the story spread, it became exaggerated, eventually to involve not only one destroyer, but battleships and cruisers as well; according to one version, a ship sent to rescue Fala was removed from the scene of battle. On August 31, Michigan representative Harold Knutson told the House of Representatives that Fala had not been discovered missing until they reached Seattle, and that a destroyer was dispatched a thousand miles to fetch him. The White House immediately denied the charge, as did House Democratic Majority Leader John McCormick, who quoted from FDR's own chief of staff, Admiral William Leahy, that the tale was false. Then, on September 13, Knutson added the additional charge that a military plane had been sent to transport Fala to the president.

None of these charges were true; and, in this case, the story backfired badly on the Republicans. As Roosevelt was preparing his speech for the Teamsters' Union dinner in Washington, D.C., he jotted down a few lines, which he described as "just a happy thought," and sent them to his speechwriter Samuel Rosenman. FDR told Rosenman over the phone that he did not think too much of them, but he should see if they could be used somewhere or another in the speech. This became the part of the speech that everyone would remember long after the speech was over—the immortal paragraph about Fala, his dog.

The speech began with an attack on the Republicans, and a recitation of all the positive accomplishments of his years in office. Then, without cracking a smile until the end, he told the audience how much Fala resented the Republicans' story that he had been left behind on an Aleutian island and rescued by a destroyer, all at considerable expense. Roosevelt went on to say, "He has not been the same dog since. I am accustomed to hearing malicious falsehoods about myself, but I think I have a right to object to libelous statements about my dog."

It can never be known how much effect this speech had on the eventual outcome of the election. Eleanor Roosevelt would later say that she thought the speech had laid the foundation for Dewey's defeat. Whatever the case, the name of Fala would be forever immortalized in American election lore, alongside Roosevelt's.

Hawaii of the danger immediately. If Dewey chose to make this news public, it potentially could have swung thousands of votes to his campaign. However, after conferring with his aides he decided to suppress it, because it could just as easily result in a backlash against him for attacking the national war effort and endangering the troops in the field.

The Communism Issue

After the "Fala" speech, Dewey also fought back by giving renewed stress to the issue of communism in America. This was by no means a new issue, as far as the Republicans were concerned; since the 1930s, they had identified the New Deal with communism.

But in 1944, they now concluded that communists were using the Congress of Industrial Organizations' Political Action Committee (CIO-PAC) to take over the Democratic Party and the country. In early July, *Time* magazine did a cover story on Sidney Hillman, leader of the CIO-PAC, that emphasized his Lithuanian Jewish background and the fact that he had socialist friends. Because Hillman was one of Roosevelt's strongest supporters, it therefore followed that communists were supporting Roosevelt. Hillman's connection with Roosevelt was the key to their strategy. According to their version of the story, at the Democratic convention Roosevelt was said to have told his people, "Clear Everything with Sidney."

JOHN WILLIAM BRICKER

PARTY: Republican

DATE OF BIRTH: September 6, 1893

PLACE OF BIRTH: Near Mt. Sterling, Madison County, Ohio

PARENTS: Lemuel and Laura King Bricker

EDUCATION: B.A., Ohio State University, 1916; Ohio State University Law School, 1920

FAMILY: Married Harriet Day; one child: John

MILITARY SERVICE: First lieutenant and chaplain, U.S. Army (during World War I)

CAREER: Admitted to Ohio bar, 1917; solicitor, Grandview Heights (Ohio), 1920–28; assistant attorney general of Ohio, 1923–27; Public Utilities Commission of Ohio, 1929–32; attorney general of Ohio, 1933–37; Ohio state attorney general, 1933–37; governor of Ohio, 1939–45; unsuccessful candidate for U.S. vice president, 1944; U.S. senator from Ohio, 1947–59; unsuccessful candidate for U.S. Senate, 1958; law practice, after 1959

DATE OF DEATH: March 22, 1986

PLACE OF DEATH: Columbus, Ohio

PLACE OF BURIAL: Columbus, Ohio

Actually, this was not quite true. Arthur Krock, who wrote the original article for the *New York Times* where the phrase had its origin, later insisted that Roosevelt only wanted Hillman's approval of the vice presidential nomination. The Republicans were exaggerating what Roosevelt originally intended to suggest that Hillman's influence extended to everything else as well. In a speech at Boston, Dewey warned that the communists were using Hillman as a front to seize control of the federal government—and that if they were successful, fundamental freedoms, including freedom of religion, would be endangered. "In America," he said, "a Communist is a man who supports the fourth term so our form of government may more easily be changed."

It was true that Roosevelt needed a big working-class turnout to win the election. Because of a light turnout by labor in 1942, the Republicans managed to win several seats in Congress. To prevent that from happening again, he counted on the CIO to get out the labor vote in 1944. Organized labor's political potential had grown enormously over the years, and in 1944 its political action committee, under Sidney Hillman, sought to get out the vote for Roosevelt. To do so they relied on registration drives and, on Election Day, made telephone calls to union members, provided babysitters to those who needed them, and even transportation to the polls. In the end, the CIO contributed more than $1.57 million to the campaign, a figure that comprised more than 30 percent of all Democratic expenditures.

It is debatable whether Republican attacks on the CIO-PAC swayed many voters. When respondents to a pre-election National Opinion Research Center (NORC) poll were asked whether they had ever heard of the PAC, only 68 percent of Americans said "yes," and almost one-third said "no." Those who said they knew about the PAC were also asked if that would make them more or less likely to vote for Roosevelt. Only 21 percent of those respondents said it would make them less likely to vote for Roosevelt, while 75 percent said it would not have any effect; the rest either said they would be more likely to vote for him, or they didn't know how it would affect their decision.

While it appears that the Republicans may have overestimated the effect the PAC had on voters, it appeared they might have hit "pay dirt" with the communism-in-government issue. In a pre-election NORC poll, more than one-third of the respondents said they thought that communists would have more influence on government if Roosevelt, rather than Dewey, were elected. The Roosevelt campaign took this issue quite seriously. They were very concerned that the communist issue might be hurting them among ethnic and Catholic voters. In retrospect, it turns out that the communism issue was highly partisan. The voters who seemed to feel that communists would be more likely to influence a Roosevelt administration were largely Protestant, white-collar workers and farmers who lived outside the South. NORC poll results showed that 51 percent of them thought that communists would have more influence in a Roosevelt than in a Dewey administration. These groups normally voted heavily Republican in elections, anyway. In contrast, the groups the party could typically rely on to vote Democratic, such as blue-collar workers, Jews, Catholics, and southerners, seemed to show little concern about communism in government if Roosevelt were reelected.

Roosevelt did his best to deflect Dewey's allegations about communism in a radio address from Washington on October 5, 1944: "I have never sought and I do not welcome the support of any person or group committed to Communism, or Fascism, or any other foreign ideology which would undermine the American system of government or the American system of free enterprise and private property."

In his final campaign speech from Boston on November 4, FDR tried to make light of the issue by ridiculing Dewey for being unable to decide whether he was fighting against a communist take-over of the government, or one-man rule which he labeled a monarchy: "Now really, which is it, communism or monarchy. I do not think we could have both in this country, even if we wanted either, which we do not."

Roosevelt must have done a good job defusing the issue, because when all the major campaign issues are weighed together in the same analysis (winning the war, making the peace, communism in government, postwar jobs, joining the United Nations, and the PAC), the issue that divided Roosevelt voters from Dewey voters the most was the question of which candidate would do the best job working with other countries to create a lasting peace. Based on findings from a NORC poll, more than 82 percent of those who preferred Roosevelt to handle the postwar world voted Democratic, and nearly 93 percent of those who thought Dewey would do a better job favored him. The fact that more than 60 percent of respondents thought that Roosevelt would do a better job of insuring the peace than Dewey was no doubt indicative of the fact that Americans could not dismiss as unimportant the fact that Roosevelt had firsthand knowledge of foreign affairs and carried great prestige with nations around the world, which the inexperienced Dewey could not claim.

The Election

Franklin D. Roosevelt won the election with 53.4 percent of the popular vote. Although his vote totals were down from the previous two elections, FDR carried thirty-six states, which gave him 432 electoral votes to just 99 for Dewey, who managed to carry only twelve states. Although Dewey was competitive everywhere except the South, the only states he won were the midwestern states of North Dakota, South Dakota, Nebraska, Kansas, Iowa, Wisconsin, Ohio, and Indiana, the New England states of Maine and Vermont, and the mountain states of Colorado and Wyoming. The popular vote was down from what, in 1940, was due in part to dislocations caused by the war. Many people had migrated to take wartime jobs and didn't meet residency requirements.

Demographically, the vote split primarily along religious lines, with Roosevelt winning the majority of the Jewish and Catholic votes (72.9 percent) and Dewey the Protestant vote (54.3 percent), although the Protestant vote was far from homogeneous. Roosevelt won most of the Protestant vote in the South (71.4 percent) and the blue-collar workers in the North (57.9 percent) while Protestant white-collar and farm voters in the North sided with Dewey (70.1 percent). Together the Catholic, Jewish, and Protestant blue-collar blocs accounted for more than 62 percent of Roosevelt's votes. Over half of Dewey's votes (56 percent) came from Protestant white-collar workers and farmers in the North.

The election revealed that Americans were not ready to entrust the presidency to anyone other than Roosevelt, at least not someone as inexperienced as Dewey was in foreign affairs. Soon after the inauguration in January 1945, Roosevelt nominated former vice president Henry Wallace as secretary of commerce as a payback for being bumped off the ticket. Soon thereafter, he was off to Yalta to confer with Churchill and Stalin on what the postwar world would look like, in order to fulfill the trust the American people had placed in him to make a lasting peace. In April, after he returned, Roosevelt went off to recuperate in Warm Springs, Georgia, as he had done so many times in the past. But on April 12, he would suffer a massive cerebral hemorrhage. Within minutes Roosevelt was dead—and Vice President Harry Truman, little known to most Americans, would become president.

James Mott

Bibliography

Burns, James MacGregor. *Roosevelt: The Soldier of Freedom 1940–1945*. New York: Harcourt Brace Javanovich, 1970.

Freidel, Frank. *Franklin D. Roosevelt: A Rendezvous with Destiny*, Boston: Little, Brown, 1990.

Gosnell, Harold. *Champion Campaigner*. New York: MacMillan, 1952.

Korchin, Sheldon. "Psychological Variables in the Behavior of Voters." Ph.D. diss., Harvard University, 1949.

McCullough, David. *Truman*. New York: Simon and Schuster, 1992.

Neal, Steve. *Dark Horse: A Biography of Wendell Willkie*. New York: Doubleday, 1984.

Rosenman, Samuel I. *Working with Roosevelt*. New York: Harper and Brothers, 1952.

Roosevelt, Eleanor. *This I Remember*. New York: Harper and Brothers, 1949.

Smith, Richard Norton. *Thomas E. Dewey and His Times*. New York: Simon and Schuster, 1982.

THE VOTE: ELECTION OF 1944

State	Total No. of Electors	Total Popular Vote	Electoral Vote D	Electoral Vote R	Margin of Victory Votes	Margin of Victory % Total Vote	Roosevelt Democrat Votes	Roosevelt Democrat %	Dewey Republican Votes	Dewey Republican %	Others Votes	Others %
Alabama	1	244,743	11		154,378	63.1%	198,918	81.3%	44,540	18.2%	1,285	0.5%
Arizona	4	137,634	4		24,639	17.9%	80,926	58.8%	56,287	40.9%	421	0.3%
Arkansas	9	212,954	9		85,414	40.1%	148,965	70.0%	63,551	29.8%	438	0.2%
California	25	3,520,875	25		475,599	13.5%	1,988,564	56.5%	1,512,965	43.0%	19,346	0.5%
Colorado	6	505,039		6	34,400	6.8%	234,331	46.4%	268,731	53.2%	1,977	0.4%
Connecticut	8	831,990	8		44,619	5.4%	435,146	52.3%	390,527	46.9%	6,317	0.8%
Delaware	3	125,361	3		11,419	9.1%	68,166	54.4%	56,747	45.3%	448	0.4%
Florida	8	482,592	8		196,162	40.6%	339,377	70.3%	143,215	29.7%	0	0.0%
Georgia	12	328,102	12		211,681	64.5%	268,187	81.7%	56,506	17.2%	3,409	1.0%
Idaho	4	208,321	4		7,262	3.5%	107,399	51.6%	100,137	48.1%	785	0.4%
Illinois	28	4,036,061	28		140,165	3.5%	2,079,479	51.5%	1,939,314	48.0%	17,268	0.4%
Indiana	13	1,672,091		13	94,488	5.7%	781,403	46.7%	875,891	52.4%	14,797	0.9%
Iowa	10	1,052,599		10	47,391	4.5%	499,876	47.5%	547,267	52.0%	5,456	0.5%
Kansas	8	733,776		8	154,638	21.1%	287,458	39.2%	442,096	60.2%	4,222	0.6%
Kentucky	11	867,921	11		80,141	9.2%	472,589	54.5%	392,448	45.2%	2,884	0.3%
Louisiana	10	349,383	10		213,814	61.2%	281,564	80.6%	67,750	19.4%	69	0.0%
Maine	5	296,400		5	14,803	5.0%	140,631	47.4%	155,434	52.4%	335	0.1%
Maryland	8	608,439	8		22,541	3.7%	315,490	51.9%	292,949	48.1%	0	0.0%
Massachusetts	16	1,960,665	16		113,946	5.8%	1,035,296	52.8%	921,350	47.0%	4,019	0.2%
Michigan	19	2,205,223	19		22,476	1.0%	1,106,899	50.2%	1,084,423	49.2%	13,901	0.6%
Minnesota	11	1,125,529	11		62,448	5.5%	589,864	52.4%	527,416	46.9%	8,249	0.7%
Mississippi	9	180,080	9		156,878	87.1%	168,479	93.6%	11,601	6.4%	0	0.0%
Missouri	15	1,572,474	15		46,280	2.9%	807,804	51.4%	761,524	48.4%	3,146	0.2%
Montana	4	207,355	4		19,393	9.4%	112,556	54.3%	93,163	44.9%	1,636	0.8%
Nebraska	6	563,126		6	96,634	17.2%	233,246	41.4%	329,880	58.6%	0	0.0%
Nevada	3	54,234	3		5,012	9.2%	29,623	54.6%	24,611	45.4%	0	0.0%
New Hampshire	4	229,625	4		9,747	4.2%	119,663	52.1%	109,916	47.9%	46	0.0%
New Jersey	16	1,963,761	16		26,539	1.4%	987,874	50.3%	961,335	49.0%	14,552	0.7%
New Mexico	4	152,225	4		10,701	7.0%	81,389	53.5%	70,688	46.4%	148	0.1%
New York	47	6,316,790	47		316,591	5.0%	3,304,238	52.3%	2,987,647	47.3%	24,905	0.4%
North Carolina	14	790,554	14		264,244	33.4%	527,399	66.7%	263,155	33.3%	0	0.0%
North Dakota	4	220,171		4	18,391	8.4%	100,144	45.5%	118,535	53.8%	1,492	0.7%
Ohio	25	3,153,056		25	11,530	0.4%	1,570,763	49.8%	1,582,293	50.2%	0	0.0%
Oklahoma	10	722,636	10		82,125	11.4%	401,549	55.6%	319,424	44.2%	1,663	0.2%
Oregon	6	480,147	6		23,270	4.8%	248,635	51.8%	225,365	46.9%	6,147	1.3%
Pennsylvania	35	3,794,793	35		105,425	2.8%	1,940,479	51.1%	1,835,054	48.4%	19,260	0.5%
Rhode Island	4	299,276	4		51,869	17.3%	175,356	58.6%	123,487	41.3%	433	0.1%
South Carolina	8	103,375	8		86,054	83.2%	90,601	87.6%	4,547	4.4%	8,227	8.0%
South Dakota	4	232,076		4	38,654	16.7%	96,711	41.7%	135,365	58.3%	0	0.0%
Tennessee	12	510,792	12		108,396	21.2%	308,707	60.4%	200,311	39.2%	1,774	0.3%
Texas	23	1,150,331	23		630,180	54.8%	821,605	71.4%	191,425	16.6%	137,301	11.9%
Utah	4	248,319	4		52,197	21.0%	150,088	60.4%	97,891	39.4%	340	0.1%
Vermont	3	125,361		3	17,707	14.1%	53,820	42.9%	71,527	57.1%	14	0.0%
Virginia	11	388,485	11		97,033	25.0%	242,276	62.4%	145,243	37.4%	966	0.2%
Washington	8	856,328	8		125,085	14.6%	486,774	56.8%	361,689	42.2%	7,865	0.9%
West Virginia	8	715,596	8		69,958	9.8%	392,777	54.9%	322,819	45.1%	0	0.0%
Wisconsin	12	1,339,152		12	24,119	1.8%	650,413	48.6%	674,532	50.4%	14,207	1.1%
Wyoming	3	101,340		3	2,502	2.5%	49,419	48.8%	51,921	51.2%	0	0.0%
TOTAL	531	47,977,156	432	99	3,598,424	7.5%	25,612,916	53.4%	22,014,492	45.9%	349,748	0.7%

For sources, see p. 1127.

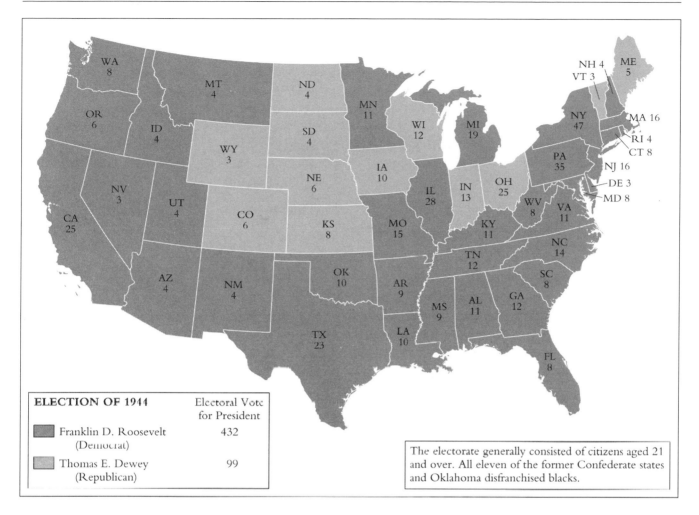

ELECTION OF 1944   Electoral Vote for President

Franklin D. Roosevelt (Democrat)   432

Thomas E. Dewey (Republican)   99

The electorate generally consisted of citizens aged 21 and over. All eleven of the former Confederate states and Oklahoma disfranchised blacks.

DOCUMENTS: ELECTION OF 1944

In the midst of World War II, a feeble and exhausted FDR sought a fourth term. Already having broken unprecedented ground in 1940 by running President Roosevelt for a third term, the Democrats believed that they needed to draft the president again in 1944 to defuse charges that Roosevelt never intended to step down. In Document 1, a letter from the chairman of the Democratic National Committee to the president, Robert Hannegan revealed to Roosevelt, and the public, that delegates were going to nominate him for a fourth term. He urged the president to accept because it was his duty to see the nation through the war's end. In Document 2, Roosevelt restated his desire to retire, but "reluctantly" agreed to be a "good soldier" and carry on as president.

Although Democrats downplayed the president's failing health, they knew that Roosevelt might not be able to survive another four years. Who was to be the vice presidential nominee became the major issue of the Democratic convention. Document 3, two letters from Roosevelt concerning his vice presidential preferences, illustrated the president's strong support for Vice President Henry Wallace. However, he did agree to accept either Senator Harry S Truman of Missouri or Supreme Court Justice William O. Douglas. The convention deemed Wallace's politics too leftist—and dumped him. They selected Truman on the second ballot. The little-known candidate did nothing to inspire Democrats with his acceptance speech, Document 4, which was one of the shortest ever delivered.

Concerns over Roosevelt's health and quest for a fourth term gave Republicans optimistic hopes for presidential success in 1944. When Republicans assembled at their convention in June, all they needed was the right man to unseat Roosevelt. Wendell Willkie wanted another opportunity, but received little support in the primaries. By the time the convention met, Governor Thomas E. Dewey of New York emerged as the choice; he earned the nomination with only one dissenting vote. In Document 5, his speech accepting the Republican nomination, Dewey pledged total commitment to winning the war and securing peace. However, he argued that the inefficient and free-spending Democrats needed to be removed from office, and the New Deal stopped, for a smooth adjustment to a peacetime economy. Dewey reiterated these themes throughout the campaign and, as in Document 6, subtly addressed Roosevelt's health. Rather than openly discussing the issue, Dewey repeatedly made reference to the "tired . . . Administration that had been in office twelve long years."

Roosevelt's personal charisma and his ability to deflect attacks helped him to win a fourth term. His personal doctor declared him fit as ever, and the president campaigned as much to prove his health as to win Americans over with policy statements. In Document 7, a Roosevelt campaign speech, the president played down his health and age. Instead, he addressed serious charges of inefficiency and exorbitant spending in his administration by taking umbrage with Republican statements about his dog, Fala. Republicans charged that Fala was left behind during an inspection tour in Alaska, and that Roosevelt sent a destroyer just to pick up his dog. In the end, Roosevelt won again; but a narrow popular majority (53 percent) signified voter concerns over the president's health and growing weariness with the Democrats.

Document 1

Letter from Democratic National Committee Chairman Robert E. Hannegan to President Franklin D. Roosevelt, July 10, 1944

Dear Mr. President:. . .
Based upon these official certifications to the National Committee, I desire to report to you that more than a clear majority of the delegates to the National Convention are legally bound by the action of their constituents to cast their ballots for your nomination as President of the United States. This action in the several States is a reflection of the wishes of the vast majority of the American people that you continue as President in this crucial period in the nation's history.

I feel, therefore, Mr. President, that it is my duty as Chairman of the Democratic National Committee to report to you the fact that the National Committee will during its deliberations in Chicago tender to you the nomination of the Party as it is the solemn belief of the rank and file of Democrats, as well as many other Americans, that the nation and the world need the continuation of your leadership.

In view of the foregoing, I would respectfully request that you send to the Convention or otherwise convey to the people of the United States an expression that you will again respond to the call of the Party and the people. I am confident that the people recognize the tremendous burdens of your office, but I am equally confident that they are determined that you must continue until the war is won and a firm basis for abiding peace among men is established.

Source: The Public Papers and Addresses of Franklin D. Roosevelt, 1944–1945 (New York: Harper and Brothers, 1950).

Document 2

Response of President Franklin D. Roosevelt to Democratic National Committee Chairman Robert E. Hannegan, July 11, 1944

Dear Mr. Hannegan:
You have written me that in accordance with the records a majority of the delegates have been directed to vote for my renomination for the office of President, and I feel that I owe to you, in candor, a simple statement of my position.

If the Convention should carry this out, and nominate me for the Presidency, I shall accept. If the people elect me, I will serve.

Every one of our sons serving in this war has officers from whom he takes his orders. Such officers have superior officers. The President is the Commander in Chief and he, too, has his superior officer—the people of the United States.

I would accept and serve, but I would not run, in the usual partisan, political sense. But if the people command me to continue in this office and in this war, I have as little right to withdraw as the soldier has to leave his post in the line.

At the same time, I think I have a right to say to you and to the delegates to the coming Convention something which is personal—purely personal.

For myself, I do not want to run. By next spring, I shall have been President and Commander in Chief of the armed forces for twelve years—three times elected by the people of this country under the American constitutional system.

From the personal point of view, I believe that our economic system is on a sounder, more human basis than it was at the time of my first inauguration.

It is perhaps unnecessary to say that I have thought only of the good of the American people. My principal objective, as you know, has been the protection of the rights and privileges and fortunes of what has been so well called the average of American citizens.

After many years of public service, therefore, my personal thoughts have turned to the day when I could return to civil life. All that is within me cries out to go back to my home on the Hudson River, to avoid public responsibilities, and to avoid also the publicity which in our democracy follows every step of the nation's Chief Executive.

Such would be my choice. But we of this generation chance to live in a day and hour when our nation has been attacked, and when its future existence and the future existence of our chosen method of government are at stake.

To win this war wholeheartedly, unequivocally and as quickly as we can is our task of the first importance. To win this war in such a way that there be no further world wars in the foreseeable future is our second objective. To provide occupations, and to provide a decent standard of living for our men in the armed forces after the war, and for all Americans, are the final objectives.

Therefore, reluctantly, but as a good soldier, I repeat that I will accept and serve in this office, if I am so ordered by the Commander in Chief of us all—the sovereign people of the United States.

Source: *The Public Papers and Addresses of Franklin D. Roosevelt, 1944–1945* (New York: Harper and Brothers, 1950).

Document 3.
Two Letters of President Franklin D. Roosevelt Regarding His Vice Presidential Preferences

Roosevelt to Indiana Senator Samuel D. Jackson, July 14, 1944

My dear Senator Jackson:
In the light of the probability that you will be chosen as Permanent Chairman of the Convention, and because I know that many rumors accompany all Conventions, I am wholly willing to give you my own personal thought in regard to the selection of a candidate for Vice President. I do this at this time because I expect to be away from Washington for the next few days.

The easiest way of putting it is this: I have been associated with Henry Wallace during his past four years as Vice President, for eight years earlier while he was Secretary of Agriculture, and well before that. I like him and I respect him, and he is my personal friend. For these reasons, I personally would vote for his renomination if I were a delegate to the Convention.

At the same time, I do not wish to appear in any way as dictating to the Convention. Obviously the Convention must do the deciding. And it should—and I am sure it will—give great consideration to the pros and cons of its choice.

Roosevelt to Democratic National Committee Chairman Robert E. Hannegan, July 19, 1944

Dear Bob:
You have written me about Harry Truman and Bill Douglas. I should, of course, be very glad to run with either of them and believe that either one of them would bring real strength to the ticket.

Source: *The Public Papers and Addresses of Franklin D. Roosevelt, 1944–1945* (New York: Harper and Brothers, 1950).

Document 4

Acceptance Speech by Senator Harry S Truman, Chicago, July 21, 1944

You don't know how much I appreciate this very great honor which has come to the great State of Missouri. There is also connected with it a very great responsibility, which I am perfectly willing to assume. It has been my privilege to be United States Senator for the past nine and one-half years, and I expect to continue the effort which I have been making in that capacity as United States Senator, to help shorten the war and win the peace under the great direction of our great leader, Franklin Delano Roosevelt.

There is not much I can say to you except that I accept the honor with all the humility that a citizen of the United States can assume in this position. Thank you very much.

Source: *New York Times*, July 22, 1944.

Document 5

Acceptance Speech by Governor Thomas E. Dewey, Chicago, June 28, 1944

I come to this great task a free man. I have made no pledges, promises or commitments, expressed or implied, to any man or woman. I shall make none, except to the American people.

These pledges I do make:

To men and women of the Republican Party everywhere I pledge my utmost efforts in the months ahead. In return, I ask for your support. Without it, I cannot discharge the heavy obligation you lay upon me.

To Americans of every party I pledge that on January 20 next year our government will again have a cabinet of the ablest men and women to be found in America. The members of that Cabinet will expect and will receive full delegation of the powers of their office. They will be capable of administering those powers. They will each be experienced in the task to be done and young enough to do it. This election will bring an end to one-man government in America.

To Americans of every party I pledge a campaign dedicated to one and above all others—that this nation under God may continue in the years ahead a free nation of free men.

At this moment on battlegrounds around the world Americans are dying for the freedom of our country. Their comrades are pressing on in the face of hardship and suffering. They are pressing on for total victory and for the liberties of all of us.

Everything we say or do today and in the future must be devoted to the single purpose of that victory. Then, when victory is won, we must devote ourselves with equal unity of purpose to re-winning at home the freedom they have won at such desperate cost abroad.

To our allies let us send from this convention one message from our hearts: The American people are united with you to the limit of our resources and our manpower, devoted to the single task of victory and the establishment of a firm and lasting peace.

To every member of the axis powers, let us send this message from this Convention: By this political campaign, which you are unable to understand, our will to victory will be strengthened, and with every day you further delay surrender the consequences to you will be more severe. . . .

But the war is being fought on the home front as well as abroad. While all of us are deeply proud of the military conduct of the war, can we honestly say that the home front could not bear improvement? The present administration in Washington has been in office for more than 11 years. Today, it is at war with Congress, and at war with itself. Squabbles between Cabinet members, feuds between rival bureaucrats and bitterness between the President and his own party members, in and out of Congress, have become the order of the day. In the vital matters of taxation, price control, rationing, labor relations, manpower, we have become familiar with the spectacle of wrangling, bungling and confusion.

Does anyone suggest that the present national administration is giving either efficient or competent government? We have not heard that claim made, even by its most fanatical supporters. . . .

In all the record of the past 11 years is there anything that suggests the present administration can bring about high-level employment after this war? Is there any reason to believe that those who have so signally failed in the past can succeed in the future? The problem of jobs will not be easily solved; but it will never be solved at all unless we get a new, progressive administration in Washington—and that means a Republican administration.

For one hundred and fifty years America was the hope of the world. Here on this great broad continent we had brought into being something for which men had longed throughout all history. Here, all men were held to be free and equal. Here, government derived its just powers from the consent of the governed. Here men believed passionately in freedom, independence—the God-given right of the individual to be his own master. Yet, with all of this freedom—I insist—because of this freedom—ours was a land of plenty. In a fashion unequalled anywhere else in the world, America grew and strengthened; our standard of living became the envy of the world. In all lands, men and women looked toward America as the pattern of what they, themselves, desired. And because we were what we were, good will flowed toward us from all corners of the earth. An American was welcomed everywhere and looked upon with admiration and regard.

At times, we had our troubles; made our share of mistakes; but we faltered only to go forward with renewed vigor. It remained for the past eleven years, under the present national administration, for continuing unemployment to be accepted with resignation as the inevitable condition of a nation past its prime.

It is the New Deal which tells us that America has lost its capacity to grow. We shall never build a better world by listening to those counsels of defeat. Is America old and worn out as the New Dealers tell us? Look to the beaches of Normandy for the answer. Look to the reaches of the wide Pacific—to the corners of the world where American men are fighting. Look to the marvels of production in the war plants in your own cities and towns. I say to you: our country is just fighting its way through to new horizons. The future of America has no limit.

Source: New York Times, June 29, 1944.

Document 6

Speech by Governor Thomas E. Dewey, New York, November 4, 1944

Openly and in plain words John Bricker and I, in the name of the Republican party, are dedicated to these propositions:

1. To speed total victory and with it the prompt return of our fighting men by putting energy and competence in Washington behind the magnificent effort of our military command.

2. To provide American leadership in the world for an effective organization among all nations to prevent future wars.

3. To direct all Government policies in the peacetime years ahead to achieving jobs and opportunity for every American.

To these ends,

We shall restore honesty and integrity to our National Government; We shall put an end to one-man rule;

We shall unite our people in teamwork and harmony behind a President and a Congress that can and will work together to realize the limitless promise of America.

These are no partisan objectives. They are in truth the objectives of the American people. They can never be attained under the tired and quarrelsome Administration that has been in office for twelve long years. They can only be attained under a new, vigorous Administration that comes fresh from the people. That's why all over the country the people are saying it's time for a change.

America is determined to win a speedy and overwhelming victory in this war. All of us have perfect confidence in our military and naval commanders. But this war cannot be won alone upon the battlefronts. It must also be won at home. And each of us must play his part. . . .

My opponent talks once again of jobs in the future, but he offers us nothing except a repetition of the New Deal policies which failed for eight straight peacetime years. This Administration took office when the worldwide depression was nearly four years old. No previous depression in the whole hundred years of our history had lasted more than five years. Yet Mr. Roosevelt contrived to make that depression last eleven years—twice as long as any depression in the whole century.

He had unlimited power; he spent 58 billion dollars; yet in March of 1940 there were still ten million unemployed. Under the New Deal it took a war to get jobs.

We dare not, we must not risk the future of our country in the hands of those who never succeeded in eight peacetime years in even approaching full employment. We need to sweep away the strangling mass of rules and regulations, of petty bureaucratic interferences. We need to sweep away the old dank, wretched atmosphere of hostility and abuse. We need once more to let the American people—industry, labor and agriculture—know that their Government believes with them in the American tradition of opportunity for all.

We need an Administration that cares more about little business than it does about big government. We need an Administration that will not be afraid of the peace—that will want to bring our fighting men home when victory is achieved—and will keep its promise to do so. And that's another reason why it's time for a change. . . .

All this is the inevitable result of too many years in power—and the desire for perpetual office. It is exactly what every great American, beginning with George Washington and Thomas Jefferson, warned against it. It is inevitable that it should have produced political leadership which today publicly defines politics as the science of "how who gets what, when and why." I say the young men of America are not fighting and dying for these corrupt and decadent practices. In the name of those men, the American people will rise up and repudiate that whole philosophy of government. The time has come to put an end to government by "who gets what, when and why." That's why it's time for a change.

Source: New York Times, November 5, 1944.

Document 7

Speech by President Franklin D. Roosevelt, Washington, September 23, 1944

You know I am actually four years older—which is a fact that seems to annoy some people. In fact, in the mathematical field there are millions of Americans who are more than eleven years older than when we started in to clear up the mess that was dumped into our laps in 1933. . . .

These Republican leaders have not been content with attacks on me, or on my wife, or on my sons—no, not content with that, they now include my little dog, Fala. Well, of course, I don't resent attacks and my family doesn't resent attacks, but Fala does resent them. You know, you know Fala's Scotch and, being a Scottie, as soon as he learned that the Republican fiction writers in Congress and out had concocted a story that I had left him behind on an Aleutian island and had sent a destroyer back to find him—at a cost to the taxpayers of two or three or eight or twenty million dollars—his Scotch soul was furious. He has not been the same dog since.

I am accustomed to hearing malicious falsehoods about myself—such as that old, worm-eaten chestnut that I have represented myself as indispensable. But I think I have a right to resent, to object to libelous statements about my dog.

Well, I think we all recognize the old technique. The people of this country know the past too well to be deceived into forgetting. Too much is at stake to forget. There are tasks ahead of us which we must now complete with the same will, the same skill and intelligence and devotion that have already led us so far along the road to victory.

There is the task of finishing victoriously this most terrible of all wars as speedily as possible and with the least cost on lives.

There is the task of setting up international machinery to assure that peace, once established, will not again be broken.

And there is the task that we face here at home—the task of reconverting our economy for the purposes of war from the purposes of war to the purposes of peace.

These peace-building tasks were faced once before, nearly a generation ago. They were botched—b-o-t-c-h-e-d—they were botched by a Republican Administration. That must not happen this time. We will not let it happen this time.

Source: The Public Papers and Addresses of Franklin D. Roosevelt, 1944–1945 (New York: Harper and Brothers, 1950).

THE ELECTION OF 1948

Historians generally consider the election of 1948 to be a transitional one. It marked a change from party-based voting to issue-based voting. It would be the last election in which the farm vote significantly altered national election results. 1948 was also the last campaign that relied on radio as the primary medium of communication. And it was the last campaign in which a major party needed more than one convention ballot to select a nominee. The 1948 election, moreover, marked the beginning of the crucial transition in the South from being a Democratic stronghold to a Republican supporter in national elections. But beyond any particular political or demographic change, the election of 1948 reflected the nation's hunger to find a moral and ideological center at a time of tremendous change and uncertainty.

Reconversion of the New Deal Coalition

The 1948 presidential election was the first in the United States after the conclusion of World War II, which had ended in 1945. In the three-year interval, the country had come to grips with its new place in the world. The earth's only nuclear power, it had engaged the Soviet Union in the Cold War. It had pulled out of the Great Depression, but had not easily converted back to a peacetime economy. And the "baby boom" had exploded as birthrates rose dramatically from 19.4 per thousand in 1940, to 24 per thousand by 1946.

Equally significant changes were made to American ideology. Adolph Hitler, the Holocaust, and the atrocities of war had fundamentally altered the American moral landscape. "Absolute evil" was no longer a biblical abstraction or a beast with horns and a tail. It was human and very real. Communism seamlessly replaced fascism as the principal source of global malevolence, as Americans quickly came to associate Moscow with all things immoral and un-American—socialism, authoritarianism, atheism, and violent revolution. With Soviet communists solidifying control of Eastern Europe and positioned to expand into Greece and Turkey, the Middle East, and Western Europe, the United States quickened its resolve to defend democratic values against the new totalitarian threat.

Elected vice president in 1944, Harry S Truman (see fact box, p. 778) became president on April 12, 1945, following the death of Franklin D. Roosevelt. The Truman administration worked diligently to address the concerns of the nation in the years just after the war. When, in March 1946, the Soviets continued the Red Army's occupation of northern Iran and threatened to merge the region with communist-controlled Azerbaijan, President Truman moved the Sixth Fleet into the eastern Mediterranean and forced Soviet leader Joseph Stalin to back down. A year later the president led a joint session of Congress in approving $400 million in emergency aid for Greece and Turkey, two countries threatened by communist expansion. He also had openly adopted George F. Kennan's "containment" strategy as official American policy toward the Soviet Union. "It must be the

CHRONOLOGY

1945

APRIL 12   Roosevelt dies; Truman becomes president.

MAY 7   Germany surrenders.

AUGUST 6   First atomic bomb dropped on Hiroshima, Japan.

AUGUST 9   Second atomic bomb dropped on Nagasaki, Japan.

AUGUST 14   Japan surrenders unconditionally, ending World War II.

1946

MARCH 2   Deadline passes for Soviet troops to withdraw from Iran.

APRIL 1   United Mine Workers join auto and steel workers in strikes.

NOVEMBER 5   Republicans win majorities in House and Senate.

DECEMBER 29   Progressive Citizens of America organized.

1947

MARCH 12   Truman asks Congress for emergency aid for Greece and Turkey.

JUNE 23   Taft-Hartley Act passed over a presidential veto.

OCTOBER 29   *To Secure These Rights* published.

1948

JUNE 5   Marshall Plan introduced at Harvard University.

JUNE 21   Republican National Convention opened.

JUNE 28   Truman decides to supply West Berlin by air.

JULY 12   Democratic National Convention opened.

JULY 17   "Dixiecrats" meet in Birmingham.

AUGUST 3   Whittaker Chambers names Alger Hiss as a communist spy.

NOVEMBER 2   Truman wins presidential election.

1949

MARCH 4   Truman inaugurated as president.

policy of the United States," Truman declared, "to support free peoples who are resisting attempted subjugation by armed minorities or by outside pressure." Under the banner of the Truman Doctrine, emergency aid for the rest of Europe was also passed by Congress in 1947. During a four-year period beginning in 1948, the Marshall Plan would deliver some $17 billion to Europe, returning the region to prosperity and bolstering its resistance to communist influence.

Domestically Truman worked to prevent a return to depression, control inflation, extend social programs, and deal with a growing civil rights movement. He supported unemployment pay, Social Security benefits, the GI Bill of Rights, and housing legislation to cushion the shock of demobilization and reconversion for veterans. He championed retention of the Fair Employment Practices Committee that had protected minority workers during the war. And he promised a national health insurance plan, public works programs, an increased minimum wage, small business assistance, and a new education initiative. The president cast himself as the new leader of the New Deal and the heir to Franklin Roosevelt.

Truman was less successful than his predecessor, however, in bolstering the Democratic coalition of labor, farmers, minorities, and liberal New Dealers. His determination to control inflation by continuing Office of Price Administration (OPA) regulations met with hostility from business leaders. The National Association of Manufacturers mounted a campaign with other groups to dismantle the OPA, and eventually gained the backing of Congress. The agency was stripped of power by the summer of 1946—and inflation soared.

Labor, meanwhile, clashed directly with the Truman administration over the strikes of 1945–46.

When electrical, automobile, steel, and meatpacking workers walked out, the president had responded by asking Congress for the power to declare an emergency and assume control over any industry that he regarded as vital to the national interest. United Auto Workers leader Walter Reuther declared that the proposal "would make slavery legal." A few months later—as strikes spread to the railroad brotherhoods and coal miners—Truman seized the mines, took over the roads, and threatened to ask Congress for legislation restricting the right of workers to strike in jobs tied to national security.

With Americans frustrated by the Democrats' handling of housing, rationing, inflation, and price controls, and with disgruntled union members choosing to stay at home rather than vote, the Republicans won House and Senate majorities in the 1946 midterm

President Harry S Truman delivers a speech during a "whistle-stop" in Waco, Texas, on October 1, 1948. With the development of travel by air, car, and bus, the day of the railroad campaign was nearing its end. *(Brown Brothers)*

elections. Under their new congressional leader, the anti-New Deal, states'-rights conservative, Senator Robert A. Taft of Ohio, the Republicans refocused Washington on rolling back the New Deal. In this vein, the 80th Congress enacted the anti-labor Taft-Hartley Act over President Truman's veto. The Taft-Hartley Act restricted labor's power by outlawing closed shops, which hired only union members. It also outlawed "bad faith" bargaining on the part of unions, secondary boycotts in which non-striking unions boycotted or picketed retailers selling the products of companies struck by its union allies, and jurisdictional strikes where unions struck to gain management recognition of their exclusive right to organize. While the passage of Taft-Hartley was an

ALBEN BARKLEY

PARTY: Democrat

DATE OF BIRTH: November 24, 1877

PLACE OF BIRTH: Near Lowes, Graves County, Kentucky

PARENTS: John Wilson Barkley and Electra Smith

EDUCATION: B.A., Marvin College, 1897; attended Emory College and University of Virginia Law School

FAMILY: Married Dorothy Brower, 1903; children: David, Marian, Laura, and Louise

CAREER: Admitted to the bar, 1901; prosecuting attorney, McCracken Co. Court (Ky.), 1905–9; judge, McCracken Co. Court, 1909–13; U.S. congressman, 1913–27; U.S. senator, 1927–49, 1955–56 (majority leader, 1937–47; minority leader, 1947–49); U.S. vice president, 1949–53

DATE OF DEATH: April 30, 1956

PLACE OF DEATH: Lexington, Virginia

CAUSE OF DEATH: Heart attack

PLACE OF BURIAL: Paducah, Kentucky

indication of Truman's waning power over Congress, the president's veto of the bill mended his relationship with labor. The Republicans, ironically, had driven labor back into Truman's camp.

Labor, though, was just one piece of the puzzle. Reestablishing the New Deal coalition would be the key to a Democratic victory in 1948. Truman's prospects for leading his party were doubtful at the beginning of the campaign season. He was not the charismatic force that President Roosevelt had been, and Roosevelt's coalition seemed to be fraying at the edges. Labor, minorities, and farmers all had reason to be suspicious of Truman's ability to deliver what

they needed. Liberals, in addition, had decided to stay home in the midterm elections, and there was little reason to anticipate their return to the polls two years later. Nevertheless Democrats remained a majority among the nation's voters, and the president had begun to work hard to bring the discontented back into the fold, and to define a new centrist vision around which they could rally.

Wallace and the Dixiecrats

Two significant challenges from within the Democratic ranks would test Truman's ability to capture his party's support. The first came from former vice president and secretary of commerce Henry A. Wallace (see fact box, p. 761). Wallace represented leftist Democrats and would run his campaign as a friend of the Soviet Union and a champion of social justice. With the help of a unified group of liberal and left-wing organizations called the Progressive Citizens of America (PCA), he criticized Truman's domestic security program for trampling on civil liberties, denounced the administration's policies in Europe, and pushed for a closer relationship with the Soviet Union. He also blasted the president's handling of labor and accused Truman of straying from New Deal traditions. Finally— and most importantly for the future of the Democratic Party— Wallace slammed Truman's lack of leadership in gaining civil rights for African Americans, and called for immediate desegregation of the armed forces.

Wallace's appearances in the South in 1947 demonstrated his commitment to the civil rights issue. The former vice president had, for the most part, refused to address segregated audiences. Where he did speak, his supporters were attacked, while the candidate himself was barraged with rotten vegetables and epithets of "communist" and "nigger lover." He carried on, however, with more than a little courage—and a sense of moral determination that liberals were searching for.

Wallace's Democratic opponents recognized his heroism in confronting Southern discrimination. Even the PCA's main organizational rival among Democrats, the Americans for Democratic Action (ADA), had to regard Wallace's efforts in the South as "tolerant," "thoughtful," and "courageous." But where Wallace marched in stride with the Democratic Party and most liberals on the race issue, his own and the PCA's association with American communists, and his criticism of the administration's foreign policy of "containment," put him at odds with party centrists. "The most violent scenes of the Dixie drama," declared an ADA analysis of the 1948 campaign, "could not obscure Wallace's sad surrender to the Communist machine" or his role as "the embittered spokesman of Soviet interests."

JAMES STROM THURMOND

PARTY: States' Rights Democrat ("Dixiecrat"); Republican

DATE OF BIRTH: December 5, 1902

PLACE OF BIRTH: Edgefield, South Carolina

PARENTS: John William Thurmond and Eleanor Gertrude Strom

EDUCATION: B.S., Clemson College, 1923

FAMILY: Married Jean Crouch, 1947; married Nancy Moore, 1968; children: Nancy Moore, J. Strom Jr., Juliana Gertrude, and Paul Reynolds

MILITARY SERVICE: Reserve officer, 1923–59; U.S. Army, 1942–46 (82nd Airborne Division, 1944)

CAREER: High School teacher (S.C.), 1923–29; admitted to bar (S.C.), 1930; county superintendent of education, 1929–33; city and county attorney, 1930–38; South Carolina state senator, 1933–38; circuit court judge, 1938–46; governor of South Carolina, 1947–51; unsuccessful candidate for U.S. president, 1948; U.S. senator, 1954–2003 (president *pro tem*, 1981–87, 1995–2001)

Wallace's vulnerability on the communist issue worked to Truman's advantage. Democrats and Republicans were in consensus on the general threat of communism, and never more so than at the height of the 1948 campaign season. The summer's headlines were dominated by the American airlift to supply West Berliners cut off by Soviet occupation authorities in Germany, and by former communist agent Whittaker Chambers's accusations that a high-ranking State Department official, Alger Hiss, had been spying for the Soviets. Where Republicans might have effectively tied these cases to "spy queen" Elizabeth Bentley's accusations that several New Dealers were involved in a spy ring, while blasting

Truman for being too soft on communism, Wallace and PCA positions served to emphasize the president's place in the anticommunist center.

In addition, the communist issue destroyed whatever inclination organized labor had to support Wallace. The Congress of Industrial Organizations (CIO) under Philip Murray, a devout Catholic, was becoming anticommunist and helped the ADA lead the charge against a Wallace nomination. Truman could sit back and focus on the Republican challenger, while the CIO and ADA attacked Wallace's pro-communist record. Many liberals backed Truman out of fear that a communist-tainted Wallace candidacy would deliver the White House to the Republicans. Many also simply preferred the president's anti-Soviet foreign policy.

Thus, in part, the Democratic coalition would gel around Truman in reaction to Wallace. But the president also brought his own credentials to the table. When it came to racial minorities, potentially Wallace's most devoted followers, Truman had already made great strides. Despite his own deep ambivalence about racial issues, the president had maintained consistent support for civil rights since 1945. He backed the retention of the FEPC, appointed blacks to high-ranking federal positions, was the first president to speak in front of the National Association for the Advancement of Colored People, and, perhaps most importantly, Truman created a federal commission to study racial violence. The path-breaking Civil Rights Committee's recommendations, published in 1947 as *To Secure These Rights*, would ultimately lead to anti-lynching legislation, abolition of the poll tax, voting rights statutes, a permanent FEPC, desegregation of the armed forces, a permanent civil rights division for the Justice Department, support for civil rights suits in federal courts, and establishment of the United States Commission on Civil Rights.

But embracing of these issues, while popular among liberals, was potentially very costly. The South had always been a key constituency for the Democrats—but the adoption of a civil rights platform ran the risk of driving white southern segregationists from the party. Truman's political instincts were to appease the South during the primary election season, then return to the civil rights issue during the general election. Therefore, he would push for an understated civil rights platform.

The ADA worried that Truman's platform would drive crucial votes to Wallace. The organization had, like Wallace, committed itself to a strong, liberal civil rights plank with an understanding that a unified minority vote would carry the party into the 1948 election—and redefine the liberal center for the future. ADA leaders, as would the Republicans, looked to the charismatic and recognizable General Dwight Eisenhower to replace Truman as the party's candidate, and pushed hard to make civil rights the key issue in the 1948 election. While a Democratic Eisenhower candidacy never emerged in 1948, the ADA was able to deliver its civil rights platform. Democrats gathered in Philadelphia in July for their national convention. Under the leadership of Minneapolis mayor Hubert Humphrey—and with the support of labor leaders, big-city bosses, and liberals—the ADA ushered through the strongest civil rights plank the Democratic Party had ever approved. Somewhat ironically, the platform adopted the specific recommendations outlined by the Truman administration in *To Secure These Rights*.

Humphrey spoke for a great many of the convention's delegates when he called for the Democratic Party "to get out of the shadow of states' rights and walk forthrightly into the bright sunshine of human rights." But in response to the platform vote the white South revolted, as Truman had feared, posing the other great challenge to Truman's quest for the presidency from within the Democratic ranks. Delegates from Alabama and Mississippi angrily walked out of the Philadelphia hall, leaving those who remained to nominate Truman and add the popular Senator Alben W. Barkley of Kentucky to the ticket. Truman had offered the job to Supreme Court justice William O. Douglas; but when the noted jurist

declined, party regulars pushed for Barkley, a relentless campaigner, respected Senate Democratic leader and civil rights moderate, who could keep Southern loyalists in the party fold. Alienated white southerners would meet separately a few days later in Birmingham, Alabama. There they would form the States' Rights Democratic Party (later labeled "Dixiecrats" by the press), and vow to preserve segregation and the "Southern way of life." The group nominated Governor J. Strom Thurmond of South Carolina for president, with Governor Fielding Wright of Mississippi as his running mate. (See "The Dixiecrat Revolt," 802.)

The Dixiecrats had little hope of winning outright; but they ran on the idea that if they could gain enough

FIELDING WRIGHT

PARTY: States' Rights Democrat ("Dixiecrat")

DATE OF BIRTH: May 16, 1895

PLACE OF BIRTH: Rolling Fork, Mississippi

PARENTS: Henry James and Fannie

EDUCATION: B.A., University of Alabama, 1915

FAMILY: Married Nan Kelly, 1917; children: Fielding Lewis and Elaine

MILITARY SERVICE: U.S. Army, 1918–19

CAREER: Admitted to bar; Mississippi state senator, 1928–32; Mississippi House of Representatives, 1932–40 (speaker, 1936–40); lieutenant governor of Mississippi, 1944–46; governor of Mississippi, 1946–48; unsuccessful candidate for U.S. vice president, 1948, practiced law, 1952–56

DATE OF DEATH: May 4, 1956

PLACE OF DEATH: Jackson, Mississippi

CAUSE OF DEATH: Heart attack

PLACE OF BURIAL: Rolling Fork, Mississippi

electoral votes, neither major party would earn a victory. The election would then be thrown to the House of Representatives, where the southerners could control the deciding votes. The Dixiecrats would also make a more lasting statement about the South's loyalty to the Democratic Party. If the Democrats were to be the party of civil rights, the South would look elsewhere for representatives. The "Solid South" had clearly begun to dissolve.

The same month that the Dixiecrats decided their ticket, Henry Wallace accepted the third-party candidacy of the Progressive Party. His running mate was Senator Glen Taylor, the "singing cowboy" of Idaho. The one-time actor and entertainer brought

The Progressive Party nominated former vice president Henry A. Wallace to run for president and Senator Glen Taylor for vice president. At their convention in Philadelphia, delegates hoped that their "new party" would soon become the nation's "first party." *(Brown Brothers)*

a charisma to the ticket that balanced Wallace's aloof personality. Taylor was also an unrelenting critic of Truman's foreign and domestic policies who supported popular liberal-left programs for postwar peace, and an economic bill of rights guaranteeing all Americans equal access to jobs, food, clothing, shelter, education, and healthcare. Under Wallace and Taylor, Progressives used their platform to identify big business as the root cause of most American evils; they also called for the dismantling of the "containment" foreign policy, and for a comprehensive program of government action to secure full rights for the mass of Americans.

Republican Challenge

While Dixiecrats and Progressives certainly drew the attention of the Democrats and Truman, the president's main concern was the Republicans. The GOP had gained significant momentum from the 1946 elections and appeared to be the more unified party. But the Republicans were struggling with their own rift between left and right. Conservatives leaned to Robert Taft. While the Ohio senator favored the prudent use of federal investments for the public welfare, he was a fiscal conservative and a unilateralist (if not an isolationist) in foreign policy.

Serving in the Senate since 1938, Taft was a power broker in Washington and a natural choice; but his personality concerned many rank-and-file members of the party. He was abrupt, cold, humorless, and stiff. He cared little for public opinion and, perhaps as a result, had a difficult time connecting with large audiences.

Others backed the progressive, former "boy governor" of Minnesota, Harold E. Stassen. Stassen, only forty years old at the time, represented the

GLEN TAYLOR

PARTY: Progressive

DATE OF BIRTH: April 12, 1904

PLACE OF BIRTH: Portland, Oregon

PARENTS: Pleasant John Taylor and Olive Higgens

EDUCATION: Left school at an early age to become a traveling entertainer

FAMILY: Married Pearl Nitkowskie, 1922; one child; married Dora Pike, 1931; three children

CAREER: Actor, dramatic stock company, 1919; owner and manager, entertainment enterprises, 1926–44; country-western singer; U.S. senator, 1944–51; unsuccessful candidate for U.S. vice president, 1948; president, Coryell Construction Co., 1950–52; president, Taylor Topper Inc.

DATE OF DEATH: April 28, 1984

PLACE OF DEATH: Millbrae, California

CAUSE OF DEATH: Natural causes

PLACE OF BURIAL: San Mateo, California

youth of the GOP. He had been elected governor of Minnesota for the first time at the age of thirty-one, and was reelected twice before resigning to serve in the military during World War II. He initiated significant labor legislation and served as a delegate to the San Francisco conference that formed the United Nations; but Stassen had accomplished little else as a public servant. He had a formidable campaign organization that ran outside of traditional Republican circles. Stassen even declared himself a liberal in his announcement speech. He was, in fact, almost as conservative as the Old Guard from whom he tried to distance himself. He opposed federal aid to housing, supported caps on federal income taxes and opposed the Marshall Plan, fearing that it would aid socialist governments in Europe. Stassen also allied himself with the emerging Republican forces hoping to outlaw communism in the United States.

Moderates favored Thomas E. Dewey (see fact box, p. 779). Although the progressive governor of New York had lost to Franklin Roosevelt in 1944, his policies seemed to put him more in the mainstream. As governor he had built highways and hospitals, established state-based reform programs, and pioneered laws against racial and religious discrimination in employment and education. He also dealt with reconversion to a peacetime economy better than Washington, establishing popular programs for GI education, small business growth, rent controls, public works financed by budget surpluses, tax cuts, and higher teacher salaries. In addition, Dewey supported collective bargaining, while denouncing public employee strikes. An internationalist, he denounced the isolationist policies of the conservative wing of the Republican Party. Personally, Dewey was impatient, sometimes tactless, arrogant (some suggested he was capable of strutting while sitting down) and stiff, though not to the same degree as Senator Taft. He was also honest and ambitious, and cared about public opinion—even using the latest polling techniques. In appearance, Dewey was formal and dignified—presidential, but also resembling the "little man on the wedding cake."

The 1948 national party conventions were the first to be broadcast on television. In part to facilitate TV coverage, the Republicans convened at the same Philadelphia venue as the Democrats and Progressives. Some 10 million viewers on the eastern seaboard would see the event as it happened. The Republican audience watched Dewey suffer through three ballots before he won the nomination. Another political centrist, Governor Earl Warren of California, was chosen as his running mate. The genial and photogenic governor had, like Dewey, gained a reputation as a prudently progressive fighter of crime and corruption in his home state. The Republicans hoped Warren's influence in California would carry that state's 25 electoral votes, the most of any state other than New York, Pennsylvania, and Ohio. They were in good shape for the general election.

Truman, however, would focus his campaign strategy and run a tight race. The president noticed that the Republican platform endorsed many of the programs he had been advocating, including civil

EARL WARREN

PARTY: Republican

DATE OF BIRTH: March 19, 1891

PLACE OF BIRTH: Los Angeles, California

PARENTS: Mathias H. and Crystal

EDUCATION: B.L., University of California, 1912; J.D., University of California, 1914

FAMILY: Married Nina Meyers, 1914; children: James C., Virginia, Earl, Dorothy, Nina Elizabeth, and Robert

MILITARY SERVICE: U.S. Army, 1917–19

CAREER: Admitted to bar, 1914; deputy city attorney, Oakland (Calif.), 1919–20; deputy district attorney, Almeda Co. (Calif.), 1920–25 (chief deputy, 1923–25); district attorney, Almeda Co., 1925–38; attorney general of California, 1939–43; governor of California, 1943–53, unsuccessful candidate for U.S. vice president, 1948; chief justice, U.S. Supreme Court, 1953–69

DATE OF DEATH: July 9, 1974

PLACE OF DEATH: Washington, D.C.

CAUSE OF DEATH: Heart attack

PLACE OF BURIAL: Arlington National Cemetery

This campaign button depicts the 1948 Republican ticket of Thomas Dewey and Earl Warren. Warren later became Chief Justice of the United States. *(Gyory Collection/Cathy Casriel Photo)*

rights, public housing, a higher minimum wage, and supports for farmers. Judging them to be insincere, Truman called the Republican 80th Congress into special session in late July to make good on these promises. The GOP leadership cried "foul"—but Congress met for two weeks and, as Truman anticipated, accomplished nothing. For the rest of the campaign, the president would hammer the 80th as the "do-nothing Congress."

Meanwhile, Truman continued his long-term plan to solidify and expand the New Deal. The general program was the one he had advanced since 1945; but in rejuvenating the New Deal coalition in 1948, his tactics were reinforced by supporters like presidential aide Clark Clifford. Clifford was "first among equals" in the so-called Wardman Park group, which had met every Monday evening since the 1946 election to discuss political strategy and the future of the Truman administration. Notables such as Oscar Ewing, a former party official and director of the Federal Security Agency, Leon Keyserling, a member of the President's Council of Economic Advisors, and David Morse, the assistant secretary of labor, attended the meetings. Taking their cue from a campaign strategy memo passed to Clifford by former Roosevelt adviser James Rowe, the group advised the president to cater to the individual needs of each group within the New Deal coalition. On a nationwide "whistle-stop" tour, Truman captured midwestern and western farmers by strongly advocating agricultural price supports; he played up his veto of Taft-Hartley to solidify the labor vote; and he touted his civil rights recommendations for minority voters. With these constituencies secured, he could afford to lose some votes in East Coast cities to Dewey, some votes in the South to Thurmond, and some minority votes to Wallace.

The GOP continued to feel the effects of party infighting during the general election. Old Guard conservatives in Congress controlled domestic policy and pushed for budget cuts in popular programs, tax reductions that favored the wealthy, and Taft-Hartley

THE DIXIECRAT REVOLT

When the chairman of the 1948 Democratic National Convention announced the adoption of the party's vigorous civil rights platform by a vote of 651½ to 582½, Alabama delegate-at-large Bull Connor frantically moved to be recognized. Ignoring Connor's pleas, the chair quickly recessed the proceedings until that evening. By the time the convention reconvened, all of Mississippi's delegates and about half of Alabama's had decided to walk out. Answering the roll call of states for the nomination of a presidential candidate, Alabama delegate Handy Ellis bade the convention goodbye and walked out of the hall, followed by the other bolters.

The southern revolt had actually been in the making since early in the year. Four days after the president delivered his civil rights message to Congress in February 1948, a meeting of the southern governors' conference had begun the movement to oppose Truman's nomination. Chaired by South Carolina governor Strom Thurmond, a committee of inquiry reported that "the virtually unanimous will of the people of the southern states is to take every possible effective action within their power, not only to prevent the enactment of the proposed legislation, but also to defeat those who have proposed it and any others advocating it." It recommended that the southern delegates propose an alternative platform in Philadelphia and, failing its adoption, meet in executive session in Birmingham, Alabama, to recommend alternative candidates to the presidential ticket.

Thomas Dewey, governor of New York, accepting the Republican nomination in Philadelphia in 1948. In his second run for the presidency, Dewey came close to unseating President Harry Truman. *(Brown Brothers)*

penalties on labor, while obstructing housing legislation. Moderate Republicans controlled foreign policy. Their support of the Truman Doctrine, Marshall Plan, Berlin Airlift, NATO, and the recognition of Israel had effectively cloned the policies of the Democrats, and offered little in the way of political capital. Dewey's campaign rode the middle ground, avoiding specifics that would generate further divisions. As a *Louisville Courier-Journal* reporter observed, Dewey himself provided little more than four "historic" sentences: "Agriculture is important. Our rivers are full of fish. You cannot have freedom without liberty. The future lies ahead."

Still, the Republicans remained confident that a victory was at hand. Pollsters agreed. In the last few surveys before the election, they all called Dewey the winner. Gallup's final poll, in late October, gave the race to Dewey, 49.5 percent to 44.5 percent. Archibald Crossley published similar numbers, as did several other pollsters. Based on this information, the press felt comfortable in predicting an overwhelming Dewey victory. *Time* and *Life* even prepared post-election editions in advance with photos of the new Republican president-elect.

States' Righters met that July in Birmingham—but not, as originally planned, to mount an insurgent action from within the Democratic Party. The Dixiecrats would formally separate into a third party in the hope that they could draw enough votes from the other parties to throw the election to the House of Representatives. There, they could trade support for promises to end civil rights initiatives.

Politicians from across the South, including governors Fielding Wright of Mississippi, Strom Thurmond of South Carolina, William Tuck of Virginia, and Ben Laney of Arkansas, as well as Mississippi senators John Stennis and James Eastland, led the convention. Bound by a conservative southern disenchantment with a changing America, they adopted a platform that would block a range of social and political reforms imposed on the South, they argued, by federal tyrants. To the right of many Republicans, States' Righters rejected the New Deal and charged that its extension amounted to an acceptance of communism. But chief among their causes was to prevent a revolution in race relations.

At every stop on the campaign trail, Dixiecrat presidential candidate Strom Thurmond stressed the need to protect segregation; but he also understood the need to distance the party from its more radical white-supremacist supporters like Gerald L. K. Smith. States' Righters could win over loyalists to the Democratic Party—but not if they were perceived as hate mongers.

Thurmond and the Dixiecrats never escaped their race-baiting image; as a result, they did not make much of an electoral impact. Southerners generally remained loyal to the Democratic Party and the New Deal. The white South was uniformly segregationist; but it was not as monolithically conservative on other issues as the States' Righters had hoped. The Dixiecrats, nevertheless, made significant showings in the plantation counties of Alabama, Mississippi, South Carolina, and Louisiana, and foreshadowed a general shift in southern political loyalties.

Truman Wins

The results were embarrassing for the prognosticators. The *Time* and *Life* editions had to be scrapped before press time. Others were not so lucky. The *Chicago Daily Tribune* went to press early in the morning, before the results were finally tabulated—printing "Dewey Defeats Truman" in a bold headline on the front page. In one of the most recognizable photographs in American political history, a gleeful President Truman can be seen holding up the newspaper at a victory celebration.

Voter turnout was low, and Truman ran behind FDR's 1944 showing. He could muster only a minority victory, 49.5 percent to Dewey's 45.1 percent. Wallace and Thurmond each earned 2.4 percent. But the incumbent president posted comfortable leads in the electoral and popular votes. Truman registered 24,105,812 popular votes to Dewey's 21,970,065. Wallace and Thurmond both won around 1,150,000. Truman took twenty-eight states and 303 electoral votes, to Dewey's sixteen states and 189 electoral votes. The Dixiecrats won only four states in the deep South—Alabama, Louisiana, Mississippi, and South Carolina—accounting for just 39 electoral votes.

Wallace did not win a single state—but he took enough votes away from Truman in New York to throw its 47 electoral votes, the largest number of any state, to Dewey.

Democrats completed their victory by retaking both houses of Congress. After the election, they would hold congressional majorities of 262 to the Republican's 171 in the House, and 54 to 42 in the Senate. While the congressional turnaround was a clear repudiation of the 80th Congress and a complete reversal of the 1946 midterm election, it was not necessarily won on Truman's coattails. In terms of his percentage margin of victory, the president ran behind most Democratic congressional candidates.

So why did Truman defy the pollsters and win in 1948? The answers to this question are many and varied. It could be said that the Republicans did as much to lose the election as Truman did to win it. The Republicans were never able to generate popular support for a platform that differed significantly from the Democrats'. But Truman also served himself well in patching up the leaky New Deal coalition. He and Barkley's late offensive on farm issues, in particular, shored up key votes in the South and Midwest that might have gone to the Republicans or Dixiecrats.

In perhaps the most famous political photograph ever taken, a grinning President Harry S Truman holds up an early—and mistaken—edition of the *Chicago Daily Tribune*. The *Tribune* relied on bad polling and, like many observers, predicted a Dewey victory. (*AP Wide World Photos*)

The Democrats also displayed an impressive organizational and fund-raising drive toward the end of the campaign. And it should be remembered that Truman was the incumbent, and that Democrats represented a clear majority of the nation's voters. Viewed in this light, his victory was certainly no upset.

Henry Wallace and the Dixiecrats, ironically, also aided Truman's cause. As Samuel Lubbell originally argued in *The Future of American Politics* (1951), Democrats concerned about the viability of the third-party candidates rallied around Truman and forced the adoption of a more compelling, universal, and stable platform that could last into the future. Democrats would continue to count on a precarious coalition of

New Dealers in the years ahead, but would no longer be wholly dependent on the South or the Left.

As historian, ADA member, and Democratic political activist Arthur Schlesinger, Jr., would observe in a book published only a few months after the 1948 election, a new "vital center" on the American political Left had emerged. This center had grown out of the New Deal and was shaped by the struggle against fascism in World War II. It then had shifted to muster the nation's "moral strength" in the face of global communism. Its principal tool in each of these struggles was an enduring commitment to a free society based on civil liberties and civil rights. Only by maintaining an "unrelenting attack" on discrimination, centrists believed, would the United States maintain its prestige and win the Cold War propaganda battle in Africa, Asia, and Latin America. Through skill, determination, circumstance, and a little luck, Truman had captured this vital moral and political center better than his opponents. His commitment to centrist issues like civil rights and anticommunism, in the end, made the difference.

Jeffrey Randall Woods

Bibliography

Barnard, William. *Dixiecrats and Democrats*. Tuscaloosa: University of Alabama Press, 1974.

Donaldson, Gary. *Truman Defeats Dewey*. Lexington: University Press of Kentucky, 1999.

Gillon, Steven. *Politics and Vision: The ADA and American Liberalism, 1947–1985*. New York: Oxford University Press, 1987.

Gullen, Harold. *The Upset That Wasn't: The Crucial Election of 1948*. Chicago: Ivan R. Dee, 1998.

Hamby, Alonzo. *Beyond the New Deal: Harry S Truman and American Liberalism*. New York: Columbia University Press, 1973.

———. *Man of the People: A Life of Harry S Truman*. New York: Oxford University Press, 1995.

Karabell, Zachary. *The Last Campaign: How Harry Truman Won the 1948 Election*. New York: Knopf, 2000.

Markowitz, Norman. *The Rise and Fall of the People's Century*. New York: Free Press, 1973.

Ross, Irwin. *The Loneliest Campaign: The Truman Victory of 1948*. Westport, CT: Greenwood, 1977.

THE VOTE: ELECTION OF 1948

State	Total No. of Electors	Total Popular Vote	Electoral Vote D	Electoral Vote R	Electoral Vote SR	Margin of Victory Votes	Margin of Victory % Total Vote	Truman Democrat Votes	Truman Democrat %	Dewey Republican Votes	Dewey Republican %	Thurmond States' Rights Votes	Thurmond States' Rights %	Wallace Progressive Votes	Wallace Progressive %	Others Votes	Others %
Alabama	11	214,980			11	130,513	60.7%	0	0.0%	40,930	19.0%	171,443	79.7%	1,522	0.7%	1,085	0.5%
Arizona	4	177,065	4			17,654	10.0%	95,251	53.8%	77,597	43.8%	0	0.0%	3,310	1.9%	907	0.5%
Arkansas	9	242,475	9			98,700	40.7%	149,659	61.7%	50,959	21.0%	40,068	16.5%	751	0.3%	1,038	0.4%
California	25	4,021,538	25			17,865	0.4%	1,913,134	47.6%	1,895,269	47.1%	1,228	0.0%	190,381	4.7%	21,526	0.5%
Colorado	6	515,237	6			27,574	5.4%	267,288	51.9%	239,714	46.5%	0	0.0%	6,115	1.2%	2,120	0.4%
Connecticut	8	883,518		8		14,457	1.6%	423,297	47.9%	437,754	49.5%	0	0.0%	13,713	1.6%	8,754	1.0%
Delaware	3	139,073		3		1,775	1.3%	67,813	48.8%	69,588	50.0%	0	0.0%	1,050	0.8%	622	0.4%
Florida	8	577,643	8			87,708	15.2%	281,988	48.8%	194,280	33.6%	89,755	15.5%	11,620	2.0%	0	0.0%
Georgia	12	418,760	12			169,591	40.5%	254,646	60.8%	76,691	18.3%	85,055	20.3%	1,636	0.4%	732	0.2%
Idaho	4	214,816	4			5,856	2.7%	107,370	50.0%	101,514	47.3%	0	0.0%	4,972	2.3%	960	0.4%
Illinois	28	3,984,046	28			33,612	0.8%	1,994,715	50.1%	1,961,103	49.2%	0	0.0%	0	0.0%	28,228	0.7%
Indiana	13	1,656,214		13		13,246	0.8%	807,833	48.8%	821,079	49.6%	0	0.0%	9,649	0.6%	17,653	1.1%
Iowa	10	1,038,264	10			28,362	2.7%	522,380	50.3%	494,018	47.6%	0	0.0%	12,125	1.2%	9,741	0.9%
Kansas	8	788,819		8		71,137	9.0%	351,902	44.6%	423,039	53.6%	0	0.0%	4,603	0.6%	9,275	1.2%
Kentucky	11	822,658	11			125,546	15.3%	466,756	56.7%	341,210	41.5%	10,411	1.3%	1,567	0.2%	2,714	0.3%
Louisiana	10	416,336			10	67,946	16.3%	136,344	32.7%	72,657	17.5%	204,290	49.1%	3,035	0.7%	10	0.0%
Maine	5	264,787		5		38,318	14.5%	111,916	42.3%	150,234	56.7%	0	0.0%	1,884	0.7%	753	0.3%
Maryland	8	596,735		8		8,293	1.4%	286,521	48.0%	294,814	49.4%	2,476	0.4%	9,983	1.7%	2,941	0.5%
Massachusetts	16	2,107,146	16			242,418	11.5%	1,151,788	54.7%	909,370	43.2%	0	0.0%	38,157	1.8%	7,831	0.4%
Michigan	19	2,109,609		19		35,147	1.7%	1,003,448	47.6%	1,038,595	49.2%	0	0.0%	46,515	2.2%	21,051	1.0%
Minnesota	11	1,212,226	11			209,349	17.3%	692,966	57.2%	483,617	39.9%	0	0.0%	27,866	2.3%	7,777	0.6%
Mississippi	9	192,190			9	148,154	77.1%	19,384	10.1%	5,043	2.6%	167,538	87.2%	225	0.1%	0	0.0%
Missouri	15	1,578,628	15			262,276	16.6%	917,315	58.1%	655,039	41.5%	42	0.0%	3,998	0.3%	2,234	0.1%
Montana	4	224,278	4			22,301	9.9%	119,071	53.1%	96,770	43.1%	0	0.0%	7,313	3.3%	1,124	0.5%
Nebraska	6	488,940		6		40,609	8.3%	224,165	45.8%	264,774	54.2%	0	0.0%	0	0.0%	1	0.0%
Nevada	3	62,117	3			1,934	3.1%	31,291	50.4%	29,357	47.3%	0	0.0%	1,469	2.4%	0	0.0%
New Hampshire	4	231,440		4		13,304	5.7%	107,995	46.7%	121,299	52.4%	7	0.0%	1,970	0.9%	169	0.1%
New Jersey	16	1,949,555		16		85,669	4.4%	895,455	45.9%	981,124	50.3%	0	0.0%	42,683	2.2%	30,293	1.6%
New Mexico	4	187,063	4			25,161	13.5%	105,464	56.4%	80,303	42.9%	0	0.0%	1,037	0.6%	259	0.1%
New York	47	6,177,337		47		60,959	1.0%	2,780,204	45.0%	2,841,163	46.0%	0	0.0%	509,559	8.2%	46,411	0.8%
North Carolina	14	791,209	14			200,498	25.3%	459,070	58.0%	258,572	32.7%	69,652	8.8%	3,915	0.5%	0	0.0%
North Dakota	4	220,716		4		19,327	8.8%	95,812	43.4%	115,139	52.2%	374	0.2%	8,391	3.8%	1,000	0.5%
Ohio	25	2,936,071	25	0		7,107	0.2%	1,452,791	49.5%	1,445,684	49.2%	0	0.0%	37,596	1.3%	0	0.0%
Oklahoma	10	721,599	10			183,965	25.5%	452,782	62.7%	268,817	37.3%	0	0.0%	0	0.0%	0	0.0%
Oregon	6	524,080		6		17,757	3.4%	243,147	46.4%	260,904	49.8%	0	0.0%	14,978	2.9%	5,051	1.0%
Pennsylvania	35	3,735,148		35		149,771	4.0%	1,752,426	46.9%	1,902,197	50.9%	0	0.0%	55,161	1.5%	25,364	0.7%
Rhode Island	4	327,702	4			52,949	16.2%	188,736	57.6%	135,787	41.4%	0	0.0%	2,619	0.8%	560	0.2%
South Carolina	8	142,571			8	68,184	47.8%	34,423	24.1%	5,386	3.8%	102,607	72.0%	154	0.1%	1	0.0%
South Dakota	4	250,105		4		11,998	4.8%	117,653	47.0%	129,651	51.8%	0	0.0%	2,801	1.1%	0	0.0%
Tennessee	12	550,283	11		1[a]	67,488	12.3%	270,402	49.1%	202,914	36.9%	73,815	13.4%	1,864	0.3%	1,288	0.2%
Texas	23	1,147,245	23			468,460	40.8%	750,700	65.4%	282,240	24.6%	106,909	9.3%	3,764	0.3%	3,632	0.3%
Utah	4	276,305	4			24,749	9.0%	149,151	54.0%	124,402	45.0%	0	0.0%	2,679	1.0%	73	0.0%
Vermont	3	123,382		3		30,369	24.6%	45,557	36.9%	75,926	61.5%	0	0.0%	1,279	1.0%	620	0.5%
Virginia	11	419,256	11			28,716	6.8%	200,786	47.9%	172,070	41.0%	43,393	10.4%	2,047	0.5%	960	0.2%
Washington	8	905,059	8			89,850	9.9%	476,165	52.6%	386,315	42.7%	0	0.0%	31,692	3.5%	10,887	1.2%
West Virginia	8	748,750	8			112,937	15.1%	429,188	57.3%	316,251	42.2%	0	0.0%	3,311	0.4%	0	0.0%
Wisconsin	12	1,276,800	12			56,351	4.4%	647,310	50.7%	590,959	46.3%	0	0.0%	25,282	2.0%	13,249	1.0%
Wyoming	3	101,425	3			4,407	4.3%	52,354	51.6%	47,947	47.3%	0	0.0%	931	0.9%	193	0.2%
TOTAL	531	48,691,199	303	189	39	2,135,747	4.4%	24,105,812	49.5%	21,970,065	45.1%	1,169,063	2.4%	1,157,172	2.4%	289,087	0.6%

[a] A Truman elector in Tennessee voted for Strom Thurmond.

For sources, see p.1127.

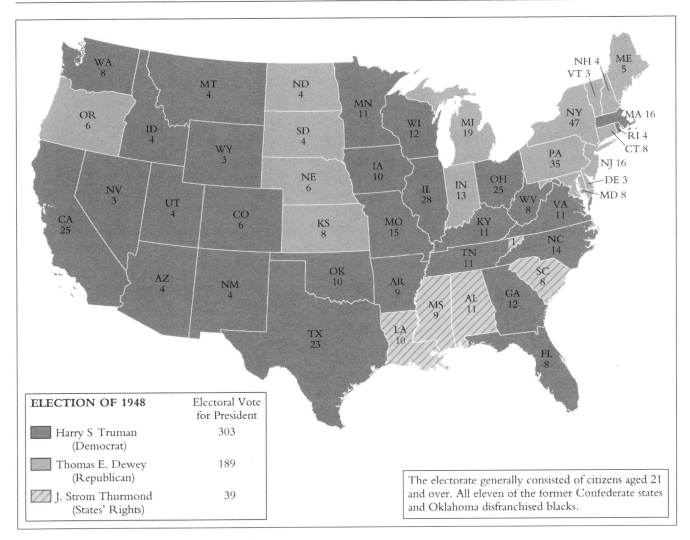

ELECTION OF 1948 — Electoral Vote for President

	Candidate	Electoral Vote
■	Harry S Truman (Democrat)	303
■	Thomas E. Dewey (Republican)	189
▨	J. Strom Thurmond (States' Rights)	39

The electorate generally consisted of citizens aged 21 and over. All eleven of the former Confederate states and Oklahoma disfranchised blacks.

DOCUMENTS: ELECTION OF 1948

In a stunning upset, President Harry S Truman overcame serious divisions within the Democratic Party to defeat his Republican opponent, Governor Thomas E. Dewey of New York. Initially, some influential Democrats believed Truman had little chance of winning and had tried to enlist General Dwight Eisenhower for the nomination. Eisenhower refused, and Truman won the nomination on the first ballot. However, liberal and conservative Democrats bolted the party and ran their own presidential candidates.

With many predicting a Dewey victory over the divided Democrats, the Republican candidate campaigned cautiously, while Truman commenced a vigorous schedule. He traveled over 30,000 miles and talked to millions of Americans. Truman gave over 300 speeches in his "whistle stop" campaign. This added to his considerable amount of personal appeal, and his attacks on the Republican-controlled Congress won support among labor and farmers. Still unconvinced, election eve polls predicted a Dewey win—and, in an early morning edition the day after the election, the Chicago Tribune *even went so far as to declare in a headline, "Dewey Defeats Truman." But Truman prevailed, with a 49.5 to 45.1 percent popular plurality and a 303 to 189 Electoral College majority.*

Document 1, a radio broadcast by former vice president Henry A. Wallace, suggested that there was little difference between the two major parties over foreign policy. A hard-line approach to the Soviet Union would lead us to war while ignoring the economic concerns of Americans. Wallace ran for president on the Progressive Party platform with a message to end the Cold War and work with the Soviet Union for peace. He received the endorsement of many left-wing groups, including the American Communist Party and huge numbers of young people who were looking for a better way than harsh confrontation. In Document 2, an editorial in the Washington Post, *Arthur Friendly attempted to undercut Wallace's appeal by revealing that Communists were using his campaign for their gain. While some Wallace supporters tried to capture more than just the far Left by lumping both Democrats and Republicans together as in Document 3, liberals like young Arthur Schlesinger, Jr., and John Kenneth Galbraith formed the Americans for Democratic Action to cut themselves free of the far Left.*

At the Democratic National Convention, Mayor Hubert H. Humphrey of Minneapolis delivered a resounding speech, Document 4, calling for civil rights for all Americans. It was his great moment in American history. Just thirty-seven years old, Humphrey helped convince Democrats to adopt a civil rights platform plank and caused southern conservatives to desert the party. These "Dixiecrats" quickly held a convention and nominated Governor Strom Thurmond of South Carolina for president, and ran on a platform emphasizing states' rights, Document 5. This committed them to segregation, but also associated their opponents with communism. However, amid the loud, racist speeches of the Dixiecrats, a Time *article, Document 6, revealed their true importance when it detailed the proceedings of their meeting and concluded it had "more lung power than political strength."*

Document 7, Truman's speech accepting the Democratic nomination, summarized the theme of his campaign. Truman attacked the Republicans in the 80th Congress, reminded voters of how much their lives had improved since Democrats had taken over from Herbert Hoover in the midst of the Depression, and lobbied for more social programs such as national healthcare. His "whistle-stop" campaign reiterated these themes, as seen in Document 8, but related to voters on a more personal level. The Republican Dewey's campaign promises remained vague and called for "national unity." Document 9, a Dewey campaign speech, exhibited his cautious posture.

Document 1

Radio Broadcast by Former Vice President Henry A. Wallace, December 29, 1947

For the past fifteen months I have traveled up and down, and back and forth across this country. I have talked with half a million people in public meetings and with thousands in private gatherings. I have been working for, and I shall continue to work for, peace and security.

Everywhere in the United States today, among farmers, workers, small businessmen and professional men and women, I find confusion, uncertainty and fear. The people don't ask, "Will there be another war?" but "When will the war come?"

Everywhere I find that people are spending so much for food and rent that they cannot afford their customary services from the doctor and dentist. They don't ask, "Will there be another depression?" but "When will the real depression start?"

Peace and abundance mean so much to me that I have said at a dozen press conferences and in many speeches when asked about a third party, "If the Democratic party continues to be a party of war and depression, I will see to it that the people have a chance to vote for prosperity and peace. . . ."

So far as the Republican party is concerned, there is no hope—as George Norris, Fiorello LaGuardia and Wendell Willkie long ago found out.

When the old parties rot, the people have a right to be heard through a new party. They asserted that right when the Democratic party was founded under Jefferson in the struggle against the Federalist party of war and privilege of his time. They won it again when the Republican party was organized in Lincoln's day. The people must again have an opportunity to speak out with their votes in 1948.

The lukewarm liberals sitting on two chairs say, "Why throw away your vote?" I say a vote for the new party in 1948 will be the most valuable vote you have ever cast or ever will cast.

The bigger the peace vote in 1948, the more definitely the world will know that the United States is not behind the bipartisan reactionary war policy which is dividing the world into two armed camps and making inevitable the day when American soldiers will be lying in their Arctic suits in the Russian snow.

There is no real fight between a Truman and a Republican. Both stand for a policy which opens the door to war in our lifetime and makes war certain for our children.

Stop saying, "I don't like it but I am going to vote for the lesser of two evils."

Rather than accept either evil, come out boldly, stand upright as men and women and say loudly, so all the world can hear:

"We are voting peace and security for ourselves and our children's children. We are fighting for old-fashioned Americanism at the polls in 1948. We are fighting for freedom of speech and freedom of assembly. We are fighting to end racial discrimination. We are fighting for lower prices. We are fighting for free labor unions, for jobs, and for homes in which we can decently live. . . ."

One thing I want to make clear to both Russia and the United States—peace requires real understanding between our peoples. Russia has as much to gain from peace as the United States, and just as we here fight against the spreaders of hate and falsehood against Russia, the Russian leaders can make a great contribution by restraining those extremists who try to widen the gap between our two great countries.

I insist that the United States be fully secure until there is a real peace between this country and Russia and until there is an international police force stronger than the military establishment of any nation, including Russia and the United States.

I am utterly against any kind of imperialism or expansionism, whether sponsored by Britain, Russia or the United States, and I call on Russia as well as the United States to look at all our differences objectively and free from that prejudice which the hate mongers have engendered on both sides.

What the world needs is a United Nations disarmament conference to rid humanity for all time of the threat not only of atomic bombs but also of all other methods of mass destruction. . . .

Source: Arthur M. Schlesinger, Jr., and Fred L. Israel, eds., *History of American Presidential Elections*, vol. 4 (New York: Chelsea House, 1971).

Document 2

Commentary by Alfred Friendly, May 2, 1948

The Communists' support of the Wallace campaign and their key roles in it have been, of course, obvious for many months. But it was not until last week that a competent authority stated flatly that the Communists were "directly responsible" for founding the third party movement. . . .

The Communists and the unions and locals they led should not be wishy-washy about supporting Wallace. The CIO, he went on, was rapidly moving toward the right and that trend must be stopped. The Communist-led unions should now "stand up and be counted. . . ."

According to one, it was admitted that Wallace was not so adhesively consistent as might be desired, but that he could be held as long as the Communists surrounded him and worked on him. The answer was to the effect that, "To the extent that we encircle him, to that extent he'll stick."

According to the second account, it was decided that it did not make much difference if Wallace finally turned against them. The argument was that Wallace was to be used as a tool or lever for the Communist foreign policy.

Source: Washington Post, May 2, 1948. Reprinted with permission.

Document 3

"A Good Man Is Hard to Find," A Pro-Wallace Cartoon

Document 4

Speech by Hubert H. Humphrey, Democratic National Convention, July 14, 1948

I realize that in speaking on behalf of the minority report on civil rights, as presented by Congressman Andrew Biemiller of Wisconsin, that I am dealing with a charged issue, with an issue which has been confused by emotionalism on all sides of the fence. . . .

It seems to me that the Democratic Party needs to make definite pledges of the kind suggested in the minority report, to maintain the trust and confidence placed in it by the people of all races and all sections of this country. Sure, we are here as Democrats; but, my good friends, we are here as Americans; we are here as the believers in the principles and the ideology of democracy, and I firmly believe that as men concerned with our country's future, we must specify in our platform the guarantees which we have mentioned in the minority report.

Yes, this is far more than a party matter. Every citizen in this country has a stake in the emergence of the United States as a leader in a free world. That world is being challenged by the world of slavery. For us to play our part effectively, we must be in a morally sound position.

We cannot use a double standard. There is no room for double standards in American politics: For measuring our own and other people's policies, our demands for democratic practices in other lands will be no more effective than the guarantee of those practices in our own country.

Friends, delegates, I do not believe that there can be any compromise on the guarantees of the civil rights which we have mentioned in the minority report. In spite of my desire for unanimous agreement on the entire platform, in spite of my desire to see everybody here in unanimous agreement, there are some matters which I think must be stated clearly and without qualification. There can be no hedging. The newspaper headlines are wrong.

There will be no hedging, and there will be no watering down, if you please, of the instruments and the principles of the civil rights program.

My friends, to those who say that we are rushing this issue of civil rights, I say to them we are 172 years late.

To those who say that this civil rights program is an infringement on States' Rights, I say this: That the time has arrived in America for leadership, and they are looking to America for precepts and example. . . .

My good friends, I ask my Party, and I ask the Democratic Party, to march down the high road of progressive democracy. I ask this Convention to say in unmistakable terms that we proudly hail and we courageously support our President and leader, Harry Truman, in his great fight for civil rights in America.

Source: PBS.org Great American Speeches Archive, www.pbs.org/greatspeeches/timeline. Reprinted with permission of the Minnesota Historical Society.

Document 5

The States' Rights Party Platform

THE PRINCIPLE OF STATES' RIGHTS

We direct attention to the fact that the first platform of the Democratic Party, adopted in 1840, resolved that: "Congress has no power under the Constitution to interfere with or control the domestic institutions of the several states, and that such states are the sole and proper judges of everything appertaining to their own affairs not prohibited by the Constitution."

Such pronouncement is the cornerstone of the Democratic Party. A long train of abuses and usurpations of power by unfaithful leaders who are alien to the Democratic parties of the states here represented has become intolerable to those who believe in the preservation of constitutional government and individual liberty in America.

The Executive Department of the government is promoting the gradual but certain growth of a totalitarian state by domination and control of a politically minded Supreme Court. . . .

PERIL TO BASIC RIGHTS

A totalitarian concept has been promulgated which threatens the integrity of the states and the basic rights of their citizens.

We have repeatedly remonstrated with the leaders of the national organization of our party but our petitions, entreaties and warnings have been treated with contempt. The latest response to our entreaties was a Democratic convention in Philadelphia rigged to embarrass and humiliate the South.

This alleged Democratic assembly called for a civil rights law that would eliminate segregation of every kind from all American life, prohibit all forms of discrimination in private employment, in public and private instruction and administration and treatment of students; in the operation of public and private health facilities; in all transportation, and require equal access to all places of public accommodation for persons of all races, colors, creeds and national origin. . . .

PAST LOYALTY

We point out that the South, with clock-like regularity, has furnished the Democratic Party approximately 50 percent of the votes necessary to nominate a President every four years for nearly a century. In 1920 the only states in the union that went Democratic were the eleven Southern states.

Notwithstanding this rugged loyalty to the party, the masters of political intrigue now allow Republican states in which there is scarcely a Democratic office holder to dominate and control the party and fashion its policies.

NEW POLICY

As Democrats who are irrevocably committed to democracy as defined and expounded by Thomas Jefferson, Andrew Jackson and Woodrow Wilson, and who believe that all necessary steps must be taken for its preservation, we declare to the people of the United States as follows:

1. We believe that the Constitution of the United States is the greatest charter of human liberty ever conceived by the mind of man.

2. We oppose all efforts to invade or destroy the rights vouchsafed by it to every citizen of this republic.

3. We stand for social and economic justice, which we believe can be vouchsafed to all citizens only by a strict adherence to our Constitution and the avoidance of any invasion or destruction of the constitutional rights of the states and individuals. We oppose totalitarian, centralized, bureaucratic government and the police state called for by the platforms adopted by the Democratic and Republican conventions.

4. We stand for the segregation of the races and the racial integrity of each race; the constitutional right to choose one's associates; to accept private employment without governmental interference, and to earn one's living in any lawful way. We oppose the elimination of segregation employment by Federal bureaucrats called for by the misnamed civil rights program. We favor home rule, local self-government and a minimum interference with individual rights.

5. We oppose and condemn the action of the Democratic convention in sponsoring a civil rights program calling for the elimination of segregation, social equality by Federal fiat, regulation of private employment practices, voting and local law enforcement.

6. We affirm that the effective enforcement of such a program would be utterly destructive of the social, economic and political life of the Southern people, and of other localities in which there may be differences in race, creed or national origin in appreciable numbers.

7. We stand for the checks and balances provided by the three departments of our Government. We oppose the usurpation of legislative functions by the executive and judicial departments. We unreservedly condemn the effort to establish nationwide a police state in this republic that would destroy the last vestige of liberty enjoyed by a citizen.

8. We demand that there be returned to the people, to whom of right they belong, those powers needed for the preservation of human rights and the discharge of our responsibility as Democrats for human welfare. We oppose a denial of those rights by political parties, a barter or sale of those rights by a political convention, as well as any invasion or violation of those rights by the Federal Government.

We call upon all Democrats and upon all other loyal Americans who are opposed to totalitarianism at home and abroad to unite with us in ignominiously defeating Harry S. Truman and Thomas E. Dewey, and every other candidate for public office who would establish a police state in the United States of America.

Source: Kirk H. Porter and Donald Bruce Johnson, comps., *National Party Platforms, 1840–1964* (Urbana: University of Illinois Press, 1966).

Document 6

"The South: Tumult in Dixie"

Three days after their walkout at Philadelphia, the rebellious Southerners met in Birmingham's red brick municipal auditorium. There they snake-danced under a portrait of Robert E. Lee, flourished Confederate battle flags, and shouted their defiance of Harry Truman and the rest of the Democratic Party.

But the meeting had more lung power than political strength. The delegates, except for those from Mississippi and Alabama, were political outsiders, has-beens, and non-mainstream Democrats. Most bigwig Southern politicos pointedly stayed away. Even Arkansas' Governor Ben Laney, who had withdrawn as the rebels' favorite son at Philadelphia, remained aloof in his downtown hotel room, contented himself with offering advice.

"This Infamous Program." In the convention hall, Southern oratory boomed out like cannon fire. In the front row, Oklahoma's doddering ex-Governor "Alfalfa Bill" Murray beamed his approval, proudly recalled that "I'm the man who introduced Jim Crow in Oklahoma." Race-baiting Gerald L. K. Smith turned up as a spectator under the pseudonym of S. Goodyear. A group of Mississippi students set up a chant: "To hell with Truman."

With shouts of triumph, the delegates endorsed a "Declaration of Principles." It condemned "this infamous and iniquitous program (of) equal access to all places of public accommodation for persons of all races, colors, creeds and national origin." Then they nominated South Carolina's Governor J. Strom Thurmond for President and Mississippi's Governor Fielding Wright for Vice President.

Not a Bolt. Just what they hoped to accomplish—or how they would go about it—no one seemed to know. So far, only Alabama and Mississippi electors were pledged against Harry Truman. Other states might be persuaded to instruct their electors for the Thurmond-Wright ticket. But most office-holding Democrats would think twice before risking their federal and state patronage by aligning themselves with the irregulars. Said Arkansas' Laney pointedly: "Whatever is done must be done through and by the official Democrat organization in each respective state."

Even the rebels themselves were careful to leave the door ajar. Candidate Wright explained, with careful ambiguity: "This is not a bolt. This is not a fourth party. I say to you that we are the true Democrats of the Southland and these United States." To be doubly sure that there was a way of scrambling back, the rebels agreed to convene again next October to see how they were doing.

Source: Time, July 26, 1948. Reprinted by permission.

Document 7

Harry Truman's Speech Accepting His Nomination, Democratic National Convention, July 15, 1948

We have been working together for victory in a great cause. Victory has become a habit of our party. It has been elected four times in succession, and I am convinced it will be elected a fifth time next November.

The reason is that the people know that the Democratic Party is the people's party, and the Republican Party is the party of special interest, and it always has been and always will be. . . .

The United States has to accept its full responsibility for leadership in international affairs. We have been the backers and the people who organized and started the United Nations, first started under that great Democratic President, Woodrow Wilson, as the League of Nations. The League was sabotaged by the Republicans in 1920. And we must see that the United Nations continues a strong and growing body, so we can have everlasting peace in the world. . . .

I would like to say a word or two now on what I think the Republican philosophy is, and I will speak from actions and from history and from experience. The situation in 1932 was due to the policies of the Republican Party control of the Government of the United States. The Republican Party, as I said a while ago, favors the privileged few and not the common everyday man. Ever since its inception, that party has been under the control of special privilege; and they have completely proved it in the 80th Congress. They proved it by the things they did to the people, and not for them. They proved it by the things they failed to do.

Now, let's look at some of them—just a few. . . . [I] recommended an increase in the minimum wage. What did I get? Nothing. Absolutely nothing.

I suggested that the schools in this country are crowded, teachers underpaid, and that there is a shortage of teachers. One of our greatest national needs is more and better schools. I urged the Congress to provide $300 million to aid the States in the present educational crisis. Congress did nothing about it. . . .

I have repeatedly asked the Congress to pass a health program. The Nation suffers from lack of medical care. That situation can be remedied any time the Congress wants to act upon it.

Now, what that worst 80th Congress does in this special session will be the test. The American people will not decide by listening to mere words, or by reading a mere platform. They will decide on the record, the record as it has been written. And in the record is the stark truth, that the battle lines of 1948 are the same as they were in 1932, when the Nation lay prostrate and helpless as a result of Republican misrule and inaction.

In 1932 we were attacking the citadel of special privilege and greed. We were fighting to drive the money changers from the temple. Today, in 1948, we are now the defenders of the stronghold of democracy and of equal opportunity, the haven of the ordinary people of this land and not of the favored classes or the powerful few. The battle cry is just the same now as it was in 1932, and I paraphrase the words of Franklin D. Roosevelt as he issued the challenge, in accepting nomination in Chicago: "This is more than a political call to arms. Give me your help, not to win votes alone, but to win in this new crusade to keep America secure and safe for its own people."

Now my friends, with the help of God and the wholehearted push which you can put behind this campaign, we can save this country from a continuation of the 80th Congress, and from misrule from now on.

I must have your help. You must get in and push, and win this election. The country can't afford another Republican Congress.

Source: *Public Papers of the Presidents of the United States: Harry S Truman, January 1 to December 31, 1948* (Washington, DC: Government Printing Office, 1961).

Document 8

"Whistle Stop" Speech, President Harry Truman, Framingham, Massachusetts, October 27, 1948

The people's campaign is rolling to victory. I can assure you of that. The West is with us, the central states are with us, and the East is swinging into line. If you would see the people I have been talking to since I came East, you would understand what I mean when I say the East is beginning to find out what side its bread is buttered on.

All I ask you to do is vote for yourself, vote for your family. When you come right down to the analysis of our government, our government is the people, and when the people exercise their right to vote on election day they control that government. When they don't exercise that right then you get—then you get an 80th Congress. So, two-thirds of the people of the United States entitled to vote in 1946 stayed at home. They didn't have energy enough to go and look after their political interests on election day—and they got the 80th Congress. Don't do that again. Don't do that again.

The Democrats are not afraid of the people. The Democrats know that when the people exercise their rights the country is safe.

Source: Public Papers of the Presidents of the United States: Harry S Truman, January 1 to December 31, 1948 (Washington, DC: Government Printing Office, 1964).

Document 9

Speech by Governor Thomas E. Dewey, Des Moines, Iowa, September 20, 1948

This is my pledge to my fellow-citizens, the declaration of the principles and purposes of your next Administration.

I pledge to you that, as President, every act of mine will be determined by one principle above all others: Is this good for our country?

I pledge to you that my administration will be made up of men and women devoted to that same principle—of men and women whose love of their country comes ahead of every other consideration. They will know how to translate their devotion to our country into constructive action.

I pledge to you a foreign policy based upon the firm belief that we can have peace. That policy will be made effective by men and women who really understand the nature of the threat to peace and who have the vigor, the knowledge and the experience required to wage that peace.

I pledge to you a Government of teamwork. The executive heads of your Government will be really qualified for their positions after January 20, and they will be given full responsibility to do their job without loose talk, factional quarreling or appeals to group prejudice. They will know how to work together as a team and one of the most important members of that team will be the distinguished Governor of California, the next Vice President of the United States, Earl Warren.

I pledge to you an Administration which will know how to work with the elected representatives of the people in the Congress, an Administration that wants to work with them and will do so. The unity we need for the nation will be practiced in the nation's Capitol.

I pledge to you that on next January 20 there will begin in Washington the biggest unraveling, unsnarling operation in our nation's history.

I pledge to you an Administration which knows in its mind and believes in its heart that every American is dependent on every other American; that no segment of our people can prosper without the prosperity of all; that in truth we must all go forward together.

This is what you may expect from your next, your Republican administration. It will be a government in which every member is enlisted to advance the well-being of all our people and is dedicated to the release of the enthusiasm, the energy and the enterprise of our people: a government that has faith in America and is resolved to prove its faith by its works.

This is the road on which I propose that we set out all together. As we advance we shall carry America's destiny with us. We shall also carry the hope of freedom and the living promise to a stricken world that men can be free and that free men can live in peace.

We're living in sorely troubled times. The unhappy difficulties of today are familiar to every one of us. Three years after the end of the war the world has still not found peace. As we wage the peace, we face problems as momentous as any nation has ever confronted in history, either in peace or in war.

Our sons and daughters—the young people in all our grade schools, our high schools and our colleges have lived—it seems impossible, but it's true—they have lived their whole lives in a troubled world. Their plans for education, for getting married, for getting ahead, are delayed and disrupted. Against the dangers of a sorely troubled world they are being called upon to keep America strong.

The wife and mother who's been out shopping today to buy meat for her family and clothes for her children has been up against the hard fact of high prices. Every married veteran living in a Quonset hut, or doubled up with his family, is up against the cruel fact that we do not have enough good homes for our people. Every family living in a crowded, unsanitary, cold-water tenement has the same urgent needs. Hard-working, frugal Americans find they don't make enough to lay anything by for a rainy day or for sickness, or unemployment, or old age.

Millions of Americans, too, face the intolerable fact that because of their race or their color or the way they choose to worship God, they are denied rights which are their birthrights and which, by American principle and law, are their just due.

These are some of the difficulties that confront us. It won't be easy to meet them, and I want no one to think that I believe it will be easy. These times require the cooperation of everyone of us and the highest order of devotion and intense labor by your Government. But it's part of my faith in America to believe that with restoration of faith in ourselves, of competence in our Government, of unity of purpose among our people, there is nothing, as a people, we cannot do.

I deeply believe that, with an administration which can unite our people, [we] will have taken the greatest single step toward solving these problems. This is our most urgent need.

Source: New York Times, September 21, 1948.

THE ELECTION OF
1952

Every election stands between the past and the future, but the 1952 contest uniquely blended elements of traditional, party-dominated contests with new forces that would shape media-dominated struggles of the end of the century. Although still relying on party leadership, conventions, and speaking tours, this contest highlighted the importance of new factors—television, advertising, polling, and computers—as well as the increasingly significant role of personality. Finally, paired with the election of 1948, it focused on the issues of the Cold War and civil rights, which would dominate politics in the next half century.

The Political Context

By 1952, the Democratic Party had controlled the national government for twenty years. Brought into office by the Great Depression, Franklin Roosevelt transformed the party through political skill and policy choices: expanding the federal government's powers, economic regulation and planning, protecting labor unions, supporting agriculture, and creating a safety net for the poor, unemployed, and elderly. This "New Deal" coalition changed electoral politics, creating a solid Democratic majority. After World War II ended in 1945, high inflation and labor strikes, plus Roosevelt's death and his replacement by Harry Truman, produced Republican congressional majorities in 1946. Two years later, Truman's surprising win and the Democratic victory in Congress demonstrated the basic and enduring appeal of New Deal domestic policies. But two new issues—race and the

Cold War—appeared during the campaign, and were harbingers of a major change in American political life.

After a seventy-year absence, race reemerged as a major political issue after 1945, particularly within the Democratic Party. When the party's 1948 convention adopted a strong civil rights plank, many delegates from deep South states walked out. In the election, those states voted for "Dixiecrat" Strom Thurmond. Some liberal Democrats defected to Progressive candidate Henry Wallace, who criticized the president's Cold War policies and supported civil rights. Ironically, these candidates counterbalanced each other and minimized the effect of these issues. With Dewey adding little to these debates, the election revolved primarily around New Deal/Fair Deal issues. Truman won by reassembling major elements of the New Deal voting coalition; but 1948 began the party's difficult struggle supporting civil rights and winning votes in the South, where most African Americans were disfranchised.

The Republican Party faced an equally serious division. A progressive/"Old Guard" split from the Progressive era was transformed after 1932 by different responses to the New Deal's expansion of the federal government and to foreign policy crises. Like Ohio's Senator Robert Taft, many mid-western conservatives who wished to scrap much of the New Deal also tended to be isolationists, opposing American involvement in Europe. This faction dominated the party's congressional forces, but eastern moderates had largely shaped national party platforms and selected the presidential candidates. Because they

CHRONOLOGY

1949

JANUARY   Chinese communist forces enter Peking.

JULY 21   Senate ratifies NATO treaty.

SEPTEMBER 23   Truman announces Russian atomic bomb test.

1950

JANUARY 21   Alger Hiss convicted of perjury.

FEBRUARY 11   Senator Joseph McCarthy announces a list of "communists" in government.

JUNE 25   North Korea invades South Korea.

JULY 1   U.S. forces land in Korea.

JULY 17   Julius and Ethel Rosenberg arrested as atomic spies.

SEPTEMBER 23   Internal Security Act passed over Truman's veto.

OCTOBER 7   U.S. forces invade North Korea.

NOVEMBER 29   Chinese troops attack U.S. forces.

1951

APRIL 4   Senate reaffirms NATO commitment.

APRIL 10   Truman fires General MacArthur.

1952

MARCH 11   New Hampshire primary.

APRIL 11   Eisenhower announces he will return June 1 to compete for GOP nomination.

JULY 7   Republican convention begins.

JULY 21   Democratic convention begins.

SEPTEMBER 12   Eisenhower and Taft hold Morningside Heights conference.

SEPTEMBER 23   Nixon delivers "Checkers" speech.

OCTOBER 24   Eisenhower promises to "go to Korea."

NOVEMBER 4   Eisenhower is elected president.

accepted an internationalist foreign policy and some of the New Deal's goals (but not its methods), conservatives denounced these moderates as a "Me Too" group. The defeats of presidential candidates Wendell Wilkie in 1940 and New York governor Thomas Dewey in 1944 and 1948 had badly weakened the moderates, leaving them without an obvious standard bearer, presaging a serious struggle in 1952.

The election of Truman and a Democratic Congress in 1948 had produced the first flurry of liberal legislation in a decade: a raise in the minimum wage, expanded Social Security coverage, money for slum clearance and public housing, and additional support for various water projects and farm loans. But the more ambitious parts of Truman's "Fair Deal" agenda failed, including aid to education, national health insurance, repeal of the Taft-Hartley labor law, and a reformed agriculture program. After 1950, the administration was shaken by charges of corruption in the Reconstruction Finance Corporation, the collection of income taxes, and the Justice Department. More directly damaging to Truman, his military adviser, Harry Vaughan, had accepted gifts from persons seeking influence in government. This reinforced arguments that Truman appointed cronies, rather than the most able persons, and that Democrats had held power for too long.

Communism posed even greater difficulties for the administration. Collapse of the Chiang Kai-shek regime in China during 1949 shocked the American public, and Republicans blamed the administration for the communists' victory. The news, in September 1949, that Russia had acquired atomic weapons fueled worries about American security, both abroad and at home. In 1947, Truman had attempted to defuse the issue of internal subversion by creating a program to reexamine the loyalty of all government employees. But the perjury conviction of former State Department official Alger Hiss, plus new cases of atomic espionage uncovered in 1949–50, heightened public fears. Seeking partisan advantage, Republicans emphasized the issue, but some conservatives went far beyond normal political tactics. Senator Joseph McCarthy (R-WI), operating with the tacit approval of Senator Taft, employed smear tactics by claiming, without evidence, that communists operated within the U.S. government and that Secretary of Defense George Marshall was implicated in a communist conspiracy. Besides changing the tone of politics, anticommunist hysteria encouraged the passage of harsh internal security and immigration laws over Truman's vetoes in 1950 and 1952.

The Korean War brought various foreign policy issues into sharp relief. On June 25, 1950, North Korean forces launched a surprise invasion. The administration sent in troops under General Douglas MacArthur, which by October had met the original goal of repelling the invasion. MacArthur then invaded the North, assuring Truman that the Chinese would not intervene. His horrendous miscalculation became evident on November 26, 1950, when a massive Chinese army drove the divided American forces back down the peninsula. In January 1951, American troops finally stopped the Chinese advance and, during the remainder of the war, inflicted enormous casualties on Chinese forces. However, the next two years saw little change in battlefield positions and no progress in peace talks, while American losses mounted and public frustration grew. In early 1951, MacArthur and his Republican supporters advocated expanding the war to China; but the Joint Chiefs and the administration rejected this as reckless

and likely to cause armed conflict with the Soviet Union.

The conflict pitted the "Asia first" views of MacArthur and Republicans like Taft, against the European emphasis of most military and administration leaders, as well as many eastern Republicans. The Korean War pushed Truman to propose major increases in military spending, with much of it going to the North Atlantic Treaty Organization (NATO), the defense pact the United States had entered with other noncommunist western nations in 1949. Congress passed the measure, and after a major debate in early 1951, reaffirmed the nation's commitment to NATO. MacArthur's disagreement, his inability to understand limited warfare, and his arrogance led him to cooperate with Republicans in publicly challenging the president's policy. Never one to dodge a fight, Truman fired the general on April 10, 1951, unleashing a political firestorm. MacArthur returned to the United States, and spent the next year denouncing Truman—and running for president. Calls for Truman's impeachment eventually dwindled, while congressional hearings reaffirmed both the correctness of the limited war policy and the importance of civilian control of the military. Still, many Americans felt frustrated by a military struggle so unlike the world war the country had recently won.

Battle for the GOP Nomination

The battle for the 1952 GOP nomination began immediately after the 1948 election. Conservatives, angered by losing to Dewey and furious about his loss to Truman, unified behind Ohio senator Robert Taft, who had failed to gain the nomination in 1940 and 1948. A midwestern patrician, the son of former president William Howard Taft, he had been the leading critic of the New Deal since winning election to the Senate in 1938, though in 1949 he had supported some federal aid to education and funding for public housing. This vigorous partisan, known as "Mr. Republican," displayed a mastery of legislative detail and dominated the GOP's stance on issues, especially as chair of the Republican Senate Policy Committee (1947–52). Before World War II., he had opposed Lend-Lease help to Britain, and after the war he had first resisted, and then reluctantly supported, the Marshall Plan to assist Western Europe. He led the fight against NATO, considering it an unreasonable expansion of American obligations; but he also demanded substantial aid for Chiang Kai-shek.

Taft's views and somber presence made some Republicans question his electability, but his overwhelming reelection to the Senate in 1950 improved his case. In October 1951, Taft formally opened his bid for president. Having substantial funds, an extensive organization and ardent supporters, especially in the Midwest and West, he began as the preemptive

DWIGHT DAVID EISENHOWER

PARTY: Republican

DATE OF BIRTH: October 14, 1890

PLACE OF BIRTH: Denison, Texas

PARENTS: David and Elizabeth Eisenhower

EDUCATION: B.S., U.S. Military Academy (1915)

FAMILY: Married Mamie Doud, 1916; children: Dwight and John

MILITARY SERVICE: U.S. Army, 1915–48, 1950–52; supreme commander of allied expeditionary forces, 1943–45; chief of staff, 1945–48; supreme allied commander, NATO, 1950–52

CAREER: President of Columbia University, 1948–52; U.S. president, 1953–61

DATE OF DEATH: March 28, 1969

PLACE OF DEATH: Washington, D.C.

CAUSE OF DEATH: Heart failure

PLACE OF BURIAL: Abilene, Kansas

favorite. MacArthur's bid quickly fizzled; former Minnesota governor Harold Stassen generated little enthusiasm; and California governor Earl Warren ran essentially as a favorite son. Less than a year before the election, the party's eastern wing had no formal candidate. But they had a "dream" candidate, whom they—and some Democrats—had pursued since 1948, and who became the object of a concerted and unique draft campaign beginning in the summer of 1951.

General Dwight David Eisenhower was a highly attractive political figure at mid-century. Victorious military leader during World War II, he was a national hero. After the war, he resisted initial efforts to involve him in politics and, as someone with no clear partisan identification and whose only policy position supported U.S. international involvement, he represented a blank slate upon which supporters could write their hopes. A professional soldier, "Ike," as he was nicknamed, differed from earlier soldier-politi-

cians. He had achieved fame not by leading men in battle, but through planning and managing vast operations, climaxing as supreme commander of the allied forces in Europe. He had also displayed considerable personal and political skills: before World War II, he navigated the army's internecine struggle between factions linked with generals John J. Pershing and Douglas MacArthur; during the war, he worked effectively with allied generals and politicians. Finally, Eisenhower's unpretentious style, his radiant smile, and his expressed concern for soldiers portrayed a democratic military style.

After retiring from the army in 1948, he served briefly as president of Columbia University. Living in New York connected him with the Council on Foreign Relations, important business leaders, and eastern Republican politicians. In private conversations and public speeches he refined his domestic policy views, warning against expanding government, but accepting its current extent. In December 1950, Truman asked Eisenhower to be military commander of NATO. This removed him from active political involvement, but it did not end his interest or stop his growing numbers of supporters—Republican leaders like Dewey, senators James Duff (R-PA) and Henry Cabot Lodge (R-MA), old army comrades, and prominent businessmen. By October 1951, convinced that Taft threatened the nation's foreign policy, Ike privately agreed to run. He accepted a secret organization and a campaign headed by Lodge; but he insisted on responding to a draft, rather than competing openly.

The suspense eased on January 6, 1952, when Lodge announced that Ike was a Republican and entered him in the New Hampshire primary. After winning that race on March 11, he competed closely as a write-in with Stassen in Minnesota and with Taft in Nebraska. On April 11, Ike announced that he would resign from NATO on June 1. Successful in most remaining primaries (Taft won the Midwest), during June he campaigned actively across the country. Coming into the convention in Chicago on July

7, neither candidate could claim a majority. Ike had generated popular enthusiasm; but because most delegates were not chosen in primaries, and because Taft controlled the party machinery, Ike trailed in the delegate count. Taft suffered from having become more conservative, negative, and partisan during the primary campaigns, and Eisenhower supporters used public opinion polls to argue that Taft could not win.

The first, and ultimately decisive, issues for the convention involved contested delegates from Texas, Louisiana, and Georgia. In the half-century since black disfranchisement, GOP state organizations had persisted in the South mainly to obtain federal patronage; but their delegates had provided key nomination victories to party regulars. Eisenhower broke this tradition by attracting independents and Democrats to local caucuses, but Taft-dominated state committees awarded the delegates to Taft. Eisenhower forces labeled the southern decisions a "steal," using slogans like "Rob with Bob." This felt eerily reminiscent of 1912, when Taft's father had won renomination using contested delegates, and Teddy Roosevelt's followers had bolted the convention declaring "Thou Shalt Not Steal." Taft felt additionally on the defensive because he had hammered on Democratic corruption.

At the convention, Eisenhower's managers shrewdly proposed a "Fair Play" rule, prohibiting contested delegations from voting on any dispute, and won. The credentials committee gave Ike the Louisiana seats, but the climax came over Georgia. Senator Everett Dirksen (R-IL) pointed to Dewey, who was not a candidate, and said: "We followed you before and you took us down the road to defeat,"

Dwight Eisenhower flashes his famous smile at the Republican nominating convention. Ike's wife, Mamie, sports a broad smile too, as do vice presidential nominee Richard Nixon and his wife Pat. *(Brown Brothers)*

prompting competing floor demonstrations. When the convention voted to award the Georgia seats to Ike, Taft conceded the Texas delegates—and, effectively, the nomination. Those forty-seven southern delegates reversed the candidates' relative strength— and on the first nominating ballot Taft tallied 500, while Ike garnered 595, only nine votes short of victory. When Minnesota switched its votes, Ike won the nomination. Picking Senator Richard Nixon (R-CA) for vice president balanced the ticket by age, geography, and ideology, but Taft and his supporters felt bitter about his defeat.

RICHARD MILHOUS NIXON

PARTY: Republican

DATE OF BIRTH: January 9, 1913

PLACE OF BIRTH: Yorba Linda, California

PARENTS: Francis and Hannah Milhous Nixon

EDUCATION: B.S., Whittier College, 1934; J.D., Duke University Law School, 1937

FAMILY: Married Thelma Catherine "Pat" Ryan, 1940; children: Patricia and Julie

MILITARY SERVICE: Navy lieutenant, 1942–46

CAREER: Attorney, U.S. Office of Emergency Management, 1942; U.S. congressman, 1947–51; U.S. senator, 1951–53; U.S. vice president, 1953–61; unsuccessful candidate for U.S. president, 1960; unsuccessful candidate for governor of California, 1962; president, 1969–74

DATE OF DEATH: April 22, 1994

PLACE OF DEATH: New York City, New York

CAUSE OF DEATH: Stroke

PLACE OF BURIAL: Yorba Linda, California

The Democratic Contest

The Democratic Party faced different choices. Although Truman's popularity had soared after his 1948 election, it soon plummeted, falling to 26 percent by March 1951. Whatever the historical assessment of his policies or ability, Truman failed badly to gain support from the American public. For this reason, and because he had served nearly two full terms, Truman seemed unlikely to run in 1952; but controlling the party machinery allowed him to influence who became the nominee. The party suffered from a lack of obvious candidates. Too few leaders had both recognized ability and national stature. Richard Russell of Georgia, an able senator who could not be nominated because of his segregationist views, ran partly to protect southern interests. Robert Kerr (D-OK) had served only four years in the Senate, and owning an oil company made him suspect. Vice President Alben Barkley was popular and moderate, but too old at 74, while a liberal favorite, Mutual Security Director W. Averell Harriman, had never held elective office.

The earliest announced candidate, Senator Estes Kefauver (D-TN), seemed the best choice. From a politically prominent Tennessee family, elected to the House of Representatives in 1939 and the Senate in 1948, he built a liberal voting record and supported civil rights. His problem and opportunity came in 1951, when his subcommittee investigated urban political corruption. These landmark televised hearings brought him considerable popularity, but they tarnished the party. Interested in becoming president, but having angered urban leaders and President Truman, Kefauver followed an alternate path to the White House: the primaries. He based his national campaign on his large network of political friends, made through the years and sustained through Christmas cards (a strategy later copied by John F. Kennedy). In the New Hampshire primary on March 11, 1952, Kefauver beat Truman, forcing the president to announce his decision not to seek reelection. Kefauver swept nearly all the primaries; but primaries selected less than one-third of the delegates who, in three states, were unpledged by law. While these wins demonstrated his popularity, party leaders remained unmoved.

Adlai Stevenson further complicated the party's decision. Like Taft, Stevenson came from midwestern patrician stock: his grandfather and namesake had been vice president under Grover Cleveland from 1893 to 1897. A Chicago lawyer, Stevenson worked in the early New Deal as a counsel in the Agricultural Adjustment Administration. In the late 1930s, he organized support for the Allies, and between 1941 and 1946 held positions in the Navy and State

ADLAI EWING STEVENSON II

PARTY: Democratic

DATE OF BIRTH: February 5, 1900

PLACE OF BIRTH: Los Angeles, California

PARENTS: Lewis and Helen Davis Stevenson

EDUCATION: B.A., Princeton University, 1922; Harvard University Law School, 1922–24; J.D., Northwestern University Law School, 1926

FAMILY: Married Ellen Borden, 1928; divorced, 1949; children: Adlai Ewing III, Borden, and John

MILITARY SERVICE: Navy cadet, 1918

CAREER: Counsel to Agricultural Adjustment Administration, 1933–34; assistant to the secretary of the Navy, 1941–44; special assistant to the secretary of state, 1945–46; delegate to the United Nations, 1946, 1947; governor of Illinois, 1949–53; unsuccessful candidate for U.S. president, 1952, 1956; United Nations ambassador, 1961–65

DATE OF DEATH: July 15, 1965

PLACE OF DEATH: London

CAUSE OF DEATH: Heart attack

PLACE OF BURIAL: Bloomington, Illinois

Adlai E. Stevenson, the Democrats' 1952 nominee for president, is captured here at a campaign stop in Chicago. Stevenson's intellectual bent and reserve contrasted with Truman's bluntness and Eisenhower's easy-going manner. *(AP Wide World Photos)*

Departments. In 1948, the Illinois Democratic Party needed an able reform candidate and slated him for governor. After a landslide victory, Stevenson attacked corruption in the state, established a professional state police, and ran a frugal administration. In January 1952, Truman offered to support him for the nomination. Stevenson demurred, and subsequently kept his name off the primary ballots.

Stevenson's reluctance to run was real: He felt guilty about his family (he was recently divorced), he enjoyed being governor and wanted a second term, and he viewed the presidential speculation about him as a "torture chamber" and asserted that he was unfit for the job. More practical reasons also affected his calculations. Accepting Truman's offer would have made him the hand-picked candidate of an unpopular president. Furthermore, 1952 looked like a Republican year, particularly if Eisenhower ran. On the other hand, Stevenson abhorred Taft's isolationism and the GOP's assault on civil liberties, and he feared outright refusal would end his political career. Thus, he avoided primaries and did nothing to suggest that he would run; but he remained publicly visible, writing articles, giving interviews, and speaking around the nation. In late June, he said he would accept a draft, which encouraged further efforts on his behalf.

When the Democratic National Convention met in Chicago on July 21, it faced the challenge of regaining political support in the South, while still supporting civil rights. Although liberals demanded a firm loyalty commitment from southern delegations, the convention required a weaker pledge. However, when Louisiana, South Carolina, and Virginia refused even that requirement, the convention eventually abandoned the effort. Similarly, although the platform endorsed civil rights, using the language of 1948, it omitted support for a compulsory Fair Employment Practices Commission (FEPC). Stevenson's eloquent welcoming speech swelled the ranks of his supporters, and by the time balloting began on July 24 he had decided to run. On the first

Adlai Stevenson was in his first term as governor of Illinois when Democrats nominated him for president in 1952. *(Gyory Collection/Cathy Casriel Photo)*

two ballots Kefauver led, followed by Stevenson, Russell, and others. The deadlock broke on the third ballot. Support for Kefauver and Russell had peaked, and their opponents remained determined. Harriman, as he had earlier promised, now switched to Stevenson, as did other favorite-son candidates, giving the Prairie State governor the nomination. The vice presidential nod, decided by Stevenson and a group of party leaders, went to Russell's floor manager, Senator John Sparkman (D-AL), in a further effort to placate the South. A supporter of New Deal

economic issues and an interventionist foreign policy, Sparkman had defended segregation; but his Northern defenders claimed that this was simply political necessity.

The Campaign: The "Great Crusade"

The Republicans initiated a major transformation in presidential campaigns by hiring the nation's largest advertising agency—Batten, Barton, Durstine and Osborn—to prepare a campaign plan. Presented to Eisenhower and the campaign leadership in August, the plan posited the primary importance of Republican voters, indicating that Ike needed to make peace with Taft. Victory required additional votes, but the "me too" independents courted by Dewey numbered too few to make a difference. The solution involved mobilizing nonvoters, and the only way to do this was by mounting a crusade. Thus, the plan explained: "The recommended strategy is: 'Attack! Attack! Attack!'" It also recommended using television to market the personalities of the candidates.

Already, in July, Ike had sought to heal party wounds by asking to meet with Taft, but the senator remained upset. Finally, on September 12, Taft went to Ike's New York home carrying position statements on domestic and foreign policy. The nominee accepted Taft's conservative description of his domestic policy objectives, and made only limited wording changes to Taft's foreign policy statements. Ike agreed to appoint Taft supporters to government posts and, privately, to exclude Dewey. Some Republican critics labeled it the "Surrender at Morningside Heights," while Stevenson quipped, "It looks as if Taft lost the nomination but won the nominee"; Taft proceeded to campaign actively for the ticket.

In his acceptance speech, Eisenhower called for a "Great Crusade," and throughout the fall campaign he repeated his largely nonpartisan appeal for change. Short on specifics and long on general themes, his approach relied on the popular belief in his integrity and managerial abilities. He also attempted

JOHN JACKSON SPARKMAN

PARTY: Democratic

DATE OF BIRTH: December 20, 1899

PLACE OF BIRTH: Morgan County, Alabama

PARENTS: Joseph and Julia Mitchell Sparkman

EDUCATION: B.A., University of Alabama, 1921; J.D., 1923

FAMILY: Married Ivo Hall, 1923; one child: Tazwell

CAREER: U.S. House of Representatives, 1937–46 (House majority whip, 1946); U.S. Senate, 1946–79; unsuccessful candidate for U.S. vice president, 1952

DATE OF DEATH: November 16, 1985

PLACE OF DEATH: Huntsville, Alabama

PLACE OF BURIAL: Huntsville, Alabama

to eliminate issues that might cause voters to reject his candidacy. Having assured conservatives that government would not expand, he also disavowed right-wing attacks on the New Deal, promising the public that he "would not turn back the clock, ever," and declaring that programs like Social Security, workers' compensation, and unemployment insurance were "rights, not issues." To prevent farm-state defections such as had occurred in 1948, he promised 100 percent parity for agricultural price supports. To attract southern support, he endorsed state control of off-shore oil lands; and while endorsing civil rights in principle, he rejected federal enforcement.

Republicans blamed Democrats for foreign policy blunders from Yalta to Korea, and Eisenhower advocated the "liberation" of communist satellite nations by unspecified peaceful means. Eisenhower usually criticized the administration in general, rather than in specific or personal terms; but he did not repudiate senators McCarthy and William Jenner (R-IN), who had charged Marshall, Ike's friend and mentor, with treason. Nixon led the ticket's sharpest attacks, perfecting the technique of innuendo he had used effectively in his previous campaigns. He suggested taking a hatchet to the "dry rot of corruption and communism" of American politics; following a style used by Dirksen, McCarthy and Jenner, who hinted that leftists and State Department officials were homosexuals, Nixon referred to Stevenson as "sidesaddle Adlai"; and, most egregiously, he accused Stevenson of having "a Ph.D. degree from [Secretary of State Dean] Acheson's College of Cowardly Communist Containment." But the effectiveness of the generic charge of corruption—that "mess in Washington"—suddenly faltered on September 18, with the revelation that Nixon had a private "slush fund"—secret monies donated by wealthy contributors. After speculation about whether he would or should quit the race, Nixon delivered an emotional defense on television—the "Checkers" speech—which won popular support and convinced Eisenhower to keep Nixon on the ticket. (See "Handling the Scandal: Richard Nixon and the 'Checkers Speech,'" p. 824.)

Stevenson, meanwhile, faced several delicate tasks in establishing his campaign. The most difficult involved separating himself from the Truman administration, while still working with it. He began by appointing new people to run the campaign, and set up his headquarters in Springfield. In mid-August, he first referred to the "mess in Washington."

This collection of Eisenhower buttons—including one from 1948—suggests the growing importance of candidate personality in presidential races. The buttons emphasize the candidate, not his party. "I Like Ike" helped to define the politics of the 1950s. *(National Museum of American History)*

Stevenson also struggled because he held different views on certain issues. He had not opposed the Taft-Hartley labor law totally, though his criticisms increased during the campaign; nor had he favored national health insurance for the aged. Importantly, he had not supported an FEPC, although his civil rights positions grew stronger after the convention. But while advocating the need to recognize the party's past mistakes, Stevenson strongly supported the Truman administration's basic domestic and foreign policies. Most important, he emphasized the Democratic argument that the current prosperity had resulted from Democratic policies, and claimed that Republicans would produce another depression.

While more moderate than Truman, Stevenson attracted strong liberal support because of his approach to politics. In his acceptance speech, he had discussed the nation's difficult challenges and said, "Let's talk sense to the American people." He matched this call with a serious focus on issues, thoughtful and eloquent speeches, and an emphasis on idealism. Stevenson accepted, even relished, chances to speak frankly, such as endorsing civil rights and federal control of tidelands oil in the South. He also added wit to the campaign. When Ike's speaking platform in Richmond collapsed, Stevenson joked: "I've been telling him for two months that nobody could stand on that platform." When Eisenhower complained about finding humor in a serious time, he quipped that "GOP" must stand for "Grouchy Old Pessimists." Stevenson delivered intelligent speeches, but he alone chose the topics. He also found it difficult to follow basic campaign strategy and repeat the same stump speech. Some observers concluded that he spent too much time on words, and not enough engaging people.

Both campaigns traveled extensively, now made much easier because of increased air travel. In fact, all four candidates traveled more miles than had Truman in 1948 (as did Truman himself in 1952). Television offered an alternative way to present one's message, but the candidates had different degrees of success. Ike took lessons from actor Ronald Coleman and came across well, seeming good-natured and trustworthy. Stevenson resisted coaching, felt uneasy using a teleprompter, and typically failed to tailor his remarks to the amount of TV time, resulting in his being unceremoniously cut off the air. While most of Stevenson's telecasts aired in September and early October, Ike appeared up to election eve. A significant Republican campaign innovation involved the use of 60-second spot ads. Rosser Reeves distilled the campaign themes into three issues: Korea, government corruption, and the cost of living and taxes. A total of 50 scripts aired in the last three weeks in 49 key counties. Democrats criticized this as Madison Avenue hucksterism: Stevenson complained, "This isn't Ivory Soap versus Palmolive." Republicans also focused heavily on Eisenhower's personality, using the slogan "I Like Ike." Democrats countered with "You never had it so good," reflecting the general level of prosperity and the real increases in GNP of 10 percent and 8 percent in 1950 and 1951, respectively. However, inflation had also risen by 13 percent between June 1950 and January 1952, and Republicans claimed that this prosperity rested on war spending.

By late October, roughly three-fourths of the newspaper and magazine endorsements picked Eisenhower, the same proportion that had chosen Dewey in 1948. The polls also showed a clear Eisenhower lead; but spooked by the 1948 upset, and concerned about the proportion of undecided voters, many analysts predicted a close race. Ike demolished that cautious prediction with his late campaign strategy of focusing on Korea, and especially his October 24 pledge that "I shall go to Korea." With the war issue becoming increasingly important, this pledge reminded voters of Ike's primary credential for the presidency: his military experience and success. Stevenson could not counter this, and his retort of "I will go to Washington" struck many voters as inadequate and not funny.

Election Results

By 8:30 on election night, CBS learned that Eisenhower would win in a landslide. It delayed broadcasting this information because it came from UNIVAC, the first commercial computer and its first use in elections, but the machine got it right. Winning 55.2 percent of the popular vote, Eisenhower took 442 electoral votes to 89 for Stevenson, carrying every state outside the South, plus Texas, Oklahoma, Florida, Virginia, and Tennessee. Compared with 1948, the Republican candidate gained in every region—roughly 6–9 percent in states from Illinois east and north, averaging well over 20 percent in the South, and 12–15 percent in the trans-Mississippi west. Ike made major gains among midwestern farmers, Catholic suburbanites, and southerners, especially those living in cities or oil states. The class differences, so important previously, were muted (partly by Stevenson's appeal to professionals), while Stevenson remained strong among union labor, blacks, and Jews. Additionally important, voter turnout had increased significantly to 63 percent. Republicans also gained control of the House and Senate, but only by narrow margins; in most areas they ran appreciably behind Eisenhower, especially in the South.

A candidate who loses so badly might be considered weak. (Stevenson reacted with a quip from Abraham Lincoln, comparing his feelings with the boy who stubbed his toe: "Too old to cry and it hurt too much to laugh.") Stevenson's campaign certainly had flaws: notably, a poor use of media and a failure to deal effectively with campaign symbolism. But in reality, he had run a surprisingly good campaign—despite inadequate funds, being shackled by a very unpopular president, struggling to unify a highly divided party, and facing a public upset by war and corruption and believing that change was needed.

HANDLING THE SCANDAL: RICHARD NIXON AND THE "CHECKERS SPEECH"

Richard Nixon's "Checkers" speech marked a turning point in the 1952 presidential campaign, Nixon's career, and the use and power of television in politics. The "crisis" began on September 18, 1952, with reports that since his 1950 Senate election, Nixon had received secret monies totaling $18,000 donated by wealthy contributors. Within two days, an avalanche of newspapers and public figures called for Nixon to resign from the ticket. Because Republicans were so strenuously denouncing corruption in the Truman administration, and because this surprise was his first political crisis, Eisenhower offered only limited support. He suggested that Nixon "present the facts" on television, after which Ike would make a decision. Nixon felt angry at the charges and Eisenhower's attitude, while Eisenhower felt wounded and in a no-win situation, since even resignation would verify that Nixon's selection had been a mistake.

The stakes were high; but Nixon had used television before, and the campaign's ad men and television people coached him on appropriate stances and gestures. On September 23, Nixon presented his defense in a half hour of prime time bought by the Republican National Committee. Seated on a "GI bedroom den" stage setting, Nixon briefly explained that the $18,000 had been for office and political needs, not personal use, and that no favors had been asked or granted. He then presented his financial biography, mentioned his wife's "Republican cloth coat," and reported that he had received one personal gift, a cocker spaniel that his daughters named "Checkers." And he announced that "regardless of what they say about it, we're gonna keep it." In the final ten minutes, Nixon demanded that the Democratic candidates reveal their finances. He claimed that the story was a smear perpetrated by supporters of Alger Hiss to stop him, and he urged support for Eisenhower. He ended by asking people to send their views to the GOP National Committee.

The extraordinary performance was witnessed by a huge audience of 60 million people—virtually two-fifths of the American public. Nixon's story had been accurate, as far as it went, but he had obscured key facts: that he had received money since 1946, that it came from a few wealthy contributors, that contributions had been requested to support him as a spokesman for free enterprise, and that Nixon had supported the interests of many contributors. While some people viewed Nixon's televised autobiography as maudlin soap opera (one observer quipped that it lacked only Checkers licking his face), his performance and emotional appeal touched many Americans. His surprise request that messages be sent to the party brought floods of telegrams and phone calls, and forced Eisenhower to keep Nixon on the ticket.

This incident created lasting distrust between the two men. More important, it demonstrated that television enabled politicians to appeal directly to the public and avoid difficult questions. And Richard Nixon, embittered by the crisis yet emboldened by the result, developed a reliance on television and a disdain for print journalists that would shape his remaining career.

Moreover, he essentially agreed with his opponent on what he considered the most vital issue: American participation in Europe. While Truman had believed that a class appeal could still work, the Depression was over and Democrats increasingly needed a stronger appeal to middle-class and educated voters. Stevenson's blend of issues and his style began that transition.

Ultimately, the election was Eisenhower's to lose. The most popular living American at mid-century, he impressed people who met him and those who saw him on television. His campaign effectively focused on his personality, not his party. He calmed fears about his being a conservative or endangering prosperity by accepting existing New Deal programs. Conservative Republicans hoped they could convert or control him—and they were desperate to win. But the key factor was Korea. Ike's campaign made this issue increasingly important: By late October, 52 percent of the voters considered it the top issue and, given Ike's military reputation, his promise to go to Korea clinched the election.

Philip R. VanderMeer

Bibliography

Ambrose, Stephen E. *Eisenhower*, vol. 1: "Soldier, General of the Army, President-Elect, 1890–1952." New York: Simon and Schuster, 1983.

Baker, Jean H. *The Stevensons: A Biography of an American Family.* New York: W. W. Norton, 1996.

Gorman, Joseph. *Kefauver: A Political Biography.* New York: Oxford University Press, 1971.

Greene, John Robert. *The Crusade: The Presidential Election of 1952.* Lanham, MD: University Press of America, 1985.

Martin, John Bartlow. *Adlai Stevenson of Illinois: The Life of Adlai E. Stevenson.* Garden City, NY: Doubleday, 1976.

Morris, Roger. *Richard Milhous Nixon: The Rise of an American Politician.* New York: Henry Holt, 1990.

Parmet, Herbert S. *Eisenhower and the American Crusades.* New York: Macmillan, 1972.

Patterson, James. *Mr. Republican: A Biography of Robert A. Taft.* Boston: Houghton Mifflin, 1972.

Pickett, William B. *Eisenhower Decides to Run: Presidential Politics and Cold War Strategy.* Chicago: Ivan R. Dee, 2000.

THE VOTE: ELECTION OF 1952

State	Total No. of Electors	Total Popular Vote	Electoral Vote R	Electoral Vote D	Margin of Victory Votes	Margin of Victory % Total Vote	Eisenhower Republican Vote	Eisenhower Republican %	Stevenson Democrat Votes	Stevenson Democrat %	Others Votes	Others %
Alabama	11	426,120		11	125,844	29.5%	149,231	35.0%	275,075	64.6%	1,814	0.4%
Arizona	4	260,570	4		43,514	16.7%	152,042	58.3%	108,528	41.7%	0	0.0%
Arkansas	8	404,800		8	49,145	12.1%	177,155	43.8%	226,300	55.9%	1,345	0.3%
California	32	5,341,603	32		777,941	14.6%	3,035,587	56.8%	2,257,646	42.3%	48,370	0.9%
Colorado	6	630,103	6		134,278	21.3%	379,782	60.3%	245,504	39.0%	4,817	0.8%
Connecticut	8	1,096,911	8		129,363	11.8%	611,012	55.7%	481,649	43.9%	4,250	0.4%
Delaware	3	174,025	3		6,744	3.9%	90,059	51.8%	83,315	47.9%	651	0.4%
Florida	10	989,337	10		99,086	10.0%	544,036	55.0%	444,950	45.0%	351	0.0%
Georgia	12	655,803		12	257,844	39.3%	198,979	30.3%	456,823	69.7%	1	0.0%
Idaho	4	276,231	4		85,626	31.0%	180,707	65.4%	95,081	34.4%	443	0.2%
Illinois	27	4,481,058	27		443,407	9.9%	2,457,327	54.8%	2,013,920	44.9%	9,811	0.2%
Indiana	13	1,955,325	13		334,729	17.1%	1,136,259	58.1%	801,530	41.0%	17,536	0.9%
Iowa	10	1,268,773	10		357,393	28.2%	808,906	63.8%	451,513	35.6%	8,354	0.7%
Kansas	8	896,166	8		343,006	38.3%	616,302	68.8%	273,296	30.5%	6,568	0.7%
Kentucky	10	993,148		10	700	0.1%	495,029	49.8%	495,729	49.9%	2,390	0.2%
Louisiana	10	651,952		10	38,102	5.8%	306,925	47.1%	345,027	52.9%	0	0.0%
Maine	5	351,786	5		113,547	32.3%	232,353	66.0%	118,806	33.8%	627	0.2%
Maryland	9	902,074	9		104,087	11.5%	499,424	55.4%	395,337	43.8%	7,313	0.8%
Massachusetts	16	2,383,398	16		208,800	8.8%	1,292,325	54.2%	1,083,525	45.5%	7,548	0.3%
Michigan	20	2,798,592	20		320,872	11.5%	1,551,529	55.4%	1,230,657	44.0%	16,406	0.6%
Minnesota	11	1,379,483	11		154,753	11.2%	763,211	55.3%	608,458	44.1%	7,814	0.6%
Mississippi	8	285,532		8	59,600	20.9%	112,966	39.6%	172,566	60.4%	0	0.0%
Missouri	13	1,892,062	13		29,599	1.6%	959,429	50.7%	929,830	49.1%	2,803	0.1%
Montana	4	265,037	4		51,181	19.3%	157,394	59.4%	106,213	40.1%	1,430	0.5%
Nebraska	6	609,660	6		233,546	38.3%	421,603	69.2%	188,057	30.8%	0	0.0%
Nevada	3	82,190	3		18,814	22.9%	50,502	61.4%	31,688	38.6%	0	0.0%
New Hampshire	4	272,950	4		59,624	21.8%	166,287	60.9%	106,663	39.1%	0	0.0%
New Jersey	16	2,418,554	16		357,711	14.8%	1,373,613	56.8%	1,015,902	42.0%	29,039	1.2%
New Mexico	4	238,608	4		26,509	11.1%	132,170	55.4%	105,661	44.3%	777	0.3%
New York	45	7,128,241	45		848,214	11.9%	3,952,815	55.5%	3,104,601	43.6%	70,825	1.0%
North Carolina	14	1,210,910		14	94,696	7.8%	558,107	46.1%	652,803	53.9%	0	0.0%
North Dakota	4	270,127	4		115,018	42.6%	191,712	71.0%	76,694	28.4%	1,721	0.6%
Ohio	25	3,700,758	25		500,024	13.5%	2,100,391	56.8%	1,600,367	43.2%	0	0.0%
Oklahoma	8	948,984	8		87,106	9.2%	518,045	54.6%	430,939	45.4%	0	0.0%
Oregon	6	695,059	6		150,236	21.6%	420,815	60.5%	270,579	38.9%	3,665	0.5%
Pennsylvania	32	4,580,969	32		269,520	5.9%	2,415,789	52.7%	2,146,269	46.9%	18,911	0.4%
Rhode Island	4	414,498	4		7,642	1.8%	210,935	50.9%	203,293	49.0%	270	0.1%
South Carolina	8	341,086		8	4,922	1.4%	168,082	49.3%	173,004	50.7%	0	0.0%
South Dakota	4	294,283	4		113,431	38.5%	203,857	69.3%	90,426	30.7%	0	0.0%
Tennessee	11	892,553	11		2,437	0.3%	446,147	50.0%	443,710	49.7%	2,696	0.3%
Texas	24	2,075,946	24		133,650	6.4%	1,102,878	53.1%	969,228	46.7%	3,840	0.2%
Utah	4	329,554	4		58,826	17.9%	194,190	58.9%	135,364	41.1%	0	0.0%
Vermont	3	153,557	3		66,362	43.2%	109,717	71.5%	43,355	28.2%	485	0.3%
Virginia	12	619,689	12		80,360	13.0%	349,037	56.3%	268,677	43.4%	1,975	0.3%
Washington	9	1,102,708	9		106,262	9.6%	599,107	54.3%	492,845	44.7%	10,756	1.0%
West Virginia	8	873,548		8	33,608	3.8%	419,970	48.1%	453,578	51.9%	0	0.0%
Wisconsin	12	1,607,370	12		357,569	22.2%	979,744	61.0%	622,175	38.7%	5,451	0.3%
Wyoming	3	129,251	3		33,113	25.6%	81,047	62.7%	47,934	37.1%	270	0.2%
TOTAL	531	61,750,942	442	89	6,699,439	10.8%	34,074,529	55.2%	27,375,090	44.3%	301,323	0.5%

For sources, see p. 1128.

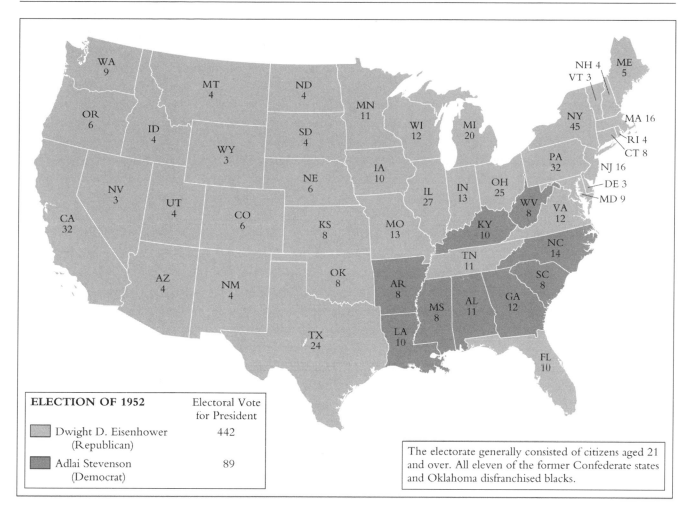

ELECTION OF 1952

Electoral Vote for President

Dwight D. Eisenhower (Republican) — 442

Adlai Stevenson (Democrat) — 89

The electorate generally consisted of citizens aged 21 and over. All eleven of the former Confederate states and Oklahoma disfranchised blacks.

DOCUMENTS: ELECTION OF 1952

After twenty years of Democratic dominance of the White House, the Republicans were finally able to regain the presidency in 1952. World War II hero Dwight D. Eisenhower, popularly known as "Ike," earned the Republican nomination after a bitter struggle with the party leadership. Meanwhile, President Truman chose to step down. Both Truman and the Korean War, which had broken out in 1950, were unpopular, making it unlikely that the president could win reelection. The Democratic nomination went to the witty and urbane Illinois governor, Adlai Stevenson, on the second ballot. Stevenson epitomized his party's liberal beliefs and had domestic and foreign policy experience, having worked for the New Deal's Agricultural Adjustment Administration in the 1930s and having helped create the United Nations in the 1940s.

Despite General Eisenhower's showing in the primaries, conservative Senator Robert A. Taft of Ohio, son of the former president, arrived at the Republican convention as the favorite for the nomination. The nomination of Eisenhower disappointed conservatives and threatened party unity. In his public statement, Document 1, Taft brought Republicans together by offering his support to General Eisenhower, assuring the conservative wing of the GOP that "Ike" was no "left-winger." Taft also promised to take an active part in the campaign.

Soon thereafter, another controversy shook the Republican Party. Eisenhower selected a young senator, Richard M. Nixon of California, as his running mate. A story broke that Nixon had taken money from supporters and was living well beyond his means. In an effort to salvage his political career, Nixon addressed a national television audience with his famous "Checkers" speech, Document 2. He denied any improprieties and pointed to a humble lifestyle as proof—stressing that his wife Pat had "a respectable Republican cloth coat," not a mink, alluding to a scandal in the Truman administration. The only gift he admitted receiving was his daughters' dog "Checkers," something he refused to give back.

Eisenhower campaigned to his perceived strengths—military and foreign policy. In Document 3, he urged Americans not to fear the Soviets. He believed that fear was the long-term goal of communist aggression, to upset worldwide economies and the normal flow of daily life. Communism would be stopped, but only if Americans would "abolish fear and build confidence." One Eisenhower speech, Document 4, in which he addressed the Korean War, proved to be the most memorable of the campaign. While criticizing Truman's mismanagement of the war, the former general pledged an "early and honorable" end to the conflict, even if it meant traveling there himself in an effort to hasten its conclusion.

In Document 5, excerpts from four of his campaign speeches, Stevenson addressed an array of domestic and foreign policy issues. He affirmed his faith in Truman's policies in Korea and in keeping the Soviet threat in check, and spoke out for patriotism and tolerance—in opposition to the aggressive anticommunism of Senator Joseph McCarthy of Wisconsin. In regard to civil rights, he conceded that many observers had misunderstood race relations in the South, but came out in favor of racial equality. Finally, he attacked his opponent for suggesting simple and confusing solutions to complex issues. In the end, however, Eisenhower's broad popularity earned the former general an electoral landslide.

Document 1

Statement by Senator Robert A. Taft, New York, September 12, 1952

I have felt, therefore, that I could be far more effective in the campaign if I could state to the people, after talking with General Eisenhower, my definite convictions regarding the character of his administration when he is elected, and the principles by which it will be guided. . . .

As I see it, there is and has been one great fundamental issue between the Republican party, and the New Deal or Fair Deal or Stevenson Deal. It is the issue of liberty against the creeping socialization in every domestic field. Liberty was the foundation of our Government, the reason for our growth, the basis of our happiness and the hope of our future. The greatest threat to liberty today is internal, from the constant growth of big Government, through the constantly increasing power and spending of the Federal Government. The price of continued liberty, including a free economic system, is the reduction of Federal spending and taxes, the repudiation of arbitrary powers in the Executive, claimed to be derived from Heaven, and the stand against statutory extension of power by the creation and extension of Federal bureaus.

The protection of the people against any arbitrary excessive power, which may be developed by big business or big labor or other pressure groups, is also essential. I recognize that some Federal Government action is necessary simply to protect liberty in our complicated modern life, but our left-wing thinkers believe that only government can solve our problems, and they present project after project, each one with plausible arguments, but all meaning a constant growth of the Federal Government.

Today, we are up against the guns. Government is taking one-third of the people's income and thereby one-third of their freedom. I wished to be sure that the new administration will be inspired with the philosophy of extending liberty before I entered into an extensive speaking campaign.

After a satisfactory discussion with General Eisenhower this morning for two hours, I am satisfied that that is his philosophy. I am convinced that he will carry out the pledges of the Republican platform. . . .

I am completely satisfied that General Eisenhower will give this country an administration inspired by the Republican principle of continued and expanding liberty for all, as against the continued growth of New Deal socialism which we would suffer under Governor Stevenson, representative of the left-wingers, if not a left-winger himself.

I urge all Americans, and particularly those who have confidence in my judgment and my principles, to vote for Eisenhower and Nixon, for all the Republican senatorial candidates and all the Republican House candidates, and to do everything possible to bring many others to the polls to do the same. I shall be glad to speak on a national broadcast or at any point throughout the country to the extent of my ability.

I believe General Eisenhower will be elected. A campaign based on the American principles in which he and I believe can arouse the enthusiasm of the people, and if that enthusiasm is properly organized we can bring to the polls 8,000,000 more voters than have ever voted the Republican ticket before. That is a sure program for success.

Source: New York Times, September 13, 1952.

Document 2

"Checkers" Speech by Senator Richard M. Nixon, Los Angeles, September 23, 1952

My fellow Americans:

I come before you tonight as a candidate for the Vice Presidency and as a man whose honesty and integrity have been questioned. Now, the usual political thing to do when charges are made against you is to either ignore them or to deny them without giving details.

I believe we've had enough of that in the United States, particularly with the present administration in Washington, D.C. To me the office of the Vice Presidency of the United States is a great office, and I feel that the people have got to have confidence in the integrity of the men who run for that office and who might obtain it. I have a theory, too, that the best and only answer to a smear or to an honest misunderstanding of the facts is to tell the truth, and that is why I'm here tonight. I want to tell you my side of the case.

I am sure that you have read the charge and you've heard it, that I, Senator Nixon, took $18,000 from a group of my supporters. Now, was that wrong? And let me say that it was wrong—I'm saying, incidentally, that it was wrong, not just illegal (because it isn't a question of whether it was legal or illegal; that isn't enough; the question is, was it morally wrong?)—I say that it was morally wrong if any of that $18,000 went to Senator Nixon for my personal use; I say that it was morally wrong if it was secretly given and secretly handled; and I say that it was morally wrong if any of the contributors got special favors for the contributions that they made.

And now to answer those questions let me say this: Not one cent of the $18,000, or any other money of that type, ever went to me for my personal use. Every penny of it was used to pay for political expenses that I did not think should be charged to the taxpayers of the United States. . . .

. . . But there are other expenses which are not covered by the Government; . . . .

Well, then the question arises: You say, "Well, how do you pay for those and how can you do it legally?"

There are several ways that it can be done, incidentally, that it is done legally in the United States Senate and in the Congress.

The first way is to be a rich man. I don't happen to be a rich man, so I couldn't use that.

Another way that is used is to put your wife on the payroll. Let me say, incidentally, that my opponent, my opposite number for the Vice Presidency on the Democratic ticket does have his wife on the payroll, and has had her on his payroll for the past ten years.

Now, just let me say this: That's his business and I'm not critical of him for doing that. You will have to pass judgment on that particular point. But I have never done that, for this reason: I have found that there are so many deserving stenographers and secretaries in Washington that needed to work that I just didn't feel it was right to put my wife on the payroll.

My wife is sitting over here. She's a wonderful stenographer. She used to teach stenography and she used to teach shorthand in high school. That was where I met her. And I can tell you folks that she has worked many hours at night and many hours on Saturdays and Sundays in my office, and she has done a fine job; and I am proud to say tonight that in the six years I have been in the House and the Senate of the United States, Pat Nixon has never been on the Government payroll. . . .

Let me say this, incidentally, that some of you may say, well, that's all right, Senator, that's your explanation, but have you got any proof?

And I would like to tell you this evening that just about an hour ago we received an independent audit of this entire fund. . . .

I should say this, that Pat doesn't have a mink coat, but she does have a respectable Republican cloth coat; and I always tell her that she'd look good in anything.

One other thing I probably should tell you, because if I don't they'll probably be saying this about me, too. We did get something, a gift, after the election. A man down in Texas heard Pat on the radio mention the fact that our two youngsters would like to have a dog; and, believe it or not, the day before we left on this campaign trip we got a message from Union Station in Baltimore saying they had a package for us.

We went down to get it. You know what it was? It was a little Cocker Spaniel dog in a crate, that he'd sent all the way from Texas; black and white spotted, and our little girl, Tricia, the 6-year-old, named it "Checkers." And, you know, the kids, like all kids, love the dog; and I just want to say this right now, that regardless of what they say about it, we are going to keep him. . . .

And now finally I know that you wonder whether or not I am going to stay on the Republican ticket or resign.

Let me say this: I don't believe that I ought to quit, because I'm not a quitter. And, incidentally, Pat is not a quitter. After all, her name was Patricia Ryan, and she was born on St. Patrick's Day—and you know the Irish never quit. . . .

Source: The Richard Nixon Library & Birthplace, Yorba Linda, California.

Document 3

Speech by General Dwight D. Eisenhower, New York, August 25, 1952

Here may I pay tribute to the American Legion for its unending, effective efforts to uproot subversion, communism from wherever it finds it in our country, and to stay on that job until it is done. And may I say you have done your work without recklessly injuring the reputations of innocent people. May I at this moment enlist with you for the duration in the great cause you have set yourselves.

Now in order to obtain their objectives, Stalin has said that there may have to be another international war unless the free nations, including America, become so convinced of the hopelessness of the struggle that they will surrender. Now is there anyone who thinks that America ever quits? Does anyone here think that America will ever surrender to that kind of threat or talk? And Stalin knows just that. Therefore I say we are in great peril because, knowing that, he is proceeding with the mobilization of the world he controls to do anything—anything—that the Kremlin finds necessary in order to subdue us.

Now Moscow is not going to make the mistake that Nazi Germany and Imperial Japan made. They were supported when they entered the war only by fractional economies. Stalin will never attack until he is certain that there has been gathered under the iron fist of the Kremlin that amount of material, human, organized military strength that he believes will bring ultimate victory.

The Nazis and the Japanese had to win instantly or not at all. But he will attack when he thinks he has a sufficient portion of the world economy in order to sustain a long and exhaustive struggle. He will never do it before then unless that war comes about by accident of the powder-keg variety.

All this means that we have some time because they do not feel ready yet to challenge in this final fashion. But it means also that to this threat we must at once find the right answer. So long as menace hangs over our heads, our peril circumscribes our industrial goal. Our agricultural program, our fiscal policies, our very attitudes are covered by this great threat.

Now fear is a climate that nourishes bankruptcy in dollars and morals alike. Those afraid seek security in a heedless extravagance that breeds waste of substance and corruption of men. Now if fear is long endured, it wastes away material resources as well as our lives. In a climate of fear long endured, we can find the death rattle of a nation.

We have no time for complacency; but I assure you, ladies and gentlemen, there is also no cause for fear.

A hundred and fifty-five million united Americans are still the greatest temporal force in the world. We must have a policy that we can understand and support with confidence. And we must not abate our efforts until we have banished from the free world that last probability of Communist aggression.

The course to peace is the establishment of conditions that will abolish fear and build confidence. . . .

First, let us tolerate nobody in our whole society who attempts to weaken and destroy the American constitutional system. . . .

Second, let us once and for all resolve that henceforth we shall be guided in our relations with our fellows by the American creed that all men are created equal and remain equal. . . .

Third, let us in every way that each of us can fight the economic inequities that still survive in our great productive system. . . .

Fourth, let us end corruption in public office at every level of government. . . .

Source: New York Times, August 26, 1952.

Document 4

Speech by General Dwight D. Eisenhower Regarding the Korean War

In this anxious autumn for America, one fact looms above all others in our people's mind. One tragedy challenges all men dedicated to the work of peace. One word shouts denial to those who foolishly pretend that ours is not a nation at war.

This fact, this tragedy, this word is: Korea.

A small country, Korea has been, for more than two years, the battleground for the costliest foreign war our nation has fought, excepting the two world wars. It has been the burial ground for 20,000 American dead. It has been another historic field of honor for the valor and skill and tenacity of American soldiers.

All these things it has been—and yet one thing more. It has been a symbol—a telling symbol—of the foreign policy of our nation.

It has been a sign—a warning sign—of the way the Administration has conducted our world affairs.

It has been a measure—a damning measure—of the quality of leadership we have been given.

Tonight I am going to talk about our foreign policy and of its supreme symbol—the Korean war. I am not going to give you elaborate generalizations—but hard, tough facts. I am going to state the unvarnished truth.

What, then, are the plain facts?

The biggest fact about the Korean war is this: It was never inevitable, it was never inescapable, no fantastic fiat of history decreed that little South Korea—in the summer of 1950—would fatally tempt Communist aggressors as their easiest victim. No demonic destiny decreed that

America had to be bled this way in order to keep South Korea free and to keep freedom itself self-respecting.

We are not mute prisoners of history. That is a doctrine for totalitarians, it is no creed for free men.

There is a Korean war—and we are fighting it—for the simplest of reasons: Because free leadership failed to check and to turn back Communist ambition before it savagely attacked us. The Korean war—more perhaps than any other war in history—simply and swiftly followed the collapse of our political defenses. There is no other reason than this: We failed to read and to outwit the totalitarian mind.

I know something of this totalitarian mind. Through the years of World War II, I carried a heavy burden of decision in the free world's crusade against the tyranny then threatening us all. Month after month, year after year, I had to search out and to weigh the strengths and weaknesses of an enemy driven by the lust to rule the great globe itself.

World War II should have taught us all one lesson. The lesson is this: To vacillate, to hesitate—to appease even by merely betraying unsteady purpose—is to feed a dictator's appetite for conquest and to invite war itself.

That lesson—which should have firmly guided every great decision of our leadership through these later years—was ignored in the development of the Administration's policies for Asia since the end of World War II. Because it was ignored, the record of these policies is a record of appalling failure. . . .

The first task of a new Administration will be to review and re-examine every course of action open to us with one goal in view: To bring the Korean war to an early and honorable end. This is my pledge to the American people.

For this task a wholly new Administration is necessary. The reason for this is simple. The old Administration cannot be expected to repair what it failed to prevent.

Where will a new Administration begin?

It will begin with its President taking a simple, firm resolution. That resolution will be: To forego the diversions of politics and to concentrate on the job of ending the Korean war—until that job is honorably done.

That job requires a personal trip to Korea.

I shall make that trip. Only in that way could I learn how best to serve the American people in the cause of peace.

I shall go to Korea. . . .

Source: "Eisenhower Speech," New York Times, October 25, 1952.

Document 5
Excerpts from Adlai E. Stevenson's Campaign Speeches, 1952

To the New York-American Legion Convention, August 27, 1952

We talk a great deal about patriotism. What do we mean by patriotism in the context of our times? . . .

Patriotism, I have said, means putting country before self. This is no abstract phrase, and unhappily, we find some things in American life today of which we cannot be proud. . . .

True patriotism, it seems to me, is based on tolerance and a large measure of humility.

There are men among us who use "patriotism" as a club for attacking other Americans. What can we say for the self-styled patriot who thinks that a Negro, a Jew, a Catholic, or a Japanese-American is less an American than he? That betrays the deepest article of our faith, the belief in individual liberty and equality which has always been the heart and soul of the American idea.

What can we say for the man who proclaims himself a patriot—and then for political or personal reasons attacks the patriotism of faithful public servants? I give you, as a shocking example, the attacks which have been made on the loyalty and the motives of our great wartime Chief of Staff, General Marshall. To me this is the type of "patriotism" which is, in Dr. Johnson's phrase, "the last refuge of scoundrels.". . .

Men who have offered their lives for their country know that patriotism is not the *fear* of something; it is the *love* of something. Patriotism with us is not the hatred of Russia; it is the love of this Republic and of the ideal of liberty of man and mind in which it was born, and to which this Republic is dedicated.

With this patriotism—patriotism in its large and wholesome meaning—America can master its power and turn it to the noble cause of peace. We can maintain military power without militarism; political power without oppression; and moral power without compulsion or complacency. . . .

Albuquerque, September 12, 1952

We have already checked Soviet aggression and perhaps saved the world from a third world war. The Truman Doctrine, the Marshall Plan and the North Atlantic Pact have restrained Soviet power in Europe. Our resistance in Korea has checked Soviet aggression in Asia. If we had let Europe fall to the Soviet, if we had acquiesced in aggression in Asia, the Soviet Union would have been emboldened into rasher and rasher adventures. By the time it occurred to the Old Guard of the Republican Party that resistance was necessary, we would have been isolated, a beleaguered garrison state in a Soviet-dominated world. . . .

Richmond, Virginia, September 20, 1952

First, I utterly reject the argument that we ought to grant all men their rights just because, if we do not, we shall give Soviet Russia a propaganda weapon. This concept is itself tainted with communist wiliness. It insultingly implies that, were it not for the communists, we would not do what is right.

The answer to this argument is that we must do right for right's sake alone. I, for one, do not propose to adjust my ethics to the values of a bloodstained despotism, scornful of all that we hold dear.

Second, I reject as equally contemptible the reckless assertions that the South is a prison in which half the people are prisoners and the other half are wardens. I view with scorn those who hurl charges that the South—or any group of Americans—is wedded to wrong and incapable of right. For this itself is an expression of prejudice compounded with hatred, a poisonous doctrine for which, I hope, there will never be room in our country.

So long as man remains a little lower than the angels, I suppose that human character will never free itself entirely from the blemish of prejudice, religious or racial. These are prejudices, unhappily, that tend to rise wherever the minority in question is large, running here against one group and there against another. Some forget this, and, in talking of the South, forget that in the South the minority is high. Some forget, too, or don't know about strides the South has made in the past decade toward equal treatment.

But I do not attempt to justify the unjustifiable, whether it is anti-Negroism in one place, anti-Semitism in another—or for that matter, anti-Southernism in many places. . . .

New York, October 31, 1952

This new proposal is simplicity itself. "Elect me President," the General says, "and you can forget about Korea; I will go there personally." I don't think for a moment that the American people are taken in by a promise without a program. It is not enough to say, "I will fix it for you." The principle of blind leadership is alien to our tradition. And, unfortunately, the ghost writer who provided the proposal failed to give it content. The General was to go to Korea, but nobody indicated what he should do when he got there. The American people were quick to realize also that the conduct of a military campaign is the task of a field commander, whereas the making of peace requires negotiation with the central adversary—and in this case the central adversary is in Moscow, not in Korea. . . .

Sources: Walter Johnson, ed., *The Papers of Adlai Stevenson, 1952–1955*, vol. 4 (Boston: Little, Brown, 1974); *New York Times,* September 13, 1952; *New York Times,* November 1, 1952.

THE ELECTION OF 1956

The presidential election of 1956 caught voters in an optimistic mood. For the first time in American history, a healthy majority of American families could be considered middle class. A mass consumer economy featuring "luxury goods at popular prices" became increasingly prevalent, owing to technological innovations, cheap imports, and declining inflation. The nation's birthrate reached a new high in 1956, symptomatic of citizens' sense of well-being. "Rarely in American history," one observer noted, "has the craving for tranquility and moderation commanded more public support." It was a good time to be an incumbent, and even better if you were President Dwight D. Eisenhower (see fact box, p. 817). Presiding over a prosperous nation at peace, Eisenhower's main task in 1956 lay in reassuring voters that his health was robust enough to withstand another four years in the White House pressure cooker.

Eisenhower's Middle Way

Eisenhower's 1952 victory over Democrat Adlai Stevenson (see fact box, p. 820) had reflected not only the Republican candidate's personal appeal but also the voters' desires to put the brakes on ever-expanding federal government. Eisenhower hit resonant notes in the campaign by attacking cronyism, ethical lapses, and fiscal mismanagement in the administration of President Harry Truman. "Ike," as he was called, promised to set things right by ending the Korean War on honorable terms, reigning in military spending, and balancing budgets. In an election that

witnessed a remarkable 26 percent rise in turnout, voters gave Eisenhower a decisive victory over Stevenson, and the Republicans control of Congress.

Often dismissed by critics as politically naive and intellectually lazy, Eisenhower in fact was neither. As author Michael Barone has observed, Eisenhower may have been "the best prepared president of the twentieth century." He knew the great leaders of the western world intimately, was familiar with congressional operations, understood budgets, and was a master at managing people. Never a rabid partisan, Eisenhower nonetheless put his stamp on the government, championing a "middle way" between laissez-faire reaction and creeping socialism. In his first term, Eisenhower was able to exert more control over military budgets and operations than any other twentieth-century president. He achieved major economies through adoption of the "New Look" defense strategy, with its emphasis on technology rather than large armies—"more bang for the buck," as the administration put it. Some of the savings went to expand Social Security coverage and benefits. Between 1953 and 1956, Ike tightened internal security, reduced taxes, raised the minimum wage from seventy-five cents to one dollar per hour, and launched the St. Lawrence Seaway and the interstate highway construction programs. He also took modest, but not insignificant, steps to enhance the rights and opportunities of African Americans—for example, by integrating military bases and public places in Washington, D.C. Eisenhower had accomplished these goals despite the fact that Republicans controlled Congress by a whisker-thin margin during

833

CHRONOLOGY

1955

SEPTEMBER 24   President Eisenhower suffers a heart attack while vacationing in Denver, Colorado.

NOVEMBER 15   Adlai Stevenson announces he will again seek the Democratic presidential nomination.

1956

FEBRUARY 29   Eisenhower announces that he will seek reelection.

JUNE 7   Eisenhower suffers an ilietis attack requiring emergency surgery, prompting speculation that he might retire.

AUGUST 11   Stevenson clinches the Democratic nomination on the first ballot.

AUGUST 22   Republicans renominate Eisenhower and Nixon in San Francisco.

OCTOBER 23   After a popular uprising ousts a communist regime, Hungarians install Imre Nagy as premier.

OCTOBER 29   Israel invades the Sinai Peninsula.

NOVEMBER 4   Soviet tanks roll into Budapest to put down the Hungarian Revolution.

NOVEMBER 5   British and French paratroopers land near the Suez Canal, deepening the Suez Crisis.

NOVEMBER 6   Eisenhower defeats Stevenson to win reelection as president.

1957

JANUARY 20   Eisenhower inaugurated for second term as president.

the 83d Congress (1953–54), and he had to contend with Democratic majorities during the 84th Congress (1955–56). Ike's cordial relations with the Democratic leadership worked to his advantage. Only in his farm policy—for example, in failing to make good on promises to revise the New Deal/Fair Deal price support system—did Eisenhower's administration noticeably stumble.

Following the censure of communist-hunting Senator Joseph R. McCarthy in December 1954 (for which the administration could claim at least partial credit), the country seemed to breathe easier. This was the real beginning of the "Ike Age." Class distinctions eased—partly because of the national consensus about the Cold War, and partly because working-class Americans (especially union members) were making enough money to live middle-class lives. No longer did that car in the driveway necessarily tell a story about the color of the collar a breadwinner wore. Not surprisingly, in an environment of material improvement that people could not fail to notice, Americans were optimistic about their prospects and happy with their president. According to the Gallup Poll, during

his first term Eisenhower's support never dipped below 57 percent approval, even during a brief recession in 1953–54.

Eisenhower's greatest frustration during his first term had been the obstinacy of a cadre of ultraconservative legislators in his own party, of whom Senator McCarthy was the most crude and reactionary. In addition to McCarthy, roughly a dozen Republican senators and several dozen representatives regularly opposed Eisenhower's moderate program. It was Eisenhower's often-expressed hope that the GOP could be remolded in his image as a forward-looking, "modern" party that would earn the loyalty of a majority of voters over the long term. By 1955, it was evident to Eisenhower that this goal was not realistic if he did not run again.

The Health Issue Clouds Republican Hopes

At age sixty-two when he entered the White House, Eisenhower was older than any first-term president

The slogan "I Like Ike" is given public display in this photograph of two supporters hugging an Eisenhower campaign poster after hearing he would seek reelection in 1956. *(AP Wide World Photos)*

since Zachary Taylor. Few voters cared much about Ike's age or work habits, or his delegation of authority to trusted aides. Americans believed their president was entitled to relaxation (golf, bridge, and long working vacations); nor did the country seem to suffer because Ike did not keep a punishing schedule or press Congress with a long list of proposals for new government programs. Nonetheless, in the autumn of 1955, Ike's health became a major concern. While vacationing in Denver, Colorado, in late September, Ike suffered a serious heart attack that sidelined him for almost four months. No crises marked the months of Eisenhower's recuperation; but the question remained: Would Ike's health permit him to run again? Would he even be willing to take on the burdens of the presidency for another four years? That topic was repeatedly mentioned in the press through the autumn of 1955 and early winter of 1956.

Ike's first preference was to step down after one term and return to his Gettysburg farm. But he remained the party's indispensable leader. At a secret White House meeting on January 13, 1956 the president's chief advisers ticked off the main reasons why

he should run again. Only his brother Milton suggested that Ike could declare that he had achieved his goals, and earned retirement in Gettysburg. Eisenhower himself gradually came to the reluctant, but firm, conviction that he was not only the best man for the job, but the best bet the Republicans had to retain the White House in 1956. He needed only a positive medical report from his heart doctor, Dr. Paul Dudley White—which arrived on his desk in mid-February—to make an affirmative decision about another campaign. As he put it when announcing his decision on February 29, "Most presidents in good health have sought, or at least made themselves available, for a second term." Besides, as Ike noted in a press conference that same day, his agenda was unfinished and he wanted to get on with the job. Eisenhower's announcement lifted Republican spirits and dashed the hopes of the most partisan Democrats.

Nixon on Tenterhooks

Weeks before Eisenhower's announcement of his reelection plans, the president had engaged his vice president in a conversation that profoundly unsettled the younger man. On December 26, 1955, Eisenhower spoke privately with Richard Nixon (see fact box, p. 819) about the vice president's options in a second Eisenhower administration. He did so mainly, Eisenhower asserted in his memoirs, to help Nixon envision alternative paths he might take to the presidency. Observing that Nixon had not been able to accumulate much executive experience as vice president, Ike advised Nixon to consider other options, such as a cabinet post like Commerce or Defense. Eisenhower wanted Nixon, as he put it in a March 7 press conference, to "chart his own course."

Nixon saw things differently. Knowing full well that the press would interpret any change in status as a demotion, he was dumbfounded by the president's counsel. For several months Nixon agonized, wondering whether Eisenhower, and perhaps a liberal "palace guard" in the White House, wanted him out of the vice presidency. "I couldn't be certain whether the President really preferred me off the ticket or sincerely believed a cabinet post could better further my career," Nixon recalled in his memoir, *Six Crises*. Nixon never seriously considered leaving the ticket. Instead, he encouraged Republican operatives to rally public opinion on his behalf. For example, conservative Senator Styles Bridges (R-NH) orchestrated a vice presidential write-in campaign for Nixon in the first primary state, New Hampshire, with impressive results. Republican pundits and party officials throughout the country raised the Nixon standard, and threatened internecine war within the GOP if Nixon was replaced. In April, when Nixon met the president and expressed his wish to remain on the ticket, Eisenhower readily acquiesced, calling a press conference and hailing Nixon as a national asset. To this day, political analysts and historians debate just what Eisenhower had wanted Nixon to do.

Stevenson's Bid for Renomination

For the putative Democratic presidential nominee, there would be no anointing. Former Illinois governor Stevenson had won the hearts of millions with his urbane and often witty speeches in 1952. "Eggheads, unite," he once quipped. "You have nothing to lose but your yolks." Stevenson's defeat in 1952 could be interpreted as no fault of his own, given two decades of Democratic rule and voters' desire for a change in government. As one scholar put it, "to his admirers, [Stevenson's] resounding defeat underscored the nobility of his sacrifice and of his refusal to compromise his own ideals." But in 1956, circumstances were different. With Ike's health a major question mark, perhaps a Democrat could win back the White House. Stevenson had remained in the public eye during the years 1953–55 through speeches, writing, and world travels. After weighing another presidential race for much of 1955, Stevenson announced his candidacy in mid-December without, as he wrote one of his friends, any huge excitement, "but with a comfortable feeling that it is right."

Not everyone thought a Stevenson candidacy was right for the Democrats. Former president Harry Truman, still active and pugnacious, had soured on his one-time protégé. Truman did not like Stevenson's cerebral campaign style and concluded that he was not electable. Meanwhile, Tennessee senator Estes Kefauver, New York governor Averell Harriman, and Missouri senator Stuart Symington positioned themselves as alternatives to another Stevenson nomination. Only the Tennessean, however, was willing to slug it out in the primaries. By January 1956, Kefauver was in the first primary state, New Hampshire, shaking hands and renewing contacts made during his unexpected victory there against President Truman in 1952. Unwilling to test

his popularity against Kefauver's in the Granite State, Stevenson instead turned his attention to Minnesota, where he had the support of Governor Orville Freeman, U.S. Senator Hubert Humphrey (who hoped to be Stevenson's running mate), and the Democratic organization. One week before Minnesotans voted, Kevauver carried New Hampshire by five to one over a Stevenson write-in. More unsettling to the party establishment, Kefauver challenged Stevenson in Minnesota and, assisted by a large Republican crossover vote, defeated him handily there as well. Wisconsin was next—and Wisconsin, too, fell to the Tennessean.

In later years, such a string of victories would have turned an upstart into a frontrunner. But primaries were not as significant in the 1950s as they would eventually become. Stevenson could count on key managers like Cook County party chairman Jacob Arvey and Pittsburgh's mayor, David Lawrence, to steer big state delegations his way. Stevenson also had substantial support in the southern states, because most party operatives there saw Kefauver as untrustworthy on the issue that most mattered to them: segregation and white supremacy. (Kefauver had declined both to filibuster against civil rights legislation and to sign the "Southern Manifesto" assailing the Supreme Court's decision in *Brown* v. *Board of Education*.) Still, Stevenson had to work for the nomination. He focused his efforts on Florida and California, campaigning with a newfound energy and making speeches that were more concrete, down to earth, and programmatic. Stevenson shook more hands, paid attention to local issues, and even kissed babies. The change of approach paid off. He won both states by decisive margins and laid claim to his party's nomination. At the close of the primary season, Kefauver's 250 delegates earned him consideration for the vice presidential nomination, but no real chance for the larger prize.

The remaining obstacle to a Stevenson steamroller was the late-blossoming candidacy of New York governor Averell Harriman, and the potential for collusion by Kefauver and "favorite son" candidates. Harriman was lured into the race in the wake of another Eisenhower health setback—an ileitis attack in early June that required emergency surgery. The president had asserted, at a March 7 press conference, that if his health was seriously impaired he would withdraw from any reelection bid. This latest reminder of the president's mortality sparked a spate of editorials suggesting that he retire—and unnerved some Republicans. When one GOP leader was asked what he would do if Ike decided not to run for health reasons, he replied, "When I get to that bridge, I will jump off it!" In fact, Eisenhower made a quick recovery from the ileitis surgery—and, on July 10, he reaffirmed his plans to run again. Still, the health issue was very much alive. It engendered reams of newspaper and magazine copy, along the lines of "What the experts say about the president's health prospects." It also encouraged the New York governor to stick more than his big toe into the presidential campaign waters.

Rich as Croesus, Harriman promised to finance a "fighting" race against the Republicans in the fall. Harriman also offered personally to pay off Kefauver's campaign debt (roughly $40,000) if the Tennessee senator would release his delegates. This gambit got Kefauver's attention; but he soon con-

---

ESTES KEFAUVER

PARTY: Democrat

DATE OF BIRTH: July 26, 1903

PLACE OF BIRTH: Madisonville, Tennessee

PARENTS: Robert Cooke Kefauver and Phredonia Bradford Estes

EDUCATION: B.A., University of Tennessee, 1924; LL.B, Yale University, 1927

FAMILY: Married Nancy Pigott, 1935; children: Eleanor, David, Diane, and Gail

CAREER: Admitted to the bar, 1927; Tennessee finance and taxation commissioner, 1939; U.S. House of Representatives, 1939–48; U.S. Senate, 1949–63; unsuccessful candidate for U.S. vice president, 1956

DATE OF DEATH: August 10, 1963

PLACE OF DEATH: Bethesda, Maryland

CAUSE OF DEATH: Heart aneurysm

PLACE OF BURIAL: Madisonville, Tennessee

---

cluded that Stevenson remained the likely nominee, and he did not want to ruin his own chances for second place on the ticket. Kefauver declined the bribe, and thereby remained on Stevenson's short list of potential running mates. Harriman won the endorsement of former president Truman, but could claim few delegates beyond his home base of New York, especially after former first lady Eleanor Roosevelt—a liberal icon if there ever was one—embraced Stevenson as the party's choice. The Harriman challenge provided copy for political reporters, but never seriously threatened the frontrunner's claim to the nomination. The Democrats' Chicago convention

became a Stevenson coronation. With the Harriman challenge blunted, Stevenson won 905 votes on the first ballot to the New Yorker's 210, with Texas senator Lyndon B. Johnson winning eighty votes and others scattering to favorite sons.

The Democrats' Vice-Presidential Free-for-All

The Democratic convention might have had a sense of *déjà vu* about it, but for Stevenson's decision to throw the vice-presidential nomination open to the delegates. The brainchild of a low-level aide, the open convention idea was meant to exemplify the Democrats' creed and to highlight the importance of the vice presidency. Stevenson embraced it, in part, because he wanted to inject some excitement into the proceedings; but, perhaps equally important, he did not want to alienate any potential running mate by choosing a rival. By most accounts, Stevenson expected the delegates to select Massachusetts senator John F. Kennedy as his running mate. Kennedy's appeal had less to do with his record in Congress, which was unimpressive, than his personal background. A handsome war hero and a youthful New England Catholic, the thirty-nine-year-old Kennedy represented the demographics Stevenson needed if he hoped to make a credible race against a popular incumbent. In what turned out to be an exciting contest featuring Kefauver, Humphrey, Kefauver's Tennessee colleague Senator Albert Gore, Sr. (father of the future vice president and 2000 Democratic presidential candidate), New York City mayor Robert F. Wagner, Jr., and Kennedy, the convention hall was electric with possibility. Kefauver could not control a majority of his home-state delegation, much less the rest of the southern states, which voted heavily for Kennedy. The Massachusetts man, his own best advocate on the convention floor, came within thirty-nine votes of the nomination on the second ballot before Missouri's delegation—and crucial momentum—shifted to Kefauver.

This photograph, taken at the Democratic National Convention, captures suggestions of Adlai E. Stevenson's urbane and witty nature. Despite the moderateness of his liberalism, Stevenson was unable to overcome the Eisenhower charisma and the drift toward the Republicans during the 1950s. *(Brown Brothers)*

Accepting the delegates' choice with good grace, Stevenson launched his campaign with what even his supporters conceded was a less-than-rousing acceptance speech. Embroidering themes he had first articulated in Bloomington, Indiana, on July 4, Stevenson called for a "New America" in which everyone had access to first-rate education and good healthcare, in which national weaknesses were addressed rather than papered over. Taking an indirect shot at Eisenhower's "Middle Way" approach to governance, Stevenson suggested that the nation was leaderless at a time of great challenge. "We are stalled in the middle of the road," he said. Precisely how Stevenson would put the nation into a different gear he did not say, in Chicago or later in the campaign. But he did offer an alternative vision to the "you've never had it so good" litany of the GOP.

Republicans Smell Victory

At the Republican convention in August, the only things in short supply were pessimism and controversy. Buoyed by incumbency and polls showing Ike running comfortably ahead of Stevenson, the party was united and confident. The only excitement in the proceedings in San Francisco were injected by Mutual Security administrator Harold Stassen. Beginning with a press conference on July 22, Stassen spearheaded a lonely crusade to convince delegates that Richard Nixon was electoral poison and needed

to be replaced on the ticket. Stassen presented polls that purportedly showed Nixon costing Eisenhower six points against a Stevenson-Kefauver ticket, enough to diminish Republican hopes to recapture the Congress and possibly even threaten Ike's re-election. Stassen proposed Massachusetts governor Christian A. Herter for the vice presidency in Nixon's stead. But party chairman Leonard Hall, Republican activists throughout the country, and Herter himself were having none of it: Nixon was their man. Stassen had been counting on Republicans in the populous northeast to join his unlikely cause; but even in New York, New Jersey, and Massachusetts delegates remained loyal to Nixon. In the end, Eisenhower forced Stassen to make a seconding speech for Nixon at the convention and pretend he liked it. The delegates, meanwhile, heartily cheered the ticket and Ike's promise to make the Republican Party the "party of the future." Ike recited the accomplishments of his administration. Republicans, he said, had proved that government could be sensitive to the "everyday needs of people, while steering clear of the paternalistic 'Big-Brother-is-watching-you' kind of interference."

If it can be fairly said that, in 1956, both parties nominated formidable candidates representing the core convictions of their faithful, it is also true that it was an unequal contest. With "everything booming except the guns," as GOP campaign ads emphasized, voters were disinclined to rock the boat by dismissing its captain. Eisenhower campaigned more than he intended, but less than any modern incumbent with the possible exception of Richard Nixon in 1972. Not until September 19, a month after his renomination, did the president make a major campaign speech. Eisenhower and his speechwriters could devote days to individual speeches. Ike even had time to spend a relaxing morning rereading his own best-selling memoir of his World War II experiences, *Crusade in Europe.* (Not so Stevenson, who wore himself out racing around the country, often making half a dozen speeches daily, often to less-than-packed auditoriums.)

The president knew that party leaders across the country wanted him to wage a vigorous campaign. But even as he admitted to close friends that he wanted to win big, Eisenhower set limits on his travels. If he could not win on his record, Eisenhower told aides, he did not want to be president anyway. Still, the president was not a hermit. He held regular press conferences and made flying trips to Oregon,

Taken at New York's Madison Square Garden, this photograph of "Ike-dressed" women atop a mechanical elephant records political advertising at its best—or wackiest—in the mid-twentieth century. The Republican Party sent six traveling "Eisenhower Bandwagon" displays around the country on campaign tours during the 1956 campaign. *(AP Wide World)*

Ohio, Kentucky, Minnesota, California, Florida, and other states to "prove" (as he put it to his friend, Swede Hazlett) "that I am a rather healthy individual." Richard Nixon would carry the main load on the campaign trail, traveling to more than half the states during the course of the fall canvass. Nixon's themes, and those of Republican officials who barnstormed the country as a GOP "truth squad," were formulaic but well received: Americans had never had it so good; and in a dangerous world, it was essential to reelect an experienced team.

In his own speeches, notably the nationally televised address opening the Republican campaign on September 19, Eisenhower asserted that his health was fine and stressed his commitment to peace and continuing prosperity. Ike listed initiatives in domestic affairs demonstrating the good things that the Republicans had made possible. Aware that the Republicans faced a possible revolt in the Midwest, where farmers were struggling to make ends meet,

Eisenhower addressed farm questions at Bradley University in Peoria, Illinois, on September 25. After noting that all Americans wanted "widening opportunity" and "an America able to guard and save the peace," Eisenhower related his administration's efforts to strengthen established farm programs and create new ones like the Soil Bank. Farmers, he asserted, would benefit greatly from expanded trade through the St. Lawrence Seaway and through a flexible-price support system.

In Cleveland on October 1, Eisenhower devoted more attention to the "remarkable" prosperity rippling through the country. He pointed to record high employment (66.8 million jobs in August), rising real wages, with unemployment and inflation below three percent. Here, and in other speeches, Eisenhower complemented his litany on economic progress with an emphasis on giving the nation a government that "is a living witness to the basic virtues in a democracy—public morality, public service, and public trust. In this Administration you cannot find those ugly marks of the past: of special favoritism, cronyism, and laxity in administration." Eisenhower made few specific promises. He suggested, however, that if voters would just elect enough Republicans to Congress, the nation would do even better in the next four years than it had in his first administration. Based on the enthusiastic response to his speeches, and poll numbers that encouraged even the most nervous Republican precinct worker, the president had struck a resonant chord.

Foreign Policy and the Campaign

As befit an underdog, Stevenson campaigned more strenuously than the president did, traveling 55,000 miles and making 300 speeches. With Democrats the out-party in presidential politics for the first time since 1932, Stevenson was much more aggressive than he had been in 1952. The trouble for Stevenson was that Eisenhower, with enormously favorable ratings in polls, was not a good target, even in the farm belt where people were hurting the most. Stevenson took aim at Eisenhower's "teflon" presidency with a wry joke. He recalled asking a farmer why his anger at the administration's agriculture policy did not extend to Eisenhower. "Oh, no one connects him with the Administration," the farmer supposedly replied. The joke was vintage Stevenson—cerebral, amusing, but politically tame. By October, Stevenson was hitting

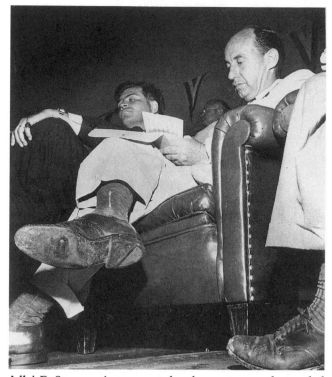

Adlai E. Stevenson's worn-out shoe became a popular symbol during the 1956 campaign. *(AP Wide World)*

harder, calling Ike a "part-time president" and arguing that a Cold War environment demanded more than smiles and complacency. Stevenson argued that the United States was falling behind in its competition with the Soviet Union. But as a liberal Cold Warrior, Stevenson had no fundamental objection to Eisenhower's containment policies. Instead, he accented his differences with the president on two issues that swung few votes his way: ending the draft, and a moratorium on testing nuclear weapons. In both cases, Eisenhower brushed off Stevenson's proposals as unrealistic in the current world climate.

The president believed that nuclear weapons testing was "far too complex and dangerous a subject to be discussed in a political campaign," his biographer Stephen Ambrose has noted. In any case, Stevenson had muddled the question by drawing no distinction between above-ground testing, which produced fallout in the form of strontium-90, and underground testing, which posed no health problems. Still, Eisenhower felt he needed to respond. In a statement issued early in October, the president pointed out that nuclear weapons were a significant element of American Cold War defense strategy. Besides, the Russians could not be trusted to adhere to a test ban.

But Eisenhower would not debate the issue with Stevenson, and he was not comfortable discussing it with reporters, either. At one point, in response to a question at a press conference on October 11, the president grew red in the face and announced that he would not discuss the matter any further. Sensing an opening, Stevenson pressed the test ban issue, pointing out that the United States already had enough nuclear weapons for deterrence and emphasizing the benefits of eliminating fallout, especially strontium-90, which Stevenson called "the most dreadful poison in the world." Unfortunately for the Democratic candidate, Soviet premier Nikolai Bulganin wrote to Eisenhower expressing his own support for a test ban, noting pointedly that "certain prominent public figures in the United States" were also advocating one. The Russian's interference in American politics provided ammunition to GOP campaigners like Vice President Nixon, who called Stevenson a "clay pigeon for Soviet sharpshooters." For his part, Eisenhower kept to the high road, confident that voters were satisfied that he would do what was in the national interest.

Disregarding his advisers, Stevenson continued to advocate "consideration" of an end to the draft and a nuclear test ban. But he shifted his rhetoric, arguing that the Republican administration was a "businessman's government" that cared little for the average guy, and making slashing attacks on Vice President Nixon, the "heir apparent" to the presidency. Stevenson's tough language energized Democrats, but won few converts among moderate Republicans or independent voters. At no point in the campaign was Stevenson ever within ten points of Eisenhower in any national poll. Stevenson was not helped by his weak stance on the issue of black civil rights and by his unwillingness or inability to master television. In paid TV ads, his speeches ran famously long (and in one instance, five minutes short). He was, at best, a half-hearted huckster and, at worst, willfully ignorant of the realities of American politics in a media age. By contrast, the Republicans spent millions on what one scholar has called a "well-ordered media operation," reminding voters that they had never had it so good. Republican ads featured Eisenhower in set-pieces that captured the president's patented smile and offered man-in-the-street testimonials to the good things that had happened during Ike's watch.

Matters did not improve for the Democrat in the midst of two international crises as the campaign was

THE SUEZ CANAL CRISIS

*A*s the campaign of 1956 moved toward its concluding days, a foreign crisis threatened to upset Eisenhower's commanding position in the presidential race. For the better part of a year, Western powers had been engaged in frustrating negotiations with Gamal Abdel Nasser, Egypt's president, over the construction of a huge dam on the Nile River. Unhappy with Nasser's alliance with the Soviet Union, the Eisenhower administration declined to help finance the dam. Nasser responded by nationalizing the Suez Canal—the crucial waterway between the Red Sea and the Mediterranean Sea—an act that annoyed the United States, but provoked no diplomatic rupture with Nasser. England and France, by contrast, were furious with Nasser. They began planning military force, as British prime minister Anthony Eden put it, to "bring Nasser to his senses." Eisenhower repeatedly warned the British and French not to do anything rash. Nonetheless, the British and French went forward, in coordination with the Israelis.

On October 29 Israel launched an assault on the Sinai. Two days later British and French planes attacked Egyptian airfields. On November 5 their paratroopers landed at Suez. The canal fell temporarily out of Nasser's control. Diplomatically, however, the Suez invasion proved a disaster for the Europeans. Eisenhower publicly criticized the military assault on Egypt and demanded that the United Nations play a role mediating issues related to the canal. Privately, Ike lambasted British prime minister Anthony Eden, threatening at one point to "break the British pound" if the British did not withdraw their troops.

Eisenhower's actions in the week before the presidential election were founded on national interest, not politics. His implicit criticism of Israel and America's World War II allies was unpopular with Jewish voters. It also offered Democratic presidential nominee Adlai Stevenson a chance to criticize an allegedly incoherent foreign policy. Yet, the Suez Crisis redounded not to Stevenson's advantage, but to Eisenhower's. Combined with public concern about the fate of Hungary and the possible outbreak of World War III, the Suez Crisis reminded voters why they had trusted Ike in the first place. Polls showing a comfortable Eisenhower lead over Stevenson never wavered; indeed, Ike's support grew as Americans rallied around their leader. In the end, as Stevenson himself acknowledged, the Suez Crisis, as well as the problems in Hungary, reinforced a result that may have been inevitable from the start. In any event, the voters registered another popular mandate for the soldier-president from Abilene.

reaching a close. Responding to Egypt's seizure in July of the Suez Canal and its subsequent nationalization, the British and French plotted a military strike to take back the canal. Invited into the cabal, Israel joined in planning an invasion, with the United States kept conspicuously out of the loop. Eisenhower smelled a rat. As one historian has noted, in Eisenhower's mind "the plot reeked of nineteenth century colonialism of the worst sort." (See "The Suez Canal Crisis," above.) The president warned against any military attack on the canal. When the attack occurred in late October, he concluded that it violated the U.N. Charter and the 1950 Tripartite Declaration. The results of the invasion could not stand. Publicly, Ike chastised the allies, insisting in a

nationally televised address that the United States would support the United Nations in seeking peace. Privately, he threatened financial retaliation if Prime Minister Anthony Eden did not withdraw British troops from Egypt. As if Mideast tensions (with the possibility of Soviet intervention on Egypt's behalf) were not enough, behind the "Iron Curtain" riots in Poland had spread to Hungary. A full-fledged Hungarian revolution against Soviet domination was in the making. In the case of Hungary, Eisenhower was as decisive as he had been in the Middle East—although this time, believing any military assistance the United States might offer the Hungarians could set off World War III, his decision was *not* to intervene. Instead, Eisenhower praised the freedom fighters and offered refuge to those able to escape to the West.

The international crises, which remained unresolved as American voters were heading to the polls on November 6, reinforced their inclination not to change horses in this election. Stevenson's last-minute speech suggesting that individuals who voted Republican were, in effect, choosing Richard Nixon for president (a veiled allusion to Eisenhower's allegedly poor chances of surviving another four years in office) also backfired. Hinting about a political opponent's mortality seemed in poor taste, even to Stevenson allies.

Eisenhower's Personal Triumph

When Americans went to the polls, Eisenhower won more convincingly than he had in 1952. Eisenhower captured nearly 58 percent of the popular vote, forty-one states, and 457 electoral votes, including those of several southern states. He even captured Louisiana, which had not voted Republican for eighty years. "That's as probable as leading in Ethiopia!" Ike exulted to associates in his campaign hotel as the votes were tallied. Catholics voted Republican in unprecedented numbers, and Eisenhower ran surprisingly well among urban black voters. Ike carried such Democratic strongholds as Chicago, Jersey City, Milwaukee, and Baltimore. In suburbia and small towns outside the South, the president won handsome majorities. Stevenson's few gains were in the farm belt and among Jewish voters, the latter angered by Ike's opposition to the Israeli seizure of the Sinai. Missouri, with a significant farm population, was the only state that shifted to Stevenson in 1956. Still, Democrats had something to be grateful for. Despite the president's assertion that his landslide victory was not a vote "merely for an individual," the truth was that Americans liked Ike more than they did the GOP. For the first time since 1848, a victorious presidential candidate failed to carry a majority in either house of Congress.

Divided government suited Americans in the 1950s. They counted on the Republican in the White House to balance the books and ensure the nation's security. They trusted the Democrats to protect the interests of the poor and working class. The 1956 election further indicated that the South could no longer be considered a one-party region. It continued the trend toward suburban political power. Last but not least, 1956 offered to the public a fresh face in national politics who would, in the next election cycle, promise to get America moving again. In his brief campaign for the vice presidency, John F. Kennedy had competed with the heavyweights in his party and held his own. He would devote much of the next four years to winning the great prize in American politics.

Eisenhower, for his part, would find his second term more trying and less rewarding than the first. Although Ike remained personally popular, his attempts to redefine the GOP as a "modern Republican" party sputtered. He was put on the defensive over *Sputnik*, and by the Democrats' claims that the Russians were surpassing the United States in development of military hardware—the celebrated (albeit nonexistent) "missile gap." Eisenhower's hopes for détente with the Soviets peaked with Nikita Khrushchev's U.S. visit in the summer of 1959, but disintegrated when a U-2 spy plane piloted by Francis Gary Powers was shot down in May 1960. Sometimes the best thing about a presidential election is not the governance that it mandates—but rather the cheering on election night.

Michael J. Birkner

Bibliography

Ambrose, Stephen E. *Eisenhower the President*. New York: Simon and Schuster, 1984.

Baker, Jean H. *The Stevensons: A Biography of an American Family*. New York: W. W. Norton, 1996.

Barone, Michael. *Our Country: The Shaping of America from Roosevelt to Reagan*. New York: Free Press, 1990.

Broadwater, Jeff. *Adlai Stevenson*. New York: Twayne, 1994.

Fontenay, Charles L. *Estes Kefauver: A Biography*. Knoxville: University of Tennessee Press, 1980.

Lubell, Samuel. *The Revolt of the Moderates*. New York: Harper & Row, 1956.

Martin, John Bartlow. *Adlai Stevenson and the World: The Life of Adlai Stevenson*. New York: Doubleday, 1978.

Parmet, Herbert. *Eisenhower and the American Crusades*. New York: Macmillan, 1972.

THE VOTE: ELECTION OF 1956

State	Total No. of Electors	Total Popular Vote	Electoral Vote R	Electoral Vote D	Electoral Vote O	Margin of Victory Votes	Margin of Victory % Total Vote	Eisenhower Republican Votes	Eisenhower Republican %	Stevenson Democrat Votes	Stevenson Democrat %	Others Votes	Others %
Alabama	11	496,861		10	1[a]	85,150	17.1%	195,694	39.4%	280,844	56.5%	20,323	4.1%
Arizona	4	290,173	4			64,110	22.1%	176,990	61.0%	112,880	38.9%	303	0.1%
Arkansas	8	406,572		8		26,990	6.6%	186,287	45.8%	213,277	52.5%	7,008	1.7%
California	32	5,466,355	32			607,533	11.1%	3,027,668	55.4%	2,420,135	44.3%	18,552	0.3%
Colorado	6	663,074	6			130,482	19.7%	394,479	59.5%	263,997	39.8%	4,598	0.7%
Connecticut	8	1,117,121	8			306,758	27.5%	711,837	63.7%	405,079	36.3%	205	0.0%
Delaware	3	177,988	3			18,636	10.5%	98,057	55.1%	79,421	44.6%	510	0.3%
Florida	10	1,124,220	10			163,478	14.5%	643,849	57.3%	480,371	42.7%	0	0.0%
Georgia	12	663,480		12		224,442	33.8%	216,652	32.7%	441,094	66.5%	5,734	0.9%
Idaho	4	272,989	4			61,111	22.4%	166,979	61.2%	105,868	38.8%	142	0.1%
Illinois	27	4,407,407	27			847,645	19.2%	2,623,327	59.5%	1,775,682	40.3%	8,398	0.2%
Indiana	13	1,974,607	13			398,903	20.2%	1,182,811	59.9%	783,908	39.7%	7,888	0.4%
Iowa	10	1,234,564	10			227,329	18.4%	729,187	59.1%	501,858	40.7%	3,519	0.3%
Kansas	8	866,243	8			270,561	31.2%	566,878	65.4%	296,317	34.2%	3,048	0.4%
Kentucky	10	1,053,805	10			95,739	9.1%	572,192	54.3%	476,453	45.2%	5,160	0.5%
Louisiana	10	617,544	10			85,070	13.8%	329,047	53.3%	243,977	39.5%	44,520	7.2%
Maine	5	351,706	5			146,770	41.7%	249,238	70.9%	102,468	29.1%	0	0.0%
Maryland	9	932,351	9			187,125	20.1%	559,738	60.0%	372,613	40.0%	0	0.0%
Massachusetts	16	2,348,506	16			445,007	18.9%	1,393,197	59.3%	948,190	40.4%	7,119	0.3%
Michigan	20	3,080,468	20			353,749	11.5%	1,713,647	55.6%	1,359,898	44.1%	6,923	0.2%
Minnesota	11	1,340,005	11			101,777	7.6%	719,302	53.7%	617,525	46.1%	3,178	0.2%
Mississippi	8	248,149		8		83,813	33.8%	60,685	24.5%	144,498	58.2%	42,966	17.3%
Missouri	13	1,832,562		13		3,984	0.2%	914,289	49.9%	918,273	50.1%	0	0.0%
Montana	4	271,171	4			38,695	14.3%	154,933	57.1%	116,238	42.9%	0	0.0%
Nebraska	6	577,137	6			179,079	31.0%	378,108	65.5%	199,029	34.5%	0	0.0%
Nevada	3	96,689	3			15,409	15.9%	56,049	58.0%	40,640	42.0%	0	0.0%
New Hampshire	4	266,994	4			86,155	32.3%	176,519	66.1%	90,364	33.8%	111	0.0%
New Jersey	16	2,484,312	16			756,605	30.5%	1,606,942	64.7%	850,337	34.2%	27,033	1.1%
New Mexico	4	253,926	4			40,690	16.0%	146,788	57.8%	106,098	41.8%	1,040	0.4%
New York	45	7,092,860	45			1,589,571	22.4%	4,340,340	61.2%	2,750,769	38.8%	1,751	0.0%
North Carolina	14	1,165,592		14		15,468	1.3%	575,062	49.3%	590,530	50.7%	0	0.0%
North Dakota	4	253,991	4			60,024	23.6%	156,766	61.7%	96,742	38.1%	483	0.2%
Ohio	25	3,702,265	25			822,955	22.2%	2,262,610	61.1%	1,439,655	38.9%	0	0.0%
Oklahoma	8	859,350	8			88,188	10.3%	473,769	55.1%	385,581	44.9%	0	0.0%
Oregon	6	735,597	6			77,189	10.5%	406,393	55.2%	329,204	44.8%	0	0.0%
Pennsylvania	32	4,576,503	32			603,483	13.2%	2,585,252	56.5%	1,981,769	43.3%	9,482	0.2%
Rhode Island	4	387,609	4			64,029	16.5%	225,819	58.3%	161,790	41.7%	0	0.0%
South Carolina	8	300,583		8		47,861	15.9%	75,700	25.2%	136,372	45.4%	88,511	29.4%
South Dakota	4	293,857	4			49,281	16.8%	171,569	58.4%	122,288	41.6%	0	0.0%
Tennessee	11	939,404	11			5,781	0.6%	462,288	49.2%	456,507	48.6%	20,609	2.2%
Texas	24	1,955,168	24			220,661	11.3%	1,080,619	55.3%	859,958	44.0%	14,591	0.7%
Utah	4	333,995	4			97,267	29.1%	215,631	64.6%	118,364	35.4%	0	0.0%
Vermont	3	152,978	3			67,841	44.3%	110,390	72.2%	42,549	27.8%	39	0.0%
Virginia	12	697,978	12			118,699	17.0%	386,459	55.4%	267,760	38.4%	43,759	6.3%
Washington	9	1,150,889	9			97,428	8.5%	620,430	53.9%	523,002	45.4%	7,457	0.6%
West Virginia	8	830,831	8			67,763	8.2%	449,297	54.1%	381,534	45.9%	0	0.0%
Wisconsin	12	1,550,558	12			368,076	23.7%	954,844	61.6%	586,768	37.8%	8,946	0.6%
Wyoming	3	124,127	3			25,019	20.2%	74,573	60.1%	49,554	39.9%	0	0.0%
TOTAL	531	62,021,114	457	73	1	9,551,152	15.4%	35,579,180	57.4%	26,028,028	42.0%	413,906	0.7%

[a] A Stevenson elector in Alabama voted for Walter Jones.

For sources, see p. 1129.

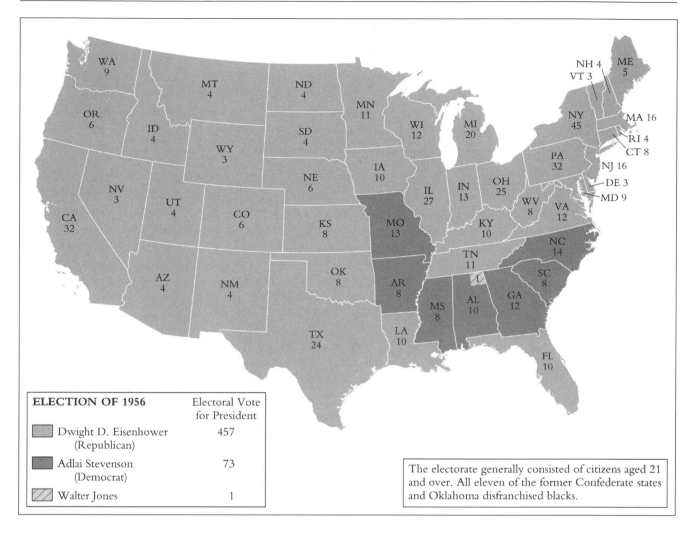

ELECTION OF 1956   Electoral Vote
                         for President

Dwight D. Eisenhower   457
(Republican)

Adlai Stevenson   73
(Democrat)

Walter Jones   1

The electorate generally consisted of citizens aged 21 and over. All eleven of the former Confederate states and Oklahoma disfranchised blacks.

DOCUMENTS: ELECTION OF 1956

The 1956 presidential election featured the same two major party candidates, Dwight Eisenhower and Adlai Stevenson, who had squared-off in 1952 and ended with a similar result: a Republican landslide. Despite having suffered a heart attack and other illnesses in his first term, President Eisenhower regained the Republican nomination without opposition. Against some opposition, he also kept his less popular running mate, Vice President Richard M. Nixon, on the ticket.

Democratic primaries reflected a weakening of Stevenson's support, but he fended off a challenge by Tennessee senator Estes Kefauver. The Democratic campaign gained some much-needed excitement and attention at the convention. Stevenson refrained from endorsing a vice presidential candidate, Document 1, requesting that the delegates select his running mate. The ensuing contest between Kefauver and a young senator from Massachusetts, John F. Kennedy, thrilled observers. Although Kefauver won, the struggle elevated Kennedy to a position as a viable national candidate. In his speech accepting the Democratic nomination, Document 2, Stevenson commenced his national campaign by attacking the Republicans for covering up foreign and domestic policy failures. Stevenson promised honesty and direction to regain the nation's leading military and economic standing in the world.

Meanwhile, in their convention Republicans celebrated their war-hero president and his popularity. In his speech accepting the Republican nomination, Document 3, Eisenhower reflected on a world divided between freedom and communism. He looked to the Republican Party's history to illustrate to Americans that it was his party that had served the nation best in times of crisis, using Lincoln's resolve to restore the Union as his model.

In the last days of the campaign, Stevenson stepped up his attacks on Eisenhower, Document 4. Although avoiding the matter of the president's health, the Democratic nominee criticized the Eisenhower administration as the "part-time Presidency," openly assaulting the president's repeated absence at times of important international crises. Still, the former general's popularity and experience in foreign policy easily deflected Stevenson's attacks.

Document 1

Adlai E. Stevenson Throws Vice Presidential Nomination to the Floor, Chicago, August 17, 1956

My heart is full.

I am deeply grateful.

But I did not come here tonight to speak of the action you have just taken. That, I shall do tomorrow night, after you have chosen a Vice President. Now, it is in connection with that choice that I have taken this unusual step of asking to be heard briefly tonight.

The American people have the solemn obligation to consider with the utmost care who will be their President, if the elected President is prevented by a higher will from serving his full term. It is a sober reminder that seven out of 34 Presidents have served as the result of such an indirect selection.

The responsibility of the Presidency has grown so great that the nation's attention has become focused as never before on the office of the Vice Presidency. The choice for that office has become almost as important as the choice for the Presidency.

Each political party has, therefore, the solemn obligation to offer the country as its choice for the Vice Presidency a person fully equipped first, to assist in the discharge of the duties of the most exacting job in the world, and, second, to himself assume, if need be, this highest responsibility.

Historically, the Presidential candidate has often designated the nominee for Vice President. Sometimes, the choice has been due to personal predilection or political expediency.

But always there is the importance of mutual confidence if they are to work together with maximum effectiveness in the interests of the nation. I recognize these considerations.

But, I respect beyond measure a convention and a party which has conferred upon me its highest honor, without there being asked of me a single commitment except faith in the program and principles of our party.

In these circumstances, I have concluded to depart from the precedents of the past. I have decided that the selection of the Vice Presidential nominee should be made through the free processes of this convention—so that the Democratic party's candidate for this office may join me before the nation not as one man's selection, but as one chosen by our great party, even as I have been chosen.

I would add only this: In taking this step, I am expressing my confidence in your choice and in the many fine men whose prominence in our party will command your consideration. The choice will be yours. The profit will be the nation's.

And now, until tomorrow night, again my heartfelt thanks and may God be with you!

Source: Walter Johnson, ed., *The Papers of Adlai Stevenson, 1955–1957*, vol. 6 (Boston: Little, Brown, 1976).

Document 2

Acceptance Speech by Adlai E. Stevenson, Chicago, August 17, 1956

I accept your nomination and your program. And I pledge to you every resource of mind and strength I possess to make your deed today a good one for our country and for our party.

Four years ago I stood in this same place and uttered those same words to you. But four years ago we lost. This time we will win! . . .

I am grateful to you for my running mate—an honorable and able American—Senator Estes Kefauver, and may

I add that I got as excited as any of you about that photo-finish between Senator Kefauver and that great young American Senator, John Kennedy. . . .

I do not propose to make political capital out of the President's illness. His ability to personally fulfill the demands of his exacting office is a matter between him and the American people. So far as I am concerned that is where the matter rests. As we all do, I wish deeply for the President's health and well being.

But if the condition of President Eisenhower is not an issue as far as I am concerned, the condition and the conduct of the President's office and of the Administration is very much an issue.

The men who run the Eisenhower administration evidently believe that the minds of Americans can be manipulated by shows, slogans and the arts of advertising. And that conviction will, I dare say, be backed up by the greatest torrent of money ever poured out to influence an American election—poured out by men who fear nothing so much as change and who want everything to stay as it is—only more so.

This idea that you can merchandise candidates for high office like breakfast cereal—that you can gather votes like box tops—is, I think, the ultimate indignity to the democratic process. And we Democrats must also face the fact that no Administration has ever before enjoyed such an uncritical and enthusiastic support from so much of the press as this one.

But let us ask the people of our country to what great purpose for the republic has the President's popularity and this unrivalled opportunity for leadership been put? Has the Eisenhower administration used this opportunity to elevate us? To enlighten us? To inspire us? Did it, in a time of headlong, worldwide, revolutionary change, prepare us for stern decisions and great risks? Did it, in short, give men and women a glimpse of the nobility and vision without which peoples and nations perish?

Or did it just reassure us that all is well, everything is all right, that everyone is prosperous and safe, that no great decisions are required of us, and that even the Presidency of the United States has somehow become an easy job?

I will have to confess that the Republican administration has performed a minor miracle. After twenty years of incessant damnation of the New Deal, they not only haven't repealed it but they have swallowed it, or most of it, and it looks as though they could keep it down at least until after the election.

I suppose we should be thankful that they have caught up with the New Deal at last, but what have they done to take advantage of the great opportunities of these times—a generation after the New Deal?

Well, I say they have smothered us in smiles and complacency while our social and economic advancement has

ground to a halt, and while our leadership and security in the world have been imperiled.

In spite of these unparalleled opportunities to lead at home and abroad, they have, I say, been wasting our opportunities and losing our world.

I say that what this country needs is not propaganda and a personality cult. What this country needs is leadership and truth, and that's what we mean to give it.

What is the truth?

The truth is that the Republican party is a house divided. The truth is that President Eisenhower, cynically coveted as a candidate but ignored as a leader, is largely indebted to Democrats in Congress for what accomplishments he can claim.

The truth is that every one is not prosperous. The truth is that the farmer, especially the family farmer who matters most, has not had his fair share of the national income and the Republicans have done nothing to help him—until an election year.

The truth is that 30,000,000 Americans live today in families trying to make ends meet on less than $2,000 a year. The truth is that the small farmer, the small business man, the teacher, the white collar worker, and the retired citizen trying to pay today's prices on yesterday's pension—all these are in serious trouble.

The truth is that in this government of big men—big financially—no one speaks for the little man.

The truth is not that our policy abroad has the Communists on the run. The truth, unhappily, is not—in the Republican President's words—that our "prestige since the last world war has never been as high as it is this day." The truth is that it has probably never been lower.

The truth is that we are losing the military advantage, the economic initiative and the moral leadership.

The truth is not that we are winning the cold war. The truth is that we are losing the cold war. . . .

What we need is a rebirth of leadership—leadership which will give us a glimpse of the nobility and vision without which peoples and nations perish. Woodrow Wilson said that "when America loses its ardor for mankind, it is time to elect a Democratic President." There doesn't appear to be much ardor in America just now for anything, and it's time to elect a Democratic administration and a Democratic Congress, yes, and a Democratic government in every state and local office across the land.

In our hearts we know that the horizons of the new America are as endless, its promise as staggering in its richness, as the unfolding miracle of human knowledge. America renews itself with every forward thrust of the human mind. . . .

Source: Walter Johnson, ed., *The Papers of Adlai Stevenson, 1955–1957,* vol. 6 (Boston: Little, Brown, 1976).

Document 3

Acceptance Speech by President Dwight D. Eisenhower, San Francisco, August 23, 1956

The Republican party is the party of the future.

I hold that the Republican party and platform are right in 1956, because they are "most closely in league with the future." And for this reason the Republican party and program are and will be decisively approved by the American people in 1956. . . .

Now, the first reason of the five I shall give you why the Republican party is the party of the future is this:

Because it is the party of long-range principle, not short-term expediency. One of my predecessors is said to have observed that in making his decisions he had to operate like a football quarterback—he could not very well call the next play until he saw how the last play turned out. Well, that may be a good way to run a football team, but in these times it is no way to run a government. . . .

My second reason for saying that the Republican party is the party of the future is this: it is the party which concentrates on the facts and issues of today and tomorrow, not the facts and issues of yesterday.

More than twenty years ago, our opponents found in the problems of the depression a battleground on which they scored many political victories. Now economic cycles have not been eliminated. Still, the world has moved on from the Nineteen Thirties: good times have supplanted depression; new techniques for checking serious recession have been learned and tested, and a whole new array of problems has sprung up. But their obsession with the depression still blinds many of our opponents to the insistent demands of today. . . .

Third: The Republican party is the party of the future because it is the party that draws people together, not drives them apart.

Our party detests the technique of pitting group against group for cheap political advantage. Republicans view as a central principle of conduct—not just as a phrase on nickels and dimes—that old motto of ours: "E Pluribus Unum"—"Out of Many-One."

Our party, as far back as 1856, began establishing a record of bringing together, as its largest element, the working people and small farmers, as well as the small businessmen. It attracted minority groups, scholars and writers, not to mention reformers of all kinds, free-soilers, independent Democrats, conscience Whigs, barnburners, "soft hunkers," teetotallers, vegetarians and transcendentalists!

Now, 100 years later, the Republican party is again the rallying point for Americans of all callings, ages, races and incomes. . . .

And now the fourth reason: The Republican party is the party of the future because it is the party through which the many things that still need doing will soonest be done—and will be done by enlisting the fullest energies of free, creative, individual people. . . .

Finally, a party of the future must be completely dedicated to peace, as indeed must all Americans. For without peace there is no future. . . .

Again the strength I speak of is not military strength alone. The heart of the collective security principle is the idea of helping other nations to realize their own potentialities—political, economic and military. The strength of the free world lies not in cementing the free worlds into a second monolithic mass to compete with that of the Communists. It lies rather in the unity that comes of the voluntary association of nations which, however diverse, are developing their own capacities and asserting their own national destinies in a world of freedom and of mutual respect.

Lincoln, speaking to a Republican state convention in 1858, began with the biblical quotation: "A house divided against itself cannot stand."

Today the world is a house divided.

But—as is sometimes forgotten—Lincoln followed this quotation with a note of hope for his troubled country:

"I do not expect the house to fall," he said, "but I do expect it will cease to be divided."

A century later, we too must have the vision, the fighting spirit, and the deep religious faith in our creator's destiny for us, to sound a similar note of promise for our divided world; that out of our time there can, with incessant work and with God's help, emerge a new era of good life, good will and good hope for all men.

One American put it this way: "Every tomorrow has two handles. We can take hold of it with the handle of anxiety or the handle of faith."

My friends, in firm faith, and in the conviction that the Republican purposes and principles are "in league" with this kind of future, the nomination that you have tendered me for the Presidency of the United States I now—humbly but confidently—accept.

Source: Public Papers of the Presidents of the United States: Dwight D. Eisenhower, January 1 to December 31, 1956 (Washington, DC: Government Printing Office, 1964).

Document 4

Speech by Adlai E. Stevenson, Los Angeles, October 27, 1956

You may gauge President Eisenhower's interest in this whole problem by another bit of history. In June of last year, by a vote of 367–0, the House of Representatives passed a resolution expressing its sympathy with the satellite nations and condemning colonialism. When asked about this resolution on June 29, President Eisenhower said: "I did not know about that. Maybe I was fishing that day. I don't know."

But this was not an isolated example. Let me give you another example where the issue of war and peace was at stake.

The winter and spring of 1954 were a time of deep trial and anxiety. Indochina was falling to the Communists. I saw that frightening war in the rice paddies and the jungles with my own eyes. The free world was divided, troubled and alarmed, hasty voices—Mr. Nixon's with characteristic volubility, was among them—were advocating armed intervention by American troops.

On February 12, the *New York Times* reported that Senate leaders "alarmed by fears of possible U.S. involvement in the Indochina war" had called high members of the Administration to an urgent secret conference. On the same day the *Times* also reported that President Eisenhower had gone South for hunting with Secretary Humphrey and had bagged his limit of quail.

Two days later the alarm had deepened in Washington and the papers reported that President Eisenhower was leaving for a six-day vacation in California. On February 19, Secretary Dulles returned from the critical four-power conference in Berlin. He couldn't report to the President. The *New York Times* said "it was golf again today for President Eisenhower" at Palm Springs.

Later, on April 13, Mr. Dulles and British Foreign Secretary Anthony Eden met to explore the possibilities of joint action—joint military action—in Indochina. The *New York Times* reported that President Eisenhower had landed in the South "to begin a golfing vacation."

Next day it was announced that we would airlift aid to Indochina; and also that the President was playing golf in Georgia.

On April 17, the *New York Times* said in a headline that the United States "weighs fighting in Indochina if necessary." The President, it said, was still vacationing in Georgia.

The next day the country learned from the papers that Nixon had said that the United States might have to intervene with military force. Less spectacular news that day was that President Eisenhower had played golf in Augusta with Billy Joe Patton.

On April 23, it was announced that the last outposts around Dienbienphu, the French stronghold, had fallen. That day the President arrived in Georgia for a new golfing holiday.

The free world suffered a severe defeat in Asia and lost a rich country and more than 10,000,000 people in Indochina. And after it was all over, Secretary Dulles boasted in an article in *Life* magazine that it had been a victory. . . .

When President Eisenhower was asked his opinion, he replied: "I have not read the article."

I could go on. The President was away golfing when it was announced early last year that our Air Force had gone on a full war footing as a result of the Formosa crisis. He was shooting quail when we evacuated the Tachen Islands. He was golfing in New Hampshire in June 1954, when the Soviets shot down a U.S. plane off Alaska. In the *New York Times*, it said "there was no visible evidence that the President had anything on his mind other than having a good time."

In February of this year, the President was golfing in Georgia during the on-again, off-again, on-again mix-up over the shipment of tanks to Saudi Arabia which so alarmed the Israeli people. Mr. Dulles as usual was out of the country. Mr. Herbert Hoover Jr. was running the store.

The President was asked this year whether Russia was leading us in guided missiles. He answered, and I quote him, that he was "astonished at the amount of information that others get that I don't."

The President was asked on April 4 of this year about an urgent message on the Middle Eastern crisis that Prime Minister Eden had sent him ten days earlier. It developed that he didn't even know the letter existed.

When asked about neutralism that long ago, the President said he thought it was fine; when Mr. Dulles was asked, he said it was immoral. After they got together, Mr. Dulles said that while he thought neutralism immoral, he didn't know any immoral neutrals.

I suppose we have to assume that the President just doesn't know, either, of his Secretary of State's incredible blunders that have shaken the Middle East and helped the Communists do in a few months what the Czars couldn't do in centuries—penetrate the Arab lands.

The President is an honorable man. So when he smilingly assures us that all is well and America's prestige has never been higher, he just must not know that in fact the American star is low on the world's horizons. . . .

Nothing can be more essential to our system of government than affirmative Presidential leadership. The President was elected to these responsibilities by the American people. He is the only officer of our Government who is elected by all the people.

These four years of a part-time Presidency have been bad enough. But what would another four be like? . . .

Beginning in 1957, if President Eisenhower should be reelected, the Republican leaders in Congress will owe him exactly nothing. He cannot help them get elected again because, under the Twenty-second Amendment, he couldn't run again even if his age and health permitted. . . .

Source: Walter Johnson, ed., *The Papers of Adlai Stevenson, 1955–1957*, vol. 6 (Boston: Little, Brown, 1976).

THE ELECTION OF 1960

After eight years of peace, prosperity, and a popular president, Dwight Eisenhower, the Republican Party seemed confident that it would continue its control of the White House in 1960 with Vice President Richard Nixon (see fact box, p. 819) as their candidate. The consummate politician, Nixon had kept himself in the public spotlight during the 1950s by vigorously campaigning for the president, fund raising, traveling, and meeting world leaders. Eisenhower's coattails, however, had never been long, while a recession and the *Sputnik* controversy revealed that Republican strength started and ended with the very popular "Ike." Republican candidates for Congress had run well behind Eisenhower's vote, and the party's hold on congressional seats decreased during the Eisenhower years. In 1958, the GOP received just 43 percent of the congressional vote, the lowest Republican tally since the Depression. By decade's end, Republicans claimed only fourteen of forty-eight state governorships and held majorities in only seven state legislatures. Democrats liked the political outlook for the presidential race of 1960.

The Primaries

Five contenders threw their hats into the ring for the Democratic nomination in 1960. For many in the party, the witty and intelligent former governor of Illinois, Adlai Stevenson, seemed the obvious first choice. Unsuccessful in his contests against Eisenhower in 1952 and 1956, Stevenson refused to state his intentions for 1960. Although those closest to him

knew that he hoped for another opportunity, Stevenson wanted party leaders to hand him the nomination. With no clear-cut frontrunner, that seemed quite possible.

Two other formidable candidates, senators Lyndon Johnson of Texas and Stuart Symington of Missouri, also refused to campaign actively for the nomination. Both hoped that a deadlocked convention might turn to one of them. Johnson, the powerful Senate majority leader, had strong support among Democratic members of Congress. Party officials, however, needed to be convinced that a southerner could gain widespread popular support in the rest of the country—particularly in the Northeast, which remained deeply anti-southern. Symington believed that he could succeed where Johnson could not. He had influential friends, hailed from a border state and won the endorsement of Harry S Truman, the former president. Yet few Americans had ever heard of him.

Lesser-known hopefuls looked to the state primaries to leverage their nomination. Senators Hubert H. Humphrey of Minnesota and John F. Kennedy of Massachusetts hoped that a few convincing primary victories would sway enough delegates to gain a first-ballot victory at the convention. Because many states still did not hold primaries, the importance of primaries in winning the Democratic nomination was largely symbolic. The Kennedy and Humphrey strategies hoped that their electoral popularity would spill over to the convention floor. Of the two candidates, Humphrey had the more impressive record. As a leader of the liberal Democratic faction of the Senate

CHRONOLOGY

1959

DECEMBER 24	Nelson Rockefeller announces he will not seek the Republican nomination for president.
DECEMBER 30	Hubert Humphrey announces his candidacy for the Democratic nomination for president.

1960

JANUARY 2	John Fitzgerald Kennedy announces his candidacy for the Democratic nomination for president.
MARCH 24	Stuart Symington announces his candidacy for the Democratic nomination for president.
APRIL 5	Kennedy wins Wisconsin Democratic primary.
MAY 1	Soviet Union shoots down American U-2 spy plane in its airspace.
MAY 8	Kennedy gives television address to West Virginia voters on his religion.
MAY 10	Kennedy wins West Virginia Democratic primary.
MAY 11	Hubert Humphrey drops out of race for Democratic nomination.
JULY 5	Lyndon Johnson announces his candidacy for the Democratic nomination for president.
JULY 13	At the Los Angeles convention, Kennedy wins Democratic nomination for president on the first ballot.
JULY 14	Lyndon Johnson accepts Democratic nomination for vice president.
JULY 15	Kennedy accepts Democratic nomination for president.
JULY 22–23	Richard Nixon meets Rockefeller in secret meeting in New York City; Rockefeller releases statement detailing their discussions and Nixon's agreement to most of his terms.
JULY 27	At the Chicago convention, Nixon wins Republican nomination for president on the first ballot.
JULY 28	Nixon accepts Republican nomination for president.
AUGUST 29–SEPTEMBER 9	Nixon hospitalized with infection in his knee.
SEPTEMBER 1	Congressional session ends, freeing Kennedy from his duties to begin active campaigning for general election.
SEPTEMBER 12	Kennedy addresses Greater Houston Ministerial Association, and puts religious issue to rest.
SEPTEMBER 26	First Kennedy-Nixon presidential debate televised from Chicago.
OCTOBER 7	Second televised presidential debate held in Washington, D.C.
OCTOBER 13	Third presidential debate televised, with Nixon in Los Angeles and Kennedy in New York.
OCTOBER 21	Fourth, and final, televised presidential debate held in New York.
OCTOBER 19	Martin Luther King, Jr., arrested in Atlanta, Georgia, and later sentenced to four months hard labor.
OCTOBER 25	Kennedy calls King's wife; JFK's brother, Robert, convinces Georgia judge to release King.
OCTOBER 25–NOVEMBER 7	Nixon commences all out television blitz.
OCTOBER 27	King released from prison.
NOVEMBER 8	Kennedy defeats Nixon in close election.

1961

JANUARY 20	Kennedy inaugurated as U.S. president.

and a long-time proponent of civil rights, Humphrey had been selected for the cover of *Time* magazine in 1958. He gained further stature when he met privately with Soviet premier Nikita Khrushchev during his tour of the United States. Money was Humphrey's biggest problem, and his lack of funds undercut his primary campaign.

Money and organization were John F. Kennedy's strengths. His family both funded and staffed a massive campaign organization. Kennedy was a Harvard graduate and had a credible war record. He was handsome, articulate, and witty. With his father's fortune behind him, Kennedy won a seat in the House of Representatives from Massachusetts in 1946, and was elected to the Senate in 1952.

JOHN FITZGERALD KENNEDY

PARTY: Democratic

DATE OF BIRTH: May 29, 1917

PLACE OF BIRTH: Brookline, Massachusetts

PARENTS: Joseph Patrick and Rose Fitzgerald

EDUCATION: B.S., Harvard University, 1940

FAMILY: Married Jacqueline Lee Bouvier, 1953; children: Caroline, John Jr., and Patrick (died in infancy)

MILITARY SERVICE: U.S. Navy, lieutenant commander, 1941–45

CAREER: Journalist, Chicago *Herald-American* (covered United Nations Conference on International Organization), and International News Service (covered Potsdam Conference), 1945; U.S. House of Representatives, 1947–53; U.S. Senate, 1953–61; author, *Profiles in Courage* (1956), which earned Pulitzer Prize for Biography; U.S. president, 1961–63

DATE OF DEATH: November 22, 1963

PLACE OF DEATH: Dallas, Texas

CAUSE OF DEATH: Assassination

PLACE OF BURIAL: Arlington National Cemetery, Arlington, Virginia

He nominated Stevenson at the Democratic convention in 1956. Over the next four years, Americans would get to know JFK from his appearances on televised programs and from his Pulitzer-Prize winning book, *Profiles in Courage*. Kennedy traveled to all fifty states and delivered hundreds of speeches in his quest for exposure. While he demonstrated an understanding and acceptance of American Cold War policy, Kennedy's political accomplishments were few, and his speeches did not broach controversial issues. Insiders knew he was inexperienced; but more than his youthfulness, they worried about his Catholicism. No person of the Catholic faith had ever been elected president.

Kennedy and Humphrey opened the primary season hoping to knock out the other candidate and establish their own nationwide appeal. Not until the Wisconsin primary, in April 1960, did they engage in a head-to-head battle. Kennedy believed that a big victory in Wisconsin, which bordered on Humphrey's home state, might open a clear route to the nomination. Humphrey knew that a win over Kennedy would result in a wave of contributions and prove to party leaders that his opponent had no appeal outside the Northeast. The Kennedy campaign established a network of offices in Wisconsin and the candidate traversed the state in his private plane.

Humphrey opened just two offices and relied heavily on weekend volunteers. Each candidate spent liberally on media advertisements.

Kennedy scored an impressive victory over Humphrey in the Wisconsin primary, taking 56 percent of the vote. But the verdict was still out on a Kennedy candidacy, in part because Catholics provided a substantial portion of his vote. Because some of them were conservative Republicans who crossed party lines in Wisconsin's open primary, that state did not prove to be the convincing victory Kennedy so desperately needed.

West Virginia became a much more decisive battleground. In a state where Protestants made up 95 percent of the population, Kennedy's hopes lay in overcoming anti-Catholic prejudices. After West Virginians began voicing concerns over whether a Catholic president would uphold the separation of church and state, Kennedy used the power of television—the medium that had made his candidacy possible—to address the religious issue. He spent much of a thirty-minute program trying to put voters' fears to rest—by pointing to his record upholding the separation of church and state, promising complete independence from church authority in all presidential decisions, and declaring his opposition to public funding for parochial schools. After the TV program, the issue disappeared from the public primary, although many voters never looked beyond Kennedy's religious affiliation. Kennedy won the primary, 61 to 39 percent, resulting in Humphrey's withdrawal from the race. Kennedy's victory in this heavily Protestant border state convinced many influential Democrats that he could be a national candidate. Although now unopposed, he kept campaigning rigorously, piling up delegates.

The Democratic Convention

On May 1, the Soviet Union shot down an American U-2 spy plane, creating an international crisis that carried over into presidential politics. The incident highlighted the seriousness of the Cold War, and reminded Democrats that experience in foreign affairs was a key factor in the presidential race. Kennedy tried to hold together his delegate base amid attacks on his inexperience in diplomacy, but stumbled when he suggested that Eisenhower should apologize to the Soviets for violating their airspace. Lyndon Johnson rekindled memories of Munich (where the British had offered unwise concessions to the Nazis on the eve of World War II), and declared that Kennedy was a "boyish appeaser of Soviets." A growing number of Democrats called for Adlai Stevenson to seek the nomination, but he refused to display an interest in the race. Former first lady Eleanor Roosevelt even suggested to Kennedy that he accept the vice presidential nomination on a Stevenson-Kennedy ticket, an arrangement that would give him an "opportunity to grow and learn."

Kennedy nervously clung to hopes of a first-ballot victory. On paper, he had enough delegates as long as those committed to him stayed loyal. The movement to draft Stevenson had gained momentum by mid-

After triumphing over Lyndon B. Johnson in securing the 1960 Democratic Party nomination for president, John F. Kennedy invited Johnson to join the ticket. Kennedy's youthful appearance in comparison to the weathered Johnson is detectable in this campaign brochure. In contrast to Nixon brochures, the Citizens for Kennedy and Johnson advertised the Democratic Party as well as its candidates.

July, when delegates met in Los Angeles. Despite noisy demonstrations, however, Stevenson could count on only a handful of delegates. Kennedy's majority held on the first ballot and he won with 806 votes, nearly twice the 409 votes that Lyndon Johnson received.

The Democratic nominee, an Irish Catholic from New England, needed to "balance" his ticket before launching a national campaign. Kennedy had gained only 13 votes from the South, while Texas senator Lyndon Johnson picked up 307 southern delegates. Despite personal differences, Kennedy asked Johnson to be the vice presidential nominee to help carry the South. On the evening of July 15, Kennedy

LYNDON BAINES JOHNSON

PARTY: Democratic

DATE OF BIRTH: August 27, 1908

PLACE OF BIRTH: Between Stonewall and Johnson City, Texas

PARENTS: Sam Early, Jr., and Rebekah Baines

EDUCATION: B.A., Southwest Texas State Teachers College, 1930; attended Georgetown University School of Law, 1934–35

FAMILY: Married Claudia Alta "Lady Bird" Taylor, 1934; children: Lynda Bird and Luci Baines

MILITARY SERVICE: U.S. Navy, lieutenant commander, 1941–42

CAREER: School teacher, 1928–31; secretary to U.S. Rep. Richard M. Kleberg of Texas, 1931–35; director, National Youth Administration in Texas, 1935–37; U.S. House of Representatives, 1937–49; U.S. Senate, 1949–61; U.S. vice president, 1961–63; U.S. president, 1963–69

DATE OF DEATH: January 22, 1973

PLACE OF DEATH: LBJ Ranch, near San Antonio, Texas

CAUSE OF DEATH: Heart attack

PLACE OF BURIAL: Johnson family plot near Johnson City, Texas

stood before the convention to accept his party's nomination, with 35 million Americans watching on television. He called for all Americans to push forward into a "New Frontier"—and to explore the "uncharted areas of science and space, unsolved problems of peace and war, unconquered pockets of ignorance and prejudice, unanswered questions of poverty and surplus."

The Republican Convention

The U-2 incident threatened to stall Nixon's path to the Republican nomination. New York governor Nelson Rockefeller, perhaps the richest man in the United States, had entertained the idea of challenging the vice president. He had flirted with a bid in the primaries, but quickly withdrew in the face of overwhelming support for Nixon among party leaders. Just prior to the convention, however, Rockefeller openly criticized Nixon and the Eisenhower administration for bungling foreign policy. A "draft Rockefeller" movement, not openly encouraged by the candidate but privately welcomed, generated significant public support. Highlighted by a massive media campaign, the Rockefeller movement claimed the allegiance of more than one-million Americans.

Rockefeller's real intention seemed to focus on influencing the party platform. Nixon feared a floor

fight on the convention floor over the party's direction, and held a secret meeting with Rockefeller to calm the waters. Nixon first offered Rockefeller the vice presidential nomination, which the governor turned down. Then they set out to find agreement on platform issues; Nixon relented on nearly every point. Rockefeller's "Fourteen Point Compact of Fifth Avenue," a public statement issued to sum up his meeting with Nixon, illustrated just how far the vice president compromised for the sake of party unity. The conservative Nixon supported planks on civil rights, and liberal positions on healthcare and education. Both moderate and conservative Republicans were outraged, believing that Nixon had contradicted Eisenhower's policies and surrendered the party's basic principles.

At the Chicago convention in late July, Nixon helped reunify Republicans with his vice presidential choice and his acceptance speech. He selected Henry Cabot Lodge, the ambassador to the United Nations and former Massachusetts senator, as his running mate. Lodge, grandson and namesake of the famous Republican senator from Massachusetts of the early twentieth century, was a moderately liberal New Englander who added weight to the Republican claim that their party was more fit to handle international crises than were Democrats. Because United Nations debates were televised in the late 1950s and early

HENRY CABOT LODGE, JR.

PARTY: Republican

DATE OF BIRTH: July 5, 1902

PLACE OF BIRTH: Nahant, Massachusetts

PARENTS: George Cabot and Mathilda Frelinghuysen Davis

EDUCATION: B.A., Harvard University, 1924

FAMILY: Married Emily Sears, 1926; children: George Cabot and Henry Sears

MILITARY SERVICE: U.S. Army, lieutenant colonel, 1941–1945

CAREER: Newspaper reporter, Boston *Evening Transcript*, 1923; newspaper reporter, New York *Herald Tribune*, 1924–32; Massachusetts state legislature, 1933–37; U.S. Senate, 1937–44 (resigned to serve in the Army), 1947–53; U.S. Representative in the United Nations, 1953–60; unsuccessful candidate for U.S. vice president, 1960; U.S. ambassador to South Vietnam, 1963–64, 1965–67; U.S. Ambassador to West Germany, 1968–69; chief U.S. representative to Paris peace talks with North Vietnam, 1969; U.S. special envoy to the Vatican, 1970–77; author, personal memoir, *The Storm Has Many Eyes*, 1973

DATE OF DEATH: February 27, 1985

PLACE OF DEATH: Beverly, Massachusetts

PLACE OF BURIAL: Mt. Auburn Cemetery, Cambridge, Massachusetts

1960s, most Americans were very familiar with Lodge, and recognized him as a foreign policy expert. Nixon's acceptance speech focused on foreign policy, promising a commitment to spread freedom to the world by a "renewed devotion to the great ideals of the American Revolution." The most memorable point of the evening came when Nixon declared: "When Mr. Khrushchev says our grandchildren will live under communism, let us say his grandchildren will live in freedom." After the conventions, the polls placed Nixon slightly ahead of Kennedy.

The General Election

The candidates pursued different strategies for winning the general election. Kennedy planned to concentrate his time and money on large electoral states such as Pennsylvania and Michigan, hoping that Johnson would help him carry the South. He assembled both party professionals and leading intellectuals, such as Arthur Schlesinger, Jr., and John Kenneth Galbraith, to coordinate his campaign and write speeches. The central theme they created was "working for a brighter future for all Americans." Kennedy's young volunteers set out to register millions of

new voters. Strategists hoped that the voter-registration drive would produce two Democratic votes for every one Republican.

Nixon maintained a Herculean campaign schedule, pledging to visit all fifty states. Since this itinerary took him to Alaska (a distant state with only three electoral votes) during the last days of the campaign, this pledge had questionable merit. Kennedy spent this time in Illinois and New Jersey, states with key blocs of electoral votes. Nixon's message emphasized his experience, and the peace and prosperity of the Eisenhower years. His campaign had a solid staff with clear strategies, but the candidate rarely took its advice. Running the race "his way" led to problems of consistency, direction, and low staff morale.

Nixon had few duties that limited his ability to campaign. He visited six states in the first ten days after the convention, stressing his experience and tough stance on communism. He met large and friendly crowds, grabbing newspaper headlines and gaining confidence everywhere he appeared. Then, in late August, Nixon banged his knee on a car door—and developed a potentially life-threatening staph infection that hospitalized him for two weeks. He lost valuable time due to his fifty-state commitment, but Nixon refused to go back on his word.

While Nixon began his campaign with a bang, Kennedy got bogged down in the Senate. Johnson, the vice presidential nominee, had scheduled a long session of Congress to highlight the Democratic legislative program for the fall congressional elections. Instead, wrangling in the upper chamber exposed deep divisions within the party over domestic issues—and kept Kennedy out of the limelight.

Once he hit the campaign trails, the religious issue reared its head again. Protestant ministers across the nation expressed concerns over his Catholicism. While he thought he had put the issue to rest in West Virginia, Kennedy realized that he needed to clarify his position on religion further. He accepted an invi-

Federal aid to needy areas for school construction, but he opposes any Federal subsidy of teachers' salaries which, he feels, would lead to Federal control of education.

He supports housing measures to help private enterprise give America the housing it needs.

He opposes the Forand Bill because it imposes direct Federal control over the individual's welfare, depriving him of freedom of choice. He favors Federal participation in a voluntary medical care program for the aged.

3) He is against segregation and discrimination.

As chairman of the President's Committee on Equal Job Opportunity, he has played an important role in eliminating discriminatory hiring by firms under Government contract.

We need a President who can get things done

Richard Nixon has the know-how

Richard Nixon is a skilled statesman with long experience both as a Congressman and a Senator. He knows how to organize the implementing action without which, under our democratic system, the noblest goals cannot be achieved. He recognizes politics as "the art of the possible."

We need a President who stands up for his beliefs

Richard Nixon's record speaks for itself

Richard Nixon has won every election in which he has run because he was willing to fight for his convictions. There was no question where he stood.

As an unknown in politics in 1946, his winning margin was 15,592 votes. His freshman term was marked by his work on foreign aid and the Taft-Hartley Act. The public's reaction? In 1948 he received not only the Republican backing for re-election but a Democratic majority as well. His margin: 141,509 votes.

In 1950, Richard Nixon won his Senate seat with a 680,847 margin, again with Democratic support. His 2.2 million vote topped the Republican registration of 1.9 million.

In 1952, Richard Nixon became Ike's running mate by popular acclamation. And in 1956 he was re-nominated by unanimous vote.

As all his victories demonstrate, Dick Nixon is as popular with Independents as he is with Republicans. He is truly the man of the people —the one man as big as the job.

With your support, Dick Nixon will win again in 1960!

Published by
NIXON VOLUNTEERS
Peter M. Flanigan, *Director*
P.O. Box 7398, Washington 4, D.C.

7560NV500M 237

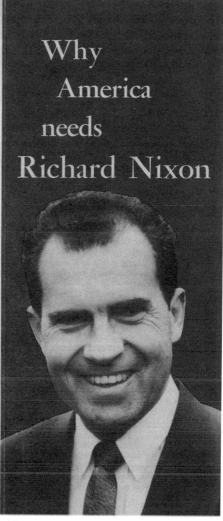

Why America needs Richard Nixon

Eisenhower's vice president in the 1950s, Richard Nixon inherited the leadership of the Republican Party in the 1960s. This brochure pictures Nixon during his run for the presidency in 1960.

tation to address the matter in Texas, at the Greater Houston Ministerial Association. With 600 people in attendance at the Rice hotel ballroom, Kennedy reaffirmed his belief in the separation of church and state. He pledged that, if elected, he would uphold the requirements of the Constitution over any claim by religious authority. In his brief speech and the question period afterward, Kennedy handled himself well. Still, the religious issue festered beneath the surface, even though it disappeared from media coverage of the campaign.

Both candidates understood the important role that television played in the election. Although of recent origin, the "tube" had become a fixture of the American way of life during the 1950s. TV set ownership increased from just over 10 percent of homes in 1950, to nearly 90 percent in 1960. Surveys indicated that the average American watched almost five hours of programming each day. Most politicians were anxious to take advantage of the new communications tool. Short and medium-length commercials were a staple of Kennedy's campaign. He bought air time in thirty-minute blocs for addresses to the nation. He participated in every national TV program that his schedule permitted. Handsome, relaxed, and genial, Kennedy came across well on television.

Nixon spent more money on television than Kennedy, but to less effect. The Republicans matched the Democrats with commercials, and then mounted a massive television campaign in the election's final week. For fifteen minutes each night, Nixon addressed the nation on live TV. The day prior to the

THE FIRST TELEVISED DEBATES

*O*n the evening of September 26, 1960, 70 million Americans tuned in to their local CBS-TV affiliates, and millions more listened on radio, as they witnessed an event that would radically alter the course of the election—and forever change presidential politics. Behind podiums on opposite sides of a television studio set stood Senator John Fitzgerald Kennedy, perceived by many as too inexperienced to be president, and Vice President Richard Milhous Nixon, a very public figure who had gained diplomatic stature by meeting and publicly debating Soviet Premier Nikita Khrushchev.

Both men appeared nervous as the lights came on, cameras rolled, and the nation's eyes focused on the first presidential debate in American history. (The famed Lincoln-Douglas debates in 1858 had been for a Senate race.) But each man had a quiet confidence. In intense practice sessions, Kennedy's campaign staff had quizzed and prepped their candidate for every possible question. Nixon, however, had spent most of the afternoon before the debate alone in his hotel room. A confident Nixon had tried to get some rest, and seemed content to rely on his knowledge of the issues and on his highly publicized debating skills.

No one knew what to expect. No precedent existed—debates would not become a regular part of the presidential campaign until 1976—and the candidates approached the evening with different styles. Kennedy spoke with a reassuring ease. Nixon debated more formally. The audience quickly warmed to

election, Republicans spent $400,000 on a four-hour afternoon telethon and on more than one hour of prime time and late-night programs featuring Hollywood celebrities, as well as politicians.

In addition to commercial air time, the major television networks offered each candidate ten hours of free time. Nixon and Kennedy agreed to use this opportunity to appear together in debates. They reasoned that this format would allow each of them to reach a cross section of Americans, especially many independent and swing voters. Ahead in the polls, Nixon initially wanted a single debate, confident that his rhetorical skills would allow him to deliver a knock-out punch in one encounter. As the underdog, and confident of his on-camera style, Kennedy pressed for five debates; the candidates compromised on four.

The debates were a key factor in the outcome of the election, although it is difficult to assess their precise effect. Seventy million Americans watched the first debate. Television audiences thought that Kennedy had won hands down. But people listening on the radio scored the contest a draw, or credited Nixon with the victory. While neither candidate made embarrassing errors or dealt impressive blows, the power of the new medium became clear. Nixon, looking tired and underweight from his hospitaliza-

tion, suffered in his visual comparison to the handsome and charismatic Kennedy. Just by holding his own against the vice president, the Massachusetts senator trumped the Republican's best card—the idea that Kennedy was an inexperienced lightweight. Republican insiders realized that their party had taken a big hit; Democrats finally recognized that their man had a real chance to win. Style mattered over substance in the television age—and first impressions on screen were difficult to change. (See "The First Televised Debates," above.)

Smaller audiences watched the final three debates, which contained few memorable moments. Kennedy did unveil a plan to create a Peace Corps, and made a pledge to close an alleged missile gap with the Soviet Union. Nixon looked much better in the final three debates, but suggested nothing new. Nor did his later appearances make up for the ground he had lost. A Gallup poll taken before the debates showed Nixon with a slight lead; Kennedy moved ahead of Nixon, by a 49 to 46 percent margin, after the second debate. When the debates concluded two weeks before the election, Kennedy's margin had increased to 51 to 45 percent. A CBS-TV poll revealed that 6 percent of those questioned had made up their minds on a candidate based solely on watching the debates—and more than 70 percent of them chose Kennedy.

Kennedy's style. Nixon's demeanor made him seem uneasy and defensive. Nonetheless, the candidates made no decisive points on the issues. Rather they reiterated campaign slogans and tried not to make mistakes. To those listening on radio, the debate was a tie, or even a Nixon victory; but Kennedy had shed the image of inexperience by holding his own against the vice president.

That night, television demonstrated its full impact. While radio listeners heard a closely matched debate without a clear-cut winner, the much larger television audience would come away with a completely different conclusion. The candidates could not have been more dissimilar in appearance. Kennedy, young and handsome, dressed in a dark suit that made him stand out prominently in front of a light-gray background, displayed grace and wit in front of the camera. His performance charmed viewers, and the message took a back seat to the messenger. Nixon, haggard from a two-week stay in the hospital, and exhausted from a frantic campaign schedule, came across poorly. Furthermore Nixon, who needed to shave twice a day to keep a clean face, chose instead to apply "Lazy Shave," a powdery-white substance that supposedly hid his "five o'clock shadow." When he began to sweat profusely beneath the hot stage lights and wiped his face, he smeared the make-up, leaving white streaks across his cheeks.

By almost a two-to-one margin, television audience polls declared Kennedy the winner. Even Nixon supporters declared that their candidate had looked tired. Gallup polls before the first debate had Nixon leading, 50 to 44 percent. After the debate, Kennedy would surge ahead, 49 to 46 percent. The television era in presidential politics had begun—and, in American elections then and since, the candidate's charisma has prevailed over the substance of the issues presented.

The first Kennedy–Nixon TV debate in 1960, pictured here, gave the relatively unknown Kennedy a boost in the presidential race, and launched television as a central tool of electioneering. *(Brown Brothers)*

The debates helped to energize the Kennedy campaign. Throngs of jubilant supporters mobbed the candidate at every stop. His strategy emphasized the large northern states during the last weeks of the race. Kennedy had avoided attacking the popular Eisenhower, but escalated his criticism of Nixon on Social Security, taxes, and farm policy. With a combination of sarcasm and reasoning, he attempted to discredit his opponent. In New Mexico, Kennedy declared:

> Mr. Nixon quoted me as having said that he and the Republicans had always opposed Social Security, and in that wonderful choice of words which distinguishes him as a great national leader, he asserted that this was a barefaced lie. Having seen him four times close up in this campaign [the debates], and made up, I would not accuse Mr. Nixon of being barefaced, but I think the American people next Tuesday can determine who is telling the truth.

Nixon parried the attack by trumpeting his diplomatic experience, and claimed that some of his recommendations to Eisenhower had become policy. To his embarrassment, reporters asked the president at one of his press conferences if he could discuss one of Nixon's important decisions. Eisenhower had shot back, "If you give me a week, I might think of one." A few weeks later, vice presidential nominee Henry Cabot Lodge promised that Nixon would appoint an African American to his cabinet. Fearing the exodus of the southern whites, a terrified and infuriated Nixon rejected the suggestion.

African-American voters were an important factor in the election's outcome. Although disfranchised in the South, many blacks supported Kennedy where they could vote. Race and civil rights remained a sensitive issue among Democrats. Northern Democrats had taken the lead in demanding an end to segregation. But southern whites remained powerful in the party, and they generally supported segregation. The Kennedy camp was fearful of the consequence of pressing civil rights too vigorously, lest the issue drive a wedge into the "solid" Democratic South. Republicans were equally cautious to not antagonize white voters.

Kennedy's role in gaining the Rev. Martin Luther King, Jr.'s release from jail in October played well with the black community. King had been given a four-month sentence for a minor traffic violation in Georgia. Kennedy's brother, Robert, persuaded the judge in the matter to suspend the sentence. The intervention received little notice in the mainstream press, but the story spread across African-American communities. Black churches distributed over 500,000 leaflets praising Kennedy's success in freeing the civil rights leader. King's father, a lifelong Republican and a powerful figure in Atlanta, announced that "I've got a suitcase full of votes, and I'm going to take them to Mr. Kennedy." The turnout of African-American voters increased by 10 percent in 1960 from the previous presidential election—and they would give a higher proportion of their votes to Kennedy than they had for Stevenson, the Democratic candidate in 1956. Illinois and Michigan, two states with sizable black votes, were pivotal in Kennedy's ability to win a majority in the Electoral College.

Sagging in the polls, Nixon decided to play the presidential card. Initially, he had refused to draw Ike into the campaign, fearing that the tactic might be perceived as a sign of his inability to win on his own. But Nixon relented in the final stretch, consenting to let the popular Eisenhower stump for him. True to form, the media and the Democrats criticized Nixon for riding the president's coattails. Nonetheless, Eisenhower's presence in the campaign contributed to a late surge in Nixon's candidacy.

The Result

Nixon's recovery made the contest too close to call on the eve of the election. Nearly sixty-nine million Americans cast ballots the next day, an 11 percent jump over 1956. In a neck-and-neck horserace, fewer than 120,000 votes separated Kennedy and Nixon at the finish line. Television networks could not pick a winner late into election night. Nixon addressed the nation at 3 A.M., but did not concede. All signs pointed to a Kennedy victory by morning, when secret service began protecting the apparent president-elect. Despite the narrowness of his plurality in the popular vote, Kennedy won convincingly in the Electoral College, 303 to 219.

The election had been full of voting irregularities. Some Republicans urged Nixon to request a recount and investigations of alleged fraud. Of nearly five million votes cast in Illinois, Kennedy's plurality stood at just 8,858, and most other states polled very close results. Nixon would have won an Electoral College victory had there been a reversal of less than 30,000 total votes in Illinois and Texas. Rumors of serious problems at the polls persisted in those states. Some claimed that Chicago mayor Richard J. Daley allowed residents of Cook County (Ill.) cemeteries to vote, and that Democratic officials in Texas threw out Nixon votes.

While most rumors simply did not withstand close inspection, there could be no certainty without lengthy investigations. As late as eight days after the election, Nixon would remain quiet while his aides, Bob Finch and Len Hall, checked into voting irregularities in eight states. Peter Flanigan, another aide, established a Nixon Recount Commission in Chicago. Nixon later claimed that many Republicans urged him to challenge the results. Some historians contend that Nixon put out the feelers for a recount, but received little support—most of his informants believed that Nixon had lost.

Nixon, a man for whom political power and the presidency meant everything, did not contest the election. He was still young, and would live to fight another day. For the rest of his life, Nixon stood by what he told New York *Herald Tribune* reporter Earl Mazo, shortly after the election: "The country can't afford the agony of a constitutional crisis, and I will not be party to creating one, just to become president." Nixon gracefully bowed out to preserve his future political prospects, and Kennedy assumed the presidency with a razor-thin mandate.

Why did Kennedy win? First, scholars probably will never know the extent of voting fraud in Chicago, what happened to ballots in Texas, or how corruption might have helped Nixon in other districts. Second, Kennedy's dynamic personality, good looks on television, and his appeal among African Americans all contributed to his success in varying, although unknown, proportions. Third, Kennedy won primarily because enough renegade Democrats returned to the party fold. Some were Catholics who had gravitated to the Republicans during the anti-Communist crusade of the late 1940s and early 1950s, appalled by Soviet repression of Catholicism in Eastern Europe. Similarly, some southern white Democrats had jumped to the Republicans and the likable Eisenhower, in part as northern Democrats gingerly embraced civil rights. Finally, new, first-time voters favored Kennedy more than Nixon.

John Kennedy's religion, however, kept the election close. Eisenhower had been able to attract Democratic votes from all parts of the country. Republican candidates for Congress lagged well behind Eisen-

hower's totals in their district. By the end of the 1950s, Democrats had a substantial majority in Congress. Had Kennedy been Protestant, he probably would have won easily. Most of the Eisenhower Democrats came back to the party in 1960, with the exception of a sizeable contingent of southern white Protestants. These white, evangelical, anti-Catholic southerners were key to the outcome of the election. One-fourth of this group refused to vote for Kennedy; four years later, they gave their votes to Lyndon Johnson. While Kennedy partially compensated for these defections by increasing his support among northern Catholics, religious prejudice nearly cost him the White House.

Craig R. Coenen

Bibliography

Brodie, Fawn. *Richard Nixon, The Shaping of His Character*. New York: W. W. Norton, 1981.

Burner, David. *John F. Kennedy and a New Generation*. Boston: Little, Brown, 1988.

David, Lester, and Irene David. *JFK: The Wit, Charm, Tears. Remembrances from Camelot*. Toronto: Paperjacks, 1988.

David, Theodore Paul. *The Presidential Election and Transition, 1960–1961*. Washington, D.C.: Brookings Institution, 1961.

Kallina, Edmund F. *Courthouse Over White House: Chicago and the Presidential Election of 1960*. Orlando: University of Central Florida Press, 1988.

Kraus, Sidney, ed. *The Great Debate: Kennedy vs. Nixon, 1960*. Bloomington: Indiana University Press, 1997.

Martin, Ralph G. *A Hero for Our Time: An Intimate Story of the Kennedy Years*. New York: Fawcett Crest, 1983.

Matthews, Chris. *Kennedy and Nixon: The Rivalry That Shaped Postwar America*. New York: Simon and Schuster, 1996.

Nixon, Richard. *RN: The Memoirs of Richard Nixon*. New York: Grosset and Dunlap, 1978.

O'Donnell, Kenneth, David F. Powers, and Joe McCarthy. *Johnny, We Hardly Knew Ye*. Boston: Little, Brown, 1970.

Parmet, Herbert S. *JFK: The Presidency of John F. Kennedy*. New York: Penguin Books, 1983.

———. *Richard Nixon and His America*. Boston: Little, Brown, 1990.

Schlesinger, Arthur, Jr. *A Thousand Days: John F. Kennedy in the White House*. Boston: Fawcett, 1965.

Sorenson, Theodore. *Kennedy*. New York: Harper and Row, 1965.

White, Theodore. *The Making of the President 1960*. New York,: Atheneum, 1961.

THE VOTE: ELECTION OF 1960

State	Total No. of Electors	Total Popular Vote	Electoral Vote D	R	O[a]	Margin of Victory Votes	% Total Vote	Kennedy Democrat Votes	%	Nixon Republican Votes	%	Others Votes	%
Alabama	11	570,225	5		6	86,069	15.1%	324,050	56.8%	237,981	41.7%	8,194	1.4%
Alaska	3	60,762		3		1,144	1.9%	29,809	49.1%	30,953	50.9%	0	0.0%
Arizona	4	398,491		4		44,460	11.2%	176,781	44.4%	221,241	55.5%	469	0.1%
Arkansas	8	428,509	8			30,541	7.1%	215,049	50.2%	184,508	43.1%	28,952	6.8%
California	32	6,506,578		32		35,623	0.5%	3,224,099	49.6%	3,259,722	50.1%	22,757	0.3%
Colorado	6	736,246		6		71,613	9.7%	330,629	44.9%	402,242	54.6%	3,375	0.5%
Connecticut	8	1,222,883	8			91,242	7.5%	657,055	53.7%	565,813	46.3%	15	0.0%
Delaware	3	196,683	3			3,217	1.6%	99,590	50.6%	96,373	49.0%	720	0.4%
Florida	10	1,544,176		10		46,776	3.0%	748,700	48.5%	795,476	51.5%	0	0.0%
Georgia	12	733,349	12			184,166	25.1%	458,638	62.5%	274,472	37.4%	239	0.0%
Hawaii	3	184,705	3			115	0.1%	92,410	50.0%	92,295	50.0%	0	0.0%
Idaho	4	300,450		4		22,744	7.6%	138,853	46.2%	161,597	53.8%	0	0.0%
Illinois	27	4,757,409	27			8,858	0.2%	2,377,846	50.0%	2,368,988	49.8%	10,575	0.2%
Indiana	13	2,135,360		13		222,762	10.4%	952,358	44.6%	1,175,120	55.0%	7,882	0.4%
Iowa	10	1,273,810		10		171,816	13.5%	550,565	43.2%	722,381	56.7%	864	0.1%
Kansas	8	928,825		8		198,261	21.3%	363,213	39.1%	561,474	60.4%	4,138	0.4%
Kentucky	10	1,124,462		10		80,752	7.2%	521,855	46.4%	602,607	53.6%	0	0.0%
Louisiana	10	807,891	10			176,359	21.8%	407,339	50.4%	230,980	28.6%	169,572	21.0%
Maine	5	421,767		5		59,449	14.1%	181,159	43.0%	240,608	57.0%	0	0.0%
Maryland	9	1,055,349	9			76,270	7.2%	565,808	53.6%	489,538	46.4%	3	0.0%
Massachusetts	16	2,469,480	16			510,424	20.7%	1,487,174	60.2%	976,750	39.6%	5,556	0.2%
Michigan	20	3,318,097	20			66,841	2.0%	1,687,269	50.9%	1,620,428	48.8%	10,400	0.3%
Minnesota	11	1,541,887	11			22,018	1.4%	779,933	50.6%	757,915	49.2%	4,039	0.3%
Mississippi	8	298,171			8	7,886	2.6%	108,362	36.3%	73,561	24.7%	116,248	39.0%
Missouri	13	1,934,422	13			9,980	0.5%	972,201	50.3%	962,221	49.7%	0	0.0%
Montana	4	277,579		4		6,950	2.5%	134,891	48.6%	141,841	51.1%	847	0.3%
Nebraska	6	613,095		6		148,011	24.1%	232,542	37.9%	380,553	62.1%	0	0.0%
Nevada	3	107,267	3			2,493	2.3%	54,880	51.2%	52,387	48.8%	0	0.0%
New Hampshire	4	295,761		4		20,217	6.8%	137,772	46.6%	157,989	53.4%	0	0.0%
New Jersey	16	2,773,111	16			22,091	0.8%	1,385,415	50.0%	1,363,324	49.2%	24,372	0.9%
New Mexico	4	311,107	4			2,294	0.7%	156,027	50.2%	153,733	49.4%	1,347	0.4%
New York	45	7,291,079	45			383,666	5.3%	3,830,085	52.5%	3,446,419	47.3%	14,575	0.2%
North Carolina	14	1,368,556	14			57,716	4.2%	713,136	52.1%	655,420	47.9%	0	0.0%
North Dakota	4	278,431		4		30,347	10.9%	123,963	44.5%	154,310	55.4%	158	0.1%
Ohio	25	4,161,859		25		273,363	6.6%	1,944,248	46.7%	2,217,611	53.3%	0	0.0%
Oklahoma	8	903,150		7	1	162,928	18.0%	370,111	41.0%	533,039	59.0%	0	0.0%
Oregon	6	776,421		6		40,658	5.2%	367,402	47.3%	408,060	52.6%	959	0.1%
Pennsylvania	32	5,006,541	32			116,326	2.3%	2,556,282	51.1%	2,439,956	48.7%	10,303	0.2%
Rhode Island	4	405,535	4			110,530	27.3%	258,032	63.6%	147,502	36.4%	1	0.0%
South Carolina	8	386,688	8			9,571	2.5%	198,129	51.2%	188,558	48.8%	1	0.0%
South Dakota	4	306,487		4		50,347	16.4%	128,070	41.8%	178,417	58.2%	0	0.0%
Tennessee	11	1,051,792		11		75,124	7.1%	481,453	45.8%	556,577	52.9%	13,762	1.3%
Texas	24	2,311,845	24			46,233	2.0%	1,167,932	50.5%	1,121,699	48.5%	22,214	1.0%
Utah	4	374,709		4		36,113	9.6%	169,248	45.2%	205,361	54.8%	100	0.0%
Vermont	3	167,324		3		28,945	17.3%	69,186	41.3%	98,131	58.6%	7	0.0%
Virginia	12	771,449		12		42,194	5.5%	362,327	47.0%	404,521	52.4%	4,601	0.6%
Washington	9	1,241,572		9		29,975	2.4%	599,298	48.3%	629,273	50.7%	13,001	1.0%
West Virginia	8	837,781	8			45,791	5.5%	441,786	52.7%	395,995	47.3%	0	0.0%
Wisconsin	12	1,729,082		12		64,370	3.7%	830,805	48.0%	895,175	51.8%	3,102	0.2%
Wyoming	3	140,782		3		14,120	10.0%	63,331	45.0%	77,451	55.0%	0	0.0%
TOTAL	537	68,838,990	303	219	15	118,550	0.2%	34,227,096	49.7%	34,108,546	49.5%	503,348	0.7%

[a] Unpledged electors won in Mississippi with 116,248 votes. These 8 electors along with 6 unpledged electors in Alabama and 1 Nixon elector in Oklahoma voted for Harry Byrd.

For sources, see p. 1130.

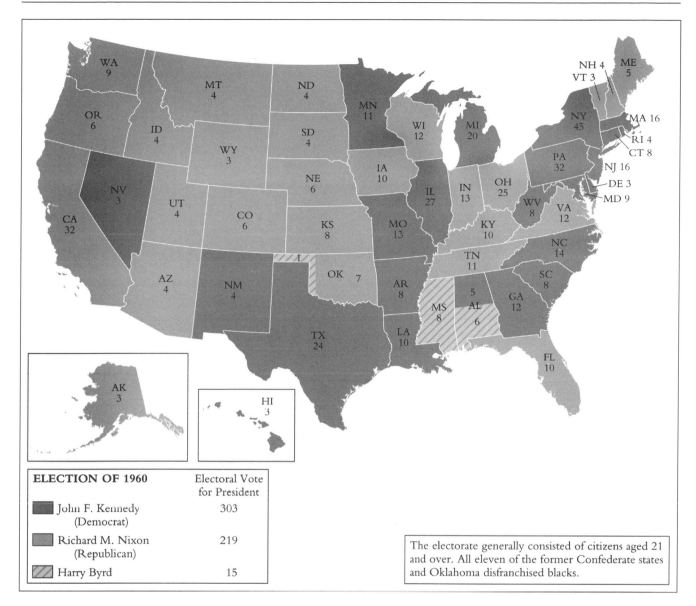

WA 9
OR 6
MT 4
ND 4
MN 11
NH 4
VT 3
ME 5
ID 4
SD 4
WI 12
MI 20
NY 45
MA 16
RI 4
CT 8
WY 3
IA 10
PA 32
NJ 16
NV 3
UT 4
NE 6
IL 27
IN 13
OH 25
DE 3
MD 9
CA 32
CO 6
KS 8
MO 13
WV 8
VA 12
KY 10
NC 14
AZ 4
NM 4
OK 7
AR 8
TN 11
SC 8
TX 24
LA 10
MS 8
AL 6
5
GA 12
FL 10

AK 3

HI 3

ELECTION OF 1960   Electoral Vote
for President

John F. Kennedy   303
(Democrat)

Richard M. Nixon   219
(Republican)

Harry Byrd   15

The electorate generally consisted of citizens aged 21 and over. All eleven of the former Confederate states and Oklahoma disfranchised blacks.

DOCUMENTS: ELECTION OF 1960

In 1960 the Democratic nominee, Massachusetts Senator John F. Kennedy, had to overcome the coattails of a popular Republican president, the experience of Vice President Richard Nixon, and concerns of many Americans about his youth and religion. (He was only 42 years old and a Catholic.) However, in an extremely close election, Kennedy prevailed by just over 100,000 votes. Kennedy echoed previous Democratic nominees Woodrow Wilson, who in 1912 had proposed a "New Freedom," and Franklin D. Roosevelt, who in 1932 had offered a "New Deal" to meet the challenges of the times. In Document 1, Kennedy's speech accepting the Democratic nomination, he offered to open a "New Frontier . . . uncharted areas of science and space, unsolved problems of peace and war, unconquered pockets of ignorance and prejudice, unanswered questions of poverty and surplus."

Document 2, a statement by Governor Nelson Rockefeller of New York, described the content of a meeting he had with Richard Nixon. In order to get Rockefeller's support for his candidacy, Nixon had accepted Rockefeller's liberal-Republican agenda. In accepting the Republican nomination, Nixon averted further party unrest with a unifying speech concentrating on foreign policy, Document 3, proclaimed "When Mr. Khrushchev [the Soviet premier] says our grandchildren will live under communism, let us say his grandchildren will live in freedom."

Kennedy was unable to quell unrest over his religion. (No Catholic had ever won the presidency, and the only Catholic ever nominated by a major party—Al Smith, in 1928—had encountered religious prejudice and personal attacks.) In an effort to put the issue behind him, Kennedy addressed the Houston Ministerial Association, Document 4, and affirmed his dedication to the separation of church and state. The first-ever televised presidential debate gave Kennedy a boost, by showing that he could hold his own against the more experienced vice president. However, all four debates offered little in terms of conflict over issues. Document 5, excerpts from the fourth presidential debate, illustrated the basic difference between the two candidates. Kennedy warned of a "missile gap" with the Soviets, while Nixon pointed to the Eisenhower administration's accomplishments and pledged more of the same. Document 6, a Kennedy campaign speech, called on America's youth to serve, in what would become the Peace Corps, to restore the nation's strength and establish freedom abroad. Meanwhile, Nixon, in a campaign speech in New York City, Document 7, warned voters that a Democratic administration would raise taxes, cause inflation, and mishandle foreign policy.

Document 1

Nomination Acceptance Speech by Senator John F. Kennedy, Los Angeles, July 15, 1960

The New Deal [President Roosevelt's remedy for the Depression] and the Fair Deal [Truman's liberal program after World War II] were bold measures for their generations—but this is a new generation.

A technological revolution on the farm has led to an output explosion—but we have not yet learned to harness that explosion usefully, while protecting our farmers' right to full parity income.

An urban population revolution has overcrowded our schools, cluttered up our suburbs, and increased the squalor of our slums.

A peaceful revolution for human rights—demanding an end to racial discrimination in all parts of our community life—has strained at the leashes imposed by timid Executive leadership.

A medical revolution has extended the life of our elder citizens without providing the dignity and security those later years deserve. And a revolution of automation finds machines replacing men in the mines and mills of America, without replacing their income or their training or their need to pay the family doctor, grocer, and landlord.

There has also been a change—a slippage—in our intellectual and moral strength. Seven lean years of drought and famine have withered the fields of ideas. Blight has descended on our regulatory agencies—and a dry rot, beginning in Washington, is seeping into every corner of America—in the payola mentality, the expense account way of life, the confusion between what is legal and what is

right. Too many Americans have lost their way, their will, and their sense of historic purpose.

It is time, in short, for a new generation of leadership—new men to cope with new problems and new opportunities. . . .

Woodrow Wilson's New Freedom promised our nation a new political and economic framework. Franklin Roosevelt's New Deal promised security and succor to those in need. But the New Frontier of which I speak is not a set of promises—it is a set of challenges. It sums up not what I intend to offer the American people, but what I intend to ask of them. It appeals to their pride, not their pocketbook—it holds out the promise of more sacrifice instead of more security.

But I tell you the New Frontier is here, whether we seek it or not. Beyond that frontier are uncharted areas of science and space, unsolved problems of peace and war, unconquered pockets of ignorance and prejudice, unanswered questions of poverty and surplus.

It would be easier to shrink back from that frontier, to look to the safe mediocrity of the past, to be lulled by good intentions and high rhetoric—and those who prefer that course should not cast their votes for me, regardless of party.

But I believe the times demand invention, innovation, imagination, decision. I am asking each of you to be new pioneers on that New Frontier. My call is to the young in heart, regardless of age—to the stout in spirit, regardless of party—to all who respond to the scriptural call:

"Be strong and of good courage; be not afraid, neither be thou dismayed." For courage—not complacency—is our need today—leadership—not salesmanship. And the only valid test of leadership is the ability to lead, and lead vigorously. A tired nation, said David Lloyd George, is a tory nation—and the United States today cannot afford to be either tired or tory.

There may be those who wish to hear more—more promises to this group or that—more harsh rhetoric about the men in the Kremlin—more assurances of a golden future, where taxes are always low and subsidies ever high. But my promises are in the platform you have adopted. Our ends will not be won by rhetoric and we can have faith in the future only if we have faith in ourselves.

For the harsh facts of the matter are that we stand on this frontier at a turning point in history. We must prove all over again whether this nation—or any nation so conceived—can long endure—whether our society—with its freedom of choice, its breadth of opportunity, its range of alternatives—can compete with the single-minded advance of the Communist system.

Can a nation organized and governed such as ours endure? That is the real question. Have we the nerve and the will? Can we carry through in an age where we will witness not only new breakthroughs in weapons of destruction—but also a race for mastery of the sky and the rain, the ocean and the tides, the far side of space, and the inside of men's minds?

Are we up to the task? Are we equal to the challenge? Are we willing to match the Russian sacrifice of the present for the future? Or must we sacrifice our future in order to enjoy the present?

That is the question of the New Frontier. That is the choice our nation must make—a choice that lies not merely between two men or two parties, but between the public interest and private comfort—between national greatness and national decline—between the fresh air of progress and the stale, dank atmosphere of "normalcy"—between determined dedication and creeping mediocrity.

Source: John Fitzgerald Kennedy Library Web site, www.cs.umb.edu/jfklibrary/j071560.htm.

Document 2

Statement by Governor Nelson A. Rockefeller, New York, July 23, 1960

The Vice President and I met today at my home in New York City. The meeting took place at the Vice President's request.

The purpose of the meeting was to discuss the platform of the Republican Party. During the course of the meeting we discussed our views with Chairman Percy and other members of the Platform Committee by telephone. The Vice President and I reached agreement on the following specific and basic positions on foreign policy and national defense:

1. The growing vigor and aggressiveness of communism demands new and profound effort and action in all areas of American life.

2. The vital need of our foreign policy is new political creativity—leading and inspiring the formation, in all great regions of the free world, of confederations, large enough and strong enough to meet modern problems and challenges. We should promptly lead toward the formation of such confederations in the North Atlantic Community and in the Western Hemisphere.

3. In the field of disarmament, we shall:
   a. Intensify the quest for better detection methods;
   b. Discontinue nuclear weapon tests in the atmosphere;
   c. Discontinue other tests as detection methods make possible; and
   d. Resume immediately underground nuclear testing for purposes of improving methods of detection.

4. In national defense, the swiftness of the technological revolution—the warning signs of Soviet aggressiveness—makes clear that new efforts are necessary, for the facts of our survival in the 1950s give no assurance of such survival, in the same military posture, in the 1960s.

5. The two imperatives of national security in the 1960s are:
   a. A powerful second-strike capacity—a nuclear retaliatory power capable of surviving surprise attacks to inflict devastating punishment on any aggressor, and
   b. A modern, flexible and balanced military establishment with forces capable of deterring or meeting any local aggression.

6. These imperatives require: more and improved bombers, airborne alert, speeded production of missiles and Polaris submarines, accelerated dispersal and hardening of bases, full modernization of the equipment of our ground forces, and an intensified program for civil defense.

7. The United States can afford and must provide the increased expenditures to implement fully this necessary program for strengthening our defense posture. There must be no price ceiling on America's security.

The Vice President and I also reached agreement on the following specific positions on domestic affairs:

1. Our government must be reorganized—especially in supporting the President in the crucial decision-making process—to cope effectively with modern problems and challenges. Specifically this calls for:
   a. Creation of a post to assist the President in the whole area of national security and international affairs;

b. Creation of a post to assist in planning and management of domestic affairs; and

c. Reorganization of defense planning and command to achieve, under the President, unified doctrine and unified direction of forces.

2. The rate of our economic growth must, as promptly as possible, be accelerated by policies and programs stimulating our free enterprise system—to allow us to meet the demands of national defense and the growing social needs and a higher standard of living for our growing population. As the Vice President pointed out in a speech in 1958, the achievement of a five percent rate of growth would produce an additional $10 billion of tax revenue in 1962.

3. Our farm programs must be realistically reoriented by:

a. Finding and encouraging ways for our low-income farmers to become more productive members of our growing economy;

b. At least doubling of the conservation reserve;

c. Use of price supports at levels best-fitted to specific commodities in order to widen markets, ease production controls, and help achieve equitable farm income;

d. Faster disposal of surpluses through an expanded "Food for Peace" program and allocation of some surplus to a stockpile for civil defense.

4. Our program for civil rights must assure aggressive action to remove the remaining vestiges of segregation or discrimination in all areas of national life—voting and housing, schools and jobs. It will express support for the objectives of the sit-in demonstrators, and will commend the action of those businessmen who have abandoned the practice of refusing to serve food at their lunch counters to their Negro customers, and will urge all others to follow their example.

5. Our program for health insurance for the aged shall provide insurance on a sound fiscal basis through a contributory system under which beneficiaries have the option of purchasing private health insurance.

6. Our program for labor, while reaffirming our efforts to support and strengthen the processes of free collective bargaining, shall provide for improved procedures for the resolution of disputes endangering the national welfare.

7. Our program for education will meet our urgent educational needs by calling for prompt and substantial grant aid for school construction, primarily on the basis of financial needs, under an equalization formula, and with matching funds by the states—including these further measures for higher education: grants-in-aid for such buildings as classrooms and laboratories, an expanded loan program for dormitories, expanded student-loan and graduate fellowship programs, and inauguration of a program of federal scholarships for the most able undergraduates.

These constitute the basic positions for which I have been fighting.

If they are embodied in the Republican Party platform, as adopted by the Convention, they will constitute a platform that I can support with pride and vigor.

Source: New York Times, July 24, 1960.

Document 3

Nomination Acceptance Speech by Vice President Richard M. Nixon, Chicago, July 28, 1960

In this campaign we are going to take no States for granted, and we are not going to concede any States to the opposition.

I announce to you tonight, and I pledge to you, that I personally will carry this campaign into every one of the 50 States of this Nation between now and November 8. And in this campaign I make a prediction—I say that, just as in 1952 and 1956, millions of Democrats will join us, not because they are deserting their party, but because their party deserted them at Los Angeles two weeks ago.

Now, I have suggested to you what our friends of the opposition offered to the American people. What do we offer? First, we are proud to offer the best eight-year record of any administration in the history of this country. But, my fellow Americans, that isn't all and that isn't enough, because we happen to believe that a record is not something to stand on, but something to build on; and in building on the record of this administration we shall build a better America, we shall build an America in which we shall see the realization of the dreams of millions of people, not only in America but throughout the world, for a fuller, freer, richer life than men have ever known in the history of mankind. . . .

The Communists proclaim over and over again that their aim is the victory of communism throughout the world. It is not enough for us to reply that our aim is to contain communism, to defend the free world against communism, to hold the line against communism; the only answer to a strategy of victory for the Communist world is a strategy of victory for the free world.

But let the victory we seek be not victory over any other nation or any other people. Let it be the victory of freedom over tyranny, of plenty over hunger, of health over disease, in every country of the world.

When Mr. Khrushchev says our grandchildren will live under communism, let us say his grandchildren will live in freedom. When Mr. Khrushchev says the Monroe Doctrine is dead in the Americas, we say the doctrine of freedom applies everywhere in the world. . . .

Let us make it clear to them that our aim in helping them is not merely to stop communism, but that in the great American tradition of concern for those less fortunate than we are, that we welcome the opportunity to work with people everywhere in helping them to achieve their aspirations for a life of human dignity. And this means that our primary aim must be not to help governments but to help people, to help people attain the life they deserve.

In essence, what I am saying tonight is that our answer to the threat of the Communist revolution is renewed devotion to the great ideals of the American Revolution, ideals that caught the imagination of the world 180 years ago and that still live in the minds and hearts of people everywhere.

Source: New York Times, July 28, 1960.

Document 4

Speech by Senator John F. Kennedy to the Houston Ministerial Association, September 12, 1960

I am grateful for your generous invitation to state my views.

While the so-called religious issue is necessarily and properly the chief topic here tonight, I want to emphasize from the outset that I believe that we have far more critical issues in the 1960 election: the spread of Communist influence, until it now festers only ninety miles off the coast of Florida—the humiliating treatment of our President and Vice President by those who no longer respect our power—the hungry children I saw in West Virginia, the old people who cannot pay their doctor's bills, the families forced to give up their farms—an America with too many slums, with too few schools, and too late to the moon and outer space.

These are the real issues which should decide this campaign. And they are not religious issues—for war and hunger and ignorance and despair know no religious barrier.

But because I am a Catholic, and no Catholic has ever been elected President, the real issues in this campaign have been obscured—perhaps deliberately in some quarters less responsible than this. So it is apparently necessary for me to state once again—not what kind of church I believe in, for that should be important only to me, but what kind of America I believe in.

I believe in an America where the separation of church and state is absolute—where no Catholic prelate would tell the President (should he be a Catholic) how to act and no Protestant minister would tell his parishioners for whom to vote—where no church or church school is granted any public funds or political preference—and where no man is denied public office merely because his religion differs from the President who might appoint him or the people who might elect him.

I believe in an America that is officially neither Catholic, Protestant nor Jewish—where no public official either requests or accepts instructions on public policy from the Pope, the National Council of Churches or any other ecclesiastical source—where no religious body seeks to impose its will directly or indirectly upon the general populace or the public acts of its officials—and where religious liberty is so indivisible that an act against one church is treated as an act against all.

For while this year it may be a Catholic against whom the finger of suspicion is pointed, in other years it has been, and may someday be again, a Jew—or a Quaker—or a Unitarian—or a Baptist. It was Virginia's harassment of Baptist preachers, for example, that led to Jefferson's statute of religious freedom. Today, I may be the victim—but tomorrow it may be you—until the whole fabric of our harmonious society is ripped apart at a time of great national peril.

Finally, I believe in an America where religious intolerance will someday end—where all men and all churches are treated as equal—where every man has the same right to attend or not to attend the church of his choice—where there is no Catholic vote, no anti-Catholic vote, no bloc voting of any kind—and where Catholics, Protestants and Jews, both the lay and the pastoral level, will refrain from those attitudes of disdain and division which have so often marred their works in the past, and promote instead the American ideal of brotherhood.

That is the kind of America in which I believe. And it represents the kind of Presidency in which I believe—a great office that must be neither humbled by making it the instrument of any religious group, nor tarnished by arbitrarily withholding it, its occupancy, from the members of any religious group. . . . For, without reservation, I can, and I quote, "solemnly swear that I will faithfully execute the office of President of the United States and will to the best of my ability preserve, protect and defend the Constitution, so help me God."

Source: John Fitzgerald Kennedy Library Web site, www.cs.umb.edu/jfklibrary/j091260.htm.

Document 5. Excerpts from the Fourth Kennedy-Nixon Presidential Debate, October 21, 1960

Kennedy's Opening Statement

The Communists say, "Come with us; look what we've done." And we've been in—on the whole, uninterested. I think we're going to have to do better. Mr. Nixon talks about our being the strongest country in the world. I think we are today. But we were far stronger relative to the Communists five years ago, and what is of great concern is that the balance of power is in danger of moving with them. They made a breakthrough in missiles, and by nineteen sixty-one, two, and three, they will be outnumbering us in missiles. I'm not as confident as he is that we will be the strongest military power by 1963. He talks about economic growth as a great indicator of freedom. I agree with him. What we do in this country, the kind of society that we build, that will tell whether freedom will be sustained around the world. . . .

Nixon's Closing Statement

Senator Kennedy has said tonight again what he has said several times in the course of this—these debates and in the campaign, that American is standing still. America is not standing still. It has not been standing still. And let's set the record straight right now by looking at the record. . . . We are first in the world in space, as I've indicated; we are first in science; we are first in education, and we're going to move even further ahead with the kind of leadership that we can provide in these years ahead.

Source: John Fitzgerald Kennedy Library Web site, www.cs.umb.edu/ jfklibrary/60-4th.htm.

Document 6

Remarks of Senator John F. Kennedy, Student Union Building Steps, University of Michigan, Ann Arbor, Michigan, October 14, 1960

I want to express my thanks to you, as a graduate of the Michigan of the East, Harvard University.

I come here tonight delighted to have the opportunity to say one or two words about this campaign that is coming into the last three weeks.

I think in many ways it is the most important campaign since 1933, mostly because of the problems which press upon the United States, and the opportunities which will be presented to us in the 1960s. The opportunity must be seized, through the judgment of the President, and the vigor of the executive, and the cooperation of the Congress. Through these I think we can make the greatest possible difference.

How many of you who are going to be doctors, are willing to spend your days in Ghana? Technicians or engineers, how many of you are willing to work in the Foreign Service and spend your lives traveling around the world? On your willingness to do that, not merely to serve one year or two years in the service, but on your willingness to contribute part of your life to this country, I think will depend the answer whether a free society can compete. I think it can! And I think Americans are willing to contribute. But the effort must be far greater than we have ever made in the past.

Therefore, I am delighted to come to Michigan, to this University, because unless we have those resources in this school, unless you comprehend the nature of what is being

asked of you, this country can't possibly move through the next ten years in a period of relative strength.

Source: John Fitzgerald Kennedy Library Web site, www.cs.umb.edu/ jfklibrary/j101460.htm.

Document 7

Richard Nixon Campaign Speech, New York City, November 2, 1960

So, my friends, the reason why the American people are going to reject our opponents and are going to elect us is that we fight for the truth, and the people know the truth, because the people live the truth. . . .

And then there's one other thing I want to set straight: I'm getting sick and tired of hearing this constant whimpering and yammering and wringing of the towel with regard to the poor United States. Oh, under Eisenhower, they say, everything's gone to pot. Our education is now second. Our science is second. We're second in space. We're running down in our economy and are going to be second there. Our military strength is being frittered away, and over across the way, the great Soviet Union, as Mr. Stevenson said recently—and I quote from *Pravda* which quoted him—and over across the way the Communist world [is] looking more dynamic than the American world. Listen, my friends, I have been to Russia, and I have seen it; I have been to the United States, and I have seen it, and there is no reason for a second-rate psychology on the part of any American.

Yes, by all means, one of the things that makes America great is that we do criticize our faults, and we improve. One of the things that makes America great is that in any campaign we hit hard; we discuss the issues, but, my friends, I say to you that the people who are asking for the opportunity to cross new frontiers should not be talking about giving up the frontiers we've already got around the world. . . .

How much is going to be spent? And this I concede: my opponent will spend more, fifteen billion a year more. Now, what does that have to do with Macy's, the price of groceries, the price of clothing in Macy's, the price of furniture in Macy's? I will tell you what it has to do. If you spend to keep the promises that have been made in my opponent's platform and in this campaign, the prices of everything that Americans will buy are going to go up and up and up. . . .

My friends, do we want a twenty-five-percent increase in our grocery bills?

Do we want to pay off these promises and pay it in higher prices and higher taxes?

Well, there's a way to do it, and that's to go with Nixon and Lodge.

Source: Theodore White, *The Making of the President 1960* (New York: Atheneum House, 1961).

THE ELECTION OF
1964

The presidential election of 1964 laid the foundation for the eventual transformation of both the Democratic and Republican parties. The rise of new challengers to the old guard leadership of both parties foreshadowed changes not just for politicians, but for the country as a whole. Compounding all of these intra-party matters, events across the country and around the world threatened to transform the everyday lives of Americans, reinforcing the political changes. Although not apparent at that time, these shifts would play a significant role in future elections.

As Americans geared up for the election, they faced several important challenges. First, there was the grief that followed President John F. Kennedy's assassination on November 22, 1963. Whether they had supported him or not, Americans struggled to deal with the loss of innocence created by the president's murder. Second, the civil rights movement, which had been gathering momentum since the end of World War II, moved to center stage. Television screens were filled with pictures of angry white mobs viciously attacking black men, women, and children, who participated in demonstrations demanding an end to the old "Jim Crow" rules of segregation. Lyndon B. Johnson (see fact box, p. 853), who became president following Kennedy's death, used Americans' guilt over Kennedy's assassination to help secure passage of the Civil Rights Act. While white Americans hoped this signaled the resolution of the situation, black Americans recognized that it was just the beginning. The movement provided a challenging backdrop to the campaign, offering opportunities to gain new voters but exposing hazards as well.

Similarly, the escalating conflict in Indochina created confusion for politicians and the public. Although not yet the full-fledged war it would become, it still served as a constant source of potential political danger to the candidates. It raised all of the questions about the Cold War that had been debated over the years since the Korean War in the early 1950s. How did you define victory in such a conflict? Who exactly was the enemy? The North Vietnamese? The Chinese? The Soviets? For the candidates, it was a delicate balancing act to insist on the application of enough force to subdue the enemy in Vietnam, but without escalating the conflict further.

Republicans: Moderates versus Conservatives

For Republicans, in particular, the war posed special problems and opportunities. On the one hand, it allowed them once again to charge their opponents with being "soft on communism." Repeating accusations they had made since 1945, Republicans lashed out at Democrats whom they felt had allowed communists to gain a foothold in Southeast Asia. Moreover, the GOP claimed that Democrats were not prosecuting the war forcefully enough. On the other hand, to insist on escalation posed a serious danger for the party. If Republicans argued too vigorously for too much conflict, they would risk looking like extremists. The trick was to focus attention on what

CHRONOLOGY

1963

FEBRUARY 17	Movement founded to draft Goldwater.
NOVEMBER 22	President John F. Kennedy assassinated.

1964

JANUARY 3	Barry Goldwater announces candidacy.
JANUARY 28	Margaret Chase Smith announces candidacy.
JUNE 2	California primary.
JUNE 19	Civil Rights Act passed.
JULY 13–16	Republican National Convention.
AUGUST 4–6	Gulf of Tonkin incident.
AUGUST 24–27	Democratic National Convention.
NOVEMBER 3	Election Day.

the Democrats were doing, without appearing to be advocating full-scale a war in Vietnam.

One unlikely Republican candidate who seemed to perform this delicate juggling act was Margaret Chase Smith. Born in a small town in Maine, Smith first arrived in Washington as the wife and secretary of a congressman. Following her husband's death, she ran for his seat and won a special election. She later won reelection in her own right, and eventually moved on to the Senate. One of very few women legislators, Smith made a name for herself by standing up to Senator Joseph McCarthy (R-WI) at the height of his power. In fact, throughout her career in the Senate, she gained a reputation for honesty and integrity. Although she never focused on her gender, she was very aware of the limitations it placed on her and other women.

In fact, her gender was one of several reasons Smith gave for throwing her hat into the presidential ring in 1964. She believed that it was time that a woman be seriously considered for the presidency. In addition, she saw herself as the compromise candidate between the various extremes of the other candidates of her party. Touting her reputation for restrained toughness against communism, she also subtly suggested that the other candidates risked nuclear war, either by being too belligerent, or by being too willing to negotiate with the Soviets. Lastly, she claimed that she wanted to see how far someone could get without the potentially influential accouterments of outside funding and a campaign organization.

Recognizing that the odds were stacked against her, she entered several primaries. She braved the cold of New Hampshire, running her campaign there as she had her senatorial ones in Maine. Her efforts earned her a disappointing fifth place, but didn't end her campaign. Instead, she moved on to the Illinois primary, where a few groups organized for her. She did better there; she still didn't win; but she cut considerably into the victor's margin. With no formal campaign staff and having returned all campaign contributions, Smith's effort was all but dead. She entered the big California primary and again lost. Still, she had the pleasure of hearing her name placed in nomination at the convention, the thrill of viewing the floor demonstration in her honor, and the satisfaction of having won twenty-seven delegate votes. The media and her colleagues treated Smith's effort with humor and derision, but she succeeded in forcing men to deal with the possibility of a woman presidential candidate.

While much of the political establishment laughed away Smith's bid, the Right posed a more serious challenge to the existing power structure. Conservative Republicans had long felt disconnected from the mainstream of their party. Frustrated by their inability to influence the party platform as well as elected officials, right-wing Republicans decided that the only way to gain access to the inner circles of power was to become the inner circle. To that end, various groups of conservatives around the country began building a base of state and local conservative leaders in the years following the 1960 election. They recognized the need to work behind the scenes until the time was right for their candidate to emerge onto center stage and claim his victory.

Emergence of Goldwater

Their choice to play the role of conservative leader was Arizona senator Barry Goldwater. In many ways, Goldwater typified the emerging power of the Southwest in the years after World War II. A businessman, military reservist, and community leader, Goldwater disliked what he and many of his fellow southwesterners saw as the expanding power of the federal government in their area. He argued that the federal bureaucracy was becoming too large and intrusive in domestic affairs, while it ignored the continuing threat of communism around the world. Moving from local politics to a seat in the U.S. Senate in 1952, Goldwater took his laissez-faire, anticommunist message on the road.

By the early 1960s, the Arizonan had an increasingly high profile as the spokesman for conservatism. He built this reputation, in part, through his service as chair of the Senate Republican Campaign Committee as he traveled the country meeting local activists and community leaders. Many more citizens came to know him through his syndicated newspaper column and his book, *The Conscience of a Conservative*, which spelled out his views on both foreign and domestic policies. In addition, Goldwater's stand on civil rights won him the support in the traditionally Democratic South. Insisting that he was not a racist, Goldwater voted against the 1964 Civil Rights Act, stating that it violated constitutional limits on federal power. Goldwater's straightforward manner and photogenic appearance made him the frontrunner in 1964.

Behind the scenes, a group of conservative activists were working to build a strong Goldwater organization. Without Goldwater's direct involvement, these men and women crisscrossed the country locating, cultivating, and securing delegates for his nomination in 1964. F. Clifton White succeeded in building a grassroots organization that, increasingly, pressured Goldwater to announce his intention to run. When Goldwater hesitated, fearing a lack of financial and political support from the urban Northeast, White's group decided to mount a draft campaign. John F. Kennedy's assassination in November 1963 increased Goldwater's reluctance to run, but did not deter his supporters.

Finally, in January 1964, despite Goldwater's concerns about financing, his own inadequacies, and the lack of party support, he announced his candidacy in Phoenix. At the same time, he named his campaign

BARRY GOLDWATER

PARTY: Republican

DATE OF BIRTH: January 1, 1909

PLACE OF BIRTH: Phoenix, Arizona

PARENTS: Baron and Josephine Williams Goldwater

EDUCATION: Staunton Military Academy, 1928; one year at University of Arizona

FAMILY: Married Margaret "Peggy" Johnson, 1934; children: Joanne, Barry Jr., Michael, and Peggy Jr.

MILITARY SERVICE: Reserve Corps officer, 1928–41; active duty, 1941–45; Arizona air national guard, 1946–67

CAREER: Appointed to Colorado River Commission, 1946; Phoenix City Council, 1949–52; U.S. senator, 1952–64, 1968–86; unsuccessful candidate for U.S. president, 1964

DATE OF DEATH: May 29, 1998

PLACE OF DEATH: Paradise Valley, Arizona

CAUSE OF DEATH: Natural causes

PLACE OF BURIAL: Cremation

staff. Shocking many of the professional politicians around him, he surrounded himself with his old advisors from Arizona, rather than the people with broader national experience who had been working with the draft movement. This decision, based on a need for the comfort of familiar faces, caused him problems during both the primary and the regular campaigns. Not wanting to lose all they had accomplished, however, many of the original group swallowed their hurt pride and continued to work for Goldwater.

As Goldwater's campaign kicked into high gear, moderates within the Republican Party expressed their surprise and concern. They feared that a Goldwater victory would lead to a more conservative platform and undermine their places in the party hierarchy. Besides, they could not believe that Goldwater would win in November. They worried that he would take the party down with him. Consequently, they looked around for candidates to challenge him.

New York governor Nelson Rockefeller posed the most serious threat to Goldwater's nomination. Grandson of the founder of Standard Oil, Rockefeller had been involved in state and national politics throughout his entire life. His wealth and East Coast background, as well as his support for the civil rights movement, put him in the more moderate wing of the Republican Party. Many conservatives, meanwhile, saw him as the embodiment of everything they despised in the GOP: privilege, a tolerance for "safety-net" programs, and a fuzzy record on communism. For his part, Rockefeller shared the dismay of his fellow moderates at Goldwater's booming campaign. The governor thought he had no choice but to join the battle.

In the various primaries against Goldwater, Rockefeller had many political assets and a few hidden liabilities. On the one hand, he obviously had a significant war chest that allowed him to flood the targeted states with television and print advertising. In addition, he had name recognition, an established reputation, and considerable party support. On the other hand, his personal situation raised concerns about his morals. Rockefeller had divorced his wife and married a recently divorced woman, who had given up custody of her four young children. Opponents charged that "Rocky," as he was called, had destroyed two families in his search for personal happiness. When his new wife gave birth to their son on the eve of the California primary, conservatives again questioned his personal morality. Goldwater won that important, winner-take-all primary by a very slim margin. Those California delegates, combined with those already committed, meant he had almost all that he needed to win the nomination.

In the meantime, other potential opponents appeared and disappeared. Michigan governor George Romney seemed poised to make a run for it, but a few misstatements about his supporters and the Vietnam situation ended his chances. Similarly,

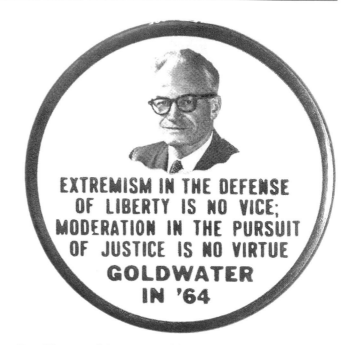

Republican candidate Barry Goldwater is shown on this 1964 campaign button, along with the most memorable phrase from his nomination acceptance speech. Goldwater's conservatism and Johnson's liberalism accentuated the ideological contrast between the candidates. (*National Museum of American History*)

former vice president Richard Nixon waited eagerly on the sidelines. Reluctant to seem too eager, he hoped for a deadlocked convention that might turn to him as a compromise candidate. Unfortunately, for him, word leaked out that he had already begun building a campaign organization, thus ending his image as disinterested bystander.

Pennsylvania governor William Scranton offered himself as the GOP's last hope. Hesitating at first, Scranton ended up joining the battle on the eve of the convention. Desperate to offer an alternative to Goldwater, however, Scranton ended up helping the Arizonan and further dividing the party. He sent Goldwater a letter insulting the senator's views, and the intelligence of his followers as well. When Goldwater released the letter, Scranton's chances, never good to begin with, vanished.

Delegates to the Republican convention in San Francisco gave Goldwater both the nomination and a badly divided party. The trouble began during the platform discussion, when delegates booed Rockefeller off the stage for supporting an anti-extremism plank. Goldwater, himself, increased the factionalization of the party. With the nomination in hand, he touted his conservative beliefs and let every-

WILLIAM EDWARD MILLER

PARTY: Republican

DATE OF BIRTH: March 22, 1914

PLACE OF BIRTH: Lockport, New York

PARENTS: Edward J. and Elizabeth Hinch Miller

EDUCATION: B.A., Notre Dame University, 1935; J.D., Union University Law School, 1938

FAMILY: Married Stephanie Wagner, 1943; children: Elizabeth Ann, Mary Karen, William E. Jr., and Stephanie Catherine

MILITARY SERVICE: U.S. army, 1942–45

CAREER: U.S. commissioner for western New York, appointed 1938; district attorney of Niagara County, appointed 1948, elected 1948–51; elected to U.S. House of Representatives, 1951–65; unsuccessful candidate for U.S. vice president, 1964

DATE OF DEATH: June 24, 1983

PLACE OF DEATH: Buffalo, New York

CAUSE OF DEATH: Natural causes

PLACE OF BURIAL: Arlington National Cemetery, Washington, D.C.

one know that they could back him up or leave the party. Tired of being the punching bag of moderates and liberals within his party, Goldwater defiantly established his control of the party structure.

Goldwater's choice of William E. Miller as his running mate further strained relations with the rest of the GOP. Without consulting party leaders, the candidate chose Miller, a Catholic congressman from upstate New York, in part because he added demographic balance to the ticket. In addition, Miller had served as Republican National Committee chair, thus bringing badly needed national experience to the campaign. Lastly, Goldwater welcomed Miller as a fellow conservative die-hard who would not be afraid to attack the liberalism of Johnson. For their part, moderate and liberal Republicans could not understand the choice. Not only had Goldwater failed to make the traditional conciliatory gesture of using the vice presidential nominee to unite the feuding party, but he had chosen a man certain to antagonize the center and left. Miller's reputation as a conservative gut-fighter appalled some Republicans almost as much as the rumors that he had exaggerated his participation in the Nuremberg trials following World War II. Liberal and moderate Republicans realized, to their dismay, that Goldwater intended to run his campaign and the party from a strictly conservative perspective.

The Democratic Convention

The Democrats, blessed with an incumbent president skilled in national politics, appeared to face many fewer problems than their Republican counterparts. Lyndon Johnson had come a long way from his days in the Texas Hill Country. Having spent his childhood watching his father practice homespun politics, Johnson absorbed many lessons in caring for a constituency and convincing political colleagues to support his legislation. Following a brief stint as a teacher, Johnson cut his teeth as a legislative aide and a New Deal bureaucrat before running for office in his own right. Johnson instantly felt at home on Capitol Hill, learning the system and polishing his communication and negotiation skills. During the 1950s, he was one of the most powerful men in Washington, serving first as Senate minority leader and later majority leader. By the end of the decade, he was ready to move onto something else. He surprised his colleagues, the public, and his closest advisors by accepting Kennedy's offer of the vice presidency in 1960. Johnson, nine years older than Kennedy, spent his years as vice president frustrated with his lack of activity and insecure about his abilities to compete with the razzle-dazzle of the "whiz kids."

Kennedy's assassination, of course, changed everything—by thrusting Johnson into the Oval Office. Moreover, the murder provided him with a powerful tool to convince Congress and the country to honor the slain president by passing his proposed legislative agenda. Thus Johnson began the 1964 campaign with two major legislative victories under his belt—creation of the War on Poverty, and passage of the Civil Rights Act.

Despite his advantages as president, Johnson did not take either his nomination or his victory in November for granted. He recognized that there were some potential traps into which he might fall. First, there was the "Bobby problem." Johnson and Robert F. Kennedy, the president's younger brother, who served as attorney general from 1961 to 1964, had never really gotten along—and the tension between them had increased following JFK's assassination. Kennedy naturally felt that Johnson was a usurper; Johnson believed that "Bobby," as many called him, wanted the presidency. The public's assumption that Johnson should make the younger Kennedy his running mate made the situation worse. After an awkward meeting, the two men agreed that there would not be a Johnson-Kennedy ticket.

Second, Johnson had to deal with the Kennedy legacy during the convention. Desperate to prove that he could win in his own right, Johnson controlled every aspect of the convention. He chose the theme, the music and, most importantly, the timing of the tribute to John F. Kennedy. Johnson won the nomination first; then, Robert Kennedy introduced the documentary on the slain president.

Racial issues posed the third, and most deadly, of the obstacles Johnson faced. Although Johnson was proud of his civil rights accomplishments, he recognized that some whites resented the changes. Understanding that racial conflicts within the party could undermine his nomination, the president wanted to keep everyone happy—or at least quiet—during the convention. The most significant threat to convention calm arose from the two rival Mississippi delegations. Excluded from registering to vote, and thus from participating in the national Democratic Party, black Mississippians formed the Mississippi Freedom Democratic Party (MFDP) and sent their own delegation to the convention. The white Mississippians refused to acknowledge the racial discrimination of their electoral process, claiming that they were the only legally authorized delegates. The credentials committee thus faced a tough decision: Which delegation should be seated? Although the white delegates had legal precedent, the MFDP won the moral high ground. Through the testimony of civil rights leaders Robert Moses, Fannie Lou Hamer, and others, the committee heard horrific stories of Americans in Mississippi being denied their basic right to vote. Hamer's eloquence, in particular, moved not only the committee members, but television viewers across the country, despite attempts by the Johnson administration to keep her off the air.

Throughout the debate, Johnson attempted to remain both in control and out of sight. He feared that the controversy would disrupt the convention and hurt his chances of election. Consequently, although

Like earlier presidents Theodore Roosevelt (TR), Franklin D. Roosevelt (FDR), and John F. Kennedy (JFK), Lyndon B. Johnson was commonly referred to by his initials. *(Gyory Collection/Cathy Casriel Photo)*

he received constant reports on the situation, he refrained from public comment and even pretended that he did not know what was going on. In the end, he got his way. The committee decided to seat the white delegation, with the understanding that the next convention would exclude all members elected through segregated procedures. In addition, they offered the MFDP two at large delegate seats. Seeing this offer as a token gesture, the MFDP refused. Thus, MFDP members left the convention angry and defeated; white southerners grumbled about the end of the Democratic Party in the South; and the rest of white America returned to its complacent view of racial tensions. Meanwhile, LBJ won the nomination.

LBJ also used the controversy to finalize his decision concerning his vice presidential running mate. Johnson had been debating his various choices for months. Having eliminated Robert Kennedy, as well as the need for a northeasterner for geographic balance, Johnson seemed to have settled on Minnesota senator Hubert Humphrey by early July. Humphrey and Johnson shared many characteristics: Both were raised in small towns and understood the hardships of poverty; both had been school teachers and continued to believe in the importance of education; most importantly, both actively supported the civil rights movement. After all, Humphrey had introduced the strong civil rights plank into the 1948 Democratic platform, causing the South to walk out and form the States' Rights, or "Dixiecrat," party. In addition, Humphrey had the backing of farmers and laborers, as well as a solid reputation with the liberal wing of the Democratic Party. More importantly, Humphrey wanted the nomination. Still, Johnson refused to announce his choice. Instead, he put Humphrey in charge of settling the dispute with the Mississippi delegation, insisting on a compromise that would not hurt Johnson's election chances with either white or black southerners. Despite his efforts in this regard, Humphrey still had to wait until almost the day of the nominations before Johnson announced his decision.

By the end of the summer, then, the major parties had their candidates and platforms in place. The two seemed in stark contrast to one another. Goldwater advocated limiting the federal government except in the area of defense, where he encouraged a vigorous foreign policy. Johnson, on the other hand, had already staked his claim to the New Deal legacy by declaring war on poverty. In addition, destroying his image as a southern conservative, he had pushed through passage of the most effective civil rights bill in American history. Goldwater, a dedicated states' rights advocate, voted against the Civil Rights Act on constitutional grounds. In terms of foreign policy, Goldwater and the Republicans wanted to intensify the war against communism, particularly in Indochina. Johnson seemed vulnerable on this issue until August 1964. Early that month, Johnson announced that the North Vietnamese had attacked American ships in the Tonkin Gulf. The bombing raids he launched, in response, seemed to show that he could be firm, but controlled.

Racial Politics

While Democrats and Republicans battled each other, they also had to deal with the wild card of Alabama governor George Wallace's (see fact box, p. 892) candidacy. Nominally a Democrat, Wallace actually posed more of a threat to Goldwater. The Alabama governor had first gained national attention with his inaugural cry of "Segregation now . . . segregation forever." In 1963, he confirmed his position as symbol of southern racism by literally standing in the schoolhouse door to prevent the integration of the University of Alabama. The following year, he proved that his brand of racism was not confined to the South by

HUBERT HORATIO HUMPHREY

PARTY: Democrat

DATE OF BIRTH: May 27, 1911

PLACE OF BIRTH: Wallace, South Dakota

PARENTS: Hubert and Christine Sannes Humphrey

EDUCATION: Denver College of Pharmacy, 1933; University of Minnesota, 1939; master's degree, Louisiana State University, 1940

FAMILY: Married Muriel Buck, 1936; children: Nancy, Hubert, Robert, and Douglas

CAREER: Mayor of Minneapolis, 1945–48; U.S. Senate, 1948–65, 1971–78; U.S. vice president, 1965–69; unsuccessful candidate for U.S. president, 1968

DATE OF DEATH: January 13, 1978

PLACE OF DEATH: Waverly, Minnesota

CAUSE OF DEATH: Natural causes

PLACE OF BURIAL: Lakewood Cemetery, Minneapolis, Minnesota

entering several northern Democratic primaries. Political pundits completely discounted his candidacy, citing his distinctive southernness, as well as the fact that he was challenging an incumbent. To the horrified surprise of many Americans, Wallace did reasonably well in the three primaries he entered. In Wisconsin, he won 34 percent of the vote; in Indiana, he got 30 percent; and in Maryland, a whopping 43 percent. After Goldwater voted against the Civil Rights Act in June 1964, Wallace, under some pressure from southern conservatives, bowed out of the race.

Wallace's campaign, albeit brief, threatened to force confrontations and raise issues neither candidate wanted to debate. In fact, Johnson and Goldwater agreed that they would avoid racial issues during the campaign. This suited both men, since the issue posed potential problems for each of them. Johnson might gain the black vote, but risked alienating white southerners. Goldwater might pick up that southern support, but feared being labeled a racist. Instead, each man allowed his supporters to carry the burden of explaining his position on civil rights matters. On a more basic level, their actions spoke louder than any speech could: Johnson had succeeded in convincing Congress to pass the Civil Rights Act, and Goldwater had voted against it. Their positions seemed perfectly clear.

The Fall Campaign

Johnson approached the fall campaign with the same cautious determination he used during the primaries. He could have avoided active politicking by claiming that he was too busy with his presidential duties. Instead, Johnson chose to run as if he were the underdog. Traveling the country, making appearances at ceremonial dedications, stopping off in small towns and mixing with the people, Johnson wore himself ragged in his quest for an overwhelming victory. He never let himself or his staff forget that they could not afford to become overconfident or to underestimate the appeal of their opponent. As a result, the Johnson people continually worked to focus attention on the weaknesses of Goldwater, rather than just on the strengths of Johnson. They very effectively used humor, sarcasm, and innuendo to insinuate that the Arizona senator was an extremist. (See "The Daisy Ad," p. 875.) This tactic kept the Republicans on the defensive and denied them the time to explain their positions to the public.

Goldwater and his staff also faced several other problems that made it difficult for them to mount an effective battle. First of all, many of the Goldwaterites lacked national campaign experience. They made sometimes foolish mistakes in terms of organizing their staffs, presenting their positions, and mobilizing their greatest asset, grass roots support. This led to a second problem—frustration and anger among the legion of "little people" working for Goldwater's election. Feeling snubbed by the people surrounding the senator and confused as to the strategy for challenging the Democrats, men and women who had been campaigning for Goldwater long before he won the nomination sometimes wondered if they had chosen the wrong candidate.

In the end, it might not have mattered what Goldwater did. Even without his extremist image and problematic campaign tactics, Goldwater would have found it difficult to defeat Johnson. After all, the Republicans also faced the slain president Kennedy. As one pundit at the time put it, the American people were not ready for three presidents in eighteen

The famous "daisy commercial" prepared by the Democrats for Lyndon B. Johnson's presidential campaign generated so much controversy that it was pulled after one airing. As the little girl picks petals from the daisy, the narrator counts down to zero. Then the screen erupts into a nuclear explosion. The message: The election of Republican candidate Barry Goldwater would increase the risk of nuclear war. *(LBJ Library, photo by Democratic National Committee)*

months. Goldwater's weaknesses did contribute to the overwhelming nature of his defeat. Winning just 27 million votes, Goldwater took only the electoral votes of the five states of the deep South and Arizona. Conservatism seemed to have been roundly defeated; liberalism looked to be triumphant.

But this seemingly clear-cut election actually hid several important shifts in the American political

THE DAISY AD

A pretty little girl with big eyes stands holding a daisy on a summer day. The wind gently blows her hair across her face. She begins plucking petals from the daisy, counting in the adorably haphazard pattern of young children. When she reaches nine, the picture freezes; the camera zooms in on her face. A man's voice begins counting down from ten. As he reaches zero, the zoom focuses on her bright eyes. Suddenly, the scene explodes into an atomic mushroom cloud. Against this backdrop, Lyndon Johnson's voice explains the severity of the issues facing Americans. He ends by urging everyone to vote on November 3rd.

Aired only once, but repeated on numerous newscasts, the "daisy commercial" epitomized the tenor of the 1964 presidential campaign. It shocked the American public; painted Goldwater as an extremist; and clouded the issues of the campaign. The Goldwater staff found it very difficult to replace that smiling little girl with a powerful symbol of their own. As a result, they constantly played defense instead of finding a good offensive game plan.

Obviously, the Johnson staff had discovered a valuable tool in their battle against Goldwater. Summoning all of their resources, the Democratic campaign utilized a public relations firm to design and produce a series of ads attacking their opponent. In addition to the "daisy" ad, which concentrated on Goldwater's foreign policy, another focused on domestic issues. In that one, a pair of disembodied hands ripped a Social Security card in half, while a voice paraphrased Goldwater's views on the issue. Such imagery reached millions of voters who would never consider reading a newspaper or a campaign pamphlet.

The Johnson staff also used humor very effectively. Goldwater's slogan was, "In your heart, you know he's right." Democrats sometimes added, "yes, extreme right!" Others changed it completely to, "In your guts, you know he's nuts!" Reinforcing the image of Goldwater the lunatic, the staff produced a book entitled *Fact: 1189 Psychiatrists Say Goldwater Is Psychologically Unfit to Be President.* Others picked up on the extremist theme. One writer created a play titled "Through a Looking Glass Darkly," in which Goldwater and some of the more conservative Republicans won office and transformed the United States into a fascist state.

The Goldwater people tried to counterattack, but lacked the skills, technical assistance, and unity of purpose necessary to succeed. Only after the campaign ended did the Republican National Committee see about hiring a public relations firm of their own to spruce up their image. During the campaign, the Goldwater staffers struggled to find time to create their own plan of attack. No matter how hard they tried, however, they could not erase the picture of the sweet little girl obliterated by the atomic bomb.

system. First of all, Goldwater might have lost the election, but conservatives won the larger battle. For the first time in a long time, they gained control of the Republican Party. Learning important lessons from their defeat, they would work to secure their new position within the GOP, and would eventually succeed in winning the Oval Office for Ronald Reagan sixteen years later. Helping them was a second development that went virtually unnoticed at the time. The candidacies of Margaret Chase Smith and George Wallace indicated that significant segments of

the population were not finding a voice within the traditional party structure. It would take a while before women were really able to break through and play a role within the leadership of the parties, but Smith's candidacy foreshadowed those days.

Wallace's strong showing similarly signaled significant changes in the political structure in the coming years. On the one hand, he proved the rising power of the South in politics, as well as the legitimation of "southerness" across the nation. On the other hand, the fact that his racist views played so well in the

President Lyndon B. Johnson greets supporters in Memphis, Tennessee, during the 1964 campaign. Johnson was most comfortable and skilled, however, at lobbying small groups of individuals. *(LBJ Library, photo by O.J. Rapp)*

North warned politicians of both parties of the growing prominence of the white backlash in reaction to the rising political power of the African American community. As more blacks voted and won political office, some whites feared losing control of their communities, and reacted with hostility. Keeping both constituencies happy would occupy the parties for the next few decades.

The circumstances facing the country during this election year also played a role in the transformations of the parties. The increasingly visible and vocal civil rights movement forced politicians of both sides to address racial issues. The reactions of some segments of white society to desegregation would strengthen the conservative wing of the Republican Party and wreak havoc on the Democrats. Conservatives won the support of racists and states'-rights adherents, as well as those upset by what seemed to them to be the violence and lawlessness of the movement. The Democrats watched as the coalition of minorities and working-class whites, which had long kept them in power, fell victim to internecine warfare. In addition,

the escalation of the war in Vietnam would raise numerous issues that played to the advantage of the conservatives and undermined the Democrats. By insisting on fighting communism in Indochina, the Johnson administration reinforced arguments that conservatives had been making for decades. Because the war did not result in an immediate victory, however, right-wingers could also use it as a battering ram against the administration. Lastly, the war would weaken Democratic unity as some party members continued to support the effort, while others questioned the methods and goals of the conflict.

In conclusion then, the election of 1964 seemed on the surface to result in a decisive victory for Johnson, the Democrats, and the traditional party structure. A closer examination, however, reveals that underlying changes during the primary and regular campaign season would eventually transform not just the result of the election, but the overall political structure of the United States. As groups such as blacks and women insisted on being heard, other constituencies such as white southerners and laborers worked to retain their position in the political sphere. For Democrats, changes threatened the unity of their party. Republicans, particularly conservatives, benefited from the assault on the status quo. With a network in place, the Right was positioned to seize control of their party and the government in the ensuing decades. For many, nothing would be the same after November 1964.

Mary C. Brennan

Bibliography

Branch, Taylor. *Pillar of Fire*. New York: Simon and Schuster, 1998.

Brennan, Mary C. *Turning Right in the Sixties*. Chapel Hill: University of North Carolina Press, 1995.

Dallak, Robert. *Flawed Giant*. New York: Oxford University Press, 1998.

Edsall, Thomas Byrne, and Mary D. Edsall. *Chain Reaction*. New York: Norton, 1991.

Goldberg, Robert Alan. *Barry Goldwater*. New Haven, CT: Yale University Press, 1995.

Herring, George. *America's Longest War*. New York: McGraw-Hill, 1996.

Matusow, Allen. *The Unraveling of America*. New York: Harper and Row, 1986.

White, F. Clifton. *Suite 3505*. New Rochelle, NY: Arlington House, 1967.

White, Theodore. *The Making of the President 1964*. New York: Atheneum, 1965.

THE VOTE: ELECTION OF 1964

State	Total No. of Electors	Total Popular Vote	Electoral Vote D	Electoral Vote R	Margin of Victory Votes	Margin of Victory % Total Vote	Johnson Democrat Votes	Johnson Democrat %	Goldwater Republican Votes	Goldwater Republican %	Others Votes	Others %
Alabama	10	689,817		10	268,353	38.9%	0	0.0%	479,085	69.5%	210,732[a]	30.5%
Alaska	3	67,259	3		21,399	31.8%	44,329	65.9%	22,930	34.1%	0	0.0%
Arizona	5	480,770		5	4,782	1.0%	237,753	49.5%	242,535	50.4%	482	0.1%
Arkansas	6	560,426	6		70,933	12.7%	314,197	56.1%	243,264	43.4%	2,965	0.5%
California	40	7,057,586	40		1,292,769	18.3%	4,171,877	59.1%	2,879,108	40.8%	6,601	0.1%
Colorado	6	776,986	6		179,257	23.1%	476,024	61.3%	296,767	38.2%	4,195	0.5%
Connecticut	8	1,218,578	8		435,273	35.7%	826,269	67.8%	390,996	32.1%	1,313	0.1%
Delaware	3	201,320	3		44,626	22.2%	122,704	60.9%	78,078	38.8%	538	0.3%
District of Columbia	3	198,597	3		140,995	71.0%	169,796	85.5%	28,801	14.5%	0	0.0%
Florida	14	1,854,481	14		42,599	2.3%	948,540	51.1%	905,941	48.9%	0	0.0%
Georgia	12	1,139,336		12	94,027	8.3%	522,557	45.9%	616,584	54.1%	195	0.0%
Hawaii	4	207,271	4		119,227	57.5%	163,249	78.8%	44,022	21.2%	0	0.0%
Idaho	4	292,477	4		5,363	1.8%	148,920	50.9%	143,557	49.1%	0	0.0%
Illinois	26	4,702,841	26		890,887	18.9%	2,796,833	59.5%	1,905,946	40.5%	62	0.0%
Indiana	13	2,091,606	13		259,730	12.4%	1,170,848	56.0%	911,118	43.6%	9,640	0.5%
Iowa	9	1,184,539	9		283,882	24.0%	733,030	61.9%	449,148	37.9%	2,361	0.2%
Kansas	7	857,901	7		77,449	9.0%	464,028	54.1%	386,579	45.1%	7,294	0.9%
Kentucky	9	1,046,105	9		296,682	28.4%	669,659	64.0%	372,977	35.7%	3,469	0.3%
Louisiana	10	896,293		10	122,157	13.6%	387,068	43.2%	509,225	56.8%	0	0.0%
Maine	4	380,965	4		143,563	37.7%	262,264	68.8%	118,701	31.2%	0	0.0%
Maryland	10	1,116,457	10		345,417	30.9%	730,912	65.5%	385,495	34.5%	50	0.0%
Massachusetts	14	2,344,798	14		1,236,695	52.7%	1,786,422	76.2%	549,727	23.4%	8,649	0.4%
Michigan	21	3,203,102	21		1,076,463	33.6%	2,136,615	66.7%	1,060,152	33.1%	6,335	0.2%
Minnesota	10	1,554,462	10		431,493	27.8%	991,117	63.8%	559,624	36.0%	3,721	0.2%
Mississippi	7	409,146		7	303,910	74.3%	52,618	12.9%	356,528	87.1%	0	0.0%
Missouri	12	1,817,879	12		510,809	28.1%	1,164,344	64.0%	653,535	36.0%	0	0.0%
Montana	4	278,628	4		51,214	18.4%	164,246	58.9%	113,032	40.6%	1,350	0.5%
Nebraska	5	584,154	5		30,460	5.2%	307,307	52.6%	276,847	47.4%	0	0.0%
Nevada	3	135,433	3		23,245	17.2%	79,339	58.6%	56,094	41.4%	0	0.0%
New Hampshire	4	286,094	4		78,036	27.3%	182,065	63.6%	104,029	36.4%	0	0.0%
New Jersey	17	2,846,770	17		903,828	31.7%	1,867,671	65.6%	963,843	33.9%	15,256	0.5%
New Mexico	4	327,615	4		62,179	19.0%	194,017	59.2%	131,838	40.2%	1,760	0.5%
New York	43	7,166,015	43		2,669,597	37.3%	4,913,156	68.6%	2,243,559	31.3%	9,300	0.1%
North Carolina	13	1,424,983	13		175,295	12.3%	800,139	56.2%	624,844	43.8%	0	0.0%
North Dakota	4	258,389	4		41,577	16.1%	149,784	58.0%	108,207	41.9%	398	0.2%
Ohio	26	3,969,196	26		1,027,466	25.9%	2,498,331	62.9%	1,470,865	37.1%	0	0.0%
Oklahoma	8	932,499	8		107,169	11.5%	519,834	55.7%	412,665	44.3%	0	0.0%
Oregon	6	786,305	6		218,238	27.8%	501,017	63.7%	282,779	36.0%	2,509	0.3%
Pennsylvania	29	4,822,690	29		1,457,297	30.2%	3,130,954	64.9%	1,673,657	34.7%	18,079	0.4%
Rhode Island	4	390,091	4		240,848	61.7%	315,463	80.9%	74,615	19.1%	13	0.0%
South Carolina	8	524,756		8	93,348	17.8%	215,700	41.1%	309,048	58.9%	8	0.0%
South Dakota	4	293,118	4		32,902	11.2%	163,010	55.6%	130,108	44.4%	0	0.0%
Tennessee	11	1,143,946	11		125,982	11.0%	634,947	55.5%	508,965	44.5%	34	0.0%
Texas	25	2,626,811	25		704,619	26.8%	1,663,185	63.3%	958,566	36.5%	5,060	0.2%
Utah	4	400,310	4		38,946	9.7%	219,628	54.9%	180,682	45.1%	0	0.0%
Vermont	3	163,089	3		53,185	32.6%	108,127	66.3%	54,942	33.7%	20	0.0%
Virginia	12	1,042,267	12		76,704	7.4%	558,038	53.5%	481,334	46.2%	2,895	0.3%
Washington	9	1,258,556	9		309,515	24.6%	779,881	62.0%	470,366	37.4%	8,309	0.7%
West Virginia	7	792,040	7		284,134	35.9%	538,087	67.9%	253,953	32.1%	0	0.0%
Wisconsin	12	1,691,815	12		411,929	24.3%	1,050,424	62.1%	638,495	37.7%	2,896	0.2%
Wyoming	3	142,716	3		18,720	13.1%	80,718	56.6%	61,998	43.4%	0	0.0%
TOTAL	538	70,639,284	486	52	15,951,287	22.6%	43,127,041	61.1%	27,175,754	38.5%	336,489	0.5%

[a] Other votes in Alabama include 210,732 votes for unpledged Democratic electors.

For sources, see p. 1130.

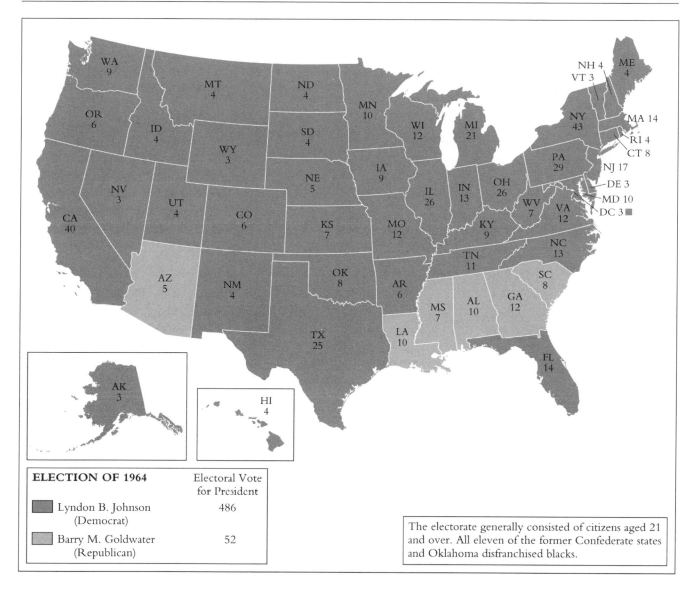

ELECTION OF 1964

Electoral Vote for President

Lyndon B. Johnson (Democrat) — 486

Barry M. Goldwater (Republican) — 52

The electorate generally consisted of citizens aged 21 and over. All eleven of the former Confederate states and Oklahoma disfranchised blacks.

DOCUMENTS: ELECTION OF 1964

After the assassination of John F. Kennedy in 1963, Lyndon Johnson became president. Johnson used Kennedy's memory to help push civil rights legislation through Congress; but he needed a mandate to further his own agenda, an all-out attack on poverty. The Republicans nominated Arizona senator Barry Goldwater, who the Democrats labeled a dangerous right-wing extremist. In the general election Johnson's strategy worked, as he polled a landslide victory.

At the Democratic convention in August 1964, Robert F. Kennedy, brother of the former president, delivered a speech, Document 1, celebrating John F. Kennedy's memory and political ideas, asking Americans to elect Johnson to complete his late brother's agenda. In his speech accepting the Democratic nomination, Document 2, Johnson proposed extensive social reforms extending the New Deal in what would become his Great Society.

Document 3, Goldwater's speech accepting the Republican nomination, detailed Democratic foreign policy failures in Berlin, Korea, Cuba, and Vietnam, and criticized his opponent for too much moderation "in the pursuit of justice." He promised a strong commitment to the military and to fighting communism. Document 4, a speech by Ronald Reagan, the future president, who was campaigning for Goldwater, extolled the Republicans' domestic agenda. Reagan proclaimed that the election was a "time for choosing" between liberal Democratic and conservative Republican ideas, the latter of which he claimed were firmly rooted in history and more closely in line with American values.

Through television advertisements and speeches, the Democrats used Goldwater's own words to portray him as an extremist. Document 5, excerpts from "Goldwater on the Record," which appeared in the Progressive, illustrates a few of his startling and contradictory statements. Just before the election, two major world events, the fall of Soviet Premier Nikita Khrushchev and China's first successful explosion of a nuclear device, raised concerns over an uncertain future and allowed Johnson to raise questions about Goldwater's ability to handle these situations. Document 6, an address to the nation by Johnson, reassured Americans that Democratic policies would work to make the world safe, while implying that Americans could not afford to elect Goldwater in such a political climate.

Document 1

Robert F. Kennedy's Address to the Democratic National Convention, August 27, 1964

I first want to thank all of you delegates to the Democratic National Convention and the supporters of the Democratic Party for all that you did for President John F. Kennedy. . . .

No matter what talent an individual possesses, what energy he might have, no matter how much integrity and how much honesty he might have, if he is by himself, and particularly a political figure, he can accomplish very little. But if he is sustained, as President Kennedy was, by the Democratic Party all over the United States, dedicated to the same things that he was attempting to accomplish, he can accomplish a great deal.. . .

So, when he became President he not only had his own principles and his own ideals, but he had the strength of the Democratic Party. As President he wanted to do something for the mentally ill and the mentally retarded; for those who were not covered by Social Security; for those who were not receiving an adequate minimum wage; for those who did not have adequate housing; for our elderly people who had difficulty paying their medical bills; for our fellow citizens who are not white and who had difficulty living in this society. To all this he dedicated himself.

But he realized also that in order for us to make progress here at home, that we had to be strong overseas, that our military strength had to be strong. He said one time, "Only when our arms are sufficient, without doubt, can we be certain, without doubt, that they will never have to be employed." So when we had the crisis with the Soviet Union and the Communist Bloc in October of 1962, the

Soviet Union withdrew their missiles and bombers from Cuba. . . .

When there were periods of crisis, you stood beside him. When there were periods of happiness, you laughed with him. And when there were periods of sorrow, you comforted him. I realize that as individuals we can't just look back, that we must look forward. When I think of President Kennedy, I think of what Shakespeare said in *Romeo and Juliet*:

"When he shall die, take him and cut him out into stars, and he shall make the face of heaven so fine that all the world will be in love with night and pay no worship to the garish sun."

I realize that as individuals, and even more important, as a political party and as a country, we can't just look to the past, we must look to the future.

So I join with you in realizing that what started four years ago—what everyone here started four years ago—that is to be sustained; that is to be continued.

The same effort and the same energy and the same dedication that was given to President John F. Kennedy must be given to President Lyndon Johnson and Hubert Humphrey. . . .

Source: John Fitzgerald Kennedy Library Web site, www.cs.umb.edu/jfklibrary/r082764.html.

Document 2

Lyndon Johnson's Nomination Acceptance Speech, August 27, 1964

. . . but the gladness of this high occasion cannot mask the sorrow which shares our hearts. So let us here tonight, each of us, all of us, rededicate ourselves to keeping burning the golden torch of promise which John Fitzgerald Kennedy set aflame.

And let none of us stop to rest until we have written into the law of the land all the suggestions that made up the John Fitzgerald Kennedy program and then let us continue to supplement that program with the kind of laws that he would have us write. . . .

Our party and our nation will continue to extend the hand of compassion, and extend the hand of affection and love, to the old and the sick and the hungry.

For who among us dares betray the command: Thou shalt open thy hand unto thy Brother, to thy poor and to thy needy in the Land?

The needs that we seek to fill, the hopes that we seek to realize, are not our needs, our hopes alone. They are the needs and hopes of most of the people. Most Americans want medical care for older citizens, and so do I.

Most Americans want fair and stable prices and decent income for our farmers, and so do I.

Most Americans want a decent home in a decent neighborhood for all, and so do I.

Most Americans want an education for every child to the limit of his ability, and so do I.

Most Americans want a job for every man who wants to work, and so do I. Most Americans want victory in our war against poverty, and so do I. Most Americans want continually expanding and growing prosperity, and so do I.

These are your goals; these are our goals; these are the goals and will be the achievements of the Democratic party.

These are the goals of this great, rich nation; these are the goals toward which I will lead if the American people choose to follow.

For 30 years, year by year, step by step, vote by vote, men of both parties have built a solid foundation for our present prosperity.

Too many have worked too long and too hard to see this threatened now by policies which promise to undo all that we have done together over all these years. . . .

I report tonight as President of the United States and as Commander in Chief of the Armed Forces on the strength of your country, and I tell you that it is greater than any adversary's.

I assure you that it is greater than the combined might of all the nations in all the wars in all the history of this planet.

And I report our superiority is growing.

Weapons do not make peace; men make peace. And peace comes not through strength alone, but through wisdom and patience and restraint.

And these qualities under the leadership of President Kennedy brought a treaty banning nuclear tests in the atmosphere, and a hundred other nations in the world joined us.

Other agreements were reached and other steps were taken. And their single guide was to lessen the danger to men without increasing the danger of freedom.

Their single purpose was peace in the world. And as a result of these policies, the world tonight knows where we stand and our allies know where we stand, too.

And our adversaries have learned again that we will never waver in the defense of freedom. . . .

Our problems are many and are great. But our opportunities are even greater. And let me make this clear. I ask the American people for a mandate, not to preside over a finished program, not just to keep things going. I ask the American people for a mandate to begin.

This nation, this generation, in this hour has man's first chance to build a great society, a place where the meaning of man's life matches the marvels of man's labor.

We seek a nation where every man can find reward in work and satisfaction in the use of his talents. We seek a nation where every man can seek knowledge and touch beauty and rejoice in the closeness of family and community.

We seek a nation where every man can work follow the pursuit of happiness—not just security, but achievement and excellence and fulfillment of the spirit. So let us join together in this great task. Will you join me tonight in starting, in rebuilding our cities to make them a decent place for our children to live in?

Will you join me tonight in starting a program that will protect the beauty of our land and the air that we breathe?

Won't you join me tonight in starting a program that will give every child education of the highest quality that he can take?

So let us, let us join together in giving every American the fullest life which he can hope for, for the ultimate test of our civilization, the ultimate test of our faithfulness to our past has not been our goods and has not been our guns. It is in the quality—the quality of our people's lives and in the men and women that we produce.

This goal can be ours. We have the resources; we have the knowledge. But tonight we must seek the courage.

Because tonight the contest is the same that we have faced at every turning point in history. It is not between liberals and conservatives, it is not between party and party or platform and platform. It is between courage and timidity.

It is between those who have visions and those who see what can be, and those who want only to maintain the status quo.

It is between those who welcome the future and those who turn away from its promise. This is the true cause of freedom. The man who is hungry, who cannot find work or educate his children, who is bowed by want—that man is not fully free. For more than 30 years, from Social Security to the war against poverty, we have diligently worked to enlarge the freedom of man, and as a result Americans tonight are freer to live as they want to live, to pursue their ambitions to meet their desires, to raise their families, than in any time in all of our glorious history.

And every American knows in his heart that this is right!

. . .

Source: *Public Papers of the Presidents of the United States: Lyndon B. Johnson, 1963–1964, Book II: July 1 to December 31, 1964* (Washington, DC: Government Printing Office, 1965).

Document 3

Barry Goldwater's Nomination Acceptance Speech, July 16, 1964

In this world no person, no party can guarantee anything, but what we can do and what we shall do is to deserve victory and victory will be ours. The Good Lord raised this mighty Republican-Republic to be a home for the Brave and to flourish as the land of the free—not to stagnate in the swampland of collectivism, not to cringe before the bully of Communism.

Now my fellow Americans, the tide has been running against freedom. Our people have followed false prophets. We must, and we shall, return to proven ways—not because they are old, but because they are true.

We must, and we shall, set the tide running again in the cause of freedom. And this party, with its every action, every word, every breath and every heart beat, has but a single resolve, and that is freedom. . . .

Now, we Americans understand freedom, we have earned it; we have lived for it, and we have died for it. This nation and its people are freedom's models in a searching world. We can be freedom's missionaries in a doubting world.

But, ladies and gentlemen, first we must renew freedom's mission in our own hearts and in our own homes.

During four futile years, the Administration which we shall replace has distorted and lost that faith. It has talked and talked and talked and talked the words of freedom, but it has failed and failed and failed in the works of freedom.

Now failure cements the wall of shame in Berlin; failures blot the sands of shame at the Bay of Pigs; failures marked the slow death of freedom in Laos; failures infest the jungles of Vietnam; and failures haunt the houses of our once great alliances and undermine the greatest bulwark ever erected by free nations, the NATO community. . . .

Yesterday it was Korea; tonight it is Vietnam. Make no bones of this. Don't try to sweep this under the rug. We are at war in Vietnam. And yet the President, who is the Commander in Chief of our forces, refuses to say, refuses to say mind you, whether or not the objective over there is victory, and his Secretary of Defense continues to mislead and

misinform the American people, and enough of it has gone by.

And I needn't remind you, but I will, it has been during Democratic years that a billion persons were cast into Communist captivity and their fate cynically sealed.

Today—today in our beloved country we have an Administration which seems eager to deal with Communism in every coin known—from gold to wheat; from consulates to confidence, and even human freedom itself.

Now the Republican cause demands that we brand Communism as the principal disturber of peace in the world today. Indeed, we should brand it as the only significant disturber of the peace. And we must make clear that until its goals of conquest are absolutely renounced, and its relations with all nations tempered, Communism and the governments it now controls are enemies of every man on earth who is or wants to be free.

Now, we here in America can keep the peace only if we remain vigilant, and only if we remain strong. Only if we keep our eyes open and keep our guard up can we prevent war.

And I want to make this abundantly clear—I don't intend to let peace or freedom be torn from our grasp because of lack of strength, or lack of will—and that I promise you Americans.

I believe that we must look beyond the defense of freedom today to its extension tomorrow. I believe that the Communism which boasts it will bury us will instead give way to the forces of freedom. And I can see in the distant and yet recognizable future the outlines of a world worthy of our dedication, our every risk, our every effort, our every sacrifice along the way. Yes, a world that will redeem the suffering of those who will be liberated from tyranny. . . .

Anyone who joins us in all sincerity we welcome. Those, those who do not care for our cause, we don't expect to enter our ranks in any case. And let our Republicanism [be] so focused and so dedicated not be made fuzzy and futile by unthinking and stupid labels.

I would remind you that extremism in the defense of liberty is no vice! And let me remind you also that moderation in the pursuit of justice is no virtue! . . .

Source: *New York Times*, July 17, 1964.

Document 4

Ronald Reagan's Speech for Goldwater, 1964

I am going to talk of controversial things. I make no apology for this.

It's time we asked ourselves if we still know the freedoms intended for us by the Founding Fathers. James Madison said, "We base all our experiments on the capacity of mankind for self government."

This idea? That government was beholden to the people, that it had no other source of power, is still the newest, most unique idea in all the long history of man's relation to man. This is the issue of this election: Whether we believe in our capacity for self-government, or whether we abandon the American Revolution and confess that a little intellectual elite in a far-distant capital can plan our lives for us better than we can plan them ourselves.

You and I are told we must choose between a left or right, but I suggest there is no such thing as a left or right. There is only an up or down. Up to man's age-old dream—the maximum of individual freedom consistent with order—or down to the ant heap of totalitarianism. Regardless of their sincerity, their humanitarian motives, those who would sacrifice freedom for security have embarked on this downward path. Plutarch warned, "The real destroyer of the liberties of the people is he who spreads among them bounties, donations and benefits."

The Founding Fathers knew a government can't control the economy without controlling people. And they knew when a government sets out to do that, it must use force and coercion to achieve its purpose. So we have come to a time for choosing.

Public servants say, always with the best of intentions, "What greater service we could render if only we had a little more money and a little more power." But the truth is that outside of its legitimate function, government does nothing as well or as economically as the private sector.

Yet any time you and I question the schemes of the do-gooders, we're denounced as being opposed to their humanitarian goals. It seems impossible to legitimately debate their solutions with the assumption that all of us share the desire to help the less fortunate. They tell us we're always "against," never "for" anything.

We are for a provision that destitution should not follow unemployment by reason of old age, and to that end we have accepted Social Security as a step toward meeting the problem. However, we are against those entrusted with this program when they practice deception regarding its fiscal shortcomings, when they charge that any criticism of the program means that we want to end payments. . . .

We are for aiding our allies by sharing our material blessings with nations which share our fundamental beliefs, but we are against doling out money government to government, creating bureaucracy, if not socialism, all over the world.

We need true tax reform that will at least make a start toward restoring for our children the American Dream that wealth is denied to no one, that each individual has the right to fly as high as his strength and ability will take him. . . . But we cannot have such reform while our tax policy is engineered by people who view the tax as a means of achieving changes in our social structure. . . .

Have we the courage and the will to face up to the immorality and discrimination of the progressive tax, and demand a return to traditional proportionate taxation? . . . Today in our country, the tax collector's share is 37 cents of every dollar earned. Freedom has never been so fragile, so close to slipping from our grasp.

Recognize that government invasion of public power is eventually an assault upon your own business. . . .

Those who ask us to trade our freedom for the soup kitchen of the welfare state are architects of a policy of accommodation.

They say the world has become too complex for simple answers. They are wrong. There are no easy answers, but there are simple answers. . . .

Source: PBS.org Great American Speeches Archive, www.pbs.org/greatspeeches/timeline.

Document 5

Excerpts from "Goldwater on the Record"

"I'd drop a low-yield atomic bomb on the Chinese supply lines in North Vietnam or maybe shell 'em with the Seventh Fleet." (*Newsweek*, May 20, 1963)

"I don't give a tinker's damn what the rest of the world thinks about the United States, as long as we keep strong militarily." (*Congressional Record*, September 23, 1963)

"The policies we have been following there for the past several years have been proven to be inadequate. . . . I predict that if these policies do not change we'll be fighting in Vietnam for a decade. And, at best, we'll end up with a draw or a slow defeat." (Interview, July 5, 1964)

"I think Social Security should be voluntary. This is the only definite position I have on it. If a man wants it, fine. If he does not want it, he can provide his own." (*New York Times Magazine*, November 24, 1963)

"We are told, however, that many people lack skills and cannot find jobs because they did not have an education. . . . The fact is that most people who have no skill have no education for the same reason—low intelligence or ambition." ([Speech at] Economic Club of New York, January 15, 1964)

"I fear Washington and centralized government more than I do Moscow." (Speech in Spartanburg, South Carolina, September 15, 1960)

"Personally, I don't believe in a graduated tax, [but] I know we can't drop it. A graduated tax is a penalty on ambition." ([Speech in] Hillsboro, New Hampshire, January 22, 1964)

"Sometimes I think this country would be better off if we could just saw off the Eastern Seaboard and let it float out to sea." (*Washington Star*, December 3, 1961)

"At best, political platforms are a packet of misinformation and lies." (Address to Young Republicans training workshop, Washington, D.C., January 24, 1964)

Source: "Goldwater on the Record," *Progressive*, September 1964.

Document 6

Broadcast by President Lyndon B. Johnson, October 18, 1964

My fellow Americans:
On Thursday of last week, from the Kremlin in Moscow, the Soviet Government announced a change in its leadership.

On Friday of last week, Communist China exploded a nuclear device on an isolated test site in Sinkiang.

Both of these important events make it right that your President report to you as fully and as clearly and as promptly as he can. That is what I mean to do this evening.

Now, let me begin with events in Moscow. We do not know exactly what happened to Nikita Khruschev last Thursday. We do know that he has been forced out of power by his former friends and colleagues. . . .

Mr. Khrushchev was clearly the dominant figure in making Soviet policy. After Lenin and Stalin, he is only the third man in history to have made himself the undisputed master of Communist Russia. . . .

But two men now share top responsibility in the Soviet Union, and their exact relation to each other and to their colleagues is not yet very clear. They are experienced, but younger men, and perhaps less rooted in the past. They are said to be realistic. We can hope that they will share with us our great objective—the prevention of nuclear war.

But what does all this mean for us in America? It means at least four things:

First, we must never forget that the men in the Kremlin remain dedicated, dangerous Communists. . . .

Second, there will be turmoil in the Communist world. It is likely that the men in the Kremlin will be concerned primarily with problems of communism. This would not be all good, because there are problems and issues that need attention between our world and theirs. But it is not all bad, because men who are busy with internal problems may not be tempted to reckless external acts.

Third, this great change will not stop the forces in Eastern Europe that are working for greater independence. Those forces will continue to have our sympathy. We will not give up our hope of building new bridges to these peoples.

Fourth, our own course must continue to prove that we on our side are ready to get on with the work of peace. . . .

That same day, the Chinese nuclear device was exploded at a test site near a lake called Lop Nor, in the Takla Makan desert of the remote Central Asian province of Sinkiang. . . .

No American should treat this matter lightly. Until this week, only four powers had entered the dangerous world of nuclear explosions. Whatever their differences, all four are sober and serious states, with long experience as major powers in the modern world.

Communist China has no such experience. . . .

Nuclear spread is dangerous to all mankind.

What if there should come to be 10 nuclear powers, or maybe 20 nuclear powers?

What if we must learn to look everywhere for the restraint which our own example now sets for a few?

Will the human race be safe in such a day?

The lesson of Lop Nor is that we are right to recognize the danger of nuclear spread; that we must continue to work against it, and we will. . . .

Source: Public Papers of the Presidents of the United States: Lyndon B. Johnson, 1963–1964, Book II: July 1 to December 31, 1964 (Washington, DC: Government Printing Office, 1965).

THE ELECTION OF
1968

Nineteen sixty-eight, Democratic presidential nominee Hubert H. Humphrey (see fact box, p. 873) once reflected, had been "no normal campaign year." In January 1968, communist troops in Vietnam launched the Tet Offensive, which energized anti-war sentiment within the United States and forced President Lyndon B. Johnson to withdraw from the presidential race. In April, the assassination of the civil rights leader Martin Luther King, Jr., rekindled urban rioting and made the need for "law and order" a central issue of the campaign. Two months later, the assassination of Senator Robert F. Kennedy, arguably the strongest Democratic presidential aspirant, allowed Humphrey to capture the party's nomination. Street unrest marred the Democratic National Convention in Chicago and damaged Humphrey's prospects in the fall campaign. Nevertheless, Humphrey's qualified pledge to work for peace in Vietnam, along with Johnson's moves toward that end, nearly lifted him to victory over Richard M. Nixon (see fact box, p. 819), the Republican nominee, and George C. Wallace, the former governor of Alabama who had run on a third-party ticket. Unlike any previous election in United States history, the paradox of violent events and efforts to achieve peace in Southeast Asia shaped the presidential campaign of 1968.

Yet the 1968 election was less unique than Humphrey had suggested. During winter and spring, candidates competed for delegates in primaries and conventions. That summer, parties convened to nominate their standard-bearers and write their platforms. Throughout the year, voters wrestled with a number of pressing issues including the Vietnam War, crime, and race. Despite talk of a "New Politics" geared to the aspirations of young people and minority groups, the existing party system produced three candidates who were middle-aged, professional politicians and sons of small-town America. Nixon had grown up in Whittier, California; Humphrey in Doland, South Dakota; and Wallace in Clio, Alabama. On Election Day, Americans trooped to the polls and elected Nixon. The "year of the barricades" ended not with revolution, but a slim triumph for the Republicans' nominee.

The 1968 campaign remains important for three reasons. First, circumstances beyond each candidate's control molded this race, making its outcome less than certain. Before Election Day, Nixon worried that a successful peace initiative by Johnson would cost him the election. Second, despite the closeness of the final tally, most voters had repudiated the party in power. Humphrey received 12 million fewer votes than Johnson had in 1964, revealing popular disaffection with liberalism and inaugurating a generation of "Grand Old Party" (GOP) dominance in presidential elections. Third, the election elevated Nixon to the presidency. The Nixon administration, which simultaneously pursued détente with the communist nations, approved liberal domestic policies, and employed "dirty tricks" against its opponents, influenced politics over the succeeding decade.

CHRONOLOGY

1967

NOVEMBER 30   Senator Eugene McCarthy announces candidacy for Democratic presidential nomination.

1968

JANUARY 30   Communists begin "Tet Offensive" in South Vietnam.

FEBRUARY 8   George C. Wallace announces candidacy for president on Independent ticket.

MARCH 12   President Johnson narrowly defeats McCarthy in New Hampshire Democratic primary; Richard Nixon wins New Hampshire primary by a wide margin.

MARCH 16   Senator Robert F. Kennedy enters presidential race.

MARCH 31   Lyndon B. Johnson withdraws from presidential contest.

APRIL 4   Dr. Martin Luther King, Jr. is assassinated.

APRIL 27   Vice President Hubert H. Humphrey announces candidacy for Democratic presidential nomination.

JUNE 4–5   Kennedy defeats McCarthy in California primary, but is later shot by assassin Sirhan Sirhan in Los Angeles.

JUNE 6   Kennedy dies from his gunshot wounds.

AUGUST 5–9   Republican National Convention meets in Miami; Richard Nixon nominated for president on first ballot.

AUGUST 26–30   Democratic National Convention meets in Chicago amid antiwar protests; Hubert Humphrey nominated for president.

SEPTEMBER 30   Humphrey vows to stop bombing of North Vietnam as an "acceptable risk for peace."

OCTOBER 29   McCarthy endorses Humphrey.

OCTOBER 31   Johnson announces peace talks to start on November 6, one day after the election.

NOVEMBER 5   Nixon narrowly elected in presidential balloting.

1969

JANUARY 20   Richard Nixon inaugurated as thirty-seventh U.S. president.

The Johnson Administration

President Johnson's record set the parameters of the 1968 campaign. LBJ had entered the White House in 1963, following the assassination of John F. Kennedy. The next year, he won the presidency in his own right, crushing his Republican opponent, conservative Senator Barry M. Goldwater of Arizona, with 61 percent of the popular vote. With huge Democratic majorities in Congress, the president secured landmark legislation in the areas of education, urban renewal, medical care, immigration, national parks, consumer and environmental protection, economic opportunity, and civil rights. Although LBJ's "Great

Society" programs improved the quality of life for millions of Americans, they only scratched the surface of racial and economic inequities. During the summers of 1965, 1966, and 1967, U.S. cities simmered with rioting, leading many whites to conclude that the civil rights movement had run its course and a period of consolidation, if not retrenchment, was in order. Across the nation, white backlash against black gains was growing.

Johnson's chief problem was the military stalemate in Vietnam. To protect the independence of South Vietnam against the Vietcong—communist rebels backed by North Vietnam—LBJ committed American combat troops in 1965. But, by the end of 1967,

U.S. bombing of North Vietnam and the introduction of nearly a half-million American soldiers had failed to defeat the communist forces. Twenty thousand Americans died in Vietnam between 1961 and 1967, and as casualties mounted, public opinion turned against the war. By the autumn of 1967, 40 percent of Americans thought the Vietnam War had been a mistake, while antiwar protestors—chanting "Hey, hey, LBJ! How many kids did you kill today?"—blamed the conflict on the president. Vietnam had become, in the eyes of millions of voters, "Lyndon Johnson's War."

The president found it hard to rally Americans behind his leadership. Johnson was often deceitful, and the press reported examples of his growing "credibility gap." He could count on little sympathy from the American public, which saw him as a vain, coarse, overbearing politician—and a Texas "wheeler-dealer," to boot. During the best of times, when the Great Society enjoyed widespread support, these sentiments puzzled him. "I'm giving them boom times and more good legislation than anybody else did, and what do they do—attack and sneer," the president privately complained. During the worst of times, as frustration over Vietnam mounted, he became distressed. LBJ once asked a friend why people did not like him. "Mr. President," the reply went, "you are not a very likeable man."

The Democrats

Weakened presidents often face opposition from inside their own parties. In November 1967, Senator Eugene McCarthy of Minnesota announced his candidacy for the Democratic presidential nomination. Intelligent, liberal, and a ten-year veteran of the Senate, he was a potential thorn in Johnson's side. McCarthy, by 1967, had turned "dove," denouncing the Vietnam War as "morally unjustifiable." Yet, in many ways, he did not represent a serious challenge. McCarthy, a Catholic, was pious, introspective, and aloof, more a scholar than a politician. Whether discussing poetry or presidents, he excelled mainly as a critic. His years in the Senate had yielded few accom-

Opposition to the war in Vietnam led Senator Eugene McCarthy to challenge Lyndon B. Johnson for the Democratic nomination for president in 1968. McCarthy failed to win the nomination but fueled the movement against the war and influenced Johnson's decision to withdraw from the race.

plishments, and the chamber's routines bored him. McCarthy's presidential bid was disorganized, and his prepared remarks left audiences cold.

But events transformed McCarthy into a formidable candidate. On January 30, 1968, during the holiday of Tet, the North Vietnamese and Vietcong unleashed a massive assault against South Vietnam. The communists occupied several cities, and penetrated the U.S. embassy compound in Saigon before American and South Vietnamese forces turned them back. Although U.S. troops eventually prevailed on the battlefield, the scale of the enemy offensive signaled that the war's end was nowhere in sight. Voters vented their frustrations at the ballot box. Three thousand university students, "shaven and shorn" in an effort to be "Clean for Gene," invaded New Hampshire, site of the first presidential primary, to campaign for McCarthy. On March 12, 1968, Johnson narrowly won the state's Democratic primary with 49.4 percent of the vote, against 42.2 percent for McCarthy. But the challenger had exceeded all expectations, capturing twenty of New Hampshire's twenty-four convention delegates. The increasingly focused McCarthy campaign had recruited only a few followers for seating at the convention, while the number of would-be delegates put up by Johnson's lieutenants (who had expected to win the primary in a "walk") exceeded the total number of seats available. As a result, popular support for the president's candidates dispersed among an array of names, allowing McCarthy voters to rally behind a small number of delegates and garner the lion's share of New Hampshire's convention seats. McCarthy's army of volunteers, buoyant and growing, marched into Wisconsin for their next showdown with the president. Within the Badger State, LBJ's supporters were either forlorn or deserting.

The tide was running against Johnson. On March 16, Senator Robert F. Kennedy of New York, brother of former president John F. Kennedy, declared his candidacy for the Democratic nomination and promised "new policies." In turning against the war, Kennedy played down his brother John's role in enhancing America's commitment to defend South Vietnam. Although Johnson continued to sound like a candidate in public, he had no stomach for a divisive fight with "Bobby," his long-time nemesis. The president's health had declined, and the burdens of office weighed heavily upon him. Fifty-two percent of Americans polled disapproved of Johnson's job per-

formance, and 63 percent opposed his handling of the war. Accordingly, LBJ decided against sending 206,000 additional troops to South Vietnam, as his military commanders had recommended. In a nationally televised address on March 31, Johnson instead announced a partial bombing halt over North Vietnam, offered to begin peace talks with the enemy, and closed with these words: "I shall not seek and I will not accept the nomination of my party for another term as your President."

Johnson's exit transformed the campaign for the Democratic nomination. McCarthy's supporters refused to forsake their candidate, the first to challenge Johnson, for Kennedy, the man who had entered the race only after McCarthy's near victory in New Hampshire. Kennedy, one columnist joked, had "come down from the hills to shoot the wounded." Vice President Hubert Humphrey, meanwhile, prepared to enter the contest. With Johnson on the sidelines, he stood to inherit the president's remaining support within the party. At fifty-six, Humphrey had wide political experience, having served as mayor of Minneapolis and a U.S. senator from Minnesota before becoming LBJ's vice president in 1965. Long associated with liberal causes, especially civil rights, Humphrey nevertheless remained tied to Johnson and his unpopular war. Since the vice president joined the race too late to compete in most primaries, he had to hunt for delegates at state conventions controlled by party bosses, many of them loyal to LBJ. The president, moreover, insisted that Humphrey refrain from criticizing the administration's Vietnam policy. "If I run," Humphrey told a friend, "Johnson's not going to make it easy."

The Republicans

The impending Democratic melee was welcome news to the Republicans. Unable to bridge the rift between its conservatives, led by Goldwater, and liberals, guided by Governor Nelson A. Rockefeller of New York, the GOP had lost the election of 1964 by landslide proportions. To avoid another round of internecine warfare in 1968, the party needed to run a centrist candidate with national appeal. Richard Nixon appeared to fit that bill. He had served in both the House and Senate and, between 1953 and 1961, was vice president under Dwight D. Eisenhower. In 1960 he had carried the GOP standard, but lost the presidency by a whisker to John F. Kennedy. Nixon was knowledgeable about foreign affairs and pragmatic regarding domestic issues. Republican Party leaders appreciated his loyalty, his willingness (unlike Rockefeller) to campaign for Goldwater, and his tireless stumping on behalf of GOP candidates in the elections of 1966.

In seeking the Republican nomination, Nixon faced several obstacles. The candidate had to overcome resentment by members of the press, political opponents, and segments of the public against his earlier "red-baiting" and negative campaigning. Having lost the presidency in 1960 and the California governorship in 1962, Nixon needed to shed his "loser" image by entering the primaries, where victory was not assured. He also had to defeat an appealing newcomer, George W. Romney, former president of American Motors and, since 1962, the governor of Michigan. Between late 1966 and the middle of 1967, polls repeatedly showed Romney, a moderate Republican, beating Johnson in a presidential trial heat.

Nixon made the most of his experience and emerged as the Republican frontrunner. His 1968 campaign was better organized than the one he had run in 1960. Nixon paced himself, delegated authority to staff members and listened to campaign aides, many of whom had studied public relations. Together, they projected the image of a "New Nixon," a mature, mellow statesman who had left his hyper-partisan past behind. The candidate used question-and-answer sessions with ordinary citizens to showcase his command of issues. In New Hampshire, he blamed the administration for the nation's domestic ills, including racial strife, lawlessness, and inflation. Regarding Vietnam, Nixon's best issue, he offered "new leadership" to "end the war." While many correspondents reported that the candidate claimed to have a "secret plan" to bring the conflict to a close, Nixon had made no such statement. Unlike Romney, he would not stumble over Vietnam.

The Romney challenge quickly fizzled out. Having visited Vietnam in 1965, the Michigan governor remarked in 1967, at the beginning of his campaign, that military officials there had given him a "brainwashing" about the war's progress. The press reported that comment, which made him appear witless and gullible. "Watching George Romney run for the presidency," Ohio governor James Rhodes later quipped, "was like watching a duck try to make love

to a football." Romney dropped out of the race on February 28, 1968, allowing Nixon to win the New Hampshire primary over his write-in opponent, Rockefeller, by a seven-to-one margin. The New York governor, in March, said that he would not seek the Republican nomination. Then, on April 30, Rockefeller proclaimed that he would indeed enter the Republican race. Nixon proceeded to score impressive, but generally uncontested, triumphs in the Indiana, Nebraska, and Oregon primaries, almost assuring his nomination.

Humphrey's Nomination

During April, Democrats had no frontrunner. McCarthy and Kennedy agreed on issues, but drew from different constituencies. Middle-class liberals leaned toward McCarthy, while blue-collar workers and racial minorities rallied to Kennedy—who became, the journalist Theodore White noted, "the most loved and most hated candidate of 1968." Kennedy's compassion and celebrity brought out frenzied crowds of the disaffected—blacks, Latinos, Native Americans, the poor, and the young. Teenage girls held up signs saying "Sock It To Me Bobby!" But Kennedy frightened many Americans, who saw him as fanning popular passions. Others thought him a ruthless opportunist, a pale imitation of his slain brother. "Jack Was Nimble, Jack Was Quick," one placard read, "But Bobby Simply Makes Me Sick." Meanwhile, Humphrey made an portentous debut. On April 27, the vice president announced his candidacy by espousing the "politics of joy." The phrase, coming three weeks after King's assassination and subsequent riots, led pundits, the public, and even Johnson to wonder whether Humphrey understood the mood of the country.

By May, Kennedy's campaign began to take off. On May 7, he defeated McCarthy in Indiana and, a week later, he garnered 52 percent of the vote in Nebraska's primary. But suburban whites in Oregon took offense at Kennedy's high-intensity campaign. That, combined with McCarthy's sharp attacks linking President Kennedy to the Vietnam War, propelled the Minnesota senator to victory. On June 4, Kennedy regrouped, winning 50 percent of the vote in South Dakota and defeating McCarthy in California by a clear, though not decisive, margin. Following his victory remarks at the Ambassador Hotel in Los Angeles, Kennedy attempted to exit via the hotel

Robert F. Kennedy delivers a speech at the Ambassador Hotel in Los Angeles upon winning the California primary on June 5, 1968. Minutes after this photograph was taken, Kennedy was shot and killed. *(AP Wide World Photos)*

kitchen—where Sirhan Sirhan, an Arab nationalist, shot him. RFK died on June 6. Kennedy's campaign had been spirited but polarizing, and his death left the nation no less divided. (See "The Assassination of Robert F. Kennedy," p. 896.)

Many Democrats believed that Kennedy, by uniting blue-collar whites and racial minorities, would have secured the nomination and prevailed in the autumn campaign. Such analysis overlooked his flagging support among suburbanites and Humphrey's successes at state conventions. On May 27, Pennsylvania's Democratic convention awarded the vice president two-thirds of its 130-vote delegation, leading his campaign manager to remark that "Humphrey was nominated in Harrisburg." Kennedy's death, and McCarthy's declining interest in his own campaign, enabled Humphrey to emerge as the party's frontrunner—and as the lightning rod for antiwar demonstrators. Greeting the vice president at campaign stops were cries of "Dump the Hump" and "Wash the blood from your hands," as well as signs

asking, "Why Change the Ventriloquist for the Dummy?" Humphrey's woes encouraged Democrats, then and later, to dream about the electoral magic that Kennedy might have worked.

Kennedy's assassination refocused attention on one of the campaign's most salient issues, "law and order." During the 1960s, Americans experienced various forms of disorder, including urban rioting, demonstrations, assassinations, and a rising crime rate. Since African Americans suffered the brunt of urban violence, the issue acquired a racial edge that left black and white liberals uneasy. Although McCarthy chose to not to discuss "law and order," the other candidates did. Kennedy, a former attorney general, reminded audiences that he once had served as the nation's chief law enforcement officer. Humphrey tried to lessen the issue's racial overtones by championing "law and order with justice." Nixon, meanwhile, exploited the issue by attacking decisions of the U.S. Supreme Court including *Miranda* v. *Arizona* (1966), which limited the ability of police to interrogate suspects and secure confessions. He later promised, as president, to appoint a new attorney general who would launch an all-out attack on both organized crime and urban violence.

Conservative Challengers

To followers of George C. Wallace, the American Independent Party candidate, "law and order" meant opposition to civil rights and antiwar demonstrations, as well as violent crime. Wallace, who launched his third-party campaign in February 1968, attacked the Supreme Court for demanding desegregation of public schools and greater rights for accused criminals. He promised that, if he were elected president

SPIRO T. AGNEW

PARTY: Republican

DATE OF BIRTH: November 9, 1918

PLACE OF BIRTH: Baltimore, Maryland

PARENTS: Theodore Spiro and Margaret Akers Agnew

EDUCATION: Johns Hopkins University, 1938–39 (withdrew); LL.B., University of Baltimore, 1947

FAMILY: Married Elinor "Judy" Judefind, 1942; children: Pamela and Kim

MILITARY SERVICE: Service officer, U.S. Army (in World War II), 1942–45

CAREER: Admitted to the Maryland bar, 1947; Baltimore County (Md.) Zoning Board of Appeals, 1957–61; chief executive, Baltimore County (Md.), 1962–66; governor of Maryland, 1967–68; U.S. vice president, 1969–73 (resigned)

DATE OF DEATH: September 17, 1996

PLACE OF DEATH: Berlin, Maryland

CAUSE OF DEATH: Leukemia

PLACE OF BURIAL: Timonium, Maryland

and "some anarchist" tried to lay in front of his car, it would be the last car the person would ever lay in front of. While his 1968 campaign was not stridently racist, Wallace, as governor, had resisted integrating the University of Alabama in 1963. A year later, after denouncing the Civil Rights Act of 1964, he won a sizeable vote in three Democratic presidential primaries. During 1968, southern whites and blue-collar workers in the North cheered his no-nonsense style. Wallace assured his supporters that "there's an awful lot of us rednecks in this country—*and they're not all in the South!*"

Another conservative politician, Governor Ronald Reagan of California, posed the chief threat to

Nixon's nomination. Although Reagan did not declare himself a candidate until August 7, at the start of the Republican National Convention in Miami, Nixon worried that southern delegates might be swayed by Reagan's "ideological siren song." An alliance between the GOP left, led by Rockefeller, and right, headed by Reagan, could then deny him the nomination. But by promising a strong national defense and a cautious approach to school desegregation, Nixon had already won over Senator Strom Thurmond of South Carolina (who had bolted the Democratic Party in 1948 and run for president as a "Dixiecrat," before joining the Republican Party in 1964). With Thurmond's backing, Nixon's southern support held, and he won the nomination with 692 first-ballot votes, against 277 for Rockefeller and 182 for Reagan. The nominee then selected a border state governor, Spiro T. Agnew of Maryland, as his running mate. Agnew's earlier endorsement of Rockefeller had pleased GOP liberals, while his denunciation of urban rioting reassured conservatives. The choice of little-known Agnew, who had served as chief executive of Baltimore County between 1962 and 1966 before being elected governor of Maryland in 1966, shocked many members of the press, who duly noted the candidate's lack of national stature. Nevertheless, the selection of Agnew underscored Nixon's careful balancing between North and South, liberals and conservatives. The party's "center" had held, and Nixon emerged from Miami with a "bounce"—a sixteen-point lead over Humphrey in the Gallup poll.

Throughout the autumn, Nixon continued to campaign as a centrist. He conceded the deep South to Wallace, and concentrated on adding the border South to the GOP's traditional base in the West and Midwest. Nixon endorsed conservative values associated with middle-income suburbanites, including hard work, traditional morality, and law and order, while hedging on other issues. He rejected coercive measures to desegregate schools, while making no promise to repeal the gains of the civil rights revolu-

With his arms outstretched, Alabama governor George Wallace stands in a limousine during a motorcade on Chicago's State Street. The size of the crowd indicates the strength of the third-party candidate's appeal in the North in 1968. *(AP Wide World Photos)*

GEORGE C. WALLACE

PARTY: Democratic; American Independent (1968)

DATE OF BIRTH: August 25, 1919

PLACE OF BIRTH: Clio, Alabama

PARENTS: George C. and Mozelle Smith Wallace

EDUCATION: LL.B., University of Alabama, 1942

FAMILY: Married Lurleen Burns (d. 1968), 1943; children: Bobbi Jo, Peggy Sue, George Jr., and Janie Lee; married Cornelia Ellis Snively, 1971 (divorced, 1978); married Lisa Taylor, 1981 (divorced, 1987)

MILITARY SERVICE: Sergeant, U.S. Air Force (in World War II), 1943–45

CAREER: Admitted to the Alabama bar, 1942; Alabama Assembly, 1947–53; judge, Third Judicial Circuit Court of Alabama, 1953–59; unsuccessful candidate for Alabama Governor, 1958; governor of Alabama, 1963–67, 1971–79, 1983–87; unsuccessful candidate for U.S. president, 1964, 1968, 1972, 1976

DATE OF DEATH: September 13, 1998

PLACE OF DEATH: Montgomery, Alabama

CAUSE OF DEATH: Bacterial blood infection

PLACE OF BURIAL: Montgomery, Alabama

tion. On Vietnam, Nixon criticized Johnson's failure to achieve victory but proposed no alternative policy, arguing that to do so might undermine ongoing efforts to achieve a peace settlement. Although slogans such as "Nixon's the One" highlighted his vague campaign message, the Republican nominee maintained a twelve to fifteen point lead over Humphrey throughout September.

Chicago and the Democratic Convention

Nixon enjoyed a comfortable lead partly because the Democratic Convention had been disastrous for Humphrey. On August 10, Senator George S. McGovern of South Dakota entered the race, presumably to hold Robert Kennedy's delegates and allow the party to draft Senator Edward M. Kennedy of Massachusetts. Meanwhile, Johnson, whose poll numbers had rebounded, flirted with accepting a draft himself. LBJ planned to attend the convention when it opened in Chicago on August 26, the eve of his sixtieth birthday. In the end, however, he decided that his appearance would only inflame tempers. Much to Humphrey's chagrin, the president's allies retained control of the convention; the platform, at LBJ's insistence, rejected any bombing halt that might endanger U.S. troops. By accepting this plank, which passed over an antiwar substitute (1,567 for, 1,041 against), Humphrey bound himself to Johnson's Vietnam policy. The vice president easily won the nomination with 1,760 votes, against 601 for McCarthy and 146 for McGovern. He then selected as his running mate Senator Edmund Muskie of Maine, an able, soft-spoken public servant who added statesmanship, but little geographical and ideological balance, to the ticket. Muskie, who had served as governor of Maine between 1955 and 1958 before being elected to the U.S. Senate in 1958, was well liked within the party and known for his steady public demeanor. "I went for the quiet man," Humphrey later reflected. "I know I talk too much, and I wanted someone who makes for a contrast in styles. Two Hubert Humphreys might be one too many."

The real drama took place outside the convention. Antiwar activists led by Abbie Hoffman and Jerry Rubin gathered in Chicago, where Mayor Richard J. Daley was prepared to quell any disturbance. The mayor, backed by 18,000 police officers and National Guard troops, cordoned the convention hall with fences and barbed wire, transforming it into "Fort Daley." On August 26, members of the Youth International Party gathered in Lincoln Park to mock the Democrats. Espousing the "politics of ecstasy," these "Yippies" proclaimed a "Festival of Life" and nominated "Pigasus," a pig, for president. The police used tear gas to evict them, though demonstrations continued throughout the week. On August 28, as the balloting for president began, approximately 3,000 demonstrators, chanting "Hey, Hey, Go Away," "Peace Now," and "Fuck You, LBJ," marched down Michigan Avenue toward the hall. Columns of police removed their badges, lobbed tear gas, and charged the throng, shouting "Kill, kill, kill." They clubbed and bloodied hundreds of young people, then dragged them into patrol wagons. Although most Americans approved of Daley's security measures, the televised spectacle of street violence suggested that Democrats were incapable of managing their own convention and, perhaps, the country as well.

The Fall Campaign

In the aftermath of Chicago, Humphrey's campaign floundered. The candidate first sided with the police against the protestors, explaining that "we ought to quit pretending that Mayor Daley did anything wrong." Days later, he conceded that Chicago had been a "catastrophe" that had left him "heartbroken" and "beaten." McCarthy, angry with the vice president's stand on the war and police treatment of "his" kids, declined to endorse his party's ticket.

EDMUND S. MUSKIE

PARTY: Democratic

DATE OF BIRTH: March 28, 1914

PLACE OF BIRTH: Rumford, Maine

PARENTS: Stephen Marciszewski and Josephine Czarnecki

EDUCATION: B.A., Bates College, 1936; LL.B., Cornell University, 1939

FAMILY: Married Jane Frances Gray, 1948; children: Stephen, Ellen, Melinda, Martha, and Edmund Jr.

MILITARY SERVICE: Lieutenant junior grade, U.S. Navy (in World War II), 1942–45

CAREER: Admitted to the Maine bar, 1939; Maine House of Representatives, 1947–51; director, Office of Price Stabilization (Maine), 1951–52; governor of Maine, 1955–58; U.S. senator, 1959–80; unsuccessful candidate for U.S. president, 1972; U.S. secretary of state, 1980–81

DATE OF DEATH: March 26, 1996

PLACE OF DEATH: Washington, D.C.

CAUSE OF DEATH: Heart attack

PLACE OF BURIAL: Arlington, Virginia

Democratic candidates Hubert Humphrey and Edmund Muskie.
(Gyory Collection/Cathy Casriel Photo)

Humphrey tried to regroup by attacking Nixon, whose "firm" stands, he sneered, made "Jell-O look like concrete." But as long as he backed Johnson's position on Vietnam, Humphrey drew scorn and limited public support. Shouts of "Murderer,"

Republican candidate Richard M. Nixon addresses a crowd outside his apartment in New York City. *(AP Wide World Photos)*

"Racist," and "Stop the War" greeted him at Oregon's Reed College. To make matters worse, Wallace had picked up steam. The Alabaman took aim at "liberals, intellectuals, and long hairs" who, he said, "have run the country for too long." Audiences applauded his assault on "over-educated, ivory tower folks with pointed heads" who were unable "to park a bicycle straight." A Gallup survey in late September found that 43 percent of the electorate backed Nixon, 28 percent were for Humphrey, and 21 percent favored Wallace.

During October, the vice president started to close the gap. In a televised address on September 30, Humphrey promised that as president he would stop the bombing of North Vietnam as "an acceptable risk for peace," because "it could lead to success in the negotiations and thereby shorten the war." He reserved the right to resume bombing if the enemy showed bad faith, making his stance only slightly more flexible than Johnson's. Nevertheless, Humphrey's words encouraged Democratic doves to "come home," and young people began waving new placards: "If You Mean It, We're with You" and "Stop the War—Humphrey, We Trust You." The vice president also began enticing union workers away from Wallace, whom he dubbed racist and anti-labor. Then, Wallace stumbled when he selected as running mate Curtis E. LeMay, a retired air force general who defended the use of atomic weapons and threatened to bomb North Vietnam "back to the Stone Age." Humphrey wondered whether Wallace and LeMay, the "bombsy twins," could be trusted to achieve peace. In the meantime, Agnew had embarrassed Nixon by making insensitive comments about Poles and Japanese and, in a crude attempt at "red-baiting," by calling the Democratic nominee "soft on communism." By October 24, the race had tightened. Forty-four percent of the electorate supported Nixon, 36 percent favored Humphrey, and 15 percent were for Wallace.

Nixon felt his lead slipping away. The campaign's longest surviving contender had exhausted his message, and editorialists were demanding more specific proposals from him. After he refused to debate Humphrey, the Democratic nominee mocked him as "Richard the Chicken-Hearted." Nixon replied with

CURTIS E. LEMAY

PARTY: American Independent

DATE OF BIRTH: November 15, 1906

PLACE OF BIRTH: Columbus, Ohio

PARENTS: Erving LeMay and Arizona Carpenter

EDUCATION: Army Air Corps School (March Field, Calif.), 1929; B.S., Ohio State University, 1934

FAMILY: Married Helen E. Maitland, 1934; one daughter

MILITARY SERVICE: Army Air Corps: lieutenant, 1935–40; captain, 1940–41; major, 1941; lieutenant colonel, 1942–43; brigadier general, 1943–44; major general, 1944–45; deputy chief of staff, Air Force Research and Development, 1945–47; head of Strategic Air Command, 1948–57; Air Force vice chief of staff, 1957–61; Air Force chief of staff, 1961–65

CAREER: Unsuccessful candidate for U.S. vice president, 1968

DATE OF DEATH: October 1, 1990

PLACE OF DEATH: Riverside, California

Like Strom Thurmond in 1948, George Wallace bolted the Democratic Party in 1968 and swept much of the South. *(Gyory Collection/ Cathy Casriel Photo)*

jabs of his own, calling Humphrey an "adult delinquent," the "fastest, loosest tongue in the West," and a big spender with "his hand in your pocket." Nevertheless, on October 29, McCarthy endorsed Humphrey as a man with "better understanding of [our] domestic needs and a strong will to act."

For Nixon, the biggest blow came two days later, when Johnson announced a bombing halt over North Vietnam and the start of peace talks on November 6, the day after the election. The Republican campaign used contacts, especially Anna Chennault, the Chinese-born widow of World War II general Claire Chennault, to discourage the South Vietnamese from joining these talks. The White House, aided by FBI surveillance, knew of such machinations but could not inform the public without disclosing how it had learned of them. When South Vietnamese President Nguyen Van Thieu declared on November 2 that his government would not negotiate with the communists, Nixon blamed the failed peace initiative on the White House. The momentum toward Humphrey quickly stopped.

The Voters Decide

The 1968 election was a cliffhanger. On November 5, Nixon won by just 511,944 votes, receiving 43.4 percent of the popular vote to 42.7 percent for Humphrey, and 13.5 percent for Wallace. His "national strategy" had worked. Nixon's 301 electoral votes came from thirty-two states including the Carolinas, Virginia, Kentucky, Tennessee, Florida, New Jersey, Illinois, Ohio, most of the Midwest, the far West, and California. Humphrey won 191 electoral votes from 13 states, mainly in the Northeast, plus the District of Columbia, while Wallace, clinging to his regional base, carried just five states in the deep South, for 46 electoral votes. Nixon won a plurality of the suburban vote, while blacks and most union workers flocked to Humphrey. When it became clear that Wallace, like earlier third-party candidates, was not going to be elected, many of his supporters returned either to the Republican or Democratic folds.

Several issues determined the election's outcome. According to Nixon, the electorate's longing for peace was the paramount issue. As the challenger, Nixon held the advantage, for he was free to attack the administration's Vietnam policies without offer-

THE ASSASSINATION OF ROBERT F. KENNEDY

*O*n June 4, 1968, Robert F. Kennedy won his greatest political victory. In California's Democratic primary, he had taken 46.3 percent of the popular vote against 41.8 percent for Minnesota senator Eugene McCarthy, his nearest rival. The Kennedy campaign had generated excitement for weeks, with large crowds of young people and racial minorities flocking to the youthful New York senator. And yet Kennedy, like his fallen brother and the recently slain Martin Luther King, Jr., evoked the best and worst of human passions. Twelve days before Kennedy's triumph in California, the *Times-Express*, an underground newspaper in San Francisco, published an eerily prophetic piece in which the ghost of the assassinated president William McKinley warned: "Don't waste your vote on Kennedy. They're going to kill him."

Shortly after midnight on June 5, Kennedy addressed supporters in the ballroom of the Ambassador Hotel in Los Angeles. The audience greeted the victor with chants of "R-F-K! R-F-K! R-F-K!" and Kennedy, flashing his toothy grin, spoke confidently: "I think we can end the divisions in the United States." He called America "a great country, an unselfish country, and a compassionate country" and closed with these words: "My thanks to all of you, and it's on to Chicago and let's win there." One observer dubbed it "his best speech of the campaign," and the throng cheered fiercely as Kennedy disappeared through a passage linking the ballroom to the annex. The crowd remained in place, and then people began running about. "What happened?" someone asked. "They shot him—Kennedy's been shot," was the answer.

Sirhan Bishara Sirhan, a twenty-four-year-old Palestinian immigrant, fired eight shots at Kennedy and his entourage. Besides the senator, four people were injured. One bullet hit Kennedy's shoulder, causing a minor wound, while another penetrated his right ear and entered his skull. He was whisked to Central Receiving Hospital, then to Good Samaritan Hospital. Kennedy press secretary Frank F. Mankiewicz, looking tired and haggard, emerged periodically to brief the nation on the senator's condition. At 5:01 A.M. on June 6, Kennedy died. His corpse was transferred to New York, where a requiem mass was said at St. Patrick's Cathedral. On the evening of June 8, Kennedy was buried in Arlington National Cemetery, not far from the grave of his brother John.

Kennedy's assassination sparked a nationwide wave of mourning. Yet the senator, known for his ruthlessness as well as his compassion, had been a polarizing candidate. President Lyndon B. Johnson seemed to embody the electorate's mixed feelings. Upon learning of the shooting, LBJ—Kennedy's nemesis—gasped that it was "too horrible for words." Together, the murders of John and Robert Kennedy formed the bookends of the Johnson presidency, and the most turbulent period of the 1960s. More importantly, Robert Kennedy's life, cut short by an assassin, led Democrats in 1968, and afterward, to ponder the eternal question: "What if . . .?"

ing specific alternatives. Since all the candidates had blurred their stances on Vietnam, the election never became a referendum on how to end the war. Meanwhile, at home, concerns about racial equality and "law and order" provided the context for the 1968 campaign. By conflating both issues, Wallace played to white backlash by suggesting that moves to promote civil rights inevitably produced civil disorder. Nixon, in contrast, addressed voters' concerns about crime, while positioning himself as a moderate on racial issues. Perhaps the Republican nominee camouflaged his appeal, as his critics later contended, by using "law and order" as a racial code word to woo disgruntled whites. In the end, he and Wallace won support from moderate and conservative Democrats, leaving the liberals to Humphrey.

In 1968 Nixon won a negative landslide; Americans rejected the incumbent administration without

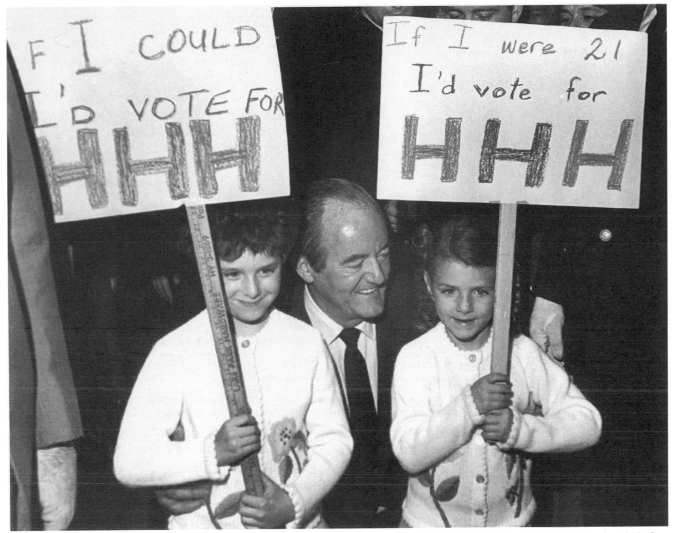

Vice president Hubert H. Humphrey, running in 1968 as the Democratic candidate for president, is pictured in Chicago shortly before Election Day. The children pictured here could not vote, but their parents could. *(AP Wide World Photos)*

giving the opposition a firm mandate. If one combines the Wallace and Nixon totals, Humphrey was walloped by the margin of 56.9 percent to 42.7 percent. The post-1945 liberal consensus, based on social reform at home and containment of communism abroad, seemed at an end. Yet, Nixon had short coattails: He was the first president since Zachary Taylor, in 1849, to enter the White House without winning a majority in either chamber of Congress.

The new president pursued a cautious agenda. Nixon gradually withdrew U.S. troops from Vietnam. In domestic affairs, he talked like a conservative, courting Wallace voters with his "southern strategy" while governing as a moderate, working with a Democratic-controlled Congress to enhance voting rights, consumer and environmental protection, occupational health and safety, and Native-American rights.

As a result, Nixon maintained his centrist base, inherited Wallace's support in Dixie, and was reelected by a landslide in 1972. Nixon's coalition helped elect Ronald Reagan in 1980 and 1984, and George Bush in 1988. In the interim, Jimmy Carter, elected in 1976 in the aftermath of Watergate, was the only Democrat to break the GOP's lock on the White House in the quarter-century from 1969 to 1993.

The Legacies of the Election

The 1968 election left the Democratic Party shattered for a generation. To avoid another fractious convention like the one in Chicago, the party became more inclusive and "democratic." To weaken the power of bosses, especially in the South, Democrats abolished the "unit rule," which had allowed the majority faction of a state delegation to control all of that state's convention votes. The party reformed the way in which it selected delegates, enabling all Democrats regardless of race, religion, or gender to participate in national conventions. Women, racial minorities, and young people became delegates in record numbers, leading one senior Democrat to lament that, at the 1972 convention, there had been too much long hair and not enough cigars. Designed to bolster the party, such reforms actually weakened it by forcing Democrats to satisfy a number of diverse and contentious constituencies. The result was a succession of mediocre nominees—George McGovern in 1972, Walter Mondale in 1984, and Michael Dukakis in 1988—who were too liberal to attract sufficient votes outside of the Northeast and Pacific Coast. The Democrats, as much as Nixon's political appeals, abetted the GOP's revival in Dixie and the nation as a whole.

The presidential campaign of 1968 reshaped U.S. politics. The assassinations of King and Robert Kennedy, the violence in Chicago, the repeated heckling of Humphrey, Nixon, and Wallace, and the election of a president with a minority of the popular vote, together suggested that large segments of the public were dissatisfied with their political options. The candidate elected in 1968 did much to diminish confidence in government. The Nixon campaign's efforts to derail Johnson's peace initiative presaged the new administration's later "dirty tricks." When Nixon and his aides learned of LBJ's surveillance of their campaign, they used this knowledge to justify their own political intelligence gathering, setting the stage for Watergate, the worst scandal in U.S. history. The "hard year," as Eugene McCarthy called 1968, helped to inaugurate a very hard decade.

Dean Kotlowski

Bibliography

Carter, Dan T. *The Politics of Rage: George Wallace, The Origins of the New Conservatism, and the Transformation of American Politics.* New York: Simon and Schuster, 1995.

Caute, David. *Year of the Barricades: A Journey Through 1968.* New York: Harper and Row, 1988.

Chester, Lewis, Godfrey Hodgson, and Bruce Page. *An American Melodrama: The Presidential Campaign of 1968.* New York: Viking, 1969.

Farber, David. *Chicago '68.* Chicago: University of Chicago Press, 1988.

Gould, Lewis. *1968: The Election That Changed America.* Chicago: Ivan Dee, 1993.

Kaiser, Charles. *1968 in America.* New York: Weidenfield and Nicolson, 1988.

Lesher, Stephan. *George Wallace: American Populist.* New York: Addison-Wesley, 1994.

Matusow, Allen J. *The Unraveling of America: A History of Liberalism in the 1960s.* New York: Harper and Row, 1984.

McGinnis, Joe. *The Selling of the President 1968.* New York: Trident Press, 1969.

Patterson, James T. *Grand Expectations: The United States, 1945–1974.* New York: Oxford University Press, 1996.

Schlesinger, Arthur M. *Robert Kennedy and His Times.* Boston: Houghton Mifflin, 1978.

Small, Melvin. *The Presidency of Richard Nixon.* Lawrence: University Press of Kansas, 1999.

Solberg, Carl. *Hubert H. Humphrey: A Biography.* New York: W. W. Norton, 1984.

Unger, Irwin, and Debi Unger. *Turning Point: 1968.* New York: Scribner's, 1988.

White, Theodore H. *The Making of the President 1968.* New York: Pocket Books, 1970.

Wicker, Tom. *One of Us: Richard Nixon and the American Dream.* New York: Random House, 1991.

THE VOTE: ELECTION OF 1968

State	Total No. of Electors	Total Popular Vote	Electoral Vote R	D	AI	Margin of Victory Votes	% Total Vote	Nixon Republican Votes	%	Humphrey Democrat Votes	%	Wallace American Independent Votes	%	Others Votes	%
Alabama	10	1,049,917			10	49,656	4.7%	146,923	14.0%	196,579	18.7%	691,425	65.9%	14,990	1.4%
Alaska	3	83,035	3			2,189	2.6%	37,600	45.3%	35,411	42.6%	10,024	12.1%	0	0.0%
Arizona	5	486,936	5			96,207	19.8%	266,721	54.8%	170,514	35.0%	46,573	9.6%	3,128	0.6%
Arkansas	6	609,590			6	4,161	0.7%	189,062	31.0%	184,901	30.3%	235,627	38.7%	0	0.0%
California	40	7,251,587	40			223,346	3.1%	3,467,664	47.8%	3,244,318	44.7%	487,270	6.7%	52,335	0.7%
Colorado	6	811,199	6			74,171	9.1%	409,345	50.5%	335,174	41.3%	60,813	7.5%	5,867	0.7%
Connecticut	8	1,256,232		8		64,840	5.2%	556,721	44.3%	621,561	49.5%	76,650	6.1%	1,300	0.1%
Delaware	3	214,367	3			7,520	3.5%	96,714	45.1%	89,194	41.6%	28,459	13.3%	0	0.0%
District of Columbia	3	170,578		3		108,554	63.6%	31,012	18.2%	139,566	81.8%	0	0.0%	0	0.0%
Florida	14	2,187,805	14			210,010	9.6%	886,804	40.5%	676,794	30.9%	624,207	28.5%	0	0.0%
Georgia	12	1,250,266			12	45,671	3.7%	380,111	30.4%	334,440	26.7%	535,550	42.8%	165	0.0%
Hawaii	4	236,218		4		49,899	21.1%	91,425	38.7%	141,324	59.8%	3,469	1.5%	0	0.0%
Idaho	4	291,183	4			76,096	26.1%	165,369	56.8%	89,273	30.7%	36,541	12.5%	0	0.0%
Illinois	26	4,619,749	26			134,960	2.9%	2,174,774	47.1%	2,039,814	44.2%	390,958	8.5%	14,203	0.3%
Indiana	13	2,123,597	13			261,226	12.3%	1,067,885	50.3%	806,659	38.0%	243,108	11.4%	5,945	0.3%
Iowa	9	1,167,931	9			142,407	12.2%	619,106	53.0%	476,699	40.8%	66,422	5.7%	5,704	0.5%
Kansas	7	872,783	7			175,678	20.1%	478,674	54.8%	302,996	34.7%	88,921	10.2%	2,192	0.3%
Kentucky	9	1,055,893	9			64,870	6.1%	462,411	43.8%	397,541	37.6%	193,098	18.3%	2,843	0.3%
Louisiana	10	1,097,450			10	52,080	4.7%	257,535	23.5%	309,615	28.2%	530,300	48.3%	0	0.0%
Maine	4	392,936		4		48,058	12.2%	169,254	43.1%	217,312	55.3%	6,370	1.6%	0	0.0%
Maryland	10	1,235,039		10		20,315	1.6%	517,995	41.9%	538,310	43.6%	178,734	14.5%	0	0.0%
Massachusetts	14	2,331,752		14		702,374	30.1%	766,844	32.9%	1,469,218	63.0%	87,088	3.7%	8,602	0.4%
Michigan	21	3,306,250		21		222,417	6.7%	1,370,665	41.5%	1,593,082	48.2%	331,968	10.0%	10,535	0.3%
Minnesota	10	1,589,095		10		199,095	12.5%	658,643	41.4%	857,738	54.0%	68,931	4.3%	3,783	0.2%
Mississippi	7	654,509			7	62,128	9.5%	88,516	13.5%	150,644	23.0%	415,349	63.5%	0	0.0%
Missouri	12	1,809,502	12			20,488	1.1%	811,932	44.9%	791,444	43.7%	206,126	11.4%	0	0.0%
Montana	4	274,404	4			24,718	9.0%	138,835	50.6%	114,117	41.6%	20,015	7.3%	1,437	0.5%
Nebraska	5	536,851	5			150,379	28.0%	321,163	59.8%	170,784	31.8%	44,904	8.4%	0	0.0%
Nevada	3	154,218	3			12,590	8.2%	73,188	47.5%	60,598	39.3%	20,432	13.2%	0	0.0%
New Hampshire	4	297,298	4			24,314	8.2%	154,903	52.1%	130,589	43.9%	11,173	3.8%	633	0.2%
New Jersey	17	2,875,395	17			61,261	2.1%	1,325,467	46.1%	1,264,206	44.0%	262,187	9.1%	23,535	0.8%
New Mexico	4	327,281	4			39,611	12.1%	169,692	51.8%	130,081	39.7%	25,737	7.9%	1,771	0.5%
New York	43	6,790,066		43		370,538	5.5%	3,007,932	44.3%	3,378,470	49.8%	358,864	5.3%	44,800	0.7%
North Carolina	13	1,587,493	12		1[a]	163,079	10.3%	627,192	39.5%	464,113	29.2%	496,188	31.3%	0	0.0%
North Dakota	4	247,882	4			43,900	17.7%	138,669	55.9%	94,769	38.2%	14,244	5.7%	200	0.1%
Ohio	26	3,959,698	26			90,428	2.3%	1,791,014	45.2%	1,700,586	42.9%	467,495	11.8%	603	0.0%
Oklahoma	8	943,086	8			148,039	15.7%	449,697	47.7%	301,658	32.0%	191,731	20.3%	0	0.0%
Oregon	6	819,622	6			49,567	6.0%	408,433	49.8%	358,866	43.8%	49,683	6.1%	2,640	0.3%
Pennsylvania	29	4,747,928		29		169,388	3.6%	2,090,017	44.0%	2,259,405	47.6%	378,582	8.0%	19,924	0.4%
Rhode Island	4	385,000		4		124,159	32.2%	122,359	31.8%	246,518	64.0%	15,678	4.1%	445	0.1%
South Carolina	8	666,978	8			56,576	8.5%	254,062	38.1%	197,486	29.6%	215,430	32.3%	0	0.0%
South Dakota	4	281,264	4			31,818	11.3%	149,841	53.3%	118,023	42.0%	13,400	4.8%	0	0.0%
Tennessee	11	1,248,617	11			121,359	9.7%	472,592	37.8%	351,233	28.1%	424,792	34.0%	0	0.0%
Texas	25	3,079,406		25		38,960	1.3%	1,227,844	39.9%	1,266,804	41.1%	584,269	19.0%	489	0.0%
Utah	4	422,568	4			82,063	19.4%	238,728	56.5%	156,665	37.1%	26,906	6.4%	269	0.1%
Vermont	3	161,404	3			14,887	9.2%	85,142	52.8%	70,255	43.5%	5,104	3.2%	903	0.6%
Virginia	12	1,361,491	12			147,932	10.9%	590,319	43.4%	442,387	32.5%	321,833	23.6%	6,952	0.5%
Washington	9	1,304,281		9		27,527	2.1%	588,510	45.1%	616,037	47.2%	96,990	7.4%	2,744	0.2%
West Virginia	7	754,206		7		66,536	8.8%	307,555	40.8%	374,091	49.6%	72,560	9.6%	0	0.0%
Wisconsin	12	1,691,538	12			61,193	3.6%	809,997	47.9%	748,804	44.3%	127,835	7.6%	4,902	0.3%
Wyoming	3	127,205	3			25,754	20.2%	70,927	55.8%	45,173	35.5%	11,105	8.7%	0	0.0%
TOTAL	538	73,200,579	301	191	46	511,944	0.7%	31,783,783	43.4%	31,271,839	42.7%	9,901,118	13.5%	243,839	0.3%

[a] A Nixon elector in North Carolina voted for George C. Wallace.

For sources, see p. 1131.

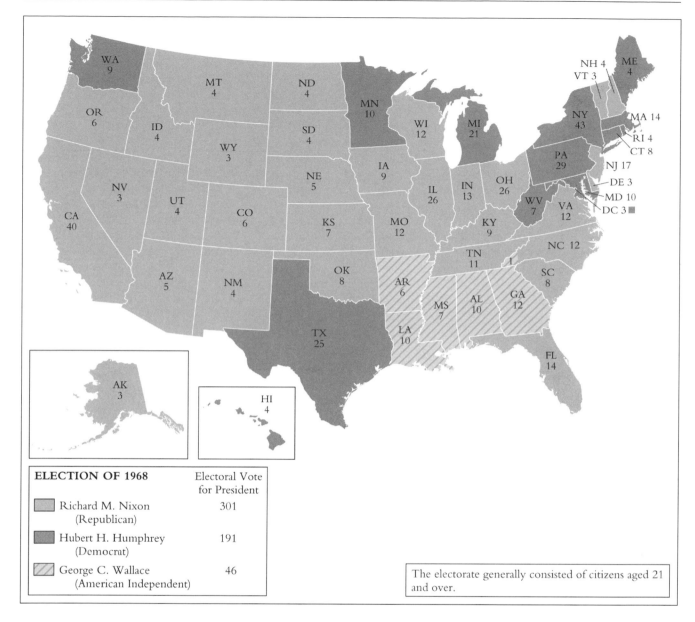

ELECTION OF 1968	Electoral Vote for President
Richard M. Nixon (Republican)	301
Hubert H. Humphrey (Democrat)	191
George C. Wallace (American Independent)	46

The electorate generally consisted of citizens aged 21 and over.

DOCUMENTS: ELECTION OF 1968

With domestic unrest over the civil rights movement and the Vietnam War, the presidential election reflected those deep divisions within the nation. The Republicans nominated former Vice President Richard Nixon, while the Democrats settled on Vice President Hubert H. Humphrey. Alabama governor George Wallace ran as an independent and garnered nearly 14 percent of the popular vote. The defection of many southern Democrats helped give Nixon a slight edge in a close election.

When the campaign began in early 1968, many assumed President Lyndon Johnson would run for reelection. However, dissatisfaction with the administration caused Senator Eugene McCarthy of Minnesota and Senator Robert F. Kennedy of New York, brother of the former president, to make a run for the nomination.

In Document 1, a speech against the Vietnam War delivered by Senator Kennedy in March, he highlights his opposition to Johnson's policies. (Less than three months later, in June, Kennedy would be assassinated.) In a surprise move, Document 2, Johnson presents a plan to scale down hostilities in Vietnam and announces that he will not seek another term.

As the Democrats selected their nominee in Chicago, violence raged in the streets. Humphrey, in his speech accepting the Democratic nomination, Document 3, asks Americans to "turn away from violence and hatred" and follow the peaceful message of slain leaders, Martin Luther King, Jr., and Robert F. Kennedy, to come together and find their "conscience."

Nixon, in his speech accepting the Republican nomination, Document 4, vows to achieve an "honorable end" to the Vietnam War and to speak for the "forgotten Americans," or silent majority, in ending the "long dark night" of social unrest and restoring faith in American institutions. Dogged by the issue throughout the campaign, Humphrey pledged to try ending the Vietnam War, but offered few specifics. In a campaign speech, Document 5, he tries to resuscitate his sagging poll numbers by proposing a "de-Americanization of the war," a policy Nixon would later use as president.

Document 1

Robert F. Kennedy Speech, March 18, 1968

Today I would speak to you . . . of the war in Vietnam. I come here . . . to discuss with you why I regard our policy here as bankrupt. . . .

I do not want—as I believe most Americans do not want—to sell out American interests, to simply withdraw, to raise the white flag of surrender. That would be unacceptable to us as a country and as a people. . . . I believe most Americans are concerned—that our present course will not bring victory; will not bring peace; will not stop the bloodshed; and will not advance the interests of the United States or the cause of peace in the world.

I am concerned that, at the end of it all, there will only be more Americans killed; more of our treasure spilled out; and because of the bitterness and hatred on every side of this war, more hundreds of thousands of Vietnamese slaughtered. . . .

The costs of the war's present course far outweigh anything we can reasonably hope to gain by it, for ourselves or for the people of Vietnam. It must be ended, and it can be ended, in a peace of brave men who have fought each other with a terrible fury, each believing that he alone was in the right. We have prayed to different gods, and the prayers of neither have been answered fully. Now, while there is still time for some of them to be partly answered, now is the time to stop.

And the fact is that much can be done. We can—as I have urged for two years, but as we have never done—negotiate with the National Liberation Front. We can—as we have never done—assure the Front a genuine place in the political life of South Vietnam. We can—as we are refusing to do today—begin to deescalate the war, concentrate on protecting populated areas, and thus save American lives and slow down the destruction of the country-side. We can—as we have never done—insist that the Government of South Vietnam broaden its base, institute real reforms, and seek an honorable settlement with their fellow countrymen. . . .

Even this modest and reasonable program is impossible while our present leadership, under the illusion that military victory is just ahead, plunges deeper into the swamp that is our present course. . . .

Source: Diane Ravitch, ed., *The American Reader* (New York: Harper Perennial, 1990).

Document 2

Lyndon Johnson's Address to the Nation, Washington, D.C., March 31, 1968

For years, representatives of our Government and others have traveled the world seeking to find a basis for peace talks. . . .

Hanoi denounced this offer, both privately and publicly. . . .

This much is clear: If they do mount another round of heavy attacks, they will not succeed in destroying the fighting power of South Vietnam and its allies.

But tragically, this is also clear. . . . Armies on both sides will take new casualties. And the war will go on.

There is no need for this to be so. There is no need to delay the talks that could bring an end to this long and this bloody war. . . .

. . . So tonight, in the hope that this action will lead to early talks, I am taking the first step to de-escalate the conflict. We are reducing—substantially reducing—the present level of hostilities, and we are doing so unilaterally and at once. . . .

Even this very limited bombing of the North could come to an early end—if our restraint is matched by restraint in Hanoi. But I cannot in good conscience stop all bombing so long as to do so would immediately and directly endanger the lives of our men and our allies. . . .

I call upon President Ho Chi Minh to respond positively, and favorably, to this new step toward peace.

But if peace does not come now through negotiations, it will come when Hanoi understands that our common resolve is unshakable, and our common strength is invincible. . . . As your President, I have put the unity of the people first. I have put it ahead of . . . divisive partisanship. And in these times, as in times before, it is true that a house divided against itself by the spirit of faction, of party, of region, of religion, of race, is a house that cannot stand.

There is division in the American house now. There is divisiveness among us all tonight. And holding the trust that is mine, as President of all the people, I cannot disregard the peril of the progress of the American people and the hope and the prospect of peace for all peoples, so I would ask all Americans whatever their personal interest or concern to guard against divisiveness and all of its ugly consequences.

Fifty-two months and ten days ago in a moment of tragedy and trauma, the duties of this office fell upon me. . . .

United we have kept that commitment. And united we have enlarged that commitment. And through all time to come, I think America will be a stronger nation, a more just society, a land of greater opportunity and fulfillment because of what we have all done together in these years of unparalleled achievement.

Our reward will come in the life of freedom and peace and hope that our children will enjoy through ages ahead.

What we won when all of our people united must not now be lost in suspicion and distrust and selfishness and politics among any of our people. And believing this as I do, I have concluded that I should not permit the Presidency to become involved in the partisan divisions that are developing in this political year. . . .

Accordingly, I shall not seek, and I will not accept, the nomination of my party for another term as your President. But let men everywhere know, however, that a strong and a confident and a vigilant America stands ready tonight to seek an honorable peace; and stands ready tonight to defend an honored cause, whatever the price, whatever the burden, whatever the sacrifice that duty may require.

Source: Public Papers of the Presidents of the United States: Lyndon B. Johnson, 1968–1969, Book I: January 1 to June 30, 1968 (Washington, DC: Government Printing Office, 1970).

Document 3

Hubert Humphrey's Nomination Acceptance Speech, Chicago, August 29, 1968

This moment—this moment is one of personal pride and gratification. Yet one cannot help but reflect the deep sadness that we feel over the troubles and the violence which have erupted, regrettably and tragically, in the streets of this great city, and for the personal injuries which have occurred.

Surely we have now learned the lesson that violence breeds counterviolence and it cannot be condoned, whatever the source.

I know that every delegate to this convention shares tonight my sorrow and my distress over these incidents. . . .

Let me speak first, then, about Vietnam. . . .

The question is not the yesterdays, but the question is what do we do now? No one knows what the situation in Vietnam will be when the next President of the United States takes that oath of office on January 20, 1969.

But every heart in America prays that by then we shall have reached a ceasefire in all Vietnam and be in serious negotiation toward a durable peace. Meanwhile, as a citizen, a candidate and Vice President, I pledge to you and to my fellow Americans that I will do everything within my power, within the limits of my capacity [and] ability, to aid the negotiations and to bring a prompt end to this war! . . .

Violence breeds more violence: disorder destroys, and only in order can we build. Riot makes for ruin; reason makes for solution. So from the White House to the courthouse to the city hall, every official has the solemn responsibility of guaranteeing to every American—black and white, rich and poor—the right to personal security—life.

Every American, black or white, rich or poor, has the right in this land of ours to a safe and decent neighborhood, and on this there can be no compromise.

I put it very bluntly—rioting, burning, sniping, mugging, traffic in narcotics, and disregard for law are the advance guard of anarchy, and they must and they will be stopped. . . . There can be no compromise on securing of human rights.

If America is to make a crucial judgment of leadership in this coming election, then let that selection be made without either candidate hedging or equivocating.

Winning the Presidency, for me, is not worth the price of silence or evasion on the issue of human rights.

And winning the Presidency—and listen well—winning the Presidency is not worth a compact with extremism.

I choose not simply to run for President. I seek to lead a great nation. . . .

And now I appeal, I appeal to those thousands—yea millions—of young Americans to join us, not simply as campaigners, but to continue as vocal, creative and even critical participants in the politics of our time. Never were you needed so much, and never could you do so much if you want to help now.

Martin Luther King, Jr. had a dream. Robert F. Kennedy as you saw tonight [in a memorial film] had a great vision. If Americans will respond to that dream and that vision, their deaths will not mark the moment when America lost its way. But it will mark the time when America found its conscience.

These men, these men have given us inspiration and direction, and I pledge from this platform tonight we shall not abandon their purpose—we shall honor their dreams by our deeds now in the days to come. . . .

And I say to America. Put aside recrimination and dissension. Turn away from violence and hatred. Believe—believe in what America can do, and believe in what America can be, and with the vast—with the help of that vast, unfrightened, dedicated, faithful majority of Americans, I say to this great convention tonight, and to this great nation of ours, I am ready to lead our country!

Source: New York Times, August 30, 1968. Reprinted with permission of the Minnesota Historical Society.

Document 4

Richard Nixon's Nomination Acceptance Speech, August 8, 1968

My fellow Americans, most important—we're going to win because our cause is right.

We make history tonight—not for ourselves but for the ages.

The choice we make in 1968 will determine not only the future of America but the future of peace and freedom in the world for the last third of the 20th century.

And the question that we answer tonight: can America meet this great challenge?

. . . let us listen to America to find the answer to that question.

As we look at America, we see cities enveloped in smoke and flame.

We hear sirens in the night.

We see Americans dying on distant battlefields abroad.

We see Americans hating each other; fighting each other; killing each other at home.

And as we see and hear these things, millions of Americans cry out in anguish:

Did we come all this way for this?

Did American boys die in Normandy and Korea and in Valley Forge for this?

Listen to the answers to those questions.

It is another voice, it is the quiet voice in the tumult and the shouting.

It is the voice of the great majority of Americans, the forgotten Americans—the non-shouters; the non-demonstrators.

They are not racists or sick; they are not guilty of the crime that plagues the land.

They are black, and they are white—they're native born and foreign born—they're young and they're old.

They work in American factories.

They run American businesses.

They serve in government.

They provide most of the soldiers who die to keep us free.

They give drive to the spirit of America.

They give lift to the American dream.

They give steel to the backbone of America.

They are good people, they are decent people; they work, and they save, and they pay their taxes, and they care.

Like Theodore Roosevelt, they know that this country will not be a good place for any of us to live in unless it is a good place for all of us to live in.

This I say to you tonight is the real voice of America. In this year 1968, this is the message it will broadcast to America and to the world.

Let's never forget that despite her faults, America is a great nation.

And America is great because her people are great.

With Winston Churchill we say: "We have not journeyed all this way across the centuries, across the oceans, across the mountains, across the prairies because we are made of sugar candy."

America is in trouble today not because her people have failed but because her leaders have failed.

And what America needs are leaders to match the greatness of her people.

And this great group of Americans, the forgotten Americans, and others know that the great question Americans must answer by their votes in November is this: Whether we shall continue for four more years the policies of the last five years. . . .

And so tonight I do not promise the millennium in the morning.

I don't promise that we can eradicate poverty, and end discrimination, eliminate all danger of war in the space of four or even eight years. But I do promise action—a new policy for peace abroad; a new policy for peace and progress and justice at home. . . .

And I pledge to you tonight that the first priority foreign policy objective of our next Administration will be to bring an honorable end to the war in Vietnam. . . .

Our goal is justice—justice for every American.

If we are to have respect for law in America, we must have laws that deserve respect.

Just as we cannot have progress without order, we cannot have order without progress, . . .

The next President of the United States will face challenges in which some ways will be greater than those of Washington or Lincoln. Because for the first time in our nation's history, an American President will face not only the problem of restoring peace abroad, but of restoring peace at home. . . .

. . . the long dark night for America is about to end.

Source: The Richard Nixon Library & Birthplace, Yorba Linda, California.

Document 5

*Hubert Humphrey Speech, Salt Lake City,
September 30, 1968*

I have pledged that my first priority as President shall be to end the war and obtain an honorable peace.

For the past four years I have spoken my mind about Vietnam, frankly and without reservation, in the Cabinet and in the National Security Council—and directly to the President.

When the President has made his decisions, I have supported them.

He has been the Commander in Chief. It has been his job to decide. And the choices have not been simple or easy.

President Johnson will continue—until January 20, 1969—to make the decisions in Vietnam. The voice at the negotiating table must be his. I shall not compete with that voice. I shall cooperate and help.

We all pray that his efforts to find peace will succeed.

But, 112 days from now, there will be a President—a new Administration—and new advisers.

If there is no peace by then, it must be their responsibility to make a complete reassessment of the situation in Vietnam—to see where we stand and to judge what we must do.

As I said in my acceptance speech: The policies of tomorrow need not be limited by the policies of yesterday.

We must look to the future. For neither vindication nor repudiation of our role in Vietnam will bring peace or be worthy of our country.

The American people have a right to know what I would do—if I am President—after January 20, 1969 to keep my pledge to honorably end the war in Vietnam. . . .

I would take the risk that South Vietnamese would meet the responsibilities they say they are now ready to assume in their own self-defense.

I would move, in other words, toward de-Americanization of the war.

I would sit down with the leaders of South Vietnam to set a specific timetable by which American forces could be systematically reduced while South Vietnamese forces took over more and more of the burden.

The schedule must be a realistic one—one that would not weaken the overall Allied defense posture. I am convinced such action would be as much in South Vietnam's interest as in ours.

What I am proposing is that it should be basic to our policy in Vietnam that the South Vietnamese take over more and more of the defense of their own country. . . .

A stopping of the bombing of the North—taking account of Hanoi's actions and assurances of prompt good faith negotiations, and keeping the option of resuming that bombing if the Communists show bad faith.

Careful, systematic reduction of American troops in South Vietnam—a de-Americanization of the war—turning over to the South Vietnamese Army a greater share of the defense of its own country.

An internationally supervised ceasefire—and supervised withdrawal of all foreign forces from South Vietnam.

Free elections, including all people in South Vietnam willing to follow the peaceful process.

Those are risks I would take for peace.

Source: New York Times, October 1, 1968. Reprinted with permission of the Minnesota Historical Society.

THE ELECTION OF
1972

*I*n 1968, Richard Nixon (see fact box, p. 819) had won a narrow victory in the presidential election over Vice President Hubert Humphrey. Nixon's victory was partially the result of dissension in the Democratic Party, which weathered challenges from the left and the right. Senator Eugene McCarthy of Minnesota represented liberal Democrats, who criticized President Lyndon Johnson's conduct of the Vietnam War. Governor George Wallace (see fact box, p. 892) of Alabama drew support from voters in the South and some northern cities, where resentment against "Great Society" liberalism festered. Wallace articulated a law-and-order protest, which some interpreted as code words for white racism and opposition to civil rights. After losing the Democratic nomination, Wallace ran for president as the candidate of the American Independent Party, forcing a schism in the Democratic Party reminiscent of the bolt of "Dixiecrats" in 1948. Robert F. Kennedy, a U.S. Senator from New York and brother of former president John F. Kennedy, appeared destined to capture the liberal wing of the party—but was killed by an assassin following the California primary.

The Republicans had turned to Nixon as their candidate following Barry Goldwater's disastrous defeat in 1964. Eisenhower's vice president for two terms, Nixon previously had been a U.S. senator and representative from California. He lost the 1960 presidential election to Democrat John Kennedy by the narrowest of margins. In 1962, Nixon ran for governor of California against Democrat Pat Brown. Losing badly, Nixon told reporters that they wouldn't have

"Nixon to kick around anymore," implying his withdrawal from politics. But Nixon returned, mended his political fences, gained the 1968 Republican presidential nomination—and went on to victory.

Nixon's first administration (1969–73) mixed moderation on domestic issues with firmness over Vietnam. Nixon's ideological instincts were fairly conservative, but as president he acted pragmatically. Facing a Congress controlled by Democrats who continued to support Great Society programs, Nixon accepted numerous domestic policy initiatives. He signed the Environmental Protection Act in 1969, congressional extension of the Voting Rights Act in 1970 and, in 1972, Educational Act amendments that prohibited sex discrimination in federal aid to schools. Defying Republican inclinations, the president ordered a wage-and-price freeze in 1971 as inflation accelerated, and consented to the indexing of Social Security benefits in 1972.

Nixon's first preoccupation as president concerned foreign policy. The president sought to ensure an American victory against the North Vietnamese and the Vietcong, while simultaneously endeavoring to negotiate a settlement to the prolonged conflict in Indochina. He approved the bombing of North Vietnam, the mining of its harbor at Haiphong, and a military incursion into Cambodia to strike at Vietcong sanctuaries. Nixon also took a hard line toward antiwar protesters, including participants in a massive rally at Washington, D.C., in 1971 that led to violence in the streets and 12,000 arrests. Seeking a way out of the quagmire that had ensnared President Lyndon Johnson, Nixon promoted "Vietnamization," which

CHRONOLOGY

1969

FEBRUARY 8   George McGovern appointed chair of the McGovern-Fraser Commission on Party Structure and Delegate Selection of Democratic National Committee.

1972

FEBRUARY 7   President Nixon signs the Federal Election Campaign Act.

FEBRUARY 15   John Mitchell becomes Nixon's campaign manager.

MAY 15   George Wallace is shot and partially paralyzed.

JUNE 17   Watergate break-in at the Democratic National Committee headquarters by Nixon's "plumbers unit."

JULY 12   George McGovern wins the Democratic nomination for President.

JULY 31   Thomas Eagleton resigns as Democratic vice presidential nominee.

AUGUST 22   Richard Nixon is renominated as Presidential nominee at the Republican Convention in Miami Beach.

NOVEMBER 7   Richard Nixon wins reelection.

DECEMBER 18   The Electoral College awards 520 votes for Nixon, 17 for McGovern and one for John Hospers of the Libertarian Party.

prepared the South Vietnamese for their own defense and allowed the gradual withdrawal of American troops. Nixon indicated late in 1972 that negotiations were close to achieving a ceasefire. This eventuality, which did not occur until January 1973, along with his earlier historic visit to China in 1972, represented the high points of Nixon's active foreign policy record.

The Primaries of 1972

One function that primaries serve is to allow candidates not favored by party leaders to prove themselves before the public. George S. McGovern won the 1972 nomination through the primaries, even though the party leadership did not support him. In the early months of 1972, the Democratic candidates were Senator George McGovern of South Dakota, Governor George Wallace of Alabama, Senator Edmund Muskie of Maine, former vice president Hubert Humphrey of Minnesota, Senator Vance Hartke of Indiana, Senator Henry Jackson of Washington, Mayor John Lindsay of New York City, Mayor Sam Yorty of Los Angeles, and New York representative Shirley Chisholm. At the start of the campaign McGovern, rated only 5 percent in the public opinion

polls. But he received strong support with his populist appeal and image as a left-of-center apostle of the "New Politics," who drew support from the followers of Eugene McCarthy and Robert Kennedy in the 1968 election. Born in 1922, McGovern had been a decorated bomber pilot in World War II, and received a Ph.D. in history from Northwestern University. He taught at Dakota Wesleyan University until he became a U.S. senator from South Dakota in 1963. He had a liberal background, having supported the Progressive Party in 1948, and served liberal causes as a senator. He was an early critic of the Vietnam War—perhaps the issue with which he was most identified—and co-chaired the McGovern-Fraser Commission to reform the Democratic National Committee.

McGovern developed a reputation as a party reformer by reshaping the rules of the Democratic convention. As a result of these reforms, the 1972 Democratic convention admitted more women, African Americans, and youths as delegates, as well as inexperienced political enthusiasts. McGovern broadened his reformist appeal by proposing that the welfare system give each person $1,000 a year. He also took liberal positions on such issues as abortion, amnesty for draft evaders, and lower defense spend-

At a news conference on May 18, 1972, Democratic candidate George McGovern met with Coretta Scott King (the widow of slain civil rights leader Martin Luther King), who endorsed his run for the presidency. *(AP Wide World Photos)*

ing—issues which, taken as a group, led some to characterize McGovern as an "extremist." Some hopeful voters viewed him as a populist promoter who would bring change to an antiquated, boss-ridden political system. He had an organization of tireless young workers who helped him win ten of twenty-three presidential primaries. On June 30, McGovern was just a few votes short of the required 1,509 delegate votes needed to win nomination.

McGovern was challenged by the surprising success of George Wallace. The former governor of Alabama, who characterized himself as a law-and-order candidate, won the Michigan and Florida primaries by campaigning against busing school children to achieve racial balance. Senator Edmund Muskie suf-

fered because, in the early primaries, the media viewed him as the frontrunner who was expected to win by large margins. Despite his nine-percentage-point lead, the media called him a "loser" because his margin of victory did not comport with a frontrunner image. Partially because of underhanded campaign tactics orchestrated by the Nixon camp, Muskie lost momentum. These "dirty tricks," as they were called, included placing false bulk orders of liquor and pizza to Muskie fund raisers, or appearing at rallies with signs reading, "IF YOU LIKED HITLER YOU'LL LOVE WALLACE—VOTE MUSKIE." On April 2, he announced his withdrawal from the presidential race after a poor showing in Wisconsin. McGovern, on the other hand, achieved the winner's label, which

George Wallace's racial appeals evoked strong comparisons.
(Gyory Collection/Cathy Casriel Photo)

resulted in a flow of financial donations, volunteers offering their services, renewed vigor from his staff, and momentum that carried the candidate on to the next primary.

Humphrey entered the 1972 contest belatedly. He decided to challenge the frontrunner in California, the last major primary. McGovern was far ahead in the delegate count and the battle looked hopeless for Humphrey, especially since a California poll showed McGovern with an overwhelming statewide vote. As in the Muskie case in New Hampshire, the polls set the measure of victory as nothing short of an overwhelming win. Humphrey's attacks on McGovern's policy positions pointed out shortcomings, and weakened his candidacy. McGovern won California; but the vote was close, which undermined McGovern's credibility.

The Minor Parties

George Wallace had won five primaries, finished second in six others, and received a total of 3,755,424 primary votes. Then, on May 15, Wallace went to campaign at a political rally in Laurel, Maryland—and was shot, and left partially paralyzed. Wallace bowed out of the race after losing the Democratic nomination, and refused renomination by the American Party. The absence of Wallace in the general election campaign benefited Nixon.

The American Party then turned to John G. Schmitz, a conservative Republican congressman from California. His running mate was Thomas J. Anderson, a farm magazine publisher from Pigeon Forge, Tennessee. Both men were members of the John Birch Society, a right-wing group that worried about communist influences in the United States. Schmitz and Anderson were chosen by the 1,500 delegates at the party's nominating convention in Louisville, Kentucky on August 4 and 5. Speaking from his room in a rehabilitation clinic, where he was undergoing treatment for paralysis, Wallace told the convention by telephone on August 4 that he could not accept a draft to run again because of his physical condition.

The American Party, formerly called the American Independent Party, made a poor showing. It placed candidates on the ballots in thirty-two states, running nine candidates for the Senate and 49 for the House. None was successful. The Schmitz-Anderson

GEORGE STANLEY MCGOVERN

PARTY: Democrat

DATE OF BIRTH: July 19, 1922

PLACE OF BIRTH: Avon, South Dakota

PARENTS: Joseph C. McGovern and Frances M. McLean

EDUCATION: B.A., Dakota Weslyan University, 1946, M.A., History, Northwestern University, 1949, Ph.D., History, Northwestern University, 1953

FAMILY: Married Eleanor Faye Stegeberg, 1943; children: Steve, Ann, Susan, Mary, and Terry (deceased)

MILITARY SERVICE: Inducted into U.S. Army Air Force, 1943–45; sent to Europe as a B-24 pilot; flew 35 missions; received the Distinguished Flying Cross and Air Medal with Oak Leaf Cluster, 1945

CAREER: History professor, South Dakota Wesleyan, 1952; executive secretary, South Dakota Democratic Party, 1953; House of Representatives, 1957–60; unsuccessful candidate for Senate, 1960; Director, Food for Peace Program, 1961–62; Senate, 1963–81; chair, McGovern-Fraser Commission of Democratic National Committee, 1969; unsuccessful candidate for president, 1972 ticket drew 1,080,541 popular votes (1.4 percent of the total) and received no electoral votes.

The second minor party was known more for its candidate than its platform ideology. Benjamin Spock, pediatrician and noted baby book author, was nominated by the People's Party, which was mostly a peace and antiwar organization. Spock became a leader in the peace movement in 1965, when the Vietnam War escalated. In 1968, a federal district court found him guilty of violating the Selective Service Act by encouraging draft resistance. The decision was reversed in 1969. The People's Party, whose main issue was the Vietnam War, collected 78,801 votes (0.1 percent of the total).

The Democratic Convention

The Democrats opened their national convention in Miami Beach, Florida, on July 10. Responding to the conflicts that marred the previous two conventions, the Democrats felt obligated to reform their party rules. At the 1964 convention, a credentials challenge had erupted over the seating of the regular delegation from Mississippi, with the result that an alternate delegation of loyal Democrats was substituted. The 1968 convention in Chicago, wracked by violence and dissension, subsequently passed resolutions that led to establishment of the McGovern-Fraser Commission on Party Structures and Delegate Selection, as well as the O'Hara Commission on Convention Rules. Recommendations by the two commissions were adopted, and governed party procedure for the 1972 election. The result reaffirmed the power of the national committee to control the procedures used in the states to select national convention delegates.

The O'Hara Commission changes provided for fewer and shorter speeches, abolished floor demonstrations, detailed the procedures for credentials challenges, and ordered that seating on the convention floor, as well as the order of state roll calls, be determined by lot. The impact of these reforms, as well as poor planning by the McGovern camp, resulted in the nominee giving his acceptance speech at the non-prime time of three o'clock in the morning, eastern time. A general thrust of the Democratic Party reforms made the party more democratic by involving more people, but appeared to transfer power to a set of citizen amateurs with a liberal ideology. Because the rules made it possible to nominate a fringe or extremist candidate, they contributed to the nomination of McGovern in 1972.

The McGovern-Fraser Commission also changed the allocation of primary delegates from winner-take-all to proportional allotment. This shift was costly for McGovern, who was initially awarded only 151 of the 271 delegates from the California primary of June 6. Ironically, McGovern, who had authored the proportional voting provision as a member of the reform commission, went on to fight for the winner-take-all allocation at the 1972 convention. The credentials committee backed the commission's position. McGovern challenged the ruling, won his point on the convention floor, and easily won a first ballot nomination on July 12.

Vice presidential nominations are usually made quickly at conventions, and almost always at the command of the presidential candidate. Sometimes the research on vice presidential candidates is not thorough. Such a scenario unfolded in 1972, causing McGovern considerable political embarrassment. McGovern chose Senator Thomas Eagleton of Missouri to be his vice president. Eagleton had the strong backing of organized labor, was Catholic, and from an urban center, all constituencies vital to a Democratic victory. On July 25, eleven days after his nomination, Eagleton told a news conference that he had been hospitalized in the 1960s for nervous exhaustion and had received shock treatments, but that his health was now excellent. McGovern quickly asserted that he stood completely by his running mate. However, columnist Jack Anderson charged on July 27 that Eagleton had a record of drunken driving arrests. Eagleton angrily denied the allegation, but some of McGovern's staff members and several newspapers called on him to withdraw. McGovern complied, and Eagleton resigned on July 31. McGovern did not realize that his decision would become one of the main issues of the contest. His flip-flop on Eagleton cost McGovern considerable credibility. (See "The Eagleton Affair," p. 910.)

McGovern recommended Sargent Shriver, John and Robert Kennedy's brother-in-law, as a replacement for Eagleton. His selection was formalized on August 8 at a special meeting of the Democratic National Committee in Washington, D.C. A former *Newsweek* editor, businessman, and president of the Chicago Board of Education, Shriver married the Kennedys' sister Eunice in 1953. He rose to national prominence after President Kennedy appointed him

THE EAGLETON AFFAIR

George McGovern's presidential campaign of 1972 got off to a bad start with his decision to drop vice presidential nominee Thomas Eagleton from the ballot. For a variety of reasons, including the desire for suspense, presidential candidates usually did not make in-depth inquiries about their running mates. For example, Walter Mondale in 1984 was not aware of the campaign irregularities and incomplete financial disclosures of his running mate Geraldine Ferraro, or the allegedly improper real estate transactions of her husband. In 1988 George Bush was surprised to find out about Dan Quayle's poor college record and his father's assistance in getting him into the National Guard to avoid service in Vietnam. Likewise George McGovern had been unaware of Eagleton's medical history when he chose him for the vice presidential nomination.

On July 25 in Custer, South Dakota, 11 days after his nomination, the 42-year-old Eagleton told a news conference that he had been hospitalized in 1960, 1964, and 1966 for nervous exhaustion and on two occasions received electric shock therapy. But he claimed his health was excellent now. McGovern said that he had not known of Eagleton's prior illnesses yet promised him "1000 percent support." Columnist Jack Anderson charged on July 27 that Eagleton had a record of drunken-driving arrests, which Eagleton angrily denied. Some of McGovern staff members and several newspapers called on Eagleton to withdraw, which the candidate did on July 31. The next day Anderson claimed that the unverified drunken-driving charge was false and publicly apologized. But the damage was done. McGovern thought the controversy interfered with the real issues of the campaign. Yet his inept handling of the affair cost him considerable credibility with the public. Eagleton was the first vice presidential candidate in history forced to resign, apparently against his own wishes.

McGovern replaced Eagleton with Sargent Shriver, a brother-in-law of President Kennedy, who rose to prominence as director of the Peace Corps and of the Office of Economic Opportunity. Despite Shriver's solid credentials, McGovern was unable to make up ground lost over his vice presidential snafu.

as first director of the Peace Corps in 1961, and President Johnson named him director of the Office of Economic Opportunity (OEO), in 1964, to fight his "war on poverty." He later served as U.S. ambassador to France (1968–70).

The Republican Convention

In control of the White House, the Republicans felt less demand for internal change of party organization than had Democrats. Republicans also experienced less fratricidal warfare than did the Democrats in 1968 and 1972, as conservatives had dominated the Republican hierarchy since the early 1960s. Nevertheless, the Republicans established two reform commissions, one emanating from the 1968 convention—the Delegates and Organizations Committee—which issued recommendations in 1970–71 similar to those of the

McGovern-Fraser Commission. But the McGovern-Fraser recommendations revolutionized the Democratic Party's presidential nominating practices, whereas the changes in the Republican Party had little impact, although they did strengthen the power of the national party.

Nixon coasted to the Republican presidential nomination on August 22, 1972, by a vote of 1,317 to one. He had easily brushed aside two weak challengers. The first came from Paul N. McCloskey, a liberal congressman from California, who argued that Nixon had not ended the Vietnam War. McCloskey received one vote at the convention. The second challenge came from John Ashbrook, a conservative congressman from Ohio, who contended that Nixon was too liberal. It was the first time in his political career that Nixon did not have to fight for his nomination.

Liberal Republicans tried to dump Spiro Agnew (see fact box, p. 891), the vice president, but Nixon stuck with him. On August 23, the convention ratified Nixon's choice. In the floor fight, liberal Republicans sponsored a delegate reform proposal to increase representation in 1976 for large-population states. Led by Senator Charles H. Percy of Illinois, moderates from the larger states wanted to stop the combination of small states and southern conservatives from ensuring Agnew's renomination in 1976. (The fight would later become a moot point when the Justice Department charged that Agnew had accepted bribes as governor of Maryland. Agnew pleaded "no contest" to one charge of income tax evasion—and resigned the vice presidency on October 16, 1973.)

The Campaign

McGovern began his campaign further behind his opponent than Humphrey had been in 1968. Unlike

President Richard Nixon (right) and Vice President Spiro Agnew (left). Despite their landslide victory, both men later resigned their offices in disgrace. *(Gyory Collection/Cathy Casriel Photo)*

ROBERT SARGENT SHRIVER, JR.

PARTY: Democrat

DATE OF BIRTH: November 9, 1915

PLACE OF BIRTH: Westminster, Maryland

PARENTS: Robert Sargent Shriver and Hilda S. Shriver

EDUCATION: B.A., Yale University, 1938; law degree, Yale University, 1941

FAMILY: Married Eunice Kennedy, 1953; children: Robert Shriver III, Maria Owings, Timothy Perry, Mark Kennedy, and Anthony Paul

MILITARY SERVICE: U.S. naval officer, World War II, 1941–45

CAREER: Assistant editor, *Newsweek* magazine, 1945–46; editor, Joseph T. Kennedy Enterprises, 1946–48; president, Chicago Board of Education, 1955–61; presidential campaign advisor to John Kennedy, 1960; first director of the Peace Corps, 1961–66; first director of the Office of Economic Opportunity (OEO), 1964–68; ambassador to France, 1968–70; member, Congressional Leadership for the Future, 1970; partner, Fried, Frank, Harris, Shriver and Jacobson law firm, 1971–86; unsuccessful candidate for vice president, 1972

Humphrey, however, McGovern was not able to close the gap. The first Gallup poll after the convention had Nixon leading McGovern by 57 to 31 percent, with 12 percent undecided. Reminiscent of 1968, the Democrats left their convention in 1972 a divided party. George Meany, head of the AFL-CIO and a traditional source of Democratic support, refused to endorse McGovern, as did other labor leaders. Later in the campaign, McGovern attempted to make peace with "regular" Democrats, such as Chicago mayor Richard Daley, who had boycotted the nominating convention and were disenchanted with their party's nominee. McGovern followers lamented that their candidate was behaving like the traditional politicians they thought they had defeated at the 1972 convention. Many McGovern loyalists were ardent opponents of the Vietnam War and passionate advocates of civil rights. Some were willing to sacrifice the chance of winning an election in the name of honoring their convictions.

McGovern encountered a number of setbacks after the convention. The first difficulty was the Eagleton affair. Sometimes voters react negatively to what might otherwise be considered minor incidents, or to those they do not understand. For example, Edward Muskie had wept in public over an insult to his wife during his bid for the nomination in 1972. The incident was interpreted as a sign that Muskie was emotionally unstable, and therefore unfit to be president. Similarly, and disastrous for his candidacy,

George Romney made an off-hand remark in the 1968 race for the Republican nomination that he had been "brainwashed" by the military regarding Vietnam. Such incidents tend to undermine the public's assessment of a candidate's leadership credibility. McGovern compounded the "Eagleton problem" by vacillating on the issue.

McGovern had alienated many Democratic Party regulars when he excluded them from the convention, costing him support among this influential group. Organized labor, a major Democratic constituency, was divided over his candidacy. Union workers supported Nixon over McGovern by a three-to-two margin. McGovern's credibility was further called into question by the "Salinger affair." McGovern had asked Pierre Salinger to be an intermediary with the North Vietnamese at the peace negotiations in Paris. However, conflicting public statements were made by both McGovern and Salinger as to whether McGovern had actually suggested the meeting. Meanwhile, Nixon received a political bonus twelve days before the election, when the North Vietnamese disclosed a breakthrough at the Vietnam peace talks. Henry Kissinger confirmed the Hanoi disclosure on October 26, claiming that "Peace is at hand."

Every flaw in the McGovern campaign received substantial media attention because he had made himself available to the media. The Nixon group, on the other hand, recognized the structural aspects of news gathering, and ran a campaign designed around the advantages of presidential incumbency. Nixon was quoted by the media mostly on foreign affairs, defense, and economic policy, while McGovern was mostly covered on domestic policy. McGovern was more interesting, because he was a new face challenging an incumbent who lacked support with most news people. Still ringing in the media's ears was the classic attack on November 13, 1969 by Spiro Agnew, who had lashed out at journalists for their adverse "instant" commentary on an address by President Nixon. Agnew charged that a tiny, anonymous group of men based in New York and Washington, who represented nobody but their own privileged fraternity, took it upon themselves to impugn the truthfulness and capabilities of the elected head of state. Media people were outraged—but people who called stations to comment on the speech sided with Agnew, two to one.

McGovern encountered a number of ironies in the campaign. For example, he benefited from the fact that journalists drew primarily on Democrats for their story sources, but the vast majority of newspapers editorially supported Nixon. McGovern worked hard to make his material newsworthy, while Nixon stayed out of the limelight. McGovern was quoted more, but Nixon received more coverage simply because he was president. Finally, despite the general

Ratification of the Twenty-sixth Amendment to the Constitution in 1971 lowered the voting age from twenty-one to eighteen years of age, and both candidates actively sought the youth vote. *(Gyory Collection/Will Gyory Photo)*

view that voters distrusted Nixon, McGovern was held in low esteem. Almost 60 percent thought Nixon could be trusted, and even Wallace was viewed as more trustworthy than McGovern. McGovern's "distrust quotient" was not due simply to his handling of the Eagleton affair.

McGovern tried to make corruption an issue in the campaign. The Republicans had changed the site of their convention from San Diego to Miami Beach. The San Diego site had become controversial because the International Telephone and Telegraph Corporation (ITT), through its Sheraton Hotel subsidiary, had given between $200,000 and $400,000 to the convention, allegedly for favorable treatment by the Department of Justice in an antitrust suit.

Surely, one of the strangest—and most consequential—events in the history of presidential campaigns was the break-in at the Democratic National Com-

This poster boosting Richard Nixon's reelection bid in 1972 emphasizes the president's domestic record. It makes no reference to the Vietnam War, perhaps because of the controversy it continued to generate. *(National Museum of American History)*

mittee, in the Watergate office complex in Washington, D.C., on June 17. Five men were apprehended as they tried to install electronic eavesdropping equipment. Among them were Bernard Barker, a Miami real estate dealer and former CIA operative, G. Gordon Liddy, a former presidential assistant on domestic affairs, E. Howard Hunt, who had worked at the White House, and James McCord, security agent for both the Committee to Reelect the President (CREEP) and the Republican National Committee. Money found on the suspects during the raid was traced by the FBI to secret Republican contributors in Houston. The money had traveled from Houston to Mexico City, returned by a Mexican lawyer to Houston, sent to Republican headquarters in Washington, D.C., and then deposited in Barker's Miami bank account. On September 15, seven individuals were indicted by a federal grand jury.

Initially, the public did not become aroused by the event. To keep the issue alive politically, the Democrats filed a $1 million lawsuit against the Watergate burglars. On September 11, they broadened their suit to include Maurice Stans, the Republican National Committee treasurer, asking for $3.2 million in damages. The Republicans filed a counter-suit for $2.5 million, and Stans filed a $5 million suit on September 14 for being "falsely and maliciously" accused. In addition John Mitchell, Nixon's attorney general, who had resigned February 15 to become Nixon's campaign manager, announced on July 1 that he was leaving politics—claiming that his wife forced his withdrawal. Clark McGregor, a former director of congressional affairs, replaced him. Although the Watergate scandal would ultimately force Nixon from the presidency in 1974, it had little impact on the 1972 campaign.

Nixon maintained an unusually low profile during the campaign, using notable surrogates like Agnew to carry the Republican message on the stump. The president refused to debate McGovern, and avoided trading partisan barbs with him in the press. He campaigned on peace and prosperity, while emphasizing the divisions in the Democratic Party. He also created CREEP (an acronym for Committee to Reelect the President), a political committee separate from the Republican National Committee, partly to attract Democratic voters.

The absence of Nixon on the campaign trail resulted in intensive scrutiny of McGovern, who was characterized as a candidate striving for office.

McGovern was not viewed as a politician in the customary sense. Nixon questioned McGovern's leadership by charging him with inconsistency: "McGovern last year . . . this year . . . what about next year?" A candidate who had changed his mind on important issues in the past gave no assurance that he would not change on those issues in the future. McGovern's message consistently criticized the nation's prolonged involvement in Vietnam. Nixon's campaign commercials consisted of edited news footage of his trips to Russia and China.

The Election Results

The most potent issues in 1972 were the Vietnam War and amnesty for draft evaders. In 1968 Nixon linked Humphrey to the Johnson administration and its involvement with the Vietnam War. Four years later Nixon varied his message painting McGovern as the "peace at any price" candidate and himself as the experienced leader who could achieve "peace with honor." Attitudes on the legalization of marijuana and campus demonstrations were strongly correlated to the vote. Political alienation peaked in 1972, a result of seemingly intractable racial and social problems. The high political alienation reading perhaps helps to explain the unprecedented rate of ticket splitting in the election. The Watergate scandal was just breaking and the Eagleton affair was given prime time coverage. Both situations increased political alienation and distrust among the voters. These factors may explain why only 55 percent of the eligible voters went to the polls, which was the lowest voter turnout in twenty-four years.

McGovern's attempt to moderate his positions on amnesty, abortion, marijuana, tax reform, and defense reductions may have backfired. Rather than reduce his image as an ultra-liberal, his shift may have undermined the voters' sense of his credibility and decisiveness. Nixon appealed to a group that he called the "new American majority," which came to be known as the "silent majority," emphasizing peace and prosperity, especially in Vietnam. He anticipated that his powers as president would help him to prevail in foreign policy and defense but he expected to have problems with the Democratic Congress on domestic programs.

The Republicans began the race with a full campaign chest of $30 million in the party's treasury. The Democrats entered the 1972 race with a $9.3 million debt left over from the 1968 campaign. Democrats charged that special interest groups were making sizeable donations for governmental favors. Nixon had signed the Federal Election Campaign Act of 1971 on February 7, 1972, which required that after April 7 all candidates must disclose the sources of the campaign funds and how the funds were disbursed. Democrats charged that Maurice Stans, the Presidents chief fundraiser and former Secretary of Commerce, encouraged large contributors, albeit legal, to submit donations before the April 7 deadline.

Nixon came out of the Republican convention with a 72–28 percent lead in the polls. By and large, he maintained this margin throughout the campaign and into the voting. Carrying 49 states, Nixon scored a landslide of historic proportions. McGovern won only Massachusetts and the District of Columbia. On December 18 the Electoral College awarded 520 votes for Nixon, 17 for McGovern, and one vote for John Hospers of the Libertarian Party. Nixon had won 60.7 percent of the popular vote and McGovern 37.5 percent.

Nixon was the first Republican to make significant inroads into the famous Roosevelt Democratic New Deal coalition composed of black, Jewish, Catholic, labor union, and old Southern Confederacy voters. He was the first Republican to carry Hawaii, the first to win Arkansas in one hundred years, and the first since Reconstruction to sweep the solid Democratic South (states of the former Confederacy). He also carried a large part of the blue-collar labor vote. A majority of Catholics had voted Democratic in all elections since 1952, but in 1972 they deserted the Democratic Party in larger numbers. Usually Jews voted 80 to 90 percent for Democrats but in 1972 they gave McGovern only 63 percent. In 1960 Nixon carried only three southern states against John F. Kennedy but in 1972 he carried all of them. The absence of Wallace, a southerner, on any ticket benefited Nixon.

Nixon's reelection kept a Republican in the presidency, but the Democrats maintained their control of Congress. Republicans hoped to gain control of the Senate but lost two seats, resulting in 56 Democrats and 42 Republicans, with one independent and one conservative. In the House the Republicans gained only 14 of the 39 seats they needed to gain control. It was the first time in any election that a party winning by such a large margin failed to take both houses of Congress. Nixon provided short coattails. He had scored a personal victory that did not translate into a mandate for the Republican Party. On the other hand, George McGovern suffered the worst defeat ever experienced by a Democratic presidential candidate. He did not even carry his home state of South Dakota.

With the exception of the presidency, 1972 was a Democratic year. Eight new Democrats and five new Republicans were elected to the Senate. Four of the Democrats upset Republican incumbents and only one Democratic incumbent lost his seat. Republicans, however, did gain seats in North Carolina, Oklahoma, and New Mexico that had been held by retiring Democratic senators. The Republicans picked up 13 House seats formerly held by Democrats with seven of them coming from the once solid Democratic South. In addition the Democrats won 11 of the 18 governors races giving the Democrats a total of 31 governorships.

Postscript

Americans have generally tended to support the forces of progressive change in the twentieth century. Yet, whenever a minority pulls them far to the right, as in 1964 and to the left, as in 1972, they have invariably moved back to the center. Apparently McGovern assumed that it was time for another period of dramatic reform. McGovern wanted an immediate cease-fire in Vietnam, a redistribution of the national wealth, major reductions in defense expenditures, and another dramatic attack on poverty. In addition, the election outcome indicated there was a powerful reaction among middle class voters against what appeared to be large government welfare payments to citizens able but seemingly not willing to take available jobs. Also there was considerable objection to proposals that advocated busing of children to create racially balanced public schools, the legalization of marijuana and abortion, and grants of amnesty to men who deserted or dodged the military draft during the Vietnam War.

Similar to Barry Goldwater in 1964, who was overwhelmingly defeated because he seemed to be moving too far to the right, McGovern lost largely because of perceptions that had moved too far to the left. President Nixon judged the mood more accurately by pounding away at McGovern's alleged radicalism and standing for slower change and law and order. This combination of pragmatism and caution awarded him the election on November 7.

Frank Colon

Bibliography

Ambrose, Stephen E. *Nixon*. 3 vols. New York: Simon and Schuster, 1987-1991.

Asher, Herbert B. *Presidential Elections and American Politics, Voters, Candidates, and Campaigns Since 1952.* 3d ed. Homewood, IL: Dorsey Press, 1984.

Blum, John Morton. *Years of Discord: American Politics and Society, 1961–1974,* New York: W.W. Norton, 1991.

Kessel, John H. *Presidential Parties.* Homewood, IL: Dorsey Press, 1984.

Perry, James M. *Us and Them: How the Press Covered the 1972 Election.* New York: C.N. Potter, 1973.

Schlesinger, Arthur M. Jr., ed., *Running for President, The Candidates and Their Images 1900–1992.* vol. II. New York: Simon and Schuster, 1994.

White, Theodore H. *The Making of the President 1972.* New York: Atheneum, 1973.

THE VOTE: ELECTION OF 1972

State	Total No. of Electors	Total Popular Vote	Electoral Vote R	D	O	Margin of Victory Votes	% Total Vote	Nixon Republican Votes	%	McGovern Democrat Votes	%	Others Votes	%
Alabama	9	1,006,093	9			471,778	46.9%	728,701	72.4%	256,923	25.5%	20,469	2.0%
Alaska	3	95,219	3			22,382	23.5%	55,349	58.1%	32,967	34.6%	6,903	7.2%
Arizona	6	653,505	6			204,272	31.3%	402,812	61.6%	198,540	30.4%	52,153	8.0%
Arkansas	6	647,666	6			246,852	38.1%	445,751	68.8%	198,899	30.7%	3,016	0.5%
California	45	8,367,862	45			1,126,249	13.5%	4,602,096	55.0%	3,475,847	41.5%	289,919	3.5%
Colorado	7	953,884	7			267,209	28.0%	597,189	62.6%	329,980	34.6%	26,715	2.8%
Connecticut	8	1,384,277	8			255,265	18.4%	810,763	58.6%	555,498	40.1%	18,016	1.3%
Delaware	3	235,516	3			48,074	20.4%	140,357	59.6%	92,283	39.2%	2,876	1.2%
District of Columbia	3	163,421		3		92,401	56.5%	35,226	21.6%	127,627	78.1%	568	0.3%
Florida	17	2,583,283	17			1,139,642	44.1%	1,857,759	71.9%	718,117	27.8%	7,407	0.3%
Georgia	12	1,174,772	12			591,967	50.4%	881,496	75.0%	289,529	24.6%	3,747	0.3%
Hawaii	4	270,274	4			67,456	25.0%	168,865	62.5%	101,409	37.5%	0	0.0%
Idaho	4	310,379	4			118,558	38.2%	199,384	64.2%	80,826	26.0%	30,169	9.7%
Illinois	26	4,723,236	26			874,707	18.5%	2,788,179	59.0%	1,913,472	40.5%	21,585	0.5%
Indiana	13	2,125,529	13			696,586	32.8%	1,405,154	66.1%	708,568	33.3%	11,807	0.6%
Iowa	8	1,225,944	8			210,001	17.1%	706,207	57.6%	496,206	40.5%	23,531	1.9%
Kansas	7	916,095	7			349,525	38.2%	619,812	67.7%	270,287	29.5%	25,996	2.8%
Kentucky	9	1,067,499	9			305,287	28.6%	676,446	63.4%	371,159	34.8%	19,894	1.9%
Louisiana	10	1,051,491	10			388,710	37.0%	686,852	65.3%	298,142	28.4%	66,497	6.3%
Maine	4	417,042	4			95,874	23.0%	256,458	61.5%	160,584	38.5%	0	0.0%
Maryland	10	1,353,812	10			323,524	23.9%	829,305	61.3%	505,781	37.4%	18,726	1.4%
Massachusetts	14	2,458,756		14		220,462	9.0%	1,112,078	45.2%	1,332,540	54.2%	14,138	0.6%
Michigan	21	3,490,325	21			502,286	14.4%	1,961,721	56.2%	1,459,435	41.8%	69,169	2.0%
Minnesota	10	1,741,652	10			95,923	5.5%	898,269	51.6%	802,346	46.1%	41,037	2.4%
Mississippi	7	645,963	7			378,343	58.6%	505,125	78.2%	126,782	19.6%	14,056	2.2%
Missouri	12	1,852,589	12			455,527	24.6%	1,154,058	62.3%	698,531	37.7%	0	0.0%
Montana	4	317,603	4			63,779	20.1%	183,976	57.9%	120,197	37.8%	13,430	4.2%
Nebraska	5	576,289	5			236,307	41.0%	406,298	70.5%	169,991	29.5%	0	0.0%
Nevada	3	181,766	3			49,734	27.4%	115,750	63.7%	66,016	36.3%	0	0.0%
New Hampshire	4	334,055	4			97,289	29.1%	213,724	64.0%	116,435	34.9%	3,896	1.2%
New Jersey	17	2,997,229	17			743,291	24.8%	1,845,502	61.6%	1,102,211	36.8%	49,516	1.7%
New Mexico	4	385,931	4			94,522	24.5%	235,606	61.0%	141,084	36.6%	9,241	2.4%
New York	41	7,161,830	41			1,241,694	17.3%	4,192,778	58.5%	2,951,084	41.2%	17,968	0.3%
North Carolina	13	1,518,612	13			616,184	40.6%	1,054,889	69.5%	438,705	28.9%	25,018	1.6%
North Dakota	3	280,514	3			73,725	26.3%	174,109	62.1%	100,384	35.8%	6,021	2.1%
Ohio	25	4,094,787	25			882,938	21.6%	2,441,827	59.6%	1,558,889	38.1%	94,071	2.3%
Oklahoma	8	1,029,900	8			511,878	49.7%	759,025	73.7%	247,147	24.0%	23,728	2.3%
Oregon	6	927,946	6			93,926	10.1%	486,686	52.4%	392,760	42.3%	48,500	5.2%
Pennsylvania	27	4,592,105	27			917,570	20.0%	2,714,521	59.1%	1,796,951	39.1%	80,633	1.8%
Rhode Island	4	415,808	4			25,738	6.2%	220,383	53.0%	194,645	46.8%	780	0.2%
South Carolina	8	677,880	8			289,157	42.7%	478,427	70.6%	189,270	27.9%	10,183	1.5%
South Dakota	4	307,415	4			26,531	8.6%	166,476	54.2%	139,945	45.5%	994	0.3%
Tennessee	10	1,201,182	10			455,854	38.0%	813,147	67.7%	357,293	29.7%	30,742	2.6%
Texas	26	3,471,281	26			1,144,607	33.0%	2,298,896	66.2%	1,154,289	33.3%	18,096	0.5%
Utah	4	478,476	4			197,359	41.2%	323,643	67.6%	126,284	26.4%	28,549	6.0%
Vermont	3	186,947	3			48,975	26.2%	117,149	62.7%	68,174	36.5%	1,624	0.9%
Virginia	12	1,457,019	11		1[a]	549,606	37.7%	988,493	67.8%	438,887	30.1%	29,639	2.0%
Washington	9	1,470,847	9			268,801	18.3%	837,135	56.9%	568,334	38.6%	65,378	4.4%
West Virginia	6	762,399	6			207,529	27.2%	484,964	63.6%	277,435	36.4%	0	0.0%
Wisconsin	11	1,852,890	11			179,256	9.7%	989,430	53.4%	810,174	43.7%	53,286	2.9%
Wyoming	3	145,570	3			56,106	38.5%	100,464	69.0%	44,358	30.5%	748	0.5%
TOTAL	538	77,742,365	520	17	1	17,995,490	23.1%	47,168,710	60.7%	29,173,220	37.5%	1,400,435	1.8%

[a] A Nixon elector in Virginia voted for Libertarian candidate John Hospers.

For sources, see p. 1132.

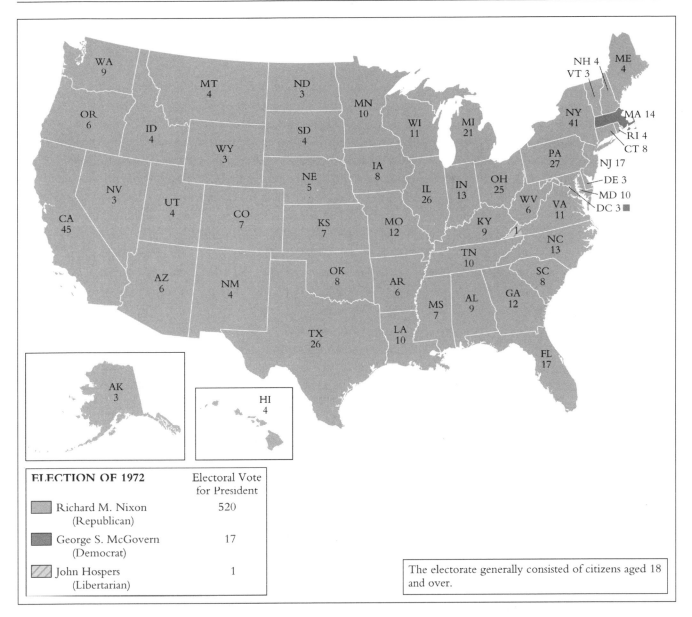

ELECTION OF 1972	Electoral Vote for President
Richard M. Nixon (Republican)	520
George S. McGovern (Democrat)	17
John Hospers (Libertarian)	1

The electorate generally consisted of citizens aged 18 and over.

DOCUMENTS: ELECTION OF 1972

The Republicans renominated President Richard M. Nixon without serious dissent. The Democrats settled on a little-known senator, George McGovern of South Dakota, after none of their frontrunners made it to the convention. Senator Edward M. Kennedy of Massachusetts had refused to run in the aftermath of his automobile accident at Chappaquiddick (on the island of Martha's Vineyard) in which a female passenger drowned. Senator Edmund Muskie of Maine, who had won the New Hampshire primary, dropped out after his support declined outside the Northeast when he cried on television. Alabama governor George Wallace, who had run as an independent in 1968, won a series of primary victories outside the South, including Maryland and Michigan, but had dropped out of the 1972 race after being shot and paralyzed by a deranged young man. McGovern, a Ph.D. in history who had studied the Populists and supported Henry Wallace's Progressive Party, was perceived as a leftist and was never able to get his campaign on track. Nixon won in a landslide.

In Document 1, his speech accepting the Democratic nomination, McGovern called for campaign finance reform, promised an honest administration (interestingly, a Time *magazine poll revealed that two-thirds of Americans thought Nixon was more trustworthy than McGovern), an immediate end to the Vietnam War, and massive cuts in defense spending. Any momentum McGovern gained from the Democratic convention, however, was soon diffused by his vice presidential choice. Document 2, excerpts from two* Time *magazine articles, examined the controversy surrounding Senator Thomas Eagleton of Missouri, McGovern's initial choice. McGovern's handling of the situation was "humiliating," and his campaign never recovered.*

Nixon, in Document 3, his speech accepting the Republican nomination, championed the "American System" of freedom and democracy against the Democratic alternative, where politicians have too much influence over people's lives. Furthermore, he promised to end the war in Vietnam on honorable terms. With a large lead in the polls, Nixon did little campaigning. Instead, he made a few television appearances and held press conferences. In Document 4, excerpts from his press conferences, Nixon responded to questions about the Watergate incident, his reelection, and Vietnam. He did not reveal very much.

In the end, McGovern was never able to convince even his own party that he was the best choice for president. Document 5, two Time *magazine articles comparing the major candidates on election issues, revealed that most voters, even Democrats, believed that McGovern was wishy-washy, and that many of his programs were "confusing" and "unrealistic." The 1972 election would prove to be one of the most ideological campaigns in American history.*

Document 1

George McGovern's Nomination Acceptance Speech, July 13, 1972

This is a nomination of the people, and I hereby dedicate this campaign to the people.

And next January we will restore the government to the people. American politics will never be the same again. . . .

To anyone in this hall or beyond who doubts the ability of Democrats to join together in common cause, I say never underestimate the power of Richard Nixon to bring harmony to Democratic ranks. He is the unwitting unifier and the fundamental issue of this campaign. And all of us together are going to help him redeem the pledge he made 10 years ago: Next year you won't have Richard Nixon to kick around any more. . . .

So let your opponents stand on the status quo, while we seek to refresh the American spirit.

Let the opposition collect their $10 million in secret money from the privileged. And let us find one million ordinary Americans who will contribute $25 to this campaign—a McGovern "million-member club" with members who will expect, not special favors for themselves, but a better land for us all. . . .

This is the time for truth, not falsehood. . . .

Truth is a habit of integrity, not a strategy of politics. And if we nurture the habit of candor in this campaign, we will continue to be candid once we are in the White House. Let us say to Americans, as Woodrow Wilson said in his first campaign: "Let me inside [the government] and I will tell you everything that is going on in there."

. . . In 1968, Americans voted to bring our sons home from Vietnam in peace—and since then, 20,000 have come home in coffins.

I have no secret plan for peace. I have a public plan.

As one whose heart has ached for 10 years over the agony of Vietnam, I will halt the senseless bombing of Indochina on Inauguration Day.

There will be no more Asian children running ablaze from bombed-out schools.

There will be no more talk of bombing the dikes or the cities of the North.

Within 90 days of my inauguration, every American soldier and every American prisoner will be out of the jungle and out of their cells and back home in America where they belong.

And then let us resolve that never again will we shed the precious young blood of this nation to perpetuate an unrepresentative client abroad.

Let us choose life, not death—this is the time.

This is also the time to turn away from excessive preoccupation overseas to rebuilding our own nation.

America must be restored to her proper role in the world. But we can do that only through the recovery of confidence in ourselves. . . .

So join with me in this campaign, lend me your strength and your support, give me your voice—and together, we will call America home to the founding ideals that nourished us in the beginning.

From secrecy and deception in high places, come home, America.

From a conflict in Indochina which maims our ideals as well as our soldiers, come home, America.

From military spending so wasteful that it weakens our nation, come home, America.

From the entrenchment of special privilege and tax favoritism, come home, America.

From the waste of idle hands to the joy of useful labor, come home, America.

From the prejudice of race and sex, come home, America.

From the loneliness of the aging poor and the despair of the neglected sick, come home, America.

Come home to the affirmation that we have a dream.

Come home to the conviction that we can move our country forward.

Come home to the belief that we can seek a newer world.

Source: "McGovern Acceptance Speech," New York Times, July 14, 1972.

Document 2.
Excerpts from *Time* on George McGovern's Vice Presidential Choices

"McGovern's First Crisis: The Eagleton Affair"

"I assume that everyone here is impressed by my control of this convention in that my choice for Vice President was challenged by only 39 other nominees. But I think we learned from watching the Republicans four years ago as they selected their vice presidential nominee, that it pays to take a little more time."—George McGovern acceptance speech, Miami Beach, Florida. . . .

The drama began early in the week when Eagleton was forced to reveal that on three occasions, in 1960, 1964, and 1966, he had been hospitalized in St. Louis or at the Mayo Clinic for nervous exhaustion. . . . McGovern and his running mate decided to break the news themselves at a press conference. . . . He spent four days at the Mayo Clinic in 1964, and about three weeks in 1966. On two of those occasions, in 1960 and 1966, he underwent electric shock therapy for depression. Now, he said, "I have every confidence that I've learned how pace myself and know the limits of my own endurance. . . ."

McGovern said: "If I had known every detail that he discussed this morning, he would still have been my choice for Vice President. . . ."

If McGovern thought that those firm words would be the end of it, he was badly mistaken. . . . The telephones and news tickers at McGovern's temporary headquarters . . . quickly relayed the anger and dismay of key Democrats round the U.S. McGovern's finance chiefs, already facing a red-ink campaign, winced in despair. Editorialists let go their thunderbolts, crying for Eagleton to quit the ticket. . . . McGovern made no effort to discourage his backers from dump-Eagleton talk.

"George McGovern Finally Finds a Veep"

The dropping of Eagleton because of the uproar over his medical history was virtually unprecedented. The rebuffs encountered by McGovern as he sought a reassuring replacement only added to the party humiliation. McGovern wooed them and practically begged, but one by one, Edward Kennedy, Abraham Ribicoff, Hubert Humphrey, Reubin Askew and Edmund Muskie all declined for various reasons their party's second highest honor. The selection of Shriver, a personable Kennedy in-law and former head of the Peace Corps and Office of Economic Opportunity, may turn out to be a good choice, but had the public aura of an act of desperation.

Sources: Time, August 7, 1972; Time, August 14, 1972. Reprinted by permission.

Document 3

Richard Nixon's Nomination Acceptance Speech, August 23, 1972

Let us commit ourselves to rule out every vestige of discrimination in this country of ours. But my fellow Americans, the way to end discrimination against some is not to begin discrimination against others.

Dividing Americans into quotas is totally alien to the American tradition.

Americans don't want to be part of a quota. They want to be part of America. This Nation proudly calls itself the United States of America. Let us reject any philosophy that would make us the divided people of America.

In that spirit, I address you tonight, my fellow Americans, not as a partisan of party, which would divide us, but as a partisan of principles, which can unite us.

Six weeks ago our opponents at their convention rejected many of the great principles of the Democratic Party. To those millions who have been driven out of their home in the Democratic Party, we say come home. We say come home not to another party, but we say come home to the great principles we Americans believe in together.

And I ask you, my fellow Americans, tonight to join us not in a coalition held together only by a desire to gain power. I ask you to join us as members of a new American majority bound together by our common ideals.

I ask everyone listening to me tonight—Democrats, Republicans, independents, to join our new majority—

not on the basis of the party label you wear in your lapel, but on the basis of what you believe in your hearts. . . .

It has become fashionable in recent years to point up what is wrong with what is called the American system. The critics contend it is so unfair, so corrupt, so unjust, that we should tear it down and substitute something else in its place.

I totally disagree. I believe in the American system.

I have traveled to 80 countries in the past 25 years, and I have seen Communist systems, I have seen Socialist systems, I have seen systems that are half Socialist and half free.

Every time I come home to America, I realize how fortunate we are to live in this great and good country. . . .

Our Administration, as you know, has provided the biggest tax cut in history, but taxes are still too high. . . .

As a result of the millions of new jobs created by our new economic policies, unemployment today in America is less than the peacetime average of the sixties, but we must continue the unparalleled increase in new jobs so that we can achieve the great goal of our new prosperity—a job for every American who wants to work, without war and without inflation. . . .

This points up one of the clearest choices in this campaign. Our opponents believe in a different philosophy.

Theirs is the politics of paternalism, where master planners in Washington make decisions for people. . . .

Peace is too important for partisanship. There have been five Presidents in my political lifetime. . . .

They had differences on some issues, but they were united in their belief that where the security of America or the peace of the world is involved we are not Republicans, we are not Democrats. We are Americans, first, last, and always.

These five Presidents were united in their total opposition to isolation for America and in their belief that the interests of the United States and the interests of world peace require that America be strong enough and intelligent enough to assume the responsibilities of leadership in the world.

They were united in the conviction that the United States should have a defense second to none in the world.

They were all men who hated war and were dedicated to peace.

But not one of these five men, and no President in our history, believed that America should ask an enemy for peace on terms that would betray our allies and destroy respect for the United States all over the world.

As your President, I pledge that I shall always uphold that proud bipartisan tradition. . . I pledged to seek an honorable end to the war in Vietnam. We have made great progress toward that end. We have brought over half a million men home, and more will be coming home. We have ended America's ground combat role. No draftees

are being sent to Vietnam. We have reduced our casualties by 98 percent. We have gone the extra mile, in fact we have gone tens of thousands of miles trying to seek a negotiated settlement of the war. We have offered a ceasefire, a total withdrawal of all American forces, an exchange of all prisoners of war, internationally supervised free elections with the Communists participating in the elections and in the supervision.

There are three things, however, that we have not and that we will not offer.

We will never abandon our prisoners of war.

Second, we will not join our enemies in imposing a Communist government on our allies—the 17 million people of South Vietnam.

And we will never stain the honor of the United States of America. . . .

We have the opportunity in our time to be the peacemakers of the world, because the world trusts and respects us and because the world knows that we shall only use our power to defend freedom, never to destroy it; to keep the peace, never to break it.

A strong America is not the enemy of peace; it is the guardian of peace.

Source: Public Papers and Addresses of the Presidents of the United States: Richard Nixon, 1972 (Washington, DC: Government Printing Office, 1974).

Document 4.
Excerpts from Nixon News Conferences, 1972

June 22, on Watergate

Q: Mr. President, can you give us some of your reasons, sir, for deciding against debating your Democratic opponent this fall?

PRESIDENT: He asked if I had any good reasons for deciding against debating my Democratic opponent this fall. As you ladies and gentlemen have often heard me say, and I will continue to hold this position, questions that deal with the campaign, questions that deal with matters that involve candidacy, are ones that I will respectfully not comment upon until after the Republican Convention. At that time I will be glad to take that question and I will give an answer then.

I have not made a decision on it yet. That is my point.

Q: Mr. O'Brien has said that the people who bugged his headquarters had a direct link to the White House. Have you had any sort of investigation made to determine whether this is true?

PRESIDENT: Mr. Ziegler and also Mr. Mitchell, speaking for the Campaign Committee, have responded to questions on this in great detail. They have stated my position and have also stated the facts accurately.

This kind of activity, as Mr. Ziegler has indicated, has no place whatever in our electoral process, or in our governmental process. And, as Mr. Ziegler has stated, the White House has had no involvement whatever in this particular incident.

As far as the matter now is concerned, it is under investigation, as it should be, by the proper legal authorities, by the District of Columbia police and by the FBI. I will not comment on those matters, particularly since possible criminal charges are involved.

August 29, on Reelection

Q: Mr. President, the confidence expressed at the Republican convention suggested that many Republicans, perhaps yourself included, consider the election a mere formality. Yet you have said, at your last press conferences, that you expected this election to be a close one. . . . Do you still feel that way?

PRESIDENT: Yes, I do. . . . I am conducting this campaign, and I have urged my colleagues in the campaign to conduct it without regard to the polls. . . . We are running on the basis of the great issues before the country. . . .

I think what we need now is a clear majority of the American people. That means a clear mandate. . . .

Q: . . . Would you be willing to debate with Senator McGovern? . . .

PRESIDENT: . . . it would not be in the national interest for the President to debate. . . . The reason does not have so much to do with confidential information that a President has. . . . What really is involved is that when a President speaks . . . he makes a policy every time he opens his mouth. . . . For a President in the heat of a partisan debate to make policy would not be in the national interest. So I have decided there will be no debates. . . .

Q: . . . Would you entertain the possibility of a debate on a lower level, between the Vice Presidential candidates?

PRESIDENT: I would be very confident as to the results on that, because I think Vice President Agnew's four years of experience, his coolness . . . would serve him in good stead in a debate. I do not believe, however, that a debate at the Vice Presidential level would serve any useful purpose. . . .

October 5, on Vietnam

Q: Mr. President, in Vietnam, do you see any possibility of a negotiated settlement before the election?

PRESIDENT: . . . I should emphasize, however, that under no circumstances will the timing of a settlement, for example, the possible negotiation of a ceasefire, the possible negotiation of, or unilateral action with regard to, a bombing halt—under no circumstances will such action be affected by the fact that there is going to be an election November 7.

If we can make the right kind of a settlement before the election, we will make it. If we cannot, we are not going to make the wrong kind of a settlement before the election. We were around that track in 1968 when well-intentioned men made a very, very great mistake in stopping the bombing without adequate agreements from the other side.

I do not criticize them for that, of course, as far as their motives are concerned. I simply said, having seen what happened then, we are not going to make that mistake now.

The election, I repeat, will not in any way influence what we do at the negotiating table. . . .

Q: Mr. President, it has been said that Hanoi may be waiting until after the election to make a settlement on the theory that if they got a Democrat elected they would get better terms for them. How do you answer that?

PRESIDENT: They could be motivated by that. There are those who believe that they were motivated to an extent in 1968 by political considerations in agreeing to a bombing halt before the election with the thought that defeating me was more in their interest than electing my opponent.

Source: Public Papers and Addresses of the Presidents of the United States: Richard Nixon, 1972 (Washington, DC: Government Printing Office, 1974).

Document 5.
Articles Comparing George McGovern and Richard Nixon

"Nixon vs. McGovern on Taxes, Prices, Jobs"

Richard Nixon and George McGovern are presenting not just contrasting programs but fundamentally different visions of what American society should be like. In a second Administration, Nixon would strive for economic stability above all else and seek to interfere as little as possible in private enterprise. . . . A McGovern Administration would take an activist lead in aiming to redistribute income and wealth more equitably among all citizens. That philosophical dispute colors the two candidates' positions on every basic aspect of the economic issue:

Nixon would try to trim federal non-military spending; McGovern would raise it by tens of billions yearly.

Nixon says that he would oppose tax increases of any kind; McGovern would press for severe tax increases on corporations, investors, and heirs.

Nixon would give the highest priority to battling inflation, even if his policies would prolong an uncomfortably steep rate of unemployment; McGovern would drive to restore full employment even at the risk of more inflation. . . .

What is surprising is that voters who are loudly and sometimes angrily dissatisfied with Nixon's economic management are at the same time often anti-McGovern. . . .

[McGovern's] plans are just not realistic and he keeps changing his position.

Resentment against McGovern's spending and welfare plans is also widespread, and it is by no means confined to people who are affluent or white or both. . . .

Economically as well as socially, Nixon is effectively appealing to rising conservative feelings. Yet to the extent that there is a pro-Nixon vote on economic issues—as distinct from an anti-McGovern vote—it reflects not so much conservative ideology as an "I'm all right, Jack" attitude among the many voters whose fortunes have improved during the exuberant upturn of the past year. . . .

"How Voters Assess George McGovern v. Richard Nixon"

Pro-McGovern Democrats: The Senator's strong stand on ending the Viet Nam War remains the most binding issue among his supporters. Surprisingly, however, half of McGovern's backers think that the Senator's own promised time-table for ending the war is impractical. . . .

McGovern's call for tax reform is favored by a solid majority of all panelists. . . . His welfare reform plan causes the most confusion. Panelists want to see the welfare "mess" straightened out, but they are dubious about the implications of a program they do not understand. . . .

Pro-Nixon Republicans and Independents: Three out of four Nixon supporters credit his trips to China and the Soviet Union as major, meaningful efforts to achieve peace. . . . Consistent with their approval of the President's foreign policies, pro-Nixon panelists strongly oppose McGovern's proposal to reduce defense spending by $32 billion over three years. . . .

Panelists who back Nixon tend to do so out of respect rather than affection. . . .

Pro-Nixon Democrats: Conservative Democrats will pose a crucial problem for McGovern. . . . Like their counterparts in the rival party, they tend view his stands on the war and some domestic problems as extreme. They make their sharpest break with the Senator on Viet Nam, fearing a settlement that would amount to a defeat for the U.S., abandonment of the South Vietnamese or the sacrifice of American prisoners of war. They criticize his proposed cut in the defense budget as jeopardizing the nation's safety and reject his welfare reform program as an expensive give-away to people who will not work.

These conservatives are more inclined to trust Nixon, a known quantity, than McGovern, whom they regard as a risky and untried leader. . . .

Sources: Time, October 30, 1972; *Time*, July 17, 1972. Reprinted by permission.

THE ELECTION OF
1976

The 1976 presidential election offered intriguing candidates, two fascinating nomination campaigns, and one of the closest general elections in the twentieth century. Yet a national mood of political disillusion clouded the entire campaign. Americans vividly remembered the Watergate scandal and President Richard Nixon's 1974 resignation, and smaller scandals continued to validate the general sense of disappointment with government. The U.S. withdrawal from Vietnam, and the subsequent unification of Vietnam under a communist government in 1975, had further diminished public confidence. More than 70 percent of Americans had expressed confidence in the federal government's handling of domestic and foreign issues in 1972, but by June 1976 less than half expressed confidence in its handling of domestic problems.

Challenges to the Ford Presidency

The nation's economic problems made Americans especially anxious. The "oil crisis" had driven the economy into recession in 1973–74. Unemployment had reached 9 percent of the workforce in May 1975, the highest rate since the beginning of World War II. Joblessness had fallen, but stubbornly remained above 7 percent during the primary and general election campaigns. The ballooning cost of oil had driven up the inflation rate to more than 12 percent in 1973; and though inflation dropped to 5 percent in 1976, many Americans had grown apprehensive about the problem. Unemployment and inflation, in turn, con-

tributed to an unprecedented federal budget deficit of $66 billion in 1976.

Social and foreign policy issues also influenced the election. Busing for the desegregation of public schools had created controversy in several cities. The Supreme Court's 1973 decision to strike down state abortion restrictions, in *Roe v. Wade*, had aroused passions on both sides of the issue. The Equal Rights Amendment, sent by Congress to the states in 1972, also had mobilized women's rights advocates and their conservative opponents. In the wake of the energy crisis, nuclear power, coal, the oil industry, and the effects of energy on the environment became campaign issues. Conservative Republicans were angered by the Strategic Arms Limitation Treaty (SALT), the policy of détente with the Soviet Union, and negotiations with Panama over rights to the Panama Canal. Secretary of State Henry Kissinger, criticized by both Republican conservatives and Democrats, especially became a lighting rod for criticisms of current foreign policy.

Major changes in the rules of delegate selection and campaign finance changed the nature of the nomination and general election games. The elections of 1968 and 1972 had already proven that presidential primaries could catapult an underdog candidate into serious contention for a party's presidential nomination. Primary election success was essential for the nomination in 1976, compared to 1968, when most delegates to the Democratic and Republican national conventions had been chosen by internal party processes, and only a third of the states had held primary elections. Thirty states now

CHRONOLOGY

1974

AUGUST 9   Gerald R. Ford sworn in as 38th president after the resignation of President Richard M. Nixon.

SEPTEMBER 8   President Ford pardons Nixon.

1975

APRIL 24   Vietnam War officially ends.

1976

JANUARY 19   Jimmy Carter finishes ahead of other Democratic candidates in Iowa caucuses.

FEBRUARY 24   Ford and Carter win Republican and Democratic primaries in New Hampshire.

MARCH 2   Carter finishes fourth in Massachusetts primary.

MARCH 9   Ford and Carter win Florida primaries.

MARCH 16   Ford wins, and Carter makes a strong showing, in Illinois primaries.

MARCH 23   Ronald Reagan wins North Carolina primary.

APRIL 6   Carter wins Wisconsin primary, but loses to Jackson in New York.

APRIL 27   Carter wins Pennsylvania primary.

MAY 1   Reagan wins Texas primary.

MAY 4   Reagan sweeps three primaries and takes the lead in delegates.

MAY 18   Ford wins Michigan primary; Brown defeats Carter in Maryland primary.

JUNE 8   Reagan and Brown win California primaries; Ford and Carter win Ohio primaries.

JULY 12–15   Carter nominated on first ballot at Democratic National Convention.

JULY 26   Reagan names Richard Schweiker as his vice presidential running mate.

AUGUST 16   Ford nominated on first ballot at Republican National Convention.

SEPTEMBER 23   First presidential debate takes place in Philadelphia.

OCTOBER 6   Second presidential debate held in San Francisco.

OCTOBER 15   Vice presidential debate takes place in Houston.

OCTOBER 22   Third presidential debate held in Williamsburg, Virginia.

NOVEMBER 2   Carter defeats Ford in general election.

1977

JANUARY 20   Carter inaugurated as U.S. president.

held primaries, and three-quarters of the delegates were chosen directly by voters. Post-Watergate campaign laws limited individual contributions and created a system of public matching funds for presidential campaigns who limited their campaign expenditures. These spending limits (about $13.1 million per candidate before the national conventions, and $21.8 million between the nomination and the November election) cramped a number of leading candidates.

At the beginning of the 1976 campaign, these developments seemed ominous for the incumbent president, Gerald R. Ford. Unlike any predecessor, Ford had never run nationwide on a presidential ticket: He had been appointed vice president to fill the vacancy left by the resignation of Vice President

Spiro T. Agnew in 1973. Ford had never been elected by a constituency larger than his House district in Grand Rapids, Michigan. A popular and partisan leader of the Republican minority in the House of Representatives, Ford had brought candor and a more relaxed atmosphere to the presidency after Nixon's resignation. Ford's controversial pardon of Nixon in September 1974 had undermined his credibility, however. Changes in the campaign laws weakened the president's natural incumbency advantages in fund raising and control of the party machinery. Ford's economic and foreign policies, along with the gradual shift of Republican strength to southern and western states, invited a challenge from within the unelected president's own party.

That challenge came from Ronald Reagan, the former actor and governor of California, who very nearly took the Republican presidential nomination from Ford. A Goldwater supporter in 1964, Reagan had become the favored candidate of the increasingly powerful conservative wing of the party. Reagan's simple, strong message criticized the excessive growth and intrusiveness of the federal government. Critics claimed that his conservative positions, like Goldwater's, were too extreme, unqualified, and uncompromising. After campaigning unofficially for months, Reagan officially declared his candidacy in November 1975, when a Gallup poll measuring presidential preferences showed Reagan trailing Ford among Republicans by 23 percent. Within three weeks, Reagan led Ford among Republicans by 8 percent. Reagan's campaign made known its intention to defeat Ford in the first primary, New Hampshire, in late February.

Carter and the Race for the Democratic Presidential Nomination

At the start of the campaign, almost none of the Democratic candidates was as familiar as either Ford or Reagan. Prominent Democrats such as George McGovern, Edmund Muskie, Edward Kennedy, and

---

GERALD RUDOLPH FORD

PARTY: Republican

DATE OF BIRTH: July 14, 1913

PLACE OF BIRTH: Omaha, Nebraska

PARENTS: Leslie Lynch King and Dorothy Ayer Gardner King Ford

EDUCATION: B.A., University of Michigan, 1935; LL.B., Yale University Law School, 1941

FAMILY: Married Elizabeth Bloomer Warren, 1948; children: Michael Gerald, John "Jack" Gardner, Steven Meigs, and Susan Elizabeth

MILITARY SERVICE: U.S. Navy, lieutenant commander, 1942–46; U.S. Naval Reserves, 1946–63

CAREER: Admitted to Michigan bar, 1941; U.S. House of Representatives, 1949–73 (minority leader, 1965–73); U.S. vice president, 1973–74; U.S. president, 1974–77

Hubert Humphrey had declined to run; Humphrey's protégé, Senator Walter Mondale, had withdrawn from the race in the fall of 1974. Eugene McCarthy, who had challenged President Lyndon Johnson in the 1968 Democratic primaries, would run in the 1976 election as an independent presidential candidate. Governor George Wallace (see fact box, p. 892) of Alabama was the best-known Democrat who declared his intention to run. Wallace continued to press the populist, anti-Washington, anti-liberal themes he had used in 1964, 1968, and 1972, but his campaign lacked some of the fiery appeal of the past, in part because a 1972 assassination attempt had confined him to a wheelchair. None of the other declared or potential Democratic contenders were well known. Senator Henry M. Jackson of Washington, a moderate on domestic affairs and conservative on foreign policy, had the most resources and seemed the frontrunner. Representative Morris K. Udall of Arizona, Senator Fred R. Harris of Oklahoma, former vice presidential candidate R. Sargent Shriver, Pennsylvania governor Milton Schapp, Senator Birch Bayh of Indiana, Senator Frank Church of Idaho, and Governor Edmund "Jerry" Brown of California all competed for—and divided—liberal support. Senator Lloyd Bentsen, Jr., of Texas and two former southern governors, Terry Sanford of North Carolina and Jimmy Carter of Georgia, appealed to moderate Democrats.

Jimmy Carter's energy, organization, and message proved especially well suited to the primary-driven

JAMES EARL (JIMMY) CARTER

PARTY: Democratic

DATE OF BIRTH: October 1, 1924

PLACE OF BIRTH: Plains, Georgia

PARENTS: James Earl Carter and Lillian Gordy Carter

EDUCATION: B.S., U.S. Naval Academy, 1946

FAMILY: Married Eleanor Rosalynn Smith, 1946; children: John William "Jack," James Earl "Chip" III, Donnel Jeffrey "Jeff," and Amy Lynn

MILITARY SERVICE: U.S. Navy, lieutenant, 1946–53

CAREER: Farmer and businessman, from 1953; Board of Education chair, Sumter Co., Georgia, 1955–62; Georgia state senator, 1963–66; governor of Georgia, 1971–75; U.S. president, 1977–81; unsuccessful candidate for president, 1980; winner of the Nobel Peace Prize, 2002

Flashing his trademark smile, Jimmy Carter greets supporters in Fort Myers, Florida, on March 2, 1976, during his quest to win the Democratic nomination for president. *(AP Wide World Photos)*

1976 Democratic nomination campaign. Bright, tenacious, and stubborn, Carter positioned himself as an honest and competent leader representing a new, more racially tolerant South, and a political outsider who could "clean up the mess in Washington." He promised an ethical administration ("I will never lie to you") and "a Government as good and as competent and as compassionate as are the American people"; he was extraordinarily candid about his Baptist faith. He emphasized government reorganization, cuts in bureaucracy, a balanced federal budget, and welfare reform. Carter had familiarized himself to some party insiders after his election as governor of Georgia in 1970 and his appointment as campaign chairman of the Democratic National Committee in 1974. In late 1972, Carter's staff, fully recognizing the importance of the primaries in 1976, had proposed that Carter aim to win the nomination by running in most of the primaries (he entered all but four), establishing strength in early contests such as the Iowa caucuses and New Hampshire and Florida primaries, then broadening his base with primary victories outside the South, and showing consistent strength in all the primaries that he entered. Because he was virtually unknown to the electorate in the fall of 1975, other Democratic candidates did not take Carter seriously and had allowed him to pursue this strategy virtually unchallenged.

The Carter campaign's hard work in Iowa and New Hampshire paid off in these initial contests. Carter won more than a quarter of the Iowa delegates selected at the January caucuses, more than twice the total of runner-up Bayh, with Harris, Udall, and Shriver winning 10 percent or less (the largest block of delegates, more than a third, was not committed to any candidate). Favorable publicity in the *New York Times* boosted media attention to Carter, giving him momentum just a month before the New Hampshire primary. This publicity, combined with his effective campaign organization, lifted Carter to another success in New Hampshire, with 30 percent of the vote to Udall's 24 percent. A week later, Carter's momentum slowed when he finished fourth in the Massachusetts primary, behind Jackson, Udall, and Wallace.

After Carter's early successes, the battle for the Democratic nomination became a extended, grinding struggle in primaries spread out across the nation and the calendar. The southern moderate Carter grasped that he had to defeat George Wallace decisively in the South, beginning in Florida. There, Carter again benefited from strong organization, while Wallace's disability clearly impeded his campaign and raised doubts about his durability. In perhaps his most important step toward the nomination, Carter won the Florida primary with 34 percent of the vote to Wallace's 31 percent, and Jackson's 24 percent. With increased momentum and national media attention, Carter won the Illinois primary a week later. When Carter confronted Wallace one-on-one in North Carolina, in late March, Carter won his first majority victory with 54 percent of the vote, effectively ending Wallace's campaign.

Each of the remaining Democrats took aim at Carter in their remaining political strongholds. Udall saw the April 6 primary in liberal Wisconsin as his best chance to stop Carter. While Udall focused on the state's urban areas, the Carter campaign targeted rural Wisconsin. A Milwaukee paper declared Udall the winner the night of the primary, but late-arriving rural votes gave Carter the victory the next morning by a single percentage point, severely wounding Udall's campaign. Jackson had poured his efforts into the New York primary, on the same day as the Wisconsin primary; Jackson won a second substantial victory over Carter, who finished third behind Udall. Jackson believed that party machinery in Pennsylvania could finish the Georgian, but Carter's own organization and momentum gave him a decisive victory in that state, ending Jackson's chances for the nomination. Scrutiny and criticism of Carter increased; a Carter comment about "ethnic purity" in urban neighborhoods had created controversy. Hubert Humphrey flirted with entering the race, but declined. Frank Church and Jerry Brown now formally declared their candidacies. Carter lost primaries to Brown in Maryland, Califor-

nia, Rhode Island, and New Jersey, while Church defeated Carter in Nebraska, Oregon, Montana, and Idaho. But Carter continued to add delegates in all these states, and he continued to win primaries in the South.

When Carter won the important Ohio primary decisively on June 8, the final day of the primaries, Chicago's Mayor Richard J. Daley described the Ohio result as "the ball game." Daley committed his Illinois delegates to Carter, putting him close to the 1,505 delegates needed for the nomination and starting an avalanche of additional endorsements and delegate shifts. After a well-publicized search, Carter chose Walter Mondale as his running mate, a selection that reassured liberals and helped bring the party together. With the party remarkably unified com-

WALTER FREDERICK MONDALE

PARTY: Democrat

DATE OF BIRTH: January 5, 1928

PLACE OF BIRTH: Ceylon, Minnesota

PARENTS: Theodore Serguaard and Claribel (Hope)

EDUCATION: B.A., University of Minnesota, 1951; LL.B., University of Minnesota, 1956

FAMILY: Married Joan Adams, 1955, children: Theodore, Eleanor Jane, and William

CAREER: Attorney general of Minnesota, 1960–64; U.S. Senate, 1964–77; U.S. vice president, 1977–81; unsuccessful candidate for vice president, 1980; unsuccessful candidate for U.S. president, 1984; U.S. ambassador to Japan, 1993–97

pared to the previous two elections, Carter received nearly three-quarters of the delegate votes at the Democratic National Convention in July. Public opinion polls showed Carter running ahead of Ford by 33 percent. Worse for the GOP, the Republican nomination was still in doubt.

Ford and Reagan Duel for the Republican Nomination

At first, President Ford's campaign for the Republican nomination seemed to have successfully turned back Ronald Reagan's challenge. Reagan had proposed returning $90 billion in federal spending to the states, but he found it difficult to explain the details of the plan to voters in New Hampshire, where the return of federal programs could result in substantial

THE NON-ELECTED PRESIDENCY

*I*n the midst of the Watergate crisis, Vice President Spiro "Ted" Agnew, the point man of the Republican's "law and order" campaign, found himself in deep legal trouble. A federal court in Maryland was about to indict him for tax evasion when, on August 6, 1973, the Justice Department announced that the former governor of Maryland was being investigated for taking bribes from public contractors. As usual, the combative Agnew defended himself, denying the charges. He insisted that they were concocted by "masochistic persons looking for all that is wrong." Although Agnew welcomed impeachment, since he thought he could beat the rap, President Richard M. Nixon feared that it would set a bad precedent in his own case. Evidence of Agnew's guilt surfaced, however, and Attorney General Elliot Richardson worked out a deal that allowed the vice president to plead "nolo contendere"—a legal term meaning "I do not wish to contest," but accepting guilt—on one count of tax evasion. In return, Agnew was fined $10,000 and resigned on October 10, 1973.

Eager to stabilize the situation, President Nixon nominated for vice president Michigan congressman Gerald R. Ford, who was the House minority leader. The Twenty-fifth Amendment, which had been added to the Constitution in 1967, provides that "whenever a vacancy occurs in the office of the Vice President, the President shall nominate a Vice President who shall take office upon confirmation by a majority vote of both Houses of Congress."

tax increases. The Ford campaign, helped by a retooled campaign organization, high turnout and favorable economic news, eked out a win over Reagan in New Hampshire by a margin of 1,317 votes, out of more than 100,000 cast. The White House geared up for a decisive victory over Reagan in Florida. The Ford campaign questioned the implications of Reagan's budget plans for Social Security, a critical issue in a state with a large proportion of retirees. The White House also began to take advantage of the benefits of incumbency, announcing a series of contracts and grants for Florida, and arranging for highly publicized presidential appearances in the state. In the Florida primary, Ford improved on his New Hampshire margin, defeating Reagan 53 to 47 percent. A week later, Ford won an even more decisive victory, winning 59 percent of the vote to Reagan's 40 percent, in the major midwestern battleground state of Illinois. Leading Republicans called on Reagan to withdraw.

Reagan refused, and the Republican nomination campaign turned in his favor as he tightened his conservative message and drove it home in the remaining southern and western primaries. In North Carolina, Reagan began to criticize Ford's policies directly. Using television effectively, and supported by con-

servatives mobilized by Senator Jesse Helms, Reagan defeated Ford in North Carolina by 6 percent. The Reagan campaign bypassed Wisconsin, New York, and Pennsylvania to focus on Texas, a conservative

Gerald Ford, who assumed the presidency in 1974 after Richard Nixon resigned, headed the Republican ticket in 1976. This photo shows him in a triumphant pose, receiving accolades from supporters in Long Island, New York. *(© Gerald R. Ford Library)*

The long-time congressman from Grand Rapids was modest—"I am a Ford not a Lincoln"—and generally liked by both Democrats and Republicans. He also had a reputation for simple honesty. Most important, from the point of view of the president, Ford represented the conservative midwestern Republicans who valued traditional morality and were becoming suspicious of Nixon's behavior. After a brief examination of his finances, political views, and mental health, Congress quickly confirmed Gerald Ford as vice president on December 6, 1973.

In a brief inaugural, he proclaimed that the United States had demonstrated to the world that our great Republic stands solid, stands strong upon the bedrock of the Constitution." But as the Watergate scandal unfolded, it became clear that nothing could be further from the truth. Just eight months later Nixon would resign—and on August 9, 1974, Ford became the president of the United States. In his inaugural, he insisted that Nixon's resignation and his elevation to the presidency showed that "Our great Republic is a government of laws and not men. Here the people rule."

Yet, ironically, Ford was the country's only non-elected president. And in accordance with the Twenty-fifth Amendment, Ford proceeded to nominate the country's second non-elected vice president. As a good party man who had never done anything politically risky, Ford secretly polled a large number of leading Republicans concerning the vice presidency. Given the choice of George H. W. Bush and Nelson Rockefeller, he went with the better-known name. Rockefeller's confirmation hearings were somewhat more confrontational than Ford's, but Congress made him vice president on December 19, 1974. For the next two years, the United States would be governed by an administration in which neither the president nor the vice president had been elected.

state strongly inclined to Reagan's message. The Texas primary, the first presidential primary in that state, permitted voters to cross over to vote for other party candidates. With Wallace effectively gone as a factor in the Democratic nomination, thousands of Texas Democrats who had supported Wallace crossed over to vote for Reagan in the Republican primary. Reagan swept the Texas primary in every part of the state, winning all of its 96 delegates. Three days later, Reagan defeated Ford in Indiana, Alabama, and Georgia, and surged ahead of Ford in the delegate count. The Republican nomination now became a war of attrition. While Ford won the West Virginia primary on May 11, Reagan won the Nebraska primary. In his home state of Michigan, Ford slowed his challenger's momentum, defeating Reagan by a two-to-one margin. Reagan and Ford each won three primaries in smaller states on May 25. On the final day of the primaries, June 8, Reagan swept the large block of delegates in his home state of California, while Ford achieved huge delegate gains in Ohio and New Jersey. At the conclusion of the primaries, newspapers estimated that President Ford was about 170 delegates short of the 1,130 needed for a first-ballot victory at the Republican convention, with Reagan only a hundred votes behind.

The Republican Convention

For the rest of the summer, the two Republican contenders struggled to win the remaining delegates necessary for a first-ballot victory. Each campaign targeted uncommitted and weakly committed delegates on an individual basis. Ford met with some delegates in the White House to win their support. On July 26, Reagan made a bold bid for moderate Republican support by announcing that Senator Richard Schweiker of Pennsylvania had agreed to serve as his vice presidential running mate. The selection of Schweiker, a liberal Republican, angered some of Reagan's conservative supporters and failed to nudge moderate Republicans in the Northeast and Midwest toward Reagan. As the Republican convention delegates arrived in Kansas City in August, Ford was thought to have sufficient support for the nomination, but no one could be certain. In a final effort to take a few delegates away from Ford, the Reagan campaign pressed the convention to force Ford to name his running mate. This maneuver alienated some Reagan supporters, however, and the proposal narrowly failed on a key procedural vote. On the first ballot, the convention nominated Ford with 1,187 votes, only 57 votes above the minimum; 1070 dele-

ROBERT JOSEPH DOLE

PARTY: Republican

DATE OF BIRTH: July 22, 1923

PLACE OF BIRTH: Russell, Kansas

PARENTS: Doran R. and Bina Talbott Dole

EDUCATION: University of Kansas, 1941-43; Washburn Municipal University, A.B., LL.B., 1952

FAMILY: Married Phyllis Holden, 1948 (divorced, 1972); one child: Robin; married Elizabeth Hanford, 1975

MILITARY SERVICE: U.S. Army, captain, 1943–48

CAREER: Kansas House of Representatives, 1951–53; Russell County attorney, 1952–60; U.S. House of Representatives, 1961–69; U.S. Senate, 1969–96 (majority leader, 1985–87, 1995–96); unsuccessful candidate for U.S. vice president, 1976; unsuccessful candidate for U.S. president, 1996

gates voted for Reagan. Ford named Senator Robert Dole of Kansas as his vice presidential running mate. Dole, an acerbic, hard-campaigning partisan, was sufficiently conservative to pacify the Reagan supporters and bring the badly fractured party back together. Ironically, the protracted battle for the Republican nomination helped the Republicans in some ways. The long nomination battle gave the Republicans extensive publicity. Ford's victory seemed to give him the national mandate he had never gained by running for national political office. Ford had trailed Carter by 23 percentage points in the Gallup poll prior to the convention, but afterward pulled within 10 points of the Democrat, who led Ford 49 to 39 percent.

The General Election Campaign

Ford and the Republican Party took positions on important issues in the general election campaign that clearly differed from the positions of Carter and the Democrats. The parties' contrasting economic prescriptions most clearly distinguished them. The Republican platform emphasized economic growth driven by private investment. It proposed that inflation was the most important problem, and that reducing inflation was a prerequisite for reducing unemployment. The most important step toward curing inflation and increasing economic growth, it argued, was the reduction of government spending and cuts in taxes. Government, implied the Republican platform, was far more a problem than a solution, stating: "All government can do is confiscate and

redistribute wealth." In contrast, the Democrats emphasized employment and equity.

For the Democrats, economic growth could be stimulated and inflation controlled by increasing the number of jobs. Its platform dedicated the Democratic candidates "to the right of all adult Americans willing, able, and seeking work to have opportunities for useful jobs, at living wages." For Carter, this promise eventually required a commitment to a large public service jobs program establishing government as an employer of last resort, and to wage and price controls, if necessary to combat inflation. The Democratic platform, describing "the present tax structure" as "welfare for the rich," promised to make taxes more fair.

On the important issue of energy, Ford argued for minimizing government intrusion in the energy industry, and advocated the expansion of nuclear power; Carter argued for strong regulation of the energy industry, and for minimizing dependence on nuclear power. On key social issues, Carter staked out positions that were moderate, but still distinct from Ford's conservative positions. Carter favored voluntary busing for desegregation, and personally opposed abortion and federal funding of abortion; Ford favored constitutional amendments banning busing and permitted states to govern abortions. Ford was forced to defend his foreign policy generally, and specifically the role of Henry Kissinger in foreign policy. Carter attacked the administration's foreign policy from both the left and right, arguing that American foreign policy should be not only more idealistic, but also tougher on the Soviet Union.

Still relatively inexperienced in national politics, Carter's mistakes frequently put him on the defensive in the first two months of the general election campaign. Most memorably, the pious Carter granted an interview to *Playboy* magazine, in which he admitted that "I've committed adultery in my heart many times." The Ford campaign took advantage of these gaffes and Carter's naïvete to define his opponent as too liberal, too inconsistent, and too inexperienced to be president. Ford used his incum-

THE PRESIDENTIAL DEBATES

*I*ncumbents rarely find it advantageous to debate their challengers. But Gerald Ford, lagging far behind Jimmy Carter in the polls and seeking opportunities to make up ground, told the delegates to the Republican national convention that he would engage Jimmy Carter in the first presidential debates since 1960. The two campaigns enlisted the respected League of Women Voters to sponsor three presidential debates and an unprecedented debate between the vice presidential candidates. The first debate would cover domestic and economic issues; the second, defense and foreign policy; and the third would be open to any relevant subject. A panel of journalists would ask a question of one candidate, and the other could respond to his opponent's answer. The campaigns negotiated the stage setting, the rules, and candidate preparation, paying close attention to the way each decision could affect the perception of its candidate.

In the first debate, in Philadelphia, Ford placed the anxious Carter on the defensive from the start. As Carter began his final statement, the studio sound failed and the program was delayed for twenty-eight uncomfortable minutes. Opinion polls after the debate gave Ford a slight edge over Carter. It was expected that the incumbent president also would enjoy a substantial advantage over the inexperienced Carter in the second debate, which would deal exclusively with foreign affairs. In that debate, in San Francisco, Ford demonstrated a solid command of foreign policy—until a *New York Times* reporter asked whether or not the United States had tacitly agreed to Soviet dominance in Eastern Europe. Ford responded: "There is no Soviet domination of Eastern Europe and there never will be under a Ford administration." Asked to clarify, Ford responded that the Yugoslavians, Rumanians, and Poles did not "consider themselves dominated by the Soviet Union." Ford continued to defend these statements in the following days, refusing to admit a mistake until October 12. Ford's campaign had made remarkable gains since the Democratic convention; but now the president was on the defensive, and the two candidates would be essentially tied for the remainder of the campaign. In the vice presidential debate in Houston, Robert Dole aggressively criticized the Democrats, charging that all the wars of the twentieth century had been "Democrat wars." Walter Mondale's much more moderate performance made him a great asset to Carter for the rest of the campaign. Guarding against another gaffe, both Ford and Carter answered questions very cautiously during their final debate in Williamsburg, Virginia.

bency to full effect. Until October, he imitated Richard Nixon's 1972 "Rose Garden" strategy by minimizing political appearances and engaging in nonpartisan White House activities such as signing bills and receiving foreign dignitaries. In 1976, with campaign finance limited and so little-known an opponent, incumbency provided Ford the valuable extra benefit of free television exposure through coverage of presidential events.

The candidates agreed to three presidential debates and a debate between the vice presidential candidates. (See "The Presidential Debates," above.) Neither candidate decisively overshadowed the other in the debates, and Ford's effective campaign steadily cut away from Carter's lead, which fell to 6 points in

mid-October. Ford's comments on Eastern Europe in the second debate slowed the president's momentum, however, as did the resignation of Agriculture Secretary Earl Butz after the revelation that Butz had made a racist joke. In the campaign's final three weeks, the president gained support among undecided voters and wavering Republicans. The perception of a worsening economy solidified Carter's support. The final polls taken before the election indicated that the contest was too close to call, and that one out of five voters remained undecided. Among those voters who decided in the campaign's final week, Carter won a slight majority, and he won 61 percent of the voters who made their decision on election day itself. Organized labor and African-

A collage of candidate buttons from the 1976 presidential election. Democrats Jimmy Carter and Walter Mondale, pictured in the lower left, narrowly defeated Republicans Gerald Ford and Robert Dole. Note the peanut imagery, drawing attention to Carter's farming activity, and the old Model-T Ford, making a visual pun on the president's name. *(National Museum of American History)*

American organizations especially aided Carter on Election Day with grassroots voting drives. Still, the election returns were too close for the television networks to call for many hours after the polls closed on November 2.

The Election

In the predawn hours of Wednesday, November 3, the television networks declared Carter the winner. The final count of the popular vote showed that Carter had defeated Ford by 2 percent nationwide, 40,831,881 votes to 39,148,634. Carter won 297 electoral votes to 240 for Ford. The Democrat carried all of the former Confederate states except for Virginia; but, in contrast to Democratic presidential candidates prior to the Voting Rights Act of 1965, Carter depended heavily on African-American voters for the winning margin in the South. Carter also won Ohio (by 11,000 votes out of 4 million), Pennsylvania, New York, Massachusetts, and Missouri. Ford took all the western and plains states, along with Illinois, Indiana, and Michigan, and several smaller midwestern and New England states. A shift of a few thousand popular votes in key states such as Ohio would have given the election to Ford. Independent candidate Eugene McCarthy received 756,691 popular votes. Though he took less than one percent of the vote nationwide, McCarthy's votes may have reduced Carter's electoral vote margin; Ford carried Iowa, Maine, Oklahoma, and Oregon by margins that were smaller than the McCarthy vote in those states. The Libertarian Party, which had been on only two state presidential ballots in 1972, had quietly built a national presence. Libertarian candidate Roger MacBride was on the ballot in thirty-two states and received 173,011 popular votes.

Exit polls showed that the 1976 presidential election had been a very partisan contest. Carter won the votes of eight out of ten self-described Democrats, while Ford won nine out of ten Republicans. Carter won back Democrats who had abandoned the party when it nominated George McGovern in 1972. Economic distress helped Carter win back these Democrats. Votes from union households contributed to narrow Carter victories in Ohio, Pennsylvania, New York, Wisconsin, and Missouri. Carter won 83 percent of the African-American vote, but narrowly lost the votes of whites, 48 percent to 52 percent for Ford. Carter made inroads into the traditionally Republican vote in suburban, small-town, and rural areas. No gender gap was evident; for the last time in the twentieth century, each presidential candidate received the same percentage of votes from men and women. Low turnout hinted at growing general political disaffection. Less than 55 percent of voters cast presidential ballots in 1976, despite its competitiveness and unusually high turnout in the southern states for Carter, a regional candidate. Many of the non-voters expressed a desire for trustworthy leaders—an ironic sentiment, given that both Carter and Ford had appealed for the voters' trust.

The 1976 election featured many of the distinctive characteristics of presidential elections for the rest of the twentieth century. Social issues, taxes, and inflation were emerging at the top of the political agenda. Reagan's near success signified a new Republican political coalition founded on conservative positions on these issues. Reagan was changing the Republican Party by drawing together the Goldwater, Wallace, and conservative Democratic constituencies. Carter proved that the Democrats could counter conservative Republicans with moderate positions and candidates with appeal in the South and the suburbs. The primary election calendar, public campaign finance, and contribution and spending limits all restricted campaign strategy. More than ever, all facets of candidates' image and message to the media required premeditation. Taken together, these developments would do little to restore public confidence in government or inspire Americans to turn out to vote.

David Brian Robertson

Bibliography

Anderson, Patrick. *Electing Jimmy Carter: The Campaign of 1976.* Baton Rouge: Louisiana State University Press, 1994.

Blitzer, Lloyd, and Theodore Rueter. *Carter vs. Ford: The Counterfeit Debates of 1976.* Madison: University of Wisconsin Press, 1980.

Drew, Elizabeth. *American Journal: The Events of 1976.* New York: Random House, 1977.

Ford, Gerald R. *A Time to Heal: The Autobiography of Gerald R. Ford.* New York : Harper and Row, 1979.

Patterson, Thomas E. *The Mass Media Election: How Americans Choose Their President.* New York: Praeger, 1980.

Pomper, Marlene M., ed. *The Election of 1976: Reports and Interpretations.* New York: Longman, 1977.

Schram, Martin. *Running for President: A Journal of the Carter Campaign.* New York: Pocket Books, 1978.

Stroud, Kandy. *How Jimmy Won: The Victory Campaign from Plains to the White House.* New York: Morrow, 1977.

Witcover, Jules. *Marathon: The Pursuit of the Presidency, 1972–1976.* New York: Viking Press, 1977.

Wooten, James. *Dasher: The Roots and the Rising of Jimmy Carter.* New York: Summit Books, 1978.

THE VOTE: ELECTION OF 1976

State	Total No. of Electors	Total Popular Vote	Electoral Vote D	Electoral Vote R	Electoral Vote O	Margin of Victory Votes	Margin of Victory % Total Vote	Carter Democrat Votes	Carter Democrat %	Ford Republican Votes	Ford Republican %	Others Votes	Others %
Alabama	9	1,182,850	9			155,100	13.1%	659,170	55.7%	504,070	42.6%	19,610	1.7%
Alaska	3	123,574		3		27,497	22.3%	44,058	35.7%	71,555	57.9%	7,961	6.4%
Arizona	6	742,719		6		123,040	16.6%	295,602	39.8%	418,642	56.4%	28,475	3.8%
Arkansas	6	769,396	6			230,861	30.0%	499,614	64.9%	268,753	34.9%	1,029	0.1%
California	45	7,867,117		45		139,960	1.8%	3,742,284	47.6%	3,882,244	49.3%	242,589	3.1%
Colorado	7	1,081,135		7		124,014	11.5%	460,353	42.6%	584,367	54.1%	36,415	3.4%
Connecticut	8	1,381,526		8		71,366	5.2%	647,895	46.9%	719,261	52.1%	14,370	1.0%
Delaware	3	235,834	3			12,765	5.4%	122,596	52.0%	109,831	46.6%	3,407	1.4%
District of Columbia	3	168,830	3			109,945	65.1%	137,818	81.6%	27,873	16.5%	3,139	1.9%
Florida	17	3,150,631	17			166,469	5.3%	1,636,000	51.9%	1,469,531	46.6%	45,100	1.4%
Georgia	12	1,467,458	12			495,666	33.8%	979,409	66.7%	483,743	33.0%	4,306	0.3%
Hawaii	4	291,301	4			7,372	2.5%	147,375	50.6%	140,003	48.1%	3,923	1.3%
Idaho	4	340,932		4		77,602	22.8%	126,549	37.1%	204,151	59.9%	10,232	3.0%
Illinois	26	4,718,833		26		92,974	2.0%	2,271,295	48.1%	2,364,269	50.1%	83,269	1.8%
Indiana	13	2,220,362		13		169,244	7.6%	1,014,714	45.7%	1,183,958	53.3%	21,690	1.0%
Iowa	8	1,279,306		8		12,932	1.0%	619,931	48.5%	632,863	49.5%	26,512	2.1%
Kansas	7	957,845		7		72,331	7.6%	430,421	44.9%	502,752	52.5%	24,672	2.6%
Kentucky	9	1,167,142	9			83,865	7.2%	615,717	52.8%	531,852	45.6%	19,573	1.7%
Louisiana	10	1,278,439	10			73,919	5.8%	661,365	51.7%	587,446	46.0%	29,628	2.3%
Maine	4	482,968		4		4,041	0.8%	232,279	48.1%	236,320	48.9%	14,369	3.0%
Maryland	10	1,432,273	10			86,951	6.1%	759,612	53.0%	672,661	47.0%	0	0.0%
Massachusetts	14	2,547,558	14			399,199	15.7%	1,429,475	56.1%	1,030,276	40.4%	87,807	3.4%
Michigan	21	3,653,749		21		197,028	5.4%	1,696,714	46.4%	1,893,742	51.8%	63,293	1.7%
Minnesota	10	1,949,931	10			251,045	12.9%	1,070,440	54.9%	819,395	42.0%	60,096	3.1%
Mississippi	7	769,360	7			14,463	1.9%	381,309	49.6%	366,846	47.7%	21,205	2.8%
Missouri	12	1,953,600	12			70,944	3.6%	998,387	51.1%	927,443	47.5%	27,770	1.4%
Montana	4	328,734		4		24,444	7.4%	149,259	45.4%	173,703	52.8%	5,772	1.8%
Nebraska	5	607,668		5		126,013	20.7%	233,692	38.5%	359,705	59.2%	14,271	2.3%
Nevada	3	201,876		3		8,794	4.4%	92,479	45.8%	101,273	50.2%	8,124	4.0%
New Hampshire	4	339,618		4		38,300	11.3%	147,635	43.5%	185,935	54.7%	6,048	1.8%
New Jersey	17	3,014,472		17		65,035	2.2%	1,444,653	47.9%	1,509,688	50.1%	60,131	2.0%
New Mexico	4	416,590		4		10,271	2.5%	201,148	48.3%	211,419	50.7%	4,023	1.0%
New York	41	6,525,225	41			288,767	4.4%	3,389,558	51.9%	3,100,791	47.5%	34,876	0.5%
North Carolina	13	1,677,906	13			185,405	11.0%	927,365	55.3%	741,960	44.2%	8,581	0.5%
North Dakota	3	297,094		3		17,392	5.9%	136,078	45.8%	153,470	51.7%	7,546	2.5%
Ohio	25	4,111,873	25			11,116	0.3%	2,011,621	48.9%	2,000,505	48.7%	99,747	2.4%
Oklahoma	8	1,092,251		8		13,266	1.2%	532,442	48.7%	545,708	50.0%	14,101	1.3%
Oregon	6	1,029,876		6		1,713	0.2%	490,407	47.6%	492,120	47.8%	47,349	4.6%
Pennsylvania	27	4,620,787	27			123,073	2.7%	2,328,677	50.4%	2,205,604	47.7%	86,506	1.9%
Rhode Island	4	411,170	4			46,387	11.3%	227,636	55.4%	181,249	44.1%	2,285	0.6%
South Carolina	8	802,594	8			104,685	13.0%	450,825	56.2%	346,140	43.1%	5,629	0.7%
South Dakota	4	300,678		4		4,437	1.5%	147,068	48.9%	151,505	50.4%	2,105	0.7%
Tennessee	10	1,476,346	10			191,910	13.0%	825,879	55.9%	633,969	42.9%	16,498	1.1%
Texas	26	4,071,884	26			129,019	3.2%	2,082,319	51.1%	1,953,300	48.0%	36,265	0.9%
Utah	4	541,198		4		155,798	28.8%	182,110	33.6%	337,908	62.4%	21,180	3.9%
Vermont	3	187,855		3		21,041	11.2%	81,044	43.1%	102,085	54.3%	4,726	2.5%
Virginia	12	1,697,094		12		22,658	1.3%	813,896	48.0%	836,554	49.3%	46,644	2.7%
Washington	9	1,555,534		8	1[a]	60,409	3.9%	717,323	46.1%	777,732	50.0%	60,479	3.9%
West Virginia	6	750,674	6			121,154	16.1%	435,914	58.1%	314,760	41.9%	0	0.0%
Wisconsin	11	2,101,336	11			35,245	1.7%	1,040,232	49.5%	1,004,987	47.8%	56,117	2.7%
Wyoming	3	156,343		3		30,478	19.5%	62,239	39.8%	92,717	59.3%	1,387	0.9%
TOTAL	538	81,531,345	297	240	1	1,683,247	2.1%	40,831,881	50.1%	39,148,634	48.0%	1,550,830	1.9%

[a] A Ford elector in Washington voted for Ronald Reagan.

For sources, see p. 1132.

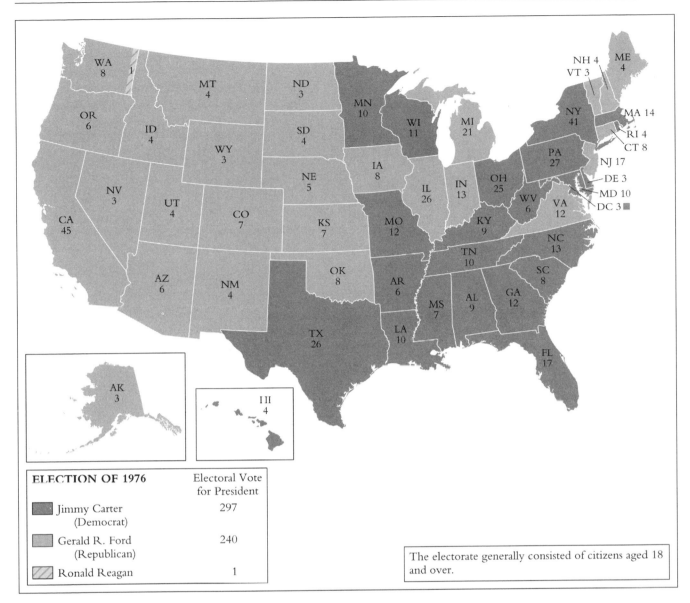

ELECTION OF 1976 — Electoral Vote for President

		Electoral Vote for President
	Jimmy Carter (Democrat)	297
	Gerald R. Ford (Republican)	240
	Ronald Reagan	1

The electorate generally consisted of citizens aged 18 and over.

DOCUMENTS: ELECTION OF 1976

After the Watergate scandal forced Richard M. Nixon to resign, Americans looked to candidates untainted by Washington. Gerald R. Ford, a long-time congressman from Michigan, had become the first non-elected president in American history. (He had been appointed vice president after Spiro Agnew resigned in 1973, and became president when Nixon resigned.) Ford had no involvement in the Watergate break-in or cover-up, but his pardon of Nixon shortly after assuming office, Document 1, hurt his popularity and led to challenges within the Republican Party for the presidential nomination.

Ronald W. Reagan, the former governor of California, posed a serious challenge to Ford. In Document 2, a speech entitled, "To Restore America," Reagan positioned himself as the conservative alternative and Wash-

ington outsider, promising to curb government spending and restore pride in American foreign policy. Reagan piled up primary victories, but lost the support of key conservatives at the convention by naming a moderate, Senator Richard Schweiker of Pennsylvania, as his proposed running mate. Ford won the nomination by a narrow 1,187-to-1,070 vote. In his speech accepting the Republican nomination, Document 3, Ford criticized the Congress (controlled by the Democrats) and declared that he needed an electoral mandate to force the Democrats to enact his programs. However, he found himself more than 20 percentage points behind his Democratic challenger, Jimmy Carter, in the polls.

Democrats realized that Watergate and Republican disunity offered them a great opportunity to regain the White House. After a scramble for the party's nomination, the former governor of Georgia, James Earl Carter, earned the nod. "Jimmy" Carter, as everyone called the peanut farmer, was moderate, southern, Christian (a devout Baptist), and a Washington outsider; he unified the Democrats after more than a decade of party divisions. Document 4, Congresswoman Barbara Jordan's keynote address at the Democratic convention, stressed unity of purpose among Democrats to clean up government and use it for the "common good." In his speech accepting the Democratic nomination, Document 5, Carter promised honesty and hard work to help all Americans live in a nation that upheld the principles of the Constitution and provided a decent life.

Down in the polls, Ford became the first president to propose debating his opponent. In the first major-ticket debates since 1960, the candidates met four times in three presidential and one vice presidential debates. Document 6, excerpts from the second and third presidential debates, offered two memorable moments. The first was Ford's mistake in declaring that there was no Soviet domination in Eastern Europe. Then, there was Carter's attempt to explain why he chose Playboy *magazine as a forum to reveal that he had looked upon women with lust in his heart. Ford closed the gap, but in the end Carter held on to win a narrow victory.*

Document 1

Gerald Ford's Pardon of Nixon, September 8, 1974

I have come to a decision which I felt I should tell you and all of my fellow American citizens, as soon as I was certain in my own mind and in my own conscience that it is the right thing to do. . . .

After years of bitter controversy and divisive national debate, I have been advised and I am compelled to conclude that many months and perhaps more years will have to pass before Richard Nixon could obtain a fair trial by jury in any jurisdiction of the United States under governing decisions of the Supreme Court. I deeply believe in equal justice for all Americans, whatever their station or former station. . . .

But it is not the ultimate fate of Richard Nixon that most concerns me, though surely it deeply troubles every decent and every compassionate person. My concern is the immediate future of this great country. . . . My conscience tells me it is my duty not merely to proclaim domestic tranquility but to use every means that I have to ensure it.

I do believe that the buck stops here, that I cannot rely upon public opinion polls to tell me what is right. . . . I feel that Richard Nixon and his loved ones have suffered enough and will continue to suffer no matter what I do, no

matter what we as a great and good nation can do together to make his goal of peace come true.

Now, therefore, I, Gerald R. Ford, president of the United States, pursuant to the pardon power conferred upon me by Article II, Section 2, of the Constitution, have granted and by these presents do grant a full, free, and absolute pardon unto Richard Nixon for all offenses against the United States which he, Richard Nixon, has committed or may have committed or taken part in during the period from July [January] 20, 1969, through August 9, 1974. . . .

Source: Public Papers and Addresses of the Presidents of the United States: Gerald R. Ford, August 9 to December 31, 1974 (Washington, DC: Government Printing Office, 1975).

Document 2

"To Restore America," Speech by Ronald Reagan, March 31, 1976

I'm a candidate for the Republican nomination for president. But I hope that you who are Independents and Democrats will let me talk to you also tonight because the problems facing our country are problems that just don't bear any party label. . . .

Inflation is the cause of recession and unemployment. And we're not going to have real prosperity or recovery until we stop fighting the symptoms and start fighting the disease. There's only one cause for inflation: government spending more than government takes in. The cure is a balanced budget. . . .

Now, let's look at Social Security. Mr. Ford says he wants to "preserve the integrity of Social Security." Well, I differ with him on one word. I would like to restore the integrity of Social Security. Those who depend on it see a continual reduction in their standard of living. Inflation strips the increase in their benefits. . . .

Before leaving this subject of our economic problems, let's talk about unemployment. Ending inflation is the only long range and lasting answer to the problem of unemployment. The Washington Establishment is not the answer. It's the problem. Its tax policies, its harassing regulation, its confiscation of investment capital to pay for its deficits keeps business and industry from expanding to meet your needs and to provide the jobs we all need. . . .

An effort has been made in this campaign to suggest that there aren't any real differences between Mr. Ford and myself. Well, I believe there are, and these differences are fundamental. . . . Mr. Ford was a Congressman for 25 years. His concern, of necessity, was the welfare of his congressional district. For most of his adult life he has been a part of the Washington Establishment. Most of my adult life has been spent outside of government. My experience in government was the eight years I served as governor of California. If it were a nation, California would be the 7th-ranking economic power in the world today. . . .

I believe that what we did in California can be done in Washington, if government will have faith in the people and let them bring their common sense to bear on the problems bureaucracy hasn't solved. I believe in the people. Now, Mr. Ford places his faith in the Washington Establishment. . . .

"Wandering without aim" describes the United States's foreign policy. . . .

Mr. Ford says détente will be replaced by "peace through strength." Well now, that slogan has a nice ring to it, but neither Mr. Ford nor his new Secretary of Defense will say that our strength is superior to all others. . . .

The Soviet Army outnumbers ours more than two-to-one and in reserves four-to-one. They out-spend us on weapons by 50 percent. Their Navy outnumbers ours in surface ships and submarines two-to-one. We're out-gunned in artillery three-to-one and their tanks outnumber ours four-to-one. Their strategic nuclear missiles are larger, more powerful and more numerous than ours. The evidence mounts that we are Number Two in a world where it's dangerous, if not fatal, to be second best. Is this why Mr. Ford refused to invite Alexander Solzhenitsyn to the White House? Or, why Mr. Ford traveled halfway 'round the world to sign the Helsinki Pact, putting our stamp of approval on Russia's enslavement of the captive nations? We gave away the freedom of millions of people, freedom that was not ours to give. . . .

Why should we become frightened? No people who have ever lived on this earth have fought harder, paid a higher price for freedom, or done more to advance the dignity of man than the Americans living in this land today. There isn't any problem we can't solve if government will give us the facts. Tell us what needs to be done. Then, get out of the way and let us have at it. . . .

I would like to go to Washington. I would like to be president, because I would like to see this country become once again a country where a little six-year old girl can grow up knowing the same freedom that I knew when I was six years old, growing up in America. If this is the America you want for yourself and your children; if you want to restore government not only of and for but by the people; to see the American spirit unleashed once again; to make this land a shining, golden hope God intended it to be. . . .

Source: American Experience Web site, www.pbs.org/wgbh/amex/presidents/nf/resource/reagan/prindocs/restore.html.

Document 3

Gerald Ford's Speech Accepting the Republican Nomination, August 19, 1976

Something wonderful happened to this country of ours the past two years. We all came to realize it on the Fourth of July. Together, out of years of turmoil and tragedy, wars and riots, assassinations and wrongdoing in high places, Americans recaptured the spirit of 1776. We saw again the pioneer vision of our revolutionary founders and our immigrant ancestors. Their vision was of free men and free women enjoying limited government and unlimited opportunity. The mandate I want in 1976 is to make this vision a reality, but it will take the voices and the votes of many more Americans who are not Republicans to make that mandate binding and my mission possible. . . .

For two years I have stood for all the people against a vote-hungry, free-spending congressional majority on Capitol Hill. Fifty-five times I vetoed extravagant and unwise legislation; 45 times I made those vetoes stick. Those vetoes have saved American taxpayers billions and billions of dollars. I am against the big tax spender and for the little taxpayer.

I called for a permanent tax cut, coupled with spending reductions, to stimulate the economy and relieve hard-pressed, middle-income taxpayers. . . . But there is one big problem—their own Congress won't act.

I called for reasonable constitutional restrictions on court-ordered busing of schoolchildren. . . . Congress won't act.

I called for a major overhaul of criminal laws to crack down on crime and illegal drugs. . . . Congress won't act.

The other party's platform talks about a strong defense. Now, here is the other side of the problem—their own Congress did act. They slashed $50 billion from our national defense needs in the last 10 years.

My friends, Washington is not the problem; their Congress is the problem.

You know, the President of the United States is not a magician who can wave a wand or sign a paper that will instantly end a war, cure a recession, or make bureaucracy disappear. A President has immense powers under the Constitution, but all of them ultimately come from the American people and their mandate to him. That is why, tonight, I turn to the American people and ask not only for your prayers, but also for your strength and your support, for your voice, and for your vote.

I come before you with a two-year record of performance without your mandate. I offer you a four-year pledge of greater performance with your mandate. . . .

We will continue winning the fight against inflation. We will go on reducing the dead weight and impudence of bureaucracy.

We will submit a balanced budget by 1978.

We will improve the quality of life at work, at play, and in our homes and in our neighborhoods. We will not abandon our cities. We will encourage urban programs which assure safety in the streets, create healthy environments, and restore neighborhood pride. We will return control of our children's education to parents and local school authorities.

We will make sure that the party of Lincoln remains the party of equal rights.

We will create a tax structure that is fair for all our citizens, one that preserves the continuity of the family home, the family farm, and the family business.

We will ensure the integrity of the Social Security system and improve Medicare so that our older citizens can enjoy the health and the happiness that they have earned. There is no reason they should have to go broke just to get well.

We will make sure that this rich Nation does not neglect citizens who are less fortunate, but provides for their needs with compassion and with dignity.

We will reduce the growth and the cost of government and allow individual breadwinners and businesses to keep more of the money that they earn.

We will create a climate in which our economy will provide a meaningful job for everyone who wants to work and a decent standard of life for all Americans. We will ensure that all of our young people have a better chance in life than we had, an education they can use, and a career they can be proud of.

We will carry out a farm policy that assures a fair market price for the farmer, encourages full production, leads to record exports, and eases the hunger within the human family. We will never use the bounty of America's farmers as a pawn in international diplomacy. There will be no embargoes.

We will continue our strong leadership to bring peace, justice, and economic progress where there is turmoil, especially in the Middle East. We will build a safer and saner world through patient negotiations and dependable arms agreements which reduce the danger of conflict and horror of thermonuclear war. While I am President, we will not return to a collision course that could reduce civilization to ashes.

We will build an America where people feel rich in spirit as well as in worldly goods. We will build an America where people feel proud about themselves and about their country.

We will build on performance, not promises; experience, not expediency; real progress instead of mysterious plans to be revealed in some dim and distant future. The American people are wise, wiser than our opponents think. They know who pays for every campaign promise. They are not afraid of the truth. We will tell them the truth.

From start to finish, our campaign will be credible; it will be responsible. We will come out fighting, and we will win. . . .

God helping me, I won't let you down.

Source: Public Papers and Addresses of the Presidents of the United States: Gerald R. Ford, August 9 to December 31, 1974 (Washington, DC: Government Printing Office, 1975).

Document 4

"Who Then Will Speak for the Common Good?"
Democratic Convention Keynote Address by Representative Barbara Jordan, July 12, 1976

One hundred and forty-four years ago, members of the Democratic Party first met in convention to select a Presidential candidate. . . .

A lot of years passed since 1832, and during that time it would have been most unusual for any national political party to ask that a Barbara Jordan deliver a keynote address. . . . But tonight here I am. And I feel that, notwithstanding the past, that my presence here is one additional bit of evidence that the American Dream need not forever be deferred. . . .

Many fear the future. Many are distrustful of their leaders, and believe that their voices are never heard. Many seek only to satisfy their private work wants. To satisfy private interests.

But this is the great danger America faces. That we will cease to be one nation and become instead a collection of interest groups: city against suburb, region against region, individual against individual. Each seeking to satisfy private wants.

If that happens, who then will speak for America?

Who then will speak for the common good?

This is the question which must be answered in 1976....

As a first step, We must restore our belief in ourselves....

A nation is formed by the willingness of each of us to share in the responsibility for upholding the common good.

A government is invigorated when each of us is willing to participate in shaping the future of this nation....

Let each person do his or her part. If one citizen is unwilling to participate, all of us are going to suffer....

What are those of us who are elected public officials supposed to do? . . . More is required of public officials than slogans and handshakes and press releases....

If we promise as public officials, we must deliver. If we as public officials propose, we must produce. If we say to the American people, it is time for you to be sacrificial, sacrifice. If the public official says that, we [public officials] must be the first to give, we must be. And again, if we make mistakes, we must be willing to admit them....

Let there be no illusions about the difficulty of forming this kind of a national community. It's tough, difficult, not easy. But a spirit of harmony will survive in America only if each of us remembers that we share a common destiny....

Source: Gifts of Speech Web site, http://gos.sbc.edu/j/jordan1.html.

Document 5

Jimmy Carter's Nomination Acceptance Speech, July 15, 1976

My name is Jimmy Carter and I'm running for President....

During this election year, we candidates will ask you for your vote. And from us will be demanded our vision. My vision of this nation and its future has been deepened and matured during the 19 months that I campaigned among you for President. I've never had more faith in America than I do today. We have an America that, in Bob Dylan's phrase, is busy being born, not busy dying.

We CAN have an American Government that has turned away from scandal and corruption and official cynicism and is once again as decent and competent as our people.

We CAN have an America that has reconciled its economic needs with its desire for an environment that we can pass on with pride to the next generation.

We CAN have an America that provides excellence in education for my child and your child and every child.

We CAN have an America that encourages and takes pride in our ethnic diversity, our religious diversity, our cultural diversity, knowing that out of our pluralistic heritage has come the strength and vitality and creativity that has made us great and will keep us great.

We CAN have an American government that does not oppress or spy on its own people.

But respect our dignity and our privacy and our right to be left alone.

We can have an America where freedom on the one hand and equality on the other hand are mutually supported and not in conflict, and where the dreams of our nation's first leaders are fully realized in our day and age.

And we can have an America which harnesses the idealism of the student, the compassion of the nurse or the social worker, the determination of a farmer, the wisdom of a teacher, the practicality of the business leader, the experience of the senior citizen and the hope of the laborer to build life for us all—and we can have and we're going to have it.

As I've said many times before, we can have an American President who does not govern with negativism and fear for the future, but with vigor and vision and aggressive leadership, a President who's not isolated from the people, but who feels your pain and shares your dreams and takes his strength and his wisdom and his courage from you.

I see an America on the move again, united, a diverse and vital and tolerant nation, entering our third century with pride and confidence, an America that lives up to the majesty of our Constitution and the simple decency of our people.

This is the America we want.

This is the America that we will have.

We will go forward from this convention with some differences of opinion, perhaps, but nevertheless, united in our calm determination to make our country large and driving and generous in spirit once again; ready to embark on great national deeds and, once again as brothers and sisters, our hearts will swell with pride to call ourselves Americans.

Source: "Carter's Acceptance Speech," *New York Times*, July 16, 1976.

Document 6.
Excerpts from Carter-Ford Presidential Debates

Second Presidential Debate, October 6, 1976

MAX FRANKEL: Mr. President, I'd like to explore a little more deeply our relationship with the Russians. . . . We've recognized the permanent Communist regime in East Germany. We've virtually signed, in Helsinki, an agreement that the Russians have dominance in Eastern Europe. . . .

FORD: There is no Soviet domination of Eastern Europe and there never will be under a Ford administration....

FRANKEL: I'm sorry, I—could I just follow—did I understand you to say, sir, that the Russians are not using Eastern Europe as their own sphere of influence in occupying mo—most of the countries there and in—and making sure with their troops that it's a—that it's a Communist zone? . . .

FORD: I don't believe—Mr. Frankel that—the Yugoslavians consider themselves dominated by the Soviet Union. I don't believe that the Rumanians consider themselves dominated by the Soviet Union. I don't believe that the Poles consider themselves dominated by the Soviet Union. Each of those countries is independent, autonomous: it has its own territorial integrity and the United States does not concede that those countries are under the domination of the Soviet Union. As a matter of fact, I visited Poland, Yugoslavia and Rumania to make certain that the people of those countries understood that the president of the United States and the people of the United—are dedicated to their independence, their autonomy and their freedom.

PAULINE FREDERICK: Governor Carter, may I have your response?

CARTER: (chuckle) I would like to see Mr. Ford convince the Polish-Americans and the Czech-Americans and the Hungarian-Americans in this country that those countries don't live under the domination and supervision of the Soviet Union behind the Iron Curtain. . . .

Third Presidential Debate, October 22, 1976

ROBERT MAYNARD: Governor, by all indications, the voters are so turned off by this election campaign so far that only half intend to vote. One major reason for this apathetic electorate appears to be the low level at which this campaign has been conducted. It has digressed frequently from important issues into allegations of blunder and brainwashing and fixations on lust and *Playboy*. What responsibility do you accept for the low level of this campaign for the nation's highest office?

CARTER: I've made some mistakes. And I think this is—part of—of just being a human being. I—I have to say that my campaign has been an open one. And—the *Playboy* thing has been of great—very great concern to me. I don't know how to deal with it exactly. I—agreed to give the interview—to *Playboy*. Other people have done it who are notable—Governor Jerry Brown—Walter Cronkite—Albert Schweitzer, Mr. Ford's own secretary of the treasury, Mr. Simon—William Buckley—many other people. But they weren't running for president, and in retrospect, from hindsight, I would not have given that—interview had I do it—had it—I to do it over again. If I should ever decide in the future to discuss my deep Christian beliefs and—condemnation and sinfulness, I'll use another forum besides *Playboy*.

Source: Gerald R. Ford Library and Museum Web site, www.ford.utexas.edu/library/speeches.htm.

THE ELECTION OF
1980

Every presidential election has unique aspects, yet a few contests possess special distinctiveness. This is the case with the election of 1980, which had three unusual features. First, President Jimmy Carter (see fact box, p. 926), was defeated in his bid for reelection. Although four other sitting presidents suffered a similar fate in the twentieth century, incumbents usually possess unbeatable advantages. Second, events drove presidential politics in 1980 more than is customary in the United States. To a large extent, all candidates are captive to circumstances beyond their control; yet a combination of events were particularly influential in the outcome of the 1980 race. And third, Ronald Reagan, the Republican challenger, won the election as much by default as by attracting voters to his conservative views. But Reagan's election provided a springboard for his sponsorship of a conservative turn in federal policy.

United States Decline in the 1970s

America of the 1970s was awash in bad news that undermined public confidence in the nation's leaders. The Vietnam War, which had divided Americans since the mid-1960s, reached a conclusion in 1973 when the United States unceremoniously abandoned Indochina. That same year, the Organization of Petroleum Exporting Countries (OPEC) embargoed petroleum shipments to the United States, causing gasoline prices to nearly double within a year and ending the country's tradition of cheap fuel. In 1974,

the Watergate scandal led to the resignation of President Richard Nixon. New York City went broke in 1975, requiring a financial bailout from the state government. In 1979, an accident at the Three Mile Island power plant in Pennsylvania spread panic about nuclear radiation. But the banner event of that year occurred in Iran, where Islamic radicals stormed the American embassy in Tehran and seized sixty-six people. The following year, President Jimmy Carter ordered a boycott of American participation in the Olympic Games in Moscow to protest the Russian invasion of Afghanistan. Few Americans could remember such a rash of bad news happening within such a brief time.

The economy was another source of trouble. The 1973 oil embargo caused an abrupt upward spike in consumer prices, unsettling economic calculations. A severe economic recession in 1975 and 1976 appeared to bring inflation under control; but a second oil crisis, triggered by the revolution in Iran, reignited inflation in 1979. The price of a gallon of gasoline doubled between 1977 and 1979. By 1980, the cost of oil on the world market was ten times higher than in 1973. Prices for consumer goods, from a loaf of bread to the purchase of a home, leapt higher. Economic conditions seemed out of control in early 1980, when inflation hit an annualized rate of 18 percent. During the year, unemployment edged up to an unacceptable level, the economy's rate of growth slowed perceptively, and incomes actually fell by an average of 5 percent. Commentators observed that the economy was wallowing in its bleakest period since the Great Depression.

CHRONOLOGY

1978

MARCH 16   Panama Canal Treaty ratified; U.S. relinquishes Canal Zone.

JUNE 6   California voters adopt Proposition 13.

1979

JANUARY 16   Shah flees Iran; second energy crisis begins.

MARCH 28   Nuclear accident shuts down Three Mile Island power plant.

JULY 15   Carter delivers "crisis of confidence" speech from Camp David.

NOVEMBER 4   Iran hostage crisis begins.

1980

JANUARY 21   Iowa party caucuses.

FEBRUARY   Inflation hits 18 percent.

FEBRUARY 12   Carter announces a boycott of the Olympic Games in Moscow.

FEBRUARY 26   New Hampshire primary.

MARCH 18   Illinois primary.

APRIL 25   Eight U.S. servicemen die in abortive hostage rescue mission.

JULY 16   Republican convention, in Detroit, nominates Reagan.

AUGUST 13   Democratic convention, in New York, nominates Carter.

OCTOBER 28   Reagan and Carter debate.

NOVEMBER 4   Reagan wins presidential election.

1981

JANUARY 20   Reagan inaugurated as president; Iran releases American hostages.

The legacy of President Lyndon Johnson's "Great Society" laid the groundwork for criticism of national politics in the 1970s. During the 1960s, government had undertaken major initiatives in civil rights and nondiscrimination policy, welfare eligibility, and legal safeguards for persons accused of a crime. The 1973 Supreme Court decision, *Roe v. Wade*, which protected a woman's right to abortion in the first trimester of pregnancy, had expanded the definition of individual privacy. Abortion and other newly articulated individual rights generated a backlash against social liberalism, particularly concerning civil rights and racial equality. Richard Nixon's 1968 and 1972 presidential victories, and George Wallace's third party challenge in 1968, benefited from this rising tide of resentment.

Carter's Presidency

Jimmy Carter's 1976 presidential victory was partially due to his ability to distance himself from Washington insiders and "Great Society" liberalism. The recession of 1975–76, lingering inflation, and the Watergate scandal also helped propel him into the White House. Although his electoral margin was thin, Carter seemed just what the times demanded. He was a moralist who pledged not to "lie" to the American people, a clear dig at Nixon's cover-up of the Republican break-in at the Democratic headquarters at the Watergate complex. He was a graduate of the Naval Academy at Annapolis with a degree in engineering, who had worked on nuclear submarines during his time in the Navy. He personally opposed abortion and the busing of children to achieve the racial integration of schools, two hot-button social issues. On budgetary matters, he was a moderate with conservative leanings. The ticket had been balanced with Walter Mondale (see fact box, p. 927), a liberal senator from Minnesota.

Despite these attributes, Carter was unable to capture the affection of most Americans, largely because he failed to solve the country's most pressing problems. The "outsider" motif, which had helped him win the White House, worked against the development of a rapport with Congress. Lacking the knack of compromise, he became ensnared between the liberal wing of the Democratic Party, led by Senator Edward Kennedy of Massachusetts, who defended social programs, and the conservative Republicans, who demanded less spending and less government regulation. When both parties agreed, such as on the deregulation of trucks, airlines, and banks, legislation resulted. But Carter experienced difficulty producing a budget that satisfied all factions, as well as an acceptable energy policy.

Carter's failures were compounded by the public's declining confidence in government. Pollsters recorded a steady increase in the proportion of people who thought that "government can not be trusted." In 1968, the figure stood at 36 percent; by 1980, it had grown to 73 percent. This dissatisfaction was linked to people's belief that government was inefficient and that taxes were unfair. Such attitudes were at play in 1978, when California voters approved Proposition 13, a referendum proposal that reduced property taxes. The passage of Proposition 13 sent shock waves through the state capitals, and fanned a "budget-cutting mentality" in Congress. Inflation continued to rise, fueled by events in Iran, and appeared beyond Carter's control. Faced with festering problems, the president's approval ratings dropped.

Frustrated and perplexed, Carter retreated to Camp David, in Maryland, in July 1979, to ponder the condition of his administration. Reemerging ten days later, the president made a major address in which he said that the nation suffered from a "crisis of confidence." The country was in "paralysis and stagnation and drift" because Congress could not legislate, and because of the obstruction of "well-financed and powerful special interests." The public was largely unmoved by Carter's diagnosis and his approval rating fell further. The taking of the American hostages in Iran, in November 1979, boosted the president's popularity temporarily, as Americans rallied behind their country; but in early 1980 his rating again sagged significantly. (See "The Iran Hostage Crisis," p. 944.)

Divided Democrats

The nomination process began as the Iranian hostage crisis erupted. Normally, a president can expect an uncontested renomination. But Carter faced two Democratic opponents. Edmund ("Jerry") G. Brown, governor of California, was first to challenge the president. Brown's candidacy persuaded Senator Edward Kennedy to enter the contest. As the younger brother of President John F. Kennedy and Senator Robert Kennedy, both of whom had been assassinated in the 1960s, "Ted" Kennedy inherited the responsibility for carrying on the family's tradition of political leadership. He also was the Democrats' most vocal defender of "Great Society" liberalism. As Carter abandoned traditional Democratic commitments during the latter half of his administration, Kennedy's criticism of the presidency mounted.

The Iowa caucuses were the first major test of the candidates' popularity. Held in January 1980, citizens of the Hawkeye state signified their candidate preferences in local party meetings. Due to the advance planning of Hamilton Jordan, the president's closest political strategist, the Carter campaign was prepared for its challengers. The president's team organized early and thoroughly, both in Iowa and in other key states such as New Hampshire. The Carter administration accelerated the release of federal grant monies to states where primaries were held, and widely publicized these expenditures. Finally, the president adopted a "Rose Garden" strategy of sticking to the White House and acting "presidential" during the Iran hostage crisis.

The Kennedy camp, by contrast, was poorly organized, under-financed, and largely directionless in its first months of activity. Moreover, Kennedy continued to be haunted by the Chappaquiddick incident. After leaving a party on Chappaquiddick Island (Martha's Vineyard, Mass.) on a summer evening in 1969, Kennedy had driven a car off a bridge into the water, which led to the drowning of a female passenger. His failure to report the accident for twenty-four hours left a residue of unanswered questions about the senator's behavior that long clouded his career. Kennedy's befuddled campaign and personal difficulties

THE IRAN HOSTAGE CRISIS

*C*hanting "Death to the Shah! Death to Carter! Death to America!" radical Islamic students seized the United States Embassy in Tehran, Iran, on November 4, 1979, and took sixty-six diplomatic personnel and visitors hostage. The crisis would drag on for 444 days, until a settlement between Iran and the United States was reached that freed the hostages on January 20, 1981 (the day of Reagan's inauguration as president). The background of the conflict was America's long support for the Shah of Iran, who had ruled his country since 1941. Discontent with the Shah's Westernization and his brutal police state had swelled during the 1970s, when Iranian-American ties were strengthened. This opposition benefited the Muslim clergy, who sought to establish a religious state and sever ties with the United States, partly to rid Iran of western cultural influences. A revolution in 1979 thrust the Ayatollah Khomeini, a Muslim religious leader who returned from exile, into power as Iran's effective leader. The Shah fled the country on January 16, 1979, and later entered the United States for treatment of lymphatic cancer. Two weeks later, the militants stormed the U.S. embassy and demanded the return of the Shah.

The Iranian hostage crisis lingered as an irritant for the Carter administration for the duration of the presidential campaign. Public figures, including Democrat Edward Kennedy, criticized the president's inability to resolve the situation. Ultimately, the crisis hurt Carter's bid for reelection in 1980; but, in the short run, the president benefited from it. His approval rating had slipped to 29 percent by November 1, 1979, three months after Carter delivered his "crisis of confidence" speech, which had addressed the problems of inflation and high gasoline prices. The hostage affair produced a rapid rebound in the president's positive rating over the next months, as the first round of presidential primaries unfolded.

Instead of actively campaigning, President Carter adopted a "Rose Garden" strategy that kept him in the White House, purportedly so he could supervise hostage negotiations. During the early months of 1980, Carter beat Kennedy in the Iowa caucuses and in the New Hampshire primary, and thus critically hindered his chief rival for the nomination. But snags in negotiations—plus an abortive military rescue mission in April that left eight American servicemen dead from an aircraft accident in the Iran desert—helped reverse the president's fortunes. By August 1980, Carter's disapproval rating was twice as large as his approval score.

Carter's failed diplomacy reinforced Ronald Reagan's charge that America's military was weak. Reagan's campaign staff was paranoid about an "October surprise." This scenario envisioned the president receiving a boost in his rating sufficient to capture the election by freeing the hostages. But it never happened. Instead Reagan, not Carter, reaped the electoral benefits from the hostage crisis.

hurt his effort in Iowa, where he lost to Carter, 59 to 31 percent. The president's momentum continued into first general primary, held in New Hampshire. Carter prevailed there, 47 to 37 percent, beating Kennedy in the senator's backyard. Brown, who was better known for dating pop singer Linda Ronstadt than for his political views, finished out of the running and soon dropped out of the race.

Victory in New Hampshire usually sets the tone for the remainder of the campaign season, for the winner gains increased press exposure and a boost in ability to raise campaign funds. Strangely, however, Kennedy's falling star did not totally expire. Rather, it gained new life. He went on to win the important New York primary in March, the Pennsylvania primary in April, and the California primary in June. During these months, inflation shot up significantly and a military mission to rescue the hostages flopped. Although Kennedy's primary campaign finished with a flurry, Carter was able to win in Florida (March 11), Illinois (March 16), and Texas (May 3). When the thirty-four Democratic primaries were concluded,

President Jimmy Carter, the Democratic candidate for president, acknowledges the cheers of supporters at a rally in Texarkana, Texas, on October 23, 1980. Beside him stands Bill Clinton, the youthful governor of Arkansas and future president of the United States. *(AP Wide World Photos)*

RONALD WILSON REAGAN

PARTY: Republican

DATE OF BIRTH: February 6, 1911

PLACE OF BIRTH: Tampico, Illinois

PARENTS: John Edward and Nellie Wilson Reagan

EDUCATION: B.A. in economics, Eureka College, 1932

FAMILY: Married Jane Wyman, 1940 (divorced, 1948); children: Maureen Elizabeth and Michael Edward; married Nancy Davis, 1952; children: Patricia Ann and Ronald Prescott

MILITARY SERVICE: U.S. Army Air Corp, captain, 1942–45

CAREER: Radio announcer; movie actor; elected president of Screen Actors Guild, 1947–52, 1959; television host of *General Electric Theater*, 1954–62; governor of California, 1967–75; U.S. president, 1981–89

Carter had accumulated enough delegates to win renomination. Hoping for a miracle, Kennedy sought to have delegates released from their primary commitments at the party's convention in New York, but Carter's forces rebuffed the gambit. Democratic delegates gave Carter 2,129 votes, while Kennedy received 1,146. Besides renominating the president, the convention kept Vice President Walter Mondale as Carter's running mate.

Rise of Reagan

Republicans faced a crowded field of presidential aspirants. They included congressman Philip Crane, a history professor and right-wing conservative from Illinois. Robert Dole, a senator from Kansas, had run as Gerald Ford's vice presidential candidate in 1976. Howard Baker of Tennessee was the minority leader in the Senate. John Anderson, a lawyer and congressman from northern Illinois, was the most liberal of the Republicans chasing the nomination. These four were joined by John Connolly, the former governor of Texas and secretary of the treasury under President Richard Nixon. Connolly spent $11 million on his presidential bid, but bagged only one delegate. Former president Gerald Ford let it be known that he would accept a draft by the convention, but did not actively pursue the nomination. George H.W. Bush (father of George W. Bush, the forty-third president), represented the party's moderate wing. Bush had a varied political career that included the oil business in Texas, election to the House of Representatives from Texas, U.S. ambassador to the United Nations under President Nixon, and director of the Central Intelligence Agency under President Ford. A Yale graduate with New England roots and a father who had been a senator from Connecticut, Bush was viewed as a scion of the northeastern elite.

All of these contestants ran in the shadow of Ronald Reagan. He was not only the most popular Republican candidate in 1980, but at 69, also the oldest. Reagan had an unconventional career for a man aspiring to the country's highest office. After graduating from Eureka College in Illinois, he broadcast baseball games in Iowa, and then became a movie actor in Hollywood. Although he never reached the top echelon of screen stars, he did win the presidency of the Screen Actors Guild, a position that provided practical lessons in politics. Reagan honed his political thinking during the years that he hosted the *General Electric Theater* on television and traveled around the country giving speeches for the firm. In 1966, he won the governorship of California, and was reelected in 1970.

Reagan had considered running for president soon after his gubernatorial victory. By late 1976, he began to prepare for the 1980 contest. Although not without flaws, Reagan possessed two assets that made him a formidable candidate. First, his message was simple. He blamed government for the country's problems, especially its weak economy. His solution for these ills was to cut taxes and spending, and to balance the budget as well. George Bush called the proposal "voodoo economics." But Reagan persisted, repeating his mantra that bureaucracy was the enemy.

Second, Reagan knew how to perform in front of the camera. He had perfected this skill during his movie and television days, and from innumerable speaking engagements around the country. During this period, Reagan had cultivated a relaxed and sincere presence that was marvelously suited to the television era of politics, where cameras focused on every move of the frontrunners. There was one additional asset that aided the Reagan campaign: The Republican Party had drifted toward the right since 1964. Originally a Democrat, Reagan was part of this Republican movement toward conservatism.

On the advice of John Sears, his campaign manager at the time, Reagan did not campaign in Iowa. The decision was a mistake, as George Bush gathered the largest number of Iowa caucus votes. But Bush did not capitalize on his momentum, while the Reagan effort regrouped. An incident three days before the polling in the New Hampshire primary critically wounded the Bush campaign. Reagan and Bush had agreed to debate in Nashua, New Hamp-

GEORGE HERBERT WALKER BUSH

PARTY: Republican

DATE OF BIRTH: June 12, 1924

PLACE OF BIRTH: Milton, Massachusetts

PARENTS: Prescott Sheldon and Dorothy Walker Bush

EDUCATION: B.A. in economics, Yale University, 1948

FAMILY: Married Barbara Pierce, 1945; children: George W., John E., Neil M., Marvin P., and Dorothy

MILITARY SERVICE: U.S. Navy bomber pilot, lieutenant (junior grade), 1942–45

CAREER: Co-founder of Zapata Oil, in Texas (president, 1956–64; board chairman, 1964–66); U.S. House of Representatives, 1966–71; U.S. ambassador to United Nations, 1971–72; chair, Republican National Committee, 1972–73; head, U.S. Liaison Office with China, 1974; director, Central Intelligence Agency, 1975–76; U.S. vice president, 1981–89; U.S. president, 1989–93; unsuccessful candidate for president, 1992

This 1980 Ronald Reagan poster shows the candidate with his movie-actor good looks and smile. Reagan's polished Hollywood style carried over to his campaigning and allowed the candidate to be relaxed and affable in public. *(National Museum of American History)*

shire, under the auspices of the local newspaper. At the last moment, John Sears invited the other four Republican contestants to join the discussion—but he failed to inform the Bush camp. When the four showed up in the auditorium of the local high school where the event was staged, indecision reigned. Bush remained grim and silent in his chair and Jon Breen, the moderator, made no effort to include the unwelcome debaters. As Reagan reached for the microphone to explain the situation, Breen commanded a technician to turn off Reagan's microphone. Reagan reacted instantly, yelling "I paid for this show. I'm paying for this microphone...." Breen backed down, the four candidates were granted a little time for statements, and Reagan was perceived as an outraged but heroic citizen who had stood up for his colleagues.

The favorable publicity helped Reagan to rout Bush in New Hampshire. The Bush campaign never recovered, nor did the rest of the field. The Reagan machine mowed down the opposition in the southern state primaries. In March, he beat John Anderson in Illinois. The defeat in his home state persuaded the congressman that his only chance for victory was by running as an Independent candidate. By May, Reagan had the nomination sewed up, and he coasted to victory in the remaining primaries. The only mystery at the Republican convention in Detroit was Reagan's choice for vice president. In one of the most bizarre plots in recent vice presidential politics, the Reagan camp initially offered the post to Gerald Ford, the former president. But Ford wanted too much authority, a kind of co-presidency, so Reagan scotched the deal and called on Bush.

Reagan had staked out his issues well before the convention. First on his agenda was inflation, which he proposed to cure by cutting government spending. The intellectual foundation for this position came from Martin Anderson of the Hoover Institute, at Stanford University, in a policy memorandum written in August 1979. "We don't have inflation because the people are living too well," Reagan said. "We have inflation because the government is living too well." Tax reduction was a second Reagan objective; he used his nomination acceptance speech in Detroit to reiterate his support of a 30 percent cut in income taxes. In addition, he criticized deficit spending, which had produced an unbalance budget.

Reagan also expressed alarm at the Soviet Union's rapid military build-up and at the deterioration of America's defense. He charged that Carter had allowed the country's military position to erode. Reagan's solution to the energy crisis was to reduce government regulations on oil companies. He rejected Carter's advocacy of energy conservation and the implication that an "era of limits" on America's high-consumption habits was inevitable. He opposed a 50-cent-per-gallon tax on gasoline, which John Anderson had advocated as a way to reduce demand for petroleum.

The Republican platform advocated numerous family-oriented social positions, such as prayer in public schools, opposition to abortion, and less government intrusion into private affairs. Republicans wanted judges to get tough with criminals and governments to allow citizens to bear arms. Reagan agreed with these social principles, but he did not make them the centerpiece of his campaign.

The Fall Campaign

Reagan's strategists believed that the route to victory lay in attracting Democrats to the Reagan ticket. Reagan's chief pollster, Richard Wirthlin, emphasized this course and pointed out that dissatisfaction with Carter was already widespread. He urged Reagan to target white southern Democrats and the ethnic, blue-collar workers in the industrial states. Several

With matching smiles, Republicans Ronald Reagan and George Bush appealed to patriotism and optimism in 1980. *(Gyory Collection/Cathy Casriel Photo)*

This photograph depicts Republican candidate Ronald Reagan and his wife Nancy campaigning in Columbia, South Carolina, in 1980. A former actress, Nancy Reagan matched her husband's poise in her public appearances. *(Courtesy Ronald Reagan Library)*

roadblocks stood in the way of executing the plan. One obstacle was the difficulty of reorienting a campaign that had focused on an intra-party struggle in the primaries, toward a national contest against the other party. The Reagan camp stumbled in its initial attempt to make this transition. A second worry was Reagan's propensity for making verbal gaffs. Sometimes he got his facts confused and sometimes he said the first thing that came to mind in response to questions. In discussing pollution, he had confused nitrogen oxides (an industrial pollutant) with nitrous oxides, which are released by decaying organic matter. Pollution, he said, was natural. A protester at a later campaign stop put a sign on a tree that read: "Chop Me Down Before I Kill Again." The Reagan

campaign hired a specialist to travel with the candidate as a gaff-preventer.

Meanwhile Patrick Caddell, Carter's pollster, painted a bleak picture of the president's chances. Caddell's data in June 1980 showed an electorate that was distressed by the country's unresolved problems, and that lacked confidence in the president. "By and large," Caddell's memo to the president concluded, "the American people did not like Jimmy Carter." Needing a dramatic countermove, Carter abandoned his "Rose Garden" strategy and came out swinging, calling Reagan incompetent and dangerous. The president implied that Reagan was trigger-happy and likely to snag the country in war, perhaps involving nuclear weapons. Carter also insinuated that Reagan

Cartoonists found much to criticize in the two candidates. One button mocks the competence of President Jimmy Carter by comparing him to the Marx Brothers, the zany comedy team of the 1930s. The other button questions the trustworthiness of his Republican challenger, Ronald Reagan, a former movie actor. *(Gyory Collection/Cathy Casriel Photo)*

was a racist and that he would deny welfare benefits to the poor. The press called this strategy Carter's "meanness phase." The new aggressive style seemed out of context for a man who had been a Sunday school teacher and was deeply religious. Perhaps it was Carter's way of compensating for his lack of dramatic rhetorical style. Yet the tactic worked. By mid-October, Reagan's competency rating with voters had slipped.

JOHN BAYARD ANDERSON

PARTY: Republican; Independent

DATE OF BIRTH: February 15, 1922

PLACE OF BIRTH: Rockford, Illinois

PARENTS: E. Albin and Martha Edna Ring Anderson

EDUCATION: B.A. in political science, University of Illinois, 1942; J.D., University of Illinois College of Law, 1946; LL.M., Harvard Law School, 1949

FAMILY: Married Keke Machakos, 1953; children: Eleanora, John B. Jr., Karen Beth, and Susan Kimberly

MILITARY SERVICE: U.S. Army, field artilleryman, 1942–45

CAREER: Staff adviser, U.S. High Commission for Germany, 1952–55; state's attorney for Winnebago County, IL, 1957–61; U.S. House of Representatives, 1961–80; unsuccessful candidate for U.S. president, 1980

Carter's attack on Reagan's character influenced the challenger to call for a debate. Reagan had debated Anderson in September, but Carter declined to participate, claiming that Anderson was not a major candidate. This time he accepted Reagan's offer. The debate was scheduled for October 28, a week before the election, and was sponsored by the League of Women Voters, an arrangement that allowed the exclusion of Anderson. The exchange showcased Reagan's capacity to toss memorable off-the-cuff one-liners. When Carter began to malign his opponent's record, Reagan cocked his head and retorted: "There you go again." It was a distinct television moment. Reagan's concluding remarks were equally effective. "Are you better off than you were four years ago?" he asked. "Is America as respected throughout the world as it was?" Clearly, many of the 100 to 110 million viewers thought not. Reagan wrapped up his monologue by pledging "to take government off the backs of the great people of this country. . . ." Intellectually,

PATRICK JOSEPH LUCEY

PARTY: Democrat; Independent (1980)

DATE OF BIRTH: March 21, 1918

PLACE OF BIRTH: La Crosse, Wisconsin

PARENTS: Gregory C. and Ella (McNamara) Lucey

EDUCATION: St. Thomas College

FAMILY: Married Jean Vlasis, 1951; children: Paul, Laurie, and David

MILITARY SERVICE: U.S. Army, discharged as captain, 1941–45

CAREER: Managed farms, 1945–51; executive director, Wisconsin Democratic Party, 1951–53; director, Lucey Investment and Continental Mortgage Insurance corporations; lieutenant governor of Wisconsin, 1965–67; governor of Wisconsin, 1971–77; U.S. ambassador to Mexico, 1977–79; unsuccessful candidate for U.S. vice president, 1980

the press rated the debate a draw. Politically, Reagan was the winner. He had demonstrated his ability to hold his own with the president, and that he was not the demon Carter had made him out to be.

Reagan Elected

Reagan's boost from the debate carried over to Election Day on November 4. He received 50.7 percent of the popular vote, compared with 41 percent for Carter. But Reagan's 91 percent of the electoral vote made his victory a landslide. Carter had won the 1976 election by carrying 23 states and the District of Columbia; he managed to win in only six states plus the District of Columbia in 1980. In 1976, Carter had held the South and taken New York, Pennsylvania, and Ohio, as well as other northeastern states. Both regions turned against the president in 1980. The West remained solidly Republican, as it had been since 1968. Besides gaining the White House, the Republicans pulled an upset in the race for Senate seats, winning a majority in the upper chamber for the first time since 1952. Democrats retained a comfortable majority in the House of Representatives despite losing thirty-three seats.

Not only did the nation reject a sitting president for the fourth time in the century (Taft, Hoover, and Ford—and later Bush, in 1992), it also witnessed a substantial third-party vote. Anderson did not come close to winning any electoral votes, but his 6.6 percent of the popular vote represented one of the better showings for a third-party candidate in a presidential race. Only Robert La Follette in 1924, George Wallace in 1968, and Ross Perot in 1992 and 1996 did better in the twentieth century. Anderson's votes were drawn disproportionately from liberal Independents. Younger, white, college-educated women, especially in the East and West, were the most likely group to vote for Anderson. Exit polls showed that Anderson drew the support of 4 percent of Republicans, 6 percent of Democrats, and 12 percent of Independents. Libertarian Party candidate Edward E. Clark received 921,128 votes. Barry Commoner—whose Citizens Party attacked corporate influence, wanted a smaller military, sought a ban on nuclear power, and supported price controls—attracted 234,294 votes.

Like Anderson, Reagan scored well among Independents and Democrats. Independents constituted a sizable block of voters, representing 23 percent of the electorate. They went for Reagan over Carter by a 58–27 percent margin. About 39 percent of the electorate identified themselves as Democrats; 26 percent of them marked their ballot for Reagan and 67 percent went for Carter. "Moderate" Democrats, the party's largest ideological block, cast 27 percent of their vote for the Republican candidate. Reagan, on the other hand, saw only 9 percent of Republican identifiers defect to Carter. "Conservative" Republicans, who represented a fifth of the electorate, favored Reagan over Carter by an 83–10 percent margin.

Reagan's support from numerous Democrats, who soon became known as "Reagan Democrats," and his large majority among Independents pinpoint the keys to his victory. A major candidate who attracts only two-thirds of his party identifiers, as Carter did in 1980, inevitably courts defeat. A second key to success in presidential elections in the late twentieth century was attracting the Independent vote. Since the 1950s, the number of voters calling themselves "Independents" had grown. As this group expanded, the stakes of winning their vote rose. Reagan's success rate over Carter among Independents was nearly two to one.

People who called themselves "conservatives," had considerable education and income, and lived in suburbs favored Reagan by substantial margins. Women, on the other hand, gave Reagan only a slight nod in their balloting, while blacks voted for Carter by a ten-to-one ratio. The pro-Carter margin was even higher among black females. Democrats also scored well among people with low incomes and education. The most pro-Republican voters were white males who were middle-aged, Protestant, and who earned more than $50,000 a year (in 1980). If they also called themselves "conservative" Republicans, they represented an automatic vote for Reagan.

Despite committed Republican and Democratic supporters, the election was won and lost among voters who made up their minds at the last minute. A high percentage of the electorate disliked both candidates. Carter was widely regarded as an inept president; but large segments of the electorate remained wary of Reagan. The low voter turnout, 52 percent of the eligible population, reinforces this finding from polling research. The president's number one problem, in the eyes of the public, was his inability to fix the economy. Reagan captured three-quarters of the voters who said they were worse-off financially in 1980 than they had been in 1976. Further underscoring the impact of the economy was the fact that Reagan voters cited this issue as the most influential one in their decision. First and foremost, the poor economy cost Carter the presidency.

The Iran hostage crisis also eroded Carter's support. Iranian militants had snubbed their noses at the United States nightly on the TV news during the campaign season. The president appeared powerless to rectify the insult. Reagan repeatedly charged that the nation's respect abroad had slipped. Voters listed Iran, after the economy and the federal budget deficit, as the issue most responsible for their decision to vote for Reagan. Carter acknowledged the image of American impotence over the Iran crisis, and inflation, as reasons for his defeat. He pointed to Ted Kennedy as the third cause. The president criticized the senator for undermining the natural Democratic base.

Kennedy's challenge to Carter in 1980 epitomized problems in the Democratic Party during in the 1970s. Since the Great Society legislation of the 1960s, critics had charged that Democrats had become the party of special interests, especially blacks and women. In this view "ivory tower" elites—not the party's traditional ethnic, working-class constituencies—had pushed experiments in social policy. A backlash against race and gender policies had emerged during the 1970s and became fused in many

people's minds with tax increases. Critics complained that the federal budget was in deficit because the government spent too much on welfare and other benefits for minorities. Middle-class taxpayers, in short, were shouldering the bill to subsidize special interest groups. Moreover, critics continued, these policies also caused runaway inflation. There is reason to believe that many white southerners and urban workers, traditionally Democratic loyalists, accepted this reasoning and abandoned their old party ties. Business also became more critical of Democratic policies in the 1970s, and stepped up political opposition to them. The flow of money to political action committees (PACs), many of which targeted their funds to conservatives and pro-business candidates, was partial confirmation of this tendency.

The backlash against social liberalism helped to fracture the Democratic Party's voter base. This long-term factor helps to explain Carter's loss in 1980, although short-term factors appear to have been equally decisive. The polls did not show a philosophic shift toward conservatism among voters during the 1980 campaign season. Voters' attitudes about political fundamentals remained largely unchanged. Rather, the fate of the election rested on undecided voters who concluded that Reagan was the lesser of two evils. However, a political turn to the right did occur—but it was manifested in the actions of government, and not in public ideology. Reagan used the power of the presidency to cut taxes, reduce spending, slow enforcement of civil rights, reaffirm traditional moral values, and fight drugs and crime. The Reagan revolution began in 1981.

Ballard C. Campbell

Bibliography

Congressional Quarterly Weekly Report, November 1, 1980.

Edsall, Thomas B. *Chain Reaction: The Impact of Race, Rights, and Taxes on American Politics.* New York: Norton, 1992.

Hargrove, Erwin C. *Jimmy Carter as President: Leadership and Politics of the Public Good.* Baton Rouge: Louisiana State University Press, 1988.

Lipset, Seymour Martin, and William Schneider. *The Confidence Gap: Business, Labor, and Government in the Public Mind.* New York: Free Press, 1983.

Pomper, Gerald, ed. *The Election of 1980: Reports and Interpretations.* Chatham, NJ: Chatham House, 1981.

White, Theodore. *America in Search of Itself: The Making of the President 1956–1980.* New York: Harper and Row, 1982.

Wills, Gary. *Reagan's America.* New York: Penguin Books, 1988.

THE VOTE: ELECTION OF 1980

State	Total No. of Electors	Total Popular Vote	Electoral Vote R	Electoral Vote D	Margin of Victory Votes	Margin of Victory % Total Vote	Reagan Republican Votes	Reagan Republican %	Carter Democrat Votes	Carter Democrat %	Anderson Independent Votes	Anderson Independent %	Clark Libertarian Votes	Clark Libertarian %	Others Votes	Others %
Alabama	9	1,341,929	9		17,462	1.3%	654,192	48.8%	636,730	47.4%	16,481	1.2%	13,318	1.0%	21,208	1.6%
Alaska	3	158,445	3		44,270	27.9%	86,112	54.3%	41,842	26.4%	11,155	7.0%	18,479	11.7%	857	0.5%
Arizona	6	873,945	6		282,845	32.4%	529,688	60.6%	246,843	28.2%	76,952	8.8%	18,784	2.1%	1,678	0.2%
Arkansas	6	837,582	6		5,123	0.6%	403,164	48.1%	398,041	47.5%	22,468	2.7%	8,970	1.1%	4,939	0.6%
California	45	8,587,063	45		1,441,197	16.8%	4,524,858	52.7%	3,083,661	35.9%	739,833	8.6%	148,434	1.7%	90,277	1.1%
Colorado	7	1,184,415	7		284,291	24.0%	652,264	55.1%	367,973	31.1%	130,633	11.0%	25,744	2.2%	7,801	0.7%
Connecticut	8	1,406,285	8		135,478	9.6%	677,210	48.2%	541,732	38.5%	171,807	12.2%	8,570	0.6%	6,966	0.5%
Delaware	3	235,668	3		5,498	2.3%	111,252	47.2%	105,754	44.9%	16,288	6.9%	1,974	0.8%	400	0.2%
District of Columbia	3	173,889		3	106,918	61.5%	23,313	13.4%	130,231	74.9%	16,131	9.3%	1,104	0.6%	3,110	1.8%
Florida	17	3,687,026	17		627,476	17.0%	2,046,951	55.5%	1,419,475	38.5%	189,692	5.1%	30,524	0.8%	384	0.0%
Georgia	12	1,597,467		12	236,565	14.8%	654,168	41.0%	890,733	55.8%	36,055	2.3%	15,627	1.0%	884	0.1%
Hawaii	4	303,287		4	5,767	1.9%	130,112	42.9%	135,879	44.8%	32,021	10.6%	3,269	1.1%	2,006	0.7%
Idaho	4	437,431	4		180,507	41.3%	290,699	66.5%	110,192	25.2%	27,058	6.2%	8,425	1.9%	1,057	0.2%
Illinois	26	4,749,721	26		376,636	7.9%	2,358,049	49.6%	1,981,413	41.7%	346,754	7.3%	38,939	0.8%	24,566	0.5%
Indiana	13	2,242,033	13		411,459	18.4%	1,255,656	56.0%	844,197	37.7%	111,639	5.0%	19,627	0.9%	10,914	0.5%
Iowa	8	1,317,661	8		167,354	12.7%	676,026	51.3%	508,672	38.6%	115,633	8.8%	13,123	1.0%	4,207	0.3%
Kansas	7	979,795	7		240,662	24.6%	566,812	57.9%	326,150	33.3%	68,231	7.0%	14,470	1.5%	4,132	0.4%
Kentucky	9	1,294,627	9		18,857	1.5%	635,274	49.1%	616,417	47.6%	31,127	2.4%	5,531	0.4%	6,278	0.5%
Louisiana	10	1,548,591	10		84,400	5.5%	792,853	51.2%	708,453	45.7%	26,345	1.7%	8,240	0.5%	12,700	0.8%
Maine	4	523,011	4		17,548	3.4%	238,522	45.6%	220,974	42.3%	53,327	10.2%	5,119	1.0%	5,069	1.0%
Maryland	10	1,540,496		10	45,555	3.0%	680,606	44.2%	726,161	47.1%	119,537	7.8%	14,192	0.9%	0	0.0%
Massachusetts	14	2,524,298	14		3,829	0.2%	1,057,631	41.9%	1,053,802	41.7%	382,539	15.2%	22,038	0.9%	8,288	0.3%
Michigan	21	3,909,725	21		253,693	6.5%	1,915,225	49.0%	1,661,532	42.5%	275,223	7.0%	41,597	1.1%	16,148	0.4%
Minnesota	10	2,051,953		10	80,933	3.9%	873,241	42.6%	954,174	46.5%	174,990	8.5%	31,592	1.5%	17,956	0.9%
Mississippi	7	892,620	7		11,808	1.3%	441,089	49.4%	429,281	48.1%	12,036	1.3%	5,465	0.6%	4,749	0.5%
Missouri	12	2,099,824	12		142,999	6.8%	1,074,181	51.2%	931,182	44.3%	77,920	3.7%	14,422	0.7%	2,119	0.1%
Montana	4	363,952	4		88,782	24.4%	206,814	56.8%	118,032	32.4%	29,281	8.0%	9,825	2.7%	0	0.0%
Nebraska	5	640,854	5		253,086	39.5%	419,937	65.5%	166,851	26.0%	44,993	7.0%	9,073	1.4%	0	0.0%
Nevada	3	247,885	3		88,351	35.6%	155,017	62.5%	66,666	26.9%	17,651	7.1%	4,358	1.8%	4,193	1.7%
New Hampshire	4	383,999	4		112,841	29.4%	221,705	57.7%	108,864	28.4%	49,693	12.9%	2,067	0.5%	1,670	0.4%
New Jersey	17	2,975,684	17		399,193	13.4%	1,546,557	52.0%	1,147,364	38.6%	234,632	7.9%	20,652	0.7%	26,479	0.9%
New Mexico	4	456,237	4		82,953	18.2%	250,779	55.0%	167,826	36.8%	29,459	6.5%	4,365	1.0%	3,808	0.8%
New York	41	6,201,959	41		165,459	2.7%	2,893,831	46.7%	2,728,372	44.0%	467,801	7.5%	52,648	0.8%	59,307	1.0%
North Carolina	13	1,855,833	13		39,383	2.1%	915,018	49.3%	875,635	47.2%	52,800	2.8%	9,677	0.5%	2,703	0.1%
North Dakota	3	301,545	3		114,506	38.0%	193,695	64.2%	79,189	26.3%	23,640	7.8%	3,743	1.2%	1,278	0.4%
Ohio	25	4,283,603	25		454,131	10.6%	2,206,545	51.5%	1,752,414	40.9%	254,472	5.9%	49,033	1.1%	21,139	0.5%
Oklahoma	8	1,149,708	8		293,544	25.5%	695,570	60.5%	402,026	35.0%	38,284	3.3%	13,828	1.2%	0	0.0%
Oregon	6	1,181,516	6		114,154	9.7%	571,044	48.3%	456,890	38.7%	112,389	9.5%	25,838	2.2%	15,355	1.3%
Pennsylvania	27	4,561,501	27		324,332	7.1%	2,261,872	49.6%	1,937,540	42.5%	292,921	6.4%	33,263	0.7%	35,905	0.8%
Rhode Island	4	416,072		4	43,549	10.5%	154,793	37.2%	198,342	47.7%	59,819	14.4%	2,458	0.6%	660	0.2%
South Carolina	8	890,083	8		13,647	1.5%	441,207	49.6%	427,560	48.0%	14,150	1.6%	4,975	0.6%	2,191	0.2%
South Dakota	4	327,703	4		94,488	28.8%	198,343	60.5%	103,855	31.7%	21,431	6.5%	3,824	1.2%	250	0.1%
Tennessee	10	1,617,616	10		4,710	0.3%	787,761	48.7%	783,051	48.4%	35,991	2.2%	7,116	0.4%	3,697	0.2%
Texas	26	4,541,637	26		629,558	13.9%	2,510,705	55.3%	1,881,147	41.4%	111,613	2.5%	37,643	0.8%	529	0.0%
Utah	4	604,222	4		315,421	52.2%	439,687	72.8%	124,266	20.6%	30,284	5.0%	7,226	1.2%	2,759	0.5%
Vermont	3	213,299	3		12,676	5.9%	94,628	44.4%	81,952	38.4%	31,761	14.9%	1,900	0.9%	3,058	1.4%
Virginia	12	1,866,032	12		237,435	12.7%	989,609	53.0%	752,174	40.3%	95,418	5.1%	12,821	0.7%	16,010	0.9%
Washington	9	1,742,394	9		215,051	12.3%	865,244	49.7%	650,193	37.3%	185,073	10.6%	29,213	1.7%	12,671	0.7%
West Virginia	6	737,715		6	33,256	4.5%	334,206	45.3%	367,462	49.8%	31,691	4.3%	4,356	0.6%	0	0.0%
Wisconsin	11	2,273,221	11		107,261	4.7%	1,088,845	47.9%	981,584	43.2%	160,657	7.1%	29,135	1.3%	13,000	0.6%
Wyoming	3	176,713	3		61,273	34.7%	110,700	62.6%	49,427	28.0%	12,072	6.8%	4,514	2.6%	0	0.0%
TOTAL	538	86,509,770	489	49	8,423,084	9.7%	43,903,260	50.7%	35,480,176	41.0%	5,719,851	6.6%	921,128	1.1%	485,355	0.6%

For sources, see p. 1133.

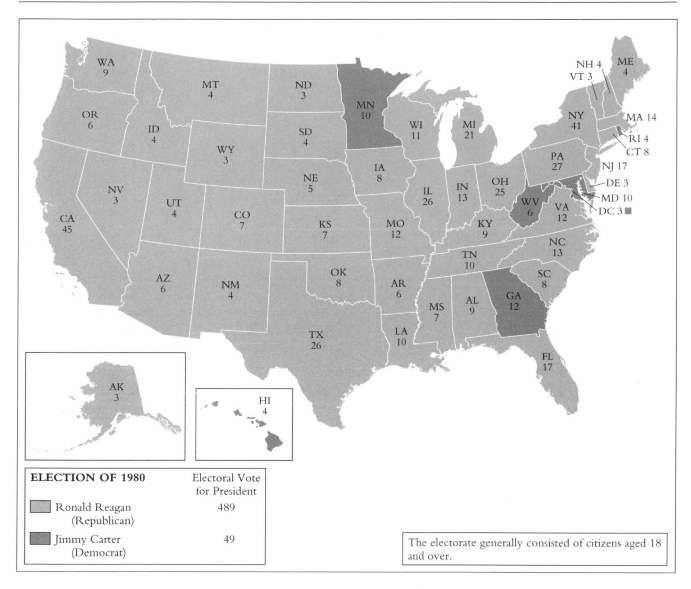

ELECTION OF 1980 — Electoral Vote for President

Ronald Reagan (Republican) — 489

Jimmy Carter (Democrat) — 49

The electorate generally consisted of citizens aged 18 and over.

DOCUMENTS: ELECTION OF 1980

By 1980 Jimmy Carter, the inexperienced one-term governor from Georgia who seemed to be the perfect solution to the post-Watergate presidency in 1976, had lost much of his support. Despite getting Egypt and Israel to agree to peace through the Camp David Accords, the sudden end of détente with the Soviet invasion of Afghanistan, an energy crisis, high unemployment and inflation, and the Iran-hostage crisis had led many Americans to believe that the job had overwhelmed Carter. In Document 1, Carter, with an approval rating below 30 percent, attempted to pinpoint the causes of this American "malaise" in an address to the nation. He argued that Americans suffered from a "crisis of confidence" that undermined the national will, but offered few remedies.

Carter's weakness led to a serious challenge for the Democratic nomination. Senator Edward M. "Ted" Kennedy, brother of John F. and Robert F. Kennedy, squared off with the president throughout the primaries, winning about one-third of the contests. Carter would fend off the challenge and receive the nomination by a two-to-one margin, but Kennedy's popularity had highlighted the president's weaknesses and divided the party. At the convention, Kennedy accepted defeat, but had earned a forum to express his vision of the Democratic Party. In Document 2, his keynote speech at the Democratic convention, Kennedy stirred the delegates by reminding them of their liberal roots and great successes of the twentieth century. He hoped to unify the party and rally Americans to a more liberal agenda. The Massachusetts senator's speech was so well received, however, that its impact took the focus off President Carter and his nomination acceptance, Document 3.

The "crisis in confidence" presented conservative Republicans with the issue they knew could get them into the White House. Emerging from the primaries as the clear-cut favorite, former governor Ronald Reagan of California earned the Republican nomination. Having nearly defeated Gerald Ford for the nomination four years earlier, in 1980 Reagan's conservative message resonated even better with large numbers of voters of both parties who were disillusioned with Carter. In his nomination acceptance speech, Document 4, Reagan proclaimed that Carter would give Americans "four more years of weakness, indecision, mediocrity and incompetence." He promised tax cuts, increased military spending, and an efficient government to lead the nation on a "crusade to make America great again."

With Democrats courting liberals and Republicans growing ever more conservative, Representative John B. Anderson of Illinois ran for president as the moderate alternative. He vied for the Republican nomination until Reagan secured it. Undaunted, Anderson bolted his party to run as an independent candidate, selecting former governor Patrick Lucey of Wisconsin, a Democrat, as his running mate. Document 5, Anderson's closing statement at the Reagan-Anderson debate, declared that both parties had offered decades of broken promises and asked Americans to give an Independent, or "coalition," party an opportunity. Anderson, however, won only 7 percent of the popular vote and earned no electoral votes.

In the Carter-Reagan debate, just a week before the election, both candidates presented their best arguments for election, Document 6. Carter portrayed himself as the mainstream candidate, insisting that Reagan represented the views of a minority of Americans. Meanwhile, Reagan simply asked, "Are you better off than you were four years ago?" Despite Reagan's conservatism and renegade image, for most Americans the question Reagan posed at the debate stayed with them as they went to the polls. Reagan received a 51–41 edge in the popular vote, but earned 489 electoral votes to Carter's 49, the lowest total for an incumbent president since Taft in 1912.

Document 1

"Crisis of Confidence," An Address to the Nation by Jimmy Carter, July 15, 1979

I want to talk to you right now about a fundamental threat to American democracy. . . . It is a crisis of confidence. It is a crisis that strikes at the very heart and soul and spirit of our national will. We can see this crisis in the growing doubt about the meaning of our own lives and in the loss of a unity of purpose for our nation. The erosion of our confidence in the future is threatening to destroy the social and the political fabric of America. . . .

In a nation that was proud of hard work, strong families, close-knit communities, and our faith in God, too many of us now tend to worship self-indulgence and consumption. Human identity is no longer defined by what one does, but by what one owns. But we've discovered that owning things and consuming things does not satisfy our longing for meaning. We've learned that piling up material goods cannot fill the emptiness of lives which have no confidence or purpose.

The symptoms of this crisis of the American spirit are all around us. For the first time in the history of our country a majority of our people believe that the next five years will be worse than the past five years. Two-thirds of our people do not even vote. The productivity of American workers is actually dropping, and the willingness of Americans to save for the future has fallen below that of all other people in the Western world. As you know, there is a growing disrespect for government and for churches and for schools, the news media, and other institutions. This is not a message of happiness or reassurance, but it is the truth and it is a warning.

These changes did not happen overnight. They've come upon us gradually over the last generation, years that were filled with shocks and tragedy. We were sure that ours was a nation of the ballot, not the bullet, until the murders of John Kennedy and Robert Kennedy and Martin Luther King Jr. We were taught that our armies were always invincible and our causes were always just, only to suffer the agony of Vietnam. We respected the presidency as a place of honor until the shock of Watergate. We remember when the phrase "sound as a dollar" was an expression of absolute dependability, until ten years of inflation began to shrink our dollar and our savings. We believed that our nation's resources were limitless until 1973, when we had to face a growing dependence on foreign oil. . . .

Restoring that faith and that confidence to America is now the most important task we face. It is a true challenge of this generation of Americans. . . .

Little by little we can and we must rebuild our confidence. We can spend until we empty our treasuries, and we may summon all the wonders of science. But we can succeed only if we tap our greatest resources: America's people, America's values, and America's confidence. I have seen the strength of America in the inexhaustible resources of our people. . . .

In closing, let me say this: I will do my best, but I will not do it alone. Let your voice be heard. Whenever you have a chance, say something good about our country. With God's help and for the sake of our nation, it is time for us to join hands in America. Let us commit ourselves together to a rebirth of the American spirit. Working together with our common faith, we cannot fail.

Source: Public Papers and Addresses of the Presidents of the United States: Jimmy Carter, 1979, Book II, June 23 to December 31, 1979 (Washington, DC: Government Printing Office).

Document 2

Edward Kennedy's Keynote Speech, 1980 Democratic Convention, New York, August 12, 1980

I have come here tonight not to argue as a candidate, but to affirm a cause. I'm asking you—I am asking you to renew the commitment of the Democratic Party to economic justice.

I am asking you to renew our commitment to a fair and lasting prosperity that can put America back to work. . . .

I speak out of a deep belief in the ideals of the Democratic Party, and in the potential of that Party and of a President to make a difference. And I speak out of a deep trust in our capacity to proceed with boldness and a common vision that will feel and heal the suffering of our time and the divisions of our Party. . . .

We dare not forsake that tradition. We cannot let the great purposes of the Democratic Party become the bygone passages of history.

We must not permit the Republicans to seize and run on the slogans of prosperity. We heard the orators at their convention all trying to talk like Democrats. . . .

The 1980 Republican convention was awash with crocodile tears for our economic distress, but it is by their long record and not their recent words that you shall know them.

The same Republicans who are talking about the crisis of unemployment have nominated a man who once said, and I quote, "Unemployment insurance is a prepaid vacation plan for freeloaders.". . .

The same Republicans who are talking about security for the elderly have nominated a man who said just four years ago that "Participation in social security should be made voluntary.". . .

The same Republicans who are talking about preserving the environment have nominated a man who last year made the preposterous statement, and I quote, "Eighty percent of our air pollution comes from plants and trees.". . .

The great adventures which our opponents offer is a voyage into the past. Progress is our heritage, not theirs. . . .

The demand of our people in 1980 is not for smaller government or bigger government, but for better government. . . .

Again and again, Democratic leaders have followed that star and they have given new meaning to the old values of liberty and justice for all.

We are the party. We are the party of the New Freedom, the New Deal and the New Frontier. We have always been the party of hope. So this year let us offer new hope, new hope to an America uncertain about the present, but unsurpassed in its potential for the future. . . .

A fair prosperity and a just society are within our vision and our grasp. . . . I have found that faith still alive wherever I have traveled across this land. So let us reject the counsel of retreat and the call to reaction. Let us go forward in the knowledge that history only helps those who help themselves.

There will be setbacks and sacrifices in the years ahead, but I am convinced that we as a people are ready to give something back to our country in return for all it has given to us.

Let this be our commitment: Whatever sacrifices must be made will be shared and shared fairly. . . .

I am confident that the Democratic Party will reunite on the basis of Democratic principles, and that together we will march towards a Democratic victory in 1980.

And someday, long after this convention, long after the signs come down, and the crowds stop cheering, and the bands stop playing, may it be said of our campaign that we kept the faith. May it be said of our Party in 1980 that we found our faith again. . . .

For me, a few hours ago, this campaign came to an end. For all those whose cares have been our concern, the work goes on, the cause endures, the hope still lives, and the dream shall never die.

Source: John Fitzgerald Kennedy Library Web site, www.cs.umb.edu/jfklibrary/e081280.htm.

Document 3

Jimmy Carter's Nomination Acceptance, August 14, 1980

The life of every human being on Earth can depend on the experience and judgment and vigilance of the person in the Oval Office. The President's power for building and his power for destruction are awesome. And the power's greatest exactly where the stakes are highest—in matters of war and peace.

And I've learned something else, something that I have come to see with extraordinary clarity: Above all, I must look ahead, because the President of the United States is the steward of the Nation's destiny. He must protect our children and the children they will have and the children of generations to follow. He must speak and act for them. That is his burden and his glory.

And that is why a President cannot yield to the shortsighted demands, no matter how rich or powerful the special interests might be that make those demands. And that's why the President cannot bend to the passions of the moment, however popular they might be. That's why the President must sometimes ask for sacrifice when his listeners would rather hear the promise of comfort.

The President is a servant of today, but his true constituency is the future. That's why the election of 1980 is so important.

Some have said it makes no difference who wins this election. They are wrong. This election is a stark choice between two men, two parties, two sharply different pictures of what America is and what the world is; but it's more than that—it's a choice between two futures. . . .

I see peace.

I see a future of economic security—security that will come from tapping our own great resources of oil and gas, coal and sunlight, and from building the tools and technology and factories for a revitalized economy based on jobs and stable prices for everyone.

I see a future of justice—the justice of good jobs, decent health care, quality education, a full opportunity for all people. We can choose the future I have been building to security and justice, regardless of color or language or religion; the simple human justice of equal rights for all men and for all women, guaranteed equal rights at last under the Constitution of the United States of America.

And I see a future of peace—a peace born of wisdom, and based on a fairness toward all countries of the world, a peace guaranteed both by American military strength and by American moral strength as well.

That is the future I want for all people, a future of confidence and hope and a good life. It's the future America must choose, and with your help and with your commitment, it is the future America will choose.

But there is another possible future. In that other future I see despair—despair of millions who would struggle for equal opportunity and a better life, and struggle alone. And I see surrender—the surrender of our energy future to the merchants of oil, the surrender of our economic future to a bizarre program of massive tax cuts for the rich, service cuts for the poor, and massive inflation for everyone. And I see risk—the risk of international confrontation, the risk of an uncontrollable, unaffordable, and unwinnable nuclear arms race.

No one, Democrat or Republican either, consciously seeks such a future, and I do not claim that my opponent does. But I do question the disturbing commitments and policies already made by him, and by those with him, who have now captured control of the Republican Party. The consequences of those commitments and policies would drive us down the wrong road. It's up to all of us to make sure America rejects this alarming and even perilous destiny. . . .

We've learned the uses and the limitations of power. We've learned the beauty and responsibility of freedom. We've learned the value and the obligation of justice. And we have learned the necessity of peace. . . .

I need for all of you to join me in fulfilling that vision. The choice, the choice between the two futures, could not be more clear. If we succumb to a dream world, then we'll wake up to a nightmare. But if we start with reality and fight to make our dreams a reality, then Americans will have a good life, a life of meaning and purpose in a nation that's strong and secure.

Above all, I want us to be what the Founders of our Nation meant us to become—the land of freedom, the land of peace, and the land of hope.

Source: Public Papers and Addresses of the Presidents of the United States: Jimmy Carter, 1980, Book II, May 24 to September 26, 1980 (Washington, DC: Government Printing Office, 1982).

Document 4

Ronald Reagan's Nomination Acceptance Speech, July 17, 1980

The major issue of this campaign is the direct political, personal and moral responsibility of Democratic Party leadership—in the White House and in Congress—for this unprecedented calamity which has befallen us. They tell us they have done the most that humanly could be done. They say that the United States has had its day in the sun, that our nation has passed its zenith. They expect you to tell your children that the American people no longer have the will to cope with their problems; that the future will be one of sacrifice and few opportunities.

My fellow citizens, I utterly reject that view. The American people, the most generous on earth, who created the highest standard of living, are not going to accept the notion that we can only make a better world for others by moving backwards ourselves. Those who believe we can have no business leading the nation.

I will not stand by and watch this great country destroy itself under mediocre leadership that drifts from one crisis to the next, eroding our national will and purpose. We have come together here because the American people deserve better from those to whom they entrust our nation's highest offices, and we stand united in our resolve to do something about it.

We need a rebirth of the American tradition of leadership at every level of government, and in private life as well. The United States of America is unique in world history because it has a genius for leaders—many leaders—on many levels. But, back in 1976, Mr. Carter said, "Trust me." And a lot of people did. Now, many of those people are out of work. Many have seen their savings eaten away by inflation. Many others on fixed incomes, especially the elderly, have watched helplessly as the cruel tax of inflation wasted away their purchasing power. And, today, a great many who trusted Mr. Carter wonder if we can survive the Carter policies of national defense.

"Trust me" government asks that we concentrate our hopes and dreams on one man; that we trust him to do what's best for us. My view of government places trust not in one person or one party, but in those values that transcend persons and parties. The trust is where it belongs—in the people. The responsibility to live up to that trust is where it belongs, in their elected leaders. That kind of relationship, between the people and their elected leaders, is a special kind of compact. . . .

The first task of national leadership is to set honest and realistic priorities in our policies and our budget, and I pledge that my administration will do that.

When I talk of tax cuts, I am reminded that every major tax cut in this century has strengthened the economy, generated renewed productivity and ended up yielding new revenues for the government by creating new investment, new jobs and more commerce among our people. . . .

For those who have abandoned hope, we'll restore hope and we'll welcome them into a great national crusade to make America great again!

When we move from domestic affairs and cast our eyes abroad, we see an equally sorry chapter on the record of the present administration. . . .

The administration which has brought us to this state is seeking your endorsement for four more years of weakness, indecision, mediocrity and incompetence. No Amer-

ican should vote until he or she has asked, is the United States stronger and more respected now than it was three-and-a-half years ago? Is the world today a safer place in which to live?

It is the responsibility of the president of the United States, in working for peace, to insure that the safety of our people cannot successfully be threatened by a hostile foreign power. As president, fulfilling that responsibility will be my Number One priority. . . .

We know only too well that war comes not when the forces of freedom are strong, but when they are weak. It is then that tyrants are tempted. . . .

Let our friends and those who may wish us ill take note: The United States has an obligation to its citizens and to the people of the world never to let those who would destroy freedom dictate the future course of human life on this planet. I would regard my election as proof that we have renewed our resolve to preserve world peace and freedom. This nation will once again be strong enough to do that. . . .

We must eliminate unnecessary functions of government. . . . We must consolidate subdivisions of government and, like the private citizen, give up luxuries which we can no longer afford.

"I propose to you, my friends, and through you that government of all kinds, big and little be made solvent and that the example be set by the president of the United States and his Cabinet."

So said Franklin Delano Roosevelt in his acceptance speech to the Democratic National Convention in July 1932.

The time is now, my fellow Americans, to recapture our destiny, to take it into our own hands. But, to do this will take many of us, working together. I ask you tonight to volunteer your help in this cause so we can carry our message throughout the land. . . .

I'll confess that I've been a little afraid to suggest what I'm going to suggest—I'm more afraid not to—that we begin our crusade joined together in a moment of silent prayer. God bless America.

Source: New York Times, July 18, 1980.

Document 5

John Anderson's Closing Statement, the Anderson-Reagan Presidential Debate, September 21, 1980

President Carter was not right a few weeks ago, when he said that the American people were confronted with only two choices, with only two men, and with only two parties. I think you've seen tonight in this debate that Governor Reagan and I have agreed on exactly one thing—we are both against the re-imposition of a peacetime draft. We have disagreed, I believe, on virtually every other issue. I respect him for showing tonight—for appearing here, and

I thank the League of Women Voters for the opportunity that they have given me. I am running for President as an Independent because I believe our country is in trouble. I believe that all of us are going to have to begin to work together to solve our problems. If you think that I am a spoiler, consider these facts: Do you really think that our economy is healthy? Do you really think that 8 million Americans being out of work and the 50 percent unemployment among the youth of our country are acceptable? Do you really think that our armed forces are really acceptably strong in those areas of conventional capability, where they should be? Do you think that our political institutions are working the way they should when, literally, only half of our citizens vote? I don't think you do think that. And therefore, I think you ought to consider doing something about it, and voting for an Independent in 1980. You know, a generation of office seekers has tried to tell the American people that they could get something for nothing. It's been a time, therefore, of illusion and false hopes, and the longer it continues, the more dangerous it becomes. We've got to stop drifting. What I wish tonight so desperately is that we had had more time to talk about some of the other issues that are so fundamentally important. A great historian, Henry Steele Commager, said that in their lust for victory, neither traditional party is looking beyond November. And he went on to cite three issues that their platforms totally ignore: atomic warfare, Presidential Directive 59 notwithstanding. If we don't resolve that issue, all others become irrelevant. The issue of our natural resources; the right of posterity to inherit the earth, and what kind of earth will it be? The issue of nationalism—the recognition, he says, that every major problem confronting us is global, and cannot be solved by nationalism here or elsewhere— that is chauvinistic, that is parochial, that is as anachronistic as states' rights was in the days of Jefferson Davis. Those are some of the great issues—atomic warfare, the use of our natural resources, and the issue of nationalism—that I intend to be talking about in the remaining six weeks of this campaign, and I dare hope that the American people will be listening and that they will see that an Independent government of John Anderson and Patrick Lucey can give us the kind of coalition government that we need in 1980 to begin to solve our problems.

Source: Commission on Presidential Debates Web site, www. debates.org/ pages/trans80a.html.

Document 6

Excerpt from the Carter-Reagan Presidential Debate, October 28, 1980

MR. CARTER: As I've studied the record between myself and Governor Reagan, I've been impressed with the stark differences that exist between us. I think the result of this debate indicates that that fact is true. I consider myself in the mainstream of my party. I consider myself in the mainstream even of the bipartisan list of Presidents who served before me. The United States must be a nation strong; the United States must be a nation secure. We must have a society that's just and fair. And we must extend the benefits of our own commitment to peace, to create a peaceful world. I believe that since I've been in office, there have been six or eight areas of combat evolved in other parts of the world. In each case, I alone have had to determine the interests of my country and the degree of involvement of my country. I've done that with moderation, with care, with thoughtfulness; sometimes consulting experts. But . . . the final judgment about the future of the nation—war, peace, involvement, reticence, thoughtfulness, care, consideration, concern—has to be made by the man in the Oval Office. It's a lonely job, but with the involvement of the American people in the process, with an open Government, the job is a very gratifying one. . . . There is a partnership involved in our nation. To stay strong, to stay at peace, to raise high the banner of human rights, to set an example for the rest of the world, to let our deep beliefs and commitments be felt by others in other nations, is my plan for the future. I ask the American people to join me in this partnership. . . .

MR. REAGAN: Next Tuesday, all of you will go to the polls, will stand there in the polling place and make a decision. I think when you make that decision, it might be well if you would ask yourself: Are you better off than you were four years ago? . . . Is America as respected throughout the world as it was? Do you feel that our security is as safe, that we're as strong as we were four years ago? . . . This country doesn't have to be in the shape that it is in. . . . All of this can be cured and all of it can be solved. . . . I know that the economic program that I have proposed for this nation in the next few years can resolve many of the problems that trouble us today. I know because we did it there [in California]. We cut the cost—the increased cost of government—in half over the eight years. We returned $5.7 billion in tax rebates, credits and cuts to our people. We, as I have said earlier, fell below the national average in inflation when we did that. And I know that we did give back authority and autonomy to the people. I would like to have a crusade today, and I would like to lead that crusade with your help. And it would be one to take Government off the backs of the great people of this country, and turn you loose again to do those things that I know you can do so well, because you did them and made this country great.

Source: Commission on Presidential Debates Web site, www. debates.org/ pages/trans80b.html.

THE ELECTION OF 1984

The first week of September, like the first day of the baseball season, is a time of hope and optimism in a presidential campaign. No matter how daunting the odds, the underdog candidate may dream freely of what could happen in the next nine weeks, buoyed by marching bands and cheering crowds. On Labor Day, all things seem possible. For Walter Mondale (see fact box, p. 927), however, even that small comfort was denied him. On Labor Day 1984, the presidential nominee of the Democratic Party and his running mate, Geraldine Ferraro, rode through the streets of New York at the head of the parade—in front of crowds only one deep. It was "an eerily inauspicious beginning for a campaign to win the votes of millions of Americans," wrote a *New York Times* reporter.

David Broder, one of the deans of American political journalism, compared the stumbling Mondale efforts to "a kazoo band trying to drown out a mighty Wurlitzer." The reelection campaign of Ronald Reagan (see fact box, p. 945) was indeed an apparatus designed for high amplification. Throughout the fall of 1984, Walter Mondale and the Democrats struggled to make themselves heard against the booming themes of Reagan's march to a second term: Peace and prosperity; "It's morning again in America." One of the most striking aspects of the 1984 presidential campaign was how little the public appeared to be affected by it: Reagan began his run with a large lead, maintained it with minor fluctuations (despite one of the worst performances of his political career in his first debate with Walter Mondale), and finished with a flourish. Article after article, filed by journalist after journalist covering the Mondale campaign, highlighted faint signs of hope for the challenger: larger-than-expected crowds at rallies, promised surges in voter registration and turnout, evidence of a closing gap in one state or another. But hope after hope was quashed, culminating in the results on Election Day: 49 states and 525 electoral votes for Ronald Reagan, who won 59 percent of the popular vote. Mondale carried only his home state of Minnesota and the District of Columbia.

One of the curious things, however, about this particular landslide is how little of the political terrain seemed to be disturbed in its aftermath. Republican House and Senate candidates, for example, found that Reagan's coattails were not long ones. In the House of Representatives, the Republicans gained 15 seats and put a small dent in a large Democratic majority, which was reduced to 253 seats out of 435. The GOP actually suffered a net loss of two seats in the Senate, dropping its majority from 55 to 53, a small advantage that the party lost in the 1986 midterm elections. Further, both conservatives and liberals complained that the president had failed to set a clear agenda for his second term, resulting in a triumph without a substantial mandate on the issues. Coupled with this criticism was a persistent contention that 1984 was a personal victory for Reagan, not an ideological one. The media dwelled on the contrast between the sunny, well-tanned president from California and his dour, gray challenger from Minnesota—and suggested that Reagan, the showman, had managed to convince Americans to like him, despite the fact that they disagreed with many of his policies.

CHRONOLOGY

1981

JANUARY 20	American hostages released from U.S. embassy in Iran; Reagan begins first term as president.
FEBRUARY 18	In address to Congress, Reagan proposes cuts in taxes and the federal budget, but asks for increases in the defense budget.
MARCH 30	Reagan survives assassination attempt.
SEPTEMBER 25	Sandra Day O'Connor becomes first female seated on U.S. Supreme Court.
DECEMBER 7	Reagan administration officials estimate federal budget deficit will rise to record $109 billion in 1982 fiscal year.

1982

JUNE 30	Effort fails to persuade states to ratify Equal Rights Amendment.
NOVEMBER 2	Democrats gain 26 seats in House; Republicans keep control of Senate.

1983

MARCH 23	Reagan proposes space-based missile defense system.
APRIL 20	Reagan signs bipartisan bill to ensure financial solvency of Social Security system.
JUNE 15	Supreme Court reaffirms *Roe v. Wade*.
OCTOBER 23	241 American troops killed in bombing of barracks in Lebanon.
OCTOBER 25	U.S. troops invade Grenada.

1984

FEBRUARY 28	Senator Gary Hart upsets Walter Mondale in New Hampshire Democratic primary.
JUNE 5	Mondale wins New Jersey primary.
JULY 19	Representative Geraldine Ferraro accepts nomination as Mondale's running mate.
AUGUST 23	Reagan accepts Republican nomination to run for reelection.
OCTOBER	Presidential and vice presidential debates held.
NOVEMBER 6	Reagan and Bush win reelection in landslide.

At most, critics charged, the voters' endorsement was an endorsement of American peace and prosperity, not a charge to the incumbent to go to the next stage of his "revolution," whatever that might be.

One way to assess whether the Reagan presidency was ephemeral or long-lasting, in its impact on American politics, is to consider it in terms of presidential electoral politics. Political scientists have debated whether the 1980 and 1984 elections represented a "realignment" in the American electorate, a tidal shift in voting patterns producing a majority coalition that controls the institutions of representative government for a significant period of time. At the end of this chapter, we will consider this question by examining the success of Republican presidential candidates, before and after Reagan, on a region-by-region basis. First, however, we turn our attention to the campaign of 1984, and Walter Mondale's path to the nomination of his party. Much like the Labor Day parade in New York City, Mondale's voyage through the primaries did not go as expected.

The Parties' Nomination Process

Everything old was new again in the 1984 Democratic primary season. George McGovern, the 1972 presidential nominee, staged another run for the nomination. McGovern ran against one of his main campaign operatives in 1972, Gary Hart, now a United States senator from Colorado. Hart ran as the candidate of "new ideas"—more specifically, he ran as the standard-bearer for a new breed of Democrat that had already made its mark in Congress: the neo-liberal who took more conservative stances on economic issues than the typical Democrat, and more liberal positions on cultural ones. In some ways, however, Hart's candidacy was not new at all, but the newest model in a line of reform-minded insurgents that dated back to Senator Eugene McCarthy in 1968.

Like McCarthy, Hart ran against a politician from Minnesota who struggled to hold together the remains of the New Deal coalition. In the 1984 remake of this old Democratic story, Walter Mondale (like his Minnesota forefather, Hubert Humphrey) was cast in the unenviable role of the "Establishment" frontrunner. Mondale, like Humphrey, was a loyal member of the Minnesota Democratic-Farmer-Labor Party. Mondale served as his state's attorney general in the early 1960s, and in 1964 was appointed to fill Humphrey's seat in the U. S. Senate when Humphrey was elected as Lyndon Johnson's vice president. Minnesotans sent Mondale back to the Senate in 1966 and 1972. In 1976, Mondale again followed in Humphrey's footsteps by serving as the running mate to a southern politician; he was given credit for helping to push Jimmy Carter over the top in a closely fought contest with Gerald Ford. But the duo had lost the White House to Reagan and George Bush in 1980.

In 1984, former vice president Mondale was forced to suffer the slings and arrows of a schedule of primaries months in length. (To bring the story full circle, this gauntlet was the product of attempts to democratize the Democratic Party's nomination process following the tumultuous intra-party battles of 1968. These reforms were devised by a party commission led by George McGovern.)

Mondale, like other Democratic frontrunners before him, had hoped that his support among the party elite would propel him through the primaries to the nomination. An easy road to the nomination would have enabled him to establish himself as a different sort of Democrat, one of sobriety and moderation. This was Mondale's aim, said political analysts Michael Barone and Grant Ujifusa in their 1986 *Almanac of American Politics*, when he declared his intent to raise taxes in his acceptance speech at the Democratic convention. Mondale wanted to be the straight-talking candidate who "was going to tell voters what he planned to do." This approach, presumably, would cast him as an attractive alternative to the smoke-and-mirrors magician occupying the White House, who had declared that the government could lower taxes, raise defense spending, and balance the budget simultaneously.

Mondale's hopes for a smooth trip to the nomination, however, disappeared in a New Hampshire blizzard. Gary Hart, fresh off a weak second-place finish to Mondale in the Iowa caucuses, reaped the benefits of a message well-tuned to the New England state's well-heeled Democrats, excellent organization (his campaign team included future governor Jeanne Shaheen), and attention from the media as the New Democrat alternative to the conventional frontrunner. Hart's nine-point victory in New Hampshire was the starting point of a textbook example of how an under-the-radar primary campaign can quickly gain that mysterious quality known as "momentum." Two weeks later, Hart's momentum nearly propelled him to a sweep of the "Super Tuesday" primaries, easily winning contests in two more New England states (Massachusetts and Rhode Island), and carrying Florida by six points. Mondale managed to avoid a knockout with two victories in the South, taking Alabama easily and pulling out a three-point squeaker in Georgia. The frontrunner's attempts to hold off the hard-charging challenger were hampered by the "rainbow coalition" candidacy of the Rev. Jesse Jackson, whose candidacy drew away large numbers of African-American voters. As a result, Mondale had little choice but to resort to a traditional message to attract traditional Democratic constituencies. This strategy paid off with victories in key primaries such as Illinois, New York, Pennsylvania, and New Jersey. Coupled with continued success among southern Democrats, Mondale was able to hold off Hart, whose candidacy was suffering growing pains as it made the difficult transition from insurgency to full-fledged candidacy. As a result, however, "Mondale appeared increasingly as the candidate of the old Democratic party," Barone concluded, "of promises and propping up old factories, of big government programs and sloppy generosity."

Mondale's struggles to unify his party continued into the summer and past the convention. Jackson remained a thorn in his side for months, refusing to

Rev. Jesse Jackson was the first African American to make a serious run for the White House. *(Gyory Collection/Cathy Casriel Photo)*

commit fully to the nominee's campaign unless his supporters received appropriate positions in the campaign apparatus. Jackson's demands, in turn, sparked anger from African-American politicians who had been with Mondale from the start. Further, Mondale's lengthy search for a running mate, covered in excruciating detail by a press corps with little other news to report, only reinforced the perception that the party was divided against itself into a loose collection of special interests.

Out of this dull, plodding procedure, however, came a small strike of lightning: Mondale's choice of Representative Geraldine Ferraro as his running mate, the first woman to be part of a major-party ticket. The representative of New York's Ninth Congressional District ignited hopes, however briefly, that her selection would reshuffle the political deck and give the Democratic ticket a fresh start. Ferraro was expected to be a magnet not only for female voters, but also for the ethnic Democrats of the Northeast, who had fled the party in droves four years earlier; such Democrats, after all, were plentiful in the constituency of her Queens district.

From the beginning of her political career, Ferraro took pains to distinguish herself from "bleeding-heart" liberal Democrats. Stressing her experience as an assistant district attorney, her campaign slogan for her Congressional run in 1978 was, "Finally, A

Tough Democrat." After her nomination as Mondale's running mate, crowds thronged to see Ferraro on the stump, and the vice presidential nominee often seemed to outshine Mondale. Ferraro exhibited a brash, no-nonsense style; she said of Reagan, for example, that he "walks around calling himself a good Christian, but I don't for one minute believe it because [his] policies are so terribly unfair." When Jackson complained that a black was not among her first three staff appointments, Ferraro chided him in turn for being impatient, saying he should "know better." Ferraro's star dimmed, however, amid a cloud of questions regarding alleged financial improprieties by her and her husband, John Zaccaro. The resulting controversy put an additional obstacle in the way of a campaign already struggling to gain momentum.

Unlike his competitor, President Ronald Reagan faced no opposition to his renomination as the Republican candidate for president—the first uncontested nomination in the GOP since Dwight Eisenhower in 1956. Reagan's strong support for his vice president, George H.W. Bush (see fact box, p. 946), ensured that his running mate also would face no opposition. The devil of discord, however, lay in the details of the party's August convention. "Young Turk" conservatives such as Representatives Jack Kemp of New York (who ran for the GOP

After a harder-than-expected battle for the Democratic nomination, former vice president Walter Mondale chose New York representative Geraldine Ferraro as his running mate. *(Gyory Collection/ Cathy Casriel Photo)*

nomination four years later against Bush, and then served as Bob Dole's running mate in 1996), Newt Gingrich of Georgia (future speaker of the House), and Trent Lott of Mississippi (future Senate majority leader) shaped a platform that embraced supply-side economics, including a new bundle of tax cut proposals, and encouraged a return to the gold standard. "I carried the water for [Reagan] on two other tax increases, and I've had enough," Lott was quoted as saying. "I may throw rocks if I have to." Republican House members did just that in Reagan's second term, during the contentious debate over tax reform.

On the closing night of the GOP convention,

GERALDINE ANNE FERRARO

PARTY: Democrat

DATE OF BIRTH: August 26, 1935

PLACE OF BIRTH: Newburgh, New York

PARENTS: Dominick and Antonetta L. Corrieri

EDUCATION: B.A., Marymount Manhattan College, 1956; J.D., Fordham University Law School, 1960

FAMILY: Married John Zaccaro, 1960; children: Donna, John, and Laura

CAREER: Lawyer; assistant district attorney for borough of Queens (New York City), 1974–78; elected to U.S. House of Representatives (NY), 1978, 1980, 1982; unsuccessful candidate for U.S. vice president (first woman vice presidential nominee of a major American political party), 1984; fellow, Harvard Institute of Politics, 1988; managing partner, Keck Mahin Cate & Koether (New York), 1993–94; appointed U.S. ambassador to United Nations Human Rights Commission, 1994–95; guest moderator and co-host, CNN *Crossfire*, 1996–97; unsuccessful New York state Democratic primary candidate for U.S. Senate, 1992, 1998; consultant, author

however, no rock-throwers were casting stones when the Goliath of the party took center stage. Reagan gave a speech that was as valedictory as it was forward-looking. He began with "a little stroll down memory lane," reminding his listeners of how the "misery index" (obtained by adding together the unemployment and inflation rates) had declined from more than 20 percent, in 1980, to 11.6 percent. He asked the same question he had raised four years earlier: "Are you better off than you were four years ago?" And he struck the contrast between his party and its opponents in these terms: "The choices this year are not just between two different personalities, or between two political parties. They are between two different visions of the future, two fundamen-

tally different ways of governing—their government of pessimism, fear, and limits, or ours of hope, confidence, and growth."

The General Campaign

Both Mondale and Reagan made early forays onto their opponent's home turf. Mondale and Ferraro officially began their campaign in Jackson, Mississippi, and then traveled to Texas—a state that every successful Democratic presidential candidate in the twentieth century carried, with the exception of Bill Clinton. For his part, Reagan made one of his first stops a Roman Catholic Church festival in Hoboken, New Jersey, accompanied by Frank Sinatra. The president's attendance at the pasta dinner was one in a series of efforts to convince white ethnic Democrats that he was more in tune with their lives and their politics than their traditional party. For Mondale, his Southern swing was the first in a number of attempts to knock his Republican opponent off balance and disrupt the rhythm of the Reagan campaign's confident stride.

In its selection of campaign issues, the Mondale campaign paralleled its geographical strategy of flying into the teeth of the storm. In a maneuver perhaps borne of necessity, Mondale aimed a frontal assault at what appeared to be the strongest sections of the Reagan campaign fortress: the peace and prosperity of the previous four years. Mondale's attacks on the Reagan record took on the tone of a series of Cassandra-like warnings: Not only were the recent good times not so good for many Americans, but they would ultimately lead to disaster just around the corner—a ballooning budget deficit, a widening gap between rich and poor, and an escalating arms race with the Soviets. Again and again, Mondale pleaded with voters to look behind the curtain and see, with their own eyes, what he claimed to see—namely, that Reagan was a modern-day Wizard of Oz, excellent only at the creation of illusions.

Accompanied by scores of union leaders and workers, Walter Mondale and Geraldine Ferraro march in New York City's 1984 Labor Day parade. To Mondale's left is New York governor Mario Cuomo. *(AP Wide World Photos)*

Taxes, the Deficit, and the Economy

Mondale is best remembered for his pledge at the Democratic convention that he would raise taxes—a breathtakingly brazen statement, in the context of today's virulent anti-tax politics. Less well recalled is the other shoe that Mondale dropped: His contention that Reagan had a secret plan to raise taxes in his second term in office, in order to come to grips with the federal budget deficit. Mondale hoped that voters would be alarmed at the prospect of deficits as far as the eye could see. During the 1980 campaign, Reagan had promised to cut taxes, increase defense spending, and balance the budget. By 1984, the government was projected to run deficits of at least $200 billion annually through the rest of the decade; the Congressional Budget Office ventured that the budget deficit might rise as high as $300 billion by 1989 if nothing was done. Once Mondale succeeded in getting the public's attention focused on the deficit, he hoped to persuade them that his prescription of austerity would

make the economy healthier in the long term than would Reagan's dangerously illusory patent medicine. The Democrat tempered his plans to increase domestic spending, in order to meet his goal of reducing the deficit by two-thirds during his administration. All in all, given the success of future presidential candidates such as Ross Perot in exploiting the issue of the deficit, Mondale's political instincts were not wholly misguided.

Reagan initially was somewhat nonplussed by Mondale's gambit. Back in January, he had in fact requested the Treasury Department to study possible modifications of the tax system, and to report back after the election. During the summer, Reagan said there was no plan to raise taxes, but left the door open to that possibility if deficits continued, even after the federal budget was cut back as far as possible. Reagan was more in command when he shifted his focus from the future to the record of his past, and from talk of deficits to talk of taxes. "I have reduced the tax burden on the American people, and I want to reduce

Geraldine Ferraro, the Democratic Party's nominee for vice president, appears here on *The Donahue Show*. She was the first woman to run on a major party presidential ticket. *(AP Wide World Photos)*

it even further," he said, adding that Mondale had been a tax-and-spender his entire political career. "For him, raising taxes is a first resort. For me, it is a last resort." Reagan and his strategists were wagering that the time-proven issue of taxes would cut more ice with voters than the more abstract economics of deficit spending.

Mondale attempted to manufacture his own wedge issue on the economy, by claiming that many working Americans were being left behind as the national economy raced forward. Responding to Reagan's frequent invocations of Democratic presidents such as Roosevelt, Truman, and Kennedy (as well as Mondale's political hero, Minnesotan Hubert Humphrey), Mondale found himself trying to call home the working-class, "lunch pail" voters who were the base of his party. He said his opponent showed "uncaring, icy indifference" toward such social programs as Social Security, Medicare, student loans, and food programs for the needy. At a rally in Boston the week before the election, Mondale told a crowd of 50,000: "I come to you today as a people's Democrat, as a full-employment Democrat in the tradition of Roosevelt and Truman and Kennedy and Humphrey." In contrast, he said, the Reagan administration had been a disaster for the underprivileged: "If you're unemployed, it's too bad. If you're old, it's tough luck. If you're sick, it's good luck. If you're

black or Hispanic, you're out of luck. And if you're handicapped, you shouldn't be."

Mondale's populist message had little bite, however, when compared to Reagan's mantra of peace and prosperity, and his warning that Mondale would lead the country back to the 1970s, and "an endless desert of worsening inflation and recession." According to Election Day exit polls, Reagan appealed across the board to the less well-off as well as the wealthy, to the yuppie and the farmer alike, to the high school graduate as well as the college educated. Mondale only had conspicuous success among blacks, Jewish voters, and families earning less than $5,000 a year.

Foreign Policy and Leadership

"My fellow Americans," Reagan said during a sound check before his weekly radio broadcast on August 11, "I'm pleased to tell you today that I've signed legislation that will outlaw Russia forever. We begin bombing in five minutes." The president's one-liner had unforeseen reverberations for him throughout the fall. With a single quip, he gave his political opponents ammunition for a broadside attack that continued for the next three months: Reagan was fundamentally untrustworthy to have his finger on the nuclear button, the Democrats charged, for reasons of policy and personal competence.

On the question of foreign policy, Mondale aimed to portray himself as a president who would be stern with the Soviet Union, but not unwilling to go to the bargaining table. While criticizing Reagan's military budgets as exorbitant, he proposed annual increases of 4 to 5 percent in defense spending, and committed himself to strengthening conventional forces. Mondale also supported new weapons systems such as the Stealth bomber and the Trident submarine, while opposing the B-1 bomber and the MX missile. He argued, however, that it took a strong leader to recognize the international peril of the arms race, and to meet the Soviets on what he called "the common ground of survival." In contrast, Mondale charged, Reagan was the first president in the nuclear age not to have negotiated on arms control. Compounding what the Democrat argued was a fundamental error in judgment, Reagan backed a space-based antimissile system, dubbed "Star Wars," as a solution to the danger of nuclear war. In October, during the candidates' second debate, Mondale asked: "Why

President Ronald Reagan and Democratic challenger Walter Mondale engaged in two televised debates during the 1984 presidential campaign. Mondale charged that Reagan would not admit it if he planned to raise taxes and then declared, "I just did." *(Courtesy Ronald Reagan Library)*

don't we stop this madness now, and draw a line to keep the heavens free of war?"

For his part, the president vowed to stick to his guns on national defense. While stating his plan to work toward the abolition of all nuclear weapons in his second term, Reagan refused to back off his assertion that the Soviet Union was an "evil empire," and maintained that America's defense build-up was a rational means of deterrence against an aggressive foe. And, as with taxes, the president drew a clear contrast between his policies and the "policies of weakness" of the past, and connected his opponent with the latter. During their second debate, Reagan referred to a Mondale commercial in which the candidate stood on the deck of the aircraft carrier Nimitz: "That's an image of strength. Except that if he had had his way when the Nimitz was being planned, he would have been deep in the water out there, because there wouldn't have been any Nimitz to stand on. He was against it."

During the course of the campaign, and especially after a first debate in which Reagan turned in an uncharacteristically poor performance, Mondale and fellow Democrats raised questions as to whether the 73-year-old president was too old to serve another term in office. (See "The Fitness Issue," p. 967.) Mondale also pointed to the 1983 terrorist bombing of a Marine barracks in Lebanon, in which 241 American soldiers were killed, as an example of Reagan being asleep at the switch. In the vice presidential debate, however, Ferraro was unable to do more than break even against Bush, who appeared more assured and comfortable on foreign policy issues than his challenger. Thanks in part to Reagan's stronger second debate, the issue of the incumbent's competence never became a serious obstacle to his reelection. Indeed, throughout the campaign, it was Mondale who had to struggle to convince the public that he had the leadership qualities necessary to be president.

THE FITNESS ISSUE

*I*n the first of two presidential debates in October 1984, Ronald Reagan turned in an uncharacteristically poor performance, appearing tentative and defensive, and lacked the command he usually displayed on television. Two days later, the *Wall Street Journal* ran a lead article with the headline, "Reagan Debate Performance Invites Open Speculation on His Ability to Serve"; in the article, a gerontologist commented that a man of Reagan's age should be watched for symptoms of senility. Democrats also seized upon the president's stumble. Representative Tony Coelho (D-CA), who chaired the Democratic Congressional Campaign Committee, said Reagan "looked old and acted old" in the debate. When asked if the 73-year-old president acted doddering, he responded, "Well, he didn't quite drool." While Reagan's opponent, Walter Mondale, was not quite so blunt, the 56-year-old Democratic presidential nominee made questions of his opponent's competence an increasingly central part of his campaign, asking: "Who's in charge?"

Not surprisingly, Reagan and his campaign downplayed the issue. Senator Paul Laxalt (R-NV), a friend of Reagan's, said the White House staff had bombarded the president with facts and figures prior to the debate, and then "brutalized" him by putting him through six dress rehearsals—all while Reagan was in the middle of meetings with Soviet foreign minister Andrei Gromyko. The White House physician declared that the president's health was "excellent." Reagan himself said he was willing to arm-wrestle his opponent anytime.

The Mondale campaign seized upon their candidate's success as a potential shift in the momentum of the race. Polls indicated that the public viewed Mondale significantly more favorably after the debate; but Reagan's favorable ratings remained very high. The second debate, two weeks later in Kansas City, was held up as Mondale's last, best chance to help himself pull off a near-miraculous comeback.

That evening, it was Henry Trewhitt, diplomatic correspondent for the *Baltimore Sun*, who threw the much-anticipated fitness question at the president. Reagan replied with one of the more memorable quips in the history of presidential debates:

TREWHITT: Mr. President, I want to raise an issue that I think has been lurking out there for two or three weeks, and cast it specifically in national security terms. You already are the oldest president in history, and some of your staff say you were tired after your most recent encounter with Mr. Mondale. I recall, yes, that President Kennedy . . . had to go for days on end with very little sleep during the Cuban missile crisis. Is there any doubt in your mind that you would be able to function in such circumstances?

REAGAN: Not at all, Mr. Trewhitt, and I want you to know that, also, I will not make age an issue of this campaign. I am not going to exploit for political purposes my opponent's youth and inexperience.

In all, Reagan turned in a significantly stronger performance in the second debate, with no major gaffes. Democratic hopes faded of cashing in on the issue of Reagan's fitness for office, and the president cruised to victory on Election Day.

Realignment, or Simply Reelection? A Look at the Election Returns

Reagan's victory ranks among the most lopsided of the twentieth century, along with Franklin Roosevelt's victory over Alfred Landon in 1936 and Richard Nixon's triumph over George McGovern in 1972. After the 1984 election, there was much talk that the results signaled a realignment of the American electorate, ensuring a Republican lock on the presidency for the foreseeable future. As is often the case in politics, however, the future is not so easily foreseen, and the GOP "lock" only lasted until 1992, when Americans refused George Bush a second term as president and turned, instead, to Arkansas Democratic governor Bill Clinton.

Was Reagan's 1984 triumph simply a function of his personal popularity, and the peace and prosperity of the 1980s? Or did it signal a long-lasting shift in presidential electoral voting patterns? To aid in studying this question, the table on the facing page of the Republican presidential vote, from 1960 to 2000, was constructed. At the top of each column is listed the year of the election, the name of the Republican candidate, and the percentage of the vote he received nationwide. Below that is listed the *difference* between the percentage of the vote the GOP candidate received in a particular state (arranged by region), and his national percentage. For example, in 1984 Reagan received 58.8 percent of the vote nationwide. In Maine, Reagan won 60.8 percent of the vote, 2 percent more than his share of the national vote; in Rhode Island, he received only 51.7 percent of the vote—7.1 percent less than his share of the national vote.

By displaying the candidate's share of the vote in this fashion, one can distinguish a Republican candidate's general strength nationwide from his particular strength in a specific region (or regions) of the country. Studying shifts in a party's strength in a particular region will offer clues as to whether significant realignment may have taken place. (Kevin Phillips made very good use of this technique in his 1969 book, *The Emerging Republican Majority*; in fact, Phillips was prescient in seeing many of the trends described here.) Over time, one may detect regions of the country where, at one point in time, GOP presidential candidates win percentages of the vote lower than their percentage nationwide, and then, at a later point in time, win percentages of the vote that are higher than their percentage nationwide.

Looking at the Republicans' performance in presidential elections before and after 1984, region by region, suggests that Ronald Reagan's presidency signaled a high tide for the GOP, but not an earthquake that caused a long-lasting shift in the American presidential electorate toward the Republican Party.

As the table indicates, the East Coast has not been an especially friendly place for Republican presidential candidates for several decades now. Before Reagan, New England, once a bastion of Republican strength, was at best neutral toward the GOP; in the middle Atlantic states, GOP presidential candidates consistently underperformed, relative to their performance nationwide. After Reagan, the electoral situation here became even worse for Republicans, as New England joined the middle Atlantic region as a general weakness for the GOP.

Before Reagan, the industrial states of the Midwest were swing states. Some years, the Republican presidential candidate performed better than nationwide in the majority of these states; in other years, the performance was worse than nationwide in most of these states. After Reagan, very little changed in this part of the Midwest. Before Reagan, GOP presidential candidates found the Great Plains a very welcoming place, typically getting larger percentages of the vote there than they did nationwide. The Great Plains states remained strongly Republican after Reagan.

Ironically, the election and reelection of Reagan, the former governor of California, also signaled the decline of the Republican Party on the West Coast at the presidential level. Before Reagan, the West Coast was a toss-up for the GOP; sometimes presidential candidates performed better there than nationwide, sometimes worse. Starting in 1984, GOP presidential candidates have underperformed on the West Coast, relative to their nationwide percentage, in every state except Alaska. The Rocky Mountain states were a GOP stronghold before Reagan, and remained so after Reagan.

The South is the one region where a positive Republican realignment may be detected after Reagan. The 1964 candidacy of Barry Goldwater, of course, signaled the beginning of significant changes in the South, though Nixon's performance there in 1968 was severely hurt by the third-party candidacy of George Wallace. Significantly, though, both Ford in 1976 and Reagan in 1980 underperformed in the South, relative to their percentage of the popular vote nationwide, when opposed by a southern Democratic candidate.

Election Year	1960	1964	1968	1972	1976	1980	1984	1988	1992	1996	2000
Republican Candidate	Nixon	Goldwater	Nixon	Nixon	Ford	Reagan	Reagan	G.H.W. Bush	G.H.W. Bush	Dole	G.W. Bush
NATIONAL PERCENTAGE	49.5	38.5	43.4	60.7	48	50.7	58.8	53.4	37.4	40.7	47.9

DIFFERENCE BETWEEN NATIONAL AND STATE PERCENTAGES

	1960	1964	1968	1972	1976	1980	1984	1988	1992	1996	2000
East											
Maine	7.5	−7.3	−0.3	0.8	0.9	−5.1	2	1.9	−7	−9.9	−3.9
New Hampshire	3.9	−2.1	8.7	3.3	6.7	7	9.9	9.1	0.2	−1.3	0.2
Vermont	9.1	−4.8	9.4	2	6.3	−6.3	−0.9	−2.3	−7	−9.6	−7.2
Massachusetts	−9.9	−15.1	−10.5	−15.5	−7.6	−8.8	−7.6	−8	−8.4	−12.6	−15.4
Rhode Island	−13.1	−19.4	−11.6	−7.7	−3.9	−13.5	−7.1	−9.5	−8.4	−13.9	−16
Connecticut	−3.2	−6.4	0.9	−2.1	4.1	−2.5	1.9	−1.4	−1.6	−6	−9.5
New York	−2.2	−7.2	0.9	−2.2	−0.5	−4	−5	−5.9	−3.5	−10.1	−12.7
New Jersey	−0.3	−4.6	2.7	0.9	2.1	1.3	1.3	2.8	3.2	−4.8	−7.6
Pennsylvania	−0.8	−3.8	0.6	−1.6	−0.3	−1.1	−5.5	−2.7	−1.3	−0.7	−1.5
Delaware	−0.5	0.3	1.7	−1.1	−1.4	−3.5	1	2.5	−2.1	−4.1	−6
Maryland	−3.1	−4	−1.5	0.6	−1	−6.5	−6.3	−2.3	−1.8	−2.4	−7.7
Midwest											
Ohio	3.8	−1.4	1.8	−1.1	0.7	0.8	0.1	1.6	0.9	0.3	2.1
Indiana	5.5	5.1	6.9	5.4	5.3	5.3	2.9	6.4	5.5	6.4	8.8
Illinois	0.3	2	3.7	−1.7	2.1	−1.1	−2.6	−2.7	−3.1	−3.9	−5.3
Michigan	−0.7	−5.4	−1.9	−4.5	3.8	−1.7	0.4	0.2	−1	−2.2	−1.8
Wisconsin	2.3	−0.8	4.5	−7.3	−0.2	−2.8	−4.6	−5.6	−0.6	−2.2	−0.3
Minnesota	−0.3	−2.5	−2	−9.1	−6	−8.1	−9.3	−7.5	−5.5	−5.7	−2.4
Iowa	7.2	−0.6	9.6	−3.1	1.5	0.6	−5.5	−8.9	−0.1	−0.8	0.3
Missouri	0.2	−2.5	1.5	1.6	−0.5	0.5	1.2	−1.6	−3.5	0.5	2.5
Kansas	10.9	6.6	11.4	7	4.5	7.2	7.5	2.4	1.5	13.6	10.1
Nebraska	12.6	8.9	16.4	9.8	11.2	14.8	11.8	6.8	9.2	13	14.4
South Dakota	8.7	5.9	9.9	−6.5	2.4	9.8	4.2	−0.6	3.3	5.8	12.4
North Dakota	5.9	3.4	12.5	1.4	3.6	13.5	6	2.6	6.8	6.2	12.8
West											
Montana	1.6	2.1	7.2	−2.8	4.8	6.1	1.7	−1.3	−2.3	3.4	10.5
Idaho	4.3	10.6	13.4	3.5	11.9	15.8	13.6	8.7	4.6	11.5	19.3
Wyoming	5.5	4.9	12.4	8.3	11.3	11.9	11.7	7.1	2.2	9.1	19.9
Colorado	5.1	−0.3	7.1	1.9	6	4.4	4.6	−0.3	−1.5	5.1	2.9
New Mexico	−0.1	1.7	8.4	0.3	2.7	4.2	0.9	−1.5	−0.1	1.2	0
Arizona	6	11.9	11.4	0.9	8.4	9.9	7.6	6.6	1.1	3.6	3.1
Utah	5.3	6.6	13.1	6.9	14.4	22.1	15.7	12.8	6	13.7	18.9
Nevada	−0.7	2.9	4.1	3	2.2	11.8	7	5.5	−2.7	2.2	1.6
California	0.6	2.3	4.4	−5.7	1.3	2	−1.3	−2.3	−4.8	−2.5	−6.2
Oregon	3.1	−2.5	6.4	−8.3	−0.2	−2.4	−2.9	−6.8	−4.9	−1.6	−1.4
Washington	1.2	−1.1	1.7	−3.8	2	−1	−3	−4.9	−5.4	−3.4	−3.3
Alaska	1.4	−4.4	1.9	−2.6	9.9	3.6	7.9	6.2	2.1	10.1	10.7
Hawaii	0.5	−17.3	−4.7	1.8	0.1	−7.8	−3.7	−8.6	−0.7	−9.1	−10.4
South											
West Virginia	−2.2	−6.4	−2.6	2.9	−6.1	−5.4	−3.7	−5.9	−2	−3.9	4
Virginia	2.9	7.7	0	7.1	1.3	2.3	3.5	4.6	6	8	8.1
North Carolina	−1.6	5.3	−3.9	8.8	−3.8	−1.4	3.1	8.1	10.6	9.1	8.9
South Carolina	−0.7	20.4	−5.3	9.9	−4.9	−1.1	4.8	6.4	5.5	6.3	6.8
Georgia	−12.1	15.6	−13	14.3	−15	−9.7	1.4	6.4	3.5	1.6	1
Florida	2	10.4	−2.9	11.2	−1.4	4.8	6.5	7.5	3.5	1.6	1
Alabama	−7.8	31	−29.4	11.7	−5.4	−1.9	1.7	5.8	10.2	9.4	8.6
Mississippi	−24.8	48.6	−29.9	17.5	−0.3	−1.3	3.1	6.5	12.3	8.5	9.7
Tennessee	3.4	6	−5.6	7	−5.1	−2	−1	4.5	5	4.9	3.3
Kentucky	4.1	−2.8	0.4	2.7	−2.4	−1.6	1.2	2.1	3.9	4.2	8.6
Arkansas	−6.4	4.9	−12.4	8.2	−13.1	−2.6	1.7	3	−1.9	−3.9	3.4
Louisiana	−20.9	18.3	−19.9	4.6	−2	0.5	2	0.9	3.6	−0.8	4.7
Texas	−1	−2	−3.5	5.5	0	4.6	4.8	2.6	3.2	8.1	11.4
Oklahoma	9.5	5.8	4.3	13	2	9.8	9.8	4.5	5.2	7.6	12.4
District of Columbia	a	−24	−25.2	−39.1	−31.5	−37.3	−45.1	−39.1	−28.3	−31.4	−38.9

a The District of Columbia received the presidential vote in 1961.

Since Reagan, however, Republican presidential candidates have consistently done better in the South than they have nationwide—even when faced by a Democratic candidate who hailed from the South, as has been the case in the past three elections. GOP strength in the South has persisted over the last five elections, even when neither the nominee nor his running mate were from the South, as was the case in 1996 with Bob Dole of Kansas and Jack Kemp of New York.

To sum up, the strongest evidence for a Reagan realignment in favor of the Republican Party appears in the South. Realignment since Reagan has gone against the GOP, however, on both the East and West coasts. The net result has been increased polarization of the American electorate in presidential contests, as shown most dramatically in the 2000 election.

Dante J. Scala

Bibliography

Abramson, Paul R., John H. Aldrich, and David W. Rohde. *Change and Continuity in the 1984 Elections*. Washington, DC: Congressional Quarterly Press, 1987.

Barone, Michael, and Grant Ujifusa. *The Almanac of American Politics 1986*. Washington, DC: National Journal, 1985.

Drew, Elizabeth. *Campaign Journal: The Political Events of 1983–1984*. New York: Macmillan, 1985.

Germond, Jack W., and Jules Witcover. *Wake Us When It's Over: Presidential Politics of 1984*. New York: Macmillan, 1985.

Nelson, Michael, ed. *The Elections of 1984*. Washington, DC: Congressional Quarterly Press, 1985.

Presidential Elections 1789–1996. Washington, DC: Congressional Quarterly, 1997.

Ranney, Austin, ed. *The American Elections of 1984*. Durham, NC: Duke University Press, 1985.

Shields, Mark. *On the Campaign Trail*. Chapel Hill, NC: Algonquin Books of Chapel Hill, 1985.

THE VOTE: ELECTION OF 1984

State	Total No. of Electors	Total Popular Vote	Electoral Vote R	Electoral Vote D	Margin of Victory Votes	Margin of Victory % Total Vote	Reagan Republican Votes	Reagan Republican %	Mondale Democrat Votes	Mondale Democrat %	Others Votes	Others %
Alabama	9	1,441,713	9		320,950	22.3%	872,849	60.5%	551,899	38.3%	16,965	1.2%
Alaska	3	207,605	3		76,370	36.8%	138,377	66.7%	62,007	29.9%	7,221	3.5%
Arizona	7	1,025,897	7		347,562	33.9%	681,416	66.4%	333,854	32.5%	10,627	1.0%
Arkansas	6	884,406	6		196,128	22.2%	534,774	60.5%	338,646	38.3%	10,986	1.2%
California	47	9,505,423	47		1,544,490	16.2%	5,467,009	57.5%	3,922,519	41.3%	115,895	1.2%
Colorado	8	1,295,381	8		366,844	28.3%	821,818	63.4%	454,974	35.1%	18,589	1.4%
Connecticut	8	1,466,900	8		321,280	21.9%	890,877	60.7%	569,597	38.8%	6,426	0.4%
Delaware	3	254,572	3		50,534	19.9%	152,190	59.8%	101,656	39.9%	726	0.3%
District of Columbia	3	211,288		3	151,399	71.7%	29,009	13.7%	180,408	85.4%	1,871	0.9%
Florida	21	4,180,051	21		1,281,534	30.7%	2,730,350	65.3%	1,448,816	34.7%	885	0.0%
Georgia	12	1,776,093	12		362,094	20.4%	1,068,722	60.2%	706,628	39.8%	743	0.0%
Hawaii	4	335,846	4		37,896	11.3%	185,050	55.1%	147,154	43.8%	3,642	1.1%
Idaho	4	411,144	4		189,013	46.0%	297,523	72.4%	108,510	26.4%	5,111	1.2%
Illinois	24	4,819,088	24		620,604	12.9%	2,707,103	56.2%	2,086,499	43.3%	25,486	0.5%
Indiana	12	2,233,069	12		535,749	24.0%	1,377,230	61.7%	841,481	37.7%	14,358	0.6%
Iowa	8	1,319,805	8		97,468	7.4%	703,088	53.3%	605,620	45.9%	11,097	0.8%
Kansas	7	1,021,991	7		344,147	33.7%	677,296	66.3%	333,149	32.6%	11,546	1.1%
Kentucky	9	1,369,345	9		282,163	20.6%	821,702	60.0%	539,539	39.4%	8,104	0.6%
Louisiana	10	1,706,822	10		385,713	22.6%	1,037,299	60.8%	651,586	38.2%	17,937	1.1%
Maine	4	553,144	4		121,985	22.1%	336,500	60.8%	214,515	38.8%	2,129	0.4%
Maryland	10	1,675,873	10		91,983	5.5%	879,918	52.5%	787,935	47.0%	8,020	0.5%
Massachusetts	13	2,559,453	13		71,330	2.8%	1,310,936	51.2%	1,239,606	48.4%	8,911	0.3%
Michigan	20	3,801,658	20		721,933	19.0%	2,251,571	59.2%	1,529,638	40.2%	20,449	0.5%
Minnesota	10	2,084,449		10	3,761	0.2%	1,032,603	49.5%	1,036,364	49.7%	15,482	0.7%
Mississippi	7	940,192	7		229,285	24.4%	581,477	61.8%	352,192	37.5%	6,523	0.7%
Missouri	11	2,122,771	11		425,605	20.0%	1,274,188	60.0%	848,583	40.0%	0	0.0%
Montana	4	384,377	4		85,708	22.3%	232,450	60.5%	146,742	38.2%	5,185	1.3%
Nebraska	5	652,090	5		272,188	41.7%	460,054	70.6%	187,866	28.8%	4,170	0.6%
Nevada	4	286,667	4		97,115	33.9%	188,770	65.8%	91,655	32.0%	6,242	2.2%
New Hampshire	4	388,953	4		146,656	37.7%	267,051	68.7%	120,395	31.0%	1,507	0.4%
New Jersey	16	3,217,862	16		672,307	20.9%	1,933,630	60.1%	1,261,323	39.2%	22,909	0.7%
New Mexico	5	514,370	5		105,332	20.5%	307,101	59.7%	201,769	39.2%	5,500	1.1%
New York	36	6,806,810	36		545,154	8.0%	3,664,763	53.8%	3,119,609	45.8%	22,438	0.3%
North Carolina	13	2,175,361	13		522,194	24.0%	1,346,481	61.9%	824,287	37.9%	4,593	0.2%
North Dakota	3	308,971	3		95,907	31.0%	200,336	64.8%	104,429	33.8%	4,206	1.4%
Ohio	23	4,547,619	23		853,120	18.8%	2,678,560	58.9%	1,825,440	40.1%	43,619	1.0%
Oklahoma	8	1,255,676	8		476,450	37.9%	861,530	68.6%	385,080	30.7%	9,066	0.7%
Oregon	7	1,226,527	7		149,221	12.2%	685,700	55.9%	536,479	43.7%	4,348	0.4%
Pennsylvania	25	4,844,903	25		356,192	7.4%	2,584,323	53.3%	2,228,131	46.0%	32,449	0.7%
Rhode Island	4	410,492	4		14,974	3.6%	212,080	51.7%	197,106	48.0%	1,306	0.3%
South Carolina	8	968,540	8		271,069	28.0%	615,539	63.6%	344,470	35.6%	8,531	0.9%
South Dakota	3	317,867	3		84,154	26.5%	200,267	63.0%	116,113	36.5%	1,487	0.5%
Tennessee	11	1,711,993	11		278,498	16.3%	990,212	57.8%	711,714	41.6%	10,067	0.6%
Texas	29	5,397,571	29		1,484,152	27.5%	3,433,428	63.6%	1,949,276	36.1%	14,867	0.3%
Utah	5	629,656	5		313,736	49.8%	469,105	74.5%	155,369	24.7%	5,182	0.8%
Vermont	3	234,561	3		40,135	17.1%	135,865	57.9%	95,730	40.8%	2,966	1.3%
Virginia	12	2,146,635	12		540,828	25.2%	1,337,078	62.3%	796,250	37.1%	13,307	0.6%
Washington	10	1,883,910	10		244,318	13.0%	1,051,670	55.8%	807,352	42.9%	24,888	1.3%
West Virginia	6	735,742	6		77,358	10.5%	405,483	55.1%	328,125	44.6%	2,134	0.3%
Wisconsin	11	2,212,016	11		202,953	9.2%	1,198,800	54.2%	995,847	45.0%	17,369	0.8%
Wyoming	3	188,968	3		79,871	42.3%	133,241	70.5%	53,370	28.2%	2,357	1.2%
TOTAL	538	92,652,116	525	13	16,877,090	18.2%	54,454,392	58.8%	37,577,302	40.6%	620,422	0.7%

For sources, see p. 1134.

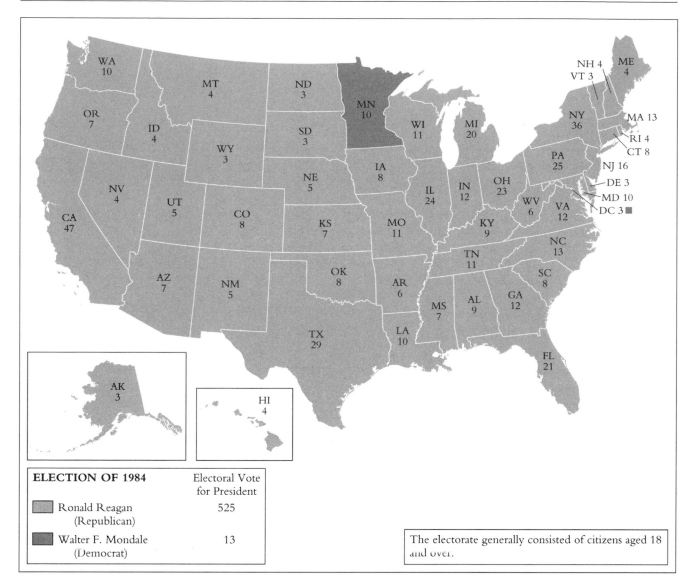

ELECTION OF 1984	Electoral Vote for President
Ronald Reagan (Republican)	525
Walter F. Mondale (Democrat)	13

The electorate generally consisted of citizens aged 18 and over.

DOCUMENTS: ELECTION OF 1984

With the United States in the midst of an economic recovery, anyone who challenged the popular Republican president, Ronald Reagan, faced a difficult task. Furthermore, many voters identified former Vice President Walter Mondale, the Democratic nominee, with the Carter administration's failures. Mondale suffered the worst Electoral College defeat in American history.

Part of Reagan's appeal was that he simplified the Cold War into a struggle between good and evil. In doing so, he restored American confidence by calling for a spiritual awakening to overcome "sin and evil in the world." Document 1, Reagan's "Evil Empire" speech given before the National Association of Evangelicals, illustrated these themes.

In order for Mondale to have a chance at victory, he needed a boost. When Mondale selected a running mate, New York Representative Geraldine Ferraro, many experts believed that it just might be the key to a surprise victory. Document 2, a New York Times *article, examined her impact on the Democratic ticket. As the first woman on a major-party ticket, Ferraro faced many questions about her being a token nominee and her qualifications. In Document 3, an excerpt from the vice presidential debate, Ferraro assailed her critics and detailed her experience.*

At the Democratic Convention, Governor Mario M. Cuomo of New York delivered a speech, Document 4, attacking Reagan's economic policies. He claimed that the nation had become a "Tale of Two Cities," where the government denied support to starving children, in order to give tax breaks and wasteful defense contracts to large corporations. Mondale's speech accepting the Democratic nomination, Document 5, further assaulted the Reagan administration's unequal, deficit-laden economic recovery and dangerous arms buildup, offering a Democratic platform of peace and prosperity for all. Most remembered was Mondale's pledge: "Mr. Reagan will raise taxes, and so will I. He won't tell you. I just did."

Document 6, Reagan's speech accepting the Republican nomination, hailed his domestic and foreign policy achievements, and requested another fours years to complete the "national crusade to make America great again." In Document 7, an excerpt from the first presidential debate, Reagan mentioned that he not ask, "Are you better off than you were four years ago?" because the answer was clear. However, Mondale challenged Americans to see beyond the shortsighted policies of the Reagan administration and ask, "Will your children be better off?"

Document 1

Ronald Reagan's "Evil Empire" Speech, Orlando, Florida, March 8, 1983

The American experiment in democracy rests on this insight. Its discovery was the great triumph of our Founding Fathers, voiced by William Penn when he said: "If we will not be governed by God, we must be governed by tyrants." Explaining the inalienable rights of men, Jefferson said, "The God who gave us life, gave us liberty at the same time." And it was George Washington who said that "of all the dispositions and habits which lead to political prosperity, religion and morality are indispensable supports."

And finally, that shrewdest of all observers of American democracy, Alexis de Tocqueville, put it eloquently after he had gone on a search for the secret of America's greatness and genius—and he said: "Not until I went into the churches of America and heard her pulpits aflame with righteousness did I understand the greatness and the genius of America. . . . America is good. And if America ever ceases to be good, America will cease to be great."

Well, I'm pleased to be here today with you who are keeping America great by keeping her good. Only through your work and prayers and those of millions of others can we hope to survive this perilous century and keep alive this experiment in liberty, this last, best hope of man. . . .

Now, I'm sure that you must get discouraged at times, but you've done better than you know, perhaps. There's a great spiritual awakening in America, a renewal of the traditional values that have been the bedrock of America's goodness and greatness. . . .

There is sin and evil in the world, and we're enjoined by Scripture and the Lord Jesus to oppose it with all our might. Our nation, too, has a legacy of evil with which it must deal. . . . For example, the long struggle of minority citizens for equal rights, once a source of disunity and civil war, is now a point of pride for all Americans. We must never go back. There is no room for racism, anti-Semitism, or other forms of ethnic and racial hatred in this country. . . .

But whatever sad episodes exist in our past, any objective observer must hold a positive view of American history, a history that has been the story of hopes fulfilled and dreams made into reality. Especially in this century, America has kept alight the torch of freedom, but not just for ourselves but for millions of others around the world. . . .

I pointed out that, as good Marxist-Leninists, the Soviet leaders have openly and publicly declared that the only morality they recognize is that which will further their cause, which is world revolution. I think I should point out I was only quoting Lenin, their guiding spirit, who said in 1920 that they repudiate all morality that proceeds from supernatural ideas—that's their name for religion—or ideas that are outside class conceptions. Morality is entirely subordinate to the interests of class war. And everything is moral that is necessary for the annihilation of the old, exploiting social order and for uniting the proletariat. . . .

This doesn't mean we should isolate ourselves and refuse to seek an understanding with them. . . . At the same time, however, they must be made to understand we will never compromise our principles and standards. We will never give away our freedom. We will never abandon our belief in God. . . .

The reality is that we must find peace through strength. . . .

A number of years ago, I heard a young father . . . addressing a tremendous gathering in California. . . . He went on: "I would rather see my little girls die now, still believing in God, than have them grow up under communism and one day die no longer believing in God."

There were thousands of young people in that audience. They came to their feet with shouts of joy. They had instantly recognized the profound truth in what he had said, with regard to the physical and the soul and what was truly important.

Yes, let us pray for the salvation of all of those who live in that totalitarian darkness—pray they will discover the joy of knowing God. But until they do, let us be aware that while they preach the supremacy of the state, declare its omnipotence over individual man, and predict its eventual domination of all peoples on the Earth, they are the focus of evil in the modern world. . . .

I urge you to beware the temptation of pride—the temptation of blithely declaring yourselves above it all and label both sides equally at fault, to ignore the facts of history and the aggressive impulses of an evil empire, to simply call the arms race a giant misunderstanding and thereby remove yourself from the struggle between right and wrong and good and evil. . . .

While America's military strength is important, let me add here that I've always maintained that the struggle now going on for the world will never be decided by bombs or rockets, by armies or military might. The real crisis we face today is a spiritual one; at root, it is a test of moral will and faith. . . .

Source: Public Papers and Addresses of the Presidents of the United States: Ronald Reagan, 1983, Book I, January 1 to July 1, 1983 (Washington, DC: Government Printing Office, 1984).

Document 2

Excerpt from the Vice Presidential Debate, October 11, 1984

[John] MASHEK [of *U.S. News & World Report*]: Congresswoman Ferraro, your opponent has served in the House of Representatives, he's been ambassador to the United Nations, ambassador to China, director of the Central Intelligence Agency and now he's been vice president for four years. How does your three terms in the House of Representatives stack up against experience like that?

FERRARO: Well, let me first say that I wasn't born at the age of forty-three, when I entered Congress. I did have a life before that as well. I was a prosecutor for almost five years in the district attorney's office in Queens County, and I was a teacher. There's not only what is

on your paper resume that makes you qualified to run for or to hold office. It's how you approach problems and what your values are. I think if one is taking a look at my career they'll see that I level with the people; that I approach problems analytically; that I am able to assess the various facts with reference to a problem, and I can make the hard decisions. . . . We are facing absolutely massive deficits. . . . People in Johnstown, Pennsylvania, are not terribly thrilled with what's happening in the economy because they're standing in the light of a closed plant because they've lost their jobs. . . . In San Jose, California, they're complaining because they can't export their high-tech qualities—goods—to Japan and other countries. . . . Things are not as great as the administration is wanting us to believe in their television commercials. My feeling, quite frankly, is that I have enough experience to see the problems, address them and make the tough decisions and level with people with reference to those problems. . . .

Being the candidate for vice president of my party is the greatest honor I have ever had. But it's not only a personal achievement for Geraldine Ferraro—and certainly not only the bond that I feel as I go across this country with women throughout the country. I wouldn't be standing here if Fritz Mondale didn't have the courage and my party didn't stand for the values that it does—the values of fairness and equal opportunity. Those values make our country strong, and the future of this country and how strong it will be is what this election is all about. . . . Fritz Mondale has said that he would rather lose a battle for decency than win one over self-interest. Now I agree with him. This campaign is not over. For our country, for our future, for the principles we believe in Walter Mondale and I have just begun to fight.

Source: Commission on Presidential Debates Web site, www.debates.org/pages/trans84b.html.

Document 3

Mario M. Cuomo's Speech to the Democratic Convention, July 17, 1984

Ten days ago, President Reagan admitted that although some people in this country seemed to be doing well nowadays, others were unhappy, even worried, about themselves, their families, and their futures. The President said that he didn't understand that fear. He said, "Why, this country is a shining city on a hill." And the President is right. In many ways we are "a shining city on a hill." But the hard truth is that not everyone is sharing in this city's splendor and glory. . . .

There's another part of the "shining city": the part where some people can't pay their mortgages and most young people can't afford one, where students can't afford the education they need and middle-class parents watch the dream they hold for their children evaporate. In this part of the city there are more poor than ever, more families in trouble. More and more people who need help but can't find it. Even worse, there are elderly people who tremble in the basements of the houses there. And there are people who sleep in the city's streets, in the gutter, where the glitter doesn't show. There are ghettoes where thousands of young people, without a job or an education, give their lives away to drug dealers every day. There is despair, Mr. President, in the faces that you don't see, in the places that you don't visit in your shining city. In fact, Mr. President, this nation is more a "Tale of Two Cities," than it is just a "Shining City on a Hill."

Maybe, Mr. President, if you visited some more places; maybe if you went to Appalachia where some people still live in sheds; maybe if you went to Lackawanna where thousands of unemployed steel workers wonder why we subsidize foreign steel while we surrender their dignity to unemployment and to welfare checks; maybe, Mr. President, if you stopped in at a shelter in Chicago and spoke to the homeless there; maybe, Mr. President, if you asked a woman who had been denied the help she needed to feed her children because you said you needed the money for a tax break for a millionaire or for a missile we couldn't afford to use—maybe then you'd understand. . . .

That struggle to live with dignity is the real story of the shining city. . . .

Source: New York Times, July 17, 1984.

Document 4

Walter Mondale's Nomination Acceptance Speech, July 19, 1984

I do not envy the drowsy harmony of the Republican Party. They squelch debate; we welcome it. They deny differences; we bridge them. They are uniform; we are united. They are a portrait of privilege; we are a mirror of America.

Just look at us at here tonight: Black and white, Asian and Hispanic, Native and immigrant, young and old, urban and rural, male and female—from yuppie to lunchpail, from sea to shining sea. We're all here tonight in this convention speaking for America. And when we in this hall speak for America, it is America speaking. . . .

So, tonight we come to you with a new realism: Ready for the future, and recapturing the best in our tradition.

We know that America must have a strong defense, and a sober view of the Soviets.

We know that government must be as well managed as it is well meaning.

We know that a healthy, growing private economy is the key to the future.

We know that Harry Truman spoke the truth when he said: "A President . . . has to be able to say yes and no, but mostly no."

Look at our platform. There are no defense cuts that weaken our security; no business taxes that weaken our economy; no laundry lists that raid our Treasury.

We are wiser, stronger, and focused on the future. If Mr. Reagan wants to re-run the 1980 campaign: Fine. Let them fight over the past. We're fighting for the American future—and that's why we're going to win this campaign.

One last word to those who voted for Mr. Reagan.

I know what you were saying. But I also know what you were not saying.

You did not vote for a $200 billion deficit.

You did not vote for an arms race.

You did not vote to turn the heavens into a battleground.

You did not vote to savage Social Security and Medicare.

You did not vote to destroy family farming.

You did not vote to trash the civil rights laws.

You did not vote to poison the environment.

You did not vote to assault the poor, the sick, and the disabled.

And you did not vote to pay fifty bucks for a fifty-cent light bulb.

Four years ago, many of you voted for Mr. Reagan because he promised you'd be better off. And today, the rich are better off. But working Americans are worse off, and the middle class is standing on a trap door. . . .

If this administration has a plan for a better future, they're keeping it a secret.

Here is the truth about the future: We are living on borrowed money and borrowed time. These deficits hike interest rates, clobber exports, stunt investment, kill jobs, undermine growth, cheat our kids, and shrink our future.

Whoever is inaugurated in January, the American people will have to pay Mr. Reagan's bills. The budget will be squeezed. Taxes will go up. And anyone who says they won't is not telling the truth to the American people. . . .

Let's tell the truth. It must be done, it must be done. Mr. Reagan will raise taxes, and so will I. He won't tell you. I just did. . . .

To the corporations and freeloaders who play the loopholes or pay no taxes, my message is: Your free ride is over. . . .

As president, I will reassert American values. I'll press for human rights in Central America, and for the removal of all foreign forces from the region. And in my first hundred days, I will stop the illegal war in Nicaragua.

We know the deep differences with the Soviets. And America condemns their repression of dissidents and Jews; their suppression of Solidarity; their invasion of Afghanistan; their meddling around the world.

But the truth is that between us, we have the capacity to destroy the planet. Every president since the bomb went off understood that and talked with the Soviets and negotiated arms control. Why has this administration failed? Why haven't they tried? Why can't they understand the cry of Americans and human beings for sense and sanity in control of these God-awful weapons? Why, why?

Why can't we meet in summit conferences with the Soviet Union at least once a year? Why can't we reach agreements to save this earth? The truth is, we can. . . .

My friends, America is a future each generation must enlarge; a door each generation must open; a promise each generation must keep. . . .

Source: *New York Times,* July 20, 1984.

Document 5

Ronald Reagan's Nomination Acceptance Speech,
August 23, 1984

The choices this year are not just between two different personalities, or between two political parties. They are between two different visions of the future, two fundamentally different ways of governing—their government of pessimism, fear, and limits, or ours of hope, confidence, and growth.

Their government—their government sees people only as members of groups. Ours serves all the people of America as individuals. Theirs lives in the past, seeking to apply the old and failed policies to an era that has passed them by. Ours learns from the past and strives to change by boldly charting a new course for the future.

Theirs lives by promises, the bigger, the better. We offer proven, workable answers. . . .

But how about taxes. They were talked about in San Francisco. Will Rogers once said he never met a man he didn't like. Well if I could paraphrase Will, our friends in the other party have never met a tax they didn't like. They didn't like, or hike. . . .

By nearly every measure, the position of poor Americans worsened under the leadership of our opponents. Teenage drug use, out-of-wedlock births and crime increased dramatically. Urban neighborhoods and schools deteriorated. Those whom Government intended to help discovered a cycle of dependency that could not be broken. Government became a drug, providing temporary relief, but addiction as well. . . .

Our country was also in serious trouble abroad. We had aircraft that couldn't fly and ships that couldn't leave port. Many of our military were on food stamps because of meager earnings, and re-enlistments were down. Ammunition was low, and spare parts were in short supply.

Many of our allies mistrusted us. In the four years before we took office, country after country fell under the Soviet yoke; since January 20, 1981, not one inch of soil has fallen to the Communists.

But worst of all, worst of all Americans were losing the confidence and optimism about the future that has made us unique in the world. Parents were beginning to doubt that their children would have the better life that has been the dream of every American generation.

We can all be proud this pessimism is ended. America is coming back and is more confident than ever about the future. . . .

America is on the move again, and expanding toward new eras of opportunity for everyone. . . . That means a future of sustained economic growth, without inflation, that's going to create for our children and grandchildren a prosperity that finally will last.

Today . . . our troops have newer and better equipment, and their morale is higher. The better armed they are, the less likely it is they will have to use that equipment. But if—but if, heaven forbid, they are ever called upon to defend this nation, nothing would be more immoral than asking them to do so with weapons inferior to those of any possible opponent. . . .

We have heard a lot about deficits this year from those on the other side of the aisle. Well, they should be experts on budget deficits. They've spent most of their political careers creating deficits. For 42—for 42 of the last 50 years, they have controlled both houses of the Congress. And for almost all of those 50 years, deficit spending has been their deliberate policy. Now, however, they call for an end to deficits, they call them ours, yet at the same time the leadership of their party resists our every effort to bring Federal spending under control.

For three years straight they have prevented us from adopting a balanced budget amendment to the Constitution. . . .

They call their policy the "new realism," but their "new realism" is just the "old liberalism." They will place higher and higher taxes on small businesses, on family farms and on every working family so that government may once again grow at the people's expense. You know, we could say they spend like drunken sailors, but that would be unfair to drunken sailors. . . .

Another part of our future, the greatest challenge of all, is to reduce the risk of nuclear war by reducing the levels of nuclear arms. . . . We ask the Soviets, who have walked out of our negotiations, to join us in reducing and, yes, ridding the earth of this awful threat. . . .

In 1980—it's getting late—in 1980 we asked the people of America: Are you better off than you were four years ago?

Well, the people answered then by choosing us to bring about a change. We have every reason now, four years later, to ask that same question again, for we have made a change—the American people joined us and helped us.

Let us ask for their help again to renew the mandate of 1980, to move us further forward on the road we presently travel, the road of common sense; of people in control of their own destiny; the road leading to prosperity and economic expansion in a world at peace. . . .

We bring to the American citizens in this election year a record of accomplishment and the promise of continuation.

We came together in a "national crusade to make America great again," and to make "a new beginning."

Well, now it's all coming together. With our beloved nation at peace, we are in the midst of a springtime of hope for America. Greatness lies ahead of us. . . .

Source: Public Papers and Addresses of the Presidents of the United States: Ronald Reagan, 1984, Book II, June 30 to December 31, 1984 (Washington, DC: Government Printing Office, 1987).

Document 6

Excerpts from First Presidential Debate, October 7, 1984

REAGAN: Four years ago in similar circumstances to this I asked you, the American people, a question. I asked, are you better off than you were four years before? The answer to that obviously was no, and as a result I was elected to this office and promised a new beginning. Now, maybe I'm expected to ask that same question again. I'm not going to because I think that all of you or, not everyone, those people that have—are in those pockets of poverty and haven't caught up, they couldn't answer the way I would want them to. But I think that most of the people in this country would say yes, they are better off than they were four years ago. . . .

I think we've given the American people back their spirit. I think there is an optimism in the land and a patriotism, and I think that we're in a position once again to heed the words of Thomas Paine, who said: "We have it in our power to begin the world over again."

MONDALE: The president's favorite question is, "Are you better off?" Well, if you're wealthy, you're better off. If you're middle income, you're about where you were, and if you're of modest income, you're worse off. That's what the economists tell us. But is that really the question that should be asked? Isn't the real question, "Will we be better off? Will our children be better off? Are we building the future that this nation needs?" . . .

The question is our future. President Kennedy once said in response to similar arguments, we are great but we can be greater. We can be better if we face our future, rejoice in our strengths, face our problems and by solving them build a better society for our children.

Source: The NewsHour with Jim Lehrer Web site, www.pbs.org/newshour/debatingourdestiny/84debates/1pres4.html.

THE ELECTION OF
1988

In 1988, Republican George Herbert Walker Bush (see fact box, p. 946), the incumbent vice president, defeated Democrat Michael Stanley Dukakis, the governor of Massachusetts, in the presidential race. It was the first time a sitting vice president had won the presidency since 1836. While President Ronald Reagan's popularity aided the Republican cause immensely, Bush succeeded in defining the terms of the election. Dukakis, the first Greek American nominated by a major party, ultimately failed to convince the electorate of the need for change.

The Context

Scholars could not help but notice the striking similarity between the 1960 and 1988 Presidential elections. In each case, a popular Republican incumbent was stepping down after the completion of two terms, with his less popular vice president left to carry the party's banner. The Democrats, in both cases, ran presidential candidates from Massachusetts with special ethnic appeal and vice presidential candidates from Texas. Yet, as perhaps the differing results indicate, 1988 was not 1960. The tensions of the Cold War had subsided considerably as Mikhail Gorbachev, a reformer, now led the Soviet Union on a path of reconciliation with the West. In short, the country was at peace. The economy was seemingly strong as well, with high employment, low inflation, and sustained growth. A context marked by peace and prosperity is a very favorable one for the incumbent party—which, in this case, was Republican.

Yet, underneath the economic surface, there were disconcerting signs. For the first time since 1914, the United States had become a net debtor in the world economy. While expensive problems such as homelessness were worsening, the national government was operating with sustained peacetime deficits. The stock market had dropped 508 points on a single day in October 1987, an event that prompted fears of a recession that was yet to come. To capitalize on these negative indicators, the Democrats would have to craft a campaign that forced voters to look below the surface and appealed to their growing sense of economic insecurity.

Developments during Reagan's second term similarly provided opportunities for both parties. Touting a creed of lower taxes, more military spending, and cuts in domestic programs, Reagan was able to claim success with the signing of the 1986 Tax Reform Act. Passed with votes from both Democrats and Republicans, the bill reduced taxes and, in so doing, undermined the potential for Democrats to build a comparable coalition in support of domestic programs. The bill virtually guaranteed that there would not be the requisite funds to entertain seriously the expansion of domestic programs, such as a campaign to eradicate homelessness. Despite this evidence of Reagan's control of the agenda, a series of events beginning with the 1986 elections pointed to an opening for the Democrats. In 1986, Democrats strengthened their control of the House of Representatives with a net gain of six seats, and regained control of the Senate for the first time since 1980. While it is typical of the president's party to lose seats in a midterm election,

CHRONOLOGY

1986

OCTOBER 22   Tax Reform Act passed.

NOVEMBER 4   Congressional midterm elections held.

1987

MARCH 4   President Reagan accepts formal responsibility for Iran-Contra Affair.

MAY 8   Hart withdraws from Democratic presidential race.

SEPTEMBER 23   Biden withdraws from Democratic presidential race.

OCTOBER 19   Stock market drops 508 points.

1988

FEBRUARY 8   Iowa caucuses held.

FEBRUARY 16   New Hampshire primaries held.

MARCH 8   Super Tuesday primaries held.

APRIL 26   Bush clinches Republican nomination.

JUNE 7   Dukakis clinches Democratic nomination.

JULY 12   Dukakis announces choice of Bentsen as running mate.

JULY 21   Dukakis accepts Democratic nomination at convention.

AUGUST 16   Bush announces choice of Quayle as running mate.

AUGUST 18   Bush accepts Republican nomination at convention.

SEPTEMBER 25   First presidential debate takes place.

OCTOBER 5   Vice presidential debate conducted.

OCTOBER 13   Second presidential debate takes place.

NOVEMBER 8   Bush defeats Dukakis in presidential election.

1989

JANUARY 20   Bush inaugurated as U.S. president.

the shift in control of the Senate was a psychological victory for the Democrats.

Shortly after the midterm election, the Democrats' improved standing was bolstered by news of a Republican scandal known as the Iran-Contra Affair. Contrary to the Republican administration's hard line about its refusal to negotiate with terrorists, it had been selling arms to the Iranian government to secure the release of American hostages in Lebanon. Even more problematical, the proceeds from those sales were then used to finance the "Contras" in Nicaragua, who were attempting to overthrow the leftist Sandinista regime. Congressional statutes had explicitly prohibited governmental support of the Contras. Although Reagan accepted formal responsibility for these policies in an address to the nation, he denied any personal knowledge of them. Vice President Bush notoriously claimed to have been "out of the loop" on these matters. As the election year approached, the Republican Party had recovered somewhat from this scandal and Reagan himself rebounded in popularity. However, the Democrats could certainly remind voters of Iran-Contra and other issues, and thereby make a case for change, despite relatively peaceful and prosperous times.

Democratic Race

While the context was inviting to candidates of both parties, the first "open" presidential seat in twenty years was even more enticing. In this election, no candidate would have the advantage of incumbency. As might be expected in this situation, several candidates in both parties vied for the nomination. With that said, the Democratic field was initially notable for those absent from it. National leaders such as New York governor Mario Cuomo, who had greatly impressed the 1984 delegates to the party's convention, opted out of the race. As a result, former Colorado senator Gary Hart was the early favorite in the Democratic camp. When he had sought the Democratic nomination in 1984 against Walter Mondale, Hart had performed "better than expected." Hailing from Colorado, Hart had the potential to make inroads in a Republican area and to bring a new perspective to the party. From the very beginning, though, he was dogged by questions about his character. In 1984, for example, reporters uncovered evidence that he had changed his name from Hartpence and his age to appear younger. It was also rumored that he was a womanizer. To put this rumor to rest in the 1988 campaign, Hart told reporters to follow him and see for themselves that it was not true. Accepting the challenge, reporters from the *Miami Herald* followed Hart and discovered that he had spent a night with Donna Rice, a twenty-nine-year-old model, while his wife was away. Days later, on May 8, 1987, Hart formally withdrew from the race.

After Hart's departure, seven Democratic candidates remained. Because none had national stature with the exception of African-American civil rights leader Jesse Jackson, who was believed at that time incapable of victory, some commentators referred to them jokingly as the "seven dwarfs." In a race with unknown candidates, money provides a critical advantage because it enables candidates to achieve name recognition via advertising. Claiming this advantage as the candidate with the most money, Dukakis campaigned on the themes of the immigrant dream, "good jobs at

good wages," and managerial expertise. In his quest for the nomination, he faced Democratic senators Paul Simon (IL), Al Gore (TN), and Joseph Biden (DE), Representative Richard Gephardt (MO), Governor Bruce Babbitt (AZ), and the Rev. Jesse Jackson. Another scandal, in the early fall of 1987, forced the withdrawal of Biden, when it was revealed that he had plagiarized the speeches of Robert Kennedy and Neill

---

MICHAEL S. DUKAKIS

PARTY: Democrat

DATE OF BIRTH: November 3, 1933

PLACE OF BIRTH: Brookline, Massachusetts

PARENTS: Panos and Euturpe (Boukis) Dukakis

EDUCATION: B.A., Swarthmore College, 1955; J.D., Harvard Law School, 1960

FAMILY: Married Katherine "Kitty" Dickerson, 1963; children: John, Andrea, and Kara

MILITARY SERVICE: U.S. Army, 1955–57; served in Korea

CAREER: Massachusetts state legislator, 1963–70; unsuccessful candidate for Massachusetts lieutenant governor, 1970; governor of Massachusetts, 1975–79, 1983–91; unsuccessful candidate for U.S. president, 1988; visiting professor/lecturer, Northeastern University and John F. Kennedy School of Government at Harvard University, 1979–82, after 1991

Kinnock, a British politician. Astonishingly, Gary Hart reentered the race in December 1987, but his campaign was not taken seriously.

Positioning himself to the right of other candidates, Gore emphasized his support of national defense and described himself as a "mainstream Democrat." While similarly characterizing himself as a "traditional Democrat," Simon sought to expand domestic spending to assist the elderly and the poor. Both Babbitt and Gephardt focused on the Midwest, with Gephardt appealing to the economic frustrations of farmers and workers in a populist style, while Babbitt stressed the need to reduce the federal deficit. Aligning himself with the progressive wing of the Democratic Party, Jackson called for justice and compassion. With a background in the ministry, Jackson invoked a different style of politics and sought to bring excluded groups, such as the poor and African Americans, into the political process.

As in any presidential campaign, the early results in the Iowa caucuses and New Hampshire primary were eagerly anticipated—but in this year, more to winnow the field than to identify frontrunners. In

Iowa, Gephardt and Simon were widely perceived to have the advantage, given their roots in the region, while Dukakis was the clear frontrunner in New Hampshire, which bordered his home state of Massachusetts. Gephardt won the Iowa caucuses on February 8, 1988, but finished 16 percentage points behind Dukakis in New Hampshire on February 16. All attention then turned to March 8, the first "Super Tuesday," the day on which every southern and border state except South Carolina and West Virginia, as well as a few non-southern states, held their primaries. Devised by the Democratic Party as a means to enhance southern influence on the choice of nominees, Super Tuesday also "frontloaded" the process by placing an increasing number of contests earlier in the calendar. Obviously, frontloading leads to the faster elimination of candidates from the contest. In this expectation, Super Tuesday did not disappoint. At the end of the day, the Democratic field had, for all practical purposes, been reduced to Michael Dukakis, Al Gore, and Jesse Jackson.

Of the three remaining contenders, Jackson was taken the most lightly—that is, until he stunned pundits with a victory in the Michigan caucuses on March 26. For the first time, Jackson finished first in a race with a predominantly white electorate, an achievement that bolstered his credibility. Dukakis, now considered the frontrunner, quickly came back with victories in Connecticut and Wisconsin. However, all eyes shifted to New York as a testing ground for the three remaining candidates. Already handicapped because of his decision to skip the crucial early contests in Iowa and New Hampshire, Gore finished with only 10 percent of the vote in New York, and then withdrew from the campaign. Because New York had a large black population and a liberal white constituency, Jackson had to demonstrate his ability to build a winning coalition there. When he finished with 37.1 percent of the vote, compared to Dukakis's 50.9 percent, it was clear that he could not win the nomination. However, it was not until June 7 that Dukakis clinched it with victories in California, Montana, New Jersey, and New Mexico.

With the presidential nomination settled, Jackson, who had won 29.2 percent of the total vote, hinted that he would accept the vice presidential nomination if offered to him. Racial politics partly explain Dukakis's reluctance to choose Jackson. While the Democratic Party counted upon the support of African Americans, it was afraid to embrace this constitu-

The 1988 Democratic ticket of Massachusetts governor Michael Dukakis and Texas senator Lloyd Bentsen echoed the "Boston-Austin" axis of 1960, when Massachusetts senator John F. Kennedy ran with Texas senator Lyndon B. Johnson. *(Gyory Collection/Cathy Casriel Photo)*

ency too openly for fear of alienating white voters, particularly in the South. To assuage this latter constituency, in fact, Dukakis chose Senator Lloyd Bentsen, Jr., of Texas as his vice presidential nominee. Because of a communications mishap, Jackson learned of the decision from the media. This slight led to a rift with the Dukakis camp, which would ultimately be healed by conceding to Jackson's demands to revise the delegate selection rules for 1992. Dukakis chose Bentsen to appeal to conservative Democrats and to force the Republicans to spend money in the South. Although Dukakis hoped that Bentsen could help him win Texas, it was an optimistic hope indeed, given Bush's strong ties to that state.

After the skirmish with Jackson was settled, the Democrats staged a unifying and successful convention in Atlanta from July 18 to 21. Electoral victory was clearly the main concern, as the platform was shortened considerably from the previous election. Instead of making specific commitments to liberal constituencies, it set general goals, though ones consistent with the party's traditional philosophy. Contrary to his reputation as an emotionless and bureaucratic leader, Dukakis delivered his acceptance speech very well and, indeed, received a substantial "bounce" in the polls after the convention. The words them-

LLOYD M. BENTSEN, JR.

PARTY: Democrat

DATE OF BIRTH: February 11, 1921

PLACE OF BIRTH: Mission, Texas

PARENTS: Lloyd and Edna Ruth (Colbath) Bentsen

EDUCATION: L.L.B., University of Texas Law School, 1942

FAMILY: Married Beryl Ann Longino, 1943; children: Lloyd III, Lan, and Tina

MILITARY SERVICE: U.S. Army, major, 1942–45; served in World War II; awarded Distinguished Flying Cross and Air Medal; Air Force Reserve, 1950–59; promoted to colonel before retirement

CAREER: U.S. Representative, 1948–55; president/CEO in business, 1955–70; U.S. senator, 1970–93; chair, Senate Finance Committee, 1987–93; unsuccessful candidate for U.S. vice president, 1988; U.S. secretary of the treasury, 1993–94; awarded Presidential Medal of Freedom, 1999

selves, however, were more emblematic of his reputation, as he sought to make the election about "competence, not ideology." He could thus tout his success at balancing budgets and creating jobs, instead of expounding a vision of justice. This emphasis was understandable, given Reagan's and Bush's claims of ignorance about the Iran-Contra scandal, as well as reports that Reagan occasionally had consulted his wife's astrologer. Dukakis's famous line, however, would enable the Republicans to define the ideological agenda around issues favorable to themselves.

Republican Race

Because the incumbent president had an heir-apparent in his vice president, the Republican contest was not as competitive as the Democratic one. From the outset, the nomination was Bush's to lose. Not only did Bush have name recognition and money, but his close association with the popular Reagan placed his competitors in a difficult spot. How could they simultaneously sing the praises of Reagan and criticize Bush? Yet Bush's upper-class background and unstinting loyalty to Reagan caused some to label him a "wimp," an association that stuck in popular culture.

Whether because of his weaknesses as a candidate or not, five candidates challenged Bush for the nomination. Of these, the most serious contender was Kansas senator and former vice presidential candidate Robert Dole, who differed with Bush more in background and personality than he did on ideology. On

the campaign trail, Dole contrasted his humble beginnings and pragmatic leadership with Bush's elitism. The most interesting of the other four candidacies was Pat Robertson, because of his role as a televangelist and his unorthodox style of campaigning. Emphasizing his conservative positions on social issues, Robertson appealed to "Christian soldiers." Despite his notoriety for hosting the *700 Club* on television, Robertson had a limited political base and inflicted wounds upon himself with his flamboyant and factually incorrect statements. For example, he maintained that Cuba was filled with Soviet missiles and insisted that AIDS was spread by casual contact. Two other candidates, Delaware senator Pierre du Pont and New York representative Jack Kemp, challenged Bush from the right, as well. And Alexander Haig, a former secretary of state and commander of NATO, campaigned on the basis of his experience in foreign policy.

Given the high expectations for Bush, his third-place finish in Iowa, on February 8, sent shockwaves through his campaign. Because Dole was a midwesterner, it was no surprise that he won the contest. But it was Pat Robertson's second-place finish that embarrassed the Bush camp and magnified the importance of the primary in New Hampshire on February 16. After provoking Dole to lose his temper and publicly tell Bush to "stop lying about my record" in his "attack" ads, Bush won the New Hampshire contest convincingly, as well as the following one in South Carolina on March 5. On Super Tuesday, Bush swept the southern primaries, basically locking up the nomination. With the momentum from that day Bush became unstoppable, and he clinched the nomination on April 26 with a victory in Pennsylvania.

Because the Republican Party's nominee was known so far in advance of the convention, the media's attention shifted to speculation about vice presidential hopefuls. Bush allowed the anticipation to build until just two days before his acceptance speech at the party's convention in New Orleans. He then announced his choice of Senator J. Danforth Quayle of Indiana. Chosen for his solid conservative credentials, loyalty, and youthful image (the senator was just 41 years old), Quayle instantly became a controversial choice. Information soon came to light about his use of family connections to gain admission to the National Guard (which was a means to avoid military service in Vietnam) and to law school. Critics also questioned Quayle's experience and qualifications for the presidency.

Despite the negative publicity surrounding his vice presidential choice, the Republican National Convention of August 15–18 gave Bush a 6-point lead in the polls. As he did in his choice of Quayle, Bush bowed to the right in the formulation of the platform and his acceptance speech. Unlike the Democratic one, the Republican platform was quite specific in its advocacy of a conservative agenda. In his speech, Bush responded to Dukakis's claim that the campaign was about "competence" by insisting, instead, that it was about "ideology." He then proceeded to malign liberalism by associating it with "tax-and-spend" policies, a reckless pursuit of individual rights, and anti-Americanism. For his part, Bush famously pledged, "Read my lips: no new taxes." To soften the ideology and thereby appeal to women, Bush professed a "kinder and gentler" brand of conservatism that encouraged volunteers to serve as a "thousand points of light" in grappling with social problems. Bush concluded his speech with the Pledge of Allegiance, to contrast his enthusiastic patriotism with the "liberal" Dukakis's alleged lack of it. The Pledge was pertinently symbolic of this issue because Dukakis, as governor, had for constitutional reasons vetoed a bill requiring Massachusetts school teachers to lead their classes in the Pledge. This not-so-implicit attack was representative of the Bush campaign strategy.

The Fall Campaign

Indeed, beginning in May, Bush launched a sustained attack on Dukakis that attempted to define him out of the mainstream. Because Dukakis was not fully known to voters, he was vulnerable to this strategy. While such attack politics can backfire, in this case it

contrarily helped to discredit the image of Bush as a wimp. The Bush campaign relied upon emotional issues and symbols to paint Dukakis as an extreme liberal, and then to associate liberalism with a carefree attitude toward crime, disrespect for the flag, and contempt for the military. In drawing this association, the Bush camp capitalized on Dukakis's prior acknowledgment that he was a "card-carrying member" of the American Civil Liberties Union (ACLU). Bush, citing Dukakis's own words, defended this labeling in the first presidential debate and then proceeded to equate Dukakis's ideology with some of the most unpopular positions advocated

J. DANFORTH QUAYLE

PARTY: Republican

DATE OF BIRTH: February 4, 1947

PLACE OF BIRTH: Indianapolis, Indiana

PARENTS: James and Corinne (Pulliam) Quayle

EDUCATION: B.A., DePauw University, 1969; J.D., Indiana University, 1974

FAMILY: Married Marilyn Tucker, 1972; children: Tucker, Benjamin, and Corinne

MILITARY SERVICE: Indiana National Guard, 1969–75

CAREER: U.S. Representative, 1977–80; U.S. senator, 1981–89; U.S. vice president, 1989–93; unsuccessful candidate for vice president, 1992; author, *Standing Firm* and other books, after 1993

by the ACLU, such as removal of the word "God" from U.S. currency and the elimination of motion picture ratings. The campaign to malign liberalism was so successful that it came to be known as the "L-word"—so evil as to be unspeakable.

In their advertisements, the Bush campaign focused particularly on crime, adding racial overtones to the issue. To prove that Dukakis was soft on crime, Republican ads repeatedly highlighted the prison furlough program in Massachusetts and subliminally reminded voters of "Willie" Horton, an African American who terrorized a white couple in Maryland after skipping furlough. (See "'Willie' Horton and Crime in the 1988 Campaign," p. 987) Capitalizing on the fears generated by these ads, Bush himself invoked Clint Eastwood's line to compare his and Dukakis's attitudes toward criminals. Bush claimed that his message to criminals would be "Go ahead and make my day," while Dukakis's would be "Go ahead and have a nice weekend." This relentless portrayal of Dukakis as soft on crime worked. Likewise, the Bush

George Bush and Dan Quayle, along with their wives, wave to supporters at the conclusion of the Republican National Convention on August 18, 1988. A youthful George W. Bush, who won the presidency twelve years later, is on the far left beside his wife. *(George Bush Presidential Library)*

campaign depicted Dukakis's positions on defense policy as dangerous to national security. Most famously, the campaign ran an unflattering video of Dukakis wearing an army tank driver's helmet and standing in the hatch of a tank, while the narrator noted that he "opposed virtually every weapon system we developed."

Why did the Dukakis campaign fail to respond effectively or to establish a competing agenda? Some of the fault lay with Dukakis and his campaign staff, who did not work well together. The campaign ran negative advertisements about Bush, but they lacked the focus of the opposing side's. Initially decrying the usefulness of labels such as "liberalism," Dukakis defended his own ideology against Bush's depiction far too late in the campaign. Additionally, Dukakis's unemotional character and cool detachment allowed the Republicans more leeway to define his image.

Precisely because Dukakis was having such a difficult time spreading his message and introducing himself to the American people, the two presidential

debates assumed great importance to his campaign. As the more articulate of the two candidates, Dukakis hoped to benefit from a format that allowed the public to compare his responses to those of Bush. In the first debate, all went according to plan and Dukakis received a boost in the polls. On the issue of abortion, Bush struggled with a question about penalties for women seeking the procedure if it were to become illegal, as he wished. However, Dukakis's surge was short-lived and, again, he found himself counting on the second debate to secure a lead. This time, Dukakis had to demonstrate his humanity and discard, once and for all, his image as a dispassionate bureaucrat. He failed miserably. Debate moderator Bernard Shaw, with one question, dashed Dukakis's hopes to counter the bureaucratic image. Posing a hypothetical scenario in which Dukakis's wife was raped and murdered, Shaw inquired whether the candidate would then support the death penalty. Instead of seizing the opportunity to express love for his wife or anger at violence, Dukakis coolly, almost

Democratic candidate Michael Dukakis donned a helmet and climbed into an M1 battle tank on September 13, 1988, to dramatize his assertion that he was not soft on defense. His opponents deemed it a ridiculous publicity stunt that only served to highlight his inexperience in national security and foreign policy. *(AP Wide World Photos)*

with impatience, responded that he had been against the death penalty all of his life and that it was not a deterrent to crime. This exchange was parodied repeatedly on *Saturday Night Live* and other late-night TV shows, thereby cementing the image of Dukakis as unemotional and bureaucratic. After the debate, the media quickly labeled Bush the "winner," and Dukakis never received the bump that he needed in the polls.

The bright spot for the Democrats came in the vice presidential debate between Bentsen and Quayle. After weathering the criticisms about Vietnam and his admission to law school, Quayle had run into trouble with some of his spontaneous remarks on the campaign trail. For example, he had referred to the Holocaust as "an obscene period in our nation's history," then tried to explain by stating, "We all live in this century. I didn't live in this century." Clearly, expectations for Quayle going into the debate were low—and, indeed, he performed poorly. When asked twice what he would do first if called upon to assume the presidency, Quayle skirted the questions. The third rendition of the inquiry prompted him to defend his youth and credentials via a comparison to those of President John F. Kennedy when he took office in 1961. In a remark that both highlighted his own maturity and ridiculed Quayle, Bentsen responded: "Senator, I served with Jack Kennedy. I knew Jack Kennedy. Jack Kennedy was a friend of mine. Senator, you're no Jack Kennedy." Quayle at this point looked like a deer in the headlights, frozen and helpless. After this fiasco, Quayle's appearances were kept to a minimum. Although the Democrats ran ads about the possibility of "President Quayle," only one in seven voters would cite running mates as a factor in their voting choice. To be sure, this number was higher than usual, but it was not high enough for Dukakis.

The campaign itself seemed to matter in this election, as Bush successfully defined Dukakis and the agenda. Despite this significance, the campaign was heavily criticized for its triviality or lack of substance. Negative advertisements that drew upon highly emotional symbols, such as the flag and criminals, dominated political discourse, while substantive differences went unnoticed. In fact, Bush and Dukakis disagreed on important issues such as the death penalty, abortion, taxation, health insurance, defense policy, and trade policies. Consistent with Republican philosophy, Bush called for tax cuts, less regulation of business, and an end to abortion. Dukakis, a mainstream Democrat, was more concerned about social equity, the maintenance of government programs, cuts in the nuclear arsenal and defense spending, and the protection of civil liberties. Ironically, Dukakis had an edge in public opinion over Bush on many issues; but, nonetheless, he would lose in a campaign allegedly dominated by ideology.

After laboring eight years in Ronald Reagan's shadow as vice president, George Bush now had a chance to shine on his own by heading the ticket. He is shown here on the campaign trail in Ohio in October in 1988. *(George Bush Presidential Library)*

Election Outcome and Analysis

In the vote that mattered most, that of the Electoral College, Bush trounced Dukakis 426 to 111. By adopting a "frostbelt" strategy, Dukakis had hoped to win in the Northeast, Midwest, and Pacific Coast. While virtually all of Dukakis's votes came from these three regions, he failed to sweep them in their entirety. Bush, on the other hand, won every state in the Rocky Mountain region and South, except West Virginia, and won selected states, such as California and Michigan, in Dukakis's targeted areas. If there was a silver lining at all for Democrats in the presidential election, it was in the results of the popular vote. To be sure, Bush was the clear victor here as well, claiming 48.8 million votes to Dukakis's 41.8 million, and carrying every region of the country. However, Bush's victory did not have the same depth as Reagan's in 1984, a fact that would prompt Gerald Pomper, in *The Election of 1988* (1989), to label it "the best loss" for Democrats in twenty years. Unlike

Mondale in 1984, Dukakis was able to secure the Democratic base with the support of blue-collar workers, those without a college education, and those with incomes below the median. Benefiting especially from the exodus of white southerners from the Democratic Party, Bush had inherited a larger base from his predecessor and he, too, was able to hold it. Bush additionally retained an advantage among men, suburbanites, Catholics, retirees, and westerners, but with a reduction from 1984. The electorate voted for continuity, then, but not with the same enthusiasm as it had in the last election. Indeed, only 50 percent of eligible citizens even bothered to vote at all in 1988, a year which saw the lowest turnout rate since 1924.

Yet another sign of the shallow nature of Bush's victory would be found in his lack of coattails. For the first time in twenty-eight years, the party winning the presidency failed to gain seats in the House of Representatives. In fact, the Republicans lost three seats in the House and one seat in the Senate. The status quo of divided government was thus affirmed in 1988, as

"WILLIE" HORTON AND CRIME IN THE 1988 CAMPAIGN

*A*fter observing the reaction of a group of targeted voters to the story of William Horton, George Bush's campaign manager reportedly promised, "By the time this election is over, Willie Horton will be a household name." William Horton, nicknamed "Willie" by the Republicans in 1988, was a convicted murderer who, while on furlough from a Massachusetts prison, traveled into Maryland, where he raped a woman and assaulted her fiancé.

An independent group with close ties to the Bush campaign produced an advertisement that linked Horton's offenses with Dukakis's policies on crime. Opening with pictures of Bush and Dukakis, the advertisement noted that Bush supported the death penalty, while Dukakis not only opposed it, but allowed first-degree murderers to have weekend passes from prison. Switching to a mug shot of Horton, who is black, the ad claimed that he "murdered a boy in a robbery, stabbing him nineteen times." "Despite a life sentence," the ad proceeded, "Horton received ten weekend passes from prison." As the words "kidnapping," "stabbing," and "raping" flashed on the screen, the ad stated: "Horton fled, kidnapping a young couple, stabbing the man and repeatedly raping his girlfriend." Concluding with an image of Dukakis, the ad explained: "Weekend prison passes. Dukakis on crime."

Because Horton's victims were white, this ad arguably appealed to racial fears. Although the ad was produced by an independent organization, the Bush campaign made repeated references to the Horton story and built upon its imagery with its own notorious "revolving door" ad. In this ad, prison inmates were shown circling through a turnstile, while the screen noted that "268 escaped" while on furlough. No mention was made of Horton in this ad, but viewers familiar with the other ad would almost certainly infer his presence. Because of their controversial nature, the media paid excessive attention to the Horton ad and the Massachusetts furlough program. The voting public thus heard the Horton story repeatedly from the commercials, the media, and the Bush camp.

The Horton story fit perfectly with Bush's campaign strategy, as it enabled him to claim a symbolic issue for himself and to associate Dukakis's liberalism with support for criminals. Ostensibly, Bush was focusing on an "issue," but in reality there was no substantive discourse sparked by this ad. For his part, Dukakis responded to the attack in characteristic fashion. He noted that his Republican predecessor had created the furlough program and that both the federal government and California, a state formerly governed by Reagan, had such programs. Citing statistics to prove the success of the program, Dukakis failed to counteract the fear elicited in the Horton ad. This narrative story, while an anomaly, resonated with voters much more than discussions about statistics. In a sense, the advertisement and Dukakis's response to it were a perfect metaphor for the campaign.

the Democrats retained control of both chambers of Congress and the Republicans held the presidency.

Given the public's support for a Democratic Congress, why was Bush able to win the presidency in such a convincing manner? To be sure, Bush reaped the benefits of his association with the popular Ronald Reagan. Throughout the campaign, there was a close relationship between Bush's standing in the polls and Reagan's job approval ratings, which were at 60 percent on the day of the election. Perhaps because of the relatively prosperous and peaceful times, voters simply opted for the status quo. Yet disturbing signs of looming economic trouble, such as the budget deficit, had created an opportunity for challengers to make the case for change. Far from making such a case effectively, however, Dukakis allowed Bush to define the terms of debate. In short, the Republicans ran a more effective campaign than the Democrats. Drawing upon an experienced pool of talent, the Bush campaign was able to plant fear in people's minds about Dukakis, who was depicted as extremely "liberal," soft on crime, and against the military. Because Dukakis failed to counteract this image convincingly, Bush, as the candidate of the status quo, emerged as the "safer" choice.

In setting the agenda of the campaign, Bush chose to focus on emotional symbols, social issues, and taxation. Racial symbols were critical to the Republican Party's success in the South, and elsewhere as well. The significance of the "Willie" Horton ad and the visual imagery of the crime ads cannot be overstated. Bush's absolute rejection of new taxes, while shoring up his conservative base, also served to frame economic issues in a manner advantageous to the Republican Party. When citizens view themselves as taxpayers, they are more apt to view the Republican Party favorably. However, when they perceive themselves as the beneficiaries of government services, they are more prone to support the Democrats. The Democrats, therefore, benefit when the discussion is about programs, rather than taxes. The conduct of the campaigns themselves, then, as well as the agenda, helped to secure Bush's victory.

Conclusion

Precisely because most of the campaign issues were symbolic in nature, the election did not endow Bush with any mandate. Democratic gains in Congress accentuated this fact. Given the lack of substance in the general election, Bush's promises to the right wing of the Republican Party during the nomination phase and at the convention took on greater importance—and later came back to haunt him. For example, when he later supported tax increases to reduce the federal deficit, he was reminded of his "Read my lips: no new taxes" pledge. Indeed, Patrick Buchanan would contest the presidential nomination in 1992, basing his crusade on Bush's failure to deliver on his promises to the right. Ironically, Bush would be haunted as well by the looming economic problems he so successfully skirted in 1988. With a posted reminder to campaign workers stating, "It's the economy, stupid," a little-known governor from Arkansas named Bill Clinton would ultimately deny Bush a second term.

Julie Walsh

Bibliography

Abramson, Paul R., John H. Aldrich, and David Rhode. *Change and Continuity in the 1988 Elections*. Washington, DC: CQ Press, 1991.

Buell, Emmett H., Jr., and Lee Sigelman, eds. *Nominating the President*. Knoxville: University of Tennessee Press, 1991.

Guth, James L., and John C. Green, eds. *The Bible and the Ballot Box: Religion and Politics in the 1988 Election*. Boulder, CO: Westview Press, 1991.

Jamieson, Kathleen Hall. *Dirty Politics: Deception, Distraction, and Democracy*. New York: Oxford University Press, 1992.

Ladd, Everett Carl. "The 1988 Elections: Continuation of the Post-New Deal System." *Political Science Quarterly* 104:1 (Spring 1989): 1–18.

Nelson, Michael, ed. *The Elections of 1988*. Washington, DC: CQ Press, 1989.

Pomper, Gerald M., et al., eds. *The Election of 1988: Reports and Interpretations*. Chatham, NJ: Chatham House, 1989.

THE VOTE: ELECTION OF 1988

State	Total No. of Electors	Total Popular Vote	Electoral Vote R	Electoral Vote D	Electoral Vote O	Margin of Victory Votes	Margin of Victory % Total Vote	Bush Republican Votes	Bush Republican %	Dukakis Democrat Votes	Dukakis Democrat %	Others Votes	Others %
Alabama	9	1,378,476	9			266,070	19.3%	815,576	59.2%	549,506	39.9%	13,394	1.0%
Alaska	3	200,116	3			46,667	23.3%	119,251	59.6%	72,584	36.3%	8,281	4.1%
Arizona	7	1,171,873	7			248,512	21.2%	702,541	60.0%	454,029	38.7%	15,303	1.3%
Arkansas	6	827,738	6			117,341	14.2%	466,578	56.4%	349,237	42.2%	11,923	1.4%
California	47	9,887,064	47			352,684	3.6%	5,054,917	51.1%	4,702,233	47.6%	129,914	1.3%
Colorado	8	1,372,394	8			106,724	7.8%	728,177	53.1%	621,453	45.3%	22,764	1.7%
Connecticut	8	1,443,394	8			73,657	5.1%	750,241	52.0%	676,584	46.9%	16,569	1.1%
Delaware	3	249,891	3			30,992	12.4%	139,639	55.9%	108,647	43.5%	1,605	0.6%
District of Columbia	3	192,877		3		131,817	68.3%	27,590	14.3%	159,407	82.6%	5,880	3.0%
Florida	21	4,302,313	21			962,184	22.4%	2,618,885	60.9%	1,656,701	38.5%	26,727	0.6%
Georgia	12	1,809,672	12			366,539	20.3%	1,081,331	59.8%	714,792	39.5%	13,549	0.7%
Hawaii	4	354,461		4		33,739	9.5%	158,625	44.8%	192,364	54.3%	3,472	1.0%
Idaho	4	408,968	4			106,609	26.1%	253,881	62.1%	147,272	36.0%	7,815	1.9%
Illinois	24	4,559,120	24			94,999	2.1%	2,310,939	50.7%	2,215,940	48.6%	32,241	0.7%
Indiana	12	2,168,621	12			437,120	20.2%	1,297,763	59.8%	860,643	39.7%	10,215	0.5%
Iowa	8	1,225,614		8		125,202	10.2%	545,355	44.5%	670,557	54.7%	9,702	0.8%
Kansas	7	993,044	7			131,413	13.2%	554,049	55.8%	422,636	42.6%	16,359	1.6%
Kentucky	9	1,322,517	9			153,913	11.6%	734,281	55.5%	580,368	43.9%	7,868	0.6%
Louisiana	10	1,628,202	10			166,242	10.2%	883,702	54.3%	717,460	44.1%	27,040	1.7%
Maine	4	555,035	4			63,562	11.5%	307,131	55.3%	243,569	43.9%	4,335	0.8%
Maryland	10	1,714,358	10			49,863	2.9%	876,167	51.1%	826,304	48.2%	11,887	0.7%
Massachusetts	13	2,632,805		13		206,780	7.9%	1,194,635	45.4%	1,401,415	53.2%	36,755	1.4%
Michigan	20	3,669,163	20			289,703	7.9%	1,965,486	53.6%	1,675,783	45.7%	27,894	0.8%
Minnesota	10	2,096,790		10		147,134	7.0%	962,337	45.9%	1,109,471	52.9%	24,982	1.2%
Mississippi	7	931,527	7			193,969	20.8%	557,890	59.9%	363,921	39.1%	9,716	1.0%
Missouri	11	2,093,228	11			83,334	4.0%	1,084,953	51.8%	1,001,619	47.9%	6,656	0.3%
Montana	4	365,674	4			21,476	5.9%	190,412	52.1%	168,936	46.2%	6,326	1.7%
Nebraska	5	662,372	5			138,801	21.0%	398,447	60.2%	259,646	39.2%	4,279	0.6%
Nevada	4	350,067	4			73,302	20.9%	206,040	58.9%	132,738	37.9%	11,289	3.2%
New Hampshire	4	450,525	4			117,841	26.2%	281,537	62.5%	163,696	36.3%	5,292	1.2%
New Jersey	16	3,099,553	16			422,840	13.6%	1,743,192	56.2%	1,320,352	42.6%	36,009	1.2%
New Mexico	5	521,287	5			25,844	5.0%	270,341	51.9%	244,497	46.9%	6,449	1.2%
New York	36	6,485,683		36		266,011	4.1%	3,081,871	47.5%	3,347,882	51.6%	55,930	0.9%
North Carolina	13	2,134,370	13			347,091	16.3%	1,237,258	58.0%	890,167	41.7%	6,945	0.3%
North Dakota	3	297,261	3			38,820	13.1%	166,559	56.0%	127,739	43.0%	2,963	1.0%
Ohio	23	4,393,699	23			476,920	10.9%	2,416,549	55.0%	1,939,629	44.1%	37,521	0.9%
Oklahoma	8	1,171,036	8			194,944	16.6%	678,367	57.9%	483,423	41.3%	9,246	0.8%
Oregon	7	1,201,694		7		56,080	4.7%	560,126	46.6%	616,206	51.3%	25,362	2.1%
Pennsylvania	25	4,536,251	25			105,143	2.3%	2,300,087	50.7%	2,194,944	48.4%	41,220	0.9%
Rhode Island	4	404,620		4		47,362	11.7%	177,761	43.9%	225,123	55.6%	1,736	0.4%
South Carolina	8	986,009	8			235,889	23.9%	606,443	61.5%	370,554	37.6%	9,012	0.9%
South Dakota	3	312,991	3			19,855	6.3%	165,415	52.8%	145,560	46.5%	2,016	0.6%
Tennessee	11	1,636,250	11			267,439	16.3%	947,233	57.9%	679,794	41.5%	9,223	0.6%
Texas	29	5,427,410	29			684,081	12.6%	3,036,829	56.0%	2,352,748	43.3%	37,833	0.7%
Utah	5	647,008	5			221,099	34.2%	428,442	66.2%	207,343	32.0%	11,223	1.7%
Vermont	3	243,333	3			8,556	3.5%	124,331	51.1%	115,775	47.6%	3,227	1.3%
Virginia	12	2,191,609	12			449,363	20.5%	1,309,162	59.7%	859,799	39.2%	22,648	1.0%
Washington	10	1,865,253		10		29,681	1.6%	903,835	48.5%	933,516	50.0%	27,902	1.5%
West Virginia	6	653,311		5	1[a]	30,951	4.7%	310,065	47.5%	341,016	52.2%	2,230	0.3%
Wisconsin	11	2,191,608		11		79,295	3.6%	1,047,499	47.8%	1,126,794	51.4%	17,315	0.8%
Wyoming	3	176,551	3			39,754	22.5%	106,867	60.5%	67,113	38.0%	2,571	1.5%
TOTAL	538	91,594,686	426	111	1	7,077,103	7.7%	48,886,588	53.4%	41,809,485	45.6%	898,613	1.0%

[a] A Dukakis elector in West Virginia voted for Lloyd Bentsen.

For sources, see p. 1134.

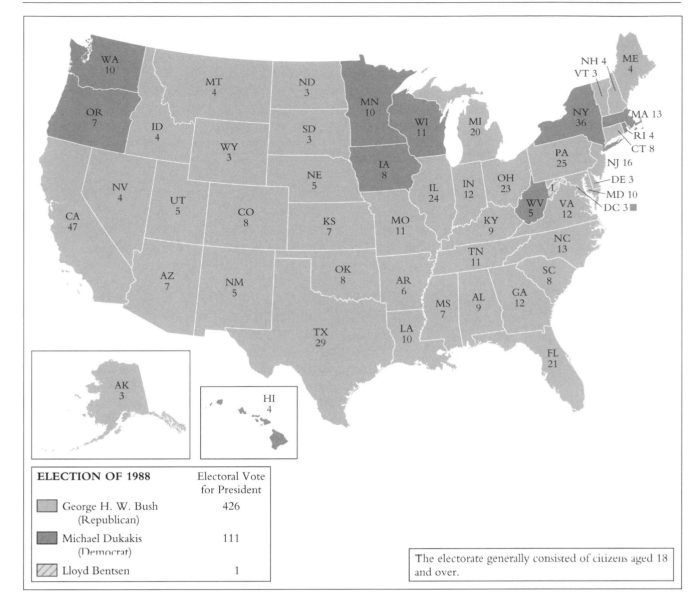

ELECTION OF 1988 — Electoral Vote for President

George H. W. Bush (Republican)	426	
Michael Dukakis (Democrat)	111	
Lloyd Bentsen	1	

The electorate generally consisted of citizens aged 18 and over.

DOCUMENTS: ELECTION OF 1988

Vice President George Bush challenged the Democratic candidate, Massachusetts governor Michael Dukakis, in one of the nastiest elections in recent history. Bush won the presidency by tying himself to President Reagan's popularity and making Dukakis's liberal ideology seem too extreme.

Document 1, Texas Governor Ann Richards's keynote address to the Democratic National Convention, praised her party's accomplishments and platform, while criticizing the Reagan-Bush administration for its inconsistencies and unwillingness to address social concerns. Governor Dukakis's speech accepting the Democratic nomination, Document 2, highlighted the Iran-Contra scandal and other Republican misdeeds. Dukakis pledged an honest administration and promised a new era "exchanging voodoo economics for can-do economics" that would offer the "American dream" to everyone, not just the privileged few.

Bush countered Dukakis in his speech accepting the Republican nomination, Document 3, by detailing Reagan's economic and foreign-policy successes. In addition to promising no new taxes, Bush cited his experience and the Democrats' inadequacies during the 1970s as reasons for his promotion to the presidency.

Dukakis selected long-time Senator Lloyd Bentsen of Texas as his running mate, while Bush chose Senator Dan Quayle of Indiana. Concerns over Quayle's military record, experience, and intelligence dogged Republicans throughout the campaign, and was a major issue in the vice presidential debate, Document 4. Quayle proved no match for Bentsen in the debate. Document 5, excerpts from the two presidential debates, illustrated the deep ideological differences between the two candidates over issues such as abortion and the death penalty. Bush struck fear in Americans by equating liberals with radical leftist ideas, and by detailing the case of Willie Horton and the Massachusetts prison furlough program. Dukakis further damaged his image by responding without apparent emotion when asked if he would change his stance on the death penalty if his wife were raped and murdered.

Document 1

Ann Richards's Democratic National Convention Keynote Address, July 18, 1988

I am delighted to be here with you this evening because after listening to George Bush all these years, I figured you needed to know what a real Texas accent sounds like. Twelve years ago, Barbara Jordan, another Texas woman, made the keynote address to this convention—and two women in 160 years is about par for the course. . . .

The greatest nation of the free world has had a leader for eight straight years that has pretended that he cannot hear our questions over the noise of the helicopter.

And we know he doesn't want to answer. But we have a lot of questions. And when we get our questions asked, or there's a leak, or an investigation, the only answer we get is, "I don't know," or "I forgot."

But you wouldn't accept that answer from your children. I wouldn't. Don't tell me "you don't know" or "you forgot." . . .

And, for eight straight years George Bush hasn't displayed the slightest interest in anything we care about.

And now that he's after a job that he can't get appointed to, he's like Columbus discovering America. He's found child care. He's found education.

Poor George. He can't help it—he was born with a silver foot in his mouth.

Well no wonder, no wonder he can't figure it out. Because the leadership of this nation is telling us one thing on TV and doing something entirely different.

They tell us, they tell us that they're fighting a war against terrorists. And then we find that the White House is selling arms to the Ayatollah. . . .

Now, they tell us that employment rates are great and that they're for equal opportunity, but we know it takes two paychecks to make ends meet today, when it used to take one. And the opportunity they're so proud of is low-wage, dead-end jobs.

And there is no major city in America where you cannot see homeless men sitting in parking lots holding signs that say, "I will work for food." . . .

I'm really glad that our young people missed the Depression, and missed the great big war. But I do regret that they missed the leaders that I knew.

Leaders who told us when things were tough, and that we would have to sacrifice, and these difficulties might last awhile.

They didn't tell us things were hard for us because we were different, or isolated, or special interests. They brought us together and they gave us a sense of national purpose. . . .

They did not lie to us.

And I think one of the saving graces of Democrats is that we are candid. We talk straight talk. We tell people what we think.

And that tradition, and those values live today in Michael Dukakis from Massachusetts.

Michael Dukakis knows that this country is on the edge of a great new era, that we're not afraid of change, that we're for thoughtful, truthful, strong leadership.

Behind his calm there's an impatience to unify this country and get on with the future. . . .

And then there's my friend and my teacher for many years, Senator Lloyd Bentsen.

And I couldn't be prouder, both as a Texan and as a Democrat, because Lloyd Bentsen understands America—from the barrio to the boardroom. He knows how to bring us together, by regions—by economics—by example.

And he's already beaten George Bush once.

So, when it comes right down to it, this election is a contest between those who are satisfied with what they have—and those who know we can do better.

That's what this election is really all about.

It's about the American dream. Those who want to keep it for the few—and those of us who know it must be nurtured and passed along. . . .

Source: Gifts of Speech Web site, http://gos.sbc.edu/r/richards.html.

Document 2

Michael Dukakis's Nomination Acceptance Speech, July 21, 1988

And my friends, if anyone tells you that the American dream belongs to the privileged few and not to all of us . . . you tell them that the Reagan era is over and that a new era is about to begin.

Because it's time to raise our sights—to look beyond the cramped ideals and the limited ambitions of the past eight years—to recapture the spirit of energy and of confidence and of idealism that John Kennedy and Lyndon Johnson inspired a generation ago. . . .

It's time to rekindle the American spirit of invention and of daring, to exchange voodoo economics for can-do economics, to build the best America by bringing out the best in every American. . . .

My friends, as President, I'm going to be setting goals for our country; not goals for our government working alone; I mean goals for our people working together. I want businesses in this country to be wise enough and innovative enough to re-train their workers, and re-tool their factories, and to help rebuild their communities. . . .

I want those of you who are bricklayers and carpenters and developers and housing advocates to work with us to help create decent and affordable housing for every family in America, so that we can once and for all end the shame of homelessness in the United States of America.

I want our young scientists to dedicate their great gifts not to the destruction of life, but to its preservation; I want them to wage war on hunger and pollution and infant mortality; and I want them to work with us to win the war against AIDS, the greatest public health emergency of our lifetime, and a disease that must be conquered.

I want a new Attorney General—I want a new Attorney General to work with me and with law enforcement officers all over America to reclaim our streets and our neighborhoods from those who commit violent crime.

And I want the members of the Congress to work with me, and I'm going to work with them, so that at long last we can make good on Harry Truman's commitment to basic health insurance for every family in America. . . .

We must be—we are—and we will be—militarily strong.

President Reagan has set the stage for deep cuts in nuclear arms—and I salute him for that.

He has said that we should judge the Soviet Union not by what it says, but by what it does—and I agree—I agree with that.

But we can do a lot more to stop the spread of nuclear and chemical arms in this world; we can do a lot more to bring peace to Central America and the Middle East; and

we can and we will do a lot more to end apartheid in South Africa. . . .

We're going to have a Justice Department that isn't the laughing stock of the nation. . . . We're going to have nominees to the Federal bench who are men and women of integrity and intelligence and who understand the Constitution of the United States.

We're going to have an Environmental Protection Agency that is more interested in stopping pollution than protecting the polluters.

We're going to have a real war and not a phony war against drugs; and, my friends, we won't be doing business with drug-running Panamanian dictators anymore.

We're going to have a Vice President who won't sit silently by when somebody at the National Security Council comes up with the cockamamie idea that we should trade arms to the Ayatollah for hostages. . . .

And as I accept your nomination tonight, I can't help recalling that the first marathon was run in ancient Greece, and that on important occasions like this one, the people of Athens would complete their ceremonies by taking a pledge.

That pledge—that covenant—is as eloquent and timely today as it was 2000 years ago.

"We will never bring disgrace to this, our country. We will never bring disgrace to this our country by any act of dishonesty or of cowardice. We will fight for the ideals of this, our country. We will revere and obey the law. We will strive to quicken our sense of civic duty. Thus, in all these ways, we will transmit this country greater, stronger, prouder and more beautiful than it was transmitted to us."

That is my pledge to you, my fellow Democrats. And that is my pledge to you, my fellow Americans. . . .

Source: New York Times, July 22, 1988.

Document 3

George Bush's Nomination Acceptance Speech, August 18, 1988

Eight years ago, I stood here with Ronald Reagan and we promised, together, to break with the past and return America to her greatness. Eight years later, look at what the American people have produced—the highest level of economic growth in our entire history and the lowest level of world tensions in more than 50 years. . . .

My friends, eight years ago this economy was flat on its back—intensive care. And we came in and gave it emergency treatment, got the temperature down by lowering regulation and got the blood pressure down when we lowered taxes. And pretty soon, the patient was up, back on his feet and stronger than ever.

And now, who do we hear knocking on the door but the same doctors who made him sick, and they're telling us to put them in charge of the case again. My friends, they're lucky we don't hit 'em with a malpractice suit. . . .

I know the liberal Democrats are worried about the economy. They're worried it's going to remain strong. And they're right. It is. With the right leadership, it will remain strong. . . .

And we have a new relationship with the Soviet Union. . . . It's a watershed. It is no accident.

It happened when we acted on the ancient knowledge that strength and clarity lead to peace; weakness and ambivalence lead to war. . . .

In 1940, when I was barely more than a boy, Franklin Roosevelt said we shouldn't change horses in midstream. . . .

My friends, these days the world moves even more quickly, and now, after two great terms, a switch will be made. But when you have to change horses in midstream, doesn't it make sense to switch to one who's going the same way? . . .

For we're a nation of community, of thousands and tens of thousands of ethnic, religious, social, business, labor union, neighborhood, regional and other organizations, all of them varied, voluntary and unique.

This is America: the Knights of Columbus, the Grange, Hadassah, the Disabled American Veterans, the Order of Ahepa, the Business and Professional Women of America, the union hall, the Bible study group, LULAC [League of United Latin American Citizens], Holy Name, a brilliant diversity spreads like stars, like a thousand points of light in a broad and peaceful sky.

Does government have a place? Yes. Government is part of the nation of communities, not the whole, just a part. . . .

Should public school teachers be required to lead our children in the Pledge of Allegiance? My opponent says no, and I say yes.

Should society be allowed to impose the death penalty on those who commit crimes of extraordinary cruelty and violence? My opponent says no, but I say yes.

And should our children have the right to say a voluntary prayer or even observe a moment of silence in the schools? My opponent says no, but I say yes.

And should free men and women have a right to own a gun to protect their home? My opponent says no, but I say yes.

And is it right to believe in the sanctity of life and protect the lives of innocent children? My opponent says no, but I say yes.

You see, we must change, we've got to change from abortion to adoption. And, let me tell you this, Barbara and I have an adopted granddaughter. The day of her christening, we wept with joy. I thank God that her parents chose life.

I'm the one who believes it is a scandal to give a weekend furlough to a hardened, first-degree killer who hasn't even served enough time to be eligible for parole.

And I'm the one who says a drug dealer who is responsible for the death of a policeman should be subject to capital punishment.

And I'm the one who will not raise taxes. My opponent now says he'll raise them as a last resort or a third resort. When a politician talks like that, you know that's one resort he'll be checking into. . . . Read my lips: no new taxes. . . .

And I hope to stand for a new harmony, a greater tolerance. . . . We've got to leave that tired old baggage of bigotry behind. . . .

The fact is: Prosperity has a purpose. It's to allow us to pursue "the better angels," to give us time to think and grow. Prosperity with a purpose means taking your idealism and making it concrete by certain acts of goodness. It means helping a child from an unhappy home learn how to read, and I thank my wife, Barbara, for all her work in helping people to read, in all her work for literacy in this country. It means teaching troubled children through your presence that there is such a thing as reliable love. Some would say it's soft and insufficiently tough to care about these things. But where is it written that we must act [as] if we do not care, as if we are not moved?

Well, I am moved. I want a kinder and gentler nation. . . .

Source: New York Times, August 19, 1988.

Document 4

Excerpts from the Bentsen-Quayle Vice Presidential Debate, October 5, 1988

[Tom] BROKAW [of NBC News]: Senator Quayle, I don't mean to beat this drum until it has no more sound in it. But to follow up on Brit Hume's question, when you said that it was a hypothetical situation. It is, sir, after all, the reason that we're here tonight, because you are running not just for vice president. And if you cite the experience that you had in Congress, surely you must have some plan in mind about what you would do if it fell to you to become president of the United States, as it has to so many vice presidents just in the last 25 years or so.

QUAYLE: Let me try to answer the question one more time. I think this is the fourth time that I've had this question.

BROKAW: The third time.

QUAYLE: Three times that I've had this question—and I will try to answer it again for you, as clearly as I can, because the question you are asking is what kind of qualifications does Dan Quayle have to be president, what kind of qualifications do I have and what would I do in this kind of a situation. And what would I do in this situation? I would make sure that the people in the cabinet and the people that are advisors to the president are called in, and I would talk to them, and I will work with them. And I will know them on a firsthand basis, because as vice president I will sit on the National Security Council. And I will know them on a firsthand basis, because I'm going to be coordinating the drug effort. I will know them on a firsthand basis because Vice President George Bush is going to recreate the Space Council, and I will be in charge of that. I will have day-to-day activities with all the people in government. And then, if that unfortunate situation happens—if that situation, which would be very tragic, happens—I will be prepared to carry out the responsibilities of the presidency of the United States of America. And I will be prepared to do that. I will be prepared not only because of my service in the Congress, but because of my ability to communicate and to lead. It is not just age; it's accomplishments, it's experience. I have far more experience than many others that sought the office of vice president of this country. I have as much experience in the Congress as Jack Kennedy did when he sought the presidency. I will be prepared to deal with the people in the Bush administration, if that unfortunate event would ever occur.

[Judy] WOODRUFF [moderator]: Senator Bentsen.

BENTSEN: Senator, I served with Jack Kennedy, I knew Jack Kennedy, Jack Kennedy was a friend of mine. Senator, you are no Jack Kennedy. (Prolonged shouts and applause) What has to be done in a situation like that is to call in the —

WOODRUFF: Please, please, once again you are only taking time away from your own candidate.

QUAYLE: That was really uncalled for, Senator. (Shouts and applause)

BENTSEN: You are the one that was making the comparison, Senator—and I'm one who knew him well. And frankly I think you are so far apart in the objectives you choose for your country that I did not think the comparison was well-taken. . . .

Sources: Commission of Presidential Debates Web site, www.debates.org/pages/trans88c.html (uncorrected transcript).

Document 5
Excerpts from the Bush-Dukakis Presidential Debates

September 25, 1988

BUSH: You see, last year in the primary, he [Dukakis] expressed his passion. He said, "I am a strong liberal Democrat"—August '87. Then he said, "I am a card-carrying member of the ACLU." That was what he said. He is out there on, out of the mainstream. He is very passionate. My argument with the governor is, do we want this country to go that far left? . . . Just take a look at the positions of the ACLU. . . . I don't want my ten-year-old grandchild to go into an X-rated movie. I like those ratings systems. I don't think they're right to try to take the tax exemption away from the Catholic Church. I don't want to see the kiddie pornographic laws repealed; I don't want to see "under God" come out from our currency. Now, these are all positions of the ACLU. And I don't agree with them. He has every right to exercise his passion, as what he said, a strong, progressive liberal. I don't agree with that. I come from a different point. And I think I'm more in touch with the mainstream of America. . . .

[Jim] LEHRER [of the *McNeil-Lehrer NewsHour*]: Governor, a response.

DUKAKIS: Well, I hope this is the first and last time I have to say this. Of course, the vice president is questioning my patriotism. I don't think there's any question about that, and I resent it. I resent it. My parents came to this country as immigrants. They taught me that this was the greatest country in the world. I'm in public service because I love this country. I believe in it. And nobody's going to question my patriotism as the vice president has now repeatedly. . . . I would hope that from this point on, we get to the issues that affect the vast majority of Americans, jobs, schools, health care, housing, the environment. Those are the concerns of the people that are watching us tonight. Not labels that we attach to each other, questions about each other's patriotism and loyalty. . . .

[Ann] GROER [of the *Orlando Sentinal*]: Governor Dukakis, is there a conflict between your opposition to the death penalty and your support for abortion on demand, even though, in the minds of many people, that's also killing?

DUKAKIS: No, I don't think there is. There are two very different issues here, and they've got to be dealt with separately. I'm opposed to the death penalty. I think everybody knows that. I'm also very tough on violent crime. . . . The issue of abortion is a very difficult issue, one that I think that we all have to wrestle with, we have to come to terms with. I don't favor abortion. I don't think it's a good thing. I don't think most people do. The question is who makes the decision. And I think it has to be the woman, in the exercise of her own conscience and religious beliefs, that makes that decision.

LEHRER: Response, Mr. Vice President.

BUSH: Well, the Massachusetts furlough program was unique. It was the only one in the nation that furloughed murderers who had not served enough time to be eligible for parole. The federal program doesn't do that. No other state programs do that. And I favor the death penalty. I know it's tough and honest people can disagree. But when a narcotics wrapped-up guy goes in and murders a police officer, I think they ought to pay with their life. And I do believe it would be inhibiting. And so I am not going to furlough men like Willie Horton, and I would meet with their, the victims of his last escapade, the rape and the brutalization of the family down there in Maryland. Maryland would not extradite Willie Horton, the man who was furloughed, the murderer, because they didn't want him to be furloughed again. And so we have a fundamental difference on this one. And I think most people know my position on the sanctity of life. I favor adoption. I do not favor abortion. . . .

October 13, 1988

[Bernard] SHAW: Governor, if Kitty Dukakis were raped and murdered, would you favor an irrevocable death penalty for the killer?

DUKAKIS: No, I don't, Bernard. And I think you know that I've opposed the death penalty during all of my life. I don't see any evidence that it's a deterrent, and I think there are better and more effective ways to deal with violent crime. . . .

SHAW: . . . if you are elected and die . . . Dan Quayle would become the 41st president of the United States. What have you to say about that possibility?

BUSH: I'd have confidence in him. And I made a good selection. And I've never seen such a pounding, an unfair pounding, on a young Senator in my entire life. And I've never seen a presidential campaign where the presidential nominee runs against my vice presidential nominee, never seen one before. . . .

But you know, Lloyd Bentsen jumped on Dan Quayle, when Dan Quayle said he's had roughly the same amount of experience. He had two terms in the Congress. He had two terms in the Senate, serving his second term. He founded, authored, the job training partnership act. . . . He, unlike my opponent, is an expert in national defense; helped amend the INF treaty. . . . I'm proud of my choice. And you know, I don't think age is the only criterion. But I'll tell you something, I'm proud that people who are 30 years old and 40 years old now have someone in their generation that is going to be vice president of the United States of America. I made a good selection. The American people are seeing it, and I'm proud of it; that's what I'd say. And he could do the job.

SHAW: Governor Dukakis, your one-minute rebuttal.

DUKAKIS: Bernard, this was the first presidential decision that we as nominees were called upon to make. And that's why people are so concerned. Because it was an opportunity for us to demonstrate what we were looking for in a running mate. . . . I picked Lloyd Bentsen, because I thought he was the best qualified person for the job. Mr. Bush picked Dan Quayle, and before he did it, he said, watch my choice for vice president, it will tell all. And it sure did. It sure did. . . .

Sources: Commission on Presidential Debates Web site, www.debates.org/pages/trans88a.html; www.debates.org/pages/trans88b.html.

1992

The 1992 presidential election held a number of surprises. The incumbent president, George H.W. Bush (see fact box, p. 946), was soundly defeated slightly more than a year-and-a-half after breaking all previous records for public approval. A political novice, Ross Perot, received the second highest proportion of votes for an independent candidate in American history. And voter turnout increased dramatically, totaling more than 100 million for the first time in U.S. history. Bush's term as president set the stage for these events.

Bush as Incumbent President

The 1992 election revolved largely around the electorate's evaluation of George Bush's performance as president. His greatest achievement had been victory in the Gulf War, in which the Iraqi military was forced out of Kuwait in 1991. However, the end of the Cold War, which came with dissolution of the Soviet Union during Bush's presidency, diminished the apparent importance of foreign affairs, leaving the electorate to concentrate on domestic policy. This was not good news for President Bush.

Although the Gulf War briefly distracted the nation's attention, helping to boost Bush's approval rating to almost 90 percent in opinion polls—the highest recorded up to that time—public discomfort with Bush's leadership was rising. The nation was in recession, economic competitors like Japan and Europe appeared much stronger than the United States, and increasing numbers of Americans feared

that their children's economic future was at risk. Whether or not it was Bush's fault, he was blamed.

In addition, Bush went back on what was arguably his most important campaign pledge. In the 1988 election campaign, Bush had repeatedly and emphatically declared, "Read my lips: No new taxes"—but barely a year-and-a-half later, the president had come out in support of raising taxes. By the beginning of the primary season, President Bush's popular support was sagging, largely because of his apparent incapacity to deal with the nation's economic problems.

The Primary Season: Republicans

In 1992, the overwhelming majority of Republican and Democratic party convention delegates—and with them, votes for the parties' presidential nominees—were distributed according to the candidates' performances in a series of state primary elections held from February 18 through June 9. In order to win the nomination and motivate his party to turn out for the general election, a candidate had to reassure voters within his own party that he was committed to their ideological and policy positions; but this had to be done carefully. Voters in Republican primaries are more conservative, and those in Democratic primaries more liberal, than the general electorate. A candidate risks frightening away moderates and independents—likely the winning margin in the general election—as a result of efforts to prove fidelity to his party during the primary season. Bill Clinton negotiated this balance more successfully than did George Bush.

CHRONOLOGY

1990

JUNE 26   Bush proposes tax increase, breaking his "no new taxes" campaign pledge.

AUGUST 2   Iraq invades and annexes Kuwait.

1991

JANUARY 16   Gulf War, Operation "Desert Storm," begins.

1992

FEBRUARY 18   Democratic and Republican parties hold first primary election in New Hampshire.

FEBRUARY 20   Perot enters presidential race.

MARCH 5–19   Kerrey, Harkin, and Tsongas withdraw from race for the Democratic nomination.

JUNE 9   Democratic and Republican parties hold last primary election in North Dakota.

JULY 13–16   Democratic Party convention nominates Clinton.

JULY 16   Perot temporarily withdraws from the presidential race.

AUGUST 17–20   Republican Party convention renominates Bush.

OCTOBER 1   Perot reenters the presidential race.

OCTOBER 11–19 Presidential and vice presidential debates held.

NOVEMBER 3   Clinton elected.

Incumbent presidents are expected to do well in their parties' primaries. Indeed, simply having significant primary opposition can be a telling sign of weakness for a sitting president. President Bush faced one significant opponent in the 1992 Republican primaries. In the first primary on February 18, in New Hampshire, Bush was opposed by Patrick Buchanan, a newspaper columnist and television commentator. Buchanan was a firebrand social conservative— opposed to women's right to choose abortion, concerned about the number of immigrants entering the country, fearful that judges were coddling criminals, and demanding a much greater role for religion in society in general, and the government in particular. In fact, he went off "the deep end" at times—calling the AIDS epidemic nature's retribution against gays, and referring to Adolf Hitler as a man of courage. But in his New Hampshire campaign, Buchanan concentrated on the economy. He charged that Bush's support of the North American Free Trade Agreement, which would lower tariffs on goods entering the United States from Canada and Mexico, amounted to exporting Americans' jobs to Latin America. He

ran ads featuring Bush making his "no new taxes" pledge during the 1988 campaign. He charged Bush with sabotaging the economy.

Unhappily for the president, New Hampshire was especially fertile ground for Buchanan's message, as the state was experiencing particularly severe economic problems. Bush's assurances that the downturn was mild and temporary were of little solace to those fearing the loss of their livelihoods, and led many to conclude that Bush was incapable of understanding their plight. The president appeared to confirm this when, at a grocers convention a few weeks before the New Hampshire primary, he appeared shocked to witness a scanner calculating the price of grocery items. Was he the only American who had not seen this in his local grocery store? Clearly, Bush seemed out of touch.

Bush won New Hampshire by what represented a narrow margin for an incumbent, garnering 53 percent of the vote to Buchanan's 37 percent. The Bush campaign was rightfully shaken by these results; but, as it turned out, Buchanan's fortunes would soon be in decline. After New Hampshire, Buchanan turned

President George Bush and Vice President Dan Quayle appear in the ears of the elephant, long a symbol of the Republican Party. *(Gyory Collection/Will Gyory Photo)*

away from economics, campaigning more on social and moral issues such as abortion and religion. His new emphasis did not serve the challenger well. Buchanan never again scored as well as he had in New Hampshire. After a few more primary defeats, Buchanan's campaign contributions were drying up and, by May 5, almost a full month before the final round of primaries, Bush had won a majority of delegates to the Republican convention, guaranteeing his nomination.

These experiences did not have the impact on President Bush one might have expected. The Republican primary results confirmed national public opinion polls: Bush's greatest weakness lay in his perceived inability to deal with the economy. His campaign operators pleaded with him to address the public's fears. Some argued that replacing the administration's leading economic advisers would demonstrate his commitment to putting the economy right—but, Bush resisted. His response to the voters' fears was continued reassurance that the nation's economic health was sound, and that any problems would soon pass.

Even though the president had faced only one serious opponent, who had sputtered out early, the Bush campaign emerged from the primaries in disarray—and he and his staff spent the weeks between the primaries and the Republican convention grappling

with questions about how to organize and fight the general election campaign. Bush had no obvious policy or personal strength on which to focus. Despite victory in the Gulf War, the end of the Cold War diminished the perceived importance of Bush's foreign policy accomplishments. Meanwhile, the president's reversal on his "no new taxes" pledge had made tax policy dangerous ground. With Bush widely perceived as incapable of action, the economy—as an issue—was the biggest loser of all.

The Primary Season: Democrats

President Bush's high level of support in public opinion polls following the Gulf War frightened off some of the strongest potential Democratic challengers. Some observers considered the declared Democratic candidates to be the party's "second string." Still, five candidates did declare and launch serious campaigns.

Paul Tsongas, a former senator from Massachusetts, was the first to declare. His message was that the economy was in trouble, and that solving the problem required sacrifice. He was popular among middle- and upper-middle-income voters. Tom Harkin, a senator from Iowa, hoped to reinvigorate the traditional Democratic coalition of economically disadvantaged voters first consolidated by Franklin D. Roosevelt in the 1930s. His strongest support (in terms of money and volunteers, as well as votes) was centered among labor unions and their members. Edmund G. "Jerry" Brown, a former California governor, relied on a liberal populist appeal. He stayed in supporters' homes, traveled without the coterie of staff that accompanied his opponents, and limited contributors to $100—setting up an 800 number to take contributors' calls—so that he would not be beholden to "monied interests." Bob Kerrey, a senator from Nebraska and a Vietnam War hero, based his campaign on healthcare reform. And finally, Bill Clinton, governor of Arkansas, was a leader in the effort to moderate the Democratic Party. While he supported government assistance for those who were struggling, Clinton stressed the need for increased individual responsibility. Within this field of Democratic contenders, Clinton could portray himself as the moderate alternative.

As with the Republicans, New Hampshire was the first test of the Democratic candidates' electoral prowess. It was a promising opening for Tsongas. He was well known in New Hampshire, and his focus on the economy promised to play well in a state suffering economic difficulties. New England was foreign territory for the other candidates; yet Clinton's staff was optimistic that their candidate's campaign skills would lead to victory. After all, little more than a

WILLIAM JEFFERSON CLINTON

PARTY: Democratic

DATE OF BIRTH: August 19, 1946

PLACE OF BIRTH: Hope, Arkansas

PARENTS: Virginia and William J. Blythe III; Roger Clinton (stepfather)

EDUCATION: B.S.F.S., Georgetown University, 1968; Rhodes Scholar, Oxford University, U.K., 1968–70; J.D., Yale University, 1973

FAMILY: Married Hillary Rodham, 1975; one child: Chelsea

CAREER: Law professor, University of Arkansas, 1974–76; unsuccessful Democratic candidate for U.S. House of Representatives, 1974; attorney general of Arkansas, 1976–78; practicing attorney, 1981–82; governor of Arkansas, 1979–81, 1983–92; U.S. president, 1993–2001

month before the February 18 primary, Clinton was leading in national public opinion polls.

The outlook for Clinton, however, soon darkened. During the month before the New Hampshire primary, newspaper stories charging an extramarital affair and questioning his Vietnam draft record were published for the first time. While rumors about extramarital affairs had hovered around Clinton for years, an article appearing in the *Star*, a supermarket tabloid, about a month before the first primary offered specifics. The article charged that Clinton had carried on a long-time affair with Gennifer Flowers. Flowers was talking—and Clinton's poll numbers were shrinking.

The Clinton campaign quickly launched a defense. Bill and his wife Hillary appeared on the CBS program *60 Minutes*. Before a huge national audience, they put "a human face" on their relationship; and while he did not specifically concede the affair, Clinton admitted difficult times in his marriage. The Clintons assured the public that their marriage was strong. This appearance was widely considered a successful effort at damage control. Much of the public seemed to conclude that possible marital infidelities were a matter of private, rather than public, concern—and Clinton's favorable ratings in the polls largely rebounded.

The next charge proved trickier to deal with. Just a week before the New Hampshire primary, a *Wall Street Journal* story alleged that Clinton had evaded the draft during the Vietnam War. Clinton at first simply denied the charge; but when polls indicated that concern over the issue was influencing people's assessments of his fitness for office, he appeared on ABC's *Nightline* program to explain. While Clinton's *Nightline* denial did not result in the kind of rise in his support that followed the *60 Minutes* appearance, it did seem to stem the decline.

The charges of infidelity and draft avoidance may have cost Clinton an outright victory in New Hampshire. He garnered 25 percent to Tsongas's 33 percent, with the other three candidates receiving about 10 percent each; but Clinton's second-place showing was not generally interpreted as a default. In fact, Clinton claimed it as something of a victory, declaring on the evening of the primary that "New Hampshire tonight has made Bill Clinton the Comeback Kid." Most media commentators decided that the New Hampshire contest had established Tsongas and Clinton as the leaders in the Democratic race.

After New Hampshire, each candidate sought out primaries he thought he could win, as victories were crucial to remaining a credible candidate. Campaign contributors and voters are not attracted to "also-rans." A number of Clinton's opponents either never caught on, or squandered their support. Tsongas, protecting his post-New Hampshire frontrunner status, didn't follow through with details of the necessary sacrifices he had earlier preached about. Instead, he began to spend more time accusing the other frontrunner, Clinton, of pandering. Indeed, Clinton's growing reputation for telling people what they wanted to hear was becoming a problem for his campaign; but the pandering charge was insufficient to sustain Tsongas's support. As he began hauling a stuffed animal to campaign stops, saying it was a "pander" bear, Tsongas's campaign began to appear increasingly hollow. Harkin's campaign also began to crumble. By the 1990s, organized labor's declining membership, and the unions' loosening grip on their members' political loyalty, proved insufficient to sustain his presidential candidacy. Kerrey's healthcare reform issue did not catch fire, and his enigmatic style bombed.

Democratic candidate Bill Clinton appeared on the *Today Show* on June 30, 1992. This photograph captures a monitor that displays an image of Clinton playing the saxophone during a previous appearance on the *Arsenio Hall Show*. The TV talk show had arrived as a factor in presidential campaigning. *(AP Wide World Photos)*

Fortunately for Clinton, a number of southern states had scheduled their primaries early in the process. The South was not only his home base, but also quite supportive of his moderate issue positions. Of the thirteen primaries scheduled for the three weeks following New Hampshire, seven were in the South. Clinton won all seven of the southern and one of the non-southern primaries held in that period, clearly establishing him as the Democratic frontrunner. With their prospects for the nomination and their campaign funds drying up, Kerrey, Harkin, and Tsongas each withdrew in turn between March 9 and 19, leaving only Clinton and Brown officially in the race for the Democratic nomination. Brown was able to continue his campaign, in large part, because his grassroots contribution system produced a small but

steady stream of money, while his low-budget campaign required few resources. Although the Clinton team did not see Brown's bare-bones campaign as a serious threat, the Californian did manage a surprise victory in Connecticut on March 24. And in New York's April 7 primary, while he won more votes than any other candidate, Clinton's total was smaller than the combined number for the next two candidates, Tsongas (still on the ballot, despite his earlier withdrawal) and Brown. While these may have been disturbing signs of discontent in the Democratic electorate, Clinton and his staff began to plan and launch their general election campaign.

An important part of that effort was enlightening the public about Clinton, the person. Polling revealed that he was generally perceived as just another son of privilege who was ready to tell people whatever they wanted to hear. To counter the perception of "pandering," Clinton set about to tell even his most ardent supporters hard truths they didn't want to hear. To that end, in a speech to the Rainbow Coalition, a group working predominantly to better the lot of African Americans, he repudiated Sister Souljah, a rap artist who had been quoted as saying that blacks would be justified in killing whites. The tactical beauty of his statement was that, by identifying a black artist who was not beloved by members of the Rainbow Coalition, he could symbolically declare his independence from the group before the national electorate, while causing limited upset to his immediate audience. This action would help inoculate him against Bush's general election charges that he was too beholden to special groups.

The public was also given an understanding of why—as he claimed Clinton did "feel [their] pain." From personal testimonials, the public learned that Clinton was born in a small Arkansas town named Hope, in which he and his mother faced economic hardships (his father had died in a car accident before he was born). Clinton's mother told of young Bill defending her against his alcoholic and abusive stepfather, and Hillary related stories describing the early years of their loving marriage. This aspect of the campaign culminated in a short film at the Democratic convention, dubbed "The Man from Hope." The implication was clear. In contrast to Bush, Clinton empathized with the pain of common citizens because he, too, had suffered.

Perot's Campaign: Phase One

While Bush and Clinton were pursuing their parties' nominations, Ross Perot, a billionaire who had never before sought elective office, was undertaking an independent campaign for president. He claimed that he didn't really want to be president. But—two days after the New Hampshire primaries—Perot implied (rather than declared) his candidacy on a television talk show, indicating that he would run if (and only if) his followers got him on the ballot in all fifty states. (See "Entertaining the Voters," p. 1003.)

The most surprising fact about Perot's candidacy was not that he was a novice at electoral politics. Political neophytes declare their intention to run during every presidential election, but they are consistently ignored. The media, however, took Perot quite seriously, as platoons of volunteers came forward to undertake the work of getting his name on state ballots. Even more shocking were the polls indicating that about a quarter of the populace supported Perot for president over either Bush or Clinton. It may, in fact, have been that Perot's status as a novice accounted for much of his popularity. Support for Perot was a way for citizens to voice their disgust with politics and politicians.

HENRY ROSS PEROT

PARTY: Independent

DATE OF BIRTH: June 27, 1930

PLACE OF BIRTH: Texarkana, Texas

PARENTS: Ross and Lulu May Perot

EDUCATION: B.S., U.S. Naval Academy, 1953

FAMILY: Married Margot Birmingham, 1956; children: Ross Jr., Nancy, Suzanne, Carolyn, and Katherine

MILITARY SERVICE: U.S. Navy, 1953–57

CAREER: Salesman, IBM, 1957–62; founder and CEO, Electronic Data Systems, 1962–84; founder, Perot Systems Corp., 1988–; unsuccessful candidate for U.S. president, 1992, 1996

Perot's skillful use of the media allowed him to cultivate the "Myth of Ross Perot," described in the special election issue of *Newsweek*, as "the tough, determined and often lonely warrior willing to take on . . . anybody . . . who got in his way." He preferred to appear on radio and TV talk shows, where the questions were friendlier and the expectations regarding specificity lower than on more traditional news shows. He talked about the problems of the national debt and the need to improve the nation's trade balance with foreign countries, illustrating his points with numerous charts. He said he would not simply spout "sound bites" like the politicians in the race. At one point, public opinion polls showed Perot leading Bush and Clinton.

Contrary to his promises, however, Perot followed through with few explanations, and by early summer

H. Ross Perot made a bid for the presidency as an Independent candidate in 1992. The highlight of his campaign were his thirty-minute television commercials, which took on the flavor of a political science classroom. *(AP Wide World Photos)*

his candidacy was beginning to show signs of weakness. Bush's and Clinton's lock on their parties' nominations left the news media with the time to focus on Perot. Stories regarding his temper, his proclivity to hire private investigators to delve into colleagues' personal lives, and his reliance on lucrative government contracts to amass his personal fortune began to take some of the luster off the Perot candidacy. On July 16, just two days after the Democrats nominated Clinton, Perot announced that he was withdrawing from the race. His campaign, he said, had done its job of waking up the major parties to the problems at hand, and his continued candidacy would simply cause a deadlocked Electoral College.

The Party Conventions

The conventions herald the beginning of the general election as much as the culmination of the nomination process. With the party's nominee known before the actual delegate balloting, the convention can be planned—almost exclusively—as a means for the nominee to present a general election message.

The Clinton campaign staff tightly controlled the Democratic convention. Their goal was to reach out to undecided voters. To do this, they muted partisan and ideological messages and underscored the party's acceptance of a wide range of views. Clinton himself was studiously balanced in his pronouncements. His

acceptance speech reflected a sensitivity to citizens' need for government help (a message which appealed to his Democratic base), but clarified that government could not solve people's problems for them (a message calculated to reassure independent, moderate voters). Clinton's choice of Al Gore, a senator from Tennessee who had vied for the Democratic presidential nomination in 1988, as his vice presidential running mate reinforced the emphasis on moderation. Like Clinton, Gore had long been a leader in attempts to moderate the party. The effort to "reach out" beyond the Democratic base paid an impressive dividend: a 10-to-15-percentage-point "bounce" in support for Clinton in polls following the convention.

The Republican convention, held three weeks later, was starkly more ideological in tone. Social conservatives played a large role, loudly voicing their displeasure with American mores. Patrick Buchanan set the tone on the opening night. He questioned Clinton's patriotism and warned that, under a Clinton presidency, the country would see more abortions, homosexual rights, women in combat, and discrimination against religion. He even attacked Clinton's wife Hillary.

Bush's decision to ignore advice that he dump Dan Quayle (see fact box, p. 983) as his vice presidential running mate heartened conservatives. Quayle, a reputed intellectual lightweight because of widely publicized incidents such as his advice to a student to spell potato with an "e," had cultivated support among social conservatives. He had campaigned hard on moral issues, going so far as to attack "Murphy Brown," a fictional television character, for bearing a child out of wedlock.

The Republican convention was very effective at reassuring the party's base—its core conservative supporters. Longstanding suspicions about the sincerity of Bush's enthusiasm for the social conservative agenda may have made this necessary. At the same time, the convention constituted a missed opportunity. With doubts about his handling of the economy overshadowing other issues, the president could not expect to win reelection on "family" values. Support from moderates and independents was crucial to a winning margin in November, and the Republican convention had done little to reassure these voters. The cost of this strategy was demonstrated by Bush's small "convention bounce"—less than half of what Clinton's had been.

ENTERTAINING THE VOTERS

During the 1992 presidential election, Bill Clinton and Ross Perot appeared on a number of television entertainment shows. While such appearances were not unprecedented, Clinton and Perot used them more often and more effectively than other candidates had. Entertainment shows offer advantages over news programs. They provide a less adversarial atmosphere with friendlier questions, furnish access to potential voters who may not tune into news shows, and may offer candidates an opportunity to present a more informal, relaxed side of themselves. Indeed, traditionalists fear that such appearances can backfire if the candidate looks so informal that he seems "unpresidential."

The most noteworthy appearances of 1992 were Perot's, on *Larry King Live*, and Clinton's, on *The Arsenio Hall Show* and MTV. Perot used Larry King's show as the forum for going public with his candidacy, and reappeared a number of times to lay out various aspects of his campaign.

Clinton's appearances on *Arsenio Hall* and MTV were especially interesting, because they were part of his strategy to target young voters. Younger Americans are less interested in politics and less likely to vote. *The Arsenio Hall Show*, a hip version of Jay Leno's *Tonight Show*, attracted a young audience. Clinton's appearance was clearly calculated to appeal to younger voters on grounds other than policy pronouncements. In addition to talking with Hall, Clinton donned wraparound sunglasses and played his saxophone, accompanied by the show's band, looking almost like a member of the "Blues Brothers." Excerpts from his appearance were then picked up for rebroadcast by news programs, increasing his exposure. While Clinton's appearance on MTV was a more traditional interview format, it was considered a bold move, given MTV's music-oriented format. His ease with the twenty-something studio audience may have made him more attractive to younger voters. And both shows allowed Clinton to use his relative youth (at forty-six, Clinton was twenty-two years younger then Bush) to advantage. Clinton's efforts to woo the young paid off. He beat Bush 44 to 34 percent among eighteen-to-twenty-nine-year-olds, a result that MTV representatives have suggested resulted in large part from his MTV appearance.

The General Election

Reaction to the conventions allowed Clinton to open a double-digit lead in the polls. As a result, for the next couple of months Clinton concentrated on avoiding missteps, while Bush searched frantically for a "silver bullet" that would kill Clinton's hopes for victory.

While a number of Republican leaders were outraged by what they saw as Clinton's usurpation of Republican positions, his balanced approach was popular well beyond Democratic ranks. Polls revealed that Clinton was the preferred candidate to deal with every major domestic policy with which the public voiced concern: the economy, healthcare, education, and the environment. At the same time, the economy was clearly *the* central issue for the Clinton campaign. As a sign in Clinton campaign headquarters read, "It's the economy, stupid."

The difficulty for Bush was that the public's concern was as much about his apparent ineptitude as the actual state of the economy. From polling and focus group results, the Bush campaign concluded that he could not win the election by touting his own virtues. The public simply didn't see the president as credible. Thus, if the electorate wasn't willing to vote *for* Bush, he would have to convince them to vote *against* Clinton. The president tried a number of themes in his effort to undermine his opponent—from attacking Clinton's wife, to implying that Clinton's youthful anti-Vietnam War activity had been seditious, to denigrating Clinton as the failed governor of an impoverished state—but nothing seemed to work.

So, for lack of a more promising alternative, Bush continually returned to the theme of trust. He was convinced that the continuing questions about the draft and rumors of Clinton's womanizing would lead the public to conclude that they simply couldn't trust "Slick Willie"—as Clinton was known in some circles. But while trust was Clinton's greatest weakness, it was also Bush's. Contrary to Bush's assertions, there was evidence that, as vice president in the 1980s, he had supported assistance to Iraq (the nation's Gulf War foe in 1991). And though he apologized and promised not to do it again, Bush had violated his "no new taxes" pledge. But most important was the president's apparent insensitivity to the public's economic fears.

On through early October, every aspect of the campaign seemed to work to Clinton's advantage—even the question of debates. When the nonpartisan commission proposed times and places for the debates to be held, Clinton quickly accepted—but Bush demurred. The president did not want to accept before he had pulled ahead in the polls; but Clinton's lead persisted, and the debates began to develop into an issue. Clinton supporters appeared at Bush rallies dressed as chickens, while Clinton took to making appearances to debate an empty chair at the times and places the commission had proposed. Vexed by the increasing perception that he was afraid to face Clinton, Bush belatedly agreed. As a result, the debates were scheduled for less than a month before the election—increasing the chance that a strong performance could carry a candidate to victory, or that a weak showing could doom him to defeat.

It was in this volatile environment that Perot reentered the race. Both Bush and Clinton had reason for concern. While Bush, trailing Clinton in the polls, might welcome anything that promised to give people reason to reconsider, Perot threatened to focus greater attention on the economy—Bush's greatest weakness. For Clinton, Perot was a possible spoiler. In Perot's absence from the race, Clinton had positioned himself as the choice for those who wanted change; but with Perot back in the race, Clinton and Bush might look like twin pillars of the status quo.

The Debates

The candidates' performances in the debates epitomized the dynamics of the three-person race. Perot

President George Bush campaigns for reelection in Colville, Washington, on September 14, 1992. Bush's wardrobe illustrates that a more casual style of dress sometimes replaced coats and ties during the 1990s. *(AP Wide World Photos)*

offered an alternative for those seeking change, threatening defections from Clinton; but more importantly, he placed blame for the nation's economic problems at Bush's feet. When Bush proclaimed that only he had presidential experience, Perot devastated him—by pointing out that, indeed, only Bush had experience running up a $4 trillion federal debt. Further undercutting Bush, Perot charged that shortly before Iraq's invasion of Kuwait, Bush had sent the Iraqi government word that he would not object to their occupation of a portion of Kuwait. Perot's charge squarely targeted Bush's one apparent success—the Gulf War.

Through most of the debates, Bush seemed lackluster. Particularly disappointing for his staff, he was unable to comprehend a question concerning how the economy had affected him. Clinton seized the opportunity, describing how as governor of a small state he knew the people who were losing their jobs, and suffered their loss personally. This move fit the Clinton campaign theme: Clinton the empathetic versus Bush the confused. Perot's attacks on Bush set

ALBERT GORE, JR.

PARTY: Democratic

DATE OF BIRTH: March 31, 1948

PLACE OF BIRTH: Washington, D.C.

PARENTS: Albert (Sr.) and Pauline Gore

EDUCATION: B.A., Harvard University, 1969; Vanderbilt School of Religion, 1971–72; Vanderbilt Law School, 1974–76

FAMILY: Married Mary Elizabeth "Tipper" Aitcheson, 1970; children: Karenna, Kristin, Sarah, and Albert III

MILITARY SERVICE: U.S. Army (served in Vietnam), 1969–71

CAREER: Reporter, *Nashville Tennessean*, 1973–76; U.S. House of Representatives, 1977–85; U.S. Senate, 1985–92; U.S. vice president, 1993–2001; unsuccessful candidate for U.S. president, 2000

the stage for this by freeing Clinton from the role of combatant, thereby allow him to assume the role of compassionate leader.

Polls revealed the public's verdict: Perot had won, Bush had lost, and Clinton had held his own. As a result, Perot began to rise in the polls—a distressing trend for the Clinton campaign, as they feared Perot's

rise would come disproportionately at Clinton's expense.

The impact of the vice presidential debates proved the reverse of the presidential exchanges. Contrary to expectations, Quayle acquitted himself well. He attacked Clinton's honesty and Gore's humorless style, and delivered his prepared ad libs with stinging success. Bush campaign staffers were as elated with Quayle's performance as they were disappointed by Bush's. Gore played it too cautiously, failing to respond to a number of Quayle's sharpest attacks on Clinton's integrity. Perot's running mate, James Stockdale—a political novice inexperienced in debate—appeared out of his depth. He often came across as confused and overwhelmed. By the end of the telecast it was clear that Quayle had scored a victory, Gore at best had held down his losses, and Stockdale appeared ill-equipped for public office.

Democratic hopefuls Bill Clinton and Al Gore are shown campaigning in Sylvester during a bus trip through south Georgia in September 1992. A consummate campaigner, Clinton connected easily with crowds. *(AP Wide World Photos)*

The only good news for Perot was that the vice presidential debates have neither the audience size nor impact on the public psyche that presidential debates command.

In the final days of the campaign, using his personal bankroll to pay for a television *blitzkrieg*, Perot rose in the polls. At the same time, the gap between Clinton

---

JAMES STOCKDALE

PARTY: Independent

DATE OF BIRTH: December 23, 1923

PLACE OF BIRTH: Abingdon, Illinois

PARENTS: Vernon and Mabel Stockdale

EDUCATION: B.S., U.S. Naval Academy, 1946; M.A., Stanford University, 1962

FAMILY: Married Sybil Bailey; children: James, Sidney, Stanford, and Taylor

MILITARY SERVICE: U.S. Navy, 1946–79; prisoner of war during Vietnam War, 1965–73; rose to rank of vice admiral

CAREER: Naval officer, 1946–79; president, Naval War College, 1976–79; president, The Citadel, 1979–80; senior research fellow, Hoover Institution on War, Revolution, and Peace, 1981–96; unsuccessful candidate for U.S. vice president, 1992

---

and Bush shrank—energizing Bush, who barnstormed across the country calling Clinton "Waffle Man," Gore "Ozone," and the Democratic ticket "those two bozos." He jubilantly reported to his campaign headquarters that he could tell from the enthusiasm of his large crowds that things had changed. Members of the Clinton campaign were nearly apoplectic. Had Clinton nursed his lead through months of turmoil to lose it mere days before the election? The answer was "no": Bush's rise was too little, too late.

The Election Outcome

Clinton won 43 percent of the popular vote, with Bush and Perot trailing at 38 and 19 percent, respectively. As usually happens, the leading candidate's margin was magnified in the Electoral College, with Clinton winning 370, Bush 168, and Perot (having carried not a single state) no electoral votes.

The most striking aspect of the 1992 election was turnout. The general decline, since the 1960s, in the proportion of eligible citizens who turned out to vote was dramatically reversed. Slightly more than 55 per-

cent of voting-age Americans, more than 104 million, turned out in 1992, compared with slightly more than 50 percent (about 92 million) in 1988. The closeness of the race, and presence of a protest option (Perot), likely contributed to this surge.

The source of support for each candidate is revealing. As Gerald Pomper wrote in his book, *The Election of 1992*, "the vote for Perot was large but hazy." While most independent candidates run more strongly among some social or ideological groups, or in a particular region, Perot's support was widely dispersed, drawn equally from Bush and Clinton, indicating a general dissatisfaction with politics.

Bush's strength was concentrated among white Protestants who considered themselves more religious, especially "born again" Christians. Voters expressing a strong concern with "family values" or "foreign affairs" leaned toward Bush; but they constituted a small proportion of the electorate and were easily overwhelmed by those concerned about the economy, who fled to Clinton and Perot.

Clinton's popularity was concentrated in the traditional "core Democratic constituency." He won overwhelmingly among blacks, Hispanics, and Jews, and ran strongly with the less-educated and those with lower incomes. The "gender gap"—the degree to which women are more supportive of Democratic candidates—is largely accounted for by their economic circumstances.

These patterns, however, should not obscure the fact that politics is about emotions, as well as substantive issues. The outcome hinged as much on concern about Bush's leadership as it did any calculated assessment of economic indicators. Statistics suggested that the economic downturn was prolonged, but not unusually severe. However, a large proportion of Americans were frightened, and Bush's efforts at reassurance sounded to many like he was either lying to secure reelection or, perhaps worse, that he was simply insensitive to the plight of "average Americans." Clinton secured his victory by convincing people that he did "feel [their] pain." But while

Bill Clinton and Al Gore made a strong—and successful—effort to gain the votes of women in 1992. *(Gyory Collection/Cathy Casriel Photo)*

Clinton's centrist campaign was effective in reassuring a large share of voters about his sensitivity, his studied moderation did not inspire most voters. Perot, by contrast, provided a means for voters to express strongly held feelings. His cultivated image, as a decisive businessman concerned with results, contrasted positively with the voters' image of professional politicians as overly prone to compromise and chronically distracted by concerns about their public images. In supporting Perot, voters could express their frustration with the apparent half-measures inherent in the practice of democratic politics, and their desire for decisiveness—but with little fear that they would actually get what they voted for, as the contest clearly turned on Clinton and Bush.

So, the 1992 election, while providing a choice among three major candidates and motivating a substantial increase in voter turnout, did not appear inherently satisfying to most members of the American electorate. Most voters seem to have been registering their opposition to, rather than support for, a particular candidate or idea.

Frank Davis

Bibliography

Abramson, Paul, John Aldrich, and David Rohde. *Change and Continuity in the 1992 Elections*. Washington, DC: CQ Press, 1995.

Alexander, Herbert, and Anthony Corrado. *Financing the 1992 Election*. Armonk, NY: M. E. Sharpe, 1995.

Matalin, Mary, and James Carville. *All's Fair*. New York: Random House, 1994.

Nelson, Michael, ed. *The Elections of 1992*. Washington, DC: CQ Press, 1993.

Pomper, Gerald, et al. *The Election of 1992*. Chatham, NJ: Chatham House, 1993.

THE VOTE: ELECTION OF 1992

State	Total No. of Electors	Total Popular Vote	Electoral Vote D	Electoral Vote R	Margin of Victory Votes	Margin of Victory % Total Vote	Clinton Democrat Votes	Clinton Democrat %	Bush Republican Votes	Bush Republican %	Perot Independent Votes	Perot Independent %	Others Votes	Others %
Alabama	9	1,688,060		9	114,203	6.8%	690,080	40.9%	804,283	47.6%	183,109	10.8%	10,588	0.6%
Alaska	3	258,506		3	23,706	9.2%	78,294	30.3%	102,000	39.5%	73,481	28.4%	4,731	1.8%
Arizona	8	1,487,006		8	29,036	2.0%	543,050	36.5%	572,086	38.5%	353,741	23.8%	18,129	1.2%
Arkansas	6	950,653	6		168,499	17.7%	505,823	53.2%	337,324	35.5%	99,132	10.4%	8,374	0.9%
California	54	11,131,721	54		1,490,751	13.4%	5,121,325	46.0%	3,630,574	32.6%	2,296,006	20.6%	83,816	0.8%
Colorado	8	1,569,180	8		66,831	4.3%	629,681	40.1%	562,850	35.9%	366,010	23.3%	10,639	0.7%
Connecticut	8	1,616,332	8		104,005	6.4%	682,318	42.2%	578,313	35.8%	348,771	21.6%	6,930	0.4%
Delaware	3	289,620	3		23,741	8.2%	126,054	43.5%	102,313	35.3%	59,213	20.4%	2,040	0.7%
District of Columbia	3	227,572	3		171,921	75.5%	192,619	84.6%	20,698	9.1%	9,681	4.3%	4,574	2.0%
Florida	25	5,314,392		25	100,612	1.9%	2,072,698	39.0%	2,173,310	40.9%	1,053,067	19.8%	15,317	0.3%
Georgia	13	2,321,133	13		13,714	0.6%	1,008,966	43.5%	995,252	42.9%	309,657	13.3%	7,258	0.3%
Hawaii	4	372,842	4		42,488	11.4%	179,310	48.1%	136,822	36.7%	53,003	14.2%	3,707	1.0%
Idaho	4	482,114		4	65,632	13.6%	137,013	28.4%	202,645	42.0%	130,395	27.0%	12,061	2.5%
Illinois	22	5,050,157	22		719,254	14.2%	2,453,350	48.6%	1,734,096	34.3%	840,515	16.6%	22,196	0.4%
Indiana	12	2,305,871		12	140,955	6.1%	848,420	36.8%	989,375	42.9%	455,934	19.8%	12,142	0.5%
Iowa	7	1,354,607	7		81,462	6.0%	586,353	43.3%	504,891	37.3%	253,468	18.7%	9,895	0.7%
Kansas	6	1,157,236		6	59,517	5.1%	390,434	33.7%	449,951	38.9%	312,358	27.0%	4,493	0.4%
Kentucky	8	1,492,900	8		47,926	3.2%	665,104	44.6%	617,178	41.3%	203,944	13.7%	6,674	0.4%
Louisiana	9	1,790,017	9		82,585	4.6%	815,971	45.6%	733,386	41.0%	211,478	11.8%	29,182	1.6%
Maine	4	679,499	4		56,600	8.3%	263,420	38.8%	206,504	30.4%	206,820	30.4%	2,755	0.4%
Maryland	10	1,985,046	10		281,477	14.2%	988,571	49.8%	707,094	35.6%	281,414	14.2%	7,967	0.4%
Massachusetts	12	2,773,700	12		513,613	18.5%	1,318,662	47.5%	805,049	29.0%	630,731	22.7%	19,258	0.7%
Michigan	18	4,274,673	18		316,242	7.4%	1,871,182	43.8%	1,554,940	36.4%	824,813	19.3%	23,738	0.6%
Minnesota	10	2,347,948	10		273,156	11.6%	1,020,997	43.5%	747,841	31.9%	562,506	24.0%	16,604	0.7%
Mississippi	7	981,793		7	87,535	8.9%	400,258	40.8%	487,793	49.7%	85,626	8.7%	8,116	0.8%
Missouri	11	2,391,270	11		242,714	10.2%	1,053,873	44.1%	811,159	33.9%	518,741	21.7%	7,497	0.3%
Montana	3	410,583	3		10,300	2.5%	154,507	37.6%	144,207	35.1%	107,225	26.1%	4,644	1.1%
Nebraska	5	739,283		5	127,002	17.2%	217,344	29.4%	344,346	46.6%	174,687	23.6%	2,906	0.4%
Nevada	4	506,318	4		13,320	2.6%	189,148	37.4%	175,828	34.7%	132,580	26.2%	8,762	1.7%
New Hampshire	4	537,215	4		6,556	1.2%	209,040	38.9%	202,484	37.7%	121,337	22.6%	4,354	0.8%
New Jersey	15	3,343,594	15		79,341	2.4%	1,436,206	43.0%	1,356,865	40.6%	521,829	15.6%	28,694	0.9%
New Mexico	5	569,986	5		48,793	8.6%	261,617	45.9%	212,824	37.3%	91,895	16.1%	3,650	0.6%
New York	33	6,926,925	33		1,097,801	15.8%	3,444,450	49.7%	2,346,649	33.9%	1,090,721	15.7%	45,105	0.7%
North Carolina	14	2,611,850		14	20,619	0.8%	1,114,042	42.7%	1,134,661	43.4%	357,864	13.7%	5,283	0.2%
North Dakota	3	308,133		3	37,076	12.0%	99,168	32.2%	136,244	44.2%	71,084	23.1%	1,637	0.5%
Ohio	21	4,939,964	21		90,632	1.8%	1,984,942	40.2%	1,894,310	38.3%	1,036,426	21.0%	24,286	0.5%
Oklahoma	8	1,390,359		8	119,863	8.6%	473,066	34.0%	592,929	42.6%	319,878	23.0%	4,486	0.3%
Oregon	7	1,462,643	7		145,557	10.0%	621,314	42.5%	475,757	32.5%	354,091	24.2%	11,481	0.8%
Pennsylvania	23	4,959,810	23		447,323	9.0%	2,239,164	45.1%	1,791,841	36.1%	902,667	18.2%	26,138	0.5%
Rhode Island	4	453,477	4		81,698	18.0%	213,299	47.0%	131,601	29.0%	105,045	23.2%	3,532	0.8%
South Carolina	8	1,202,527		8	97,993	8.1%	479,514	39.9%	577,507	48.0%	138,872	11.5%	6,634	0.6%
South Dakota	3	336,254		3	11,830	3.5%	124,888	37.1%	136,718	40.7%	73,295	21.8%	1,353	0.4%
Tennessee	11	1,982,638	11		92,221	4.7%	933,521	47.1%	841,300	42.4%	199,968	10.1%	7,849	0.4%
Texas	32	6,154,018		32	214,256	3.5%	2,281,815	37.1%	2,496,071	40.6%	1,354,781	22.0%	21,351	0.3%
Utah	5	743,998		5	119,232	16.0%	183,429	24.7%	322,632	43.4%	203,400	27.3%	34,537	4.6%
Vermont	3	289,701	3		45,470	15.7%	133,592	46.1%	88,122	30.4%	65,991	22.8%	1,996	0.7%
Virginia	13	2,558,665		13	111,867	4.4%	1,038,650	40.6%	1,150,517	45.0%	348,639	13.6%	20,859	0.8%
Washington	11	2,287,565	11		261,803	11.4%	993,037	43.4%	731,234	32.0%	541,780	23.7%	21,514	0.9%
West Virginia	5	683,677	5		89,027	13.0%	331,001	48.4%	241,974	35.4%	108,829	15.9%	1,873	0.3%
Wisconsin	11	2,531,114	11		110,211	4.4%	1,041,066	41.1%	930,855	36.8%	544,479	21.5%	14,714	0.6%
Wyoming	3	199,884		3	11,187	5.6%	68,160	34.1%	79,347	39.7%	51,263	25.6%	1,114	0.6%
TOTAL	538	104,424,029	370	168	5,805,256	5.6%	44,909,806	43.0%	39,104,550	37.4%	19,742,240	18.9%	667,433	0.6%

For sources, see p. 1135.

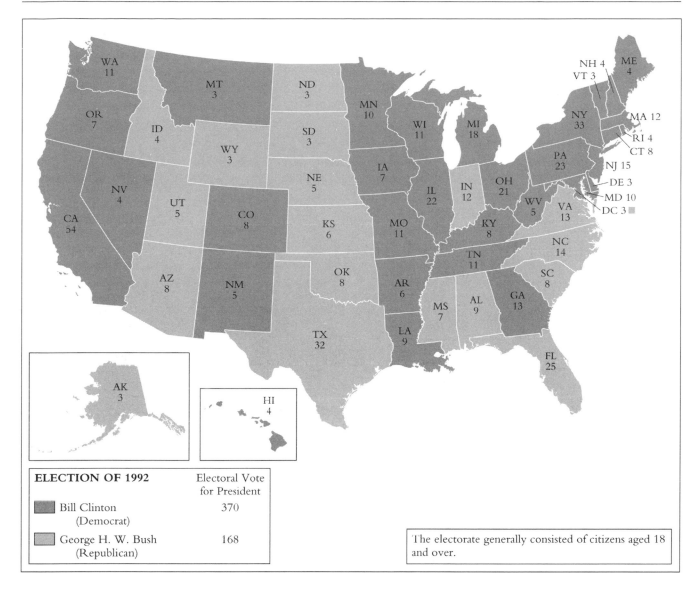

ELECTION OF 1992 | Electoral Vote for President

Bill Clinton (Democrat) — 370

George H. W. Bush (Republican) — 168

The electorate generally consisted of citizens aged 18 and over.

DOCUMENTS: ELECTION OF 1992

For the first time in a generation, a third-party candidate had a major effect on a presidential election. Texas businessman Ross Perot organized the Reform Party and presented himself as an alternative to Republican President George Bush and Arkansas Governor Bill Clinton, the Democratic nominee. Although Perot led briefly in some early polls, he failed to carry a single state in November. However, Perot's attempt to exploit unease with the major parties through a populist appeal took enough votes away from the Republicans to help give Clinton the presidency. Claiming to be a "new" Democrat, Bill Clinton, in accepting the Democratic nomination, Document 1, criticized Republican "trickle-down" economics and big business. He promised a "New Covenant," offering empowerment in place of entitlements and a more efficient government that worked for the interests of the middle class over the wealthy.

Bush fended off a surprising primary challenge by conservative commentator Pat Buchanan. However, at the Republican Convention, Buchanan's speech, Document 2, the ideology of the ultra-conservative faction of the Republican Party, coming out against homosexuality and abortion. President Bush, in his speech accepting the Republican nomination, Document 3, celebrated his foreign policy achievements and admitted a mistake in breaking his pledge not to raise taxes. He acknowledged the poor economy but blamed it on a Democratic Congress, and reminded voters how bad the economy was the last time they elected a southern Democratic governor as president, commenting that "America does not need Carter 2."

In Document 4, opening statements in the vice presidential debate, Tennessee Senator Al Gore, Clinton's running mate, made sure to bring up Dan Quayle's poor performance four years earlier. Meanwhile, Perot's vice presidential choice, retired Vice-Admiral James Stockdale, opened with, "Who am I? Why am I here?" in what would be a damaging performance. Document 5, excerpts from the first presidential debate, focused on what distinguished the three major candidates from each other and personal character, an issue that dogged Clinton throughout the campaign.

Document 1

*Bill Clinton's Nomination Acceptance Speech,
July 16, 1992*

We meet at a special moment in history, you and I. The cold war is over; Soviet Communism has collapsed, and our values—freedom, democracy, individual rights, free enterprise—they have triumphed all around the world. And yet just as we have won the cold war abroad, we are losing the battles for economic opportunity and social justice here at home. Now that we have changed the world, it's time to change America.

I have news for the forces of greed and the defenders of the status quo: your time has come—and gone. It's time for a change in America.

Tonight, ten million of our fellow Americans are out of work. Tens of millions more work harder for lower pay. The incumbent President says unemployment always goes up a little before a recovery begins. But unemployment only has to go up by one more person before a real recovery can begin—and Mr. President, you are that man. . . .

A President ought to be a powerful force for progress. But right now I know how President Lincoln felt when General McClellan wouldn't attack in the Civil War. He asked him, "If you're not going to use your army, may I borrow it?" And so I say, George Bush, if you won't use your power to help America, step aside. I will. . . .

What is George Bush doing about our economic problems?

Well, four years ago he promised 15 million new jobs by this time, and he's over 14 million short. Al Gore and I can do better.

He has raised taxes on the people driving pickup trucks and lowered taxes on the people riding in limousines. We can do better.

He promised to balance the budget, but he hasn't even tried. . . .

The Republicans have campaigned against big government for a generation. But have you noticed? They've run this big government for a generation, and they haven't changed a thing. They don't want to fix government, they still want to campaign against it, and that's all.

But, my fellow Democrats, it's time for us to realize that we've got some changing to do, too. There is not a program in government for every problem. And if we really want to use government to help people, we have got to make it work again.

Because we are committed in this convention and in this platform to making these changes, we are as Democrats, in the words that Ross Perot himself spoke today, a revitalized Democratic Party. I am well aware that all those millions of people who rallied to Ross Perot's cause wanted to be in an army of patriots for change. Tonight I say to them: Join us, and together we will revitalize America.

Now, I don't have all the answers. But I do know the old ways don't work. Trickle down economics has sure failed. And big bureaucracies, both public and private, they've failed too.

That's why we need a new approach to government. A government that offers more empowerment and less entitlement, more choices for young people in the schools they attend, in the public schools they attend. And more choices for the elderly and for people with disabilities in long-term care they receive. A government that is leaner, not meaner, a government that expands opportunity, not bureaucracy, a government that understands that jobs must come from growth in a vibrant and vital system of free enterprise. I call this approach a New Covenant, a solemn agreement between the people and their government, based not simply on what each of us can take, but what all of us must give to our nation. . . .

Of all the things George Bush has ever said that I disagree with, perhaps the thing that bothers me most is how he derides and degrades the American tradition of seeing and seeking a better future. He mocks it as "the vision thing." But just remember what the scripture says: "Where there is no vision, the people perish."

What is the vision of our New Covenant?

An America with millions of new jobs. . . .

An America in which the doors of college are thrown open once again to the sons and daughters of stenographers and steelworkers. . . .

An America in which health care is a right, not a privilege. . . .

An America in which middle-class incomes—not middle-class taxes—are going up. . . .

An America where we end welfare as we know it. . . . Welfare should be a second chance, not a way of life. . . .

An America with the world's strongest defense, ready and willing to use force, when necessary. . . .

In the end, my fellow Americans, this New Covenant simply asks us all to be Americans again. Old-fashioned Americans for a new time. Opportunity. Responsibility. Community. When we pull together, America will pull ahead. . . .

Source: *New York Times*, July 17, 1992.

Document 2

Patrick Buchanan's Republican National Convention Address, August 17, 1992

Like many of you last month, I watched that giant masquerade ball at Madison Square Garden—where 20,000 radicals and liberals came dressed up as moderates and centrists—in the greatest single exhibition of cross-dressing in American political history.

One by one, the prophets of doom appeared at the podium. The Reagan decade, they moaned, was a terrible time in America; and the only way to prevent even worse times, they said, is to entrust our nation's fate and future to the party that gave us McGovern, Mondale, Carter and Michael Dukakis.

No way, my friends. The American people are not going to buy back into the failed liberalism of the 1960s and '70s—no matter how slick the package in 1992. . . .

Out of Jimmy Carter's days of malaise, Ronald Reagan crafted the longest peacetime recovery in US history—three million new businesses created, and twenty million new jobs.

Under the Reagan Doctrine, one by one, the communist dominos began to fall. . . .

Most of all, Ronald Reagan made us proud to be Americans again. . . .

George Bush has been U.N. ambassador, CIA director, envoy to China. As vice president, he coauthored the policies that won the Cold War. . . . And Mr. Clinton? Well, Bill Clinton couldn't find 150 words to discuss foreign policy in an acceptance speech that lasted an hour. . . .

George Bush is a defender of right-to-life, and lifelong champion of the Judeo-Christian values and beliefs upon which this nation was built.

Mr. Clinton, however, has a different agenda.

At its top is unrestricted abortion on demand. When the Irish-Catholic governor of Pennsylvania, Robert Casey, asked to say a few words on behalf of the 25 million unborn children destroyed since *Roe v. Wade*, he was told there was no place for him at the podium of Bill Clinton's convention, no room at the inn.

Yet a militant leader of the homosexual rights movement could rise at that convention and exult: "Bill Clinton and Al Gore represent the most pro-lesbian and pro-gay ticket in history." And so they do. . . .

Elect me, and you get two for the price of one, Mr. Clinton says of his lawyer-spouse. And what does Hillary believe?

Well Hillary believes that 12-year-olds should have a right to sue their parents, and she has compared marriage as an institution to slavery—and life on an Indian reservation.

Well, speak for yourself, Hillary.

Friends, this is radical feminism. The agenda Clinton & Clinton would impose on America—abortion on demand, a litmus test for the Supreme Court, homosexual rights, discrimination against religious schools, women in combat—that's change, all right. But it is not the kind of change America wants. . . .

George Bush was 17 when they bombed Pearl Harbor. He left his high school class, walked down to the recruiting office, and signed up to become the youngest fighter pilot in the Pacific war. And Mr. Clinton? When Bill Clinton's turn came in Vietnam, he sat up in a dormitory in Oxford, England, and figured out how to dodge the draft. . . .

My friends, this election is about much more than who gets what. It is about who we are. It is about what we believe. It is about what we stand for as Americans. There is a religious war going on in our country for the soul of America. It is a cultural war, as critical to the kind of nation we will one day be as was the Cold War itself. And in that struggle for the soul of America, Clinton & Clinton are on the other side, and George Bush is on our side. . . .

Source: Internet Brigade Web site, www.buchanan.org/pa-92-0817-rnc.html.

Document 3

George Bush's Nomination Acceptance Speech, August 20, 1992

Just pause for a moment to reflect on what we've done.

Germany has united, and a slab of the Berlin wall sits right outside this Astrodome.

Arabs and Israelis now sit face-to-face and talk peace.

And every hostage held in Lebanon is free.

The conflicts, the conflict, in El Salvador is over, and free elections brought democracy to Nicaragua.

Black and white South Africans cheered each other at the Olympics.

The Soviet Union can only be found in history books.

The captive nations of Eastern Europe and the Baltics are captive no more.

And today, and today, on the rural streets of Poland, merchants sell cans of air labeled "the last breath of Communism."

If I had stood, if I had stood before you four years ago and described this as the world we would help to build, you would have said, "George Bush, you must have been smoking something, and you must have inhaled." . . .

Now, the Soviet bear may be gone, but there are still wolves in the woods. And we saw that when Saddam Hussein invaded Kuwait. The Mideast might have become a nuclear powder keg, our energy supplies held hostage.

So we did what was right and what was necessary. We destroyed a threat, freed a people and locked a tyrant in the prison of his own country.

Well, what about the leader of the Arkansas National Guard, the man who hopes to be commander in chief? Well, while I bit the bullet, and he bit his nails. . . .

My opponent, my opponent says America is a nation in decline. . . .

Maybe he hasn't heard, maybe he hasn't heard that we are still the world's largest economy. . . .

My opponent, my opponent won't mention that. He won't remind you that interest rates are the lowest they've been in 20 years, and millions of Americans have refinanced their homes. And you just won't hear that inflation, the thief of the middle class, has been locked in a maximum-security prison. . . .

You don't hear a lot about progress in America. So let me tell you about some good things we've done together.

Just two weeks ago, all three nations of North America agreed to trade freely from Manitoba to Mexico. And this will bring good jobs to Main Street U.S.A.

We passed the Americans with Disabilities Act. . . .

Our children will breathe easier because of our new clean air pact.

We are rebuilding our roads, providing jobs for more than half a million Americans.

And we passed a childcare law. . . . And one more thing of vital importance to all. Today, cocaine use has fallen by 60 percent among young people. . . .

Do I want to do more? You bet. Nothing hurts me more than to meet with soldiers home from the Persian Gulf, who can't find a job. Or workers who have a job, but worry that the next day will bring a pink slip. . . .

We start with a simple fact: Government is too big and spends too much.

And I have asked Congress to put a lid on mandatory spending except Social Security. And I've proposed doing away with over 200 programs and 4,000 wasteful projects and to freeze all other spending.

The gridlock Democrat Congress said, "No."

So, beginning tonight, I will enforce the spending freeze on my own. And if Congress sends me a bill spending more than I asked for in my budget, I will veto it fast. . . .

My opponent has a different experience: He has been in government nearly all his life. His passion to expand government knows no bounds.

And he has already proposed—and listen to this carefully—he has already proposed $220 billion in new spending, along with the biggest tax increase in history, $150 billion. And that's just to start.

He says he wants to tax the rich, but, folks, he defines rich as anyone who has a job. . . .

Now let me say this: When it comes to taxes, I've learned the hard way. . . .

Two years ago, I made a bad call on the Democrats' tax increase. . . .

Well, it was a mistake to go along with the Democratic tax increase. And I admit it.

But here's the question for the American people. Who do you trust in this election? The candidate who's raised taxes one time and regrets it, or the other candidate who raised taxes and fees 128 times, and enjoyed it every time? . . .

Look, we tried this once before, combining the Democratic Governor of a small Southern state with a very liberal Vice President and a Democratic Congress. America does not need "Carter 2."

We do not want to take America back to those days of malaise. . . .

Forty-four years ago, in another age of uncertainty, a different President embarked on a similar mission. His name was Harry S. Truman.

And as he stood before his party to accept their nomination, Harry Truman knew the freedom I know this evening, the freedom to talk about what's right for America and let the chips fall where they may.

Harry Truman said this: "This is more than a political call to arms. Give me your help, not to win votes alone, but to win this new crusade and keep America safe and secure for its own people. . . .

Source: Public Papers and Addresses of the Presidents of the United States: George Bush, 1992–1993, Book II, August 1, 1992 to January 20, 1993 (Washington, DC: Government Printing Office, 1993).

Document 4

Opening Statements in the Vice Presidential Debate, October 13, 1992

SENATOR GORE: Good evening. It's great to be here in Atlanta for this debate where America will be showcased to the world, when the 1996 Olympics are put on right here. It's appropriate because in a real sense, our discussion this evening will be about what kind of nation we want to be four years from now. It's also a pleasure to be with my two opponents this evening. Admiral Stockdale, may I say it's a special honor to share this stage with you. Those of us who served in Vietnam looked at you as a national hero even before you were awarded the Congressional Medal of Honor.

And Mr. Vice President—Dan, if I may—it was 16 years ago that you and I went to the Congress on the very first day together. I'll make you a deal this evening. If you don't try to compare George Bush to Harry Truman, I won't compare you to Jack Kennedy. . . .

But our real discussion is going to be about change. Bill Clinton and I stand for change because we don't believe our nation can stand four more years of what we've had under George Bush and Dan Quayle.

When the recession came they were like a deer caught in the headlights—paralyzed into inaction, blinded to the suffering and pain of bankruptcies and people who were unemployed. . . .

QUAYLE: Well, thank you, Senator Gore, for reminding me about my performance in the 1988 vice presidential debate. This is 1992, Bill Clinton is running against President George Bush. There are two things that I'm going to stress during this debate: One, Bill Clinton's economic plan and his agenda will make matters much, much worse—he will raise your taxes, he will increase spending, he will make government bigger, jobs will be lost; second, Bill Clinton does not have the strength nor the character to be president of the U.S. . . . Bill Clinton wants to empower government, we want to empower people. . . . You need to have a president you can trust. Can you really trust Bill Clinton?

ADMIRAL STOCKDALE: Who am I? Why am I here? (Laughter and applause)

I'm not a politician—everybody knows that. So don't expect me to use the language of the Washington insider. Thirty-seven years in the Navy, and only one of them up there in Washington. And now I'm an academic. . . .

And I know how governments, how American governments can be—can be courageous, and how they can be callow. And that's important. That's one thing I'm an insider on. . . .

Why am I here tonight? I am here because I have in my brain and in my heart what it takes to lead America through tough times. . . .

Source: Commission on Presidential Debates Web site, www.debates.org/pages/trans92d.html (uncorrected transcript).

Document 5
Excerpts from the First Presidential Debate, October 11, 1992

Differences

[Jim] LEHRER [of the *McNeil-Lehrer NewsHour*]: What do you believe tonight is the single most important separating issue of this campaign?

PEROT: I think the principle that separates me is that five and a half million people came together on their own and put me on the ballot. I was not put on the ballot by either of the two parties; I was not put on the ballot by any PAC money, by any foreign lobbyist money, by any special interest money. This is a movement that came from the people. This is the way the framers of the Constitution intended our government to be, a government that comes from the people. . . .

CLINTON: The most important distinction in this campaign is that I represent real hope for change, a departure from trickle-down economics, a departure from tax-and-spend economics, to invest in growth. . . .

PRESIDENT BUSH: Well, I think one thing that distinguishes is experience. I think we've dramatically changed the world. . . . Kids go to bed at night without the same fear of nuclear war. . . .

LEHRER: How do you respond to the President . . . on the question of experience? He says that is what distinguishes him from the other two of you. . . .

PEROT: I don't have any experience in running up a $4 trillion debt. I don't have any experience in gridlock government where nobody takes responsibility for anything and everybody blames everybody else. . . .

On Character

LEHRER: Are there important issues of character separating you? . . .

BUSH: I think the American people should be the judge of that. I think character is a very important question. . . . They get on me—Bill's gotten on me about "Read my lips." When I make a mistake I'll admit it. But he has made—not admitted a mistake and I just find it impossible to understand how an American can demonstrate against his own country in a foreign land—organizing demonstrations against it when young men are held prisoner in Hanoi or kids out of the ghetto were drafted. . . .

PEROT: I would say just, you know, look at all three of us. Decide who you think will do the job. Pick that person in November because believe me, as I've said before, "The party's over and it's time for the clean-up crew." . . .

CLINTON: Ross gave a good answer but I've got to respond directly to Mr. Bush. You have questioned my patriotism. . . . Now, I honor your service in World War II, I honor Mr. Perot's service in uniform and the service of every man and woman who ever served, including Admiral Crowe, who was your Chairman of the joint Chiefs and who's supporting me. But when Joe McCarthy went around this country attacking people's patriotism he was wrong. He was wrong. And a senator from Connecticut stood up to him named Prescott Bush. Your father was right to stand up to Joe McCarthy, you were wrong to attack my patriotism. I was opposed to the war but I loved my country, and we need a president who will bring this country together, not divide it. We've had enough division. I want to lead a unified country. . . .

Source: Commission on Presidential Debates Web site, www.debates.org/pages/trans92a2.html (uncorrected transcript).

THE ELECTION OF 1996

On its face, the 1996 presidential election appears quite straightforward. After leading in the polls throughout a seemingly run-of-the-mill campaign, the Democratic incumbent, Bill Clinton (see fact box, p. 999), scored a solid if not overwhelming victory in his contest with the Republican challenger, Robert Dole (see fact box, p. 930). But, closer inspection reveals the rich topography of the 1996 election. Its distinguishing features are evident when judged in the context of the times.

Prior to the 1992 election, a pattern of divided government had prevailed. For all but six of the preceding twenty-four years, Republican presidents had contended with Democratic majorities in the House and Senate. For that reason, the election of a Democratic president was a significant break with the past. The surprise of Clinton's 1992 victory, however, paled by comparison to the change wrought by the midterm elections that followed. In 1994, Republicans gained majorities in both the House and Senate for the first time in forty years. This shocking turn of events prompted an extensive reassessment of expectations for the 1996 elections.

Clinton's First Term as President

The 1994 election results appeared particularly threatening to President Clinton. His first two years had been difficult. Soon after assuming office, he abandoned the middle-class tax cut promised during the 1992 campaign, became embroiled in a dispute over the role of gays in the military, and angered members of his own party by forging a coalition composed predominantly of Republican legislators to pass the North American Free Trade Agreement. Clinton's highly touted healthcare reform proposal was rejected. He was dogged by rumors of infidelity, and by investigations of his wife's former law firm, firings in the White House travel office, and Arkansas land dealings referred to as "Whitewater." President Clinton's approval ratings in public opinion polls confirmed his difficulties, falling precipitously in his first few months in office and rising above 50 percent only sporadically.

The Democratic president's prospects for reelection seemed further impaired by the 1994 midterm results. In electing Republican majorities to the House and Senate, pundits reasoned, voters were repudiating all things Democratic—including, by implication, Bill Clinton. In this context, Clinton's 1996 reelection efforts seemed vulnerable to serious challenges from both Republican and Democratic hopefuls. Democrats were expected to blame him for their 1994 losses and, it was widely assumed, a popular Republican would be attracted to run against the weakened president. Conventional wisdom, however, would prove to be wrong. Ironically, Clinton's 1996 electoral success was made possible in no small measure by the Republicans' midterm congressional victories.

The 1994 election outcome was not so much an endorsement of Republicans' conservative ideology, as it was an expression of anger over what voters saw as the Democrats' petty corruption and complacency. While the country did seem to be moving in a conser-

CHRONOLOGY

1994

NOVEMBER 8   Midterm congressional elections shift control of House and Senate to Republicans.

1995

SEPTEMBER 25   Perot announces formation of Reform Party.

FALL   Clinton ads attack "Dolegingrich."

NOVEMBER 14–21 Budget stand-off causes first federal government shutdown.

DECEMBER 15   Second federal government shutdown begins, continuing through January 6, 1996.

1996

FEBRUARY 12   Iowa caucuses held.

FEBRUARY 20   New Hampshire Republican primary held.

FEBRUARY 27   Arizona Republican primary held.

MARCH 26   Dole achieves majority of delegates, clinching Republican nomination.

MAY 15   Dole announces his resignation from the Senate.

AUGUST 12–15   Republican Party convention meets.

AUGUST 18   Reform Party convention occurs.

AUGUST 26–29   Democratic Party convention meets.

NOVEMBER 5   Clinton beats Dole in general election.

1997

JANUARY 20   Clinton inaugurated for second term as U.S. president.

---

vative direction during the 1980s and into the 1990s, the public—in contrast to political leaders—do not tend to see the world through an ideological prism. But Republican congressional leaders—especially Georgia representative Newt Gingrich, who would become the speaker of the House of Representatives—read the 1994 election as a mandate to force their conservative principles on the Democratic president.

While the Republicans had begun by passing popular proposals laid out in their 1994 campaign, known as "Contract with America," they soon moved on to more contentious issues. They invited business lobbyists to write sections of legislation reducing the scope of government regulation. In the House of Representatives Republican leaders set out to roll back (opponents said "gut") popular environmental legislation. As their efforts to force their preferences

on the Democratic president intensified, however, the president's back stiffened, and Republican congressional leaders sought ways to force him to accept their will. In late 1995, they had decided on what they thought was a foolproof method: They would refuse to compromise with the president on the budget. Clinton would be forced to accept the Republican budget, and with it their policies, in order to keep the government in operation. As it turned out, this was a fateful miscalculation.

Clinton did respond to the 1994 election results. Adopting a strategy of "triangulation," the president aimed to set himself apart from both congressional Republicans and Democrats. He would define the "dynamic center," where practicality would win over ideology. Clinton began to declare support for popular Republican policies, calling for balancing the budget in ten years and coming out in support of welfare reform.

The button says "leadership," but the images emphasize the youth and energy of the Democratic ticket of Bill Clinton and Al Gore. *(Gyory Collection/Cathy Casriel Photo)*

But he held firm on issues with strong public backing, such as ensuring abortion rights, environmental protection, and educational opportunities.

To help define his position in contrast with Republicans, Clinton seized upon a proposal by House Speaker Gingrich to stop the growth in Medicare spending. He ran ads accusing the Republican congressional leadership of trying to end healthcare assistance for the elderly. The ads worked. Clinton's favorable rating in the polls seemed to tick up, and that of the Republican Congress down, with every broadcast of the commercials.

So when, in November 1995, the Republican Congress sent him its budget legislation, Clinton was prepared to respond. He charged that the Republican budget would impair Americans' health, safety, and security, and said he had no choice but to veto it, thereby closing down "nonessential" federal government operations. The Republican congressional leadership was surprised, but not deterred. They were so convinced that Clinton would ultimately accept their terms that they refused to compromise—and, in December, passed a second budget bill crafted to force their policies on the president. Again, Clinton vetoed the legislation. As a result, the government was shut down for six days in November, and twenty-one days from December 1995 into January 1996.

The high-stakes gamble paid off for the president. The combination of Clinton's efforts to moderate his positions, his counterattack on Medicare, and Speaker Gingrich's tendency to make intemperate public statements convinced most of the public that the Republican Congress was to blame for the government shutdown. The Republican leadership had no choice but to back down, compromising with the president on the budget. It was Clinton's first significant victory since the period before the 1994 elections and, as observed in *Newsweek's* Special Election Issue, "the first engagement in the [1996] presidential campaign. By exaggerating the GOP's mandate in 1994, Newt Gingrich dramatically lengthened the odds against" the Republicans' eventual presidential nominee. But this would not noticeably reduce the number of candidates seeking the Republican presidential nomination.

The Republican Campaign

Although ten candidates entered the race for the Republican nomination, none seemed to excite great enthusiasm among the electorate. Some of the candidates simply were not taken seriously. Alan Keyes, an obscure conservative African American, had no electoral experience. Congressman Robert Dornan was considered such a right-wing extremist that he was shunned even by his conservative congressional colleagues. Others, while more credible, lacked the spark to ignite a serious challenge. Senator Richard Lugar was highly respected by his colleagues, but had little gift for exciting voters. Two of the announced candidates—Senator Arlen Specter of Pennsylvania and Governor Pete Wilson of California—pulled out even before the first primary, citing a shortage of campaign funds.

To be viable in the 1996 primaries, a candidate had to amass a large treasury early in the campaign process. In each presidential election cycle over the previous couple of decades, states had scheduled their contests earlier in the primary season. With a large proportion of contests compressed into the early weeks of the primary calendar, a candidate simply had insufficient time between races to rely on contributions generated by early victories to fund his campaign in the later contests.

At the same time, money did not guarantee success. Senator Phil Gramm of Texas amassed an enormous treasury, bragging: "I have the most reliable friend you can have in American politics, and that is ready money." His financial strength had gone a long way in convincing pundits that he was a contender. And yet his large bankroll did not translate to electoral support—and Gramm withdrew after embarrassing losses in the first two contests.

Four of the original ten candidates—Bob Dole, Lamar Alexander, Steve Forbes, and Patrick Buchanan—proved to be serious competitors. Dole, the 1976 vice presidential candidate and Senate Republican leader since 1984, was the candidate generally expected to win the nomination. While conservative, he tended to seek compromise. Perhaps alone among Republican congressional leaders, he had been skeptical about open warfare with Clinton over the budget. Dole had no grand policy scheme, but rather ran more as the party's elder statesman. Some said that at seventy-two—among the oldest presidential candidates in U.S. history—Dole was too much of an elder. Others saw in him traditional virtues that America had lost.

Lamar Alexander, former Tennessee governor and U.S. secretary of education, campaigned against the "Washington establishment," portraying himself as the outsider in the race. He wore a red flannel shirt— an emblem of his "down home" origins, according to some, or an affectation of a well-connected politician, according to others.

Pat Buchanan, a firebrand social conservative who had sought the Republican nomination in 1992, was a television commentator and newspaper columnist. Buchanan stressed what he saw as moral positions on social issues: opposition to abortion, a larger role for religion, harsher penalties for criminals, and tighter restrictions on immigration.

Steve Forbes was a novice at electoral politics. A magazine publisher, his chief asset was an inherited fortune in the hundreds of millions of dollars, from which he was prepared to spend lavishly. While he took positions on a number of issues, the core of his campaign was a proposal to vastly lower income taxes and impose a single "flat" rate, in place of the traditional progressive tax structure.

In Iowa, the first contest with a full complement of candidates, the serious winnowing began. As expected, given that he was from a neighboring state with similar agricultural interests, Dole led the pack. Unexpectedly, however, his lead was small: Dole received 26 percent of the vote to Buchanan's 23 percent, Alexander's 18 percent, and Forbes's 10 percent.

Just eight days later, Buchanan scored an upset victory over Dole in New Hampshire. While Buchanan beat Dole by only one percentage point—27 to 26 percent—that was enough to shake the Dole campaign, which had expected an unimpeded march to the nomination. As things were developing, it appeared that they were in for a struggle. Alexander came in third in New Hampshire with 23 percent— not strong, but respectable. The only apparent casualty seemed to be Forbes, who again trailed badly with only 12 percent of the vote. His candidacy was unexpectedly revived, however, when he scored victories in two out of the four state elections held within the following week.

One of Forbes's victories was easily explained and largely discounted. In Delaware, most candidates had not campaigned. As a result, Forbes's personal appearances and large media expenditure paid off. His Arizona win seemed more convincing, as all the candidates had contested the state. By the end of the week it was Alexander, rather than Forbes, who withdrew.

So, after just three weeks the Republican race seemed to have narrowed to three candidates—Dole,

Giving a "thumbs up," 1996 Republican candidate Robert Dole appears here with his wife Elizabeth and Governor Tom Ridge of Pennsylvania. The prop held by his wife suggests the major issue of Dole's campaign. *(AP Wide World Photos)*

Buchanan, and Forbes—each of whom had scored credible victories. But appearances were deceptive. Both the Buchanan and Forbes campaigns had seen their best days.

As the political scientist William Mayer pointed out in Pomper's book, *The 1996 Election*, Buchanan had a strong core of motivated supporters who accounted for 20 to 30 percent of the Republican primary electorate. With the large field of candidates in the earliest primaries, Buchanan could win with less than a 30 percent share of the vote. But with fewer candidates left in contention, he needed a larger share for victory. The problem for Buchanan was that his foes were as numerous as his supporters. While his vote share persisted through most of the remaining primaries, it was simply too little to win in a smaller field of candidates.

Forbes's strength—his wealth—was also his weakness. He spent lavishly on his campaign, swamping the states in which he ran with expensive television ads and direct mail appeals. He could overwhelm opponents with advertising and mailings in primaries with small media markets, like Delaware and Arizona; but Forbes could not drown out the opposition's message in more populous states with much larger media markets. (See "Forbes and Campaign Finance," p. 1020.)

Dole's strength—long evident in national public opinion polls—began to exert itself. He won every primary after Arizona, 80 percent of them with a majority of the vote. Within one month after the Arizona primary, Dole had secured well over the majority of convention delegates he needed to guarantee his nomination.

But this was not a rosy picture. While the primaries would continue for another six weeks, Dole needed to turn his attention to the general election. He was trailing Clinton in the polls, and his "rotunda strat-

This photograph of President Bill Clinton and Vice President Al Gore includes their wives, Hillary Rodham Clinton and Tipper Gore, who were highly visible during the first Clinton administration. The two candidates were in Gore's home state of Tennessee in 1996 after a two-day bus tour, an event that indicated their close political relationship at the time. *(AP Wide World Photos)*

FORBES AND CAMPAIGN FINANCE

While contributions to presidential candidates are subject to strict limits, federal law allows presidential candidates to spend unlimited amounts of their own money, unless they accept federal funds. Steve Forbes financed his own campaign with more than $37 million of inherited wealth. Among the Republican primary contenders, only Bob Dole had a larger treasury.

Had Forbes been forced to rely on contributions to fund his campaign, it's unlikely that he could have launched a serious effort. As the longtime publisher of *Forbes*, a financial magazine, he had no electoral experience, few campaign skills, and little apparent support. With his self-financed campaign, however, he was able not only to buy name recognition and electoral support, but also to reshape the entire character of the Republican primaries and the general election effort of the party's eventual nominee.

Since Forbes did not rely on federal matching funds, he was also free from the spending limits imposed on his opponents. His expenditures, which began well before the primaries, totaled $14 million by the fourth quarter of 1995, to which Forbes added $7 million more in January 1996. Forbes saturated the early primary states of Iowa, New Hampshire, and Arizona with ads, spending more than $4 million in Iowa alone—about $400 for every vote he received in the state's caucuses.

Forbes's record-breaking expenditures forced other candidates to increase spending well above their budgeted amounts, pushing them toward their legal limits. In his effort to keep pace, Lamar Alexander, borrowed millions against anticipated funds he had yet to receive from the federal government. Dole was forced to spend virtually his entire treasury to win the delegates necessary to clinch the nomination. With no reserves, Dole was unable to respond to President Clinton's media campaign from mid-March until he received federal funds in August. While this may not be the reason Dole lost the election, it was a major disadvantage.

Forbes's thin record of accomplishment left him limited options for a positive campaign. As a result, he devoted much of his expenditures to ads attacking his opponents—especially Dole, the leading Republican candidate. His ads were notable for distortions and half-truths, and earned Forbes the journalists' label of "most negative" candidate. The difficulty with negative ads, especially in the primaries, is that they lower the public's support for everyone involved, potentially weakening the party's eventual nominee.

By buying himself a campaign, Forbes unquestionably made the Republican primary race more expensive and, probably, the entire election less edifying. His barrage of negative ads spawned the same among his opponents, leading to greater confusion and animosity. And while Forbes's campaign is not necessarily an argument against candidates spending their own fortunes, it does seem to indicate that qualities beyond personal wealth are important to electoral success.

egy"—using his Senate position to demonstrate his leadership qualities—was not working. Most people were unaware of Dole's legislative accomplishments. His campaign staff was in disarray, and he had depleted his campaign treasury in the early primaries. The question loomed: What was Dole to do, during the four-and-a-half months until the Republican convention, when he would be officially anointed and granted federal funds for the fall campaign?

The Democratic Campaign

Clinton's experience was in direct contrast to Dole's. The president had no serious opposition for the Democratic nomination. Rather than turning on him due to the party's midterm losses, Democrats had rallied around the president as their only hope against Republican majorities in both houses of Congress. As a result, he was neither distracted from the general election, nor did he need to finance a serious primary battle. Clinton had worked out his general election strategy, and had inaugurated an effective ad campaign the previous year. With his strategy of "triangulation," the president would appear compassionate and moderate, while his ads attacked the ideological excesses of "Dolegingrich" (one word, as *Newsweek* observed)—linking the eventual Republican nominee Dole with the increasingly unpopular House Speaker Gingrich. In the spring of 1996, Clinton was hitting his stride.

The four-and-a-half months between the time Clinton and Dole secured the necessary convention delegates to win their parties' nominations, and the parties' conventions in August, became a sort of unofficial beginning for the general election campaign, a time to finish tinkering with and launch (or, in Clinton's case, continue) the campaign against the other party's future nominee. Dole took some important steps toward his general election campaign during this period. Convinced that, in his position as Senate majority leader, voters were likely to see him as just another Washington politician (or worse, another inflexible congressional leader), Dole announced his resignation from the Senate in mid-May. But he did not fully capitalize on this action. During campaign appearances, he was prone to reminiscing about his past in the Senate, rather than explaining his future as president.

Dole's campaign style frequently got in the way of his message. He often spoke "off the cuff," ignoring his prepared text and the ideas contained therein. This not only blunted efforts to communicate his ideas, but also led to distracting controversies. Dole questioned whether cigarettes were actually addictive, and charged that an invitation he received to address the NAACP's annual convention was an effort "to set me up." His discomfort in talking about emotions impeded his efforts to explain his heroic actions as a soldier, his successes in the Senate, and his vision for American society.

Again, in stark contrast to Dole, Clinton's campaigning skills were never in doubt. Where Dole tended to lose his message by wandering from his prepared text, Clinton's improvisations worked to embroider his campaign themes, enriching his basic message with personal testimony. Where Dole was uncomfortable and, therefore, unconvincing in relating his feelings and discussing his values, Clinton drew in his audience by appearing to bare his soul.

The Clinton campaign, though, was not without its troubles. The greatest threats were questions of impropriety and ethical lapses, which swirled continuously around the president and his wife. Near the end of May, three of the president's old friends were convicted on fraud charges related to Whitewater business dealings; but prosecutor Kenneth Starr, widely perceived as a partisan "out to get the president," was unable to tie the Clintons to the case. In late June, another charge of marital infidelity arose. *The Washington Times* headlined a story alleging that Clinton was carrying on an affair with an unidentified movie star. Fortunately for the president, the source for the story had suspicious connections to Gingrich and to conservative organizations that were pursuing the Clintons. To many, allegations of the Clintons' misdeeds began to look like part of what First Lady Hillary Clinton would later identify as a "right wing conspiracy" to "get" her and her husband.

At the same time, the public did not trust President Clinton. Dole easily won on questions of "character." But, in 1996, the public didn't seem to care much about personal ethics and values. Clinton's pollsters assured him that his expressed support for "public values" (such as his stands against drugs, crime, and depictions of violence on television, and his support for preserving the environment and nurturing educational opportunities) trumped the "character" issue. Working on that principle, the president proposed a series of modest—very modest—policies. For his advocacy of school uniforms, curfews for teenagers, tobacco ad bans, and "V-chips" to censor violence and adult material on television, journalists dubbed Clinton "mayor in chief." But these proposals had their intended effect: Among young suburban parents—classic "swing" voters whose support he needed to win the election—Clinton's approval ratings rose dramatically.

The National Conventions

Moving into the summer, the Dole campaign was becoming increasingly anxious. Dole had, at times, reduced Clinton's lead in the polls to single digits, but he was unable to close the gap. He needed some way to break through if he was to have a chance of victory in November. The Dole campaign planned their move for early August: Their candidate would announce his economic plan and his vice presidential running mate the week before the Republican convention. These announcements, followed closely by the convention, would provide him sustained media attention on his terms. Unfortunately for Dole, this plan, like so much of his campaign, met with mixed success.

The centerpiece of Dole's economic plan was an across-the-board cut in income taxes. Both the media and the public reacted skeptically. Journalists noted that Dole had put aside his traditional concern with the federal deficit, perhaps in search of electoral support. Most of the public ignored the proposal, dismissing it as an empty election-year promise.

Dole's announcement of Jack Kemp, a former New York congressman and U.S. secretary of housing and urban development, as his vice presidential running mate prompted a much more positive response. Kemp was widely popular within the party, and had long been an enthusiastic supporter of tax cuts like the one Dole proposed; and, even at sixty-one, the former pro-football quarterback projected an image of vitality the ticket needed.

Finally, Dole and his staff were determined to avoid the mistakes of 1992, when the party's most strident conservatives had seemed to hijack the convention. The Dole campaign wanted the 1996 convention to demonstrate that the Republican Party

lifers" would have none of it. After numerous attempts at compromise, Dole yielded. But the controversy had stretched over several weeks preceding the convention, and developed into a prominent news story.

Clinton's experience benefited his campaign, as did Vice President Al Gore (see fact box, p. 1005), whom he again selected as his running mate. Like the Dole team, Clinton and his staff set about to produce the Democratic convention as a television spectacular, starring an inclusive party in which a wide range of views were welcome; but, in contrast to Dole, they largely succeeded. Even the first lady's speech was well received. While members of the campaign had feared that she might come across as strident or preachy, Hillary Clinton struck the proper tone, and her pro-family theme raised Clinton's support among members of a key group: working women, ages twenty-five to fifty.

The Reform Party

While Clinton and Dole pursued the Democratic and Republican nominations, a possible third-party candidacy loomed. Ross Perot (see fact box, p. 1001), who had accumulated an impressive 18 percent of the vote as an independent candidate in the last election, appeared to be a credible threat. Apparently in preparation for another run, Perot had announced the formation of the Reform Party in September 1995, but would not declare his candidacy until the following July—two days after former governor Richard Lamm of Colorado announced his intention to seek the new party's nomination.

Perot had promised an open and democratic nomination process in which anyone who wished could participate. In practice, the openness of this process was very debatable. Perot's

---

JACK FRENCH KEMP

PARTY: Republican

DATE OF BIRTH: July 13, 1935

PLACE OF BIRTH: Los Angeles, California

PARENTS: Paul R. Kemp and Francis Pope

EDUCATION: B.A., Occidental College, 1957; post-graduate studies at Long Beach State University and California Western University

FAMILY: Married Joanne Main, 1958; children: Jeffrey, Jennifer, Judith, and James

MILITARY SERVICE: U.S. Army, active duty, 1958; U.S. Army Reserve, 1958–62

CAREER: Professional football quarterback, San Diego Chargers and Buffalo (N.Y.) Bills, 1957–70; cofounder and president, AFL Players Association, 1965–70; U.S. congressman from New York, 1971–89; U.S. secretary of housing and urban development, 1989–92; cofounder and codirector, Empower America, starting 1993; unsuccessful candidate for U.S. vice president, 1996

---

welcomed diverse views. This strategy was essential to making uncommitted voters feel welcome, and appeared to be working—until Dole announced that he wanted a "declaration of tolerance" regarding abortion to be included in the party platform. "Pro-

people kept tight control over the party organization, allowed the press little access, and provoked numerous complaints from those denied party ballots. Not surprisingly, Perot won his party's nomination; but publicity about the Reform Party's questionable

PAT CHOATE

PARTY: Reform

DATE OF BIRTH: April 27, 1941

PLACE OF BIRTH: Maypearl, Texas

PARENTS: Betty Choate

EDUCATION: B.A., University of Texas at Arlington, 1963, M.A., 1964; Ph.D., University of Oklahoma, 1969

FAMILY: Married Kay Casey (second wife); children: two stepsons

MILITARY SERVICE: U.S. Army officer, 1963–65

CAREER: Regional administrator, Economic Development Administration. U.S. Department of Commerce, 1965–73; Tennessee Department of Economic and Community Development, 1973–75; director, Office of Economic Research, U.S. Economic Development Administration, 1975–76; U.S. Office of Management and Budget, 1976–77; director, Office of Economic Analysis, TRW Corporation, 1981–90; founder and head, Manufacturing Policy Project, starting 1992; unsuccessful candidate for U.S. vice president, 1996; author

nomination process, and Perot's apparently arrogant and erratic behavior over the previous four years, alienated a large proportion of his 1992 supporters.

The net affect of the August conventions was not good news for Dole or Perot. By the beginning of September, Clinton had a 15 percentage point lead over Dole in the polls. And the fallout from the Reform Party's controversial nomination had stalled Perot at 7 percent.

The General Election

The general election campaign began in earnest following the conventions. But the Dole campaign continued to be plagued by internal dissension and uncertainty. Some members of the campaign were convinced that Dole had to "go negative"—and attack Clinton for personal immorality and ethical lapses. Others feared that such a tactic might cost Dole more support than it won. While there was widespread support within the Republican campaign for labeling Clinton a committed "tax-and-spend" liberal, Dole had already been charging that Clinton was a man without principle.

Choices needed to be made, but Dole procrastinated. In fact, his entire style exacerbated disagreements among the staff, as the candidate gave little guidance about what he wanted or which approach he preferred. Dole was unwilling to commit to any one

strategy. Throughout the remainder of the campaign, he would move from one approach to another every few days. And, as a result, the campaign's ads were often out of sync with the candidate's message.

The Dole campaign faced a similar dilemma regarding the distribution of resources. By early September, his advisers had determined that contesting every region would stretch resources too thin, thereby ensuring defeat. Dole, they argued, needed to decide whether to concede California or the East Coast. But he resisted, and the campaign continued to spread its efforts nationwide.

Again, in contrast, Clinton's campaign was going well. He had two decisive advantages over his opponent. First, the economy was widely perceived to have improved greatly under Clinton's leadership. Second, while Dole consistently ignored his advisers' counsel, Clinton followed his. The Clinton campaign's pollsters were constantly probing for shifts in opinion. When they found such changes, they immediately went to work to understand the cause and prescribe an appropriate response. On the advice of pollsters and consultants, Clinton continued his vigorous pursuit of moderation and frequent advocacy of narrowly focused proposals. With a strong economy, Clinton's task was to appear competent and to counsel restraint, as precipitous change (such as electing a new president) might threaten the nation's future. He reassured those concerned about traditional values with his support for the death penalty and school prayer, and his opposition to homosexual marriage. The president took credit for bipartisan legislation imposing restrictions on immigration, reforming welfare, raising the minimum wage, and ensuring safe drinking water. At the same time, he distinguished himself from "Dolegingrich" on Social Security, Medicare, education, and the environment. There seemed only one possible cloud on Clinton's horizon.

The greatest threat faced by the Clinton campaign was the string of news stories regarding apparently illegal foreign contributions to the Democratic Party.

While these "soft money" donations were not officially given to the Clinton campaign, but rather were directed to the party (specifically, the Democratic National Committee), the possible indirect benefit to the Clinton campaign was clear. Though the stories persisted throughout most of 1996, they did not rise to the level of a visible campaign issue until October, when a story in the *Wall Street Journal* suggested a clear link between Clinton and donations from Asian business interests. This intensified news media interest and, in turn, threatened increased campaign coverage of questions regarding Clinton's character, an area he wished to avoid. Clinton's and Gore's response was to stress that the Democratic Party was separate from their campaign, and to focus on those issues that were working for them.

The presidential debates turned out like much of the rest of the campaign. Dole did an adequate job, but Clinton clearly won. In the second debate, following an adviser's suggestion, Clinton stepped from behind his podium to center stage—literally upstaging Dole. Clinton was in his element, taking questions from average Americans, as Dole stood uncomfortably behind his lectern.

During the closing days of the campaign, Dole—like Bush, in 1992—just could not accept that voters might support Clinton. And also, like Bush, he intensified his attacks on Clinton's character. He began to take increasingly desperate steps. Dole's campaign manager tried to persuade Perot to withdraw from the race, but Perot's only response was to publicly ridicule the idea as "weird and totally inconsequential," while basking in the media attention that it brought. Dole tossed aside his prepared speeches, and relied on snippets of ideas he had developed in the primaries and related stories from his long legislative career. Reacting to what he saw as the professionally unethical and personally immoral behavior of his opponent, Dole repeatedly asked his audiences, "Where's the outrage?" and called on America to "wake up." The public did not respond well. Dole's continued attacks on Clinton's integrity led to perceptions of negative campaigning, and from there to questions about Dole's character. His legislative stories reminded people of his age. The only glimmer of hope was increasing media coverage of the Democrats' questionable campaign finance practices. But, while the news may have denied Clinton his coveted majority, it came too late save Dole's candidacy.

Clinton Reelected President

On Election Day, Clinton received 49 percent of the popular vote, compared to Dole's 41 percent and Perot's 8 percent. Perot drew more support from Dole than Clinton; but, because of his relatively weak showing, Perot's candidacy did not change the election outcome. Carrying most of the states in the Northeast, Pacific Coast, and industrial Midwest, Clinton garnered 379 electoral votes. Dole, who won most states in the South, agricultural Midwest, and inter-mountain West, received 159. Perot failed to win a majority any state, and thus won no electoral votes.

Demographically, Clinton and Dole each drew from their parties' usual constituencies. Clinton's victory came from those with lower incomes and less education, blacks, Hispanics, Jews, Catholics, and women. Conversely, Dole's strength was centered on those with higher incomes, more education, whites, and Protestants (especially fundamentalists).

A few aspects of the vote are of particular interest. Republican opposition to government services for immigrants cost Dole even more support among Hispanics than might otherwise have been expected. The "gender gap"—women's tendency to support Democratic candidates more strongly than men—was greater in 1996 than in past elections because Clinton so effectively aligned himself on "compassion" issues such as health and government services, about which women are generally more concerned than men. And finally, Clinton seems to have blunted the loyalty to Dole of fundamentalist Christians with his adoption of more conservative stands on some social issues.

From one perspective, President Clinton's heavy reliance on campaign professionals and polling technology proved extremely successful. He achieved a broad-based victory, gaining more support from most groups than any recent Democratic candidate. In fact, he was the first Democratic president to be reelected to a second full term since Franklin D. Roosevelt, over a half-century before. Clinton's victory, however, may have been less than it seemed. By constructing a campaign on modest, noncontroversial policies that "polled well," he won the election—but to what end? What vision had the voters endorsed? On what policy could Clinton expect the populace to support him in battles with Congress? Further, in running not only against the Republicans in Congress, but also largely apart from the Democrats, the president risked further limiting his influence in the House and Senate during his second term. Thus, candidate Clinton's effectiveness may have come at the expense of President Clinton's influence.

Frank Davis

Bibliography

Abramson, Paul, John Aldrich, and David Rohde. *Change and Continuity in the 1996 Elections*. Washington, DC: CQ Press, 1998.

Green, John, ed. *Financing the 1996 Election*. Armonk, NY: M. E. Sharpe, 1999.

Nelson, Michael, ed. *The Elections of 1996*. Washington, DC: CQ Press, 1997.

Pomper, Gerald, et al. *The Election of 1996*. Chatham, NJ: Chatham House, 1997.

Weisberg, Herbert, and Janet Box-Steffensmeier, eds. *Reelection 1996: How Americans Voted*. Chatham, NJ: Chatham House, 1999.

THE VOTE: ELECTION OF 1996

State	Total No. of Electors	Total Popular Vote	Electoral Vote D	Electoral Vote R	Margin of Victory Votes	Margin of Victory % Total Vote	Clinton Democrat Votes	Clinton Democrat %	Dole Republican Votes	Dole Republican %	Perot Reform Votes	Perot Reform %	Nader Green Votes	Nader Green %	Others Votes	Others %
Alabama	9	1,534,349		9	106,879	7.0%	662,165	43.2%	769,044	50.1%	92,149	6.0%	0	0.0%	10,991	0.7%
Alaska	3	241,620		3	42,366	17.5%	80,380	33.3%	122,746	50.8%	26,333	10.9%	7,597	3.1%	4,564	1.9%
Arizona	8	1,404,405	8		31,215	2.2%	653,288	46.5%	622,073	44.3%	112,072	8.0%	2,062	0.1%	14,910	1.1%
Arkansas	6	884,262	6		149,755	16.9%	475,171	53.7%	325,416	36.8%	69,884	7.9%	3,649	0.4%	10,142	1.1%
California	54	10,019,484	54		1,291,455	12.9%	5,119,835	51.1%	3,828,380	38.2%	697,847	7.0%	237,016	2.4%	136,406	1.4%
Colorado	8	1,510,704		8	20,696	1.4%	671,152	44.4%	691,848	45.8%	99,629	6.6%	25,070	1.7%	23,005	1.5%
Connecticut	8	1,392,614	8		252,631	18.1%	735,740	52.8%	483,109	34.7%	139,523	10.0%	24,321	1.7%	9,921	0.7%
Delaware	3	270,845	3		41,293	15.2%	140,355	51.8%	99,062	36.6%	28,719	10.6%	18	0.0%	2,691	1.0%
District of Columbia	3	185,726	3		140,881	75.9%	158,220	85.2%	17,339	9.3%	3,611	1.9%	4,780	2.6%	1,776	1.0%
Florida	25	5,303,794	25		302,334	5.7%	2,546,870	48.0%	2,244,536	42.3%	483,870	9.1%	4,101	0.1%	24,417	0.5%
Georgia	13	2,299,071		13	26,994	1.2%	1,053,849	45.8%	1,080,843	47.0%	146,337	6.4%	0	0.0%	18,042	0.8%
Hawaii	4	360,120	4		91,069	25.3%	205,012	56.9%	113,943	31.6%	27,358	7.6%	10,386	2.9%	3,421	0.9%
Idaho	4	491,719		4	91,152	18.5%	165,443	33.6%	256,595	52.2%	62,518	12.7%	0	0.0%	7,163	1.5%
Illinois	22	4,311,391	22		754,723	17.5%	2,341,744	54.3%	1,587,021	36.8%	346,408	8.0%	1,447	0.0%	34,771	0.8%
Indiana	12	2,135,842		12	119,269	5.6%	887,424	41.5%	1,006,693	47.1%	224,299	10.5%	1,121	0.1%	16,305	0.8%
Iowa	7	1,234,075	7		127,614	10.3%	620,258	50.3%	492,644	39.9%	105,159	8.5%	6,550	0.5%	9,464	0.8%
Kansas	6	1,074,300		6	195,586	18.2%	387,659	36.1%	583,245	54.3%	92,639	8.6%	914	0.1%	9,843	0.9%
Kentucky	8	1,388,708	8		13,331	1.0%	636,614	45.8%	623,283	44.9%	120,396	8.7%	701	0.1%	7,714	0.6%
Louisiana	9	1,783,959	9		215,251	12.1%	927,837	52.0%	712,586	39.9%	123,293	6.9%	4,719	0.3%	15,524	0.9%
Maine	4	605,897	4		126,410	20.9%	312,788	51.6%	186,378	30.8%	85,970	14.2%	15,279	2.5%	5,482	0.9%
Maryland	10	1,780,870	10		284,677	16.0%	966,207	54.3%	681,530	38.3%	115,812	6.5%	2,606	0.1%	14,715	0.8%
Massachusetts	12	2,556,785	12		853,656	33.4%	1,571,763	61.5%	718,107	28.1%	227,217	8.9%	4,565	0.2%	35,133	1.4%
Michigan	18	3,848,844	18		508,441	13.2%	1,989,653	51.7%	1,481,212	38.5%	336,670	8.7%	2,322	0.1%	38,987	1.0%
Minnesota	10	2,192,640	10		353,962	16.1%	1,120,438	51.1%	766,476	35.0%	257,704	11.8%	24,908	1.1%	23,114	1.1%
Mississippi	7	893,857		7	45,816	5.1%	394,022	44.1%	439,838	49.2%	52,222	5.8%	0	0.0%	7,775	0.9%
Missouri	11	2,158,065	11		135,919	6.3%	1,025,935	47.5%	890,016	41.2%	217,188	10.1%	534	0.0%	24,392	1.1%
Montana	3	407,261		3	11,730	2.9%	167,922	41.2%	179,652	44.1%	55,229	13.6%	0	0.0%	4,458	1.1%
Nebraska	5	677,415		5	126,706	18.7%	236,761	35.0%	363,467	53.7%	71,278	10.5%	0	0.0%	5,909	0.9%
Nevada	4	464,279	4		4,730	1.0%	203,974	43.9%	199,244	42.9%	43,986	9.5%	4,730	1.0%	12,345	2.7%
New Hampshire	4	499,175	4		49,682	10.0%	246,214	49.3%	196,532	39.4%	48,390	9.7%	0	0.0%	8,039	1.6%
New Jersey	15	3,075,807	15		549,251	17.9%	1,652,329	53.7%	1,103,078	35.9%	262,134	8.5%	32,465	1.1%	25,801	0.8%
New Mexico	5	556,074	5		40,744	7.3%	273,495	49.2%	232,751	41.9%	32,257	5.8%	13,218	2.4%	4,353	0.8%
New York	33	6,316,129	33		1,822,685	28.9%	3,756,177	59.5%	1,933,492	30.6%	503,458	8.0%	75,956	1.2%	47,046	0.7%
North Carolina	14	2,515,807		14	118,089	4.7%	1,107,849	44.0%	1,225,938	48.7%	168,059	6.7%	2,108	0.1%	11,853	0.5%
North Dakota	3	266,411		3	18,145	6.8%	106,905	40.1%	125,050	46.9%	32,515	12.2%	0	0.0%	1,941	0.7%
Ohio	21	4,534,434	21		288,339	6.4%	2,148,222	47.4%	1,859,883	41.0%	483,207	10.7%	2,962	0.1%	40,160	0.9%
Oklahoma	8	1,206,713		8	94,210	7.8%	488,105	40.4%	582,315	48.3%	130,788	10.8%	0	0.0%	5,505	0.5%
Oregon	7	1,377,760	7		111,489	8.1%	649,641	47.2%	538,152	39.1%	121,221	8.8%	49,415	3.6%	19,331	1.4%
Pennsylvania	23	4,506,118	23		414,650	9.2%	2,215,819	49.2%	1,801,169	40.0%	430,984	9.6%	3,086	0.1%	55,060	1.2%
Rhode Island	4	390,284	4		128,367	32.9%	233,050	59.7%	104,683	26.8%	43,723	11.2%	6,040	1.5%	2,788	0.7%
South Carolina	8	1,151,689		8	67,175	5.8%	506,283	44.0%	573,458	49.8%	64,386	5.6%	0	0.0%	7,562	0.7%
South Dakota	3	323,826		3	11,210	3.5%	139,333	43.0%	150,543	46.5%	31,250	9.7%	0	0.0%	2,700	0.8%
Tennessee	11	1,894,105	11		45,616	2.4%	909,146	48.0%	863,530	45.6%	105,918	5.6%	6,427	0.3%	9,084	0.5%
Texas	32	5,611,644		32	276,484	4.9%	2,459,683	43.8%	2,736,167	48.8%	378,537	6.7%	4,810	0.1%	32,447	0.6%
Utah	5	665,629		5	140,278	21.1%	221,633	33.3%	361,911	54.4%	66,461	10.0%	4,615	0.7%	11,009	1.7%
Vermont	3	258,449	3		57,542	22.3%	137,894	53.4%	80,352	31.1%	31,024	12.0%	5,585	2.2%	3,594	1.4%
Virginia	13	2,416,642		13	47,290	2.0%	1,091,060	45.1%	1,138,350	47.1%	159,861	6.6%	0	0.0%	27,371	1.1%
Washington	11	2,253,837	11		282,611	12.5%	1,123,323	49.8%	840,712	37.3%	201,003	8.9%	60,322	2.7%	28,477	1.3%
West Virginia	5	636,459	5		93,866	14.7%	327,812	51.5%	233,946	36.8%	71,639	11.3%	0	0.0%	3,062	0.5%
Wisconsin	11	2,196,169	11		226,942	10.3%	1,071,971	48.8%	845,029	38.5%	227,339	10.4%	28,723	1.3%	23,107	1.1%
Wyoming	3	211,571		3	27,454	13.0%	77,934	36.8%	105,388	49.8%	25,928	12.3%	0	0.0%	2,321	1.1%
TOTAL	538	96,277,633	379	159	8,203,602	8.5%	47,402,357	49.2%	39,198,755	40.7%	8,085,402	8.4%	685,128	0.7%	905,991	0.9%

For sources, see p. 1136.

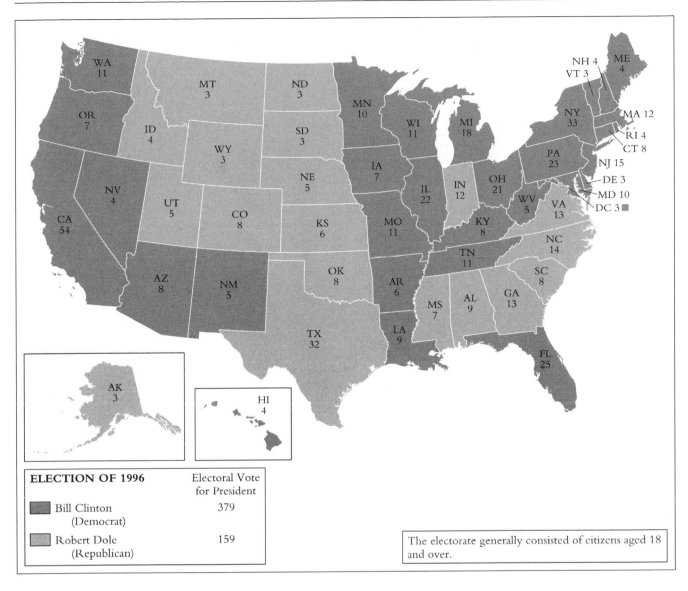

ELECTION OF 1996 — Electoral Vote for President

		Electoral Vote for President
▓	Bill Clinton (Democrat)	379
▓	Robert Dole (Republican)	159

The electorate generally consisted of citizens aged 18 and over.

DOCUMENTS: ELECTION OF 1996

Reform Party candidate Ross Perot and long-time Kansas senator Bob Dole, the Republican nominee, challenged Democratic president Bill Clinton for the presidency. Unlike four years earlier, Perot had little appeal and played no role as a spoiler. Meanwhile, Dole could not generate enthusiasm for his campaign among Republicans, much less the nation, and never mounted a serious threat to Clinton. Clinton rode a robust economy to reelection, receiving 49 percent of the popular vote. In Document 1, Clinton's fourth annual message to Congress, the president claimed the Republicans' main issue for himself: eliminating big government.

With peace, prosperity, and Clinton courting moderates, the Republicans were forced to contrast the personal credibility of the two candidates. Elizabeth Dole, wife of the Republican nominee, in Document 2, her speech at the Republican convention, focused on her husband's integrity and character. After four years of scandals over Clinton's behavior, she commented that Democrats and Republicans knew Bob Dole "is honest, trustworthy, a man of his word." In Document 3, Bob Dole's speech accepting the Republican nomination, he told the American people that the election was about more than the economy: It was about morals, trust, and the future of American families.

First Lady Hillary Clinton responded to Dole's speech in Document 4, her speech at the Democratic convention. She reiterated a claim that families can only be strong in a "village" where community leaders, teachers, clergy, and business people work together to create an American family. In his speech accepting the Democratic nomination, Document 5, President Clinton simply compared the economic successes of his administration to the failures of the Republicans in the early 1990s. Although his clamoring for reform fell upon deaf ears, Ross Perot stayed in the race to the end and kept trying to point out how both major parties were similar in their corruption and shortsightedness.

Document 1

President Bill Clinton's Fourth Annual Message to Congress, January 23, 1996

We must answer here three fundamental questions: First, how do we make the American dream of opportunity for all, a reality for all Americans who are willing to work for it? Second, how do we preserve our old and enduring values as we move into the future? And third, how do we meet these challenges together, as one America?

We know big Government does not have all the answers. We know there's not a program for every problem. We know, and we have worked to give the American people a smaller, less bureaucratic Government in Washington. And we have to give the American people one that lives within its means. The era of big Government is over. But we cannot go back to the time when our citizens were left to fend for themselves.

Instead, we must go forward as one America, one nation working together to meet the challenges we face together. Self-reliance and teamwork are not opposing virtues; we must have both. I believe our new, smaller Government must work in an old-fashioned American way, together with all of our citizens through State and local governments, in the workplace, in religious, charitable, and civic associations. Our goal must be to enable all our people to make the most of their own lives, with stronger families, more educational opportunity, economic security, safer streets, a cleaner environment in a safer world.

To improve the state of our Union, we must ask more of ourselves, we must expect more of each other, and we must face our challenges together. . . .

Our responsibility begins with balancing the budget. . . .

Source: Public Papers and Addresses of the Presidents of the United States: William J. Clinton, 1996, Book I, January 1 to June 30, 1996 (Washington, DC: Government Printing Office, 1997).

Document 2

Elizabeth Dole's Republican National Convention Address, August 14, 1996

This election is about the vision and the values that will shape America as we move into the next century. It's about the character of the man who will lead us there. Now, Bob Dole, as you know was born in Kansas, in a small town. . . .

His parents were poor. In fact at one point, when Bob was a boy, they had to move their family parents and four children into the basement, and rent out their small home upstairs just to make ends meet. But while they were perhaps poor in material things, they were rich in values. Values like honesty, decency, respect, personal responsibility, hard work, love of God, love of family, patriotism—these are the values that led Bob to risk life in battlefields of Italy.

And these are the values that enabled him to sustain over three years in the hospital. . . .

When Bob was totally paralyzed and people thought he wouldn't walk again, he literally willed himself to walk. He was a person of great perseverance, determination and drive. And he recovered fully except for the use of his right arm in the three years at the hospital.

And during that period of time, I think Bob's sensitivity to the problems of others certainly was deepened as well, because he's been there. He's been through adversity. He's known pain and suffering. . . .

Dr. Kelikian . . . had to say to Bob, "You're not going to find a miracle. Now the choice is up to you Bob, you can continue to feel sorry for yourself, or you can get on with your life and make the most of what you do have." . . .

And I certainly will never forget his last day as majority leader of the United States Senate. I was seated up in the balcony, you know, and I was watching as senator after senator, Democrats and Republicans stood and paid tribute to my husband on the Senate floor.

They talked about his countless legislative achievements. . . .

They talked about Bob's incredible ability to bring people together and his tremendous sense of humor. . . .

That's Bob Dole. But above all, these senators, Democrats and Republicans, talked about Bob's character, his honesty, his integrity. . . .

And Diane Feinstein, Democrat of California, said Bob Dole's word, listen to this now, Bob Dole's word is his commitment, and his commitment is a matter of honor. "We often disagree on issues," she said. "But even when we disagree, I know where I stand with Bob Dole and I know I can trust his word. I can trust his word."

And that's why, ladies and gentlemen, that's why Bob Dole's fellow senators elected him six times to be their leader, because they know he is honest, trustworthy, a man of his word, his word is his bond, and they know he has exceptional leadership skills. And isn't that exactly what we want in the president of the United States? . . .

Source: New York Times, August 15, 1996.

Document 3

Bob Dole's Nomination Acceptance Speech, August 15, 1996

. . . What we have in the opinion of millions of Americans is crime and drugs, illegitimacy, abortion, the abdication of duty, and the abandonment of children.

And after the virtual devastation of the American family, the rock upon this country—on which this country was founded, we are told that it takes a village, that is, the collective, and thus, the state, to raise a child.

The state is now more involved than it has ever been in the raising of children, and children are now more neglected, abused, and more mistreated than they have been in our time. This is not a coincidence. This is not a coincidence, and, with all due respect, I am here to tell you, it does not take a village to raise a child. It takes a family to raise a child.

If I could by magic restore to every child who lacks a father or a mother, that father or that mother, I would. And though I cannot, I would never turn my back on them, and I shall as president, promote measures that keep families whole.

I am here to tell you that permissive and destructive behavior must be opposed, that honor and liberty must be restored, and that individual accountability must replace collective excuse. And I am here to say to America, do not abandon the great traditions that stretch to the dawn of our history, do not topple the pillars of those beliefs—God, family, honor, duty, country—that have brought us through time and time and time and time again. . . .

Now, which is more important? Wealth or honor?

It is not, as was said by the victors four years ago, "the economy, stupid." It's the kind of nation we are. . . .

All things do not flow from wealth or poverty. . . .

The high office of the presidency requires not a continuous four-year campaign for re-election, but, rather, broad oversight and attention to three essential areas—the material, the moral, and the nation's survival, in that ascending order of importance. . . .

Make no mistake about it: My economic program is the right policy for America and for the future and for the next century. And here's what it'll mean to you. Here's what it will mean to you.

It means you will have a president who will urge Congress to pass and send to the states for ratification a balanced budget amendment to the Constitution.

It means you will have a president and a Congress who will have the will to balance the budget by the year 2002.

It means you will have a president who will reduce taxes 15 percent across-the-board for every taxpayer in America. . . .

It means you'll have a president who will help small businesses. . . .

It means you will have a president who will end the IRS as we know it.

It means you will have a president who will expand Individual Retirement Accounts, repeal President Clinton's Social Security tax increase, provide estate tax relief, reduce government regulation, reform our civil justice system, provide educational opportunity scholarships, and a host of other proposals that will create more opportunity, and security for all Americans and all across America. . . .

There is no reason why those who live on any street in America should not have the same right as the person who lives at 1600 Pennsylvania Avenue—the right to send your child to the school of your choice. . . .

I mean to attack the root cause of crime—criminals, criminals, violent criminals. And as our many and voracious criminals go to bed tonight, at, say six in the morning, they had better pray that I lose the election. Because if I win, the lives of violent criminals are going to be hell.

And I have been asked if I have a litmus test for judges. I do. My litmus test for judges is that they be intolerant of outrage, that their passion is not to amend but to interpret the Constitution. . . .

Because of misguided priorities, there have been massive cuts in funding for our national security. I believe President Clinton has failed to adequately provide for our defense. And for whatever reason his neglect, it is irresponsible. . . .

Though he [Clinton] has of late tried to be a good Republican . . . there are, there are certain distinctions that even he cannot blur. . . .

He and his party who brought us the biggest tax increase in the history of America.

We are the party of lower taxes and greater opportunity.

We are the party whose resolve did not flag as the Cold War dragged on, we did not tremble before a Soviet giant that was just about to fall, and we did not have to be begged to take up arms against Saddam Hussein.

We're not the party that, as drug use has soared among the young, hears no evil, sees no evil, and just cannot say, "Just say no."

We are the party that trusts in the people. I trust in the people. That is the heart of all I have tried to say tonight. . . .

Source: New York Times, August 16, 1996.

Document 4

Hillary Rodham Clinton's Democratic National Convention Speech, August 27, 1996

I know and you know that Chicago is my kind of town. And Chicago is my kind of village. . . .

I want to talk about what matters most in our lives and in our nation, children and families. . . .

Right now, in our biggest cities and our smallest towns, there are boys and girls being tucked gently into bed, and there are boys and girls who have no one to call mom or dad and no place to call home.

Right now there are mothers and fathers just finishing a long day's work and there are mothers and fathers just going to work, some to their second or third jobs of [the] day. Right now there are parents worrying, what if the babysitter is sick tomorrow or how can we pay for college this fall. And right now there are parents despairing about gang members and drug pushers on the corners in their neighborhoods. Right now there are parents questioning a popular culture that glamorizes sex and violence, smoking and drinking, and teaches children that the logos on their clothes are more valued than the generosity in their hearts.

But also, right now, there are dedicated teachers preparing their lessons for the new school year.

There are volunteers tutoring and coaching children. There are doctors and nurses caring for sick children, police officers working to help kids stay out of trouble and off drugs. Of course, parents first and foremost are responsible for their children. But we are all responsible for ensuring that children are raised in a nation that doesn't just talk about family values, but acts in ways that values families.

Just think—as Christopher Reeve so eloquently reminded us last night, we are all part of one family, the American family, and each one of us has value. . . .

Bill was with me when Chelsea was born in the delivery room, in my hospital room and when we brought our baby daughter home. Not only did I have lots of help, I was able to stay in the hospital as long as my doctor thought I needed to be there. . . .

For Bill and me, there has been no experience more challenging, more rewarding and more humbling than raising our daughter. And we have learned that to raise a happy, healthy, and hopeful child, it takes a family. It takes teachers. It takes clergy.

It takes business people. It takes community leaders. It takes those who protect our health and safety. It takes all of us. Yes, it takes a village. And it takes a president. . . .

It takes a president who not only holds these beliefs, but acts on them. It takes Bill Clinton.

Source: The NewsHour with Jim Lehrer Web site, www.pbs.org/newshour/convention96/floor_speeches/hillary_clinton.html.

Document 5

Bill Clinton's Nomination Acceptance Speech, August 29, 1996

Look at the facts. Just look at the facts: 4.4 million Americans now living in a home of their own for the first time. Hundreds of thousands of women have started their own new businesses. More minorities own businesses than ever before. Record numbers of new small businesses and exports. Look at what's happened. We have the lowest combined rates of unemployment, inflation and home mortgages in 28 years.

Look at what happened. Ten million new jobs, over half of them high-wage jobs. Ten million workers getting the raise they deserve with the minimum wage law. Twenty-five million people now having protection in their health insurance because the Kennedy-Kassebaum bill says you can't lose your insurance anymore when you change jobs, even if somebody in your family's been sick.

Forty million Americans with more pension security, a tax cut for 15 million of our hardest working, hardest pressed Americans and all small businesses. Twelve million Americans—12 million of them taking advantage of the Family and Medical Leave Law so they could be good parents and good workers.

Ten million students have saved money on their college loans. . . .

We have increased our investments in research and technology. . . .

Our country is still the strongest force for peace and freedom on earth.

On crime, we're putting 100,000 police on the streets. We made three-strikes-and-you're-out the law of the land. We stopped 60,000 felons, fugitives and stalkers from getting handguns under the Brady Bill. We banned assault rifles. We supported tougher punishment and prevention programs to keep our children from drugs and gangs and violence. Four years now—for four years now, the crime rate in America has gone down.

On welfare, we worked with states to launch a quiet revolution. Today, there are 1.8 million fewer people on welfare than there were the day I took the oath of office. . . . And the deficit has come down for four years in a row for the first time since before the Civil War—down 60 percent, on the way to zero. We will do it.

We are on the right track to the 21st century. We are on the right track, but our work is not finished. What should we do? First, let us consider how to proceed. Again, I say the question is no longer, "Who's to blame?" but "What to do?" . . .

I propose a $1,500 a year tuition tax credit for Americans. . . .

We must demand excellence at every level of education. . . .

We should reward teachers that are doing a good job, remove those who don't measure up. . . .

We need schools that will take our children into the next century. . . .

Tonight, let us proclaim to the American people we will balance the budget, and let us also proclaim we will do it in a way that preserves Medicare, Medicaid, education, the environment, the integrity of our pensions, the strength of our people.

Now, last year last year when the Republican Congress sent me a budget that violated those values and principles, I vetoed it, and I would do it again tomorrow. . . . It doesn't matter if they try again, as they did before, to use the blackmail threat of a shutdown of the federal government to force these things on the American people. We didn't let it happen before. We won't let it happen again. . . .

Do we really want to start piling up another mountain of debt?

[CROWD: No.]

Do we want to bring back the recession of 1991 and '92?

[CROWD: No.]

Do we want to weaken our bridge to the 21st century?

[CROWD: No.]

Of course, we don't. We have an obligation, you and I, to leave our children a legacy of opportunity, not a legacy of debt. Our budget would be balanced today—we would have a surplus today—if we didn't have to make the interest payments on the debt run up in the 12 years before the Clinton-Gore administration took office. . . .

Our bridge to the future must include bridges to other nations, because we remain the world's indispensable nation to advance prosperity, peace and freedom and to keep our own children safe from the dangers of terror and weapons of mass destruction. . . .

The real choice is whether we will build a bridge to the future, or a bridge to the past; about whether we believe our best days are still out there, or our best days are behind us; about whether we want a country of people all working together, or one where you're on your own.

Let us commit ourselves this night to rise up and build the bridge we know we ought to build all the way to the 21st century. . . .

Source: Public Papers and Addresses of the Presidents of the United States: William J. Clinton, 1996, Book II, July 1 to December 31, 1996 (Washington, DC: Government Printing Office, 1998).

THE ELECTION OF
2000

The 2000 election witnessed one of the least dramatic campaigns in decades, and yet ended as perhaps the most controversial presidential contest in American history. The race for the presidency was set amid a period of rising prosperity. It seemed that everyone with a few hundred dollars in savings was buying stocks. Technology was booming and thousands of Internet start-up companies sprouted up, looking to be the next Microsoft, Yahoo, or Amazon.com. Technology also crept into politics, as Americans struggled to protect online privacy, strengthen law enforcement of Internet crimes, and shield children from pornography on the World Wide Web. Then in 1998, a twenty-three-year-old White House intern named Monica Lewinsky burst into the national spotlight. Her romantic affair with President Bill Clinton captured media headlines and nearly cost the president his job. Morality became the central focus of the election of 2000.

Throughout his presidency, Clinton had been plagued by accusations of sexual harassment, harking back to his days as governor of Arkansas. But the country's economic prosperity, combined with Clinton's frequent trips abroad, kept his personal struggles in the background. Between 1997 and 1999, Clinton traveled across Africa and pledged a national commitment to build resources in the world's poorest and most isolated regions. He visited China and managed to build U.S. relations with the country, while maintaining a firm stance against its human rights abuses. Clinton authorized U.S. military support for United Nations' peace-keeping efforts in Kosovo, and continued to push for peace in Northern Ireland and Israel. Confronted with a narrow Republican majority in the House, the Clinton administration made little progress on its goals for Social Security and health care reform.

Clinton's real problem began on January 17, 1998, when the story broke that Attorney General Janet Reno had granted independent counsel Kenneth Starr authority to investigate President Clinton's relationship with Monica Lewinsky. The lurid details of their sexual affair leaked to the press. But it was Clinton's public denial and attempted cover-up that disturbed the nation's lawmakers. Democrats and Republicans alike condemned Clinton's actions. In August, Clinton publicly apologized to the nation in a televised address, but this act of contrition was not sufficient to stave off calls for his impeachment. Largely on the strength of Republican votes, the House of Representatives voted on December 19, 1998, to impeach Clinton. The Senate held impeachment proceedings in early 1999, but acquitted the president. Nonetheless, the bitter partisanship that had characterized the hearings, combined with the embarrassment felt by many of Clinton's Democratic colleagues over his handling of the situation, undermined the president's influence during his remaining months in the White House. (See "Sex and the White House," p. 1036.)

The Democrats: Primary and Convention

The Lewinsky scandal had a major impact on Vice President Al Gore's (see fact box, p. 1005) campaign

CHRONOLOGY

1998

JANUARY   Investigation begins into President Bill Clinton's affair with Monica Lewinsky; Clinton publicly denies the allegations.

AUGUST 17   Clinton apologizes to nation for his "inappropriate relationship" with Lewinsky.

DECEMBER 19   U.S. House of Representatives votes to impeach Clinton for perjuring himself during grand jury testimony, and for obstructing special counsel Kenneth Starr's investigation into the Lewinsky affair.

1999

FEBRUARY 12   Clinton acquitted by U.S. Senate on both impeachment charges.

2000

MARCH 7   "Super Tuesday" primary elections held.

JULY 31–AUGUST 3   Republican National Convention held in Philadelphia; George W. Bush nominated for president, Richard Cheney for vice president.

AUGUST 14–17   Democratic National Convention held in Los Angeles; Al Gore nominated for president, Joseph Lieberman for vice president.

NOVEMBER 7   Presidential balloting held on Election Day.

NOVEMBER 8   Presidential races in Florida, Oregon, and New Mexico declared too close to call.

NOVEMBER 9   Gore campaign sues to overturn Bush's election victory in Florida, demanding manual recounts in several Florida counties.

NOVEMBER 12   Bush campaign goes to court to stop the Florida hand count.

NOVEMBER 14   A 5 P.M. deadline set by Florida's Republican secretary of state, Katherine Harris, for counties to report election returns; Gore's request for complete hand recount granted in Broward County; circuit court judge Terry Lewis rules that Harris may enforce deadline, but requires her to use flexibility.

NOVEMBER 15   Harris announces that Bush leads by 300 votes, and sets 2 P.M. deadline for counties to justify late returns; Florida Supreme Court rejects Bush's bid to block all Florida hand counts of votes, and Palm Beach County proceeds with its hand count.

NOVEMBER 22   Miami-Dade County stops its recount because of disputes over standards for counting ballots; Bush appeals Florida Supreme Court ruling (allowing hand recounts) to U.S. Supreme Court.

NOVEMBER 25   Bush drops Florida Supreme Court lawsuit (to block counting of late military absentee ballots or those without postmarks); Bush then sues to have these late ballots counted in five counties across Florida.

NOVEMBER 26   Florida certifies state's election results; Bush declared the winner by 536 votes, but Palm Beach County recount not included in total.

DECEMBER 12   At 10 P.M., U.S. Supreme Court rules 5–4 in favor of George W. Bush, barring any further recounts in Florida.

DECEMBER 13   Al Gore concedes election to George W. Bush.

2001

JANUARY 20   George W. Bush inaugurated as U.S. president.

for the presidency. Gore first won election to the House of Representatives in 1976, representing a district in his home state of Tennessee, and served on the House Intelligence Committee. He was elected to the Senate in 1984 and to the vice presidency in 1992. Had Clinton's last days in office not been marred by the impeachment scandal, Gore would likely have shaped his campaign around promises of four more years of economic prosperity, and coasted to the Democratic nomination. Like many Democrats, however, he was personally disgusted by the Lewinsky affair. Declaring that "I am my own man," Gore chose to distance himself from Clinton altogether. The path he chose was a call for a "new morality" and an appeal to political moderates. Although Gore pushed for environmental protection measures, his signature issue, he was vague about controversial topics like abortion and capital punishment.

Gore's biggest challenger for the Democratic nomination was Bill Bradley, a former U.S. senator from New Jersey (1978–97) and star basketball player for the New York Knicks (1967–77). Bradley was more personable and outgoing than Gore in his public appearances. His campaign emphasized an end to capital punishment, continued support for affirmative action policies, gun control, and a more significant push for national healthcare. Still, groups such as African Americans and labor, who had long supported Clinton, tended to favor Gore over Bradley.

In the months leading up to the Democratic National Convention, charges against Maria I Isia, a Los Angeles immigration attorney, and John Huang, a Democratic Party fund raiser, dogged Gore's campaign. Hsia and Huang raised more than $100,000 for Clinton's 1996 campaign at a function held in a California Buddhist Temple. Prosecutors alleged that donors had received illegal reimbursements from temple funds. Federal charges were brought against Hsia in March 2000. Gore denied any knowledge of wrongdoing, although he had attended the function.

Support for Bradley remained strong among Democratic voters through the early months of 2000. In the New Hampshire primary, held on February 1, Bradley trailed Gore by only 5 percent, receiving 47 percent of the vote compared to Gore's 52 percent. Then Bradley's support began to wane. In Delaware, Bradley received 40.3 percent of the vote, compared to Gore's 57.2 percent.

Gore swept the Democratic primaries on "Super Tuesday," March 7. While Bradley's more radical stance on affirmative action seemed likely to woo minority voters, African-American, Hispanic and working-class Americans who had supported Clinton rallied behind Gore, Clinton's chosen successor. The Associated Press estimated that Gore's support was six-to-one over Bradley among African-American voters, eight-to-one among Hispanic voters, and three-to-one among blue-collar workers. One day later, Bradley withdrew from the race.

With the nomination locked up, Gore began seriously to consider whom he might name as his running mate. Even before the national convention gathered in Los Angeles, Gore selected Joseph I. Lieberman of Connecticut to run for vice president. Since his election to the Senate in 1988, Lieberman enjoyed a reputation as one of the most centrist Democrats, maintaining good relations with Republican as well as Democratic members. Long vocal on moral issues, he was the first Democratic senator publicly to criticize Clinton's affair with Lewinsky. Lieberman was the first Jewish American to run on a major presidential ticket.

Democrats held their nominating convention in Los Angeles from August 14 to 17. Although demonstrators outside protested the low pay and long work-

The 2000 Democratic ticket of Al Gore and Joe Lieberman captured a half-million more popular votes than the Republican ticket of George W. Bush and Dick Cheney, but came up short in the Electoral College by five votes. It was the first time since 1888 that the candidate winning the popular vote lost the election. *(Gyory Collection/Will Gyory Photo)*

ing hours demanded of immigrant workers, and carried signs reading "Old Navy, Banana Republic, Gap: Stop Sweatshops" and "Human Need Not Corporate Greed," delegates inside maintained harmony. With Lieberman at his side, Gore outlined his political platform for the upcoming election and accepted the party's nomination. His speech focused on what he called "the needs of working families," including lowering the cost of prescription drugs, improving quality of and access to public education, welfare, healthcare, and Social Security reform. "This election is not an award for past performance," Gore told the crowd. "Tonight I ask for your support on the basis of the better, fairer, more prosperous America we can build together."

The Republicans

The Clinton-Lewinsky affair gave Republicans an opening to emphasize conservative issues like religion and national security. Republican leaders also saw 2000 as a window of opportunity to rebuild a "new" Republican coalition. Moving away from divisive issues like abortion and prayer in public schools, the Republican Party sought a platform that would attract a greater range of voters, especially women and Hispanics. Like the Democrats, Republicans sought to attract the broad center of the political spectrum.

George W. Bush seemed well suited to meet these aims. A former businessman and the governor of Texas since 1995, he was also the son of former president George Bush. Coining the phrase "compassionate conservatism," Governor Bush pledged to "usher in the Responsibility Era in America." Despite this effort to stake out new ground, Bush's approach mirrored past Republican campaigns in many respects. He promised to cut taxes, emphasized the importance of national security and military spending, and championed privatization of services. Bush also emphasized the reform of education, Social Security, and healthcare, phrased in ways that would appeal to moderate Republican voters, conservative Democrats, and Independents.

Praising the honor and hard work of his father's generation, Bush promised to strengthen the nation's military, while enacting limited domestic reforms. Although opposed to abortion, Bush shied away from controversial topics. However, he did take a strong pro-immigration stance.

Bush's praise of the World War II and Cold War generation resonated with many Americans who were soured by Clinton's indiscretions. Bush himself lacked any national or international political experience. While Gore was perceived as being too stiff in his public appearances, Bush appeared more "folksy," but was criticized for his use of profanity with reporters, verbal gaffs in public speeches, and limited knowledge of world events. In an election year when morality took center stage in the campaign, Bush's alleged drug use in the late 1970s—and an arrest for drunk driving, revealed in the campaign's final days—were potential stumbling blocks. Yet his easy manner and willingness to poke fun at his own mistakes overcame some of these shortcoming. Moreover, Bush's admission of his "born-again Christian experience" won him further support.

GEORGE W. BUSH

PARTY: Republican

DATE OF BIRTH: July 6, 1946

PLACE OF BIRTH: Hartford, Connecticut

PARENTS: George Bush and Barbara Pierce

EDUCATION: B.A., Yale University, 1968; M.B.A., Harvard University, 1975

FAMILY: Married Laura Welch, 1977; children: Jenna and Barbara (twins)

MILITARY SERVICE: Fighter pilot, Texas Air National Guard.

CAREER: Founded Arbusto Energy, 1975; founder and CEO, Bush Exploration; unsuccessful candidate for 19th Congressional District (West Texas), 1978; founder, Spectrum Energy Corp. (later merged with Harkin Energy Corp.), 1986; managing general partner, Texas Rangers Baseball Team, 1989–94; governor of Texas, 1995–2000; elected U.S. president, 2000

Other early contenders for the GOP presidential nomination included Arizona senator John McCain, former secretary of labor Elizabeth Dole, publisher Steve Forbes, Family Research Council president Gary Bauer, former secretary of education Lamar Alexander, Utah senator Orrin Hatch, and former ambassador Alan Keyes. Of these candidates, the wealthy Forbes was in the best position financially to support a protracted race in large states like New York and California. Bauer and Hatch enjoyed a solid base

SEX AND THE WHITE HOUSE

The 23-year-old woman who sat in a bar, pouring out her heart to a friend and co-worker about a frustrating love affair with a married man in 1997, could have been any young professional in one of the many cities situated around the United States. But this woman was White House intern Monica Lewinsky. Her affair was with the president of the United States. And her friend, Linda Tripp, was secretly taping their conversations and turning them over to Special Counsel Kenneth Starr, to aid his investigation into President Bill Clinton's alleged abuse of office.

Clinton's and Lewinsky's affair made national headlines in January 1998. Within days, Clinton made a national television appearance and told Americans, "I have never had sexual relations with that woman, Ms. Lewinsky." Over the next six months, Americans heard an almost daily installment of intimate details about the affair. These driblets of information ranged from the book of Whitman poems and trinkets from Martha's Vineyard that Clinton had given to Lewinsky, to banter about jobs, hair styles, and word-by-word, he-said-she-said accounts of Lewinsky's and Tripp's phone conversations. By the end of January, a blue dress with traces of the president's semen on it, which Lewinsky had saved as a souvenir, had been introduced into evidence and was making headlines.

Americans responded to Clinton's affair in a variety of ways. For some Americans, the fact that their president had committed adultery was clearly upsetting. For others, Clinton's public denial of the affair, while clearly untruthful, was understandable and even predictable. But this was the first time in history that the most intimate and graphic details of a president's sexuality were laid out for public scrutiny. When Starr's report was made available over the Internet in August 1998, thousands of Americans downloaded

of support among social and Christian conservatives in Iowa and Utah, respectively. As an African American, Keyes hoped to draw minority voters who traditionally voted Democratic. Yet of these candidates, only Dole and McCain presented a serious challenge to Bush.

The wife of former senator and GOP presidential candidate Bob Dole, Elizabeth Dole enjoyed national name recognition. Dole appealed to women voters who had moved away from the GOP because of the party's hard-line stance on issues like abortion. Her platform combined a controversially liberal stance on gun control with more traditionally Republican positions on education, national defense, and foreign policy. By late 1999, however, she had dropped out of the race, citing lack of funds.

Bush's biggest challenge for the Republican nomination came from Senator McCain. As a former prisoner of war in Vietnam, McCain garnered great respect from many Americans who were tired of political insiders. McCain also had more national political experience than Bush, having served in the

House of Representatives from 1983 to 1987 before moving up to the Senate. Promising "straight talk," McCain based his campaign on a pledge to curb the influence of special interests and to enact campaign finance reform. Through the early primaries, Bush and McCain were neck and neck. McCain won the New Hampshire primary in February by more than 19 percent of the vote. Bush roared back, however, and campaigned hard against McCain in South Carolina. On February 17, Bush won the South Carolina primary with 53 percent of the vote, to McCain's 42 percent. Across the country, Bush continued to garner the most support among Republican voters, while McCain appealed to many Independents and Democrats.

McCain dominated open Republican primaries in states like New Hampshire and Michigan, but he managed to win only seven states and 231 delegates. He dropped out of the race in early March 2000.

When the Republican National Convention convened in Philadelphia in August, Bush had long since sewn up the nomination. Like Gore, he spent consid-

and read all 450 pages. From Lewinsky's dress, to play-by-play reports of foreplay and seduction, Starr's document was explicit and detailed. Clinton's defense that he had not lied, but rather did not consider the relationship between himself and Lewinsky "sexual" because they had never had sexual intercourse, further fueled a national discourse about when to call sex "sex."

Clinton apologized to the nation in August 1998. In December, the Republican-controlled House of Representatives voted to impeach the president, but the Democrat-controlled Senate refused to convict Clinton the following February. Nonetheless, Democrats and Republicans both condemned Clinton's actions. Al Gore refused to allow Clinton to campaign on his behalf during the election. And both presidential hopefuls in 2000 shaped much of their campaign rhetoric around calls for a "new morality," and promised to usher in a new "Era of Responsibility," free of sexual scandal in the White House.

Author Toni Morrison saw things differently. In a much quoted article, she called Clinton "America's first black president," and compared his poor, working-class upbringing and subsequent humiliation on account of his sexuality to the situation of many African-American men who seek positions of power. The message was clear, she argued: "No matter how smart you are, how hard you work, how much coin you earn for us, we will put you in your place or put you out of the place you have somehow, albeit with our permission, achieved." Although Morrison's perspective offered one extreme view, it underscored the level of discomfort and repulsion most Americans felt over the episode.

One thing was clear: Clinton's affair with Monica Lewinsky eclipsed attention of nearly all of the social reforms, economic growth, and world leadership that the president had achieved during his first six years in office. Although he had escaped removal, the hearings undercut his influence during the remainder of his administration. In a surprising turn of events, First Lady Hillary Clinton launched her own political career in the wake of the scandal. She announced her intent to run for the United States Senate in 1999, won election from New York in 2000, and assumed office in 2001.

erable time choosing a running mate. He ultimately selected Richard Cheney to run for vice president. A former representative from Wyoming and secretary of defense in the first Bush administration, Cheney had long experience in Washington. In the 1970s, he had served as chief of staff under President Gerald R. Ford. A solid conservative, Cheney was outspoken about his belief in limited government, a constitutional right to bear arms, and a strong national defense. These conservative views were seen as attractive to right-wing Republicans, who were less enthusiastic about Bush than were moderate Republicans. Moreover, Cheney possessed national political experience, whereas Bush had none. The Cheney selection, in short, bolstered support among Republicans who were skeptical about the qualifications of their party's presidential nominee.

Repeating the Democratic experience, thousands protested outside the convention hall in Philadelphia, calling for more attention to the environment, globalization, immigration, and the rights of labor. But inside the hall, the new GOP leaders promised to usher in a new era of leadership focused on national security and national might. Bush told the crowd at the Republican convention:

> Our current president embodied the potential of a generation. So many talents. So much charm. But in the end, to what end? Little more than a decade ago the Cold War thawed . . . but instead of seizing the moment, the Clinton/Gore administration has squandered it. We have seen a steady erosion of American power and an unsteady exercise of American influence.

The Campaign

The pace of the campaign accelerated in the months following the national conventions. Yet as November 7 drew closer, many voters saw less and less difference between the two major candidates. Both Gore and Bush talked frequently about religion and morality. Each appealed to moderate voters and tailored their public appearances accordingly. This performance exacerbated the frustration of many younger voters and Independents with big-party politics.

In a throwback to an earlier era, Republican candidate George W. Bush and his running mate Dick Cheney wave from their campaign train during a stop in Battle Creek, Michigan, on August 5, 2000. *(AP Wide World Photos)*

Fearing Clinton would alienate voters or steal the spotlight, Gore refused to allow the president to campaign on his behalf. In truth, there was little chance of confusing Gore and Lieberman with Clinton. Lieberman was well known for his moral positions. On many political issues, in fact, he was situated on the Democratic Party's far right. Gore was also well recognized for his views on morality, in part through his wife Tipper Gore. She had been actively involved in a campaign to have warning labels placed on music, films, and video games that contained violence or sexual content. Gore's decision to keep his distance from the president, because of the morality issue, may not have helped his campaign. Clinton was much better at establishing a rapport with voters than was his vice president, who appeared wooden in public appearances. Yet Gore still wanted to claim credit for the prosperity and the domestic reforms of the past seven years. Gore resolved his dilemma by campaigning heavily on religion and "moral principles."

As a self-described "born-again Christian," Bush made religion a frequent topic of his speeches. Religion had various political overtones among Republicans. Bush and Cheney used the theme as a buffer against criticism over allegations of Bush's past drug and alcohol abuse. Yet religion also provided a way to package their message of "compassionate conservatism," which they hoped would appeal to moderates and a broader segment of voters. As Gore and Lieberman moved toward the right during the course of the campaign, Bush and Cheney moved leftward, heading toward the political center. It became increasingly difficult to distinguish between the candidates' views.

The media was fixated on the candidates' backgrounds and personalities. Both Gore and Bush were sons of prominent political figures and hailed from distinguished political families. Gore's father had been a senator. Bush's father had been president and his grandfather a senator. Yet the candidates' posi-

JOSEPH ISIDORE LIEBERMAN

PARTY: Democratic

DATE OF BIRTH: February 24, 1941

PLACE OF BIRTH: Stamford, Connecticut

PARENTS: Henry Lieberman and Marcia Manger

EDUCATION: B.A., Yale University, 1964; L.L.B., 1967

FAMILY: Married Betty Haas, 1967 (divorced, 1981); married Hadassah Freilich, 1983; children: Matthew, Rebecca, Ethan, and Hana

CAREER: Connecticut state senator, 1970–81 (majority leader, 1975–81); unsuccessful candidate for U.S. Congress, 1980; attorney general of Connecticut, 1982–88; U.S. senator (Conn.), elected 1988; Senate Armed Services Committee; Senate Environment and Public Works Committee; Senate Small Business Committee; chairman, Democratic Leadership Council, elected 1995; ranking Democrat, Senate Governmental Affairs Committee, appointed 1999; unsuccessful candidate for U.S. vice president, 2000 (first Jewish American on major party ticket); reelected to U.S. Senate, 2000

tions on issues did get some attention. Environmental issues remained one clear flashpoint for the candidates. Bush favored drilling for oil in the Alaskan wildlife refuge—an idea vehemently opposed by Gore and environmental groups. But as Gore and Bush sparred over the finer points of their Social Security and healthcare plans, the majority of Americans had trouble following the details. Gore promised to protect Social Security by keeping its funds "in a lock box," while Bush urged partial privatization of the system. Gore promised a range of reforms and took pains to describe his plan in great detail. But for many Americans, the more the candidates talked, the more they began to sound alike.

Americans appeared to have become increasingly cynical about big-party politics and its dependence on corporate financing. Signs of this trend had surfaced in 1992 and 1996, when Ross Perot captured large numbers of voters in his runs for president and in 1998, when former professional wrestler Jesse Ventura was elected governor of Minnesota as an Independent. The most formidable independent challenge in 2000 came from Ralph Nader, who ran for president on the Green Party ticket. Nader, who had run a lackluster campaign for president in 1996, was nationally known as a consumer rights activist, and had been a passionate advocate of auto safety and environmental protection since the 1960s. In 1999, as concern over globalization and human rights became a focus of many younger voters, Nader again made national headlines by supporting protests at the World Trade Organization meeting in Seattle. He had never held political office. But he was a familiar figure in Congress, where he had testified on numerous occasions. His forthright criticism of American corporations, and the politicians who catered to them, appealed to many voters who had grown jaundiced about the operation of the political system.

RICHARD BRUCE CHENEY

PARTY: Republican

DATE OF BIRTH: January 30, 1941

PLACE OF BIRTH: Lincoln, Nebraska

PARENTS: Richard H. Cheney and Marjorie Dickey

EDUCATION: B.A., University of Wyoming, 1965; M.A., 1966

FAMILY: Married Lynne Ann Vincent, 1974; children: Elizabeth and Mary

CAREER: Congressional fellow, 1968–69; special assistant to the director (Donald Rumsfeld), U.S. Office of Economic Opportunity (Nixon administration), 1969–70; White House staff assistant, 1971; assistant director, U.S. Cost of Living Council, 1971–73; vice president, Bradley, Woods and Co., 1973–74; deputy assistant to President Gerald R. Ford, 1974–75; White House chief of staff, 1975–76; U.S. representative at large (Wyoming), 1979–89; House Republican Policy Committee, 1981–88 (chairman, 1987); chairman, House Republican Conference, 1988; House Republican whip, 1988; ranking Republican, House select committees to investigate covert arms deals with Iran; member, House Committee on Interior and Insular Affairs; House Permanent Select Committee on Intelligence; secretary of defense under President George Bush, Sr., 1989–93; chief executive officer, Halliburton Co., Dallas (Tex.), 1995–2000; elected U.S. vice president, 2000

RALPH NADER

PARTY: Green

DATE OF BIRTH: February 27, 1934

PLACE OF BIRTH: Winsted, Connecticut

PARENTS: Nathra and Rose Nader

EDUCATION: B.A., Princeton University, 1955; L.L.B., Harvard University, 1958

FAMILY: Unmarried

CAREER: Consumer advocate, attorney, author; consultant to U.S. Department of Labor, 1963; founder, Center for the Study of Responsive Law, Public Interest Research Group, Center for Auto Safety, Public Citizen, Clean Water Action Project, the Disability Rights Center, Pension Rights Center, and Project for Corporate Responsibility; launched *The Multinational Monitor*, an investigative journal focusing on international corporate behavior, 1980; gained national attention for opposing the General Agreement on Tariffs and Trade negotiations, 1999; unsuccessful candidate for U.S. president, 1996, 2000

The consumer advocate and political reformer Ralph Nader ran as a third-party candidate in the election of 2000. His small vote in Florida may have tipped the state to Bush and thus cost Gore the election. *(AP Wide World Photos)*

A fourth candidate for president was Patrick Buchanan, a former senior advisor to President Richard Nixon, and White House communications director for Ronald Reagan. Buchanan had become familiar to many Americans as a political commentator. Central issues for him included: a strong anti-abortion stance in all cases, including rape or incest; opposition to gun control, immigration, and free-trade agreements; and his belief that both federal taxes and the Department of Education should be abolished. After he failed to win the Republican nomination in 1992

and 1996, Buchanan left the Republican Party in late 1999 to run on the Reform Party ticket.

As the race between Gore and Bush tightened, Democratic strategists feared that Nader would siphon crucial votes from their party. In the final analysis, Nader received 2.7 percent of the total vote. Nader picked up 5 percent or more of the vote in Alaska, Colorado, the District of Columbia, Hawaii, Maine, Massachusetts, Minnesota, Montana, Oregon, Rhode Island, and Vermont. He attracted his largest support from liberal Independents, a group that normally leaned Democratic.

Gore and Bush met at the University of Massachusetts, on October 3, for the first of three presidential debates. All three debates were carefully structured with sites and dates determined by the Commission on Presidential Debates. A single moderator directed questions to the candidates. They had two minutes to answer each question and sixty seconds for rebuttal. At the end of the debates, each candidate gave a two-minute closing statement. The commission allowed only candidates who had their names on enough state ballots to have a mathematical chance of receiving a majority of Electoral College votes, and who could demonstrate a support base of at least 15 percent of American voters as determined by a national polling organization, to participate in the nationally televised debates. As a result, no third-party candidates were allowed to participate.

Medicare, taxes, and energy dominated the substance of the first debate. But public interest focused as much on how the candidates' personalities came across as on the issues. For Bush, who had little experience in public debates, his primary challenge was to appear articulate and competent, demonstrating a firm grasp of the issues he would face as president. For Gore, who was well informed, but tended to come off as lecturing and aggressive in public debates, the biggest challenge was to appear relaxed and likable. Both vice presidential hopefuls faired well in their October 5 debate, as well. Rather than helping to decide the election for voters, Cheney's and Lieberman's strong performances only seemed to emphasize just how close the election had grown.

When the presidential candidates met for a second time on October 11, at Wake Forest University in Winston-Salem, North Carolina, it was Bush who appeared to be the most relaxed and in control of the debate. Topics of discussion focused again on energy, but taxes and foreign policy received much more attention than in the earlier meeting. Although most observers agreed that Gore was more clear and persuasive in his discussion of healthcare issues, he also appeared stiff and agitated. Bush continued to perform well, delivering clear and well-modulated responses to questions. By the final debate on October 17, at Washington University in St. Louis, Missouri, the election remained in a dead heat. Both candidates appealed to moderate voters in their discussions on healthcare, education, and even affirmative action. Although most critics argued that George W. Bush tended to connect better with audiences, they divided almost equally on whether Bush or Gore had ultimately won the debates.

WINONA LADUKE

PARTY: Green

DATE OF BIRTH: 1959

PLACE OF BIRTH: Los Angeles, California

PARENTS: Vincent LaDuke and Betty Bernstein

EDUCATION: B.A., Harvard University, 1982; M.A., Antioch College, 1995

FAMILY: Married Randy Kapashesit, 1987 (separated); children: Waseyabin, Ajuawak, and Gwekaanimad

CAREER: Principal, White Earth Reservation high school, 1982; winner, Reebok Human Rights Award, 1988; founded White Earth Land Recovery Project, 1989; co-chair, Indigenous Women's Network; program director, Honor the Earth Fund; board of directors, Greenpeace; spokesperson for Chippewa Peoples of Northern Minnesota; unsuccessful candidate for U.S. vice president, 2000; author

The Election

Throughout the fall, Bush had held a slender lead in most public opinion polls; but as Election Day neared, pollsters considered the race too close to call. November 7, 2000 began like most other Election Days in recent history. Throughout the day, Democrats and Republicans focused on states with significant numbers of electoral votes and where the race was tight. Civil rights activist Jesse Jackson spent the day traveling to large black voting districts in Philadelphia to encourage residents to vote. Both presidential and vice presidential hopefuls made personal visits to polling sites in close states.

For weeks leading up to the election, analysts had declared Florida the key to the election. With 25 electoral votes, the state could clearly make the difference in a close race. Bush's brother, Jeb Bush, was governor of Florida and had taken an active role in the campaign, right up through Election Day. But the outcome in Florida was difficult to predict. Republicans had won the state in 1992, but lost it in 1996. Most rural portions of the state and the cities in the north tended to favor Republicans. Yet Florida also had one of the high-

PATRICK BUCHANAN

PARTY: Reform

DATE OF BIRTH: November 2, 1938

PLACE OF BIRTH: Washington, D.C.

PARENTS: William Buchanan and Catherine E. Crum

EDUCATION: B.A., Georgetown University, 1961; M.A. in journalism, Columbia University, 1962

FAMILY: Married Shelley Ann Scarney, 1971; no children

MILITARY SERVICE: Exempted from military service due to rheumatoid arthritis

CAREER: Editorial writer and assistant editorial page editor, *St. Louis Globe-Democrat*, 1962–65; executive assistant to President Richard Nixon, 1966–69; White House special assistant and Nixon speechwriter, 1969–74; columnist and radio-TV commentator, 1975–85, 1987–91, after 1993; communications director in Reagan White House, 1985–87; unsuccessful candidate for U.S. president, 2000; author

Democratic presidential candidate Al Gore and his wife Tipper wave to a crowd on October 30, 2000, at a rally in Fond Du Lac, Wisconsin. Behind them are Senator Joseph Lieberman, the Democratic candidate for vice president, and his wife Hadassah. *(AP Wide World Photos)*

est concentrations of Jewish and African-American voters, who generally favored the Democrats. They were concentrated in small, rural pockets, city centers, and the southeast corner of the state in Miami-Dade, Broward, and Palm Beach counties. Miami-Dade's Cuban voters were also among one of the most important voting blocs in the state, with high rates of overall turnout. Cuban Americans tended to vote Republican, largely on account of the party's consistent anticommunism stance and support of the Cuban embargo.

Based on recent experience, voters assumed that they would learn the results of the balloting in a state almost instantly after the polls closed. Using data from exit polls supplied by consortia like Voter News Service and computerized models, the news media had developed the capacity to estimate the outcome of the election. The 2000 race was no exception. As the polls in the Eastern time zone—those on the eastern edge of the nation—began closing, the networks announced their predictions. "If we say somebody's carried the state, you can take that to the bank," vet-

eran CBS anchorman Dan Rather reassured viewers. At 7:50 P.M. EST, the first calls came in. Rather was the first to tell the nation that Florida had gone for Gore. The other major networks—ABC, NBC, and CNN—soon followed suit.

From that moment forward, nothing about the 2000 election was typical or predictable. Exit polls suggested that while Bush had won a majority of states, Gore had won enough large states, including New York, Pennsylvania, Michigan, Illinois, and California, to make the electoral contest a virtual dead heat. With 25 electoral votes, victory hinged on Florida. As the actual vote tallies (rather than just exit poll data) began to come in for Florida, it seemed that Bush, not Gore had won the state. By 10 P.M. EST, Bush appeared to have carried Florida by 140,000 votes. Soon, all of the networks were changing their earlier calls. "Clearly we were wrong to make the call as soon as we did," Rather told viewers later that night. "To err is human, but to really foul up requires a computer." Gore and Lieberman prepared to concede. Gore phoned Bush to congratulate him and

Dick Cheney on their victory, and to concede the race. One hour later, however, as the Florida race tightened, Gore called Bush back and retracted his concession.

Americans went to bed not knowing who had won. The election was far from over. By Wednesday, November 8, the only thing that was clear was that the Florida, Oregon, and New Mexico votes were too close to call. Although Gore won a half-million more popular votes, he and Bush split the electoral votes, so that the three doubtful states would determine the outcome of the election. Then Oregon and New Mexico fell into Gore's column, focusing the spotlight fully on Florida. According to first set of election returns, Bush led Gore in Florida by roughly 1,210 votes out of the nearly 6 million votes cast across the state. Recounts were ordered in several Florida counties. The final results had to be certified by the Florida secretary of state, however, in order to be valid. Secretary of State Katherine Harris, a Republican, set a deadline of 5 P.M., November 14, for all Florida counties to report election returns. An automatic recount was completed for the state by November 10. By this count, Bush enjoyed a lead of 327 votes. As examination of Florida's ballots continued, however, a whole range of problems and questions arose. In Palm Beach County, preliminary election returns indicated a large number of votes in predominantly Jewish voting districts went for Buchanan, the Reform Party candidate whose anti-Semitic and staunch right-wing views made him a very unlikely choice for Jewish-American voters. Questions were raised about the way candidates were listed on the Palm Beach County ballots, as well as about its basic design. This "butterfly" ballot listed candidates on two sides of a folded page, making it difficult for voters to know which candidate one was voting for. Election officials determined that some voters had erroneously voted for the wrong name, or had voted more than once.

In other districts, antiquated voting methods that required voters to punch out little holes, or "chads," caused problem ballots. If holes were not punched completely and cleanly, so that they left indentations or "hanging chads," the ballots were not counted. More serious, some voters complained of being turned away from the polls, particularly in heavily student-populated and African-American districts. Elsewhere, missing ballots were later found. Missing or late postmarks on military and overseas absentee

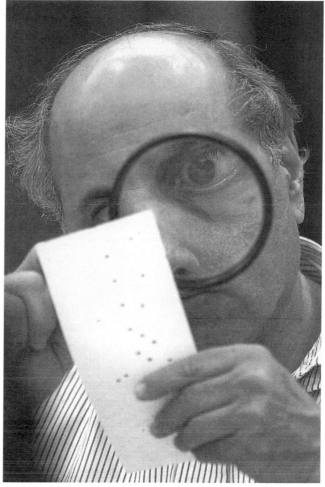

Bush or Gore? A controversy over voting procedure led to the recounting of thousands of ballots in several Florida voting districts after Election Day. This photograph shows an election official in Broward County inspecting the punch holes on a disputed ballot on November 24, 2000. *(AP Wide World Photos)*

ballots received considerable attention as election officials and Florida lawmakers worked to certify the state's election totals. Although controversies over balloting procedure and the counting of votes were not new to American elections, the closeness of this race underscored the importance of each and every vote. The issue of fairness in the Florida vote became a matter of national discussion.

Gore and Bush volleyed back and forth with lawsuits to extend or limit hand counting of ballots in specific counties. Gore's team requested hand recounts of nearly 1.8 million ballots in Broward, Miami-Dade, Palm Beach, and Volusia counties, which had long been Democratic strongholds. Bush's team, led by former U.S. secretary of state James Baker, filed a suit in federal court on November 11 to block the hand count. With these lawsuits pending, Florida secretary of state Katherine Harris refused to extend the deadline for submission of recounts, but allowed the counties an extra day to justify the hand recounts. On November 15, Harris decided that she did not find the explanations for mandated hand recounts convincing, and appealed to the Florida Supreme Court to block the hand counts. Absentee ballots received from overseas without postmarks or after the deadline were accepted, however.

While the Florida Supreme Court denied Harris's request, certification of the Florida vote was again postponed, as Bush's lawyers presented arguments before the 11th Circuit Court of Appeals, in Atlanta, on November 16. The court, however, denied the Bush team's request to block the hand recounts on constitutional grounds. The November 21 decision by the Florida Supreme Court further required that recounts from Broward, Miami-Dade, Palm Beach, and Volusia counties be included in the state-certified vote, but only if those counts were completed by November 26. The counts were not completed. And on November 26, Harris certified the Florida vote. Bush led by 537 votes.

Gore's team again filed a lawsuit with the Leon County Circuit Court, requesting that the ballots from Miami-Dade and Palm Beach counties be sent to the state capital in order to decide whether a hand count was necessary, and whether these votes should be included in the final tally. On December 4, the court found against Gore. His legal team then appealed to the Florida Supreme Court. At the same time, the Bush team appealed to the U.S. Supreme Court to halt the recount. For days, Americans waited for news of who would become their next president. The answer came on December 12, at 10 P.M. For the first time in history, the U.S. Supreme Court decided the outcome of a presidential election. The high court ruled, in a five-to-four decision, that no further recounts should take place in the state of Florida, reversing the earlier Florida Supreme Court decision. The election results certified by the Florida secretary of state stood. Florida's official count gave Bush a 537 vote lead over Gore, out of nearly 6 million ballots cast. Thus, the Republicans won Florida—and the 2000 presidential election—by a margin of electoral votes.

Election Outcome and Analysis

Portraits of Bush and Gore voters, assembled from exit polls on Election Day, indicate that each party's strength rested with groups that had traditionally leaned Republican or Democratic. Bush did best in the South, among white Protestants, men, and upper-income voters. Ninety-five percent of voters who identified themselves as conservative Republicans went for Bush. Ninety-one percent of liberal Democrats, on the other hand, supported Gore. He did best among Easterners, women, members of union households, blacks, Hispanics, urban, and low-income voters. He also outscored Bush among voters who claimed their financial situation was better currently than four years earlier (61 to 36 percent). Bush, on the other hand, had a decisive edge among voters who claimed their financial situation had gotten worse (63 to 33 percent). But voters who were age 60 or older, a sizeable fraction of the total electorate, favored Gore by a 51-to-47 percent margin.

Beyond these characteristics, journalists and political analysts spent much of 2001 trying to make sense of the election. The Democrats lost, according to one line of argument, because Gore refused to let Clinton campaign on his behalf. These critics charged that by focusing more on Clinton's infidelities than his political record, Gore had let his personal feelings interfere with an effort to broaden his coalition, as Clinton had done in 1992 and 1996. Others cited Nader's failure to withdraw from the election as fatal to Democrats. Nader's 97,488 votes in Florida may well have cost Gore the election. Although Buchanan received less than three-tenths of one percent of the vote in Florida and nationwide, the votes he received, both intended and accidentally through poorly designed ballots, may also have helped shift the election to Bush.

Another line of analysis pointed to flaws in the operation of the American electoral system. First, the Electoral College played a more decisive role in determining the outcome of the election than in any other presidential contest in living memory. For most Americans, the Electoral College was not something they thought about, outside of high school and college classrooms. Instead, they believed that it was their individual votes—in principle, if not in reality—that determined their nation's leaders. Although Gore and Lieberman received a majority of the popular votes—50,999,897, compared to 50,456,002 for the Republican candidates—Bush won because he gained a majority of electoral votes. It was the first time since 1888 that the candidate who received the most popular votes had lost the election.

Amid falling snow, President-elect George W. Bush shakes hands with Vice President Al Gore on December 19, 2000, shortly after the Supreme Court had ruled on the controversy over the vote in Florida. The scene symbolizes the capacity of the political system to maintain civility despite the invectives hurled during the campaign. *(AP Wide World Photos)*

Second, the legal and public relations campaign in the weeks after November 7 affected the election's outcome. By demanding strict enforcement of Florida state election laws in largely Democratic counties like Broward, while pushing election officials to count all overseas and military ballots in largely Republican counties like Santa Rosa, Bush was able to win a significant number of votes. A study published by the *New York Times* on July 15, 2001, which examined thousands of military and overseas absentee ballots, documented the importance of these votes to the final tally. Ballots dated after November 7 may have been counted in Santa Rosa but not in Broward, even though they possessed the same flaws. These discrep-

ancies were less the result of fraud than of political efforts, which varied among counties in Florida.

Other studies, such as ones conducted by the *Miami Herald* and *USA Today*, concluded that even if the U.S. Supreme Court had not stopped the hand count of ballots in counties where challenges occurred, Bush would have won the majority in Florida. Yet, the studies noted, if a fresh recount had been allowed in all Florida counties, using the most liberal standards of determining voter intent, Gore would have won by a narrow majority.

And third, a 2001 report on voting activities by the U.S. Commission on Civil Rights disclosed a disturbing finding. After conducting a lengthy investigation, the commission found numerous violations of the Voting Rights Act in Florida. The report concluded:

> The disenfranchisement of Florida voters fell most harshly on the shoulders of black voters. The number of votes cast by poor and minority residents that were not counted was significantly higher than those cast by white voters. Voting equipment in predominantly minority districts was old and ill-maintained. As a result, these districts saw much higher numbers of flawed ballots. Minority voters, particularly black voters, were turned away at the polls more often than white voters. And a significant number of polls were either moved or closed at irregular times, without notifying the voters they were meant to serve.

Dr. Martin Luther King, Jr.'s dream of equality has yet to come true," NAACP president Kweisi Mfume said. "The most recent proof is in Florida." Although Florida enacted an Election Reform Act in the wake of the commission's report, the new law failed to address all flaws in the system.

Conclusion

The election of 2000 confirmed the apprehensions of Americans who were disenchanted with big-party politics. Turnout figures confirm that many voters remained distant from the political system. Although young people came to the polls in greater numbers in the 1990s, still only 50 percent of all eligible Americans voted in national elections. Turnout in local and state elections was considerably lower.

Yet, by focusing national attention on flawed aspects of the electoral system, the 2000 election stimulated renewed interest in the democratic process. The flap in Florida highlighted the importance of the Electoral College, the need for improved voting machines, better voter education, and adequate staffing at the polls. The election also reiterated the inequities in campaign finance, and the influence of state legislatures on the design of electoral procedures. From John McCain's continued push for campaign finance reform in the U.S. Senate, to Florida's Election Reform Act, 2000 marked a step toward fairer elections.

While conflict over the election dogged Bush through his first months in office, a new national crisis would change the complexion of his administration. On the morning of September 11, 2001, four commercial airliners were hijacked and rerouted toward New York City and Washington, D.C. The nation reacted in horror as the planes crashed into the World Trade Center towers ,the Pentagon, and a field in Pennsylvania, killing several thousand people. "Today our nation saw evil, the worst of human nature," President Bush told the nation in an address on the evening of September 11. "America and our friends and allies join with all of those who want peace and security in the world, and we stand together to win the war against terrorism." In the months after the attack, Bush's approval rating rose to more than 90 percent, higher than any president had ever received. Although Bush's approval rating later subsided, it remained extremely high in 2002. Bush may have entered the presidency under a cloud of uncertainty, but ultimately the system prevailed. Americans accepted the results and began preparing for the 2004 campaign.

Melanie Shell Weiss

Bibliography

"Black Election: 2000," *The Black Scholar* (special edition) 31:2 (summer 2001).

Dershowitz, Alan. *How the High Court Hijacked Election 2000.* New York: Oxford University Press, 2001.

Greene, Abner. *Understanding the 2000 Election: A Guide to the Legal Battles That Decided the Presidency.* New York: New York University Press, 2001.

Posner, Richard A. *Breaking the Deadlock: The 2000 Election, the Constitution and the Courts.* Princeton, NJ: Princeton University Press, 2001.

Rakove, Jack, Alex Keyssar, and Henry Brady. *The Unfinished Election of 2000.* New York: Basic Books, 2001.

Sunstein, Cass, and Richard Epstein, eds. *The Vote: Bush, Gore, and the Supreme Court.* Chicago: University of Chicago Press, 2001.

Toobin, Jeffrey. *Too Close to Call: The Thirty-Six-Day Battle to Decide the 2000 Election.* New York: Random House, 2001.

THE VOTE: ELECTION OF 2000

State	Total No. of Electors	Total Popular Vote	Electoral Vote R	D	A[a]	Margin of Victory Votes	% Total Vote	Bush Republican Votes	%	Gore Democrat Votes	%	Nader Green Votes	%	Buchanan Reform Votes	%	Others Votes	%
Alabama	9	1,666,272	9			248,562	14.9%	941,173	56.5%	692,611	41.6%	18,323	1.1%	6,351	0.4%	7,814	0.5%
Alaska	3	285,560	3			88,394	31.0%	167,398	58.6%	79,004	27.7%	28,747	10.1%	5,192	1.8%	5,219	1.8%
Arizona	8	1,532,016	8			96,311	6.3%	781,652	51.0%	685,341	44.7%	45,645	3.0%	12,373	0.8%	7,005	0.5%
Arkansas	6	921,781	6			50,172	5.4%	472,940	51.3%	422,768	45.9%	13,421	1.5%	7,358	0.8%	5,294	0.6%
California	54	10,965,856		54		1,293,774	11.8%	4,567,429	41.7%	5,861,203	53.4%	418,707	3.8%	44,987	0.4%	73,530	0.7%
Colorado	8	1,741,368	8			145,521	8.4%	883,748	50.8%	738,227	42.4%	91,434	5.3%	10,465	0.6%	17,494	1.0%
Connecticut	8	1,459,525		8		254,921	17.5%	561,094	38.4%	816,015	55.9%	64,452	4.4%	4,731	0.3%	13,233	0.9%
Delaware	3	327,622		3		42,780	13.1%	137,288	41.9%	180,068	55.0%	8,307	2.5%	777	0.2%	1,182	0.4%
District of Columbia	3	201,894		2	1	153,850	76.2%	18,073	9.0%	171,923	85.2%	10,576	5.2%	0	0.0%	1,322	0.7%
Florida	25	5,963,110	25			537	0.0%	2,912,790	48.8%	2,912,253	48.8%	97,488	1.6%	17,484	0.3%	23,095	0.4%
Georgia	13	2,596,804	13			303,490	11.7%	1,419,720	54.7%	1,116,230	43.0%	13,432	0.5%	10,926	0.4%	36,496	1.4%
Hawaii	4	367,951		4		67,441	18.3%	137,845	37.5%	205,286	55.8%	21,623	5.9%	1,071	0.3%	2,126	0.6%
Idaho	4	501,621	4			198,300	39.5%	336,937	67.2%	138,637	27.6%	12,292	2.5%	7,615	1.5%	6,140	1.2%
Illinois	22	4,742,123		22		569,605	12.0%	2,019,421	42.6%	2,589,026	54.6%	103,759	2.2%	16,106	0.3%	13,811	0.3%
Indiana	12	2,199,302	12			343,856	15.6%	1,245,836	56.6%	901,980	41.0%	18,531	0.8%	16,959	0.8%	15,996	0.7%
Iowa	7	1,315,563		7		4,144	0.3%	634,373	48.2%	638,517	48.5%	29,374	2.2%	5,731	0.4%	7,568	0.6%
Kansas	6	1,072,216	6			223,056	20.8%	622,332	58.0%	399,276	37.2%	36,086	3.4%	7,370	0.7%	7,152	0.7%
Kentucky	8	1,544,187	8			233,594	15.1%	872,492	56.5%	638,898	41.4%	23,192	1.5%	4,173	0.3%	5,432	0.4%
Louisiana	9	1,765,656	9			135,527	7.7%	927,871	52.6%	792,344	44.9%	20,473	1.2%	14,356	0.8%	10,612	0.6%
Maine	4	651,817		4		33,335	5.1%	286,616	44.0%	319,951	49.1%	37,127	5.7%	4,443	0.7%	3,680	0.6%
Maryland	10	2,025,480		10		331,985	16.4%	813,797	40.2%	1,145,782	56.6%	53,768	2.7%	4,248	0.2%	7,885	0.4%
Massachusetts	12	2,702,984		12		737,985	27.3%	878,502	32.5%	1,616,487	59.8%	173,564	6.4%	11,149	0.4%	23,282	0.9%
Michigan	18	4,232,711		18		217,279	5.1%	1,953,139	46.1%	2,170,418	51.3%	84,165	2.0%	2,061	0.0%	22,928	0.5%
Minnesota	10	2,438,685		10		58,607	2.4%	1,109,659	45.5%	1,168,266	47.9%	126,696	5.2%	22,166	0.9%	11,898	0.5%
Mississippi	7	994,184	7			168,230	16.9%	572,844	57.6%	404,614	40.7%	8,122	0.8%	2,265	0.2%	6,339	0.6%
Missouri	11	2,359,892	11			78,786	3.3%	1,189,924	50.4%	1,111,138	47.1%	38,515	1.6%	9,818	0.4%	10,497	0.4%
Montana	3	410,997	3			103,052	25.1%	240,178	58.4%	137,126	33.4%	24,437	5.9%	5,697	1.4%	3,559	0.9%
Nebraska	5	697,019	5			202,082	29.0%	433,862	62.2%	231,780	33.3%	24,540	3.5%	3,646	0.5%	3,191	0.5%
Nevada	4	608,970	4			21,597	3.5%	301,575	49.5%	279,978	46.0%	15,008	2.5%	4,747	0.8%	7,662	1.3%
New Hampshire	4	569,081	4			7,211	1.3%	273,559	48.1%	266,348	46.8%	22,198	3.9%	2,615	0.5%	4,361	0.8%
New Jersey	15	3,187,226		15		504,677	15.8%	1,284,173	40.3%	1,788,850	56.1%	94,554	3.0%	6,989	0.2%	12,660	0.4%
New Mexico	5	598,605		5		366	0.1%	286,417	47.8%	286,783	47.9%	21,251	3.6%	1,392	0.2%	2,762	0.5%
New York	33	6,821,999		33		1,704,323	25.0%	2,403,374	35.2%	4,107,697	60.2%	244,030	3.6%	31,599	0.5%	35,299	0.5%
North Carolina	14	2,911,262	14			373,471	12.8%	1,631,163	56.0%	1,257,692	43.2%	0	0.0%	8,874	0.3%	13,533	0.5%
North Dakota	3	288,256	3			79,568	27.6%	174,852	60.7%	95,284	33.1%	9,486	3.3%	7,288	2.5%	1,346	0.5%
Ohio	21	4,705,457	21			165,019	3.5%	2,351,209	50.0%	2,186,190	46.5%	117,857	2.5%	26,724	0.6%	23,477	0.5%
Oklahoma	8	1,234,229	8			270,061	21.9%	744,337	60.3%	474,276	38.4%	0	0.0%	9,014	0.7%	6,602	0.5%
Oregon	7	1,533,968		7		6,765	0.4%	713,577	46.5%	720,342	47.0%	77,357	5.0%	7,063	0.5%	15,629	1.0%
Pennsylvania	23	4,913,119		23		204,840	4.2%	2,281,127	46.4%	2,485,967	50.6%	103,392	2.1%	16,023	0.3%	26,610	0.5%
Rhode Island	4	409,112		4		118,953	29.1%	130,555	31.9%	249,508	61.0%	25,052	6.1%	2,273	0.6%	1,724	0.4%
South Carolina	8	1,382,717	8			220,376	15.9%	785,937	56.8%	565,561	40.9%	20,200	1.5%	3,519	0.3%	7,500	0.5%
South Dakota	3	316,269	3			71,896	22.7%	190,700	60.3%	118,804	37.6%	0	0.0%	3,322	1.1%	3,443	1.1%
Tennessee	11	2,076,181	11			80,229	3.9%	1,061,949	51.1%	981,720	47.3%	19,781	1.0%	4,250	0.2%	8,481	0.4%
Texas	32	6,407,637	32			1,365,893	21.3%	3,799,639	59.3%	2,433,746	38.0%	137,994	2.2%	12,394	0.2%	23,864	0.4%
Utah	5	770,754	5			312,043	40.5%	515,096	66.8%	203,053	26.3%	35,850	4.7%	9,319	1.2%	7,436	1.0%
Vermont	3	294,308		3		29,247	9.9%	119,775	40.7%	149,022	50.6%	20,374	6.9%	2,192	0.7%	2,945	1.0%
Virginia	13	2,739,447	13			220,200	8.0%	1,437,490	52.5%	1,217,290	44.4%	59,398	2.2%	5,455	0.2%	19,814	0.7%
Washington	11	2,487,433		11		138,788	5.6%	1,108,864	44.6%	1,247,652	50.2%	103,002	4.1%	7,171	0.3%	20,744	0.8%
West Virginia	5	648,124	5			40,978	6.3%	336,475	51.9%	295,497	45.6%	10,680	1.6%	3,169	0.5%	2,303	0.4%
Wisconsin	11	2,598,607		11		5,708	0.2%	1,237,279	47.6%	1,242,987	47.8%	94,070	3.6%	11,471	0.4%	12,800	0.5%
Wyoming	3	218,351	3			87,466	40.1%	147,947	67.8%	60,481	27.7%	4,625	2.1%	2,724	1.2%	2,574	1.2%
TOTAL	538	105,405,308	271	266	1	543,895	0.5%	50,456,002	47.9%	50,999,897	48.4%	2,882,955	2.7%	449,105	0.4%	617,349	0.6%

[a] Abstention.

For sources, see p. 1137.

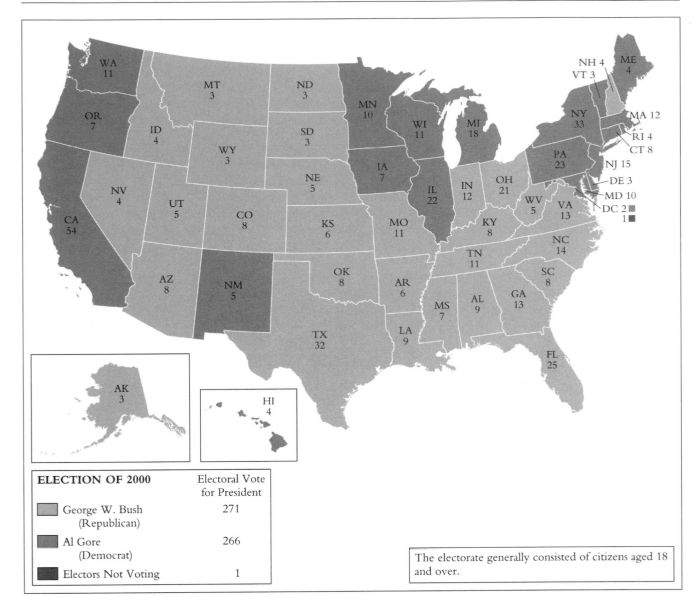

ELECTION OF 2000 | Electoral Vote for President
George W. Bush (Republican) — 271
Al Gore (Democrat) — 266
Electors Not Voting — 1

The electorate generally consisted of citizens aged 18 and over.

DOCUMENTS: ELECTION OF 2000

It took over a month of recounts and court rulings in 2000 to decide who won the presidency. Even then, uncertainty remained. In one of the closest elections in American history, Democratic vice president Al Gore polled more popular votes, but Texas governor George W. Bush, son of the former president, earned a major- ity in the Electoral College. Although the Reform Party with former Republican Pat Buchanan as the nomi- nee had little effect on the outcome, Green Party candidate Ralph Nader drew enough Democratic voters to swing the election in several key states.

Document 1, Governor Bush's speech accepting the Republican nomination, closely tied Gore to President Bill Clinton, and argued that the Democratic administration "coasted through prosperity," leaving a woefully unprepared military force and destroying the morality of America and the office of president. Vice President

Gore, in his speech accepting the Democratic nomination, Document 2, celebrated the economic prosperity of the Clinton-Gore years, but tried to distance himself from President Clinton. He declared, "I stand here tonight as my own man" and detailed a platform to offer a better future for all Americans.

Document 3, campaign speeches by Ralph Nader and Pat Buchanan, revealed the political ideology of the far left and far right. While Nader advocated national healthcare, free college tuition, and campaign finance reform, Buchanan campaigned against an activist Supreme Court that ruled in favor of abortionists and homosexuals.

Many assumed Gore had the upper hand in the debates, but Bush held his own. Document 4, an excerpt from the first presidential debate, demonstrated Gore's aggressive style, which he changed for the remaining debates because of considerable criticism. There was no clear-cut winner on Election Day, and partisan rhetoric ran high. It seemed that neither Bush nor Gore would be able to claim a legitimate presidency. However, after the Supreme Court handed down a ruling that effectively gave Bush the presidency, Gore conceded, Document 5, calling for an end to partisanship and keeping alive his future political prospects. Document 6, Bush's speech accepting the presidency, focused on the same theme of bringing the nation together after a stormy political battle.

Document 1

George W. Bush's Nomination Acceptance Speech, August 3, 2000

Prosperity can be a tool in our hands—used to build and better our country. Or it can be a drug in our system—dulling our sense of urgency, of empathy, of duty. . . .

For eight years, the Clinton-Gore administration has coasted through prosperity. And the path of least resistance is always downhill. But America's way is the rising road. This nation is daring and decent and ready for change.

Our current president embodied the potential of a generation. So many talents. So much charm. Such great skill. But, in the end, to what end? So much promise, to no great purpose.

Little more than a decade ago, the Cold War thawed and, with the leadership of Presidents Reagan and Bush, that wall came down. But instead of seizing this moment, the Clinton-Gore administration has squandered it. We have seen a steady erosion of American power and an unsteady exercise of American influence.

Our military is low on parts, pay and morale. If called on by the commander-in-chief today, two entire divisions of the Army would have to report . . . "Not ready for duty, sir."

This administration had its moment. They had their chance. They have not led. We will.

This generation was given the gift of the best education in American history. Yet we do not share that gift with everyone. Seven of ten fourth-graders in our highest-poverty schools cannot read a simple children's book.

And still this administration continues on the same old path with the same old programs—while millions are trapped in schools where violence is common and learning is rare. . . .

America has a strong economy and a surplus. We have the public resources and the public will—even the bipartisan opportunities—to strengthen Social Security and repair Medicare.

But this administration—during eight years of increasing need—did nothing. They had their moment. . . .

They had their chance. They have not led. We will. . . .

Tonight, in this hall, we resolve to be, not the party of repose, but the party of reform. . . .

To seniors in this country . . . You earned your benefits, you made your plans, and President George W. Bush will keep the promise of Social Security . . . no changes, no reductions, no way. Our opponents will say otherwise. This is their last, parting ploy, and don't believe a word of it. . . .

For younger workers, we will give you the option—your choice—to put a part of your payroll taxes into sound, responsible investments. . . .

One size does not fit all when it comes to educating our children, so local people should control local schools.

And those who spend your tax dollars must be held accountable.

When a school district receives federal funds to teach poor children, we expect them to learn. And if they don't, parents should get the money to make a different choice. . . .

Today, our high taxes fund a surplus. Some say that growing federal surplus means Washington has more money to spend. But they've got it backwards.

The surplus is not the government's money. The surplus is the people's money. . . .

On principle . . . every family, every farmer and small businessperson, should be free to pass on their life's work to those they love. So we will abolish the death tax. . . .

We will give our military the means to keep the peace, and we will give it one thing more . . . a commander-in-chief who respects our men and women in uniform, and a commander-in-chief who earns their respect. . . .

Now is the time, not to defend outdated treaties, but to defend the American people. A time of prosperity is a test of vision. And our nation today needs vision. That is a fact . . . or as my opponent might call it, a "risky truth scheme."

Every one of the proposals I've talked about tonight, he has called a "risky scheme," over and over again. It is the sum of his message—the politics of the roadblock, the philosophy of the stop sign.

If my opponent had been there at the moon launch, it would have been a "risky rocket scheme." If he'd been there when Edison was testing the light bulb, it would have been a "risky anti-candle scheme."

And if he'd been there when the Internet was invented—well, I understand he actually was there for that. He now leads the party of Franklin Delano Roosevelt. But the only thing he has to offer is fear itself. . . .

I will lead our nation toward a culture that values life—the life of the elderly and the sick, the life of the young, and the life of the unborn.

I know good people disagree on this issue, but surely we can agree on ways to value life by promoting adoption and parental notification, and when Congress sends me a bill against partial-birth abortion, I will sign it into law. . . .

Our nation's leaders are responsible . . . to confront problems, not pass them on to others.

And to lead this nation to a responsibility era, a president himself must be responsible.

And so, when I put my hand on the Bible, I will swear to not only uphold the laws of our land, I will swear to uphold the honor and dignity of the office to which I have been elected, so help me God.

I believe the presidency—the final point of decision in the American government—was made for great purposes.

It is the office of Lincoln's conscience and Teddy Roosevelt's energy and Harry Truman's integrity and Ronald Reagan's optimism.

For me, gaining this office is not the ambition of a lifetime, but it IS the opportunity of a lifetime.

And I will make the most of it. I believe great decisions are made with care, made with conviction, not made with polls.

I do not need to take your pulse before I know my own mind. I do not reinvent myself at every turn. I am not running in borrowed clothes.

When I act, you will know my reasons. . . . When I speak, you will know my heart. I believe in tolerance, not in spite of my faith, but because of it. . . .

An era of tarnished ideals is giving way to a responsibility era. . . .

Source: New York Times, August 4, 2000.

Document 2

Al Gore's Nomination Acceptance Speech, August 17, 2000

For almost eight years now, I've been the partner of a leader who moved us out of the valley of recession and into the longest period of prosperity in American history. I say to you tonight, millions of Americans will live better lives for a long time to come because of the job that's been done by President Bill Clinton. . . .

But now we turn the page and write a new chapter. And that's what I want to speak about tonight. This election is not an award for past performance. I'm not asking you to vote for me on the basis of the economy we have. Tonight I ask for your support on the basis of the better, fairer, more prosperous America we can build together. . . .

The future should belong to everyone in this land—everyone, all families.

We could squander this moment, but our country would be the poorer for it. Instead, let's lift our eyes and see how wide the American horizon has become. We're entering a new time. We're electing a new president. And I stand here tonight as my own man. . . .

So this is not just an election between my opponent and me, it's about our people, our families and our future, and whether forces standing in your way will keep you from living a better life. . . .

You ought to be able to know and then judge for yourself. If you entrust me with the presidency, I will put our democracy back in your hands and get all the special interest money, all of it, out of our democracy by enacting campaign finance reform.

At a time when most Americans will live to know even their great grandchildren, we will save and strengthen Social Security and Medicare, not only for this generation but for generations to come. At a time of almost unimaginable medical breakthroughs, we will fight for affordable healthcare for all, so patients and ordinary people are not left powerless and broke. We will move toward universal health coverage, step by step, starting with all children.

Let's get all children covered by 2004. . . .

We will double the federal investment in medical research. We will find new medicines and new cures, not just for cancer but for everything from diabetes to HIV/AIDS. . . .

I will fight for the greatest single commitment to education since the G.I. Bill. . . .

I will not go along with any plan that would drain taxpayer money away from our public schools and give it to private schools in the form of vouchers. . . .

All of this—all of this is the change we wish to see in America. Not so long ago, a balanced budget seemed impossible. Now our budget surpluses make it possible to give a full range of targeted tax cuts to working families; not just to help you save for college, but to pay for health insurance and child care, to reform the estate tax so people can pass on a small business or a family farm, and to end the marriage penalty the right way, the fair way because we should not force couples to pay more in income taxes just because they're married.

But let me say it plainly: I will not go along with a huge tax cut for the wealthy at the expense of everyone else and wreck our good economy in the process. . . .

I'll fight for tax cuts that go to the right people, to the working families who have the toughest time paying taxes and saving for the future.

I'll fight for a new tax-free way to help you save and build a bigger nest egg for your retirement. I'm talking about something extra that you can save and invest for yourself, something that will supplement Social Security, not be subtracted from it. . . .

They're for the powerful. We're for the people. . . .

We will honor families by expanding child care and after-school care, and family and medical leave, so working families have the help they need to care for their children, because one of the most important jobs of all is raising our children.

And we'll support the right of parents to decide that one of them will stay home longer with their babies, if that's what they believe is best for their families.

We will honor the ideal of equality by standing up for civil rights and defending affirmative action.

We will honor—we will honor equal rights, and we will fight for an equal day's pay for an equal day's work.

And let there be no doubt. I will protect and defend a woman's right to choose. The last thing this country needs is a Supreme Court that overturns *Roe v. Wade*. . . .

And hear me well: We will pass the Employment Non-Discrimination Act. . . .

I'll fight to toughen penalties on those who misuse the Internet to prey on our children and violate our privacy.

And I'll fight to make every school in this nation drug free and gun free.

I believe in the right of sportsmen and hunters and law-abiding citizens to own firearms. But I want mandatory background checks to keep guns away from criminals and mandatory child-safety locks to protect our children. . . .

We must always have the will to defend our enduring interests, from Europe to the Middle East to Japan and Korea. We must strengthen our partnerships with Africa, Latin America and the rest of the developing world.

We must confront the new challenges of terrorism, new kinds of weapons of mass destruction, global environmental problems, and new diseases that know no national boundaries and can threaten national security. We must welcome and promote truly free trade. But I say to you: It must be fair trade. . . .

If you entrust me with the presidency, I know I won't always be the most exciting politician. But I pledge to you tonight, I will work for you every day, and I will never let you down. . . .

Source: New York Times, August 18, 2000.

Document 3
Campaign Speeches by Ralph Nader and Pat Buchanan

Ralph Nader's Speech in Milwaukee, September 20, 2000

The Green Party stands for a major democratic movement against the extremism of concentrated power and abuse. . . . One, universal accessible health insurance for everybody. . . . Every student at a public university or a college in the United States can get free tuition for a total bill of $32 billion. $32 billion is half of what we're spending defending Western Europe and East Asia against nonexistent enemies, when they're able to defend themselves. . . .

The Green Party stands for tough law enforcement against corporate crime, fraud, and abuse. . . . We are pushing for campaign finance reform, not only by urging it—public funding and public campaigns—but by behaving in the proper way. We are the only party, the only candidacy that does not take corporate interest money, does not take political action committee money, and doesn't come close to the corrupt soft money that's going into the two-party coffers in the tens of millions of dollars from the corporate lobbyists. . . . We are practicing what we preach, so we can preach what we practice. And we are also succeeding, and that after November, the millions of people who vote for this ticket, and there will be millions of people voting for this ticket. . . . After November, we will emerge as a significant progressive third party that will be a burgeoning watchdog against the two-party system.

Pat Buchanan's Speech in Warren, Michigan, September 19, 2000

Look at the decisions they [the Supreme Court] have imposed upon America which have overthrown our traditional code of morality. They have driven God out of the public schools. They have made abortion, which was a felony in 50 states, a so-called "constitutional right." Since "*Roe v. Wade*"—in this country we call God's country—38 million unborn children have been done to death, and neither of these other two parties will talk about that. And a new issue has risen and the Supreme Court is moving to support the idea that homosexuality is a commendable lifestyle on an equal with marriage. And now the Supreme Court, by one vote—just by one vote—almost ordered the Boy Scouts to admit active homosexuals as scoutmasters for Cub Scout troops and Boy Scout troops. . . . Now that's where America is headed, and that is downhill.

This is a revolution that's been imposed upon you and me, not because we voted for it, or we wanted it, or we demanded it, it's been imposed from above by a Supreme Court, which has become a judicial dictatorship in America. And Mr. Gore says he will appoint Justices who will provide that next vote to go after the Boy Scouts. He says he will appoint justices like Ruth Bader-Ginsburg who will guarantee . . . that "*Roe* v. *Wade*" is never overturned. Mr. Bush [father of candidate George W. Bush] . . . appointed three judges to the Supreme Court that overturned his own parental notification law. I don't think Mr. Bush can be trusted. . . . In my administration, in my White House, only pro-life constitutionalists and conservatives will be elevated to the Supreme Court, and no liberal judicial activists need apply. . . .

I still dream that one day I will be up there, and I will take that oath of office, and I'll give my inaugural address, and then you take the oath, and then I will turn to Bill Clinton, and I will say to him, "Sir, you have the right to remain silent." . . .

Source: The NewsHour with Jim Lehrer Web site, wysiwyg://78/ http://www.pbs.org/newshour/bb/politics/july-dec00/stump_9-21.html.

Document 4

Excerpt from First Presidential Debate, Boston, October 3, 2000

GORE: I will balance the budget every year. I will pay down the national debt. I will put Medicare and Social Security in a lockbox and protect them. And I will cut taxes for middle-class families. . . . I will make sure that we invest in our country and our families, and I mean investing in education, healthcare, the environment, and middle-class tax cuts and retirement security. That's my agenda, and that's why I think that it's not just a question of experience.

[Jim] LEHRER [of the *NewsHour with Jim Lehrer*]: Governor Bush, one minute rebuttal.

BUSH: I want to take one-half of the surplus and dedicate it to Social Security, one quarter of the surplus for important projects. And I want to send one-quarter of the surplus back to the people who pay the bills.

I want everybody who pays taxes to have their tax rates cut, and that stands in contrast to my worthy opponent's plan, which will increase the size of government dramatically. . . .

GORE: Jim, if I could just respond.

LEHRER: Quick, and then we need to move on. Yes, sir.

GORE: He [Bush] spends more money for tax cuts for the wealthiest one percent than all of his new spending proposals for healthcare, prescription drugs, education and national defense all combined.

I agree that the surplus is the American people's money. It's your money. That's why I don't think we should give nearly half of it to the wealthiest one percent, because the other 99 percent have had an awful lot to do with building this surplus and our prosperity.

LEHRER: Our three-and-a-half minutes is up. New question.

BUSH: I hope it's about wealthy people. (Laughter) . . .

GORE: Under my plan, I will put Medicare in an iron-clad lock box and prevent the money from being used for anything other than Medicare. The governor has declined to endorse that idea, even though the Republican as well as Democratic leaders of Congress have endorsed it. I'd be interested if this—if he would this evening say that he would put Medicare in a lock box. . . .

BUSH: I—I cannot let this go by. The old-style Washington politics of "We're going to scare you in the voting booth." Under my plan, the man gets immediate help with prescription drugs. It's called immediate helping hand. Instead of squabbling and finger-pointing, he gets immediate help. . . .

LEHRER: Excuse me, gentlemen.

GORE: Jim, can I—

LEHRER: Our three and a half minutes is up, but we'll finish this.

GORE: Could I make one other point?

LEHRER: Yes.

BUSH: Wait a minute!

GORE: $25,000 a year income. That makes them ineligible.

BUSH: Look. This is a man who's got great numbers. He talks about numbers. I'm beginning to think not only did he invent the Internet, but he invented the calculator. (Laughter) It's fuzzy math. It's a scaring—trying to scare people in the voting booth. Under my tax plan, that he continues to criticize, I said a third. The federal government should take no more than a third of anybody's check. . . .

LEHRER: Let me ask you both this, and we'll move on. On this subject, as a practical matter, both of you want to bring prescription drugs to seniors. Correct?

BUSH: Correct.

GORE: Correct. But the difference is–the difference is, I want to bring it to 100 percent—

LEHRER: Yes, I know. (Laughter) All right. All right. All right.

GORE:—and he brings it only to 5 percent.

LEHRER: All right.

BUSH: That's just totally false.

GORE: That doesn't make—(laughs)—

BUSH: Wait a minute, that's just totally false for him to stand up there and say that. Let me make sure the seniors hear me loud and clear. They've had their chance to get something done. I'm going to work with both Republicans and Democrats to reform the system. All seniors will be covered. All poor seniors will have their prescription drugs paid for.

In the meantime, we're going to have a plan to help poor seniors. And in the meantime could be one year or two years.

GORE: Okay.

BUSH: I don't know—

GORE: Let me call your attention to the key word there. He said all "poor" seniors.

BUSH: No, wait a minute. All seniors are covered under prescription drugs in my plan.

GORE: In the first year? In the first year?

BUSH: If we can get it done in the first year, you bet. Yours is phased in eight years.

GORE: No, no, no. No, no. It's a two-phase plan, Jim, and for the first four years—it takes a year to pass it, and then for the first four years, only the poor are covered.

Middle-class seniors, like George McKinney [sp] and his wife, are not covered for four to five years.

LEHRER: I've got an idea.

GORE: Okay.

LEHRER: If you have any more to say about this, you can say it in your closing statement, so we'll move on, okay.

GORE: (Chuckles) Okay.

LEHRER: New question.

Source: Commission on Presidential Debates Web site, www.debates.org/pages/trans2000a.html (uncorrected transcript).

Document 5

Al Gore's Address to the Nation, December 13, 2000

Just moments ago, I spoke with George W. Bush and congratulated him on becoming the 43rd president of the United States, and I promised him that I wouldn't call him back this time.

I offered to meet with him as soon as possible so that we can start to heal the divisions of the campaign and the contest through which we just passed.

Almost a century and a half ago, Senator Stephen Douglas told Abraham Lincoln, who had just defeated him for the presidency, "Partisan feeling must yield to patriotism. I'm with you, Mr. President, and God bless you."

Well, in that same spirit, I say to President-elect Bush that what remains of partisan rancor must now be put aside, and may God bless his stewardship of this country.

Neither he nor I anticipated this long and difficult road. Certainly neither of us wanted it to happen. Yet it came, and now it has ended, resolved, as it must be resolved, through the honored institutions of our democracy.

Over the library of one of our great law schools is inscribed the motto, "Not under man but under God and law." That's the ruling principle of American freedom, the source of our democratic liberties. I've tried to make it my guide throughout this contest as it has guided America's deliberations of all the complex issues of the past five weeks.

Now the U.S. Supreme Court has spoken. Let there be no doubt, while I strongly disagree with the court's decision, I accept it. I accept the finality of this outcome which will be ratified next Monday in the Electoral College. And tonight, for the sake of our unity of the people and the strength of our democracy, I offer my concession. . . .

I've seen America in this campaign and I like what I see. It's worth fighting for and that's a fight I'll never stop.

Source: New York Times, December 14, 2000.

Document 6

George W. Bush's Address to the Nation,
December 13, 2000

Our country has been through a long and trying period, with the outcome of the presidential election not finalized for longer than any of us could ever imagine.

Vice President Gore and I put our hearts and hopes into our campaigns. We both gave it our all. We shared similar emotions, so I understand how difficult this moment must be for Vice President Gore and his family. . . .

Tonight I chose to speak from the chamber of the Texas House of Representatives because it has been a home to bipartisan cooperation. Here in a place where Democrats have the majority, Republicans and Democrats have worked together to do what is right for the people we represent.

We've had spirited disagreements. And in the end, we found constructive consensus. It is an experience I will always carry with me, an example I will always follow. . . .

The spirit of cooperation I have seen in this hall is what is needed in Washington, D.C. It is the challenge of our moment. After a difficult election, we must put politics behind us and work together to make the promise of America available for every one of our citizens.

I am optimistic that we can change the tone in Washington, D.C. . . .

I was not elected to serve one party, but to serve one nation.

The president of the United States is the president of every single American, of every race and every background.

Whether you voted for me or not, I will do my best to serve your interests and I will work to earn your respect.

I will be guided by President Jefferson's sense of purpose, to stand for principle, to be reasonable in manner, and above all, to do great good for the cause of freedom and harmony.

The presidency is more than an honor. It is more than an office. It is a charge to keep, and I will give it my all. . . .

Source: New York Times, December 14, 2000.

Appendixes

U.S. Constitution: Excerpts on the Electoral College and the Presidency

*I*n 1787, delegates gathered at the Constitutional Convention in Philadelphia to suggest revisions to the Articles of Confederation, which had served as the governing document of the United States during and immediately after the American Revolution. Delegates decided to scrap the Articles and draft an entirely new document, the Constitution. The Constitution called for three branches of government—legislative, executive, and judicial—each with separate powers and responsibilities. The thorniest issue that delegates faced was how to choose the executive, and they spent many days discussing different methods of electing the president and vice president. Delegates ultimately created a system known as the Electoral College, which entitled each state to a certain number of electoral votes proportionate to its population. The Constitution gave states control over defining the electorate and the mode of choosing the presidential electors. Subsequently the original Constitution, ratified in 1788, was amended several times, modifying the Electoral College and restricting the power of states to limit the right to vote. The Twelfth Amendment (1804) addressed what Alexander Hamilton had called a "defect" by ensuring that electoral votes would be cast separately for the president and the vice president. Later amendments barred states from denying the vote to various groups of people: black males, women, and those over eighteen.

The following passage includes the preamble to the Constitution and a selection of the clauses and amendments relating to the choice of the president and vice president and to their powers. It also includes parts of the Constitution defining the electorate for presidential elections and elections for the members of Congress. The Fourteenth Amendment is included because it declared that the whole Constitution, including the Bill of Rights and the other amendments, were applicable to the states. Those sections enclosed by brackets are ones no longer in effect because of subsequent amendments.

THE CONSTITUTION

We the People of the United States, in Order to form a more perfect Union, establish Justice, insure domestic Tranquility, provide for the common defence, promote the general Welfare, and secure the Blessings of Liberty to ourselves and our Posterity, do ordain and establish this Constitution for the United States of America.

Article I

Section 1. All legislative Powers herein granted shall be vested in a Congress of the United States, which shall consist of a Senate and House of Representatives.

Section 2. The House of Representatives shall be composed of Members chosen every second Year by the People of the several States, and the Electors in each State shall have the Qualifications requisite for Electors of the most numerous Branch of the State Legislature.

No Person shall be a Representative who shall not have attained to the Age of twenty five Years, and been seven Years a Citizen of the United States, and who shall not, when elected, be an Inhabitant of that State in which he shall be chosen.

Representatives and direct Taxes shall be apportioned among the several States which may be included within this Union, according to their respective Numbers, [which shall be determined by adding to the whole Number of free Persons, including those bound to Service for a Term of Years, and excluding Indians not taxed, three fifths of all other Persons]. The actual Enumeration shall be made within three Years after the first Meeting of the Congress of the United States, and within every subsequent Term of ten Years, in such Manner as they shall by Law direct. The Number of Representatives shall not exceed one for every thirty Thousand, but each State shall have at Least one Representative; and until such enumeration shall be made, the State of New Hampshire shall be entitled to chuse three, Massachusetts eight, Rhode-Island and Providence Plantations one, Connecticut five, New-York six, New Jersey four, Pennsylvania eight, Delaware one, Maryland six, Virginia ten, North Carolina five, South Carolina five, and Georgia three. . . .

Section 3. The Senate of the United States shall be composed of two Senators from each State, [chosen by the Legislature thereof,] for six Years; and each Senator shall have one Vote. . . .

No Person shall be a Senator who shall not have attained to the Age of thirty Years, and been nine Years a Citizen of the United States, and who shall not, when elected, be an Inhabitant of that State for which he shall be chosen.

The Vice President of the United States shall be President of the Senate, but shall have no Vote, unless they be equally divided. . . .

Judgment in Cases of Impeachment shall not extend further than to removal from Office, and disqualification to hold and enjoy any Office of honor, Trust or Profit under the United States: but the Party convicted shall nevertheless be liable and subject to Indictment, Trial, Judgment and Punishment, according to Law.

Section 4. The Times, Places and Manner of holding Elections for Senators and Representatives, shall be prescribed in each State by the Legislature thereof; but the Congress may at any time by Law make or alter such Regulations, except as to the Places of chusing Senators. . . .

Article II

Section 1. The executive Power shall be vested in a President of the United States of America. He shall hold his Office during the Term of four Years, and, together with the Vice President, chosen for the same Term, be elected, as follows.

Each State shall appoint, in such Manner as the Legislature thereof may direct, a Number of Electors, equal to the whole Number of Senators and Representatives to which the State may be entitled in the Congress: but no Senator or Representative, or Person holding an Office of Trust or Profit under the United States, shall be appointed an Elector.

[The Electors shall meet in their respective States, and vote by Ballot for two Persons, of whom one at least shall not be an Inhabitant of the same State with themselves. And they shall make a List of all the Persons voted for, and of the Number of Votes for each; which List they shall sign and certify, and transmit sealed to the Seat of the Government of the United States, directed to the President of the Senate. The President of the Senate shall, in the Presence of the Senate and House of Representatives, open all the Certificates, and the Votes shall then be counted. The Person having the greatest Number of Votes shall be the President, if such Number be a Majority of the whole Number of Electors appointed; and if there be more than one who have such Majority, and have an equal Number of Votes, then the House of Representatives shall immediately chuse by Ballot one of them for President; and if no Person have a Majority, then from the five highest on the List the said House shall in like Manner chuse the President. But in chusing the President, the Votes shall be taken by States, the Representation from each State having one Vote; A quorum for this Purpose shall consist of a Member or Members from two thirds of the States, and a Majority of all the States shall be necessary to a Choice. In every Case, after the Choice of the President, the Person having the greatest Number of Votes of the Electors shall be the Vice President. But if there should remain two or more who have equal Votes, the Senate shall chuse from them by Ballot the Vice President.]

The Congress may determine the Time of chusing the Electors, and the Day on which they shall give their Votes; which Day shall be the same throughout the United States.

No Person except a natural born Citizen, or a Citizen of the United States, at the time of the Adoption of this Constitution, shall be eligible to the Office of President; neither shall any Person be eligible to that Office who shall not have attained to the Age of thirty five Years, and been fourteen Years a Resident within the United States.

In Case of the Removal of the President from Office, or of his Death, Resignation, or Inability to discharge the Powers and Duties of the said Office, the Same shall devolve on the Vice President, and the Congress may by Law provide for the Case of Removal, Death, Resignation or Inability, both of the President and Vice President, declaring what Officer shall then act as President, and such Officer shall act accordingly, until the Disability be removed, or a President shall be elected.

The President shall, at stated Times, receive for his Services, a Compensation, which shall neither be increased nor diminished during the Period for which he shall have been elected, and he shall not receive within that Period any other Emolument from the United States, or any of them.

Before he enter on the Execution of his Office, he shall take the following Oath or Affirmation:—"I do solemnly swear (or affirm) that I will faithfully execute the Office of President of the United States, and will to the best of my Ability, preserve, protect and defend the Constitution of the United States."

Section 2. The President shall be Commander in Chief of the Army and Navy of the United States, and of the Militia of the several States, when called into the actual Service of the United States; he may require the Opinion, in writing, of the principal Officer in each of the executive Departments, upon any Subject relating to the Duties of their respective Offices, and he shall have Power to grant Reprieves and Pardons for Offenses against the United States, except in Cases of Impeachment.

He shall have Power, by and with the Advice and Consent of the Senate, to make Treaties, provided two thirds of the Senators present concur; and he shall nominate, and by and with the Advice and Con-

sent of the Senate, shall appoint Ambassadors, other public Ministers and Consuls, Judges of the supreme Court, and all other Officers of the United States, whose Appointments are not herein otherwise provided for, and which shall be established by Law: but the Congress may by Law vest the Appointment of such inferior Officers, as they think proper, in the President alone, in the Courts of Law, or in the Heads of Departments.

The President shall have Power to fill up all Vacancies that may happen during the Recess of the Senate, by granting Commissions which shall expire at the End of their next Session.

Section 3. He shall from time to time give to the Congress Information of the State of the Union, and recommend to their Consideration such Measures as he shall judge necessary and expedient; he may, on extraordinary Occasions, convene both Houses, or either of them, and in Case of Disagreement between them, with Respect to the Time of Adjournment, he may adjourn them to such Time as he shall think proper; he shall receive Ambassadors and other public Ministers; he shall take Care that the Laws be faithfully executed, and shall Commission all Officers of the United States.

Section 4. The President, Vice President and all civil Officers of the United States, shall be removed from Office on Impeachment for, and Conviction of, Treason, Bribery, or other high Crimes and Misdemeanors. . . .

AMENDMENTS TO THE CONSTITUTION

Amendment XII (1804)

The electors shall meet in their respective states, and vote by ballot for President and Vice-President, one of whom, at least, shall not be an inhabitant of the same state with themselves; they shall name in their ballots the person voted for as President, and in distinct ballots the person voted for as Vice-President, and they shall make distinct lists of all persons voted for as President, and of all persons voted for as Vice-President, and of the number of votes for each, which lists they shall sign and certify, and transmit sealed to the seat of the government of the United States, directed to the President of the Senate;—The President of the Senate shall, in the presence of the Senate and House of Representatives, open all the certificates and the votes shall then be counted;—The person having the greatest number of votes for President, shall be the President, if such number be a majority of the whole number of electors appointed; and if no person have such majority, then from the persons having the highest numbers not exceeding three on the list of those voted for as President, the House of Representatives shall choose immediately, by ballot, the President. But in choosing the President, the votes shall be taken by states, the representation from each state having one vote; a quorum for this purpose shall consist of a member or members from two-thirds of the states, and a majority of all the states shall be necessary to a choice. [And if the House of Representatives shall not choose a President whenever the right of choice shall devolve upon them, before the fourth day of March next following, then the Vice-President shall act as President, as in the case of the death or other constitutional disability of the President.] The person having the greatest number of votes as Vice-President, shall be the Vice-President, if such number be a majority of the whole number of electors appointed, and if no person have a majority, then from the two highest numbers on the list, the Senate shall choose the Vice-President; a quorum for the purpose shall consist of two-thirds of the whole number of Senators, and a majority of the whole number shall be necessary to a choice. But no person constitutionally ineligible to the office of President shall be eligible to that of Vice-President of the United States.

Amendment XIV (1868)

Section 1. All persons born or naturalized in the United States, and subject to the jurisdiction thereof, are citizens of the United States and of the state wherein they reside. No state shall make or enforce any law which shall abridge the privileges or immunities of citizens of the United States; nor shall any state deprive any person of life, liberty, or property, without due process of law; nor deny to any person within its jurisdiction the equal protection of the laws.

Section 2. Representatives shall be apportioned among the several states according to their respective numbers, counting the whole number of persons in each state, excluding Indians not taxed. But when the right to vote at any election for the choice of electors for President and Vice President of the United States,

Representatives in Congress, the Executive and Judicial officers of a State, or the members of the Legislature thereof, is denied to any of the male inhabitants of such state, being twenty-one years of age, and citizens of the United States, or in any way abridged, except for participation in rebellion, or other crime, the basis of representation therein shall be reduced in the proportion which the number of such male citizens shall bear to the whole number of male citizens twenty-one years of age in such State.

Section 3. No person shall be a Senator or Representative in Congress, or elector of President and Vice President, or hold any office, civil or military, under the United States, or under any State, who, having previously taken an oath, as a member of Congress, or as an officer of the United States, or as a member of any State legislature, or as an executive or judicial officer of any State, to support the Constitution of the United States, shall have engaged in insurrection or rebellion against the same, or given aid and comfort to the enemies thereof. But Congress may by a vote of two-thirds of each House, remove such disability.

Section 4. The validity of the public debt of the United States, authorized by law, including debts incurred for payment of pensions and bounties for services in suppressing insurrection or rebellion, shall not be questioned. But neither the United States nor any state shall assume or pay any debt or obligation incurred in aid of insurrection or rebellion against the United States, or any claim for the loss or emancipation of any slave; but all such debts, obligations, and claims shall be held illegal and void.

Section 5. The Congress shall have power to enforce, by appropriate legislation, the provisions of this article.

Amendment XV (1870)

Section 1. The right of citizens of the United States to vote shall not be denied or abridged by the United States or by any state on account of race, color, or previous condition of servitude.

Section 2. The Congress shall have power to enforce this article by appropriate legislation.

Amendment XVII (1913)

The Senate of the United States shall be composed of two Senators from each State, elected by the people thereof, for six years; and each Senator shall have one vote. The electors in each State shall have the qualifications requisite for electors of the most numerous branch of the State legislatures.

When vacancies happen in the representation of any State in the Senate, the executive authority of such State shall issue writs of election to fill such vacancies: *Provided*, That the legislature of any State may empower the executive thereof to make temporary appointments until the people fill the vacancies by election as the legislature may direct.

This amendment shall not be so construed as to affect the election or term of any Senator chosen before it becomes valid as part of the Constitution.

Amendment XIX (1920)

The right of citizens of the United States to vote shall not be denied or abridged by the United States or by any State on account of sex.

Congress shall have power to enforce this article by appropriate legislation.

Amendment XX (1933)

Section 1. The terms of the President and Vice President shall end at noon on the 20th day of January, and the terms of Senators and Representatives at noon on the 3d day of January, of the years in which such terms would have ended if this article had not been ratified; and the terms of their successors shall then begin.

Section 2. The Congress shall assemble at least once in every year and such meetings shall begin at noon on the 3d day of January, unless they shall by law appoint a different day.

Section 3. If, at the time fixed for the beginning of the term of the President, the President elect shall have died, the Vice President elect shall become President. If a President shall not have been chosen before the time fixed for the beginning of his term, or if the President elect shall have failed to qualify, then the Vice President elect shall act as President until a President shall have qualified; and the Congress may by law provide for the case wherein neither a President elect nor a Vice President elect shall have qualified, declaring who shall then act as President, or the manner in which one who is to act shall be selected, and such person shall act accordingly until a President or Vice President shall have qualified.

Section 4. The Congress may by law provide for the case of the death of any of the persons from whom the House of Representatives may choose a President whenever the right of choice shall have devolved upon them, and for the case of the death of any of the persons from whom the Senate may choose a Vice President whenever the right of choice shall have devolved upon them.

Section 5. Sections 1 and 2 shall take effect on the 15th day of October following the ratification of this article

Section 6. This article shall be inoperative unless it shall have been ratified as an amendment to the Constitution by the legislatures of three-fourths of the several States within seven years from the date of its submission.

Amendment XXII (1951)

Section 1. No person shall be elected to the office of the President more than twice, and no person who has held the office of President, or acted as President, for more than two years of a term to which some other person was elected President shall be elected to the office of the President more than once. But this article shall not apply to any person holding the office of President when this article was proposed by the Congress, and shall not prevent any person who may be holding the office of President, or acting as President, during the term within which this article becomes operative from holding the office of President or acting as President during the remainder of such term.

Section 2. This article shall be inoperative unless it shall have been ratified as an amendment to the Constitution by the legislatures of three-fourths of the several states within seven years from the date of its submission to the States by the Congress.

Amendment XXIII (1961)

Section 1. The district constituting the seat of government of the United States shall appoint in such manner as the Congress may direct:

A number of electors of President and Vice President equal to the whole number of Senators and Representatives in Congress to which the District would be entitled if it were a State, but in no event more than the least populous state; they shall be in addition to those appointed by the States, but they shall be considered, for the purpose of the election of President and Vice President, to be electors appointed by a State; and they shall meet in the District and perform such duties as provided by the twelfth article of amendment.

Section 2. The Congress shall have power to enforce this article by appropriate legislation.

Amendment XXIV (1964)

Section 1. The right of citizens of the United States to vote in any primary or other election for President or Vice President, for electors for President or Vice President, or for Senator or Representative in Congress, shall not be denied or abridged by the United States or any state by reason of failure to pay any poll tax or other tax.

Section 2. The Congress shall have power to enforce this article by appropriate legislation.

Amendment XXV (1967)

Section 1. In case of the removal of the President from office or of his death or resignation, the Vice President shall become President.

Section 2. Whenever there is a vacancy in the office of the Vice President, the President shall nominate a Vice President who shall take office upon confirmation by a majority vote of both Houses of Congress.

Section 3. Whenever the President transmits to the President pro tempore of the Senate and the Speaker of the House of Representatives his written declaration that he is unable to discharge the powers and duties of his office, and until he transmits to them a written declaration to the contrary, such powers and duties shall be discharged by the Vice President as Acting President.

Section 4. Whenever the Vice President and a majority of either the principal officers of the execu-

tive departments or of such other body as Congress may by law provide, transmit to the President pro tempore of the Senate and the Speaker of the House of Representatives their written declaration that the President is unable to discharge the powers and duties of his office, the Vice President shall immediately assume the powers and duties of the office as Acting President.

Thereafter, when the President transmits to the President pro tempore of the Senate and the Speaker of the House of Representatives his written declaration that no inability exists, he shall resume the powers and duties of his office unless the Vice President and a majority of either the principal officers of the executive department or of such other body as Congress may by law provide, transmit within four days to the President pro tempore of the Senate and the Speaker of the House of Representatives their written declaration that the President is unable to discharge the powers and duties of his office. Thereupon Congress shall decide the issue, assembling within forty-eight hours for that purpose if not in session. If the Congress, within twenty-one days after receipt of the latter written declaration, or, if Congress is not in session, within twenty-one days after Congress is required to assemble, determines by two-thirds vote of both Houses that the President is unable to discharge the powers and duties of his office, the Vice President shall continue to discharge the same as Acting President; otherwise, the President shall resume the powers and duties of his office.

Amendment XXVI (1971)

Section 1. The right of citizens of the United States, who are eighteen years of age or older, to vote shall not be denied or abridged by the United States or by any State on account of age.

Section 2. The Congress shall have the power to enforce this article by appropriate legislation.

Glossary

Absentee Ballot. Ballot submitted, usually by mail, in advance of an election by a voter unable to be present at the polls on Election Day.

Albany Regency. A small group of New York Democratic-Republican politicians, headed by Martin Van Buren, who controlled the party from Albany, the state capital, in the 1810s and 1820s.

Australian Ballot. The secret ballot introduced in Australia and then the United States in the 1890s and the first decade of the twentieth century. Its introduction was a Progressive reform designed to undermine the influence of parties.

Barnburners. The radical faction of the New York Democratic Party in the 1840s associated with Martin Van Buren. Because of their fierce opposition to compromise, opponents called them "Barnburners" after the farmer who burned his barn to get rid of the rats.

Bosses. The term is usually associated with urban politicians like William M. Tweed of New York in the nineteenth century or Mayor Richard J. Daley of Chicago in the twentieth, but can apply to anyone who controls a political party or machine.

Bull Moose. The common term used for the Progressive Party in 1912 when Theodore Roosevelt was their candidate.

Carpetbagger. Derisive term used by white southern Democrats to describe any northern-born Republican, black or white, during the Recon-

struction era. The term implied that these presumably corrupt politicians could carry all their belongings in a suitcase—called at the time a "carpetbag" because of the material from which it was made. The term would later be applied to Robert Kennedy, who moved from Massachusetts to New York in 1964 to run for the U.S. Senate, as well as to other politicians who moved from one place to another to run for office.

Caucus. A meeting of party leaders to choose candidates for an upcoming election. Initially this term referred to a meeting of Democratic-Republicans or Federalists in Congress to choose presidential and vice presidential candidates in the early nineteenth century. In the 1820s, advocates of national conventions opposed what they called "King Caucus" as being undemocratic.

Coalition. Alliance among competing groups for a mutual aim.

Coattails. The influence that a presidential or other top candidate has on those running for lower offices. Senators, representatives, and other officials are said to "come in on the coattails" of a charismatic presidential nominee. Candidates whose presence at the head of the ticket affect even minor offices are said to have "long coattails."

Conscience Whigs. The faction of the Massachusetts Whig Party in the 1840s that was antislavery. Their opponents were called "Cotton Whigs," because of their connection with the cotton mills and support of the South.

Cotton Whigs. *See* Conscience Whigs.

Critical Election. As defined by political scientist V. O. Key, a presidential election in which there are major shifts in the behavior of voters. Most elections in Key's paradigm are maintaining, or normal, elections in which the social coalitions that make up the parties remain stable for long periods. *See also* Deviating Election; Maintaining Election; Realigning Election.

Dark Horse. A candidate who is not expected to be nominated. The first dark horse nominated and elected president was James K. Polk in 1844.

Deviating Election. In V.O. Key's paradigm, an election that deviates from the norm, but only once or twice, after which the normal voting patterns return. An example is Democrat Woodrow Wilson's victories in 1912 and 1916 when the country had a Republican majority, both before and after his presidency. *See also* Critical Election; Maintaining Election; Realigning Election.

Dirty Tricks. Incorrect and critical information given to the press in the midst of a campaign. This term is associated with the activities of Nixon campaign worker Donald Segretti during the 1972 campaign and the Watergate scandal.

Dixiecrats. The southern faction of the Democratic Party that broke off in 1948 to form the States' Rights Party.

Electoral College. Constitutional system by which the president is elected in the United States. The Electoral College itself refers to the set of electors chosen in each state and who in fact never get together. Their votes are cast in their home states and sent to the president of the Senate to be counted.

Electoral Votes. Votes cast by electors that officially determine who is elected president. Each state's number of electoral votes is based on the total of its senators and representatives in Congress.

Era of Good Feelings. The period of James Monroe's administrations (1817–25) in which the Democratic-Republicans were the only viable national party. The term comes from a Boston newspaper in 1817. Sometimes these years are called the "One-Party Period" of American history, because only Democratic-Republicans received electoral votes during these years.

Faction. Group of people organized for political purposes. It refers to competing groups in the 1790s before political parties were formally organized. It also refers to dissident groups within a party.

Federal Election Commission. Government agency that oversees presidential electors and monitors campaign spending.

Federalist Papers. The series of newspaper editorials written by Alexander Hamilton, James Madison, and John Jay in defense of the Constitution in 1787–88.

Floaters. Voters who (usually for a price) move from one party to the other. It is a term associated with the Gilded Age. At the time, supposedly paid voters went from one polling place to another and voted "early and often."

Fusion Candidate. A candidate supported by two different parties that have temporarily joined or have a common goal.

GOP. *See* Grand Old Party.

Grand Old Party (GOP). Term used for the Republican Party. It was probably first used in 1876 by a Cincinnati newspaper, but it became common in the 1880s. There were mentions of the "Gallant Old Party" in the 1870s.

Grandfather Clause. This was one of the ways to disfranchise black voters in the Jim Crow era following the end of Reconstruction. These racist clauses were put into southern constitutions to deny the vote to anyone whose grandfather had been a slave.

Hunkers. The conservative faction of the New York Democratic Party in the 1840s. Led by William Marcy, they opposed the Barnburners and tended to "hunker" down.

Inauguration. The ceremony in which a president is officially installed. The traditional address at the time is often referred to simply as the "Inaugural."

Inauguration Day. The day the president is formally sworn into office following his or her election. The Constitution originally set March 4 as Inauguration Day. The Twentieth Amendment changed it to January 20.

Jacksonian Democracy. The movement supposedly initiated by President Andrew Jackson and which drew more voters into the electorate and established policies in the interest of the "common man" in the 1830s and 1840s.

Lame Duck. Any candidate who continues to serve in office after he or she has lost an election. Traditionally there was a session of Congress after the election in which the previous Congress enacted legislation, such as the Judiciary Act of 1801 or the Civil Rights Act of 1875. Until the Twentieth Amendment moved the date of inauguration from March 4 to January 20, presidents served four months after an election in which they might have been defeated (like John Adams in 1800). That period is now two-and-a-half months.

Landslide. A huge victory by a large number of votes.

Lobbyist. The representative of a business or special-interest group who is said to work in the "lobby" of the halls of Congress or a state legislature. In the nineteenth century, Whig and Republican political operator Thurlow Weed was called the "Wizard of the Lobby."

Maintaining Election. The most common kind of election in political scientist V.O. Key's typology simply maintains the status quo and returns the majority party's candidates to office. It is a "normal" election. For all of its unusual characteristics, the election of 1948 was a maintaining election. Truman won because most of the same people who voted for Roosevelt in 1944 voted for him. *See also* Critical Election, Deviating Election, Realigning Election.

Majority. One more than half. To be elected president, a candidate must win a majority of electoral votes.

Media Consultants. Experts who provide candidates with political advice on how to interact with news outlets and how to present their ideas, speeches, and messages.

Midterm Elections. The congressional elections midway between presidential elections. In the nineteenth century, these mostly came in even years in the North and odd years in the South. Today they are in nonpresidential-election, even-numbered years nationwide.

Minority President. A president who fails to win a majority of the popular vote. George W. Bush and Bill Clinton were both minority presidents.

Mudslinging. Nasty commentary by one candidate against an opponent. Jefferson was probably the first recipient in 1800 when he was attacked by Federalists as an "atheist" and associated with the radical faction of the French Revolution called the Jacobins. Recently people have called this American tradition "negative campaigning."

Mugwumps. The derisive name for the civil service reformers in the 1880s who broke with the Republican Party. Supposedly this was an American Indian term applied to those who had their "mug" on one side of the fence and their "wump" on the other. They were also called "Goo-Goos" since they favored what they called "good government."

National Convention. In the 1830s these meetings replaced the congressional caucus as the way in which presidential and vice presidential candidates were chosen. The first was that of the Anti-Masons in 1831, but there was a secret meeting of Federalists in 1812 that some historians would argue was actually the first.

Nativism. Anti-immigrant sentiment; the idea that native-born Americans should be privileged in the political system.

Old Republicans. The faction of the Democratic-Republican Party—mostly from Virginia and North Carolina—who thought they were more pure in their advocacy of states' rights and strict construction of the Constitution than Thomas Jefferson or James Madison. The most famous was the eccentric John Randolph. Some were called "Quids" in 1808 when they supported James Monroe against Madison.

PAC (Political Action Committee). Group set up by candidates to raise election funds.

Party Identification. A social-psychological term for an emotional commitment to one party or the other. It was described in the classic study of American voting behavior, *The American Voter* (1960) by Angus Campbell, Philip E. Converse, Warren E. Miller, and Donald E. Stokes.

Party Machine. What opponents call the party organization. "Machines" are political organizations usually run by "bosses."

Party Systems. Political scientists following V.O. Key have defined American political development in terms of a series of "party systems" of two competitive parties. During the dominance of a party system, the patterns of voting remain relatively stable. The first party system refers to the period between 1789 and the early 1820s, dominated by the Federalist and Democratic-Republican parties. The second party system refers to the period from the 1820s to the early 1850s, dominated by the Whig and Democratic parties. The third party system refers to the period from the 1850s to 1896, when the Democrats and Republicans were largely balanced in power. The fourth party system refers to the period from 1896 to 1932 and the hegemony of the Republican Party. The fifth party system refers to the period from 1932 to 1980 and the dominance of liberalism. And the sixth party system refers to the rising conservatism of the period since 1980.

Plank. Specific policy advocated by a candidate or party. The various planks together comprise a platform.

Platform. Formal, written description of a party's positions on political issues. Parties began issuing platforms—made up of "planks"—in 1840.

Plurality. The largest number of votes received in an election in which no one wins a majority.

Political Action Committee. *See* PAC.

Pollsters. People who sample public opinion during an election season to track candidates' standings. The worst example of polling in American presidential history was in 1936 when a telephone poll indicated that Alf Landon might defeat Franklin Roosevelt. Modern polls are more accurate than their critics acknowledge.

Poll Tax. A tax on voters that was used in the South to disfranchise both blacks and poor whites. There were similar taxes in some northern states. These taxes were outlawed for presidential and congressional elections by the Twenty-fourth Amendment.

Popular Vote. Votes cast by people in an election.

Populist. The term came from the People's Party in the late nineteenth century, but it has been used in the twentieth and twenty-first centuries to refer to anyone who appeals to the common people.

Presidential Elector. A person chosen in a state to vote for the president and vice president as a member of the Electoral College. Each political party chooses its slate, although their names are not on the ballot and are largely unknown.

Primary Elections. Popular statewide elections to choose delegates for presidential (or other) candidates. Delegates attend national nominating conventions to select a nominee. Held in the winter and spring of a presidential election year, primary elections help to gauge the support and popularity of various candidates. Since the 1960s, primaries have determined the candidates for the major parties.

Realigning Election. A part of the V.O. Key paradigm that describes an election in which the coalitional structure of the voters changes in a major way. The classic realigning election was in 1896, when Republicans became the dominant national party. *See also* Critical Election; Deviating Election; Maintaining Election.

Republicanism. The ideology of the American Revolution, which emphasized representative popular government. Subsequently it served to provide phrases and metaphors for most American political rhetoric through the nineteenth century.

Retrospective Voting. A concept developed by political scientist Morris Fiornia to describe the voters' tendency to weigh the candidates' and parties' records in their voting decision more heavily than their proposed programs.

Richmond Junto. The central committee of the Democratic-Republican Party based in Richmond, Virginia, in the early 1800s. In many ways comparable to the New York–based Albany Regency, the Richmond Junto was centered in a state capital, based on kin relationships, and reflected a preparty era of politics. The young Thomas Ritchie edited its newspaper, the *Richmond Enquirer,* which Thomas Jefferson regarded as the only newspaper that anyone needed to read.

Running Mate. In presidential elections, the vice president. Before there were organized parties and the Twelfth Amendment, this term had little meaning. Presidential candidates and party leaders have generally chosen the president's running mate, usually not until the national convention. Traditionally, running mates were selected to "balance the ticket" sectionally.

Scalawags. Southern-born whites who became Republicans in the Reconstruction Era. They were a mixed group, mostly comprised of former Whigs, who were either from the back country or the urban business class and had passively opposed the Civil War. They had an uneasy relationship with their new black and northern-born white allies.

Sectionalism. Strong devotion to a specific geographic region of the country, such as the South or the West. Sectionalism based on conflict over slavery and other issues led to the Civil War.

Solid South. Voting pattern in the South from the late 1800s to the 1960s when former Confederate states tended to vote solidly Democratic. Since the 1960s, this pattern has changed, and these states are now dominated by Republicans. No other section of the country has ever been so clearly or uniformly unified.

Suffrage. The ability to legally vote. Early in the nineteenth century, reformers pushed for universal manhood suffrage. From the 1840s until 1920, women fought for the right to vote in presidential elections. The Fifteenth Amendment, ratified in 1870 and intended to grant African-American men the right to vote, was subverted in the 1880s and not made effective until the Voting Rights Act of 1965.

Tammany Hall. The political club that long dominated Democratic politics in New York City. It dates back to the days of Aaron Burr and is often associated with the legendary Boss Tweed in the 1860s.

Third Parties. Minor political parties. Since the United States has nearly always had a two-party system because of its voting laws, third parties are the "others," even though there are sometimes more than three. The most significant third parties have been the Free Soilers in 1848, the Populists in 1892, the Progressives in 1912 and 1924, and the Dixiecrats in 1948.

Three-Fifths Clause. The compromise in the Constitution that provided that congressional representation would be based on both the white population and three-fifths of the slave population. This clause gave southern states an advantage because it affected the number of electoral votes a state had.

Ticket. In presidential elections, each party's candidates for president and vice president. But more generally the term refers to each party's entire slate of candidates running for office in an election. The term comes from the lists of candidates that used to be published in newspapers and distributed by each party on small pieces of paper that resembled railroad or theater tickets.

Turnout. The proportion of the eligible voters who actually vote. The United States has one of the lowest turnouts of any democracy.

Two-Thirds Rule. This rule derived from the first Democratic convention in 1832, which decided that a candidate must receive two-thirds of the delegates' votes to be nominated. This rule remained in effect for a century and gave the South enormous power in the Democratic Party.

Unit Rule. The idea that in national conventions, the majority within a state delegation could cast all of the state's votes for their candidate. It is related to the winner-take-all format of the voting in the Electoral College.

Virginia Dynasty. The series of five presidents, from George Washington through James Monroe (1789–1825), who mainly came from Virginia. Only John Adams of Massachusetts, president from 1797 to 1801, interrupted the Virginia Dynasty.

Waving the Bloody Shirt. The term comes from the Reconstruction period, when Representative Benjamin F. Butler (R-MA) held up in Congress the bloody shirt of a Republican whipped by the Ku Klux Klan. It came to mean an emotional appeal by Republicans to attack Democrats for their prior support of secession and their disloyalty during the Civil War.

White Primary. Part of the Jim Crow system of segregation that circumvented the Fifteenth Amendment—which guaranteed black suffrage—by prohibiting blacks from voting in primary elections, which were the most important elections in the South.

Write-in Ballot. Voters are able to literally write in with a pencil the name of a candidate who is not on the official list they are presented with.

Chronology of Political Parties

1787–89 Federalists are the supporters and defenders of the Constitution. Those associated with the Washington and Adams administrations in the 1790s continue to use the name "Federalist." After 1801, the Federalists will never again control the national government, although they will contest presidential elections through 1816, and they will exist in state politics into the 1820s.

Anti-Federalists are those who oppose ratification of the new Constitution. They never officially become a party contesting either the presidency or Congress, although a number are members of the first Congress, and George Clinton later will become vice president, and James Monroe will become president.

1796 The Democratic-Republican Party emerges during Washington's administration and puts forth Jefferson for president in 1796. Referred to as the Republican Party and the Jeffersonian-Republicans, the Democratic-Republicans succeed in capturing the presidency and Congress in the elections of 1800–1801.

1828 The Democratic-Republican Party splits into the followers of Jackson, who maintain the Democratic-Republican label, and the supporters of John Quincy Adams, who are called National Republicans.

1832 After holding the first national nominating convention in 1831, the Anti-Masonic Party becomes the first American "third party" to contest the presidency.

1836 The National Republicans and other groups, such as the Anti-Masons, become known as the Whig Party in 1834 and contest the presidency from 1836 to 1852.

1840 By 1840 the Democratic-Republicans are generally called the Democratic Party and will continue under that name to the present. The Liberty Party, established in 1839 as an antislavery party, runs presidential candidates in 1840 and 1844. In 1840, the two major parties call themselves "The American Democracy" and "The Democratic Whigs." Throughout the antebellum era, the Democrats are often referred to as "The Democracy."

1848 The Free Soil Party is organized to oppose expansion of slavery in the territories. In 1852, it takes on the name "Free Democratic Party."

1852 The Whig Party runs its last presidential candidate.

1854 Whigs, Free Soilers, and antislavery Democrats organize the Republican Party, which will continue to contest elections under that name to the present.

1856 The Republican Party runs its first presidential candidate. The nativist American Party, called the Know-Nothings, contests the election of 1856 against the Democrats and the new Republican Party, which opposes the extension of slavery. Most Know-Nothings will eventually be absorbed into the Republican Party.

1860 The Democratic Party essentially splits into two groups: a northern faction that supports Stephen Douglas for president and a southern faction that supports Vice President John C. Breckenridge. A fourth candidate, John

Bell, is nominated by the Constitutional Union Party. Abraham Lincoln becomes the first Republican elected president.

1864   To promote national unity, the Republican Party calls itself the National Union Party.

1872   A Republican faction called the Liberal Republican Party fuses with the Democrats to contest the presidential election.

1876   Two small third parties, the Greenback Party and the Prohibition Party, appear in the presidential election. The National Greenback–Labor Party will run candidates in 1880 and 1884. Prohibition Party candidates will run in every election until the present.

1892   The People's Party, also known as the Populists, which had begun earlier in the states, gains 22 electoral votes and more than 1 million popular votes for president. In 1896 the party splits, and the majority fuse with the Democrats. The party continues to run candidates in 1900, 1904, and 1908. The Socialist Labor Party makes its first showing. The party never gains more than a token vote but continues to run candidates in presidential elections until the 1980s.

1900   The Social Democratic Party runs Eugene V. Debs for president.

1904   The renamed Socialist Party runs Eugene V. Debs again for president. The Socialist Party reaches the height of its popularity in 1912 but will continue to run candidates throughout the twentieth century.

1912   The Progressive Party appears as a major third party supporting Theodore Roosevelt for president. In this election, it is also called the "Bull Moose" Party.

1924   The Progressive Party runs Robert La Follette, who receives 13 electoral votes and nearly 5 million popular votes. The Communist Party makes its first appearance and will continue to run candidates for president throughout the twentieth century, although for a time it will be outlawed.

1936   Union Party candidate William Lemke receives nearly 900,000 votes as the nominee of a protest party.

1948   The States' Rights Party, or Dixiecrats, splits off from the Democratic Party, and its candidate, Strom Thurmond, receives more than 1 million votes. The Progressive Party represents a coalition of liberal Democrats and Communists. Its candidate, former vice president Henry Wallace, also receives more than 1 million votes. They will be much less successful in 1952.

1952   The tiny Socialist Workers Party puts forth its first presidential candidate and will continue to run candidates throughout the twentieth century.

1968   The American Independent Party nominates George Wallace, who receives 46 electoral votes and nearly 10 million popular votes. Two tickets run under the name Peace and Freedom Party.

1972   The conservative American Party, whose candidate is John G. Schmitz, receives more than 1 million popular votes. The party again runs a candidate in 1976, with less success.

1976   The Libertarian Party runs its first candidate. Subsequently it will enter candidates in every presidential election.

1980   The Independent, or National Unity, Party supports a ticket of Republican John B. Anderson and Democrat Patrick Lucey. They receive nearly 6 million votes. The Citizens Party represents left-wing Democrats and runs Barry Commoner for president.

1992   The Independent Party supports Ross Perot, who receives 18.9 percent of the popular vote—nearly 20 million votes. He will do less well in 1996 when he runs as the candidate of the Reform Party. The Independent Party will run Pat Buchanan in 2000.

1996   The Green Party runs Ralph Nader, but receives less than 1 percent of the popular vote.

2000   Nader runs again as the Green Party candidate and receives nearly 3 million popular votes. Buchanan runs as the Reform Party candidate.

Chronology of Events

1787

MAY 25	Opening of the Constitutional Convention.
SEPTEMBER 17	Final approval of the Constitution.
SEPTEMBER 28	Congress sends Constitution to the states for ratification.
DECEMBER 7	Delaware ratifies.
DECEMBER 12	Pennsylvania ratifies.
DECEMBER 18	New Jersey ratifies.

1788

JANUARY 2	Georgia ratifies.
JANUARY 9	Connecticut ratifies.
FEBRUARY 7	Massachusetts ratifies, with nine recommended amendments.
MARCH 24	Rhode Island referendum rejects the Constitution.
APRIL 28	Maryland ratifies.
MAY 23	South Carolina ratifies.
JUNE 21	New Hampshire ratifies, the ninth state.
JUNE 25	Virginia ratifies, with twenty recommended amendments and other changes.
JULY 2	President of Congress announces that nine states have ratified, and chooses committee to prepare the change of government.
JULY 26	New York ratifies.
AUGUST 2	North Carolina withholds ratification without certain amendments.
SEPTEMBER 13	Congress adopts ordinance to make New York the site of the new government and sets dates for the appointment of electors, their balloting, and the meeting of the first Congress.
DECEMBER 7	First popular election for presidential electors in Pennsylvania.
DECEMBER 15	Popular election for presidential electors in New Hampshire.
DECEMBER 18	Popular election for electors in Massachusetts.

1789

JANUARY 5	Popular election for electors in Maryland.
JANUARY 7	Popular elections for electors in Delaware and Virginia.
JANUARY 7	Date set by Congress for states to choose electors.
FEBRUARY 4	Presidential electors cast their ballots.
MARCH 4	First Congress meets with a quorum.
APRIL 1	House of Representatives organized.
APRIL 6	Senate organized and ballots of the electors counted.
APRIL 21	John Adams sworn in as president of the Senate.
APRIL 30	George Washington inaugurated president.
JUNE 2	Adams takes oath of office as vice president.

1792

FEBRUARY 19	Washington notifies James Madison of intention to retire.
MAY 5	Washington seeks advice on publicizing his retirement from Madison, who remonstrates against the decision.
MAY 9	Madison advises Washington to issue a farewell address.
MAY 20	Washington asks Madison to draft a farewell address.
JUNE 20	Madison drafts a farewell address.
AUGUST 23–26	Washington appeals to Thomas Jefferson and Alexander Hamilton to settle their differences.
SEPTEMBER	Washington decides to serve a second term.
OCTOBER 16	Democratic-Republican Party caucus nominates Aaron Burr for vice president.
DECEMBER 5	Electors cast votes, electing Washington president and Adams vice president.

1793

MARCH 4	George Washington inaugurated for second term.
APRIL 8	Edmond Genêt, first minister of French Republic to the United States, arrives in Charleston.
APRIL 11	The first Democratic-Republican society, the German Republican Society, is formed in Philadelphia.

1794

OCTOBER	Army led by President Washington and former treasury secretary Hamilton puts down the Whisky Rebellion in western Pennsylvania.
NOVEMBER 19	Jay Treaty signed; Washington blames Whisky Rebellion on Democratic-Republican societies.

1795

JUNE 24	U.S. Senate approves Jay Treaty.
AUGUST 14	President Washington signs Jay Treaty.
AUGUST 23	John Beckley's "Calm Observer" attacks on Washington begin running in the Philadelphia *Aurora*.
OCTOBER 27	Treaty of San Lorenzo (Pinckney's Treaty) signed.

1796

FEBRUARY 26	James Madison informs James Monroe that Democratic-Republicans intend to "push" Thomas Jefferson for president.
FEBRUARY 29	Washington declares Jay Treaty ratified, sends it to House of Representatives.
MARCH	Federalist victory in New York legislative elections guarantees that state's electoral votes will not go to Jefferson.
MAY 3	House passes appropriations for Jay Treaty after long battle.
MAY 18	Around this date, caucus of Democratic-Republican congressmen meets to consider Aaron Burr as candidate for vice president.
SEPTEMBER 17	Washington announces retirement, issues "Farewell Address."
NOVEMBER 2	French minister Pierre Adet publishes announcement of the suspension of diplomatic relations with the United States and other hostile measures, in effort to influence Pennsylvania election.
NOVEMBER 6	Pennsylvania chooses electors by popular vote, all but one of which eventually go to Jefferson.
DECEMBER 5	Electors meeting in their respective states give John Adams 71 votes, Thomas Jefferson 68.

1797

MARCH 4	John Adams inaugurated president.

1799

OCTOBER	Pennsylvania state legislative elections return a Federalist state senate and a Democratic-Republican state assembly.

1800

APRIL 29–MAY 1	New York legislative election won by Democratic-Republicans.
MAY 5–10	James McHenry and Timothy Pickering, arch-Federalist secretaries of war and state, asked to resign by President Adams.
MAY 11	Federalists meet in congressional caucus to nominate John Adams for president and Charles Cotesworth Pinckney for vice president; Democratic-Republicans meet in congressional caucus to nominate Thomas Jefferson for president and Aaron Burr for vice president.
OCTOBER	"Letter from Alexander Hamilton, Concerning the Public Conduct and Character of John Adams, Esq., President of the United States" published in Democratic-Republican newspapers.
NOVEMBER 29	Pennsylvania state senate and state assembly agree to compromise electoral vote of 8 for Jefferson and Burr, 7 for Adams and Pinckney.
DECEMBER 2	South Carolina legislature votes to select electors.

1801

FEBRUARY 11	U.S. House of Representatives meets to count electoral votes officially.
FEBRUARY 14	Thomas Jefferson encounters President John Adams on a street in Washington, D.C.
FEBRUARY 17	House of Representatives elects Thomas Jefferson as president of the United States on 36th ballot.
MARCH 4	Thomas Jefferson inaugurated president.

1803

SEPTEMBER 5	Democratic-Republican newspaper *Wilmington Gazette* proclaims that "elective democracy" is a "good form of government responsive to the people."

1804

FEBRUARY 25	Democratic-Republicans, in congressional caucus, nominate Thomas Jefferson and George Clinton as presidential and vice presidential candidates for 1804.
MARCH	Boston *Columbian Centinel* endorses Charles Cotesworth Pinckney of South Carolina and Rufus King of New York as Federalist candidates for president and vice president. No Federalist nominating caucus is held in 1804.
APRIL 25	Incumbent vice president Aaron Burr is defeated in New York gubernatorial election.
JULY 11	Aaron Burr kills Alexander Hamilton in a duel.
SEPTEMBER 25	Twelfth Amendment to the Constitution is officially ratified, changing the method of electing president and vice president.
DECEMBER 3	Electors meet in state capitals to vote for both president and vice president.

1805

MARCH 4	Thomas Jefferson inaugurated for second term.

1806

DECEMBER 31	Monroe-Pinkney Treaty signed.

1807

JUNE 22	*Chesapeake-Leopard* incident occurs.
DECEMBER 22	Embargo enacted.

1808

JANUARY 21	Rival caucuses endorse Madison and Monroe in Richmond.
JANUARY 23	Republican congressional caucus nominates Madison and George Clinton.
AUGUST 8	Madisonians distribute "Address to Citizens."
AUGUST	Federalists representing eight states meet in New York City and nominate Charles Cotesworth Pinckney and Rufus King.
OCTOBER	Federalists in Virginia shift support from Pinckney to Monroe.
DECEMBER 7	Electors meet in state capitals to cast their ballots.

1809

FEBRUARY 8	Congress canvasses the Electoral College returns.
MARCH 3	Embargo repealed.
MARCH 4	James Madison inaugurated president.

1812

APRIL 20	Vice President George Clinton dies in office.
MAY 18	James Madison renominated by Republican caucus. Elbridge Gerry nominated for vice president.
MAY 29	Antiwar New York Republicans nominate DeWitt Clinton for President.
JUNE 18	War declared on Great Britain following separate votes by the House of Representatives (79–49) and Senate (19–13).
AUGUST 16	General William Hull surrenders Detroit to British forces.

AUGUST 17	New York Committee of Correspondence for DeWitt Clinton publishes "An Address to the People of the United States," representing the Fusion platform.
AUGUST 26	Pennsylvania delegates nominate Jared Ingersoll, a Federalist, for vice president on the fusion ticket with DeWitt Clinton.
SEPTEMBER 15	Federalist delegates from eleven states meet in New York for party convention and agree to support DeWitt Clinton.
SEPTEMBER 21	Virginia Federalists meet and nominate Rufus King for president.
OCTOBER 30	Balloting begins for presidential electors with Pennsylvania the first state to open the process. Other states follow over the next several weeks.
DECEMBER 3	Electoral College votes counted with Madison winning 128 to Clinton's 89.

1813

MARCH 4	James Madison inaugurated for second term.

1814

AUGUST 24	Battle of Bladensburg waged.
AUGUST 24–25	Washington, D.C., captured and burned by British.
AUGUST–NOVEMBER	State and congressional elections held in ten states.
SEPTEMBER 11	British defeated on Lake Champlain.
SEPTEMBER 12–14	British attack Baltimore unsuccessfully.
DECEMBER 5	Hartford Convention opens.

1815

JANUARY 5	Hartford Convention adjourns.
JANUARY 8	Jackson wins victory at New Orleans.
APRIL–NOVEMBER	State and congressional elections held in every state except South Carolina.
DECEMBER 5	President Madison delivers seventh Annual Address to Congress.

1816

FEBRUARY 14	New York Democratic-Republicans hold caucus.
FEBRUARY 18	Virginia Democratic-Republican hold caucus.
MARCH 16	Democratic-Republican congressional caucus nominates James Monroe.
MARCH 19	Compensation Act enacted.
APRIL 10	Second Bank of the United States is chartered.
APRIL 27	Tariff of 1816 passed.
DECEMBER 4	Monroe elected president.

1817

FEBRUARY 12	Debate held on Indiana's electoral votes.
MARCH 4	James Monroe inaugurated as U.S. president in first outdoor ceremony.

1820

FEBRUARY 17   Virginia Democratic-Republican caucus meets and chooses presidential electors favorable to Monroe.

MARCH 2   Monroe signs the Missouri Enabling Act, which includes the Thomas amendment restricting slavery above latitude 36°30'.

APRIL 8   Congressional caucus meets and decides that it is inappropriate to make any nominations.

NOVEMBER   Electors favoring Monroe win in Pennsylvania, which has the only popular election in which there is an opposing ticket.

NOVEMBER   New York legislature chooses a slate of electors committed to Monroe and Daniel D. Tompkins.

DECEMBER 6   Electors meet in their states and all cast their votes for Monroe, except for William Plumer of New Hampshire, who votes for John Quincy Adams.

1821

FEBRUARY 14   Congress meets to count the electoral votes; after a debate over counting the votes of Missouri, which has not yet entered the Union, Monroe is declared the winner by either 231 or 228 votes.

MARCH 5   James Monroe inaugurated for second term.

1822

JULY 20   Andrew Jackson nominated by the Tennessee legislature.

NOVEMBER 7   Henry Clay nominated by the Missouri legislature.

1823

JANUARY 19   John Quincy Adams nominated by the Maine legislature.

SEPTEMBER   William H. Crawford suffers cerebral stroke.

NOVEMBER 29   John C. Calhoun nominated by the South Carolina legislature.

1824

JANUARY 8   John Quincy Adams and wife hold reception honoring Andrew Jackson.

FEBRUARY 14   Congressional caucus nominates William H. Crawford, but few attend.

MARCH 4   John C. Calhoun withdraws as a presidential candidate, but will accept the vice presidency.

DECEMBER 6   Electoral votes counted; no candidate has a majority.

1825

JANUARY 8   Henry Clay pledges support for John Quincy Adams.

FEBRUARY 9   House of Representatives elects John Quincy Adams president.

MARCH 4   John Quincy Adams inaugurated president.

OCTOBER   Tennessee Legislature nominates Andrew Jackson for president.

DECEMBER 6   President John Quincy Adams delivers his Annual Message.

1826

JUNE 4   Vice President Calhoun allies himself with Andrew Jackson.

SEPTEMBER 18   William Morgan disappears in upstate New York.

DECEMBER   Martin Van Buren allies himself with Andrew Jackson.

1827

MARCH 23   Charges of Andrew Jackson's "adultery" are first launched.

JULY-AUGUST   Protectionist convention meets at Harrisburg, Pennsylvania.

DECEMBER 4   Andrew Stevenson, a Jacksonian, elected Speaker of the House of Representatives.

1828

JANUARY   Charges of John Quincy Adams's procuring sex for Tsar Alexander I first launched.

MAY 13   "Tariff of Abominations" passed by Congress.

OCTOBER–
NOVEMBER   Presidential election results in Jackson victory.

DECEMBER 1   Electoral votes counted: Jackson 178, Adams 83.

DECEMBER 22   Rachel Jackson dies.

1829

MARCH 4   Andrew Jackson inaugurated president.

DECEMBER 8   President Jackson's first State of the Union Address questions the usefulness and constitutionality of the Bank of the United States.

1830

MARCH 31   Pennsylvania legislature nominates Jackson for a second term as president.

APRIL 13   Jackson and Calhoun clash at a Jefferson Day Dinner.

MAY 27   Maysville Road veto.

MAY 28   Jackson signs the Indian Removal Act.

1831

FEBRUARY 15   Newspaper war between President Jackson and Vice President Calhoun.

SEPTEMBER 26   Anti-Masons hold first nominating convention in Baltimore.

DECEMBER 12   National Republicans hold convention in Baltimore.

1832

MAY 21-22   Jacksonians hold convention in Baltimore.

JULY 10   Jackson vetoes the Recharter bill for the Bank of the United States.

NOVEMBER 24   State convention in South Carolina nullifies Tariff Acts of 1828 and 1832.

DECEMBER 5   Jackson elected president.

DECEMBER 10   President Jackson issues proclamation against South Carolina's efforts at "nullification."

DECEMBER 12   John C. Calhoun is elected to the U.S. Senate.

DECEMBER 28   Calhoun resigns as vice president to become a senator from South Carolina.

1833

FEBRUARY 12   Senator Henry Clay introduces "Compromise of 1833," which lowers tariff rates and also gives the president, through the "Force Bill," power to impose federal law upon a reluctant state.

FEBRUARY 20   Compromise of 1833 is passed.

MARCH 4   Andrew Jackson inaugurated for second term.

SEPTEMBER 10   President Jackson announces that the government will no longer use Bank of the United States for its deposits—and that he will remove them.

SEPTEMBER 23   President Jackson fires Secretary of the Treasury William J. Duane after he refuses to remove government deposits from the Bank of the United States.

1834

MARCH 28   Senate passes a resolution introduced by Henry Clay censuring President Jackson for removing the deposits and firing the secretary of the treasury without congressional approval.

APRIL 15   President Jackson protests to the Senate against his censure.

1835

JANUARY 1   Massachusetts legislature nominates Daniel Webster for president; Tennessee congressional delegation nominates Hugh Lawson White for president.

MAY 20   Democratic convention in Baltimore nominates Martin Van Buren for president and Col. Richard M. Johnson for vice president.

DECEMBER 16   Anti-Masons nominate General William H. Harrison for president and Francis Granger for vice president in Harrisburg, Pennsylvania.

1836

DECEMBER 7   Electoral College elects Van Buren president.

1837

FEBRUARY 8   U.S. Senate elects Richard M. Johnson as vice president.

MARCH 4   Martin Van Buren inaugurated president; Democrats control both chambers in Congress with 128–114 advantage in House and 35–17 majority in Senate.

MAY 10   New York banks suspend specie payments, marking beginning of the Panic of 1837.

SEPTEMBER 5   President Van Buren proposes Independent Treasury to special session of Congress.

1838

AUGUST 1   Hugh Lawson White announces that he will not be a presidential candidate in 1840, endorses Henry Clay's election.

1839

JUNE 12   Daniel Webster declines Massachusetts legislature's nomination for presidency.

DECEMBER 4-7   First Whig National Convention held in Harrisburg, Pennsylvania, nominates Harrison for president and John Tyler for vice president.

1840

APRIL 1   Meeting of the "Friends of Immediate Emancipation" in Albany, New York, nominates James G. Birney as candidate of Liberty Party.

MAY 4-5   Convention of "The Whig Young Men of the Several States" in Baltimore kicks off the "Log Cabin Campaign."

MAY 5–6	Democratic National Convention in Baltimore nominates Van Buren for reelection as president, but disagreement over Richard M. Johnson prevents nomination of a vice presidential candidate.
JULY 4	President Van Buren signs the Independent Treasury Act.
OCTOBER 30–NOVEMBER 23	Harrison defeats Van Buren by 234–60 vote in Electoral College, wins 53 percent–47 percent majority in popular vote; Whigs gain 142–100 majority in House and 29–22 majority in Senate.

1841

MARCH 4	William Henry Harrison inaugurated president.
APRIL 4	President Harrison dies; John Tyler becomes president.
AUGUST 16	President Tyler vetoes bill to establish a Bank of the United States.
SEPTEMBER 9	Tyler vetoes a second bill to create a central financial institution.
SEPTEMBER 11	Members of Tyler's cabinet, except Secretary of State Daniel Webster, resign in protest over bank bill vetoes.
SEPTEMBER 13	Whig members of Congress publish a manifesto renouncing Tyler's association with the Whig Party.

1842

| MAY 31 | Henry Clay resigns from U.S. Senate. |
| AUGUST 30 | Congress passes Tariff Act of 1842, reestablishing high taxes on foreign goods imported into the United States. |

1843

MAY 8	Daniel Webster resigns as U.S. secretary of state.
JULY 24	Abel P. Upshur becomes secretary of state.
AUGUST 30–31	Liberty Party convention in Buffalo nominates James G. Birney for president and Thomas Morris for vice president.
SEPTEMBER	Democrats begin holding conventions over next five months in eighteen states to declare support for presidential nomination of Martin Van Buren, leading John C. Calhoun and James Buchanan to withdraw as candidates.
OCTOBER 16	Upshur opens negotiations with Texas representative Isaac Van Zandt for an annexation treaty.

1844

FEBRUARY 28	Upshur killed in accident on USS *Princeton*.
MARCH 6	Calhoun appointed secretary of state.
APRIL 12	Calhoun announces that United States has signed a treaty providing for the annexation of Texas.
APRIL 18	Calhoun informs British minister Richard Pakenham that the administration considers Texas annexation necessary for the protection of slavery.
APRIL 27	Washington *National Intelligencer* publishes Clay's "Raleigh letter"; Washington *Globe* publishes Van Buren's "Hammet letter."
MAY 1	Whig National Convention in Baltimore nominates Clay for president and Theodore Frelinghuysen for vice president.
MAY 27–30	Democratic national convention in Baltimore nominates James K. Polk for president and George M. Dallas for vice president.
JUNE 8	Senate rejects the Texas treaty by 35–16 vote against ratification.
JUNE 9	Polk writes letter to John K. Kane explaining his position on the tariff issue.

JULY 1	Clay writes first "Alabama letter."
JULY 27	Clay writes second "Alabama letter."
AUGUST 20	Tyler announces his withdrawal from consideration for reelection.
SEPTEMBER 2	A Lexington, Kentucky, newspaper publishes Clay's letter declaring that he is not an abolitionist.
SEPTEMBER 23	Washington *National Intelligencer* publishes Clay's letter reiterating his initial position on Texas annexation.
NOVEMBER 1–8	Voting in the states gives Polk a narrow majority in popular votes, and he is elected president by a 170–105 margin over Clay in the Electoral College.

1845

MARCH 4	James K. Polk inaugurated president.

1846

APRIL 24–26	United States and Mexican troops clash along disputed border; Mexican War begins.
JUNE 11	Zachary Taylor nominated by Trenton, New Jersey, "people's convention."
AUGUST 8	Wilmot Proviso introduced to Congress.

1847

FEBRUARY 22–23	Battle of Buena Vista occurs.
DECEMBER 24	Cass authors "Nicholson letter."

1848

FEBRUARY 2	Treaty of Guadalupe Hidalgo ends Mexican War.
APRIL 22	Taylor authors his first "Allison letter."
MAY 22	Democratic National Convention convenes in Baltimore.
JUNE 7	Whig National Convention opens in Philadelphia.
AUGUST 9	Free Soil convention held in Buffalo.
NOVEMBER 7	Voters elect Taylor president.

1849

MARCH 4	Zachary Taylor inaugurated president.

1850

JULY 9	President Taylor dies.
JULY 10	Millard Fillmore sworn in as president.
SEPTEMBER 9	California admitted as a free state.
SEPTEMBER 18	Congress passes Fugitive Slave Act, Texas and New Mexico Act, and Utah Act.
SEPTEMBER 20	Congress abolishes slave trade in Washington, D.C.
DECEMBER 14	"Georgia Platform," adopted by state convention, declares state will abide by Compromise of 1850 "as a permanent adjustment of this sectional controversy."

1851

JANUARY   Resolution supporting Compromise of 1850 signed by forty-four members of House of Representatives.

APRIL   Fugitive Slave Act enforced in Boston for the first time.

1852

MARCH   *Uncle Tom's Cabin* published.

JUNE 1–4   Democratic Convention meets in Baltimore and nominates Franklin Pierce for president.

JUNE 16–21   Whig Convention meets in Baltimore and nominates Winfield Scott for president.

JUNE 29   Henry Clay dies.

AUGUST 11–12   Free Democratic Convention meets in Pittsburgh and nominates John P. Hale for president.

OCTOBER 24   Daniel Webster dies.

NOVEMBER 2   Election Day; Pierce elected president.

1853

JANUARY 6   Benjamin Pierce, son of president-elect, killed in railway accident.

MARCH 4   Franklin Pierce inaugurated president.

APRIL 18   Vice President William R. King dies.

1854

MARCH 3   Kansas-Nebraska Act passes in U.S. Senate.

MAY 22   Kansas-Nebraska Act passes in U.S. House of Representatives.

MAY 30   President Pierce signs Kansas-Nebraska Act, repealing Missouri Compromise of 1820 and permitting slavery in territories above the line of 36°30'.

JULY 6–13   New sectional party takes "Republican" name at a mass meeting in Jackson, Michigan. Republican organizations spread quickly through northern states.

1856

FEBRUARY 22   American ("Know-Nothing") Party meets in Philadelphia and nominates Millard Fillmore for president and Andrew J. Donelson for vice president. Its platform promotes both nativism and union.

MAY 20–21   Senator Charles Sumner delivers his "Crime Against Kansas" speech, denouncing "Slave Oligarchy" and the "rape" of Kansas.

MAY 21   Conflicts between antislavery and pro-slavery forces in Kansas Territory escalate as town of Lawrence is attacked by pro-slavery forces, with homes and businesses burned and one man killed.

MAY 22   U.S. Representative Preston Brooks assaults Senator Sumner at his desk, beating him senseless with a heavy cane, thereby provoking enormous reaction throughout the nation.

MAY 24–25   John Brown and six companions (four of them his sons), revengeful about attacks on Lawrence, murder five pro-slavery men at Pottawatomie Creek.

JUNE 2   Democrats meeting in Cincinnati nominate James Buchanan for president on 17th ballot. John C. Breckinridge named as Buchanan's running mate. Party platform affirms support for Kansas-Nebraska Act.

JUNE 17   Republicans meeting in Philadelphia nominate John Charles Frémont for president and William L. Dayton for vice president on an antislavery-expansion platform.

NOVEMBER 4   Election Day; Voters elect Buchanan president.

1857

MARCH 4   James Buchanan inaugurated president.

MARCH 6   *Dred Scott* decision announced.

JUNE   Hinton Rowan Helper's *The Impending Crisis of the South: How to Meet It* published.

AUGUST 24   Financial panic begins in New York City.

DECEMBER 21   Pro-slavery constitution approved by fraudulent vote in Kansas; George Fitzhugh's *Cannibals All! or, Slaves without Masters* published.

1858

FEBRUARY 2   Buchanan recommends Lecompton Constitution to Congress.

JUNE 16   Abraham Lincoln delivers "House Divided" speech to Illinois Republican Convention.

AUGUST 21–   Lincoln-Douglas debates held in Illinois U.S. Senate race.
OCTOBER 15

AUGUST 27   Douglas outlines "Freeport Doctrine" in debate with Lincoln.

AUGUST–   Congressional elections held: Republicans sweep northern states, gaining 18 seats in the House;
OCTOBER   opposition gains in border South.

OCTOBER 25   William Henry Seward delivers "Irrepressible Conflict" speech at Rochester, New York.

1859

FEBRUARY 24   Buchanan vetoes Land-Grant College Act.

MAY 9–19   Southern Commercial Convention calls for restoration of slave importations.

OCTOBER 16   John Brown leads raid at Harper's Ferry, Virginia.

DECEMBER 2   John Brown hanged in Charles Town, Virginia.

1860

FEBRUARY 1   William Pennington (R-NJ) elected Speaker of the House after a two-month sectional deadlock.

FEBRUARY 1   President Buchanan vetoes internal improvements bill.

FEBRUARY 2   Davis Resolutions in U.S. Senate demand a federal slave code for the territories.

FEBRUARY 27   Abraham Lincoln delivers speech at Cooper Union in New York City.

APRIL 23   Democratic National Convention begins in Charleston, South Carolina.

MAY 10   Constitutional Union Party nominates John Bell and Edward Everett in Baltimore.

MAY 16   Republican National Convention nominates Abraham Lincoln and Hannibal Hamlin in Chicago.

JUNE 11   Southern bolters reconvene in Richmond, Virginia.

JUNE 16   Covode House committee report on corruption published.

JUNE 18   Democratic National Convention reconvenes in Baltimore.

JUNE 22   Stephen A. Douglas and Herschel V. Johnson are nominated at the Democratic National Convention; Buchanan vetoes homestead bill.

JUNE 28   Southern Democrats nominate John C. Breckinridge and Joseph Lane in Baltimore.

SEPTEMBER 6   Breckinridge gives campaign speech at barbeque in Ashland, Kentucky.

SEPTEMBER–   Republicans win victories in Maine, Vermont, Indiana, Ohio, and Pennsylvania state elections.
OCTOBER

OCTOBER 19–   Douglas campaigns in the deep South.
NOVEMBER 6

NOVEMBER 6   Election Day; Lincoln elected president.

1861

MARCH 4   Abraham Lincoln inaugurated president.

1863

DECEMBER   Copies of *Miscegenation: The Theory of the Blending of the Races, Applied to the American White Man and Negro* mailed to abolitionist and antislavery leaders.

DECEMBER 9   President Lincoln's third Annual Message to Congress includes his Proclamation of Amnesty and Reconstruction.

1864

FEBRUARY 17   During the debate on the Freedman's Bureau Bill, Democratic representative Samuel "Sunset" Cox of Ohio delivers a tirade against "miscegenation" and its supporters.

FEBRUARY 22   Pomeroy Circular is printed in the *National Intelligencer*, embarrassing Secretary of the Treasury Salmon P. Chase.

MAY 5   Lieutenant General Ulysses S. Grant launches the spring military campaign. Simultaneously, Union armies in northern Georgina, on the James River peninsula, and in the Shenandoah Valley also undertake offensive operations.

MAY 5–6   Battle of the Wilderness takes place.

MAY 17   President Lincoln drafts order for the conscription of 300,000 additional soldiers.

MAY 18   Anticipating Lincoln's order, would-be stock-market manipulators Howard and Mallsion foist a forged proclamation on New York's two leading Democratic newspapers.

MAY 31   Group of radical German abolitionists meet at Cleveland and, calling themselves the Radical Democrats, nominate John Charles Frémont as their candidate for president.

JUNE 1–3   Battle of Cold Harbor takes place.

JUNE 7   Republicans, calling themselves the National Union Party, meet in convention in Baltimore, along with a number of "War" Democrats, and renominate Lincoln for president and Andrew Johnson, a Tennessee Democrat, as his running mate.

JUNE 15–18   Battle of Petersburg fought.

JUNE 28   Secretary of the Treasury Salmon P. Chase resigns.

JULY 4   Lincoln pocket-vetoes the Wade-Davis bill.

JULY 5   Lincoln suspends the right of *habeas corpus* and establishes martial law in Kentucky.

JULY 18   Lincoln issues a new call for 500,000 volunteers; the president also issues "To Whom It May Concern" memorandum stating his conditions for meeting with Confederate peace commissioners.

AUGUST 5   Wade-Davis Manifesto published in the *New York Tribune*.

AUGUST 28–31   Democrats meet in Chicago in convention and nominate General George B. McClellan and George Pendleton, of Ohio, as their candidates for president and vice president.

SEPTEMBER 1   Confederate General John Bell Hood and the Army of Tennessee retreat from Atlanta.

SEPTEMBER 3   General William T. Sherman reports to Lincoln that "Atlanta is ours, and fairly won."

OCTOBER 11   State and congressional elections held in the states of Pennsylvania, Ohio, and Indiana, resulting in Republican victories.

NOVEMBER 8   Election Day; Lincoln carries all but three states; his electoral majority is 212 to 21 over McClellan.

NOVEMBER 14–DECEMBER 22   Sherman pursues his March to the Sea.

1865

JANUARY 16–MARCH 23	Sherman moves up through the Carolinas.
MARCH 4	Abraham Lincoln inaugurated for second term.
APRIL 2	Petersburg and Richmond are abandoned by Confederates.
APRIL 9	Lee surrenders the Army of Northern Virginia to Grant at Appomattox.
APRIL 14	Lincoln is shot by assassin John Wilkes Booth.
APRIL 15	Lincoln dies; Andrew Johnson becomes president.
MAY 29	President Johnson issues proclamations outlining policies on readmission and amnesty.
DECEMBER 18	Thirteenth Amendment ratified.

1866

FEBRUARY 19	Johnson vetoes Freedmen's Bureau Bill (veto sustained).
MARCH 27	Johnson vetoes Civil Rights Act (veto overridden, April 9).
JUNE 13	Fourteenth Amendment passes Congress.
JULY 23	Tennessee readmitted to Union.
AUGUST 20–SEPTEMBER 15	Johnson conducts "Swing Around the Circle" tour.

1867

MARCH 2	Reconstruction Act and Tenure of Office Act enacted over Johnson's vetoes.

1868

FEBRUARY 24	House of Representatives impeaches President Andrew Johnson.
MAY 16	Senate votes 35–19 to convict President Johnson on one charge, short of a two-thirds majority.
MAY 20–21	Republicans, meeting in Chicago, nominate Ulysses S. Grant and Schuyler Colfax.
MAY 26	Senate twice votes 35–19 to convict Johnson on two charges, short of a two-thirds majority; impeachment trial ends.
JUNE 22	Arkansas readmitted to Union.
JUNE 25	Alabama, Florida, Georgia, Louisiana, North Carolina, and South Carolina readmitted to Union.
JULY 4-9	Democrats, meeting in New York, nominate Horatio Seymour and Francis P. Blair.
JULY 20	Fourteenth Amendment ratified.
NOVEMBER 3	Election Day: Grant elected president.

1869

MARCH 4	Ulysses S. Grant inaugurated president.

1870

JANUARY 26	Virginia readmitted to Union.
FEBRUARY 8	*Hepburn* v. *Griswold* rules the Legal Tender Act of 1862 unconstitutional.
FEBRUARY 23	Mississippi readmitted to Union.
MARCH 30	Fifteenth Amendment ratified; Texas readmitted to Union.
MAY 31	Enforcement Act passed.

| JUNE 30 | Treaty to annex the Dominican Republic fails to win Senate ratification. |
| JULY 15 | Georgia readmitted to Union. |

1871

MARCH 3	Civil Service Commission established.
APRIL 20	Ku Klux Klan Act passes Congress.
MAY 1	In *Legal Tender Cases*, U.S. Supreme Court upholds constitutionality of Legal Tender Act of 1862.
MAY 8	Treaty of Washington signed.
DECEMBER 28	William M. Tweed steps down as president of Board of Supervisors in New York City; overthrow of "Tweed Ring."

1872

JANUARY 24	Meeting in Jefferson City, Missouri, anti-Grant Republicans call for a convention to meet at Cincinnati on May 1.
MARCH 1	President Grant signs bill establishing Yellowstone National Park.
MAY 1–3	Liberal Republican convention at Cincinnati, Ohio, nominates newspaper editor Horace Greeley and Senator B. Gratz Brown.
MAY 22	Amnesty Act passed.
MAY 30	Tariff reduction bill passes Congress.
JUNE 5–6	Republican convention meets at Philadelphia and renominates Grant, with Senator Henry Wilson as his running mate.
JULY 9	Democrats meet in Baltimore and nominate Greeley.
AUGUST 1	Republicans win in North Carolina state elections.
SEPTEMBER 14	Geneva tribunal awards $15.5 million in *Alabama* claims.
OCTOBER 8	Republicans win in Pennsylvania, Ohio, and Indiana state elections.
NOVEMBER 5	Election Day; Grant is reelected.

1873

| MARCH 4 | Ulysses S. Grant inaugurated for second term. |
| SEPTEMBER 18 | Failure of investment banking firm Jay Cooke & Company triggers panic on Wall Street. |

1874

| NOVEMBER 3 | Democrats score major victories in the "Tidal Wave of 1874," gaining control of the U.S. House of Representatives for the first time since before the Civil War, picking up eight seats in the U.S. Senate, and winning key governorships in New York and Indiana. |

1875

| MAY 1 | *St. Louis Democrat* exposes the Whisky Ring. |
| SEPTEMBER 14 | President Grant declines to send U.S. troops to quell violence in Mississippi election. |

1876

| MARCH 2 | U.S. House of Representatives impeaches Secretary of War William W. Belknap for taking bribes. |

JUNE 5	Former Speaker of the House James G. Blaine defends himself on the floor against allegations of influence-peddling; but "Mulligan letters," suggesting his guilt, go into the public record, to bedevil his campaign thereafter.
JUNE 16	Republican National Convention nominates Governor Rutherford B. Hayes of Ohio for president and Representative William A. Wheeler of New York for vice president.
JUNE 28–29	Democratic National Convention nominates Governor Samuel J. Tilden of New York for president and Governor Thomas A. Hendricks of Indiana for vice president.
NOVEMBER 7	Election Day; Tilden and Hendricks win the popular vote nationally by almost 250,000, but are one electoral vote short of clinching the victory.

1877

JANUARY 29	President Grant signs into law the act to create the electoral commission.
MARCH 2	Hayes and Wheeler officially declared elected.
MARCH 5	Rutherford B. Hayes inaugurated president.

1879

| SEPTEMBER | General Ulysses S. Grant returns from two-year world tour; the third-term "boom" begins. |

1880

JUNE 8	Republican National Convention breaks deadlock and nominates Representative James A. Garfield for president and Chester Alan Arthur for vice president.
JUNE 11	Greenback convention in Chicago nominates General James Baird Weaver for president and B. J. Chambers for vice president.
JUNE 24	Democratic National Convention in Cincinnati nominates Winfield Scott Hancock for president and William H. English for vice president.
JULY 10	Garfield issues his letter of acceptance.
JULY 13	Democratic delegation formally notifies Hancock of his nomination.
JULY 29	General Hancock issues his letter of acceptance.
SEPTEMBER 13	Maine state elections give Democratic-Greenbacker fusion a stunning win over Republicans.
OCTOBER 13	Ohio and Indiana state elections go narrowly Republican, taking the heart out of the Democratic campaign.
OCTOBER 20	Democrats issue forged Morey letter purportedly showing Garfield's apparent willingness to flood U.S. factories with Chinese workers.
OCTOBER 23	Garfield's statement issued, declaring the Morey letter a forgery.
NOVEMBER 2	Election Day; Garfield is elected.

1881

MARCH 4	James A. Garfield inaugurated president; he brings in James G. Blaine as secretary of state, and opens bitter war with the New York Stalwarts.
JULY 2	President Garfield shot.
SEPTEMBER 19	Garfield dies, making Vice President Chester Alan Arthur, a Stalwart, president.
DECEMBER 12	Blaine resigns as secretary of state, and begins a three-year campaign to supplant Arthur in the presidential chair.

1882

NOVEMBER   Midterm elections bring in a Democratic House, give a severe setback to Stalwart machines in Pennsylvania and New York, and give Democrats a bright political star as Grover Cleveland is elected governor of New York.

1884

APRIL 18   Republican state convention in New York delivers a near-fatal blow to President Arthur's election chances by splitting its delegation.

MAY 29   The Greenback/People's Party convention in Indianapolis tenders its presidential nomination to Benjamin Butler.

JUNE 6   Republican National Convention in Chicago nominates James G. Blaine for president and John A. Logan for vice president.

JULY 10   Democratic National Convention in Chicago nominates Grover Cleveland for president and Thomas A. Hendricks for vice president.

JULY 21   Buffalo *Telegraph* reveals "A Terrible Tale," the Cleveland sex scandal.

JULY 23   Prohibition Party holds national convention in Pittsburgh and nominates former Kansas governor John P. St. John for president.

SEPTEMBER 4 Democrats publish a new installment of the notorious "Mulligan letters," proving Blaine's conflict of interest as House speaker.

SEPTEMBER 17 Blaine begins campaign tour of the Midwest—very nearly a political first, and the first successful such campaign swing in history.

OCTOBER 12   Ohio goes narrowly Republican, Indiana narrowly Democratic, in state elections.

OCTOBER 29   Rev. Samuel Burchard declares Democrats the party of "rum, Romanism, and rebellion," and Blaine attends controversial fund-raising banquet at Delmonico's restaurant.

NOVEMBER 4   Election Day; Cleveland is elected president—thanks to Burchard's remarks, the banquet, the "Solid South," and St. John's Prohibition voters having drawn off crucial Republican votes in upstate New York.

1885

MARCH 4   Grover Cleveland inaugurated president.

1886

MAY 4   Haymarket Affair.

OCTOBER 28   Dedication of Statue of Liberty.

1887

FEBRUARY 4   Interstate Commerce Act.

FEBRUARY 8   Dawes Severalty Act.

FEBRUARY 11 Dependent pension bill veto.

FEBRUARY 16 Texas seed bill veto.

JUNE 7   President Cleveland approves order for return of Confederate battle flags.

JUNE 16   Cleveland revokes order for return of Confederate battle flags.

DECEMBER 6   Cleveland delivers annual message devoted to the tariff issue.

1888

JUNE 6	President Cleveland renominated.
JUNE 25	Benjamin Harrison nominated.
JULY 21	House passes Mills tariff bill.
AUGUST 23	Cleveland delivers special message to Congress requesting retaliatory powers in Canadian fishing dispute.
SEPTEMBER 8	Cleveland's letter of acceptance.
SEPTEMBER 11	Harrison's letter of acceptance.
OCTOBER 31	Publication of Dudley "Blocks-of-Five" letter.
NOVEMBER 4	"Murchison letter" is published in the *New York Tribune*, leading to the rejection of British minister Sackville-West.
NOVEMBER 6	Election Day; Harrison is elected.

1889

MARCH 4	Benjamin Harrison inaugurated president.

1890

MAY–SEPTEMBER	Senate debates "McKinley Tariff."
JULY 2	House of Representatives passes elections bill enforcing voting rights in the South. Bill later fails in the Senate.
OCTOBER 1	President Harrison signs McKinley Tariff bill.
NOVEMBER 4	Democrats win control of House of Representatives.

1892

JUNE 4	James G. Blaine resigns as secretary of state.
JUNE 10	Republican convention renominates Harrison.
JUNE 22	Democratic convention nominates Grover Cleveland.
JULY 4	Populist convention, meeting in Omaha, nominates James B. Weaver.
JULY 6	Gun battle ensues between workers and Pinkerton guards at Carnegie Steel Works in Homestead, Pennsylvania.
SEPTEMBER 8	Cleveland meets with New York State party leaders.
NOVEMBER 8	Election Day; Cleveland elected president; William Jennings Bryan reelected to House of Representatives.

1893

MARCH 4	Grover Cleveland inaugurated president.
MARCH 20	Reading Railroad declares bankruptcy; financial panic begins.
MAY 4–JUNE 27	Stock market crashes; economic depression begins.
OCTOBER 30	Sherman Silver Purchase Act repealed.
NOVEMBER 7	McKinley reelected as governor of Ohio.

1894

MARCH 25	"Coxey's Army" begins march on Washington.
JUNE–JULY	Pullman strike cripples the railroads.
AUGUST 27	Wilson-Gorman Tariff becomes law without Cleveland's signature.

1895

JANUARY	McKinley and Hanna organize campaign for Republican presidential nomination.
FEBRUARY	Revolution breaks out in Cuba against Spanish rule.
JULY	Bryan starts traveling the country, speaking in favor of silver coinage.

1896

JUNE 16	Republican National Convention nominates McKinley.
JULY 11	Democratic National Convention nominates Bryan.
JULY 25	Populist National Convention also nominates Bryan.
SEPTEMBER 2	"Gold" Democrats National Convention nominates John M. Palmer.
NOVEMBER 3	Election Day; McKinley elected president.

1897

| MARCH 4 | William McKinley inaugurated president. |
| JULY 24 | Congress approves Dingley Tariff. |

1898

FEBRUARY 15	USS *Maine* explodes and sinks in Havana, Cuba.
MARCH 27	President McKinley seeks to achieve Cuban independence through diplomacy.
APRIL 11	McKinley asks Congress for authority to go to war.
APRIL 19	Congress declares war against Spain.
MAY 1	Battle of Manila Bay takes place in the Philippines.
JUNE 1	Erdman Act is enacted.
JUNE 10	U.S. troops land in Cuba.
JULY	Battles take place around Santiago, Cuba; Spanish fleet is destroyed.
JULY 7	U.S. annexes Hawaii.
DECEMBER 10	Treaty of Paris signed between the United States and Spain.

1900

MARCH 14	Gold Standard Act enacted.
JUNE 19	Republican convention nominates William McKinley and Theodore Roosevelt.
JULY 4	Democratic convention nominates William Jennings Bryan and Adlai Stevenson.
NOVEMBER 6	Election Day; McKinley wins reelection.

1901

MARCH 4	William McKinley inaugurated for second term.
SEPTEMBER 6	President McKinley shot.
SEPTEMBER 14	McKinley dies; Vice President Roosevelt becomes president.

1904

| FEBRUARY 15 | Republican national chairman Marrus Hanna dies of typhoid fever. |
| FEBRUARY 23 | Sixteen Democrats join Senate Republicans in ratifying Panama Canal treaty. |

MARCH 14	Supreme Court orders dissolution of Northern Securities Company.
APRIL 18	After divisive debate, New York Democrats endorse Alton Parker.
MAY 30	American warships arrive at Tangier to demand release of Ion Perdicaris.
JUNE 20	In speech at New York's Cooper Union, Bryan denounces Parker as candidate of "plutocracy."
JUNE 21–23	Republican convention in Chicago nominates Theodore Roosevelt and Charles Fairbanks.
JULY 9	Hours after his nomination, Parker's "gold standard" telegram creates turmoil at Democratic convention in St. Louis.
AUGUST 10	During his acceptance speech, Parker disheartens Democrats with his position on trusts.
SEPTEMBER 12	In his acceptance letter, Roosevelt dares Democrats to object to his policies.
OCTOBER	During a midwestern speaking tour, Bryan offers tepid support for Parker.
NOVEMBER 1–4	Parker accuses Republican national chairman Cortelyou of bribing and extorting contributions from big business.
NOVEMBER 8	Election Day; Roosevelt reelected by largest popular vote margin to date.

1905

MARCH 4	Theodore Roosevelt inaugurated president.

1906

AUGUST 31	Bryan, upon returning from world tour, calls for government ownership of railroads in a speech at Madison Square Garden.
DECEMBER 3	President Roosevelt nominates William H. Moody to Supreme Court seat earlier offered to Taft, thereby ensuring Taft's presidential run.

1907

JANUARY 26	In front of reporters at Gridiron Club dinner, President Roosevelt and Joseph Foraker quarrel over Brownsville affair.
SEPTEMBER 28	Taft arrives at Yokohama on second mission to Japan as secretary of war.
OCTOBER 21–22	Withdrawals by worried depositors in the Knickerbocker Trust Company sets off Panic of 1907.
DECEMBER 12	White House statement reaffirms Roosevelt's pledge not to run for reelection.
DECEMBER 16	Great White Fleet leaves on world cruise.

1908

JANUARY 31	President Roosevelt times contentious message on business and labor to draw attention away from Charles Evans Hughes speech outlining his own agenda.
JUNE 17	Henry Cabot Lodge rebukes delegates after 47-minute demonstration for Roosevelt at Republican convention in Chicago; William Howard Taft nominated the next day on first ballot.
JULY 8–10	Democrats, meeting in Denver, renominate William Jennings Bryan with a pro-labor platform.
AUGUST 30	Eugene V. Debs's campaign train, the Red Special, leaves Chicago.
SEPTEMBER 6	Bryan begins three-week eastern tour, launching two months of extensive campaigning.
SEPTEMBER 25	C. N. Haskell resigns as treasurer of Democratic National Committee, after Hearst papers document his dealings with Standard Oil.
OCTOBER 15	Democrats reveal that "popular subscription" fund raising had, to date, yielded only $248,567.55.
OCTOBER 28	Nearing the end of several surprisingly effective speaking tours, Taft defends his labor record at New York's Cooper Union.
NOVEMBER 3	Election Day; Bryan suffers the worst defeat of his three presidential runs, 162 electoral votes to Taft's 321.

1909

MARCH 4   William Howard Taft inaugurated president.

SEPTEMBER 17   In a speech at Winona, Minnesota, Taft defends new tariff as "best tariff" ever passed, angering reformers in his party.

1910

AUGUST 31   Theodore Roosevelt delivers "New Nationalism" speech at Oswatomie, Kansas.

NOVEMBER 8   Midterm congressional elections result in gains for Democrats and progressive-minded Republicans.

1911

OCTOBER 26   President Taft's attorney general begins anti-trust prosecution against United States Steel.

1912

FEBRUARY 2   Robert M. La Follette gives rambling, incoherent speech, leading to rumors of his "breakdown" and the effective end of his candidacy.

FEBRUARY 24   Roosevelt formally declares entry into race for Republican presidential nomination.

MARCH 16   America's first presidential primary held in North Dakota.

JUNE 18   Republican Party committee on credentials rules against Roosevelt.

JUNE 22   Roosevelt and followers "bolt" from Republican Party; Taft renominated as Republican candidate for president.

JULY 2   Woodrow Wilson nominated for presidency by Democratic Party.

AUGUST 6   Roosevelt accepts Progressive Party presidential nomination.

AUGUST 28   Louis Brandeis meets with Wilson at Sea Girt, New Jersey.

OCTOBER 14   A would-be assassin shoots and wounds Roosevelt in Milwaukee, Wisconsin.

NOVEMBER 5   Election Day; Wilson elected.

1913

MARCH 4   Woodrow Wilson inaugurated president.

APRIL 11   Racial segregation of federal employees begins.

1914

MARCH 19   Woman suffrage amendment fails to get two-thirds Senate vote.

APRIL 21   U.S. Navy occupies Vera Cruz, Mexico.

AUGUST 18   President Wilson officially proclaims neutrality toward European conflict.

1915

JANUARY 12   Woman suffrage defeated in first House vote on the issue since 1887.

MAY 7   128 Americans killed in German torpedoing of the *Lusitania*.

1916

JANUARY 28   President Wilson nominates Louis Brandeis to Supreme Court.

MARCH 15   General John J. Pershing is sent to Mexico with "Punitive Expedition."

MAY 16	Congress agrees to army build-up legislation.
JUNE 7	Republican and Progressive nominating conventions begin. Republicans nominate Charles Evans Hughes for president and Charles W. Fairbanks for vice president. Progressives nominate Theodore Roosevelt for president and John M. Parker for vice president.
JUNE 14	Democratic nominating convention begins.
AUGUST 8	Senate passes Keating-Owen child labor bill.
SEPTEMBER 3	Wilson signs Adamson Act.
OCTOBER 2	Republican women's campaign train departs from New York City.
NOVEMBER 7	Election Day; Wilson reelected.

1917

| MARCH 4 | Woodrow Wilson inaugurated for second term. |
| APRIL 6 | U.S. declares war on Germany, enters World War I. |

1918

| NOVEMBER 11 | World War I ends. |

1919

JANUARY 6	Theodore Roosevelt dies.
JANUARY 29	Eighteenth Amendment ratified, prohibiting transportation and sale of alcohol.
JUNE 2	Bomb partially destroys Attorney General A. Mitchell Palmer's home, fueling an anti-radical campaign.
SUMMER	"Red Summer" sees a series of violent race riots across the nation.
SEPTEMBER 2	Woodrow Wilson's health fails during western speaking tour.
DECEMBER	Warren G. Harding decides to run for Republican nomination.

1920

MAY 1	Attorney General A. Mitchell Palmer's anti-radical raids end.
JUNE 12	Republicans nominate Warren G. Harding for president on the 10th ballot, and Calvin Coolidge for vice president.
JULY 6	Democrats nominate James M. Cox for president on the 44th ballot, and Franklin D. Roosevelt for vice president.
AUGUST 26	Nineteenth Amendment ratified, granting women the right to vote.
NOVEMBER 2	Election Day: Harding wins; election results first broadcast, from radio station KDKA in Pittsburgh, Pennsylvania.

1921

| MARCH 4 | Warren G. Harding inaugurated president. |
| AUGUST | Ku Klux Klan begins new campaign. |

1922

| APRIL | First investigations begin of Teapot Dome oil leases. |

1923

AUGUST 2   Warren Harding dies, and Calvin Coolidge becomes president.

SEPTEMBER 15   Oklahoma placed under martial law because of KKK activity.

OCTOBER 25   U.S. Senate begins Teapot Dome investigation.

1924

APRIL 9   Dawes Plan to reorganize German war debts announced.

MAY 26   Immigration Restriction Act passed.

JUNE–JULY   Smith-McAdoo deadlock at Democratic Party convention.

JUNE 12   Republican National Convention nominates Calvin Coolidge for president.

JUNE 30   Teapot Dome indictments begin.

JULY 4   Conference for Progressive Political Action nominates Robert La Follette for president.

JULY 9   Democratic National Convention nominates John W. Davis for president.

NOVEMBER 4   Election Day; Coolidge reelected.

1925

MARCH 4   Calvin Coolidge inaugurated president.

1927

MAY   Smith's *Atlantic Monthly* article on politics and Catholicism.
                Hoover directs Mississippi flood relief.

AUGUST 2   President Coolidge chooses not to run for another term.

1928

JUNE 14   Herbert Hoover nominated by Republican convention.

JUNE 28   Al Smith nominated by Democratic convention.

JUNE 29   Smith telegram calls for revising platform plank on Prohibition.

AUGUST 11   Hoover gives acceptance speech at Stanford University, on national radio.

AUGUST 21   Hoover recalls small town boyhood in West Branch, Iowa, speech.

SEPTEMBER 7   Willebrandt urges Methodists to defend Prohibition and oppose Smith.

SEPTEMBER 20   Smith responds to "bigotry" in Oklahoma City address.

OCTOBER 22   Hoover calls Smith's policies "state socialism."

OCTOBER 25   Smith's eastern tour climaxes in Boston.

NOVEMBER 6   Election Day; Hoover elected.

1929

MARCH 4   Herbert Hoover inaugurated president.

1930

NOVEMBER 4   Franklin D. Roosevelt elected to second term as New York governor; Democrats win big gains in congressional elections.

DECEMBER   Unemployment exceeds level of 1921 recession; drought hits agricultural regions.

1931

FALL   Demands mount for federal relief and public works programs.

1932

JANUARY 23   Franklin D. Roosevelt announces candidacy for U.S. president.

JUNE 16   Republican convention renominates President Hoover.

JUNE 27   Democratic convention opens in Chicago.

JULY 2   Democrats nominate Roosevelt, who accepts in person.

JULY 29   Federal troops clear "bonus marchers" from metropolitan Washington, D.C.

AUGUST 11   Hoover accepts Republican nomination.

SEPTEMBER 9   Roosevelt pledges to reduce federal spending.

SEPTEMBER 23   Roosevelt advances liberal agenda in San Francisco.

OCTOBER 31   In New York City, Hoover attacks Roosevelt's "economic radicalism."

NOVEMBER 8   Election Day; Roosevelt elected in a landslide.

DECEMBER 22   Reconstruction Finance Corporation created.

1933

MARCH 4   Franklin D. Roosevelt (FDR) inaugurated president.

MAY 18   Roosevelt signs bill creating Tennessee Valley Authority.

1934

JANUARY 1   Townsend founds Old Age Revolving Pensions organization.

AUGUST 22   Liberty League announced to the press.

1935

FEBRUARY 23   Huey Long delivers "Every Man a King" address.

MAY 6   President Roosevelt creates Works Progress Administration by executive order.

JULY 5   Roosevelt signs Wagner National Labor Relations Act.

AUGUST 14   Roosevelt signs Social Security Act.

SEPTEMBER 10   Senator Long shot on steps of Louisiana capitol.

1936

APRIL 4   Labor's Non-Partisan League announced.

JUNE 9   Republican convention begins in Cleveland, nominates Alf Landon for president.

JUNE 19   Father Charles Coughlin calls for Union Party.

JUNE 23   Democratic convention begins in Philadelphia.

JULY   Norman Thomas calls on workers to support Socialist Party.

OCTOBER 9   Landon criticizes Roosevelt for breaking 1932 promises.

OCTOBER 14   Roosevelt notes successes of New Deal.

OCTOBER 29   Landon charges FDR with plan to "pack" U.S. Supreme Court.

OCTOBER 31   Roosevelt highlights benefits of New Deal measures.

NOVEMBER 3   Election Day; landslide elects Roosevelt and endorses the New Deal.

1937

JANUARY 20   Franklin D. Roosevelt inaugurated for second term.

1939

SEPTEMBER 1   Germany invades Poland.

SEPTEMBER 3   Britain and France declare war against Germany.

NOVEMBER 4   "Cash and Carry" revision to the Neutrality Act enacted.

1940

MAY 16   Roosevelt asks Congress for additional appropriations for defense preparedness.

JUNE 17   German army overruns France.

JUNE 24–28   Republican nominating convention meets in Philadelphia.

JUNE 28   Republicans nominate Wendell Willkie for president.

JULY 10   Battle of Britain begins.

JULY 15–18   Democratic nominating convention meets in Chicago.

JULY 17   Democrats renominate Roosevelt.

AUGUST 17   Willkie delivers acceptance speech in Elwood, Indiana.

SEPTEMBER 3   Destroyer base deal signed with Britain.

SEPTEMBER 16   Selective Service Act passed.

SEPTEMBER 27   Mutual defense pact signed between Germany and Japan.

NOVEMBER 5   Roosevelt reelected.

1941

JANUARY 20   Franklin D. Roosevelt inaugurated for an unprecedented third term.

DECEMBER 7   Japan attacks Pearl Harbor.

1944

JUNE 6   D-Day invasion of France by the Allies.

JUNE 26–28   Republican National Convention nominates Thomas E. Dewey for president.

JULY 11   President Roosevelt announces that he will run for a fourth term, if nominated.

JULY 19–21   Democratic National Convention nominates Roosevelt for president.

AUGUST 12   Roosevelt delivers speech at Bremerton Navy Yard.

SEPTEMBER 23   Roosevelt delivers the "Fala" speech at Teamsters Union dinner.

OCTOBER 8   Wendell Willkie dies in New York City.

NOVEMBER 7   Election Day; Roosevelt reelected.

1945

JANUARY 20   Franklin D. Roosevelt inaugurated for fourth term.

FEBRUARY 4–11   At Yalta conference, Roosevelt confers with Winston Churchill and Josef Stalin.

APRIL 12   Franklin D. Roosevelt dies at Warm Springs, Georgia; Harry S Truman becomes president.

MAY 7   Germany surrenders.

AUGUST 6   First atomic bomb dropped on Hiroshima, Japan.

| AUGUST 9 | Second atomic bomb dropped on Nagasaki, Japan. |
| AUGUST 14 | Japan surrenders unconditionally, ending World War II. |

1946

MARCH 2	Deadline passes for Soviet troops to withdraw from Iran.
APRIL 1	United Mine Workers join auto and steel workers in strikes.
NOVEMBER 5	Republicans win majorities in House and Senate.
DECEMBER 29	Progressive Citizens of America organized.

1947

MARCH 12	President Truman asks Congress for emergency aid for Greece and Turkey.
JUNE 23	Taft-Hartley Act passed over a presidential veto.
OCTOBER 29	*To Secure These Rights* published.

1948

JUNE 5	Marshall Plan introduced at Harvard University.
JUNE 21	Republican National Convention opened, Thomas E. Dewey nominated for president.
JUNE 28	Truman decides to supply West Berlin by air.
JULY 12	Democratic National Convention opened, Harry S Truman nominated for president.
JULY 17	"Dixiecrats" meet in Birmingham, nominate Strom Thurmond for president.
AUGUST 3	Whittaker Chambers names Alger Hiss as a communist spy.
NOVEMBER 2	Election Day; Truman wins.

1949

JANUARY	Chinese communist forces enter Peking.
JANUARY 20	Harry S Truman inaugurated president.
JULY 21	Senate ratifies NATO treaty.
SEPTEMBER 23	President Truman announces Russian atomic bomb test.

1950

JANUARY 21	Alger Hiss convicted of perjury.
FEBRUARY 11	Senator Joseph McCarthy announces a list of "communists" in government.
JUNE 25	North Korea invades South Korea.
JULY 1	U.S. forces land in Korea.
JULY 17	Julius and Ethel Rosenberg arrested as atomic spies.
SEPTEMBER 23	Internal Security Act passed over President Truman's veto.
OCTOBER 7	U.S. forces invade North Korea.
NOVEMBER 29	Chinese troops attack U.S. forces.

1951

| APRIL 4 | Senate reaffirms NATO commitment. |
| APRIL 10 | Truman fires General Douglas MacArthur. |

1952

MARCH 11	New Hampshire primary.
APRIL 11	Dwight D. Eisenhower announces he will return June 1 to compete for GOP nomination.
JULY 7	Republican convention begins, Eisenhower nominated for president, Richard M. Nixon for vice president.
JULY 21	Democratic convention begins, Adlai Stevenson nominated for president, John Sparkman for vice president.
SEPTEMBER 12	Eisenhower and Robert Taft hold Morningside Heights conference.
SEPTEMBER 23	Nixon delivers "Checkers" speech.
OCTOBER 24	Eisenhower promises to "go to Korea."
NOVEMBER 4	Election Day; Eisenhower is elected.

1953

JANUARY 20	Dwight D. Eisenhower inaugurated president.

1955

SEPTEMBER 24	President Eisenhower suffers a heart attack while vacationing in Denver, Colorado.
NOVEMBER 15	Adlai Stevenson announces he will again seek the Democratic presidential nomination.

1956

FEBRUARY 29	President Eisenhower announces that he will seek reelection.
JUNE 7	Eisenhower suffers an ileitis attack requiring emerging surgery, prompting speculation that he might retire.
AUGUST 11	Stevenson clinches the Democratic nomination on the first ballot.
AUGUST 22	Republicans renominate Eisenhower and Nixon in San Francisco.
OCTOBER 23	After a popular uprising ousts a communist regime, Hungarians install Imre Nagy as premier.
OCTOBER 29	Israel invades the Sinai Peninsula.
NOVEMBER 4	Soviet tanks roll into Budapest to put down the Hungarian Revolution.
NOVEMBER 5	British and French paratroopers land near the Suez Canal, deepening the Suez Crisis.
NOVEMBER 6	Election Day; Eisenhower defeats Stevenson to win reelection.

1957

JANUARY 20	Dwight D. Eisenhower inaugurated for second term.

1959

DECEMBER 24	Nelson Rockefeller announces he will not seek the Republican nomination for president.
DECEMBER 30	Hubert Humphrey announces his candidacy for the Democratic nomination for president.

1960

JANUARY 2	John Fitzgerald Kennedy announces his candidacy for the Democratic nomination for president.
MARCH 24	Stuart Symington announces his candidacy for the Democratic nomination for president.
APRIL 5	Kennedy wins Wisconsin Democratic primary.

MAY 1	Soviet Union shoots downs American U-2 spy plane in its airspace.
MAY 8	Kennedy gives television address to West Virginia voters on his religion.
MAY 10	Kennedy wins West Virginia Democratic primary.
MAY 11	Humphrey drops out of race for Democratic nomination.
JULY 5	Lyndon Johnson announces his candidacy for the Democratic nomination for president.
JULY 13	At the Los Angeles convention, Kennedy wins Democratic nomination for president on the first ballot.
JULY 14	Johnson accepts Democratic nomination for vice president.
JULY 15	Kennedy accepts Democratic nomination for president.
JULY 22–23	Richard Nixon meets Rockefeller in secret meeting in New York City; Rockefeller releases statement detailing their discussions and Nixon's agreement to most of his terms.
JULY 27	At the Chicago convention, Nixon wins Republican nomination for president on the first ballot.
JULY 28	Nixon accepts Republican nomination for president.
AUGUST 29–SEPTEMBER 9	Nixon hospitalized with infection in his knee.
SEPTEMBER 1	Congressional session ends, freeing Kennedy from his duties to begin active campaigning for general election.
SEPTEMBER 12	Kennedy addresses Greater Houston Ministerial Association, and puts religious issue to rest.
SEPTEMBER 26	First Kennedy-Nixon presidential debate televised from Chicago.
OCTOBER 7	Second televised presidential debate held in Washington, D.C.
OCTOBER 13	Third presidential debate televised, with Nixon in Los Angeles and Kennedy in New York.
OCTOBER 19	Martin Luther King, Jr., arrested in Atlanta, Georgia, and later sentenced to four months hard labor.
OCTOBER 21	Fourth, and final, televised presidential debate held in New York.
OCTOBER 25	Kennedy calls King's wife; JFK's brother, Robert, convinces Georgia judge to release King.
OCTOBER 25–NOVEMBER 7	Nixon commences all-out television blitz.
OCTOBER 27	King released from prison.
NOVEMBER 8	Election Day; Kennedy defeats Nixon in close election.

1961

JANUARY 20	John F. Kennedy inaugurated president.

1963

FEBRUARY 17	Movement founded to draft Barry Goldwater.
NOVEMBER 22	President John F. Kennedy assassinated. Johnson becomes president.

1964

JANUARY 3	Barry Goldwater announces candidacy.
JANUARY 28	Margaret Chase Smith announces candidacy.
JUNE 2	California primary.
JUNE 19	Civil Rights Act passed.
JULY 13–16	Republican National Convention, Barry Goldwater nominated for president.
AUGUST 4–6	Gulf of Tonkin incident.
AUGUST 24–27	Democratic National Convention, Lyndon B. Johnson nominated for president.
NOVEMBER 3	Election Day; Johnson wins in huge landslide.

1965

JANUARY 20   Lyndon B. Johnson inaugurated president.

1967

NOVEMBER 30   Senator Eugene McCarthy announces candidacy for Democratic presidential nomination.

1968

JANUARY 30   Communists begin "Tet Offensive" in South Vietnam.

FEBRUARY 8   George C. Wallace announces candidacy for president on Independent ticket.

MARCH 12   President Johnson narrowly defeats McCarthy in New Hampshire Democratic primary; Richard Nixon wins New Hampshire primary by a wide margin.

MARCH 16   Senator Robert F. Kennedy enters presidential race.

MARCH 31   President Johnson withdraws from presidential contest.

APRIL 4   Martin Luther King, Jr., is assassinated.

APRIL 27   Vice President Hubert H. Humphrey announces candidacy for Democratic presidential nomination.

JUNE 4–5   Kennedy defeats McCarthy in California primary, but is later shot by assassin Sirhan Sirhan in Los Angeles.

JUNE 6   Robert F. Kennedy dies from his gunshot wounds.

AUGUST 5–9   Republican National Convention meets in Miami; Nixon nominated for president on first ballot.

AUGUST 26–30 Democratic National Convention meets in Chicago amid antiwar protests; Humphrey nominated for president.

SEPTEMBER 30 Humphrey vows to stop bombing of North Vietnam as an "acceptable risk for peace."

OCTOBER 29   McCarthy endorses Humphrey.

OCTOBER 31   Johnson announces peace talks to start on November 6, one day after the election.

NOVEMBER 5   Election Day; Nixon narrowly elected.

1969

JANUARY 20   Richard Nixon inaugurated president.

FEBRUARY 8   George McGovern appointed chair of the McGovern-Fraser Commission on Party Structure and Delegate Selection of Democratic National Committee.

1972

FEBRUARY 7   President Nixon signs the Federal Election Campaign Act.

FEBRUARY 15   John Mitchell became Nixon's campaign manager.

MAY 15   George Wallace is shot and partially paralyzed.

JUNE 17   Watergate break-in at the Democratic National Committee headquarters by Nixon's "plumbers unit."

JULY 12   George McGovern wins the Democratic nomination for president.

JULY 31   Thomas Eagleton resigns as Democratic vice presidential nominee.

AUGUST 22   Richard Nixon is renominated as presidential nominee at the Republican Convention in Miami Beach.

NOVEMBER 7   Election Day; Nixon wins reelection.

DECEMBER 18   The Electoral College awards 520 votes for Nixon, 17 for McGovern, and 1 for John Hospers of the Libertarian Party.

1973

JANUARY 20   Richard M. Nixon inaugurated for second term.

1974

AUGUST 9   Gerald R. Ford sworn in as president after the resignation of President Nixon.

SEPTEMBER 8   President Ford pardons Nixon.

1975

APRIL 24   Vietnam War officially ends.

1976

JANUARY 19   Jimmy Carter finishes ahead of other Democratic candidates in Iowa caucuses.

FEBRUARY 24   Ford and Carter win Republican and Democratic primaries in New Hampshire.

MARCH 2   Carter finishes fourth in Massachusetts primary.

MARCH 9   Ford and Carter win Florida primaries.

MARCH 16   Ford wins, and Carter makes a strong showing, in Illinois primaries.

MARCH 23   Ronald Reagan wins North Carolina primary.

APRIL 6   Carter wins Wisconsin primary, but loses to Henry Jackson in New York.

APRIL 27   Carter wins Pennsylvania primary.

MAY 1   Reagan wins Texas primary.

MAY 4   Reagan sweeps three primaries and takes the lead in delegates.

MAY 18   Ford wins Michigan primary; Jerry Brown defeats Carter in Maryland primary.

JUNE 8   Reagan and Brown win California primaries; Ford and Carter win Ohio primaries.

JULY 12–15   Carter nominated on first ballot at Democratic National Convention, Walter Mondale nominated for vice president.

JULY 26   Reagan names Richard Schweiker as his vice presidential running mate.

AUGUST 16   Ford nominated on first ballot at Republican National Convention, Robert Dole nominated for vice president.

SEPTEMBER 23   First presidential debate takes place in Philadelphia.

OCTOBER 6   Second presidential debate held in San Francisco.

OCTOBER 15   Vice presidential debate takes place in Houston.

OCTOBER 22   Third presidential debate held in Williamsburg, Virginia.

NOVEMBER 2   Election Day; Carter defeats Ford.

1977

JANUARY 20   Jimmy Carter inaugurated president.

1978

MARCH 16   Panama Canal Treaty ratified; U.S. relinquishes Canal Zone.

JUNE 6   California voters adopt Proposition 13.

1979

JANUARY 16	Shah flees Iran; second energy crisis begins.
MARCH 28	Nuclear accident shuts down Three Mile Island power plant.
JULY 15	Carter delivers "crisis of confidence" speech from Camp David.
NOVEMBER 4	Iran hostage crisis begins.

1980

JANUARY 21	Iowa party caucuses
FEBRUARY	Inflation hits 18 percent.
FEBRUARY 12	Carter announces a boycott of the Olympic Games in Moscow.
FEBRUARY 26	New Hampshire primary.
MARCH 18	Illinois primary.
APRIL 25	Eight U.S. servicemen die in abortive hostage rescue mission.
JULY 16	Republican convention, in Detroit, nominates Ronald Reagan for president, George H.W. Bush for vice president.
AUGUST 13	Democratic convention, in New York, renominates Carter for president, Walter Mondale for vice president.
OCTOBER 28	Reagan and Carter debate.
NOVEMBER 4	Election Day; Reagan wins.

1981

JANUARY 20	Ronald Reagan inaugurated president; Iran releases American hostages.
FEBRUARY 18	In address to Congress, Reagan proposes cuts in taxes and the federal budget, but asks for increases in the defense budget.
MARCH 30	President Reagan survives assassination attempt.
SEPTEMBER 25	Sandra Day O'Connor becomes first woman seated on U.S. Supreme Court.
DECEMBER 7	Reagan administration officials estimate federal budget deficit will rise to record $109 billion in 1982 fiscal year.

1982

JUNE 30	Effort fails to persuade states to ratify Equal Rights Amendment.
NOVEMBER 2	Democrats gain 26 seats in House; Republicans keep control of Senate.

1983

MARCH 23	President Reagan proposes space-based missile defense system.
APRIL 20	Reagan signs bipartisan bill to ensure financial solvency of Social Security system.
JUNE 15	Supreme Court reaffirms *Roe* v. *Wade*.
OCTOBER 23	241 American troops killed in bombing of barracks in Lebanon.
OCTOBER 25	U.S. troops invade Grenada.

1984

FEBRUARY 28	Senator Gary Hart upsets Walter Mondale in New Hampshire Democratic primary.

JUNE 5	Mondale wins New Jersey primary.
JULY 19	Representative Geraldine Ferraro accepts nomination as Mondale's running mate.
AUGUST 23	Reagan accepts Republican nomination to run for reelection.
OCTOBER	Presidential and vice presidential debates held.
NOVEMBER 6	Election Day; Reagan reelected in landslide.

1985

| JANUARY 20 | Ronald Reagan inaugurated for second term. |

1986

| OCTOBER 22 | Tax Reform Act passed. |
| NOVEMBER 4 | Congressional midterm elections held. |

1987

MARCH 4	President Reagan accepts formal responsibility for Iran-Contra Affair.
MAY 8	Gary Hart withdraws from Democratic presidential race.
SEPTEMBER 23	Joseph Biden withdraws from Democratic presidential race.
OCTOBER 19	Stock market drops 508 points.

1988

FEBRUARY 8	Iowa caucuses held.
FEBRUARY 16	New Hampshire primaries held.
MARCH 8	Super Tuesday primaries held.
APRIL 26	Vice President George H.W. Bush clinches Republican nomination.
JUNE 7	Massachusetts governor Michael S. Dukakis clinches Democratic nomination
JULY 12	Dukakis announces choice of Senator Lloyd M. Bentsen as running mate.
JULY 21	Dukakis accepts Democratic nomination at convention.
AUGUST 16	Bush announces choice of Senator Dan Quayle as running mate.
AUGUST 18	Bush accepts Republican nomination at convention.
SEPTEMBER 25	First presidential debate takes place.
OCTOBER 5	Vice presidential debate conducted.
OCTOBER 13	Second presidential debate takes place.
NOVEMBER 8	Election Day; Bush defeats Dukakis.

1989

| JANUARY 20 | George H.W. Bush inaugurated president. |

1990

| JUNE 26 | President Bush proposes tax increase, breaking his "no new taxes" campaign pledge. |
| AUGUST 2 | Iraq invades and annexes Kuwait. |

1991

JANUARY 16   Gulf War, Operation "Desert Storm," begins.

1992

FEBRUARY 18   Democratic and Republican parties hold first primary election in New Hampshire.

FEBRUARY 20   Ross Perot enters presidential race.

MARCH 5–19   Bob Kerrey, Tom Harkin, and Paul Tsongas withdraw from race for the Democratic nomination.

JUNE 9   Democratic and Republican parties hold last primary election in North Dakota.

JULY 13–16   Democratic Party convention nominates Bill Clinton for president and Al Gore for vice president.

JULY 16   Perot temporarily withdraws from the presidential race.

AUGUST 17–20   Republican Party convention renominates President Bush—and Vice President Dan Quayle.

OCTOBER 1   Perot reenters the presidential race.

OCTOBER 11–19   Presidential and vice presidential debates held.

NOVEMBER 3   Election Day; Clinton elected.

1993

JANUARY 20   Bill Clinton inaugurated president.

1994

NOVEMBER 8   Midterm congressional elections shift control of House and Senate to Republicans.

1995

SEPTEMBER 25   Ross Perot announces formation of Reform Party.

FALL   President Clinton ads attack "Dolegingrich."

NOVEMBER 14–21   Budget stand-off causes first federal government shutdown.

DECEMBER 15   Second federal government shutdown begins, continuing through January 6, 1996.

1996

FEBRUARY 12   Iowa caucuses held.

FEBRUARY 20   New Hampshire Republican primary held.

FEBRUARY 27   Arizona Republican primary held.

MARCH 26   Robert Dole achieves majority of delegates, clinching Republican nomination.

MAY 15   Dole announces his resignation from the Senate.

AUGUST 12–15   Republican Party convention meets, nominates Dole for president and Jack Kemp for vice president.

AUGUST 18   Reform Party convention occurs, nominates Perot for president..

AUGUST 26–29   Democratic Party convention meets, renominates President Clinton and Vice President Al Gore.

NOVEMBER 5   Election Day; Clinton beats Dole.

1997

JANUARY 20   Bill Clinton inaugurated for second term.

1998

JANUARY   Investigation begins into President Clinton's affair with Monica Lewinsky; Clinton publicly denies the allegations.

AUGUST 17   Clinton apologizes to nation for his "inappropriate relationship" with Lewinsky.

DECEMBER 19   U.S. House of Representatives votes to impeach Clinton for perjuring himself during grand jury testimony, and for obstructing special counsel Kenneth Starr's investigation Lewinsky affair.

1999

FEBRUARY 12   President Clinton acquitted by U.S. Senate on both impeachment charges.

2000

MARCH 7   "Super Tuesday" primary elections held.

JULY 31–AUGUST 3   Republican National Convention held in Philadelphia; George W. Bush nominated for president, Richard Cheney for vice president.

AUGUST 14–17   Democratic National Convention held in Los Angeles; Al Gore nominated for president, Joseph Lieberman for vice president.

NOVEMBER 7   Election Day.

NOVEMBER 8   Presidential races in Florida, Oregon, and New Mexico declared too close to call.

NOVEMBER 9   Gore campaign sues to overturn Bush's election victory in Florida, demanding manual recounts in several Florida counties.

NOVEMBER 12   Bush campaign goes to court to stop the Florida hand count.

NOVEMBER 14   A 5 P.M. deadline set by Florida's Republican secretary of state, Katherine Harris, for counties to report election returns; Gore's request for complete hand recount granted in Broward County; circuit court judge Terry Lewis rules that Harris may enforce deadline, but requires her to use flexibility.

NOVEMBER 15   Harris announces that Bush leads by 300 votes, and sets 2 P.M. deadline for counties to justify late returns; Florida Supreme Court rejects Bush's bid to block all Florida hand counts of votes, and Palm Beach County proceeds with its hand count.

NOVEMBER 22   Miami-Dade County stops its recount because of disputes over standards for counting ballots; Bush appeals Florida Supreme Court ruling (allowing hand recounts) to U.S. Supreme Court.

NOVEMBER 25   Bush drops Florida Supreme Court lawsuit (to block counting of late military absentee ballots or those without postmarks); Bush then sues to have these late ballots counted in five counties across Florida.

NOVEMBER 26   Florida certifies state's election results; Bush declared the winner by 536 votes, but Palm Beach County recount not included in total.

DECEMBER 12   At 10 P.M., U.S. Supreme Court rules 5–4 in favor of George W. Bush, barring any further recounts in Florida.

DECEMBER 13   Al Gore concedes election to George W. Bush.

2001

JANUARY 20   George W. Bush inaugurated president.

Bibliography

General Works

Aldrich, John H. *Why Parties?: The Origin and Transformation of Party Politics in America.* Chicago: University of Chicago Press, 1995.

Blaisdell, Thomas C., Jr. *The American Presidency in Political Cartoons, 1776–1976.* Berkeley, CA: University Art Museum, 1976.

Boller, Paul F. *Presidential Campaigns.* New York: Oxford University Press, 1984.

Burnham, Walter Dean. *Critical Elections and the Mainsprings of American Politics.* New York: W.W. Norton, 1970.

———. *The Current Crisis in American Politics.* New York: Oxford University Press, 1982.

Burns, James McGregor. *The American Experiment.* New York: Alfred Knopf, 1982–89.

Chambers, William N., and W.D. Burnham, eds. *The American Party Systems: Stages of Political Development.* 2d ed. New York: Oxford University Press, 1975.

Clubb, Jerome, Wm. H. Flanigan, and Nancy Zingale. *Partisan Realignment: Voters, Parties, and Government in American History.* Beverly Hills, CA: Sage, 1980.

Garraty, John A., and Mark C. Carnes, eds. *American National Biography.* 24 vols. New York: Oxford University Press, 1999.

Grantham, Dewey W. *The Democratic South.* New York: W.W. Norton, 1963.

Jamieson, Kathleen Hall. *Packaging the Presidency: A History and Criticism of Presidential Campaign Advertising.* New York: Oxford University Press, 1984.

Jensen, Richard. "Armies, Admen, and Crusaders: Types of Presidential Election Campaigns." *The History Teacher* 2 (January 1969): 33–50.

Johnson, Allen, and Dumas Malone, eds. *Dictionary of American Biography.* 20 vols., 7 supps. New York: Charles Scribner's Sons, 1943–81.

Key, V.O., Jr. *Southern Politics in State and Nation.* New York: Alfred A. Knopf, 1949.

Kleppner, Paul, ed. *The Evolution of American Electoral Systems.* Westport, CT: Greenwood Press, 1981.

Kleppner, Paul. *Who Voted? The Dynamics of Electoral Turnout, 1879–1980.* New York: Praeger, 1982.

Ladd, Everett Carl, Jr. *American Political Parties: Social Change and Political Response.* New York: W.W. Norton, 1970.

Layman, Geoffrey. *The Great Divide: Religious and Cultural Conflict in American Party Politics.* Baltimore: Johns Hopkins University Press, 2001.

Leish, Kenneth, editor in charge. *The American Heritage Pictorial History of the Presidents of the United States.* 2 vols. New York: American Heritage, 1968.

Lichtman, Allan J. *Thirteen Keys to the Presidency.* Lanham, MD: Madison Books, 1990.

Maisel, L. Sandy, and William G. Shade, eds. *Parties and Politics in American History: A Reader.* New York: Garland, 1994.

Marcus, Robert D. "Presidential Elections in the American Political System." *The Review of Politics* 33 (January 1971): 3–23.

Mayhew, David R. *Placing Parties in American Politics: Organizations, Electoral Settings, and Government Activity in the Twentieth Century.* Princeton, NJ: Princeton University Press, 1986.

Mazmanian, Daniel. *Third Parties in Presidential Elections.* Washington, DC: Brookings, 1974.

McCormick, Richard P. *The Presidential Game: The Origins of American Presidential Politics.* New York: Oxford University Press, 1982.

Mieczkowski, Yanek. *The Routledge Historical Atlas of Presidential Elections.* New York: Routledge, 2000.

Reiter, Howard L. *Selecting the President: The Nominating Process in Transition.* Philadelphia: University of Pennsylvania Press, 1985.

Roseboom, Eugene H. *A History of Presidential Elections.* New York: Macmillan, 1964.

Schlesinger, Arthur M. *Running for President: The Candidates and their Images*. New York: Simon and Schuster, 1994.

Schlesinger, Arthur M., Jr., and Fred L. Israel, eds. *History of American Presidential Elections*. 4 vols. New York: Chelsea House, 1971.

Schumacker, Paul D., and Burdett A. Loomis, eds. *Choosing a President: The Electoral College and Beyond*. New York: Chatham House, 2001.

Shafer, Byron E., ed. *The End of Realignment? Interpreting American Electoral Eras*. Madison: University of Wisconsin Press, 1991.

Shafer, Byron E., and Anthony J. Badger, eds. *Contesting Democracy: Substance & Structure in American Political History, 1775–2000*. Lawrence: University Press of Kansas, 2001.

Skowronek, Stephen. *The Politics Presidents Make: Leadership from John Adams to Bill Clinton*. Cambridge, MA: Belknap Press of Harvard University Press, 1997.

Southwick, Leslie H. *Presidential Also-Rans and Running Mates, 1788–1980*. Jefferson, NC: McFarland, 1984.

Stanley, Harold W., and R.G. Niemi. *Vital Statistics on American Politics*. 5th ed. Washington, DC: Congressional Quarterly, 1995.

Stanwood, Edward. *A History of the Presidency*. 2 vols. Boston and New York: Houghton, Mifflin, 1928.

Sundquist, James L. *Dynamics of the Party System: Alignment and Realignment of Political Parties in the U.S.* Washington, DC: Brookings Institute, 1973.

Urosky, Melvin I. *The American Presidents: Critical Essays*. London and New York: Routledge, 2000.

The Early Republic, 1789–1860

Benson, Lee. *The Concept of Jacksonian Democracy: New York as a Test Case*. Princeton, NJ: Princeton University Press, 1961.

Chambers, William N. *Political Parties in a New Nation*. New York: Oxford University Press, 1963.

Chase, James S. *Emergence of the Presidential Nominating Convention, 1789–1832*. Urbana: University of Illinois Press, 1973.

Cunningham, Noble. *The Jeffersonian Republicans: The Formation of Party Organization, 1789–1801*. Chapel Hill: University of North Carolina Press, 1957.

———. *The Jeffersonian Republicans in Power: Party Operations, 1801–1809*. Chapel Hill: University of North Carolina Press, 1963.

Formisano, Ronald P. *The Transformation of Political Culture: Massachusetts Parties, 1790s-1840s*. New York: Oxford University Press, 1982.

Hanyan, Craig. *DeWitt Clinton and the Rise of the People's Men*. Montreal and Kingston: McGill/Queen's University Press, 1996.

Heale, M.J. *The Presidential Quest: Candidates and Images in American Political Culture, 1787–1852*. London and New York: Longman, 1982.

Hofstadter, Richard. *The Idea of a Party System: The Rise of Legitimate Opposition in the United States*. Berkeley: University of California Press, 1969.

Holt, Michael F. *The Rise and Fall of the American Whig Party: Jacksonian Politics and the Onset of the Civil War*. New York: Oxford University Press, 1999.

Howe, Daniel Walker. *The Political Culture of the American Whigs*. Chicago: University of Chicago Press, 1979.

Ketcham, Ralph. *Presidents Above Party: The First American Presidency, 1789–1829*. Chapel Hill: University of North Carolina Press, 1984.

McCormick, Richard P. *The Second American Party System*. Chapel Hill: University of North Carolina Press, 1966.

Nichols, Roy F. *The Invention of Political Parties: A Study in Political Improvisation*. New York: Macmillian, 1967.

Sisson, Daniel. *The American Revolution of 1800*. New York: Alfred A. Knopf, 1974.

Sydnor, Charles S. *Gentleman Freeholders: Political Practices in Washington's Virginia*. Chapel Hill: University of North Carolina Press, 1952.

The Era of the Civil War and Reconstruction, 1860–1876

Altschuler, Glenn C., and Stuart M. Blumin. *Rude Republic: Americans and their Politics in the Nineteenth Century*. Princeton, NJ: Princeton University Press, 2000.

Baker, Jean H. *Affairs of Party: The Political Culture of Northern Democrats in the Mid-Nineteenth Century*. Ithaca, NY: Cornell University Press, 1983.

Fogel, Robert William. *Without Consent or Contract: The Rise and Fall of American Slavery*. New York: Norton, 1989.

Gienapp, William E. *The Origins of the Republican Party, 1852–1856*. New York: Oxford University Press, 1987.

———. "Who Voted For Lincoln?" In *Abraham Lincoln and the American Political Tradition,* ed. John L. Thomas, pp. 50–97. Amherst: University of Massachusetts Press, 1986.

Holt, Michael F. *The Political Crisis of the 1850s*. New York: Wiley, 1978.

———. *Political Parties and American Political Development from the Age of Jackson to the Age of Lincoln*. Baton Rouge: Louisiana State University Press, 1993.

Nichols, Roy F. *The Disruption of American Democracy*. New York: Macmillan, 1948.

Renda, Lex. *Running on the Record: Civil War-Era Politics in New Hampshire*. Charlottesville: University Press of Virginia, 1997.

Silbey, Joel. *The American Political Nation, 1858–1893*. Stanford, CA: Stanford University Press, 1992.

Thornton, J. Mills, III. *Politics and Power in a Slave Society: Alabama, 1800–1860*. Baton Rouge: Louisiana State University Press, 1978.

The Gilded Age and Progressive Era, 1877–1932

Allswang, John M. *A House for All Peoples: Ethnic Politics in Chicago.* Lexington: University of Kentucky Press, 1971.

Burner, David. *The Politics of Provincialism: The Democratic Party in Transition, 1918–1932.* New York: W.W. Norton, 1967.

Cherny, Robert W. *American Politics in the Gilded Age, 1868–1900.* Wheeling, IL: Harlan Davidson, 1997.

Connolly, James J. *The Triumph of Ethnic Progressivism: Urban Political Culture in Boston, 1900–1925.* Cambridge, MA: Harvard University Press, 1998.

Degler, Carl. "American Politics Parties and the Rise of the City: An Intepretation." *Journal of American History* 51:1 (June 1964): 41–59.

Edwards, Rebecca. *Angels in the Machinery: Gender in American Party Politics from the Civil War to the Progressive Era.* New York: Oxford University Press, 1997.

Jensen, Richard J. *The Winning of the Midwest: Social Political Conflicts, 1888–1896.* Chicago: University of Chicago Press, 1971.

Kleppner, Paul. *Continuity and Change in Electoral Politics, 1893–1928.* New York: Greenwood, 1987.

———. *The Third Electoral System, 1853–1892: Parties, Voters, and Political Culture.* Chapel Hill: University of North Carolina Press, 1979.

Kornbluh, Mark Lawrence. *Why America Stopped Voting: The Decline of Participatory Democracy and the Emergence of Modern American Politics.* New York: New York University Press, 2000.

Kousser, J. Morgan. *The Shaping of Southern Politics: Suffrage Restriction and the Establishment of the One-Party South, 1880–1910.* New Haven, CT: Yale University Press, 1974.

Marcus, Robert. *Grand Old Party: Political Structure in the Gilded Age, 1880–1896.* New York: Oxford University Press, 1971.

McGerr, Michael E. *The Decline of Popular Politics: The American North, 1865–1928.* New York: Oxford University Press, 1986.

Ostler, Jeffrey. *Prairie Populism: The Fate of Agrarian Radicalism in Kansas, Nebraska, and Iowa, 1880–1892.* Lawrence: University Press of Kansas, 1933.

Perman, Michael. *Struggle for Mastery: Disfranchisement in the South, 1888–1908.* Chapel Hill: University of North Carolina Press, 2001.

Reynolds, John F. *Testing Democracy: Electoral Behavior and Progressive Reform in New Jersey.* Chapel Hill: University of North Carolina Press, 1998.

Sarasohn, David. *Party of Reform: Democrats in the Progressive Era.* Jackson: University of Mississippi Press, 1989.

Wright, James D. *The Politics of Populism: Dissent in Colorado.* New Haven, CT: Yale University Press, 1974.

New Deal, World War, and the Postwar Era, 1932–1968

Allswang, John M. *The New Deal and American Politics: A Study in Political Change.* New York: John Wiley and Sons, 1978.

Anderson, Kristi. *Creation of a Democratic Majority, 1928–1936.* Chicago: University of Chicago Press, 1979.

Axelrod, Robert. "Where the Votes Come From: An Analysis of Electoral Coalitions, 1952–1968." *American Political Science Review* 66 (March 1972).

Campbell, Angus, Philip E. Converse, Warren E. Miller, and Donald E. Stokes. *The American Voter: An Abridgement.* New York: John Wiley and Sons, 1960.

Campbell, Angus, et al., eds. *Elections and the Political Order.* New York: John Wiley and Sons, 1966.

Fiorina, Morris P. *Retrospective Voting in American National Elections.* New Haven, CT: Yale University Press, 1981.

Free, Lloyd A., and Hadley Cantril. *The Political Beliefs of Americans: A Study of Public Opinion.* New Brunswick, NJ: Rutgers University Press, 1967.

Key, V.O., Jr. *The Responsible Electorate: Rationality in Presidential Voting, 1936–1960.* New York: Vintage Books, 1966.

———. *Southern Politics in State and Nation.* New York: Knopf, 1949.

Knoke, David, and Richard Felson. "Ethnic Stratification and Political Cleavage in the United States, 1952–1968." *American Journal of Sociology* 80 (November 1974).

Ladd, Everett Carll. *Transformation of the American Party System: Political Conditions from the New Deal to the 1970s.* New York: Norton, 1975.

Miller, Warren E. *American National Election Studies Data Sourcebook, 1953–1986.* Cambridge, MA: Harvard University Press, 1989.

Nie, Norman H., Sidney Verba, and Hohn R. Petrocik. *The Changing American Voters.* Cambridge, MA: Harvard University Press, 1976.

Shover, John L. "The Emergence of a Two-Party System in Republican Philadelphia, 1924–1936." *Journal of American History* 60:4 (March 1974): 985–1002.

Modern Politics, 1968–Present

Berman, William C. *America's Right Turn: From Nixon to Bush.* Baltimore: Johns Hopkins University Press, 1994.

Carter, Daniel T. *The Politics of Rage: George Wallace, the Origins of the New Conservatism, and the Transformation of American Politics.* New York: Simon and Schuster, 1995.

Dionne, E.J., Jr. *Why Americans Hate Politics.* New York: Simon and Schuster, 1991.

Edsall, Thomas B. *Chain Reaction: The Impact of Race, Rights, and Taxes on American Politics.* New York: W.W. Norton, 1992.

Ferguson, Thomas, and Joel Rodgers. *Right Turn: The Decline of the Democrats and the Future of American Politics.* New York: Hill and Wang, 1986.

Ginsberg, Benjamin, and Martin Shefter. *Politics By Other Means.* New York: Basic Books, 1990.

Hibbs, Douglas. *The American Political Economy: Macroeconomics and Electoral Politics.* Cambridge, MA: Harvard University Press, 1987.

Mayer, William G. *The Changing American Mind: How and Why American Public Opinion Changed between 1960 and 1988.* Ann Arbor: University of Michigan Press, 1992.

Phillips, Kevin. *The Emerging Republican Majority.* New Rochelle, NY: Arlington House, 1969.

———. *The Politics of the Rich and the Poor: Wealth and the American Electorate in the Reagan Aftermath.* New York: Random House, 1990.

Piven, Frances Fox, and R.A. Cloward. *Why Americans Don't Vote.* New York: Pantheon, 1998.

Rosenstone, Steven J. *Who Votes?* New Haven, CT: Yale University Press, 1980.

Speel, Robert W. *Changing Patterns of Voting in the Northern States: Electoral Realignment 1952–1996.* University Park: Pennsylvania State University Press, 1998.

Wattenberg, Martin P. *The Decline of American Political Parties, 1952–1994.* Cambridge, MA: Harvard University Press, 1996.

White, Theodore. *America in Search of Itself: The Making of the President, 1956–1980.* New York: Harper and Row, 1982.

Wilson, Carey McWilliams. *The Politics of Disappointment: American Elections, 1976–1994.* Chatham House, 1995.

Elections, Campaigns, and Politics

Abramson, Paul R., John H. Aldrich, and David W. Rohde. *Change and Continuity in the 1984 Elections.* Washington, DC: Congressional Quarterly Press, 1987.

———. *Change and Continuity in the 1992 Elections.* Washington, DC: Congressional Quarterly Press, 1995.

———. *Change and Continuity in the 1996 Elections.* Washington, DC: Congressional Quarterly Press, 1998.

Adams, Henry. *History of the United States of America during the Second Administration of Thomas Jefferson.* 2 vols. New York: Charles Scribner's Sons, 1890.

Adams, John Quincy. *Memoirs of John Quincy Adams, Comprising Portions of His Diary from 1795 to 1848*, ed. Charles Francis Adams, vols. 6 and 7. Freeport, NY: Books for Libraries Press, 1969.

Aldrich, John. *Before the Convention.* Chicago: University of Chicago Press, 1980.

Alexander, Herbert. *Financing Politics.* 4th ed. Washington, DC: Congressional Quarterly Press, 1992.

Alexander, Herbert, and Anthony Corrado. *Financing the 1992 Election.* Armonk, NY: M.E. Sharpe, 1995.

Allen, Frederick Lewis. *Only Yesterday: An Informal History of the 1920s.* New York: Harper and Row, 1931.

Ambrose, Stephen E. *Eisenhower.* 2 vols. "Soldier, General of the Army, President-Elect, 1890–1952." New York: Simon and Schuster, 1983–84.

Ambrose, Stephen E. *Nixon.* 3 vols. New York: Simon and Schuster, 1987-1991.

Ammon, Harry. "James Monroe and the Election of 1808 in Virginia." *William and Mary Quarterly* 3:20 (1963): 33–56.

———. *James Monroe: The Quest for National Identity.* New York: McGraw-Hill, 1971.

Anbinder, Tyler. *Nativism and Slavery: The Northern Know Nothings and the Politics of the 1850s.* New York: Oxford University Press, 1993.

Anderson, Donald F. *William Howard Taft: A Conservative's Conception of the Presidency.* Ithaca, NY: Cornell University Press, 1973.

Anderson, Patrick. *Electing Jimmy Carter: The Campaign of 1976.* Baton Rouge: Louisiana State University Press, 1994.

Asher, Herbert B. *Presidential Elections and American Politics, Voters, Candidates, and Campaigns Since 1952.* 3d ed. Homewood, IL: Dorsey Press, 1984.

Baker, Jean H. *The Stevensons: A Biography of an American Family.* New York: W.W. Norton, 1996.

Baker, Jean H., ed. *Votes for Women: The Struggle for Suffrage Revisited.* New York: Oxford University Press, 2002.

Baldasty, Gerald J. *The Commercialization of News in the Nineteenth Century.* Madison: University of Wisconsin Press, 1992.

Banner, James M. *To the Hartford Convention: Federalists and the Origins of Party Politics in Massachusetts, 1789–1815.* New York: Harper, 1970.

Barnard, William. *Dixiecrats and Democrats.* Tuscaloosa: University of Alabama Press, 1974.

Barone, Michael. *Our Country: The Shaping of America From Roosevelt to Reagan.* New York: Free Press, 1990.

Barone, Michael, and Grant Ujifusa. *The Almanac of American Politics 1986.* Washington, DC: National Journal, 1985.

Bartels, Larry M. *Presidential Primaries and the Dynamics of Public Choice.* Princeton, NJ: Princeton University Press, 1988.

Bauer, K. Jack. *Zachary Taylor: Soldier, Planter, Statesman of the Old Southwest.* Baton Rouge: Louisiana State University Press, 1985.

Beckley, John James. *Justifying Jefferson: The Political Writings of John James Beckley*, ed. Gerard W. Gawalt. Washington, DC: Library of Congress, 1995.

Belmont, Perry. *Return to Secret Party Funds: Value of Reed Committee.* New York: G. P. Putnam's Sons, 1927.

Bemis, Samuel Flagg. *Jay's Treaty: A Study in Commerce and Diplomacy*, rev. ed. New Haven, CT: Yale University Press, 1962.

———. *John Quincy Adams and the Union.* New York: Knopf, 1956.

Ben-Atar, Doron, and Barbara B. Oberg, eds. *Federalists Reconsidered.* Charlottesville: University Press of Virginia, 1998.

Benedict, Michael Les. *A Compromise of Principle: Congressional Republicans and Reconstruction, 1863–1869.* New York: W.W. Norton, 1974.

Berns, Walter, ed. *After the People Vote.* Washington, DC: AEI Press, 1992.

Best, Judith A. *The Choice of the People? Debating the Electoral College.* Lanham, MD: Rowman and Littlefield, 1996.

Bingham, Duncan. *Whitelaw Reid: Journalist, Politician, Diplomat.* Athens: University of Georgia Press, 1995.

Birkner, Michael J., ed. *James Buchanan and the Political Crisis of the 1850s.* Selinsgrove, PA: Susquehanna University Press, 1996.

Birnbaum, Jeffrey. *The Money Men: The Real Story of Fund-Raising's Influence on Political Power in America.* New York: Crown, 2000.

"Black Election: 2000," *The Black Scholar* (special edition) 31:2 (Summer 2001).

Blee, Kathleen M. *Women of the Klan: Racism and Gender in the 1920s.* Berkeley: University of California Press, 1991.

Bliss, Edward, Jr. *Now the News: The Story of Broadcast Journalism.* New York: Columbia University Press, 1991.

Blitzer, Lloyd, and Theodore Rueter. *Carter vs. Ford: The Counterfeit Debates of 1976.* Madison: University of Wisconsin Press, 1980.

Blue, Frederick J. *The Free Soilers: Third Party Politics, 1848–1854.* Urbana: University of Illinois Press, 1973.

Blum, John Morton. *The Republican Roosevelt.* Cambridge, MA: Harvard University Press, 1954.

———. *Years of Discord: American Politics and Society, 1961–1974,* New York: W.W. Norton, 1991.

Branch, Taylor. *Pillar of Fire.* New York: Simon and Schuster, 1998.

Brand, Irving. *James Madison: Secretary of State, 1800–1809.* Indianapolis, IN: Bobbs-Merrill, 1953.

Brands, H.W. *T. R.: The Last Romantic.* New York: Basic Books, 1997.

Brennan, Mary C. *Turning Right in the Sixties.* Chapel Hill: University of North Carolina Press, 1995.

Bridges, Amy. *Morning Glories : Municipal Reform in the Southwest.* Princeton, NJ: Princeton University Press, 1997.

Brinkley, Alan. *Voices of Protest: Huey Long, Father Coughlin, and the Great Depression.* New York: Alfred A. Knopf, 1982.

Broadwater, Jeff. *Adlai Stevenson.* New York: Twayne, 1994.

Broderick, Francis. *Progressivism at Risk: Electing a President in 1912.* New York: Greenwood Press, 1989.

Brodie, Fawn. *Richard Nixon, The Shaping of His Character.* New York: W.W. Norton, 1981.

———. *Thomas Jefferson: An Intimate History.* New York: W.W. Norton, 1974.

Broussard, James. *The Southern Federalists, 1800–1815.* Baton Rouge: Louisiana State University Press, 1978.

Brown, Courtney. "Mass Dynamics of U.S. Presidential Competitions, 1928–1936." *American Political Science Review* 82:4 (December 1988): 1153–81.

Brown, Everett S. "The Presidential Election of 1824–25." *Political Science Quarterly* 40 (September 1925): 384–403.

Brown, Roger. *The Republic in Peril: 1812.* New York: W.W. Norton, 1971.

Buell, Emmett H., Jr., and Lee Sigelman, eds. *Nominating the President.* Knoxville: University of Tennessee Press, 1991.

Burner, David. *Herbert Hoover: A Public Life.* New York: Atheneum, 1984.

———. *John F. Kennedy and a New Generation.* Boston: Little, Brown, 1988.

Burns, James MacGregor. *Roosevelt: The Lion and the Fox, 1882–1940.* New York: Harcourt Brace and World, 1956.

———. *Roosevelt: The Soldier of Freedom 1940–1945.* New York: Harcourt Brace Jovanovich, 1970.

———. *The Workshops of Democracy: From Emancipation Proclamation to the Era of the New Deal.* New York: Vintage Books, 1985.

Caute, David. *Year of the Barricades: A Journey Through 1968.* New York: Harper and Row, 1988.

Ceaser, James W. *Presidential Selection: Theory and Development.* Princeton, NJ: Princeton University Press, 1979.

Chambers, William Nisbet. *The First Party System.* New York: John Wiley, 1972.

Cherny, Robert W. *A Righteous Cause: The Life of William Jennings Bryan.* Boston: Little, Brown, 1985.

Chester, Lewis, Godfrey Hodgson, and Bruce Page. *An American Melodrama: The Presidential Campaign of 1968.* New York: Viking, 1969.

Clancy, Herbert S. *The Presidential Election of 1880.* Chicago: Loyola University Press, 1958.

Clubb, Jerome M., and Howard Allen. "The Cities and the Election of 1928: Partisan Realignment?" *American Historical Review* 74:4 (April 1969): 1205–20.

Cole, Donald B. *Martin Van Buren, and the American Political System.* Princeton, NJ: Princeton University Press, 1984.

———. *The Presidency of Andrew Jackson.* Lawrence: University of Kansas Press, 1993.

Coleman, Charles H. *The Election of 1868: The Democratic Effort to Regain Control.* New York: Columbia University Press, 1933.

Coletta, Paolo. *The Presidency of William Howard Taft.* Lawrence: University Press of Kansas, 1973.

———. *William Jennings Bryan.* 3 vols. Lincoln: University of Nebraska Press, 1964–69.

Combs, Jerald A. *The Jay Treaty: Political Battleground of the Founding Fathers.* Berkeley: University of California Press, 1970.

Cooper, John Milton. *Pivotal Decades: The United States, 1900–1920.* New York: W.W. Norton, 1990.

———. *The Warrior and the Priest: Woodrow Wilson and Theodore Roosevelt.* Cambridge, MA: Harvard University Press, 1983.

Cornog, Evan. *The Birth of Empire: De Witt Clinton and the American Experience, 1769–1828.* New York: Oxford University Press, 1998.

Cox, James M. *Journey Through My Years.* New York: Simon and Schuster, 1946.

Craig, Douglas B. *After Wilson: The Struggle for the Democratic Party, 1920–1934.* Chapel Hill: University of North Carolina Press, 1992.

Crichton, Judy. *America 1900: The Turning Point.* New York: Henry Holt, 1998.

Crofts, Daniel. *Reluctant Confederates: Upper South Unionists in the Secession Crisis.* Chapel Hill: University of North Carolina Press, 1989.

Crotty, William, and John S. Jackson III. *Presidential Primaries and Nominations*. Washington, DC: Congressional Quarterly, 1985.

Cunningham, Noble E. *The Presidency of James Monroe*. Lawrence: University Press of Kansas, 1996.

Dallak, Robert. *Flawed Giant*. New York: Oxford University Press, 1998.

Dangerfield, George. *The Awakening of American Nationalism, 1815–1828*. New York: Harper and Row, 1965.

Daniels, Roger. *The Bonus March: An Episode of the Great Depression*. Westport, CT: Greenwood Press, 1971.

Dauer, Manning J. *The Adams Federalists*. Baltimore: Johns Hopkins University Press, 1953.

David, Lester, and Irene David. *JFK: The Wit, Charm, Tears. Remembrances from Camelot*. Toronto: Paperjacks, 1988.

David, Theodore Paul. *The Presidential Election and Transition, 1960–1961*. Washington, DC: Brookings Institution, 1961.

Davis, James W. *U. S. Presidential Primaries and the Caucus-Convention System*. Westport, CT: Greenwood, 1997.

Davis, Kenneth S. *FDR: Into the Storm, 1937–1940*. New York: Random House, 1993.

Degregorio, William A. *The Complete Book of U.S. Presidents*. New York: Wings Books, 1991.

Dershowitz, Alan. *How the High Court Hijacked Election 2000*. New York: Oxford University Press, 2001.

Donald, David Herbert. *Lincoln*. New York: Simon and Schuster, 1995.

Donaldson, Gary. *Truman Defeats Dewey*. Lexington: University Press of Kentucky, 1999.

Drew, Elizabeth. *American Journal: The Events of 1976*. New York: Random House, 1977.

———. *Campaign Journal : The Political Events of 1983–1984*. New York: Macmillan, 1985.

———. *The Corruption of American Politics: What Went Wrong and Why*. Woodstock, NY: Overlook Press, 2000.

Dumenil, Lynn. *The Modern Temper: American Culture and Society in the 1920s*. New York: Hill and Wang, 1995.

Eisenhower, John S. D. *Agent of Destiny: The Life and Times of General Winfield Scott*. Norman: University of Oklahoma Press, 1999.

Elkins, Stanley, and Eric McKittrick. *The Age of Federalism: The Early American Republic, 1788–1800*. New York: Oxford University Press, 1993.

Farber, David. *Chicago '68*. Chicago: University of Chicago Press, 1988.

Fauzald, Martin, and George Mazuzan, eds. *The Hoover Presidency: A Reappraisal*. Albany: State University of New York Press, 1974.

Feller, Daniel. *The Jacksonian Promise*. Baltimore, MD: Johns Hopkins University Press, 1995.

Ferling, John. *The First of Men: A Life of George Washington*. Knoxville: University of Tennessee Press, 1988.

———. *John Adams: A Life*. Knoxville: University of Tennessee Press, 1992.

Final Report of the National Commission on Federal Election Reform. Online at *www.reformelections.org*.

Fischer, David Hackett. *The Revolution of American Conservatism: The Federalist Party in the Era of Jeffersonian Democracy*. New York: Harper and Row, 1965.

Fite, Emerson D. *The Presidential Campaign of 1860*. New York: MacMillan, 1911.

Flexner, James Thomas. *George Washington*. 4 vols. Boston: Little, Brown, 1965–72.

———. *Washington: The Indispensable Man*. New York: New American Library, 1984.

Flick, Alexander Clarence. *Samuel Jones Tilden: A Study in Political Sagacity*. New York: Dodd, Mead, 1939.

Fontenay, Charles L. *Estes Kefauver: A Biography*. Knoxville: University of Tennessee Press, 1980.

Ford, Gerald R. *A Time to Heal: The Autobiography of Gerald R. Ford*. New York : Harper and Row, 1979.

Freeman, Douglas Southall. *George Washington: A Biography*. 6 vols. New York: Charles Scribner's Sons, 1954.

Freeman, Jo. *A Room at a Time: How Women Entered Party Politics*. Lanham, MD: Rowman and Littlefield, 2000.

Freidel, Frank. *Franklin D. Roosevelt: A Rendez-vous with Destiny*, Boston: Little, Brown, 1990.

———. *Franklin D. Roosevelt: The Triumph*. Boston: Little, Brown, 1956.

Gammon, Samuel R. *The Presidential Campaign of 1832*. Baltimore, MD: Johns Hopkins University Press, 1922.

Gara, Larry. *The Presidency of Franklin Pierce*. Lawrence: University Press of Kansas, 1991.

Garment, Suzanne. *Scandal: The Culture of Mistrust in American Politics*. New York: Anchor Books, 1991.

Garrison, Webb. *Love, Lust, and Longing in the White House*. Nashville: Cumberland House, 2000.

Germond, Jack W., and Jules Witcover. *Wake Us When It's Over: Presidential Politics of 1984*. New York: Macmillan, 1985.

Gillespie, J. David. *Politics at the Periphery: Third Parties in Two-Party America*. Columbia: University of South Carolina Press, 1993.

Gillette, William. *Retreat from Reconstruction, 1869–1879*. Baton Rouge: Louisiana State University Press, 1979.

Gillon, Steven. *Politics and Vision: The ADA and American Liberalism, 1947–1985*. New York: Oxford University Press, 1987.

Glad, Paul W. *McKinley, Bryan, and the People*. Philadelphia: Lippincott, 1964.

Goldberg, Robert Alan. *Barry Goldwater*. New Haven, CT: Yale University Press, 1995.

Gorman, Joseph. *Kefauver: A Political Biography*. New York: Oxford University Press, 1971.

Gosnell, Harold. *Champion Campaigner*. New York: MacMillan, 1952.

Gould, Lewis L. *1968: The Election That Changed America*. Chicago: Ivan Dee, 1993.

———. *The Presidency of William McKinley*. Lawrence: Regents Press of Kansas, 1980.

———. *The Presidency of Theodore Roosevelt*. Lawrence: Regents Press of Kansas, 1991.

———. *Regulation and Reform: American Politics from Roosevelt to Wilson*. 2d ed. New York: Alfred A. Knopf, 1986.

Gould, Lewis L., and Craig H. Roell. *William McKinley: A Bibliography*. Westport, CT: Meckler, 1988.

Govan, Thomas P. *Nicholas Biddle, Nationalist and Public Banker, 1786–1844*. Chicago: University of Chicago Press, 1959.

Greene, Abner. *Understanding the 2000 Election: A Guide to the Legal Battles That Decided the Presidency*. New York: New York University Press, 2001.

Greene, John Robert. *The Crusade: The Presidential Election of 1952*. Lanham, MD: University Press of America, 1985.

Green, John, ed. *Financing the 1996 Election*. Armonk, NY: M.E. Sharpe, 1999.

Greene, Julie. *Pure and Simple Politics: The American Federation of Labor and Political Activism, 1881–1917*. New York: Cambridge University Press, 1998.

Gullen, Harold. *The Upset That Wasn't: The Crucial Election of 1948*. Chicago: Ivan R. Dee, 1998.

Gunderson, Robert G. *The Log-Cabin Campaign*. Lexington: University of Kentucky Press, 1957.

Gustafson, Melanie, Kristie Miller, and Elisabeth Israels Perry, eds. *We Have Come to Stay: American Women and Political Parties, 1860–1960*. Albuquerque: University of New Mexico Press, 1999.

Guth, James L., and John C. Green, eds. *The Bible and the Ballot Box: Religion and Politics in the 1988 Election*. Boulder, CO: Westview, 1991.

Hagedorn, Hermann, ed. *The Works of Theodore Roosevelt*. National ed. 20 vols. New York: Charles Scribner's Sons, 1926.

Hamby, Alonzo. *Beyond the New Deal: Harry S Truman and American Liberalism*. New York: Columbia University Press, 1973.

———. *Man of the People: A Life of Harry S Truman*. New York: Oxford University Press, 1995

Hamilton, Holman. *Zachary Taylor: Soldier in the White House*. Indianapolis, IN: Bobbs-Merrill, 1951.

Harbaugh, William H. *Lawyer's Lawyer: The Life of John W. Davis*. New York: Oxford University Press, 1973.

———. *The Life and Times of Theodore Roosevelt*. Rev. ed. New York: Collier, 1963.

Hargreaves, Mary W. M. *The Presidency of John Quincy Adams*. Lawrence: University Press of Kansas, 1985.

Hargrove, Erwin C. *Jimmy Carter as President: Leadership and Politics of the Public Good*. Baton Rouge: Louisiana State University Press, 1988.

Hay, Robert P. "The Case for Andrew Jackson in 1824: Eaton's 'Wyoming Letters.'" *Tennessee Historical Quarterly* 29 (Winter/Spring 1970): 139–51.

Haynes, Emory. *James Baird Weaver*. Iowa City: State Historical Society of Iowa, 1919.

Herring, George. *America's Longest War*. New York: McGraw-Hill, 1996.

Herzberg, Donald, and Gerald M. Pomper, ed. *American Party Politics*. New York: Holt, Rinehart, and Winston, 1966.

Hesseltine, William B. *Third-Party Movements in the United States*. Princeton, NJ: Van Nostrand, 1962.

Hesseltine, William B., and Rex G. Fisher, eds. *Trimmers, Trucklers & Temporizers: Notes of Murat Halstead from the Political Conventions of 1856*. Madison: State Historical Society of Wisconsin, 1961.

Hicks, John D. "The Third Party Tradition in American Politics." *Mississippi Valley Historical Review* 20 (June 1933): 3–28.

Higginbotham, Sanford. *The Keystone in the Democratic Arch: Pennsylvania Politics, 1800–1816*. Harrisburg: Pennsylvania Historical and Museum Commission, 1952.

Higham, John. *Strangers in the Land: Patterns of American Nativism, 1860–1925*. New Brunswick, NJ: Rutgers University Press, 1955.

Hirsch, Mark D. *William C. Whitney: Modern Warwick*. New York: Dodd, Mead, 1948.

Holli, Melvin G. *The Wizard of Washington: Emil Hurja, Franklin Roosevelt, and the Birth of Public Opinion Polling*. New York: Palgrave, 2002.

Hollingsworth, J. Rogers. *The Whirligig of Politics: The Democracy of Cleveland and Bryan*. Chicago: University of Chicago Press, 1963.

Holt, James. *Congressional Insurgents and the Party System, 1909–1916*. Cambridge, MA: Harvard University Press, 1967.

Hoogenboom, Ari. *Outlawing the Spoils: A History of the Civil Service Reform Movement, 1865–1883*. Urbana: University of Illinois Press, 1961.

———. *Rutherford B. Hayes: Warrior and Statesman*. Lawrence: University Press of Kansas, 1995.

Jamieson, Kathleen Hall. *Dirty Politics: Deception, Distraction, and Democracy*. New York: Oxford University Press, 1992.

Jensen, Merrill, et al., eds. *The Documentary History of the First Federal Elections, 1788–1790*. 4 vols. Madison: University of Wisconsin Press, 1989.

Jensen, Richard. "The Cities Reelect Roosevelt: Ethnicity, Religion and Class in 1940." *Ethnicity* 8:2 (1981): 189–95.

Johannsen, Robert W. *Stephen A. Douglas*. New York: Oxford University Press, 1973.

Jones, Stanley. *The Presidential Election of 1896*. Madison: University of Wisconsin Press, 1964.

Jordan, David. *Winfield Scott Hancock: A Soldier's Life*. Bloomington: Indiana University Press, 1988.

Kaiser, Charles. *1968 in America*. New York: Weidenfeld and Nicolson, 1988.

Kallina, Edmund F. *Courthouse Over White House: Chicago and the Presidential Election of 1960*. Orlando: University of Central Florida Press, 1988.

Kaminski, John. *George Clinton: Yeoman Politician of the New Republic*. Madison, WI: Madison House, 1993.

Karabell, Zachary. *The Last Campaign: How Harry Truman Won the 1948 Election*. New York: Knopf, 2000.

Kazin, Michael. *The Populist Persuasion: An American History*. New York: Basic Books, 1995.

Kehl, James A. "The Unmaking of a President, 1889–1892." *Pennsylvania History* 39:4 (October 1972): 469–84.

Kellor, Frances. "Women in the Campaign." *Yale Review* 6 (January 1917): 233–40.

Kennedy, Roger G. *Burr, Hamilton and Jefferson: A Study in Character*. New York: Oxford University Press, 2000.

Kent, Noel J. *America in 1900*. Armonk, NY: M.E. Sharpe, 2000.

Kerber, Linda. *Federalists in Dissent: Imagery and Ideology in Jeffersonian America*. Ithaca, NY: Cornell University Press, 1970.

Kessel, John H. *Presidential Parties*. Homewood, IL: Dorsey, 1984.

Keyssar, Alexander. *The Right to Vote: The Contested History of Democracy in the United States*. New York: Basic Books, 2000.

Klein, Philip S. *President James Buchanan*. University Park: Pennsylvania State University Press, 1962.

Klunder, William Carl. *Lewis Cass and the Politics of Moderation*. Kent, OH: Kent State University Press, 1996.

Koenig, Louis W. *Bryan: A Political Biography of William Jennings Bryan*. New York: G.P. Putnam's Sons, 1971.

Korchin, Sheldon. "Psychological Variables in the Behavior of Voters." Ph.D. diss., Harvard University, 1949.

Kraus, Sidney, ed. *The Great Debate: Kennedy vs. Nixon, 1960*. Bloomington: Indiana University Press, 1997.

Kuroda, Tadahisa. *The Origins of the Twelfth Amendment: The Electoral College in the Early Republic, 1787–1804*. Westport, CT: Greenwood, 1994.

Kurtz, Stephen G. *The Presidency of John Adams: The Collapse of Federalism, 1795–1800*. New York: A.S. Barnes, 1961.

Ladd, Everett Carl. "The 1988 Elections: Continuation of the Post-New Deal System." *Political Science Quarterly* 104:1 (Spring 1989): 1–18.

Lazarfeld, Paul, Bernard Berelson, and Hazel Gaudet. *The People's Choice: How the Voter Makes Up His Mind in a Presidential Campaign*. New York: Duell, Sloan and Pearce, 1994.

Leibiger, Stuart. *Founding Friendship: George Washington, James Madison, and the Creation of the American Republic*. Charlottesville and London: University Press of Virginia, 1999.

Leonard, Thomas C. *News for All: America's Coming-of-Age with the Press*. New York: Oxford University Press, 1995.

———. *The Power of the Press: The Birth of American Political Reporting*. New York: Oxford University Press, 1986.

Lesher, Stephan. *George Wallace: American Populist*. New York: Addison-Wesley, 1994.

Leuchtenburg, William E. *The FDR Years: On Roosevelt and His Legacy*. New York: Columbia University Press, 1995.

———. *Franklin D. Roosevelt and the New Deal*. New York: Harper and Row, 1963.

Lichtman, Allan J. *Prejudice and the Old Politics: The Election of 1928*. Chapel Hill: University of North Carolina Press, 1979.

Link, Arthur S., ed. *Papers of Woodrow Wilson*. 69 vols. Princeton, N.J.: Princeton University Press, 1966–94.

Link, Arthur S. *Woodrow Wilson and the Progressive Era, 1910–1917*. New York: Harper and Brothers. 1954.

Link, Eugene Perry. *Democratic-Republican Societies, 1790–1800*. 1942. Reprint, New York: Octagon Books, 1973.

Lipset, Seymour Martin, and William Schneider. *The Confidence Gap: Business, Labor, and Government in the Public Mind*. New York: Free Press, 1983.

Long, David E. *The Jewel of Liberty: Abraham Lincoln's Re-election and the End of Slavery*. Mechanicsburg, PA: Stackpole Books, 1994.

Longley, Lawrence D., and Neal R. Peirce. *Electoral College Primer 2000*. New Haven, CT: Yale University Press, 1999.

Lorant, Stefan. *The Glorious Burden*. Crawfordsville, IN: R.R. Donnelley, 1976.

"Loud in their Praise of Marion Hospitality." *Marion Star*, October 2, 1920.

Lubell, Samuel. *The Revolt of the Moderates*. New York: Harper & Row, 1956.

Luthin, Reinhard H. *The First Lincoln Campaign*. Cambridge, MA: Harvard University Press, 1944.

MacKay, Kenneth C. *The Progressive Movement of 1924*. New York: Columbia University Press, 1947.

Malone, Dumas. *Jefferson and His Time*. 6 vols. Boston: Little, Brown, 1948–81.

———. *Jefferson the President, Second Term, 1805–1809*. Boston: Little, Brown, 1974.

Maney, Patrick. *The Roosevelt Presence: A Biography of Franklin Delano Roosevelt*. New York: Twayne, 1992.

Markowitz, Norman. *The Rise and Fall of the People's Century*. New York: Free Press, 1973.

Martin, John Bartlow. *Adlai Stevenson and the World: The Life of Adlai Stevenson*. Garden City, NY: Doubleday, 1977.

Martin, Ralph G. *A Hero for Our Time: An Intimate Story of the Kennedy Years*. New York: Fawcett Crest, 1983.

Masur, Louis P. *1831 Year of Eclipse*. New York: Hill and Wang, 2001.

Matalin, Mary, and James Carville. *All's Fair*. New York: Random House, 1994.

Matthews, Chris. *Kennedy and Nixon: The Rivalry That Shaped Postwar America*. New York: Simon and Schuster, 1996.

Matusow, Allen J. *The Unraveling of America: A History of Liberalism in the 1960s*. New York: Harper and Row, 1984.

Mayer, William G., ed. *In Pursuit of the White House*. Chatham, NJ: Chatham House, 1996.

———. *In Pursuit of the White House 2000*. New York: Chatham House, 2000.

McCormick, Richard P. "New Perspectives on Jacksonian Politics." *American Historical Review* 65 (January 1960): 288–301.

McCoy, Donald R. *Calvin Coolidge: The Quiet President*. Lawrence: University Press of Kansas, 1988.

———. *Landon of Kansas*. Lincoln: University of Nebraska Press, 1966.

McCullough, David. *John Adams*. New York: Simon and Schuster, 2001.

———. *Truman*. New York: Simon and Schuster, 1992.

McDonald, Forrest. *The Presidency of George Washington*, Lawrence: University Press of Kansas, 1974.

McElvaine, Robert S. *The Great Depression: America, 1929–1941.* New York: Times Books, 1993.

McFarland, Gerald. *Mugwumps, Morals and Politics.* Amherst: University of Massachusetts Press, 1975.

McGinnis, Joe. *The Selling of the President 1968.* New York: Trident, 1969.

McMath, Robert C., Jr. *American Populism: A Social History, 1877–1898.* New York: Hill and Wang, 1993.

McPherson, James M. *Abraham Lincoln and the Second American Revolution.* New York: Oxford University Press, 1991.

Merk, Frederick. *Manifest Destiny and Mission in American History.* New York: Random House, 1963.

Miller, John C. *The Federalist Era, 1789–1801.* New York: Harper and Row, 1963.

Mooney, Chase C. *William H. Crawford, 1772–1834.* Lexington: University Press of Kentucky, 1974.

Moore, Edmund A. *A Catholic Runs for President: The Campaign of 1928.* New York: Ronald, 1956.

Morello, John A. *Selling the President, 1920: Albert D. Lasker, Advertising, and the Election of Warren G. Harding.* Westport, CT: Praeger, 2001.

Morgan, H. Wayne. *Eugene V. Debs: Socialist for President.* Syracuse, NY: Syracuse University Press, 1962.

———. *From Hayes to McKinley: National Party Politics, 1877–1896.* Syracuse, NY: Syracuse University Press, 1969.

———. *William McKinley and His America.* Syracuse, NY: Syracuse University Press, 1963.

Morris, Roger. *Richard Milhous Nixon: The Rise of an American Politician.* New York: Henry Holt, 1990.

Morrison, Chaplain W. *Democratic Politics and Sectionalism: The Wilmot Proviso Controversy.* Chapel Hill: University of North Carolina Press, 1967.

Morrison, Michael A. "Martin Van Buren, the Democracy, and the Partisan Politics of Texas Annexation." *Journal of Southern History* 61 (November 1995): 695–724.

———. *Slavery and the American West: The Eclipse of Manifest Destiny and the Coming of the Civil War.* Chapel Hill: University of North Carolina Press, 1997.

Mowry, George E. *The Era of Theodore Roosevelt and the Birth of Modern America, 1900–1912.* New York: Harper and Row, 1958.

Murray, Robert K. *The Harding Era: Warren G. Harding and His Administration.* Minneapolis: University of Minnesota, 1969.

———. *The Politics of Normalcy: Governmental Theory and Practice in the Harding-Coolidge Era.* New York: W.W. Norton, 1973.

Muzzey, David Saville. *James G. Blaine: A Political Idol of Other Days.* New York: Dodd, Mead, 1934.

Nagel, Paul C. "The Election of 1824: A Reconsideration Based on Newspaper Opinion." *Journal of Southern History* 26 (August 1960): 315–29.

Nasaw, David. *The Chief: The Life of William Randolph Hearst.* Boston: Houghton Mifflin, Mariner Books, 2001.

Neal, Donn C. *The World Beyond the Hudson: Alfred E. Smith and National Politics, 1918–1928.* New York: Garland, 1983.

Neal, Steve. *Dark Horse: A Biography of Wendell Willkie.* Garden City, NY: Doubleday, 1984.

Neely, Mark E., Jr. *The Last Best Hope of Earth: Abraham Lincoln and the Promise of America.* Cambridge, MA: Harvard University Press, 1993.

Nelson, Michael, ed. *The Elections of 1984.* Washington, DC: Congressional Quarterly Press, 1985.

———. *The Elections of 1992.* Washington, DC: Congressional Quarterly Press, 1993.

———. *The Elections of 1996.* Washington, DC: Congressional Quarterly Press, 1997.

Nevins, Allan. *The Emergence of Lincoln.* 2 vols. New York: Charles Scribner's Sons, 1950.

———. *Franklin Pierce, Young Hickory of the Granite Hills.* Philadelphia: University of Pennsylvania Press, 1958.

———. *Grover Cleveland: A Study in Courage.* New York: Dodd, Mead, 1948.

Niven, John. *Martin Van Buren: The Romantic Age of American Politics.* New York and Oxford: Oxford University Press, 1983.

Nixon, Richard. *RN: The Memoirs of Richard Nixon.* New York: Grosset and Dunlap, 1978.

Noggle, Burl. *Teapot Dome: Oil and Politics in the 1920s.* New York: Norton, 1962.

Oates, Stephen B. *With Malice Toward None: A Life of Abraham Lincoln.* New York: Harper and Row, 1977.

O'Donnell, Kenneth, David F. Powers, and Joe McCarthy. *Johnny, We Hardly Knew Ye.* Boston: Little, Brown, 1970.

Painter, Nell Irvin. *Standing at Armageddon: The United States, 1877–1919.* New York: W.W. Norton, 1987.

Palmer, Niall. *The New Hampshire Primary and the American Electoral Process.* Boulder, CO: Westview Press, 2000.

Parmet, Herbert. *The Democrats: The Years After FDR.* New York: MacMillan, 1976.

———. *Eisenhower and the American Crusades.* New York: Macmillan, 1972.

———. *JFK: The Presidency of John F. Kennedy.* New York: Penguin Books, 1983.

———. *Richard Nixon and His America.* Boston: Little, Brown, 1990.

Parmet, Herbert S., and Marie B. Hecht. *Never Again: A President Runs for a Third Term.* New York: Macmillan, 1968.

Parsons, Lynn Hudson. *John Quincy Adams.* Madison, WI: Madison House, 1998.

Pasley, Jeffrey L. "'A Journeyman, Either in Law or Politics': John Beckley and the Social Origins of Political Campaigning." *Journal of the Early Republic* 16 (1996): 531–69.

———. *"The Tyranny of Printers": Newspaper Politics in the Early American Republic.* Charlottesville: University Press of Virginia, 2001.

Patterson, James T. *Grand Expectations: The United States, 1945–1974.* New York: Oxford University Press, 1996.

———. *Mr. Republican: A Biography of Robert A. Taft.* Boston: Houghton Mifflin, 1972.

Patterson, Thomas E. *The Mass Media Election: How Americans Choose Their President*. New York: Praeger, 1980.

———. *Out of Order*. 2d ed. New York: Vintage, 1994.

Peel, Roy V., and Thomas Donnelly. *The 1932 Campaign: An Analysis*. New York: Farrar and Rinehart, 1935.

Perman, Michael. *The Road to Redemption: Southern Politics, 1869–1879*. Chapel Hill: University of North Carolina Press, 1984.

Perry, James M. *Us and Them: How the Press Covered the 1972 Election*. New York: C.N. Potter, 1973.

Peskin, Allan. *Garfield: A Biography*. Kent, OH: Kent State University Press, 1978.

Peterson, Norma Lois. *The Presidencies of William Henry Harrison and John Tyler*. Lawrence: University Press of Kansas, 1989.

Pickett, William B. *Eisenhower Decides to Run: Presidential Politics and Cold War Strategy*. Chicago: Ivan R. Dee, 2000.

Polakoff, Keith Ian. *The Politics of Inertia: The Election of 1876 and the End of Reconstruction*. Baton Rouge: Louisiana State University Press, 1973.

Polsby, Nelson W. *Consequences of Party Reform*. Oxford: Oxford University Press, 1983.

Polsby, Nelson W., and Aaron Wildavsky. *Presidential Elections*, 10th ed. New York: Chatham House, 2000.

Pomper, Gerald M. *Nominating the President*. Evanston, IL: Northwestern University Press, 1966.

Pomper, Gerald M., et al., eds. *The Election of 1976: Reports and Interpretations*. New York: Longman, 1977.

———. *The Election of 1980: Reports and Interpretations*. Chatham, NJ: Chatham House, 1981.

———. *The Election of 1988: Reports and Interpretations*. Chatham, NJ: Chatham House, 1989.

———. *The Election of 1992: Reports and Interpretations*. Chatham, NJ: Chatham House, 1993.

———. *The Election of 1996: Reports and Interpretations*. Chatham, NJ: Chatham House, 1997.

Posner, Richard A. *Breaking the Deadlock: The 2000 Election, the Constitution and the Courts*. Princeton, NJ: Princeton University Press, 2001.

Potter, David Morris. *The Impending Crisis, 1848–1861*. Completed and edited by Don E. Fehrenbacher. New York: Harper and Row, 1976.

Presidential Elections 1789–1996. Washington, DC: Congressional Quarterly, 1997.

Pringle, Henry F. *The Life and Times of William Howard Taft*. 2 vols. New York: Farrar and Rinehart, 1939.

Rakove, Jack. *James Madison and the Creation of the American Republic*. Glenview, IL: Harper Collins, 1990.

Rakove, Jack, Alex Keyssar, and Henry Brady. *The Unfinished Election of 2000*. New York: Basic Books, 2001.

Randall, J.G., and Richard N. Current. *Lincoln the President: Last Full Measure*. Urbana and Chicago: University of Illinois Press, 1991.

Ranney, Austin, ed. *The American Elections of 1984*. Durham, NC: Duke University Press, 1985.

Rayback, Joseph G. *Free Soil: The Election of 1848*. Lexington: University Press of Kentucky, 1970.

Rayback, Robert J. *Millard Fillmore: Biography of a President*. Buffalo, NY: Buffalo Historical Society, 1959.

Reeves, Thomas C. *Gentleman Boss: The Life of Chester Alan Arthur*. New York: Knopf, 1975.

———. *A Question of Character: A Life of John F. Kennedy*. New York: Free Press, 1991.

Reitano, Joanne. *The Tariff Question in the Gilded Age: The Great Debate of 1888*. University Park: Pennsylvania State University Press, 1994.

Remini, Robert V. *Andrew Jackson and the Course of American Freedom, 1822–1832*. New York: Harper and Row, 1981.

———. *Daniel Webster, The Man and His Times*. New York and London: W.W. Norton, 1997.

———. *The Election of 1828*. Philadelphia: J. B. Lippincott, 1963.

———. *Henry Clay, Statesman for the Union*. New York: W.W. Norton, 1991.

———. *Martin Van Buren and the Making of the Democratic Party*. New York: W.W. Norton, 1970.

———. "New York and the Presidential Election of 1816." *New York History* 31 (July 1950): 308–22.

Risjord, Norman K. *Chesapeake Politics, 1781–1800*. New York: Columbia University Press, 1978.

Roosevelt, Eleanor. *This I Remember*. New York: Harper and Brothers, 1949.

Rosenman, Samuel I., comp. *The Public Papers and Addresses of Franklin D. Roosevelt, 1882–1945*. 13 vols. New York: Russell & Russell, 1938–50.

Rosenman, Samuel I. *Working with Roosevelt*. New York: Harper and Brothers, 1952.

Rosenstone, Steven J., Roy L. Behr, and Edward H. Lazarus. *Third Parties in America: Citizen Response to Major Party Failure*. 2d ed. Princeton, NJ: Princeton University Press, 1996.

Ross, Earl Dudley. *The Liberal Republican Movement*. New York: Columbia University Press, 1919.

Ross, Hugh. "Was the Nomination of Wendell Willkie a Political Miracle?" *Indiana Magazine of History* 57:2 (June 1962): 80–99.

Ross, Irwin. *The Loneliest Campaign: The Truman Victory of 1948*. Westport, CT: Greenwood, 1977.

Rusk, Jerrold G. *A Statistical History of the American Electorate*. Washington, DC: Congressional Quarterly, 2001.

Russell, Francis. *The Shadow of Blooming Grove: Warren G. Harding and His Times*. New York: McGraw-Hill, 1968.

Rutland, Robert Allen. *The Presidency of James Madison*. Lawrence: Kansas University Press, 1990.

Salvatore, Nick. *Eugene V. Debs: Citizen and Socialist*. Urbana: University of Illinois Press, 1982.

Savage, Sean. *Roosevelt: The Party Leader, 1932–1945*. Lexington: University Press of Kentucky, 1991.

Schlesinger, Arthur M., Jr. *The Age of Roosevelt: The Politics of Upheaval*. Boston: Houghton Mifflin, 1960.

———. *Robert Kennedy and His Times*. Boston: Houghton Mifflin, 1978.

———. *A Thousand Days: John F. Kennedy in the White House.* Boston: Fawcett, 1965.

Schlup, Leonard. "Adlai E. Stevenson and Southern Politics in 1892." *Mississippi Quarterly* 47:1 (Winter 1993–94): 57–78.

Schram, Martin. *Running for President: A Journal of the Carter Campaign.* New York: Pocket Books, 1978.

Schwarz, Jordan A. *The Interregnum of Despair: Hoover, Congress and the Depression.* Urbana: University of Illinois Press, 1970.

Seip, Terry L. *The South Returns to Congress: Men, Economic Measures, and Intersectional Relationships, 1868–1879.* Baton Rouge: Louisiana State University Press, 1983.

Sellers, Charles. *James K. Polk: Continentalist, 1843–1846.* Princeton, NJ: Princeton University Press, 1966.

———. *The Market Revolution: Jacksonian America, 1815–1846.* New York: Oxford University Press, 1991.

Sewell, Richard H. *Ballots for Freedom: Antislavery Politics in the United States, 1837–1860.* New York: Oxford University Press, 1976.

———. *John P. Hale and the Politics of Abolition.* Cambridge, MA: Harvard University Press, 1965.

Sharp, James Roger. *American Politics in the Early Republic: The New Nation in Crisis.* New Haven and London: Yale University Press, 1993.

Sherman, Richard B. *The Republican Party and Black America: From McKinley to Hoover, 1896–1933.* Charlottesville: University Press of Virginia, 1973.

Shields, Mark. *On the Campaign Trail.* Chapel Hill, NC: Algonquin Books of Chapel Hill, 1985.

Shklar, Judith. *American Citizenship: The Quest for Inclusion.* Cambridge, MA: Harvard University Press, 1991.

Sievers, Harry J. *Benjamin Harrison, Hoosier Statesman: From the Civil War to the White House, 1865–1888.* New York: University Publishers, 1959.

Silbey, Joel H. *A Respectable Minority: The Democratic Party in the Civil War Era, 1860–1868.* New York: W.W. Norton, 1977.

Simpson, Brooks D. *Let Us Have Peace: Ulysses S. Grant and the Politics of War and Reconstruction, 1861–1868.* Chapel Hill: University of North Carolina, 1991.

———. *The Political Education of Henry Adams.* Columbia: University of South Carolina Press, 1996.

———. *The Reconstruction Presidents.* Lawrence: University Press of Kansas, 1998.

Small, Melvin. *The Presidency of Richard Nixon.* Lawrence: University Press of Kansas, 1999.

Smallwood, Frank. *The Other Candidates: Third Parties in Presidential Elections.* Hanover, NH: University Press of New England, 1983.

Smelser, Marshall. *The Democratic Republic: 1801–1815.* New York: Harper and Row, 1968.

Smith, Bradley A. *Unfree Speech: The Folly of Campaign Finance Reform.* Princeton, NJ: Princeton University Press, 2001.

Smith, Culver H. *The Press, Politics, and Patronage: The American Government's Use of Newspapers, 1789–1875.* Athens: University of Georgia Press, 1977.

Smith, James Morton. *The Republic of Letters: The Correspondence Between Thomas Jefferson and James Madison, 1776–1826.* 3 vols. New York: W.W. Norton, 1995.

Smith, Richard Norton. *Thomas E. Dewey and His Times.* New York: Simon and Schuster, 1982.

Sobel, Robert. *Coolidge: An American Enigma.* Washington, DC: Regnery, 1998.

Socolofsky, Homer E., and Allan B. Spetter. *The Presidency of Benjamin Harrison.* Lawrence: University Press of Kansas, 1987.

Solberg, Carl. *Hubert H. Humphrey: A Biography.* New York: W.W. Norton, 1984.

Sorauf, Frank. *Inside Campaign Finance.* New Haven, CT: Yale University Press, 1992.

Sorenson, Theodore. *Kennedy.* New York: Harper and Row, 1965.

Spivac, Burton. *Jefferson's English Crisis: Commerce, Embargo, and the Republican Revolution.* Charlottesville: University of Virginia Press, 1979.

Sproat, John G. *"The Best Men": Liberal Reformers in the Gilded Age.* New York: Oxford University Press, 1968.

Steeples, Douglas W., and David O. Whitten. *Democracy in Desperation: The Depression of 1893.* Westport, CT: Greenwood, 1998.

Stroud, Kandy. *How Jimmy Won: The Victory Campaign from Plains to the White House.* New York: Morrow, 1977.

Summers, Mark W. *The Era of Good Stealings.* New York: Oxford University Press, 1992.

———. *The Plundering Generation: Corruption and the Crisis of the Union, 1849–1861.* New York: Oxford University Press, 1987.

———. *The Press Gang: Newspapers and Politics, 1865–1878.* Chapel Hill: University of North Carolina Press, 1994.

———. *Rum, Romanism, & Rebellion: The Making of a President, 1884.* Chapel Hill: University of North Carolina, 2000.

Sunstein, Cass, and Richard Epstein, eds. *The Vote: Bush, Gore, and the Supreme Court.* Chicago: University of Chicago Press, 2001.

Sydnor, Charles S. "The One-Party Period of American History." *American Historical Review* 51 (April 1946): 439–51.

Tagg, James D. *Benjamin Franklin Bache and the Philadelphia "Aurora."* Philadelphia: University of Pennsylvania Press, 1991.

Tansill, Charles Callan. *The Secret Loves of the Founding Fathers.* New York: Devin-Adair, 1964.

Tebbel, John, and Sarah Miles Watts. *The Press and the Presidency: From George Washington to Ronald Reagan.* New York: Oxford University Press, 1985.

Toobin, Jeffrey. *Too Close to Call: The Thirty-Six-Day Battle to Decide the 2000 Election.* New York: Random House, 2001.

Turner, Lynn W. *William Plumer of New Hampshire.* Chapel Hill: University of North Carolina Press, 1962.

Unger, Irwin, and Debi Unger. *Turning Point: 1968.* New York: Scribner's, 1988.

Unger, Nancy C. *Fighting Bob La Follette: The Righteous Reformer.* Chapel Hill: University of North Carolina Press, 2000.

Van Deusen, Glyndon G. *The Jacksonian Era, 1828–1848*. New York: Harper Torchbooks, 1959.

Volpe, Vernon L. "The Liberty Party and Polk's Election, 1844." *The Historian* 53 (Summer 1991): 691–710.

Voss-Hubbard, Mark. "The 'Third Party Tradition' Reconsidered: Third Parties and American Public Life, 1830–1900." *Journal of American History* 86 (June 1999): 121–50.

Ward, John William. *Andrew Jackson, Symbol for an Age*. New York: Oxford University Press, 1955.

Watson, Harry T. *Liberty and Power: The Politics of Jacksonian America*. New York: Noonday, 1990.

Waugh, John C. *Reelecting Lincoln: The Battle for the 1864 Presidency*. New York: Crown, 1997.

Webber, Michael J. *New Deal Fat Cats: Business, Labor, and Campaign Finance in the 1936 Presidential Election*. New York: Fordham University Press, 2000.

Weinstein, James. *The Decline of Socialism in America, 1912–1925*. New York: Random House, 1967.

Weisberg, Herbert, and Janet Box-Steffensmeier, eds. *Reelection 1996: How Americans Voted*. Chatham, NJ: Chatham House, 1999.

Weisberger, Bernard A. *America Afire: Jefferson, Adams, and the Revolutionary Election of 1800*. New York: William Morrow, 2000.

Welch, Richard E., Jr. *The Presidencies of Grover Cleveland*. Lawrence: University Press of Kansas, 1988.

West, Darrell W. *Checkbook Democracy: How Money Corrupts Political Campaigns*. Boston: Northeastern University Press, 2000.

White, F. Clifton. *Suite 3505*. New Rochelle, NY: Arlington House, 1967.

White, Theodore. *The Making of the President 1960*. New York,: Atheneum, 1961.

———. *The Making of the President 1964*. New York: Atheneum, 1965.

———. *The Making of the President 1968*. New York: Pocket Books, 1970.

Wicker, Tom. *One of Us: Richard Nixon and the American Dream*. New York: Random House, 1991.

Williams, R. Hal. *Years of Decision: American Politics in the 1890s*. New York: John Wiley and Sons, 1978.

Williamson, Chilton. *American Suffrage: From Property to Democracy, 1760–1860*. Princeton, NJ: Princeton University Press, 1960.

Wills, Gary. *Reagan's America*. New York: Penguin Books, 1988.

Wilmarth, Mary Hawes, to Ellen Gates Starr, October 21, 1916. Ellen Gates Starr Manuscript Collection, in the Sophie Smith Collection, Smith College Library, Northampton, MA.

Wilson, Major L. *The Presidency of Martin Van Buren*. Lawrence: University Press of Kansas, 1984.

Witcover, Jules. *Marathon: The Pursuit of the Presidency, 1972–1976*. New York: Viking, 1977.

Wooten, James. *Dasher: The Roots and the Rising of Jimmy Carter*. New York: Summit Books, 1978.

Sources for Election Statistics

1788-1820

U.S. National Archives and Records Administration, Washington, DC (www.nara.gov)

1824

Indiana Legislative Reference Bureau, "Indiana's Electoral and Popular Vote for President from 1816 to Date," *Year Book of the State of Indiana for the Year 1917* (Indianapolis, 1918); State Administrative Board of Election Laws, *Review of the Meetings of Presidential Electors in Maryland, 1789–1980* (Baltimore: 20th Century Printing, 1981); "New Jersey Presidential Voting Popular Vote, Since 1824," *New Jersey Legislative Manual 1995* (Trenton, 1995); Ohio Secretary of State, "Vote Cast in Ohio for President . . . at the Presidential and State Elections from 1803 to 1938, Inclusive," *Ohio Election Statistics, The General Election Held on the Eighth Day of November 1938* (Columbus, 1939); Pennsylvania Department of Property and Supplies, "Popular Vote of Pennsylvania for President 1789–1972," *The 1972–1973 Pennsylvania Manual* (Harrisburg, 1973); *Presidential Elections, 1789–1992* (Washington: Congressional Quarterly, 1995); Rhode Island Secretary of State, "R.I. Vote at Presidential Elections," *Rhode Island Manual 1985–86* (Providence, 1986)

1828

Indiana Legislative Reference Bureau, "Indiana's Electoral and Popular Vote for President from 1816 to Date," *Year Book of the State of Indiana for the Year 1917* (Indianapolis, 1918); State Administrative Board of Election Laws, *Review of the Meetings of Presidential Electors in Maryland, 1789–1980* (Baltimore: 20th Century Printing, 1981); "New Jersey Presidential Voting Popular Vote, Since 1824," *New Jersey Legislative Manual 1995* (Trenton, 1995); Ohio Secretary of State, "Vote Cast in Ohio for President . . . at the Presidential and State Elections from 1803 to 1938, Inclusive," *Ohio Election Statistics, The General Election Held on the Eighth Day of November 1938* (Columbus, 1939); Pennsylvania Department of Property and Supplies, "Popular Vote of Pennsylvania for President 1789–1972," *The 1972–1973 Pennsylvania Manual* (Harrisburg, 1973); *Presidential Elections, 1789–1992* (Washington: Congressional Quarterly, 1995); Rhode Island Secretary of State, "R.I. Vote at Presidential Elections," *Rhode Island Manual 1985–86* (Providence, 1986); Vermont Secretary of State, ed., "Presidential Elections in Vermont Since 1828," *Vermont Legislative Directory and State Manual 1981–1982* (Montpelier, 1981)

1832

Indiana Legislative Reference Bureau, "Indiana's Electoral and Popular Vote for President from 1816 to Date," *Year Book of the State of Indiana for the Year 1917* (Indianapolis, 1918); State Administrative Board of Election Laws, *Review of the Meetings of Presidential Electors in Maryland, 1789–1980* (Baltimore: 20th Century Printing, 1981); "New Jersey Presidential Voting Popular Vote, Since 1824," *New Jersey Legislative Manual 1995* (Trenton, 1995); Ohio Secretary of State, "Vote Cast in Ohio for President . . . at the Presidential and State Elections from 1803 to 1938, Inclusive," *Ohio Election Statistics, The General Election Held on the Eighth Day of November 1938*

(Columbus, 1939); Pennsylvania Department of Property and Supplies, "Popular Vote of Pennsylvania for President 1789–1972," *The 1972–1973 Pennsylvania Manual* (Harrisburg, 1973); *Presidential Elections, 1789–1992* (Washington: Congressional Quarterly, 1995); Rhode Island Secretary of State, "R.I. Vote at Presidential Elections," *Rhode Island Manual 1985–86* (Providence, 1986); Vermont Secretary of State, ed., "Presidential Elections in Vermont Since 1828," *Vermont Legislative Directory and State Manual 1981–1982* (Montpelier, 1981)

1836

Indiana Legislative Reference Bureau, "Indiana's Electoral and Popular Vote for President from 1816 to Date," *Year Book of the State of Indiana for the Year 1917* (Indianapolis, 1918); State Administrative Board of Election Laws, *Review of the Meetings of Presidential Electors in Maryland, 1789–1980* (Baltimore: 20th Century Printing, 1981); Michigan Department of State, comp., "Presidential Vote in Michigan from 1836 to 1916," *Michigan Official Directory and Legislative Manual 1917–1918* (Lansing, 1917); "New Jersey Presidential Voting Popular Vote, Since 1824," *New Jersey Legislative Manual 1995* (Trenton, 1995); Ohio Secretary of State, "Vote Cast in Ohio for President . . . at the Presidential and State Elections from 1803 to 1938, Inclusive," *Ohio Election Statistics, The General Election Held on the Eighth Day of November 1938* (Columbus, 1939); Pennsylvania Department of Property and Supplies, "Popular Vote of Pennsylvania for President 1789–1972," *The 1972–1973 Pennsylvania Manual* (Harrisburg, 1973); *Presidential Elections, 1789–1992* (Washington: Congressional Quarterly, 1995); Rhode Island Secretary of State, "R.I. Vote at Presidential Elections," *Rhode Island Manual 1985–86* (Providence, 1986); Vermont Secretary of State, ed., "Presidential Elections in Vermont Since 1828," *Vermont Legislative Directory and State Manual 1981–1982* (Montpelier, 1981)

1840

Indiana Legislative Reference Bureau, "Indiana's Electoral and Popular Vote for President from 1816 to Date," *Year Book of the State of Indiana for the Year 1917* (Indianapolis, 1918); State Administrative Board of Election Laws, *Review of the Meetings of Presidential Electors in Maryland, 1789–1980* (Baltimore: 20th Century Printing, 1981); Michigan Department of State, comp., "Presidential Vote in Michigan from 1836 to 1916," *Michigan Official Directory and Legislative Manual 1917–1918* (Lansing, 1917); "New Jersey Presidential Voting Popular Vote, Since 1824," *New Jersey Legislative Manual 1995* (Trenton, 1995); Ohio Secretary of State, "Vote Cast in Ohio for President . . . at the Presidential and State Elections from 1803 to 1938, Inclusive," *Ohio Election Statistics, The General Election Held on the Eighth Day of November 1938* (Columbus, 1939); Pennsylvania Department of Property and Supplies, "Popular Vote of Pennsylvania for President 1789–1972," *The 1972–1973 Pennsylvania Manual* (Harrisburg, 1973); *Presidential Elections, 1789–1992* (Washington: Congressional Quarterly, 1995); Rhode Island Secretary of State, "R.I. Vote at Presidential Elections," *Rhode Island Manual 1985–86* (Providence, 1986); Vermont Secretary of State, ed., "Presidential Elections in Vermont Since 1828," *Vermont Legislative Directory and State Manual 1981–1982* (Montpelier, 1981)

1844

Indiana Legislative Reference Bureau, "Indiana's Electoral and Popular Vote for President from 1816 to Date," *Year Book of the State of Indiana for the Year 1917* (Indianapolis, 1918); State Administrative Board of Election Laws, *Review of the Meetings of Presidential Electors in Maryland, 1789–1980* (Baltimore: 20th Century Printing, 1981); Michigan Department of State, comp., "Presidential Vote in Michigan from 1836 to 1916," *Michigan Official Directory and Legislative Manual 1917–1918* (Lansing, 1917); "New Jersey Presidential Voting Popular Vote, Since 1824," *New Jersey Legislative Manual 1995* (Trenton, 1995); Ohio Secretary of State, "Vote Cast in Ohio for President . . . at the Presidential and State Elections from 1803 to 1938, Inclusive," *Ohio Election Statistics, The General Election Held on the Eighth Day of November 1938* (Columbus, 1939); Pennsylvania Department of Property and Supplies, "Popular Vote of Pennsylvania for President 1789–1972," *The 1972–1973 Pennsylvania Manual* (Harrisburg, 1973); *Presidential Elections, 1789–1992* (Washington: Congressional Quarterly, 1995); Rhode Island Secretary of State, "R.I. Vote at Presidential Elections," *Rhode Island Manual 1985–86* (Providence, 1986); Vermont Secretary of State, ed., "Presidential Elections in Vermont Since 1828," *Vermont Legislative Directory and State Manual 1981–1982* (Montpelier, 1981)

1848

Indiana Legislative Reference Bureau, "Indiana's Electoral and Popular Vote for President from 1816 to Date," *Year Book of the State of Indiana for the Year 1917* (Indianapolis, 1918); State Administrative Board of Election Laws, *Review of the Meetings of Presidential Electors in Maryland, 1789–1980* (Baltimore: 20th Century Printing, 1981); Michigan Department of State, comp., "Presidential Vote in Michigan from 1836 to 1916," *Michigan Official Directory and Legislative Manual 1917–1918* (Lansing, 1917); "New Jersey Presidential Voting Popular Vote, Since 1824," *New Jersey Legislative Manual 1995* (Trenton, 1995); Ohio Secretary of State, "Vote Cast in Ohio for President . . . at the Presidential and State Elections from 1803 to 1938, Inclusive," *Ohio Election Statistics, The General Election Held on the Eighth Day of November 1938* (Columbus, 1939); Pennsylvania Department of Property and Supplies, "Popular Vote of Pennsylvania for President 1789–1972," *The 1972–1973 Pennsylvania Manual* (Harrisburg, 1973); *Presidential Elections, 1789–1992* (Washington: Congressional Quarterly, 1995); Rhode Island Secretary of State, "R.I. Vote at Presidential Elections," *Rhode Island Manual 1985–86* (Providence, 1986); Texas Secretary of State, Elections Division, *Presidential Election Results* (www.sos.state.tx.us/elections/index.shtml) (accessed February 1, 2002); Vermont Secretary of State, ed., "Presidential Elections in Vermont since 1828," *Vermont Legislative Directory and State Manual 1981-1982* (Montpelier, 1981); "Presidential Vote in Wisconsin from 1848 to 1884," *The Blue Book for the State of Wisconsin, for 1885* (Madison, 1885)

1852

Indiana Legislative Reference Bureau, "Indiana's Electoral and Popular Vote for President from 1816 to Date," *Year Book of the State of Indiana for the Year 1917* (Indianapolis, 1918); State Administrative Board of Election Laws, *Review of the Meetings of Presidential Electors in Maryland, 1789–1980* (Baltimore: 20th Century Printing, 1981); Michigan Department of State, comp., "Presidential Vote in Michigan from 1836 to 1916," *Michigan Official Directory and Legislative Manual 1917–1918* (Lansing, 1917); New Hampshire Secretary of State, *The New Hampshire Manual of Useful Information 1889* (Manchester, 1889); "New Jersey Presidential Voting Popular Vote, Since 1824," *New Jersey Legislative Manual 1995* (Trenton, 1995); Ohio Secretary of State, "Vote Cast in Ohio for President . . . at the Presidential and State Elections from 1803 to 1938, Inclusive," *Ohio Election Statistics, The General Election Held on the Eighth Day of November 1938* (Columbus, 1939); Pennsylvania Department of Property and Supplies, "Popular Vote of Pennsylvania for President 1789–1972," *The 1972–1973 Pennsylvania Manual* (Harrisburg, 1973); *Presidential Elections, 1789–1992* (Washington: Congressional Quarterly, 1995); Rhode Island Secretary of State, "R.I. Vote at Presidential Elections," *Rhode Island Manual 1985–86* (Providence, 1986); Texas Secretary of State, Elections Division, *Presidential Election Results* (www.sos.state.tx.us/elections/index.shtml) (accessed February 1, 2002); Vermont Secretary of State, ed., "Presidential Elections in Vermont Since 1828," *Vermont Legislative Directory and State Manual 1981–1982* (Montpelier, 1981); "Presidential Vote in Wisconsin from 1848 to 1884," *The Blue Book for the State of Wisconsin, for 1885* (Madison, 1885)

1856

State of Connecticut Secretary of State, *Connecticut State Register and Manual 1905* (Hartford, 1905); Indiana Legislative Reference Bureau, "Indiana's Electoral and Popular Vote for President from 1816 to Date," *Year Book of the State of Indiana for the Year 1917* (Indianapolis, 1918); State Administrative Board of Election Laws, *Review*

---

of the Meetings of Presidential Electors in Maryland, 1789–1980 (Baltimore: 20th Century Printing, 1981); Michigan Department of State, comp., "Presidential Vote in Michigan from 1836 to 1916," *Michigan Official Directory and Legislative Manual 1917–1918* (Lansing, 1917); New Hampshire Secretary of State, *The New Hampshire Manual of Useful Information 1889* (Manchester, 1889); "New Jersey Presidential Voting Popular Vote, Since 1824," *New Jersey Legislative Manual 1995* (Trenton, 1995); Ohio Secretary of State, "Vote Cast in Ohio for President . . . at the Presidential and State Elections from 1803 to 1938, Inclusive," *Ohio Election Statistics, The General Election Held on the Eighth Day of November 1938* (Columbus, 1939); Pennsylvania Department of Property and Supplies, "Popular Vote of Pennsylvania for President 1789–1972," *The 1972–1973 Pennsylvania Manual* (Harrisburg, 1973); *Presidential Elections, 1789–1992* (Washington: Congressional Quarterly, 1995); Rhode Island Secretary of State, "R.I. Vote at Presidential Elections," *Rhode Island Manual 1985–86* (Providence, 1986); Texas Secretary of State, Elections Division, *Presidential Election Results* (www.sos.state.tx.us/elections/index.shtml) (accessed February 1, 2002); Vermont Secretary of State, ed., "Presidential Elections in Vermont Since 1828," *Vermont Legislative Directory and State Manual 1981–1982* (Montpelier, 1981); "Presidential Vote in Wisconsin from 1848 to 1884," *The Blue Book for the State of Wisconsin, for 1885* (Madison, 1885)

1860

State of Connecticut Secretary of State, *Connecticut State Register and Manual 1905* (Hartford, 1905); Indiana Legislative Reference Bureau, "Indiana's Electoral and Popular Vote for President from 1816 to Date," *Year Book of the State of Indiana for the Year 1917* (Indianapolis, 1918); State Administrative Board of Election Laws, *Review of the Meetings of Presidential Electors in Maryland, 1789–1980* (Baltimore: 20th Century Printing, 1981); Michigan Department of State, comp., "Presidential Vote in Michigan from 1836 to 1916," *Michigan Official Directory and Legislative Manual 1917–1918* (Lansing, 1917); Minnesota Secretary of State, "Presidential Vote," *The Legislative Manual of the State of Minnesota 1885* (St. Paul, 1885); New Hampshire Secretary of State, *The New Hampshire Manual of Useful Information 1889* (Manchester, 1889); "New Jersey Presidential Voting Popular Vote, Since 1824," *New Jersey Legislative Manual 1995* (Trenton, 1995); Ohio Secretary of State, "Vote Cast in Ohio for President . . . at the Presidential and State Elections from 1803 to 1938, Inclusive," *Ohio Election Statistics, The General Election Held on the Eighth Day of November 1938* (Columbus, 1939); Oregon Office of the Secretary of State, "Votes Cast in Oregon for U.S. President 1860–2000," *Oregon Blue Book 2001–2002* (Salem, 2001); Pennsylvania Department of Property and Supplies, "Popular Vote of Pennsylvania for President 1789–1972," *The 1972–1973 Pennsylvania Manual* (Harrisburg, 1973); *Presidential Elections, 1789–1992* (Washington: Congressional Quarterly, 1995); Rhode Island Secretary of State, "R.I. Vote at Presidential Elections," *Rhode Island Manual 1985–86* (Providence, 1986); Texas Secretary of State, Elections Division, *Presidential Election Results* (www.sos.state.tx.us/elections/index.shtml) (accessed February 1, 2002); Vermont Secretary of State, ed., "Presidential Elections in Vermont Since 1828," *Vermont Legislative Directory and State Manual 1981–1982* (Montpelier, 1981); "Presidential Vote in Wisconsin from 1848 to 1884," *The Blue Book for the State of Wisconsin, for 1885* (Madison, 1885)

1864

State of Connecticut Secretary of State, *Connecticut State Register and Manual 1905* (Hartford, 1905); Indiana Legislative Reference Bureau, "Indiana's Electoral and Popular Vote for President from 1816 to Date," *Year Book of the State of Indiana for the Year 1917* (Indianapolis, 1918); Iowa Secretary of State, "Popular Vote in Iowa for U.S. President," *Iowa Official Register 1985–86* (Des Moines, 1986); State Administrative Board of Election Laws, *Review of the Meetings of Presidential Electors in Maryland, 1789–1980* (Baltimore: 20th Century Printing, 1981); Massachusetts: *Aggregate of Votes for Presidential Electors for 1864 At Large, November 8, 1864* (Boston, 1864); Michigan Department of State, comp., "Presidential Vote in Michigan from 1836 to 1916," *Michigan Official Directory and Legislative Manual 1917–1918* (Lansing, 1917); Minnesota Secretary of State, "Presidential Vote," *The Legislative Manual of the State of Minnesota 1885* (St. Paul, 1885); Nevada Secretary of State, *Political History of Nevada, 1996* (Carson City, 1996); New Hampshire Secretary of State, *The New Hampshire Manual of Useful Information 1889* (Manchester, 1889); "New Jersey Presidential Voting Popular Vote, Since 1824," *New Jersey Legislative Manual 1995* (Trenton, 1995); Ohio Secretary of State, "Vote Cast in Ohio for President . . . at the Presidential and State Elections from 1803 to 1938, Inclusive," *Ohio Election Statistics, The General Election Held on the Eighth Day of November 1938* (Columbus, 1939); Oregon Office of the Secretary of State, "Votes Cast in Oregon for U.S. President 1860–2000," *Oregon Blue Book 2001–2002* (Salem, 2001); Pennsylvania Department of Property and Supplies, "Popular Vote of Pennsylvania for President 1789–1972," *The 1972–1973 Pennsylvania Manual* (Harrisburg, 1973); *Presidential Elections, 1789–*

1992 (Washington: Congressional Quarterly, 1995); Rhode Island Secretary of State, "R.I. Vote at Presidential Elections," *Rhode Island Manual 1985–86* (Providence, 1986); Vermont Secretary of State, ed., "Presidential Elections in Vermont Since 1828," *Vermont Legislative Directory and State Manual 1981–1982* (Montpelier, 1981); "Presidential Vote in Wisconsin from 1848 to 1884," *The Blue Book for the State of Wisconsin, for 1885* (Madison, 1885)

1868

State of Connecticut Secretary of State, *Connecticut State Register and Manual 1905* (Hartford, 1905); Indiana Legislative Reference Bureau, "Indiana's Electoral and Popular Vote for President from 1816 to Date," *Year Book of the State of Indiana for the Year 1917* (Indianapolis, 1918); Iowa Secretary of State, "Popular Vote in Iowa for U.S. President," *Iowa Official Register 1985–86* (Des Moines, 1986); State Administrative Board of Election Laws, *Review of the Meetings of Presidential Electors in Maryland, 1789–1980* (Baltimore: 20th Century Printing, 1981); Massachusetts: *Aggregate of Votes for Presidential Electors for 1868 At Large, November 3, 1868* (Boston, 1868); Michigan Department of State, comp., "Presidential Vote in Michigan from 1836 to 1916," *Michigan Official Directory and Legislative Manual 1917–1918* (Lansing, 1917); Minnesota Secretary of State, "Presidential Vote," *The Legislative Manual of the State of Minnesota 1885* (St. Paul, 1885); Nebraska Secretary of State, "Nebraska Presidential Election Statistics, 1868–2000," *Nebraska Blue Book 2001–2002* (Lincoln, 2001); Nevada Secretary of State, *Political History of Nevada, 1996* (Carson City, 1996); New Hampshire Secretary of State, *The New Hampshire Manual of Useful Information 1889* (Manchester, 1889); "New Jersey Presidential Voting Popular Vote, Since 1824," *New Jersey Legislative Manual 1995* (Trenton, 1995); Ohio Secretary of State, "Vote Cast in Ohio for President . . . at the Presidential and State Elections from 1803 to 1938, Inclusive," *Ohio Election Statistics, The General Election Held on the Eighth Day of November 1938* (Columbus, 1939); Oregon Office of the Secretary of State, "Votes Cast in Oregon for U.S. President 1860–2000," *Oregon Blue Book 2001–2002* (Salem, 2001); Pennsylvania Department of Property and Supplies, "Popular Vote of Pennsylvania for President 1789–1972," *The 1972–1973 Pennsylvania Manual* (Harrisburg, 1973); *Presidential Elections, 1789–1992* (Washington: Congressional Quarterly, 1995); Rhode Island Secretary of State, "R.I. Vote at Presidential Elections," *Rhode Island Manual 1985–86* (Providence, 1986); Vermont Secretary of State, ed., "Presidential Elections in Vermont Since 1828," *Vermont Legislative Directory and State Manual 1981–1982* (Montpelier, 1981); Wisconsin, comp., "Comparative Vote of Wisconsin for President in 1872 . . ." *The Legislative Manual of the State of Wisconsin 1873* (Madison, 1873)

1872

State of Connecticut Secretary of State, *Connecticut State Register and Manual 1905* (Hartford, 1905); Indiana Legislative Reference Bureau, "Indiana's Electoral and Popular Vote for President from 1816 to Date," *Year Book of the State of Indiana for the Year 1917* (Indianapolis, 1918); State Administrative Board of Election Laws, *Review of the Meetings of Presidential Electors in Maryland, 1789–1980* (Baltimore: 20th Century Printing, 1981); Massachusetts: *Aggregate of Votes for Presidential Electors for 1872 Electors At Large: Data for Highest Elector At Large, November 5, 1872* (Boston, 1872); Michigan Department of State, comp., "Presidential Vote in Michigan from 1836 to 1916," *Michigan Official Directory and Legislative Manual 1917–1918* (Lansing, 1917); Minnesota Office of the Secretary of State, Elections Division, "Vote for President and Vice President: November 7, 2000, General Election," *The Minnesota Legislative Manual 2001–2002* (St. Paul, 2001); Nebraska Secretary of State, "Nebraska Presidential Election Statistics, 1868–2000," *Nebraska Blue Book 2001–2002* (Lincoln, 2001); Nevada Secretary of State, *Political History of Nevada, 1996* (Carson City, 1996); New Hampshire Secretary of State, *The New Hampshire Manual of Useful Information 1889* (Manchester, 1889); "New Jersey Presidential Voting Popular Vote, Since 1824," *New Jersey Legislative Manual 1995* (Trenton, 1995); New York Secretary of State, *Manual for the Use of the Legislature of the State of New York 1873* (Albany, 1873); Ohio Secretary of State, "Abstract of Votes Cast at the Presidential Election of 1872, and for Governor in 1873," *Annual Report of the Secretary of State to the Governor of the State of Ohio . . . for the Year 1874* (Columbus: Nevins & Myers, 1875); Oregon Office of the Secretary of State, "Votes Cast in Oregon for U.S. President 1860–2000," *Oregon Blue Book 2001–2002* (Salem, 2001); Pennsylvania Department of Property and Supplies, "Popular Vote of Pennsylvania for President 1789–1972," *The 1972–1973 Pennsylvania Manual* (Harrisburg, 1973); *Presidential Elections, 1789–1992* (Washington: Congressional Quarterly, 1995); Rhode Island Secretary of State, "R.I. Vote at Presidential Elections," *Rhode Island Manual 1985–86* (Providence, 1986); Texas Secretary of State, Elections Division, *Presidential Election Results* (www.sos.state.tx.us/elections/index.shtml) (accessed February 1, 2002); Vermont Secretary of State, ed., "Presidential Elections in Vermont Since 1828," *Vermont Legislative Directory and State Manual 1981–1982* (Montpelier, 1981); "Presidential Vote

in Wisconsin from 1848 to 1884," *The Blue Book for the State of Wisconsin, for 1885* (Madison, 1885)

1876

Indiana Legislative Reference Bureau, "Indiana's Electoral and Popular Vote for President from 1816 to Date," *Year Book of the State of Indiana for the Year 1917* (Indianapolis, 1918); State Administrative Board of Election Laws, *Review of the Meetings of Presidential Electors in Maryland, 1789–1980* (Baltimore: 20th Century Printing, 1981); Massachusetts: *Aggregate of Votes for Presidential Electors for 1876 Electors At Large, November 7, 1876* (Boston, 1876); Michigan Department of State, comp., "Presidential Vote in Michigan from 1836 to 1916," *Michigan Official Directory and Legislative Manual 1917–1918* (Lansing, 1917); Minnesota Office of the Secretary of State, Elections Division, "Vote for President and Vice President: November 7, 2000, General Election," *The Minnesota Legislative Manual 2001–2002* (St. Paul, 2001); Nebraska Secretary of State, "Nebraska Presidential Election Statistics, 1868–2000," *Nebraska Blue Book 2001–2002* (Lincoln, 2001); Nevada Secretary of State, *Political History of Nevada, 1996* (Carson City, 1996); New Hampshire Secretary of State, *The New Hampshire Manual of Useful Information 1889* (Manchester, 1889); Ohio Secretary of State, "Abstract of Votes for Governor in 1875 and President in 1876," *Annual Report of the Secretary of State to the Governor of the State of Ohio . . . for the Year 1876* (Columbus: G.J. Brand, 1877); Oregon Office of the Secretary of State, "Votes Cast in Oregon for U.S. President 1860–2000," *Oregon Blue Book 2001–2002* (Salem, 2001); Pennsylvania Department of General Services, comp., "Official Vote of Pennsylvania, November 7, 1876, by Counties, for President of the United States," *Smull's Legislative Handbook, 1877 Manual of the Rules of the General Assembly of Pennsylvania and Legislative Directory* (Harrisburg, 1877); *Presidential Elections, 1789–1992* (Washington: Congressional Quarterly, 1995); Rhode Island Secretary of State, "R.I. Vote at Presidential Elections," *Rhode Island Manual 1985–86* (Providence, 1986); Texas Secretary of State, Elections Division, *Presidential Election Results* (www.sos.state.tx.us/elections/index.shtml) (accessed February 1, 2002); Vermont Secretary of State, ed., "Presidential Elections in Vermont Since 1828," *Vermont Legislative Directory and State Manual 1981–1982* (Montpelier, 1981); "The Presidential Vote of 1876, 1872, and 1868," *The Legislative Manual of the State of Wisconsin 1877* (Madison, 1877)

1880

Indiana Legislative Reference Bureau, "Indiana's Electoral and Popular Vote for President from 1816 to Date," *Year Book of the State of Indiana for the Year 1917* (Indianapolis, 1918); Kansas Secretary of State, "Official Vote of the State of Kansas for 1880," *Secretary of State Report* (Topeka, 1881); State Administrative Board of Election Laws, *Review of the Meetings of Presidential Electors in Maryland, 1789–1980* (Baltimore: 20th Century Printing, 1981); Massachusetts: *Aggregate of Votes for Presidential Electors for 1880 At Large, November 2, 1880* (Boston, 1880); Michigan Department of State, comp., "Presidential Vote in Michigan from 1836 to 1916," *Michigan Official Directory and Legislative Manual 1917–1918* (Lansing, 1917); Minnesota Office of the Secretary of State, Elections Division, "Vote for President and Vice President: November 7, 2000, General Election," *The Minnesota Legislative Manual 2001–2002* (St. Paul, 2001); Nebraska Secretary of State, "Nebraska Presidential Election Statistics, 1868–2000," *Nebraska Blue Book 2001–2002* (Lincoln, 2001); Nevada Secretary of State, *Political History of Nevada, 1996* (Carson City, 1996); New Hampshire Secretary of State, *The New Hampshire Manual of Useful Information 1889* (Manchester, 1889); Ohio Secretary of State, "Abstract of Votes for President and Vice President of the United States, at the Election Held November 2, 1880, in the State of Ohio," *Annual Report of the Secretary of State to the Governor of the State of Ohio for the Year 1880* (Columbus: G.J. Brand, 1881); Oregon Office of the Secretary of State, "Votes Cast in Oregon for U.S. President 1860–2000," *Oregon Blue Book 2001–2002* (Salem, 2001); Pennsylvania Department of General Services, comp., "Official Vote of Pennsylvania, November 2, 1880, by Counties, for President of the United States," *Smull's Legislative Handbook and Manual of the State of Pennsylvania 1881* (Harrisburg, 1881); *Presidential Elections, 1789–1992* (Washington: Congressional Quarterly, 1995); Rhode Island Secretary of State, *Rhode Island Manual 1882–83* (Providence, 1883); Texas Secretary of State, Elections Division, *Presidential Election Results* (www.sos.state.tx.us/elections/index.shtml) (accessed February 1, 2002); Vermont Secretary of State, ed., "Presidential Elections in Vermont Since 1828," *Vermont Legislative Directory and State Manual 1981–1982* (Montpelier, 1981); "Presidential Vote in Wisconsin from 1848 to 1884," *The Blue Book for the State of Wisconsin, for 1885* (Madison, 1885)

1884

State of Connecticut Secretary of State, *Connecticut State Register and Manual 1905* (Hartford, 1905); Indiana Secretary of State, "Recapitulation of Votes Polled for

Presidential Electors, November Election, A.D. 1884," *Biennial Report of William R. Myers, Secretary of State of the State of Indiana for the Two Years Ending October 31st, 1886* (Indianapolis, 1887); Kansas Secretary of State, "Official Vote of the State of Kansas for 1884," *Fifth Biennial Report of the Secretary of State of the State of Kansas* (Topeka, 1885); State Administrative Board of Election Laws, *Review of the Meetings of Presidential Electors in Maryland, 1789–1980* (Baltimore: 20th Century Printing, 1981); Massachusetts: *Aggregate of Votes for Presidential Electors 1884 At Large, November 4, 1884* (Boston, 1884); Michigan Department of State, comp., "Presidential Vote in Michigan from 1836 to 1916," *Michigan Official Directory and Legislative Manual 1917–1918* (Lansing, 1917); Minnesota Secretary of State, "Presidential Vote," *The Legislative Manual of the State of Minnesota 1885* (St. Paul, 1885); Nebraska Secretary of State, "Nebraska Presidential Election Statistics, 1868–2000," *Nebraska Blue Book 2001–2002* (Lincoln, 2001); Nevada Secretary of State, *Political History of Nevada, 1996* (Carson City, 1996); New Hampshire Secretary of State, *The New Hampshire Manual of Useful Information 1889* (Manchester, 1889); "Names of Counties and Number of Votes Received by Each Elector in Each County," *Manual of the Legislature of New Jersey 1885* (Trenton, 1885); New York Secretary of State, *Manual for the Legislature of the State of New York 1885* (Albany, 1885); Ohio Secretary of State, "Name of Candidates for Presidential Electors of Ohio, and the Number of Votes Cast for Each, November 4, 1884," *Annual Report of the Secretary of State to the Governor of the State of Ohio for the Year 1888* (Columbus: Westbote, 1885); Oregon Office of the Secretary of State, "Votes Cast in Oregon for U.S. President 1860–2000," *Oregon Blue Book 2001–2002* (Salem, 2001); Pennsylvania Department of Property and Supplies, "Popular Vote of Pennsylvania for President 1789–1972," *The 1972–1973 Pennsylvania Manual* (Harrisburg, 1973); *Presidential Elections, 1789–1992* (Washington: Congressional Quarterly, 1995); Rhode Island Secretary of State, *Rhode Island Manual 1886–87* (Providence, 1887); Texas Secretary of State, Elections Division, *Presidential Election Results* (www.sos.state.tx.us/elections/index.shtml) (accessed February 1, 2002); Vermont Secretary of State, ed., "Presidential Elections in Vermont Since 1828," *Vermont Legislative Directory and State Manual 1981–1982* (Montpelier, 1981); "Vote for President, 1884—by Counties," *The Blue Book for the State of Wisconsin, for 1885* (Madison, 1885)

1888

State of Connecticut Secretary of State, *Connecticut State Register and Manual 1893* (Hartford, 1893); Indiana Secretary of State, "Vote Polled for Presidential Electors—November, 1888," *Biennial Report of Charles F. Griffin, Secretary of State of the State of Indiana for the Two Years Ending October 31st, 1888* (Indianapolis, 1888); Kansas Secretary of State, "Official Vote of the State of Kansas, 1888," *Sixth Biennial Report of the Secretary of State of the State of Kansas* (Topeka, 1889); State Administrative Board of Election Laws, *Review of the Meetings of Presidential Electors in Maryland, 1789–1980* (Baltimore: 20th Century Printing, 1981); Massachusetts: *Aggregate of Votes for Presidential Electors At Large for 1889, November 6, 1888* (Boston, 1888); Michigan Department of State, comp., "Presidential Vote in Michigan from 1836 to 1916," *Michigan Official Directory and Legislative Manual 1917–1918* (Lansing, 1917); Minnesota Office of the Secretary of State, Elections Division, "Vote for President and Vice President: November 7, 2000, General Election," *The Minnesota Legislative Manual 2001–2002* (St. Paul, 2001); Missouri Secretary of State, "Vote of Missouri for President Vote of 1888," *Official Manual of the State of Missouri for the Years 1889–1890* (Jefferson City, 1889); Nebraska Secretary of State, "Nebraska Presidential Election Statistics, 1868–2000," *Nebraska Blue Book 2001–2002* (Lincoln, 2001); Nevada Secretary of State, *Political History of Nevada, 1996* (Carson City, 1996); "Names of Counties and Number of Votes Received by Each Elector in Each County," *Manual of the Legislature of New Jersey 1889* (Trenton, 1889); New York Secretary of State, *Manual for the Use of the Legislature of the State of New York 1889* (Albany, 1889); Ohio Secretary of State, "Abstract of Votes Cast for Presidential and State Officers at the Election Held November 6, 1888," *Annual Report of the Secretary of State to the Governor of the State of Ohio for the Year 1888* (Columbus: Westbote, 1889); Oregon Office of the Secretary of State, "Votes Cast in Oregon for U.S. President 1860–2000," *Oregon Blue Book 2001–2002* (Salem, 2001); Pennsylvania Department of General Services, comp., "Official Vote of Pennsylvania for Presidential Electors, 1888," *Smull's Legislative Handbook and Manual of the State of Pennsylvania 1889* (Harrisburg, 1889); *Presidential Elections, 1789–1992* (Washington: Congressional Quarterly, 1995); Rhode Island Secretary of State, *Rhode Island Manual 1888–89* (Providence, 1889); Texas Secretary of State, Elections Division, *Presidential Election Results* (www.sos.state.tx.us/elections/index.shtml) (accessed February 1, 2002); Vermont Secretary of State, ed., "Presidential Elections in Vermont Since 1828," *Vermont Legislative Directory and State Manual 1981–1982* (Montpelier, 1981); "Vote for President, 1884–1888, by Counties," *The Blue Book for the State of Wisconsin, for 1889* (Madison, 1889)

1892

California Secretary of State, comp., "Presidential Electors," *Statement of Vote of the State of California at the General Election Held November 8, A.D. 1892* (Sacramento, 1892); Connecticut Secretary of State, *Connecticut State Register and Manual 1893* (Hartford, 1893); Idaho Secretary of State. Election Division, *State of Idaho Presidential Vote Cast at the General Election November 8, 1892* (Boise, 1913); Indiana Secretary of State, "Recapitulation of Vote on Presidential Electors, November Election, 1892," *Biennial Report of W. R. Myers, Secretary of State of the State of Indiana, for the Two Years Ending October 31st, 1894* (Indianapolis, 1894); Kansas Secretary of State, "Official Vote of the State of Kansas, 1892," *Eighth Biennial Report of the Secretary of State of the State of Kansas* (Topeka, 1893); State Administrative Board of Election Laws, *Review of the Meetings of Presidential Electors in Maryland, 1789–1980* (Baltimore: 20th Century Printing, 1981); Massachusetts: *Aggregate of Votes for Presidential Electors at Large for 1893, November 8, 1892* (Boston, 1893); Michigan Department of State, comp., "Presidential Vote in Michigan from 1836 to 1916," *Michigan Official Directory and Legislative Manual 1917–1918* (Lansing, 1917); Minnesota Secretary of State, "Official Canvass by the State Board of Canvassers for Presidential Electors, Election Held November 8, 1892," *The Legislative Manual of the State of Minnesota 1893* (St. Paul, 1893); Missouri Secretary of State, "Vote of Missouri for President Vote of 1892," *Official Manual of the State of Missouri for the Years 1893–1894* (Jefferson City, 1894); Nebraska Legislative Reference Bureau, "Popular Vote by Counties for Presidential Candidates in Nebraska, 1868–1916," *The Nebraska Blue Book and Historical Register 1918* (Lincoln, 1918); Nevada Secretary of State, *Political History of Nevada, 1996* (Carson City, 1996); New Hampshire Department of State, *State of New Hampshire Manual for the General Court 1893* (Concord, 1893); "Names of Counties and Number of Votes Received by Each Elector in Each County," *Manual of the Legislature of New Jersey 1893* (Trenton, 1893); New York Secretary of State, *Manual for the Use of the Legislature of the State of New York for the Year 1893* (Albany, 1893); Ohio Secretary of State, "Election Statistics of Ohio Table No. 1—President," *Annual Report of the Secretary of State to the Governor of the State of Ohio for the Year Ending November 15, 1892* (Norwalk: Laning Printing, 1893); Oregon Office of the Secretary of State, "Votes Cast in Oregon for U.S. President 1860–2000," *Oregon Blue Book 2001–2002* (Salem, 2001); Pennsylvania Department of General Services, comp., "Official Vote of Pennsylvania for Presidential Electors, 1892," *Smull's Legislative Handbook and Manual of the State of Pennsylvania 1893* (Harrisburg, 1893); *Presidential Elections, 1789–1992* (Washington: Congressional Quarterly, 1995); Rhode Island Secretary of State, *Rhode Island Manual 1893–1894* (Providence, 1913); South Dakota Secretary of State, comp., "Official Vote of South Dakota by Counties, November Election, 1892," *South Dakota Legislative Manual 1909* (Pierre: State Publishing, 1909); Texas Secretary of State, Elections Division, *Presidential Election Results* (www.sos.state.tx.us/elections/index.shtml) (accessed February 1, 2002); Vermont Secretary of State, ed., "Presidential Elections in Vermont Since 1828," *Vermont Legislative Directory and State Manual 1981–1982* (Montpelier, 1981); Washington Secretary of State, *State Election, November 8, 1892* (Olympia, 1892); "Comparative Vote for President, 1892–1896, by Counties, with Population," *The Blue Book for the State of Wisconsin, for 1897* (Madison, 1897); "General Election—November 8, 1892," *Wyoming Historical Blue Book: A Legal and Political History of Wyoming 1868–1943* (Denver: Bradford-Robinson Printing, 1913)

1896

California Secretary of State, comp., "Presidential Electors," *Statement of Vote of California for Presidential Electors and Congressmen November 3, 1896* (Sacramento, 1896); Connecticut Secretary of State, *Connecticut State Register and Manual 1902* (Hartford, 1902); Idaho Secretary of State, Election Division, *State of Idaho Presidential Vote Cast at the General Election November 3, 1896* (Boise, 1913); Indiana Secretary of State, "Recapitulation of Vote on Presidential Electors, November Election, 1896," *Biennial Report of William D. Owen, Secretary of State of the State of Indiana, for the Two Years Ending October 31, 1896* (Indianapolis, 1897); Iowa Secretary of State, "Vote for President and Vice President by Counties, Based upon Vote Cast for Electors at Large," *Iowa Official Register 1897* (Des Moines, 1897); Kansas Secretary of State, "Statement of Official Vote, State of Kansas, 1896," *Tenth Biennial Report of the Secretary of State of the State of Kansas* (Topeka, 1897); State Administrative Board of Election Laws, *Review of the Meetings of Presidential Electors in Maryland, 1789–1980* (Baltimore: 20th Century Printing, 1981); Michigan Department of State, comp., "Presidential Vote in Michigan from 1836 to 1916," *Michigan Official Directory and Legislative Manual 1917–1918* (Lansing, 1917); Minnesota Secretary of State, "Official Canvass by the State Board of Canvassers for Presidential Electors, Election Held November 3, 1896," *The Legislative Manual of the State of Minnesota 1897* (St. Paul, 1897); Nebraska Legislative Reference Bureau, "Popular Vote by Counties for Presidential Candidates in Nebraska, 1868–1916," *The Nebraska Blue Book and Historical Register 1918* (Lincoln, 1918); Nevada Secretary of State, *Political History of Nevada, 1996* (Carson

City, 1996); New Hampshire Department of State, *State of New Hampshire Manual for the General Court, 1897* (Concord, 1897); "Number of Votes Received by Each Elector in Each County," *Manual of the Legislature of New Jersey 1897* (Trenton, 1897); New York Secretary of State, *Manual for the Use of the Legislature of the State of New York for the Year 1897* (Albany, 1897); Ohio Secretary of State, "Vote for Presidential Electors at the Election Held November 3, 1896," *Annual Report of the Secretary of State to the Governor of the State of Ohio for the Year Ending November 15, 1896* (Norwalk: Laning Printing, 1897); Oregon Office of the Secretary of State, "Votes Cast in Oregon for U.S. President 1860–2000," *Oregon Blue Book 2001–2002* (Salem, 2001); Pennsylvania Department of General Services, comp., "Official Vote of Pennsylvania for Presidential Electors, 1896," *Smull's Legislative Handbook and Manual of the State of Pennsylvania 1897* (Harrisburg, 1897); *Presidential Elections, 1789–1992* (Washington: Congressional Quarterly, 1995); Rhode Island Secretary of State, *Rhode Island Manual 1896–1897* (Providence, 1913); South Dakota Secretary of State, comp., "Official Vote of South Dakota by Counties, November Election, 1896," *South Dakota Legislative Manual 1909* (Pierre: State Publishing, 1909); Texas Secretary of State, Elections Division, *Presidential Election Results* (www.sos.state.tx.us/elections/index.shtml) (accessed February 1, 2002); Vermont Secretary of State, "State of Vermont Canvass of Votes for Electors of President and Vice President" (Rutland, 1896); Washington Secretary of State, "Electors of President and Vice President," *Abstract of Votes Polled in the State of Washington, at the General Election Held November 3, 1896* (Olympia, 1896); "Comparative Vote for President, 1892–1896, by Counties, with Population," *The Blue Book for the State of Wisconsin, for 1897* (Madison, 1897); "General Election—November 3, 1896," *Wyoming Historical Blue Book: A Legal and Political History of Wyoming 1868–1943* (Denver: Bradford-Robinson Printing, 1913)

1900

State of Connecticut Secretary of State, *Connecticut State Register and Manual 1905* (Hartford, 1905); Idaho Secretary of State, Election Division, *State of Idaho Presidential Vote Cast at the General Election November 6, 1900* (Boise, 1913); Indiana Secretary of State, "Certificate of Vote Cast for Presidential Electors, November 6, 1900," *Biennial Report of Union B. Hunt, Secretary of State of the State of Indiana, for the Two Years Ending October 31, 1900* (Indianapolis, 1900); Iowa Secretary of State, "Vote for President and Secretary of State by Counties," *Iowa Official Register 1901* (Des Moines, 1901); Kansas Secretary of State, "Statement of Official Vote State of Kansas, 1900," *Twelfth Biennial Report of the Secretary of State of the State of Kansas* (Topeka, 1901); Maryland Secretary of State, comp., "Electors for President and Vice President," *Maryland Manual 1900* (Baltimore: Wm. J.C. Dulany, 1901); Massachusetts Secretary of State, "Number of Votes Received by Each Candidate for a State Office at the Annual State Election, Nov. 6, 1900," *Public Document #43, 1900* (Boston, 1901); Michigan Department of State, comp., "Presidential Vote in Michigan from 1836 to 1916," *Michigan Official Directory and Legislative Manual 1917–1918* (Lansing, 1917); Minnesota Secretary of State, "Official Canvass by the State Board of Canvassers for Presidential Electors, Election Held November 6, 1900," *The Legislative Manual of the State of Minnesota, 1901* (St. Paul, 1901); Missouri Secretary of State, "Vote for President and Governor, 1900," *Official Manual of the State of Missouri for the Years 1901–1902* (Jefferson City, 1901); Nebraska Legislative Reference Bureau, "Popular Vote by Counties for Presidential Candidates in Nebraska, 1868–1916," *The Nebraska Blue Book and Historical Register 1918* (Lincoln, 1918); Nevada Secretary of State, *Political History of Nevada, 1996* (Carson City, 1996); New Hampshire Department of State, *State of New Hampshire Manual for the General Court 1901* (Concord, 1901); "Average Vote for Electors—By Counties," *Manual of the Legislature of New Jersey 1901* (Trenton, 1901); New York Secretary of State, "Statement of the Whole Number of Votes Cast for All the Candidates for the Office of Electors of President and Vice-President at a General Election Held in the State of New York on the 6th Day of November, in the Year 1900," *Manual for the Use of the Legislature of the State of New York for the Year 1901* (Albany, 1901); Oregon Office of the Secretary of State, "Votes Cast in Oregon for U.S. President 1860–2000," *Oregon Blue Book 2001–2002* (Salem, 2001); Pennsylvania Department of General Services, comp., "Official Vote of Pennsylvania for Presidential Electors, 1900," *Smull's Legislative Handbook and Manual of the State of Pennsylvania 1901* (Harrisburg, 1901); *Presidential Elections, 1789–1992* (Washington: Congressional Quarterly, 1995); Rhode Island Secretary of State, *Rhode Island Manual 1902* (Providence, 1913); South Dakota Secretary of State, comp., "Official Vote of South Dakota by Counties, November Election, 1900," *South Dakota Legislative Manual 1909* (Pierre: State Publishing, 1909); Texas Secretary of State, Elections Division, *Presidential Election Results* (www.sos.state.tx.us/elections/index.shtml) (accessed February 1, 2002); Vermont Secretary of State, "State of Vermont Canvass of Votes for Electors of President and Vice President" (Rutland, 1900); Washington Secretary of State, "Electors for President and Vice President," *Abstract of Votes Polled in the State of Washington, at the General Election Held November 6, 1900* (Olympia, 1900); "Comparative Vote for President, 1900 and

1896," *The Blue Book for the State of Wisconsin, for 1901* (Madison, 1901); "General Election—November 6, 1900," *Wyoming Historical Blue Book: A Legal and Political History of Wyoming 1868–1943* (Denver: Bradford-Robinson Printing, 1913)

1904

California Secretary of State, comp., "Presidential Electors," *Statement of Vote of California at the General Election, Held November 8, 1904* (Sacramento: State Printing Office, 1904); Connecticut Secretary of State, *Connecticut State Register and Manual 1905* (Hartford, 1905); Idaho Secretary of State, Election Division, *State of Idaho Presidential Vote Cast at the General Election November 8, 1904* (Boise, 1913); Indiana Secretary of State, "Vote Cast for Presidential Electors and State Officers, November 8, 1904," *Biennial Report of Daniel E. Storms, Secretary of State of the State of Indiana, for the Two Years Ending October 31, 1904* (Indianapolis, 1904); Iowa Secretary of State, "Vote for President by Counties—1900 and 1904," *Iowa Official Register 1905* (Des Moines, 1905); Kansas Secretary of State, "Statement of Official Vote, State of Kansas, 1904," *Fourteenth Biennial Report of the Secretary of State of the State of Kansas* (Topeka, 1905); Maryland Secretary of State, comp., "Returns of the Election Held on Tuesday, November 8, 1904," *Maryland Manual 1904* (Baltimore: Wm. J.C. Dulany, 1905); Massachusetts Secretary of State, "Number of Votes Received by Each Candidate for a State Office at the Annual State Election, Nov. 8, 1904," *Public Document #43, 1904* (Boston, 1905); Michigan Department of State, comp., "Presidential Vote in Michigan from 1836 to 1916," *Michigan Official Directory and Legislative Manual 1917–1918* (Lansing, 1917); Minnesota Secretary of State, "Abstract of Votes Polled in the State of Minnesota for Presidential Electors," *The Legislative Manual of the State of Minnesota 1905* (St. Paul, 1905); Missouri Secretary of State, "Vote for President and Governor, 1904 (by Counties)," *Official Manual of the State of Missouri for the Years 1905–1906* (Jefferson City, 1905); Montana Secretary of State, *Official Vote of the State of Montana Cast at the Regular Election Held on the 8th Day of November, A.D. 1904, as Canvassed by the State Board of Canvassers* (Helena: Allied Printing, 1904); Nebraska Legislative Reference Bureau, "Popular Vote by Counties for Presidential Candidates in Nebraska, 1868–1916," *The Nebraska Blue Book and Historical Register 1918* (Lincoln, 1918); Nevada Secretary of State, comp., *State of Nevada Official Returns of the Election of November, 1904* (Carson City, 1904); New Hampshire Department of State, *State of New Hampshire Manual for the General Court 1905* (Concord, 1905); New Jersey, "Vote for President, 1904—Highest Electors' Vote," *Manual of the Legislature of New Jersey 1905* (Trenton, 1905); New York Secretary of State, "Statement of the Whole Number of Votes Cast for All the Candidates for the Office of Electors of President and Vice-President at a General Election Held in the State of New York on the 8th Day of November, in the Year 1904," *Manual for the Use of the Legislature of the State of New York for the Year 1905* (Albany, 1905); Ohio Secretary of State, "Vote for Presidential Electors at the Election Held November 8, 1904," *Annual Report of the Secretary of State to the Governor of the State of Ohio for the Year Ending November 15, 1904* (Springfield: Springfield Publishing, 1905); Oregon Secretary of State, *Abstract of Votes Cast at a General Election in the State of Oregon, on the Eighth Day of November, A.D. 1904, for Electors of President and Vice-President of the United States* (Salem, 1904); Pennsylvania Department of General Services, comp., "Official Vote of Pennsylvania for Presidential Electors, 1904," *Smull's Legislative Handbook and Manual of the State of Pennsylvania 1906* (Harrisburg, 1906); *Presidential Elections, 1789–1992* (Washington: Congressional Quarterly, 1995); Rhode Island Secretary of State, *Rhode Island Manual 1905* (Providence, 1913); South Dakota Secretary of State, comp., "Official Vote of South Dakota by Counties, November Election, 1904," *South Dakota Legislative Manual 1909* (Pierre: State Publishing, 1909); Texas Secretary of State, Elections Division, *Presidential Election Results* (www.sos.state.tx.us/elections/index.shtml) (accessed February 1, 2002); Vermont Secretary of State, "State of Vermont Canvass of Votes for Electors of President and Vice President" (Rutland, 1904); Washington Secretary of State, "Electors for President and Vice President," *Abstract of Votes Polled in the State of Washington, at the General Election Held November 8, 1904* (Olympia, 1904); "Comparative Vote for President, 1904 and 1908, by Counties, with Population, 1900," *The Blue Book for the State of Wisconsin, for 1909* (Madison, 1909); "General Election—November 8, 1904," *Wyoming Historical Blue Book: A Legal and Political History of Wyoming 1868–1943* (Denver: Bradford-Robinson Printing, 1913)

1908

California Secretary of State, comp., "Presidential Electors," *Statement of Vote of California at the General Election, Held November 3, 1908* (Sacramento: State Printing Office, 1908); Connecticut Secretary of State, "Election Statistics Vote for President—1908 and 1912," *Connecticut State Register and Manual 1913* (Hartford, 1913); Idaho Secretary of State, Election Division, *State of Idaho Presidential Vote Cast at the General Election November 3, 1908* (Boise, 1913); Illinois Office of the Secretary of State, "Vote for President—Nov. 5, 1912," *Official Vote of the State of Illinois Cast at the*

General Election November 5, 1912 (Springfield, 1912); Indiana Secretary of State, "Vote by Counties for Presidential Electors First Elector," *Biennial Report of Fred A. Sims, Secretary of State of the State of Indiana, for the Fiscal Term Ending September 30, 1908* (Indianapolis, 1908); Iowa Secretary of State, "Official Canvass of Vote by Counties for President 1908–1904 and Governor 1908–1906," *Iowa Official Register 1909* (Des Moines, 1909); Kansas Secretary of State, "Statement of Official Vote, State of Kansas, 1908," *Sixteenth Biennial Report of the Secretary of State of the State of Kansas* (Topeka, 1909); Maryland Secretary of State, comp., "Tabulated Vote for Presidential Electors," *Maryland Manual 1908–1909* (Baltimore: John Murphy, 1909); Massachusetts Secretary of State, "Number of Votes Received by Each Candidate for a State Office at the Annual State Election, Nov. 3, 1908," *Public Document #43, 1908* (Boston, 1909); Michigan Department of State, comp., "Presidential Vote in Michigan from 1836 to 1916," *Michigan Official Directory and Legislative Manual 1917–1918* (Lansing, 1917); Minnesota Secretary of State, "Vote for Presidential Electors," *The Legislative Manual of the State of Minnesota 1909* (St. Paul, 1909); Missouri Secretary of State, "Total Vote, by Counties, for President and Governor, November 3, 1908," *Official Manual of the State of Missouri for the Years 1909–1910* (Jefferson City, 1909); Montana Secretary of State, *Official Vote of the State of Montana Cast at the Regular Election Held on the 3d Day of November, A.D. 1908, Canvassed by the State Board of Canvassers* (Helena: Allied Printing, 1913); Nebraska Legislative Reference Bureau, "Popular Vote by Counties for Presidential Candidates in Nebraska, 1868–1916," *The Nebraska Blue Book and Historical Register 1918* (Lincoln, 1918); Nevada Secretary of State, comp., *State of Nevada Official Returns of the Election of November, 1908* (Carson City, 1908); New Hampshire Department of State, *State of New Hampshire Manual for the General Court 1909* (Concord, 1909); "Vote for President, 1908—Highest Electors' Vote," *Manual of the Legislature of New Jersey 1909* (Trenton, 1909); New York Secretary of State, "Statement of the Whole Number of Votes Cast for All the Candidates for the Office of Electors of President and Vice-President at a General Election Held in the State of New York on the 3rd Day of November, in the Year 1908," *Manual for the Use of the Legislature of the State of New York for the Year 1909* (Albany, 1909); Ohio Secretary of State, "Vote for Presidential Electors at the Election Held November 8, 1904," *Annual Report of the Secretary of State to the Governor of the State of Ohio for the Year Ending November 15, 1908* (Springfield: Springfield Publishing, 1909); Oklahoma Department of Libraries, *Directory of Oklahoma State Almanac 1989-90* (Oklahoma City, 1990); Oregon Secretary of State, *Abstract of Votes Cast at a General Election in the State of Oregon, on the Third Day of November, A.D. 1908, for Electors of President and Vice-President of the United States* (Salem, 1908); Pennsylvania Department of General Services, comp., "Official Vote of Pennsylvania for Presidential Electors, 1908," *Smull's Legislative Handbook and Manual of the State of Pennsylvania 1909* (Harrisburg, 1909); *Presidential Elections, 1789–1992* (Washington: Congressional Quarterly, 1995); Rhode Island Secretary of State, *Rhode Island Manual 1909* (Providence, 1913); South Dakota Secretary of State, comp., "Official Vote of South Dakota by Counties, November Election, 1908," *South Dakota Legislative Manual 1909* (Pierre: State Publishing, 1909); Texas Secretary of State, Elections Division, *Presidential Election Results* (www.sos.state.tx.us/elections/index.shtml) (accessed February 1, 2002); Vermont Secretary of State, "State of Vermont Canvass of Votes for Electors of President and Vice President" (Rutland, 1908); Washington Secretary of State, "Presidential Electors," *Abstract of Votes Polled in the State of Washington at the General Election Held November 3, 1908* (Olympia, 1908); "Comparative Vote for President, 1904 and 1908, by Counties, with Population, 1900," *The Blue Book for the State of Wisconsin, for 1909* (Madison, 1909); Wyoming Secretary of State, comp., "Official Vote for State on November 3rd, 1908," *Legislative Manual and Official Directory of Wyoming 1909* (Cheyenne, 1909)

1912

Alabama Department of Archives and History, "Presidential Election, November 5, 1912, Vote for Electors for President and Vice President," *Alabama Official and Statistical Register 1913* (Montgomery, 1913); Arizona Secretary of State, *General Election Returns, November 5th, 1912, State of Arizona* (Phoenix, 1913); California Secretary of State, comp., "Electors of President and Vice-President of the United States," *Statement of Vote of California at the General Election Held November 5, 1912* (Sacramento: State Printing Office, 1912); Connecticut Secretary of State, "Election Statistics Vote for President—1908 and 1912," *Connecticut State Register and Manual 1913* (Hartford, 1913); Florida Department of State, Division of Elections, *Official Vote, General Election, 1912, Tabulated by Counties* (Tallahassee, 1912); Idaho Secretary of State, Election Division, *State of Idaho Presidential Vote Cast at the General Election November 5, 1912* (Boise, 1913); Illinois Office of the Secretary of State, "Vote for President—Nov. 5, 1912," *Official Vote of the State of Illinois Cast at the General Election November 5, 1912* (Springfield, 1912); Indiana Secretary of State, "Vote by Counties for Presidential Electors First Elector," *Biennial Report of L. G. Ellingham, Secretary of State of the State of Indiana, for the Fiscal Term Ending September 30, 1912* (Indianapolis,

1912); Iowa Secretary of State, "Official Canvass of Vote by Counties for President 1912, Governor 1910–1912–1914," *Iowa Official Register 1915* (Des Moines, 1915); Kansas Secretary of State, "General Election, November 5, 1912. Official Statement of Votes Cast," *Eighteenth Biennial Report of the Secretary of State of the State of Kansas 1911-12* (Topeka: State Printing Office, 1912); Maryland Secretary of State, comp., "Electors of President and Vice-President of the United States," *Maryland Manual 1912–1913* (Annapolis, 1913); Massachusetts Secretary of State, "Number of Votes Received by Each Candidate for a State Office at the Annual State Election, Nov. 5, 1912," *Public Document #43, 1912* (Boston, 1913); Michigan Department of State, comp., "Presidential Vote in Michigan from 1836 to 1916," *Michigan Official Directory and Legislative Manual 1917–1918* (Lansing, 1917); Minnesota Secretary of State, "Vote for President, 1912," *The Legislative Manual of the State of Minnesota 1913* (St. Paul, 1913); Missouri Secretary of State, comp., "Vote for President, 1912 (by Counties)," *Official Manual of the State of Missouri for the Years 1913–1914* (Jefferson City, 1913); Montana Secretary of State, *Official Vote of the State of Montana Cast at the Regular Election Held on the 5th Day of November, A.D. 1912, as Canvassed by the State Board of Canvassers* (Helena: State Publishing, 1913); Nebraska Legislative Reference Bureau, "Popular Vote by Counties for Presidential Candidates, 1868–1916," *The Nebraska Blue Book and Historical Register 1918* (Lincoln, 1918); Nevada Secretary of State, comp., *State of Nevada Official Returns of the Election of November, 1912* (Carson City, 1912); New Hampshire Department of State, *State of New Hampshire Manual for the General Court 1913* (Concord, 1913); "Vote for President, 1912—Highest Electors," *Manual of the Legislature of New Jersey 1913* (Trenton, 1913); New Mexico Secretary of State, comp., "Presidential Election, November 5, 1912," *The New Mexico Blue Book or State Official Register* (Santa Fe, 1915); "Vote for Electors of President in 1912," *The New York Red Book 1913* (Albany, 1913); Ohio Secretary of State, comp., "Vote Cast for Presidential Electors, November Election, 1912 (First Elector)," *Annual Statistical Report of the Secretary of State to the Governor and General Assembly of the State of Ohio for the Year Ending November 15, 1912* (Springfield: Springfield Publishing, 1913); Oklahoma Department of Libraries, *Directory of Oklahoma State Almanac 1989-90* (Oklahoma City, 1990); Oregon Secretary of State, *Abstract of Votes Cast in the Several Counties in the State of Oregon at a General Election Held on the Fifth Day of November, A.D. 1912, for Electors of President and Vice-President of the United States . . .* (Salem, 1912); Pennsylvania Department of General Services, comp., "Official Vote of Pennsylvania for Presidential Electors, 1912," *Smull's Legislative Handbook and Manual of the State of Pennsylvania 1914* (Harrisburg, 1914); *Presidential Elections, 1789–1992* (Washington: Congressional Quarterly, 1995); Rhode Island Secretary of State, "Presidential Election, November 5, 1912, Vote of Rhode Island by Cities and Towns," *Rhode Island Manual 1913–1914* (Providence, 1913); South Carolina Secretary of State, "Statement of the Whole Number of Votes Cast for Presidential and Vice Presidential Electors at the General Election Held November 3, 1912 as Appears from Certified Returns of County Boards of Canvassers," *Report of the Secretary of State to the General Assembly of South Carolina for the Fiscal Year Beginning January 1, 1912, and Ending December 31, 1912, Part II* (Columbia, 1913); South Dakota Secretary of State, comp., "Official Vote—November Election, 1912, Presidential Electors," *South Dakota Legislative Manual 1913* (Pierre: State Publishing, 1913); Texas Secretary of State, Elections Division, *Presidential Election Results* (www.sos.state.tx.us/elections/index.shtml) (accessed February 1, 2002); Utah Bureau of Immigration and Statistics, "Votes Cast for Presidential Electors, 1912," *Bureau of Immigration & Statistics, 1911–1912* (Salt Lake City, 1913); Vermont Secretary of State, *State of Vermont Canvass of Votes for Electors of President and Vice President A.D. 1912* (Rutland, 1912); Washington Secretary of State, "For Presidential Electors," *Abstract of Votes Polled in the State of Washington at the General Election Held November 5, 1912* (Olympia, 1912); Wisconsin Industrial Commission, comp., "Summary of Vote for President, 1912, by Counties," *The Wisconsin Blue Book 1913* (Madison, 1913); Wyoming Secretary of State, comp., "Official Vote, General Election, November 5, 1912, Presidential Electors," *Official Directory of Wyoming 1913* (Cheyenne, 1913)

1916

Arizona Secretary of State, *General Election Returns, State of Arizona, November 7, 1916* (Phoenix: 1917); California Secretary of State, "Electors of President and Vice-President of the United States," *Statement of Vote at General Election Held on November 7, 1916, in the State of California* (Sacramento, 1916); State of Connecticut Secretary of State, *Connecticut State Register and Manual 1932* (Hartford, 1932); Idaho Secretary of State, Election Division, *State of Idaho Presidential Vote Cast at the General Election, November 7, 1916* (Boise, 1913); Indiana Secretary of State, "Vote by Counties for Presidential Electors First Elector," *Biennial Report of Homer L. Cook, Secretary of State of the State of Indiana, for the Fiscal Term Ending September 30, 1916* (Indianapolis, 1916); Iowa Secretary of State, "General Election Comparative Vote Cast at General Election of 1916 and 1920 by Counties Official Canvass," *Iowa Official Register 1921–1922*

(Des Moines, 1921); Kansas Secretary of State, "General Election, November 7, 1916. Official Statement of Votes Cast," *Twentieth Biennial Report of the Secretary of State of the State of Kansas 1915-'16* (Topeka: Kansas State Printing Plant, 1916); Maryland Secretary of State, comp., "For Electors of President and Vice-President of the United States," *Maryland Manual 1916-1917* (Annapolis, 1917); Massachusetts Secretary of State, "Presidential Electors at Large," *Public Document #43, 1916* (Boston, 1917); Michigan Department of State, comp., "Presidential Vote in Michigan from 1836 to 1916," *Michigan Official Directory and Legislative Manual 1917-1918* (Lansing, 1917); Minnesota Secretary of State, "Abstract of Votes Polled for President by Counties, 1916," *The Legislative Manual of the State of Minnesota 1917* (St. Paul, 1917); Missouri Secretary of State, "Vote for President, 1916 (by Counties)," *Official Manual of the State of Missouri for the Years 1917-1918* (Jefferson City, 1917); Montana Secretary of State, *Official Vote of the State of Montana at an Election Held November 7th, 1916* (Helena, 1916); Nebraska Secretary of State, comp., *Official Report of the Nebraska State Canvassing Board, General Election Held November 7th, 1916* (Lincoln, 1916); Nevada Secretary of State, comp., *State of Nevada Official Returns of the Election of November, 1916* (Carson City, 1917); New Hampshire Department of State, *State of New Hampshire Manual for the General Court 1917* (Concord, 1917); "Vote for President—U.S. Senator—Governor, 1916," *Manual of the Legislature of New Jersey 1917* (Trenton, 1917); New Mexico Secretary of State, "Election Results Compilation of Election, November 7, 1916," *The New Mexico Blue Book State Official Register 1917* (Santa Fe, 1917); "Vote for Electors of President in 1916," *The New York Red Book 1917* (Albany, 1917); North Dakota Secretary of State, ed., "Party Votes, General Election, November 7, 1916," *Compilation of Election Returns, National and State, 1914-1928* (Bismarck, 1930); Ohio Secretary of State, comp., "Votes Cast by Counties for Electors of President and Vice President at the Election Held November 7, 1916 (First Elector)," *Ohio Election Statistics, General Election Held on the Seventh Day of November 1916* (Columbus, 1916); Oklahoma Department of Libraries, *Directory of Oklahoma State Almanac 1989-90* (Oklahoma City, 1990); Oregon Secretary of State, *Abstract of Votes Cast in the Several Counties in the State of Oregon at a General Election Held on the Seventh Day of November, A.D. 1916, for Presidential Electors . . .* (Salem, 1916); Pennsylvania Department of General Services, comp., "Official Vote of Pennsylvania for Presidential Electors, November 7, 1916," *Smull's Legislative Handbook and Manual of the State of Pennsylvania 1917* (Harrisburg, 1917); *Presidential Elections, 1789–1992* (Washington: Congressional Quarterly, 1995); Rhode Island Secretary of State, "Presidential Election, November 7, 1916, Vote of Rhode Island by Cities and Towns," *Rhode Island Manual 1917* (Providence, 1913); South Carolina Secretary of State, "Statement of the Whole Number of Votes Cast for Presidential and Vice Presidential Electors at the General Election Held November 7, A.D. 1916," *Report of the Secretary of State to the General Assembly of South Carolina for the Fiscal Year Beginning January 1, 1916, and Ending December 31, 1916 Part II* (Columbia, 1917); South Dakota Secretary of State, comp., "Presidential Electors," *Official Election Returns for South Dakota General Election, November 7, 1916* (Pierre, 1916); Texas Secretary of State, Elections Division, *Presidential Election Results* (www.sos.state.tx.us/elections/index.shtml) (accessed February 1, 2002); Vermont Secretary of State, "Summary Vote for Electors, 1916" (Rutland, 1913); Washington Secretary of State, comp., "Presidential Electors," *Abstract of Votes Polled in the State of Washington at the General Election Held November 7, 1916* (Olympia, 1916); Wisconsin Industrial Commission, comp., "Summary of Vote for President, November 7, 1916, by Counties," *The Wisconsin Blue Book 1917* (Madison, 1917); Wyoming Secretary of State, *General Election, November 7, 1916* (Cheyenne, 1913)

1920

Alabama: Clerk of the House of Representatives, comp., *Statistics of the Congressional and Presidential Election of November 2, 1920* (Washington, DC, 1921); Arizona Secretary of State, *General Election Returns, State of Arizona, November 2, 1920* (Phoenix, 1921); Arkansas: Clerk of the House of Representatives, comp., *Statistics of the Congressional and Presidential Election of November 2, 1920* (Washington, DC, 1921); California Secretary of State, "Electors of President and Vice-President of the United States," *Statement of Vote at General Election Held on November 2, 1920, in the State of California* (Sacramento, 1920); Colorado Secretary of State, comp., *State of Colorado Abstract of Votes Cast at the . . . General Election Held on the Second Day of November, A.D. 1920 . . .* (Denver, 1920); State of Connecticut Secretary of State, *Connecticut State Register and Manual 1921* (Hartford, 1921); Delaware: Clerk of the House of Representatives, comp., *Statistics of the Congressional and Presidential Election of November 2, 1920* (Washington, DC, 1921); Florida: Clerk of the House of Representatives, comp., *Statistics of the Congressional and Presidential Election of November 2, 1920* (Washington, DC, 1921); Georgia: Clerk of the House of Representatives, comp., *Statistics of the Congressional and Presidential Election of November 2, 1920* (Washington, DC, 1921); Idaho Secretary of State, Election Division, *State of Idaho Presidential Vote Cast at the General Election, November 2, 1920* (Boise, 1921);

Illinois Office of the Secretary of State, "Vote for President—Nov. 2, 1920," *Official Vote of the State of Illinois Cast at the General Election, November 2, 1920* (Springfield, 1920); Indiana Legislative Reference Bureau, "Abstract of Vote for Presidential Electors . . . At the General Election held on November 2, 1920," *Year Book of the State of Indiana for the Year 1920* (Indianapolis, 1921); Iowa Secretary of State, "General Election, Comparative Vote Cast at General Election of 1916 and 1920 by Counties, Official Canvass," *Iowa Official Register 1921-1922* (Des Moines, 1921); Kansas Secretary of State, "General Election, November 2, 1920, Official Statement of Votes Cast," *Twenty-second Biennial Report of the Secretary of State 1919–1920* (Topeka: Kansas State Printing Plant, 1920); Kentucky: Clerk of the House of Representatives, comp., *Statistics of the Congressional and Presidential Election of November 2, 1920* (Washington, DC, 1921); Louisiana: Clerk of the House of Representatives, comp., *Statistics of the Congressional and Presidential Election of November 2, 1920* (Washington, DC, 1921); Maine: Clerk of the House of Representatives, comp., *Statistics of the Congressional and Presidential Election of November 2, 1920* (Washington, DC, 1921); Maryland Secretary of State, comp., "Maryland Election Returns, 1920," *Maryland Manual 1921* (Annapolis, 1921); Massachusetts Secretary of State, "Presidential Electors at Large," *Public Document #43, 1920* (Boston, 1921); Michigan Department of State, "Presidential Vote by Counties, 1920," *Michigan Official Directory and Legislative Manual 1921-1922* (Lansing, 1921); Minnesota Secretary of State, "Vote by Counties on Presidential Electors," *The Legislative Manual of the State of Minnesota 1921* (St. Paul, 1921); Mississippi Secretary of State, "General Election, November 2, 1920—for Presidential Electors," *Biennial Report of the Secretary of State to the Legislature of Mississippi Oct. 1, 1917, to Oct. 1, 1921* (Jackson, 1921); Missouri Secretary of State, "Missouri Vote for President, November, 1920, by Counties," *State of Missouri Official Manual for the Years 1921–1922* (Jefferson City, 1921); Montana Secretary of State, *Official Vote of the State of Montana at the General Election Held November 2nd, 1920* (Helena, 1921); Nebraska Secretary of State, comp., *Official Report of the Nebraska State Canvassing Board and Joint Session of the Legislature General Election Held November 2, 1920* (Lincoln, 1921); Nevada Secretary of State, comp., *State of Nevada Official Returns of the Election of November, 1920* (Carson City, 1920); New Hampshire Department of State, *State of New Hampshire Manual for the General Court 1921* (Concord, 1921); New Jersey: Clerk of the House of Representatives, comp., *Statistics of the Congressional and Presidential Election of November 2, 1920* (Washington, DC, 1921); New Mexico Secretary of State, "Election Returns, November 2, 1920," *The New Mexico Blue Book State Official Register 1921–1922* (Santa Fe, 1922); "Vote for Electors of President in 1920," *The New York Red Book 1921* (Albany, 1921); North Carolina: Clerk of the House of Representatives, comp., *Statistics of the Congressional and Presidential Election of November 2, 1920* (Washington, DC, 1921); North Dakota Secretary of State, ed., "Party Votes, General Election, Nov. 2, 1920," *Compilation of Election Returns, National and State, 1914-1928* (Bismarck, 1930); Ohio Secretary of State, comp., *Vote for President . . . Polled in the Several Counties of the State of Ohio at the Election Held . . . Second Day of November, 1920* (Springfield, 1920); Oklahoma: Clerk of the House of Representatives, comp., *Statistics of the Congressional and Presidential Election of November 2, 1920* (Washington, DC, 1921); Oregon Secretary of State, *Abstract of Votes Cast in the Several Counties in the State of Oregon at a General Election Held on the Second Day of November, A.D. 1920, for Presidential Electors . . .* (Salem, 1920), Pennsylvania Bureau of Publications, "Official Vote of Pennsylvania for Presidential Electors, November 2, 1920," *Pennsylvania State Manual 1923–24* (Harrisburg, 1923); Rhode Island Secretary of State, "Presidential Election, November 2, 1920, Vote of Rhode Island by Cities and Towns," *Rhode Island Manual 1921-1922* (Providence, 1921); South Carolina Secretary of State, "Statement of the Whole Number of Votes Cast for President of the United States at the General Election Held November 3, 1920," *Report of the Secretary of State to the General Assembly of South Carolina for the Fiscal Year Beginning January 1, 1920, and Ending December 31, 1920, Part II* (Columbia, 1921); South Dakota Secretary of State, "Presidential Electors," *Official Election Returns for South Dakota General Election, November 2, 1920* (Pierre, 1920); Tennessee Secretary of State, comp., "Presidential Election, 1920," *Tennessee Hand-Book and Official Directory, Official Vote, 1920 . . .* (Nashville, 1921); Texas Secretary of State, Elections Division, *Presidential Election Results* (www.sos.state.tx.us/elections/index.shtml) (accessed February 1, 2002); Utah: Clerk of the House of Representatives, comp., *Statistics of the Congressional and Presidential Election of November 2, 1920* (Washington, DC, 1921); Vermont Secretary of State, "Presidential Election," *Vermont Legislative Directory Biennial Session 1921* (Montpelier, 1921); Virginia: Clerk of the House of Representatives, comp., *Statistics of the Congressional and Presidential Election of November 2, 1920* (Washington, DC, 1921); Washington Secretary of State, comp., "Presidential Electors," *Abstract of Votes Polled in the State of Washington at the General Election Held November 2, 1920* (Olympia, 1920); West Virginia Secretary of State, "Vote for President of the United States," *General Election Returns, 1920* (Charleston, 1920); Wisconsin Legislative Reference Library, comp., "Summary of

Vote for President," *The Wisconsin Blue Book 1921* (Madison, 1921); Wyoming Secretary of State, comp., "Total Vote by Counties, General Election, November 2, 1920," *1920 Official Directory of Wyoming and Election Returns for 1920* (Sheridan: Mills Company, 1921)

1924

Alabama: Clerk of the House of Representatives, comp., *Statistics of the Congressional and Presidential Election of November 4, 1924* (Washington, DC, 1925); Arizona Secretary of State, *General Election Returns, State of Arizona, November 4, 1924* (Phoenix, 1925); Arkansas: Clerk of the House of Representatives, comp., *Statistics of the Congressional and Presidential Election of November 4, 1924* (Washington, DC, 1925); California Secretary of State, "Electors of President and Vice-President of the United States," *Statement of Vote at General Election Held on November 4, 1924, in the State of California* (Sacramento, 1924); Colorado Secretary of State, comp., *State of Colorado Abstract of Votes Cast at the . . . General Election Held on the Fourth Day of November, A.D. 1924 . . .* (Denver, 1924); State of Connecticut, comp., "Summary—Vote for President of the United States and State Officers November 4, 1924," *State of Connecticut Public Document No. 26, Statement of Vote, General Election, November 4, 1924* (Hartford, 1924); Delaware: Clerk of the House of Representatives, comp., *Statistics of the Congressional and Presidential Election of November 4, 1924* (Washington, DC, 1925); Florida Department of State, *Official Vote, State of Florida, General Election, 1924* (Tallahassee, 1924); Georgia: Clerk of the House of Representatives, comp., *Statistics of the Congressional and Presidential Election of November 4, 1924* (Washington, DC, 1925); Idaho Secretary of State, Election Division, *State of Idaho Presidential Vote Cast at the General Election, November 4, 1924* (Boise, 1925); Illinois Office of the Secretary of State, "Vote for President—Nov. 4, 1924," *Official Vote of the State of Illinois Cast at the General Election, November 4, 1924* (Springfield, 1924); Indiana Legislative Reference Bureau, "Abstract of Vote for Presidential Electors . . . at the General Election Held on November 4, 1924," *Year Book of the State of Indiana for the Year 1924* (Indianapolis, 1925); Iowa: Clerk of the House of Representatives, comp., *Statistics of the Congressional and Presidential Election of November 4, 1924* (Washington, DC, 1925); Kansas Secretary of State, "General Election, November 2, 1924, Electors of President and Vice President," *Twenty-fourth Biennial Report of the Secretary of State 1923–1924* (Topeka: Kansas State Printing Plant, 1924); Kentucky: Clerk of the House of Representatives, comp., *Statistics of the Congressional and Presidential Election of November 4, 1924* (Washington, DC, 1925); Louisiana Secretary of State, *Election Returns for Electors for President and Vice-President of the United States* (Baton Rouge, 1924); Maryland Secretary of State, comp., "General Election, Nov. 4, 1924," *Maryland Manual 1925* (Annapolis, 1925); Massachusetts Secretary of State, "Presidential Electors at Large," *Public Document #43, 1924* (Boston, 1925); Michigan Department of State, "Presidential Vote by Counties, 1924," *Michigan Official Directory and Legislative Manual 1925–1926* (Lansing, 1925); Minnesota Secretary of State, *The Legislative Manual of the State of Minnesota 1925* (St. Paul, 1925); Mississippi Secretary of State, *Biennial Report of the Secretary of State to the Legislature of Mississippi Oct. 1, 1923, to Oct. 1, 1925* (Jackson, 1925); Missouri Secretary of State, "Missouri Vote for President, November, 1924, by Counties," *State of Missouri Official Manual for the Years 1925–1926* (Jefferson City, 1925); Montana Secretary of State, *Montana General Election Returns, Official Abstract of Votes Cast at the General Election Held in Montana Nov. 4, 1924* (Helena, 1924); Nebraska Secretary of State, comp., *Official Report of the Nebraska State Canvassing Board, General Election Held November 4th, 1924* (Lincoln, 1924); Nevada Secretary of State, comp., *State of Nevada Official Returns of the Election of November, 1924* (Carson City, 1924); New Hampshire Department of State, *State of New Hampshire Manual for the General Court 1925* (Concord, 1925); New Jersey: Clerk of the House of Representatives, comp., *Statistics of the Congressional and Presidential Election of November 4, 1924* (Washington, DC, 1925); New Mexico Secretary of State, "Canvass of Returns of Election Held November 7, 1924—State of New Mexico," *The New Mexico Blue Book State Official Register 1925–1926* (Santa Fe, 1926); New York Secretary of State, "Presidential Vote, New York State by Counties, November 4, 1924," *Manual for the Use of the Legislature of the State of New York for the Year 1925* (Albany, 1925); North Carolina: Clerk of the House of Representatives, comp., *Statistics of the Congressional and Presidential Election of November 4, 1924* (Washington, DC, 1925); North Dakota Secretary of State, ed., "Party Votes, General Election, November 4, 1924," *Compilation of Election Returns, National and State 1914–1928* (Bismarck, 1930); Ohio Secretary of State, comp., *Vote for President . . . Polled in the Several Counties of the State of Ohio at the Election Held . . . Fourth Day of November, 1924* (Springfield, 1924); Oklahoma Department of Libraries, *Directory of Oklahoma State Almanac 1989-90* (Oklahoma City, 1990); Oregon Secretary of State, *Abstract of Votes Cast in the Several Counties in the State of Oregon at a General Election Held on the Fourth Day of November, A.D. 1924, for Presidential Electors . . .* (Salem, 1924); Pennsylvania Bureau of Publications, "Official Vote of Pennsylvania for Presidential Electors, 1924," *Pennsylvania State Manual 1925–26* (Harrisburg, 1925); Rhode Island

Secretary of State, "Presidential Election, November 4, 1924, Vote of Rhode Island by Cities and Towns," *Rhode Island Manual 1925–1926* (Providence, 1925); South Carolina Secretary of State, "Statement of the Whole Number of Votes Cast for President of the United States, at the General Election Held November 4th, 1924," *Report of the Secretary of State to the General Assembly of South Carolina for the Fiscal Year Beginning January 1, 1924, and Ending December 31, 1924, Part II* (Columbia, 1925); South Dakota Secretary of State, comp., "Presidential Electors," *Official Election Returns for South Dakota General Election, November 4, 1924* (Pierre, 1924); Tennessee: Clerk of the House of Representatives, comp., *Statistics of the Congressional and Presidential Election of November 4, 1924* (Washington, DC, 1925); Texas Secretary of State, Elections Division, *Presidential Election Results* (www.sos.state.tx.us/elections/index.shtml) (accessed February 1, 2002); Utah: Clerk of the House of Representatives, comp., *Statistics of the Congressional and Presidential Election of November 4, 1924* (Washington, DC, 1925); Vermont Secretary of State, "Presidential Election," *Vermont Legislative Directory Biennial Session 1925* (Montpelier, 1925); Virginia: Clerk of the House of Representatives, comp., *Statistics of the Congressional and Presidential Election of November 4, 1924* (Washington, DC, 1925); Washington Secretary of State, comp., "Presidential Electors," *Abstract of Votes Polled in the State of Washington at the General Election Held November 4, 1924* (Olympia, 1924); West Virginia Secretary of State, "Vote for President of the United States," *General Election Returns, 1924* (Charleston, 1924); Wisconsin Legislative Reference Library, comp., "Summary Vote for Presidential Electors Nov. 4, 1924," *The Wisconsin Blue Book 1925* (Madison, 1925); Wyoming Secretary of State, comp., "Total Vote by Counties, General Election, November 4, 1924," *1924 Official Directory of Wyoming and Election Returns for 1924* (Cheyenne: Wyoming Labor Journal, 1925)

1928

Alabama: Clerk of the House of Representatives, comp., *Statistics of the Congressional and Presidential Election of November 6, 1928* (Washington, DC, 1929); Arizona Secretary of State, *Official Canvass General Election Returns, November 6, 1928* (Phoenix, 1929); Arkansas: Clerk of the House of Representatives, comp., *Statistics of the Congressional and Presidential Election of November 6, 1928* (Washington, DC, 1929); California Secretary of State, "Electors of President and Vice-President of the United States," *Statement of Vote at General Election Held on November 6, 1928, in the State of California* (Sacramento, 1928); Colorado Secretary of State, comp., *State of Colorado Abstract of Votes Cast at the . . . General Election Held on the Sixth Day of November, A.D. 1928 . . .* (Denver, 1928); State of Connecticut, comp., "Summary—Vote for President of the United States, State Officers, and U.S. Senators, November 6, 1928," *State of Connecticut Public Document No. 26, Statement of Vote General Election, November 6, 1928* (Hartford, 1928); Delaware: Clerk of the House of Representatives, comp., *Statistics of the Congressional and Presidential Election of November 6, 1928* (Washington, DC, 1929); Florida: Clerk of the House of Representatives, comp., *Statistics of the Congressional and Presidential Election of November 6, 1928* (Washington, DC, 1929); Georgia: Clerk of the House of Representatives, comp., *Statistics of the Congressional and Presidential Election of November 6, 1928* (Washington, DC, 1929); Idaho Secretary of State, Election Division, *State of Idaho Presidential Vote Cast at the General Election, November 6, 1928* (Boise, 1929); Illinois Office of the Secretary of State, "Vote for President—Nov. 6, 1928," *Official Vote of the State of Illinois Cast at the General Election, November 6, 1928* (Springfield, 1928); Indiana Legislative Bureau, "Abstract of Vote for Presidential Electors . . . at the general election held on November 6, 1928," *Year Book of the State of Indiana for the Year 1928* (Indianapolis, 1929); Iowa: Clerk of the House of Representatives, comp., *Statistics of the Congressional and Presidential Election of November 6, 1928* (Washington, DC, 1929); Kansas Secretary of State, "General Election, November 6, 1928, Electors of President and Vice President," *Twenty-sixth Biennial Report of the Secretary of State 1927–1928* (Topeka: Kansas State Printing Plant, 1928); Kentucky: Clerk of the House of Representatives, comp., *Statistics of the Congressional and Presidential Election of November 6, 1928* (Washington, DC, 1929); Louisiana Secretary of State, *Election Returns for Electors for President and Vice-President of the United States* (Baton Rouge, 1928); Maine: Clerk of the House of Representatives, comp., *Statistics of the Congressional and Presidential Election of November 6, 1928* (Washington, DC, 1929); Maryland Secretary of State, comp., "General Election Returns, November 6th, 1928," *Maryland Manual 1929* (Annapolis, 1929); Massachusetts Secretary of State, "Presidential Electors at Large," *Public Document #43, 1928* (Boston, 1929); Minnesota Secretary of State, "Vote by Counties of Presidential Electors," *The Legislative Manual of the State of Minnesota 1929* (St. Paul, 1929); Mississippi Secretary of State, "General Election Presidential Electors, November 6th, 1928," *Biennial Report of the Secretary of State to the Legislature of Mississippi Oct. 1, 1927, to Oct. 1, 1929* (Jackson, 1929); Missouri Secretary of State, "Missouri Vote for President, November 6, 1928, by Counties," *State of Missouri Official Manual for the Years 1929–1930* (Jefferson City, 1929); Montana Secretary of State, *Montana General Election Returns, Official Abstract of Votes Cast at the General Election Held in Montana Nov. 6,*

1928 (Helena, 1928); Nebraska Secretary of State, comp., *Official Report of the Nebraska State Canvassing Board, General Election Held November 6th, 1928* (Lincoln, 1928); Nevada Secretary of State, comp., *State of Nevada Official Returns of the Election of November, 1928* (Carson City, 1928); New Hampshire Department of State, *State of New Hampshire Manual for the General Court 1929* (Concord, 1929); New Jersey: Clerk of the House of Representatives, comp., *Statistics of the Congressional and Presidential Election of November 6, 1928* (Washington, DC, 1929); New Mexico Secretary of State, "Canvass of Returns of Election Held November 6, 1928—State of New Mexico," *The New Mexico Blue Book State Official Register 1929–1930* (Santa Fe, 1930); New York State Department of State, "Presidential Vote, New York State by Counties, November 6, 1928," *Manual for the Use of the Legislature of the State of New York 1929* (Albany, 1929); North Carolina Secretary of State, "Vote for President by Counties 1928–1948," *North Carolina Manual 1949* (Raleigh, 1929); North Dakota Secretary of State, ed., "Party Votes, General Election, November 6, 1928," *Compilation of Election Returns, National and State 1914–1928* (Bismarck, 1930); Ohio Secretary of State, *Ohio Election Statistics, the General Election Held on the Eighth Day of November 1938* (Cleveland, 1939); Oklahoma Department of Libraries, *Directory of Oklahoma State Almanac 1989-90* (Oklahoma City, 1990); Oregon Secretary of State, *Abstract of Votes Cast in the Several Counties in the State of Oregon at a General Election Held on the Sixth Day of November, A.D. 1928, for Presidential Electors . . .* (Salem, 1928); Pennsylvania Bureau of Publications, "Votes Cast for Presidential Electors at General Election November 6, 1928," *The Pennsylvania Manual 1929* (Harrisburg, 1929); Rhode Island Secretary of State, "Presidential Election, November 6, 1928, Vote of Rhode Island by Cities and Towns," *Rhode Island Manual 1929–1930* (Providence, 1929); South Carolina Secretary of State, "Statement of the Whole Number of Votes Cast for President of the United States, at the General Election Held in South Carolina on November 6th, 1928," *Supplemental Report of the Secretary of State to the General Assembly of South Carolina for the Fiscal Year Beginning January 1, 1923, and Ending December 31, 1928, Part II* (Columbia, 1929); South Dakota Secretary of State, "Presidential Electors," *Official Election Returns for South Dakota General Election November 6, 1928* (Pierre, 1928); Tennessee: Clerk of the House of Representatives, comp., *Statistics of the Congressional and Presidential Election of November 6, 1928* (Washington, DC, 1929); Texas Secretary of State, Elections Division, *Presidential Election Results* (www.sos.state.tx.us/elections/index.shtml) (accessed February 1, 2002); Utah: Clerk of the House of Representatives, comp., *Statistics of the Congressional and Presidential Election of November 6, 1928* (Washington, DC, 1929); Vermont Secretary of State, "Presidential Election," *Vermont Legislative Directory Biennial Session 1929* (Montpelier, 1929); Virginia: Clerk of the House of Representatives, comp., *Statistics of the Congressional and Presidential Election of November 6, 1928* (Washington, DC, 1929); Washington Secretary of State, comp., "Presidential Electors," *Abstract of Votes Polled in the State of Washington at the General Election Held November 6, 1928* (Olympia, 1928); West Virginia Secretary of State, "Vote for President of the United States," *General Election Returns, 1928* (Charleston, 1928); Wisconsin Legislative Reference Library, comp., "Summary Vote for President Nov. 6, 1928," *The Wisconsin Blue Book 1929* (Madison, 1929); Wyoming Secretary of State, comp., "Total Vote by Counties, General Election, November 6, 1928," *1929 Official Directory of Wyoming and Election Returns for 1928* (Cheyenne, 1929)

1932

Alabama: Clerk of the House of Representatives, comp., *Statistics of the Congressional and Presidential Election of November 8, 1932* (Washington, DC, 1933); Arizona Secretary of State, *Official Canvass General Election Returns, State of Arizona, November 8th, 1932* (Phoenix, 1933); Arkansas: Clerk of the House of Representatives, comp., *Statistics of the Congressional and Presidential Election of November 8, 1932* (Washington, DC, 1933); California Secretary of State, "Electors of President and Vice-President of the United States," *Statement of Vote at General Election Held on November 8, 1932, in the State of California* (Sacramento, 1932); Colorado Secretary of State, comp., *State of Colorado Abstract of Votes Cast at the . . . General Election Held on the Eighth Day of November A.D., 1932 . . .* (Denver, 1932); State of Connecticut, comp., "Summary—Vote for President of the United States, United States Senator and State Officers, November 8, 1932," *State of Connecticut Public Document No. 26, Statement of Vote, General Election November 8, 1932* (Hartford, 1932); Delaware: Clerk of the House of Representatives, comp., *Statistics of the Congressional and Presidential Election of November 8, 1932* (Washington, DC, 1933); Florida Department of State, Division of Elections, *Official Vote—State of Florida General Election—1932* (Tallahassee, 1932); Georgia: Clerk of the House of Representatives, comp., *Statistics of the Congressional and Presidential Election of November 8, 1932* (Washington, DC, 1933); Idaho Secretary of State, Election Division, *State of Idaho Presidential Vote Cast at the General Election, November 8, 1932* (Boise, 1933); Illinois Office of the Secretary of State, "Vote for President—Nov. 8, 1932," *Official Vote of the State of Illinois Cast at the General Election, November 8, 1932* (Springfield, 1932); Indiana Legislative Bureau, "Abstract of Vote

for Presidential Electors . . . held on November 8, 1932," *Year Book of the State of Indiana for the Year 1932* (Indianapolis, 1933); Iowa: Clerk of the House of Representatives, comp., *Statistics of the Congressional and Presidential Election of November 8, 1932* (Washington, DC, 1933); Kansas Secretary of State, "General Election, November 8, 1932, for President and Vice President," *Twenty-eighth Biennial Report of the Secretary of State 1931–1932* (Topeka: Kansas State Printing Plant, 1932); Kentucky: Clerk of the House of Representatives, comp., *Statistics of the Congressional and Presidential Election of November 8, 1932* (Washington, DC, 1933); Louisiana Secretary of State, *Election Returns for Electors for President and Vice-President of the United States* (Baton Rouge, 1932); Maryland Secretary of State, comp., "General Election Returns, November 8, 1932," *Maryland Manual 1933* (Annapolis, 1933); Massachusetts Secretary of State, "Presidential Electors of President and Vice President," *Public Document #43, 1932* (Boston, 1933); Michigan Department of State, "Presidential Vote by Counties, 1932," *Michigan Official Directory and Legislative Manual 1933–1934* (Lansing, 1933); Minnesota Secretary of State, "Vote by Counties of Presidential Electors," *The Legislative Manual of the State of Minnesota 1933* (St. Paul, 1933); Mississippi Secretary of State, "Official Returns, General Election, 1932," *Mississippi Blue Book Biennial Report of the Secretary of State to the Legislature of Mississippi July 1, 1931, to July 1, 1933* (Jackson, 1933); Missouri Secretary of State, "General Election Returns, Vote for President, by Counties, at General Election, November 8, 1932," *State of Missouri Official Manual for the Years 1933–1934* (Jefferson City, 1933); Montana Secretary of State, *Official Montana General Election Returns, November 8, 1932* (Helena, 1933); Nebraska Secretary of State, comp., *Official Report of the Nebraska State Canvassing Board, General Election Held November 8th, 1932* (Lincoln, 1932); Nevada Secretary of State, comp., *State of Nevada Official Returns of the Election of November, 1932* (Carson City, 1932); New Hampshire Department of State, *State of New Hampshire Manual for the General Court 1933* (Concord, 1933); New Jersey: Clerk of the House of Representatives, comp., *Statistics of the Congressional and Presidential Election of November 8, 1932* (Washington, DC, 1933); New Mexico Secretary of State, "Canvass of Returns of Election Held November 8, 1932—State of New Mexico," *The New Mexico Blue Book State Official Register 1933–1934* (Santa Fe, 1934); "Vote, New York State, by Counties, November 8, 1932, for President and Vice President," *The New York Red Book 1933* (Albany, 1933); North Carolina Secretary of State, "Vote for President by Counties 1928–1948," *North Carolina Manual 1949* (Raleigh, 1933); North Dakota Secretary of State, comp., "Official Abstract of Votes Cast at the General Election Held November 8th, 1932," *Compilation of Election Returns, National and State, 1930-1944* (Bismarck, 1945); Ohio Secretary of State, *Ohio Election Statistics, the General Election Held on the Eighth Day of November 1932* (Cleveland, 1933); Oklahoma Department of Libraries, *Directory of Oklahoma State Almanac 1989-90* (Oklahoma City, 1990); Oregon Secretary of State, *Electors of President and Vice President of the United States* (Salem, 1932); Pennsylvania Bureau of Publications, "Official Vote for Presidential Electors, November 8, 1932," *The Pennsylvania Manual 1933* (Harrisburg, 1933); Rhode Island Secretary of State, "Presidential Election, November 8, 1932, Vote of Rhode Island by Cities and Towns," *Rhode Island Manual 1933–1934* (Providence, 1933); South Carolina Secretary of State, "Statement of the Whole Number of Votes Cast for Presidential and Vice-Presidential Electors at the General Election Held in South Carolina on November 8th, 1932," *Supplemental Report of the Secretary of State to the General Assembly of South Carolina, Election, Nov. 8, 1932* (Columbia, 1933); South Dakota Secretary of State, "Presidential Electors," *Official Election Returns for South Dakota General Election, November 8, 1932* (Pierre, 1932); Tennessee: Clerk of the House of Representatives, comp., *Statistics of the Congressional and Presidential Election of November 8, 1932* (Washington, DC, 1933); Texas Secretary of State. Elections Division, *Presidential Election Results* (www.sos.state.tx.us/elections/index.shtml) (accessed February 1, 2002); Utah: Clerk of the House of Representatives, comp., *Statistics of the Congressional and Presidential Election of November 8, 1932* (Washington, DC, 1933); Vermont Secretary of State, "Presidential Election," *Vermont Legislative Directory Biennial Session 1933* (Montpelier, 1933); Virginia: Clerk of the House of Representatives, comp., *Statistics of the Congressional and Presidential Election of November 8, 1932* (Washington, DC, 1933); Washington Secretary of State, comp., "Presidential Electors," *Abstract of Votes Polled in the State of Washington at the General Election Held November 8, 1932* (Olympia, 1932); West Virginia Secretary of State, "Vote for President of the United States," *General Election Returns, 1932* (Charleston, 1932); Wisconsin Legislative Reference Library, comp., "Summary Vote for President November, 1932," *The Wisconsin Blue Book 1933* (Madison, 1933); Wyoming Secretary of State, comp., "Total Vote by Counties, General Election, November 8, 1932," *1933 Official Directory of Wyoming and Election Returns for 1932* (Casper: S.E. Boyer & Co., 1933)

1936

Alabama: Clerk of the House of Representatives, comp., *Statistics of the Congressional Election of November 3, 1936* (Washington, DC, 1937); Arizona Secretary of State,

General Election Returns, State of Arizona, November 3, 1936 (Phoenix, 1937); Arkansas: Clerk of the House of Representatives, comp., *Statistics of the Congressional Election of November 3, 1936* (Washington, DC, 1937); California Secretary of State, "Electors of President and Vice-President of the United States," *Statement of Vote at General Election Held on November 3, 1936, in the State of California* (Sacramento, 1936); Colorado Secretary of State, comp., *State of Colorado Abstract of Votes Cast at the . . . General Election Held on the Third Day of November, A.D. 1936 . . .* (Denver, 1936); State of Connecticut, comp., "Summary—Vote for President of the United States . . . , November 3, 1936," *State of Connecticut Public Document No. 26, Statement of Vote, General Election November 3, 1936* (Hartford, 1936); Delaware: Clerk of the House of Representatives, comp., *Statistics of the Congressional Election of November 3, 1936* (Washington, DC, 1937); Florida Department of State, Division of Elections, *Official Vote—State of Florida General Election—1936* (Tallahassee, 1936); Georgia: Clerk of the House of Representatives, comp., *Statistics of the Congressional Election of November 3, 1936* (Washington, DC, 1937); Idaho Secretary of State, Election Division, *State of Idaho Presidential Vote Cast at the General Election, November 3, 1936* (Boise, 1937); Illinois Office of the Secretary of State, "Vote for President—Nov. 3, 1936," *Official Vote of the State of Illinois Cast at the General Election, November 3, 1936* (Springfield, 1936); Indiana Division of Accounting and Statistics, "General Election Returns, November 3, 1936, Presidential Electors at Large," *Year Book of the State of Indiana for the Year 1936* (Indianapolis, 1937); Iowa: Clerk of the House of Representatives, comp., *Statistics of the Congressional Election of November 3, 1936* (Washington, DC, 1937); Kansas Secretary of State, "General Election, November 3, 1936, for President and Vice President," *Thirtieth Biennial Report of the Secretary of State 1935–1936* (Topeka: Kansas State Printing Plant, 1936); Kentucky: Clerk of the House of Representatives, comp., *Statistics of the Congressional Election of November 3, 1936* (Washington, DC, 1937); Louisiana Secretary of State, *Election Returns for Electors for President and Vice-President of the United States* (Baton Rouge, 1937); Maine: Clerk of the House of Representatives, comp., *Statistics of the Congressional Election of November 3, 1936* (Washington, DC, 1937); Maryland Secretary of State, comp., "General Election Returns, November 3, 1936," *Maryland Manual 1937* (Annapolis, 1937); Massachusetts Secretary of State, "Presidential Electors of President and Vice President," *Public Document #43, 1936* (Boston, 1937); Michigan Department of State, "Official Canvass of Votes, Election November 3, 1936, President of the United States," *Michigan Official Directory and Legislative Manual 1937–1938* (Lansing, 1937); Minnesota Secretary of State, "Vote by Counties of Presidential Electors," *The Legislative Manual of the State of Minnesota 1937* (St. Paul, 1937); Mississippi: Clerk of the House of Representatives, comp., *Statistics of the Congressional Election of November 3, 1936* (Washington, DC, 1937); Missouri Secretary of State, comp., "Vote for Candidates for President and Vice-President at General Election, November 3, 1936," *State of Missouri Official Manual for the Years 1937–1938* (Jefferson City, 1937); Montana Secretary of State, *Official Montana General Election Returns, November 3, 1936* (Helena, 1937); Nebraska Secretary of State, comp., "Election Statistics, 1936 President, Vice-President, and United States Senator," *Nebraska Blue Book, 1936* (Lincoln, 1936), Nevada Secretary of State, comp., *State of Nevada Official Returns of the Election of November, 1936* (Carson City, 1936); New Hampshire Department of State, *State of New Hampshire Manual for the General Court 1937* (Concord, 1937); New Jersey: Clerk of the House of Representatives, comp., *Statistics of the Congressional Election of November 3, 1936* (Washington, DC, 1937); New Mexico Secretary of State, "Canvass of Returns of Election Held November 3, 1936, State of New Mexico," *The New Mexico Blue Book State Official Register 1937–1938* (Santa Fe, 1938); "Vote, New York State, by Counties, November 3, 1936, for Highest Elector for President and Vice President," *The New York Red Book 1937* (Albany, 1937); North Carolina Secretary of State, "Vote for President by Counties 1928–1948," *North Carolina Manual 1949* (Raleigh, 1937); North Dakota Secretary of State, comp., "Party Ballot—Presidential Electors General Election, November 3rd, 1936," *Compilation of Election Returns, National and State, 1930-1944* (Bismarck, 1945); Ohio Secretary of State, *Ohio Election Statistics, the General Election Held on the Eighth Day of November 1938* (Cleveland, 1939); Oklahoma Department of Libraries, *Directory of Oklahoma State Almanac 1989-90* (Oklahoma City, 1990); Oregon Secretary of State, *Abstract of Votes Cast in the several counties in the State of Oregon at the Regular General Election held on the Third Day of November, A.D. 1936, for Candidates for Presidential Electors . . .* (Salem, 1936); Pennsylvania Bureau of Publications, "Votes Cast for President and Vice-President at General Election, November 3, 1936," *The Pennsylvania Manual 1937* (Harrisburg, 1937); Rhode Island Secretary of State, "Presidential Election, November 3, 1936 Vote of Rhode Island by Cities and Towns," *Rhode Island Manual 1937–1938* (Providence, 1937); South Carolina Secretary of State, "Statement of the Whole Number of Votes Cast for Presidential and Vice-Presidential Electors at the General Election Held in South Carolina on November 3rd, 1936," *Supplemental Report of the Secretary of State to the General Assembly of South Carolina, Election, Nov. 3, 1936* (Columbia, 1937); South Dakota Secretary of State, comp., "Presidential Electors," *Official Election Returns for South Dakota General Elec-

tion, November 3, 1936* (Pierre, 1936); Tennessee: Clerk of the House of Representatives, comp., *Statistics of the Congressional Election of November 3, 1936* (Washington, DC, 1937); Texas Secretary of State. Elections Division. *Presidential Election Results* (http://www.sos.state.tx.us/elections/index.shtml) (accessed February 1, 2002); Utah: Clerk of the House of Representatives, comp., *Statistics of the Congressional Election of November 3, 1936* (Washington, DC, 1937); Vermont Secretary of State, "Presidential Election, 1936," *Vermont Legislative Directory Biennial Session 1937* (Montpelier, 1937); Virginia: Clerk of the House of Representatives, comp., *Statistics of the Congressional Election of November 3, 1936* (Washington, DC, 1937); Washington Secretary of State, comp., "Presidential Candidates," *Abstract of Votes Polled in the State of Washington at . . . General Election, Nov. 3, 1936* (Olympia, 1936); West Virginia Secretary of State, "Vote for President of the United States," *General Election Returns, 1936* (Charleston, 1936); Wisconsin Legislative Reference Library, comp., "Summary Vote for President by Counties November 1936," *The Wisconsin Blue Book 1937* (Madison, 1937); Wyoming Secretary of State, comp., "Total Vote by Counties, General Election, November 3, 1936," *1937 Official Directory of Wyoming and 1936 Election Returns* (Sheridan: Mills Company, 1937);

1940

Alabama: Clerk of the House of Representatives, comp., *Statistics of the Presidential and Congressional Election of November 5, 1940* (Washington, DC, 1941); Arizona Secretary of State, *Returns, General Election, Nov. 5, 1940* (Phoenix, 1941); Arkansas: Clerk of the House of Representatives, comp., *Statistics of the Presidential and Congressional Election of November 5, 1940* (Washington, DC, 1941); California Secretary of State, comp., "Presidential Electors," *State of California Statement of Vote, General Election, November 5, 1940* (Sacramento, 1940); Colorado Secretary of State, comp., *State of Colorado Abstract of Votes Cast at the . . . General Election Held on the Fifth Day of November A.D., 1940 . . .* (Denver, 1940); State of Connecticut, comp., "Summary—Vote for President of the United States . . . November 5, 1940," *State of Connecticut Public Document No. 26, Statement of Vote General Election, November 5, 1940* (Hartford, 1940); Delaware: Clerk of the House of Representatives, comp., *Statistics of the Presidential and Congressional Election of November 5, 1940* (Washington, DC, 1941); Florida: Clerk of the House of Representatives, comp., *Statistics of the Presidential and Congressional Election of November 5, 1940* (Washington, DC, 1941); Georgia: Clerk of the House of Representatives, comp., *Statistics of the Presidential and Congressional Election of November 5, 1940* (Washington, DC, 1941); Idaho Secretary of State, Election Division, *State of Idaho Presidential Vote Cast at the General Election, November 5, 1940* (Boise, 1941); Illinois Office of the Secretary of State, "Vote for President—Nov. 5, 1940," *Official Vote of the State of Illinois Cast at the General Election, November 5, 1940* (Springfield, 1940); Indiana Division of Accounting and Statistics, "General Election Returns, November 5, 1940, Presidential Electors at Large," *Year Book of the State of Indiana for the Year 1940* (Indianapolis, 1941); Iowa Secretary of State, "General Election Vote Cast at General Election, November 5, 1940, by Counties for President and Vice President," *Iowa Official Register 1941–1942* (Des Moines, 1941); Kansas Secretary of State, "General Election, November 5, 1940, for President and Vice President," *Thirty-second Biennial Report of the Secretary of State 1939–1940* (Topeka: Kansas State Printing Plant, 1940); Kentucky: Clerk of the House of Representatives, comp., *Statistics of the Presidential and Congressional Election of November 5, 1940* (Washington, DC, 1941); Louisiana Secretary of State, *Election Returns for Electors for President and Vice-President of the United States* (Baton Rouge, 1940); Maine: *State Year Book and Legislative Manual No. 73* (Fred L. Towers, 1942); Maryland Secretary of State, "Maryland General Election Returns, November 5, 1940," *Maryland Manual 1940–41* (Annapolis, 1942); Massachusetts Secretary of State, "Presidential Electors of President and Vice President," *Public Document #43, 1940* (Boston, 1941); Michigan Department of State, "Official Canvass of Votes, Election November 5, 1940, President of the United States," *Michigan Official Directory and Legislative Manual 1941–1942* (Lansing, 1941); Minnesota Secretary of State, "Vote by Counties of Presidential Electors," *The Legislative Manual of the State of Minnesota 1941* (St. Paul, 1941); Mississippi Secretary of State, "Vote for Presidential Electors, November 5, 1940," *Mississippi Blue Book Biennial Report of the Secretary of State to the Legislature of Mississippi July 1, 1939, to July 1, 1941* (Jackson, 1941); Missouri Secretary of State, "General Election Returns, Vote for President, by Counties, at General Election, November 5, 1940," *State of Missouri Official Manual for the Years 1941–1942* (Jefferson City, 1941); Montana Secretary of State, *Official Montana General Election Returns, November 5, 1940* (Helena, 1941); Nebraska Secretary of State, comp., *Official Report of the Nebraska State Canvassing Board, General Election Held November 5, 1940* (Lincoln, 1940); Nevada Secretary of State, comp., *State of Nevada Official Returns of the Election of November, 1940* (Carson City, 1940); New Hampshire Department of State, *State of New Hampshire Manual for the General Court 1941* (Concord, 1941); New Jersey: Clerk of the House of Representatives, comp., *Statistics of the Presidential and Congressional Election of November 5, 1940* (Washington, DC, 1941); New Mexico

Secretary of State, "Canvass of Returns of Election Held November 5, 1940, State of New Mexico," *The New Mexico Blue Book State Official Register 1941-1942* (Santa Fe, 1942); "Vote, New York State, by Counties, November 5, 1940, for Highest Elector for President and Vice President," *The New York Red Book 1941* (Albany, 1941); North Carolina Secretary of State, "Vote for President by Counties 1928-1948," *North Carolina Manual 1949* (Raleigh, 1941); North Dakota Secretary of State, comp., "Official Abstract of Votes Cast at the General Election Held November 5, 1940," *Compilation of Election Returns, National and State 1930-1944* (Bismarck, 1945); Ohio Secretary of State, *Ohio Election Statistics, the General Election Held on the Second Day of November 1948* (Cleveland, 1949); Oklahoma Department of Libraries, *Directory of Oklahoma State Almanac 1989-90* (Oklahoma City, 1990); Oregon Secretary of State, *Abstract of Votes Cast in the Several Counties in the State of Oregon at the Regular General Election Held on the Fifth Day of November, A.D. 1940, for Candidates for Presidential Electors . . .* (Salem, 1940); Pennsylvania Bureau of Publications, "Votes Cast for Presidential Electors at General Election, November 5, 1940," *The Pennsylvania Manual 1941* (Harrisburg, 1941); Rhode Island Secretary of State, "Presidential Election, November 5, 1940, Vote of Rhode Island by Cities and Towns," *Rhode Island Manual 1941-1942* (Providence, 1941); South Carolina Secretary of State, "Statement of the Whole Number of Votes Cast for Presidential and Vice-Presidential Electors at the General Election Held in South Carolina, on November 5th, 1940," *Supplemental Report of the Secretary of State to the General Assembly of South Carolina, Election, Nov. 5, 1940* (Columbia, 1941); South Dakota Secretary of State, comp., "Presidential Electors," *Official Election Returns for South Dakota General Election, November 5, 1940* (Pierre, 1940); Tennessee: Clerk of the House of Representatives, comp., *Statistics of the Presidential and Congressional Election of November 5, 1940* (Washington, DC, 1941); Texas Secretary of State, Elections Division, *Presidential Election Results* (www.sos.state.tx.us/elections/index.shtml) (accessed February 1, 2002); Utah: Clerk of the House of Representatives, comp., *Statistics of the Presidential and Congressional Election of November 5, 1940* (Washington, DC, 1941); Vermont Secretary of State, "Presidential Election, 1940," *Vermont Legislative Directory Biennial Session 1941* (Montpelier, 1940); Virginia: Clerk of the House of Representatives, comp., *Statistics of the Presidential and Congressional Election of November 5, 1940* (Washington, DC, 1941); Washington Secretary of State, comp., "Presidential Candidates," *Abstract of Votes Polled in the State of Washington at . . . General Election, Nov. 5, 1940* (Olympia, 1940); West Virginia Secretary of State, "Vote for President of the United States," *General Election Returns, 1940* (Charleston, 1940); Wisconsin Legislative Reference Library, comp., "Summary Vote for President by Counties, November 1940," *The Wisconsin Blue Book 1942* (Madison, 1942); Wyoming Secretary of State, comp., "Total Vote by Counties, General Election, November 5, 1940," *1941 Wyoming Official Directory and 1940 Election Returns* (Casper: Prairie Publishing Co., 1941)

1944

Alabama: Clerk of the House of Representatives, comp., *Statistics of the Presidential and Congressional Election of November 7, 1944* (Washington: U.S. Government Printing Office, 1949); Arizona Secretary of State, *Official Canvass General Election Returns, November 7, 1944* (Phoenix, 1945); Arkansas: Clerk of the House of Representatives, comp., *Statistics of the Presidential and Congressional Election of November 7, 1944* (Washington: U.S. Government Printing Office, 1949); California Secretary of State, "Presidential Electors," *State of California Statement of Vote, General Election, November 7, 1944* (Sacramento, 1944); Colorado Secretary of State, comp., *State of Colorado Abstract of Votes Cast at the . . . General Election Held on the Seventh Day of November, A.D. 1944 . . .* (Denver, 1944); State of Connecticut, comp., "Summary—Vote for President of the United States . . . November 7, 1944," *State of Connecticut Public Document No. 26, Statement of Vote, General Election, November 7, 1944* (Hartford, 1945); Delaware Secretary of State, "Vote by Counties—Election of 1944," *Delaware State Manual 1945* (Dover, 1945); Florida Department of State, Division of Elections, *Official Vote—State of Florida General Election—1944* (Tallahassee, 1944); Georgia: Clerk of the House of Representatives, comp., *Statistics of the Presidential and Congressional Election of November 7, 1944* (Washington: U.S. Government Printing Office, 1949); Idaho Secretary of State. Election Division, *State of Idaho Presidential Vote Cast at the General Election, November 4, 1944* (Boise, 1945); Illinois Office of the Secretary of State, "Vote for President—Nov. 7, 1944," *Official Vote of the State of Illinois Cast at the General Election, November 7, 1944* (Springfield, 1944); Indiana Division of Accounting and Statistics, "General Election Returns, November 7, 1944, Presidential Electors at Large," *Year Book of the State of Indiana for the Year 1944* (Indianapolis, 1945); Iowa Secretary of State, "General Election Vote Cast at General Election, November 7, 1944, by Counties for President and Vice President," *Iowa Official Register 1945-1946* (Des Moines, 1945); Kansas Secretary of State, "General Election, November 7, 1944, for Electors of President and Vice President," *Thirty-fourth Biennial Report of the Secretary of State 1943-1944* (Topeka: Kansas State Printing Plant,

1944); Kentucky: Clerk of the House of Representatives, comp., *Statistics of the Presidential and Congressional Election of November 7, 1944* (Washington: U.S. Government Printing Office, 1949); Louisiana Secretary of State, *Election Returns for Electors for President and Vice-President of the United States* (Baton Rouge, 1944); Maine: *State Year Book and Legislative Manual No. 78* (Fred L. Towers, 1946); Maryland State Board of Elections, "For President of the United States," *General Election Returns—November 7, 1944* (Annapolis, 1944); Massachusetts Secretary of State, "Presidential Electors of President and Vice President," *Public Document #43, 1944* (Boston, 1945); Michigan Department of State, "Official Canvass of Votes, Election November 7, 1944, President of the United States," *Michigan Official Directory and Legislative Manual 1945-1946* (Lansing, 1945); Minnesota Secretary of State, "Vote by Counties of Presidential Electors," *The Legislative Manual of the State of Minnesota 1945* (St. Paul, 1945); Mississippi Secretary of State, "Vote for Presidential Electors, General Election, November 7, 1944," *Mississippi Blue Book Biennial Report of the Secretary of State to the Governor and Legislature of Mississippi, July 1, 1943, to July 1, 1945* (Jackson, 1945); Missouri Secretary of State, "General Election Returns, Vote for President, by Counties, at General Election, November 7, 1944," *State of Missouri Official Manual for the Years 1945-1946* (Jefferson City, 1945); Montana Secretary of State, *Official Montana General Election Returns, November 7, 1944* (Helena, 1945); Nebraska Secretary of State, comp., *Official Report of the Nebraska State Canvassing Board, General Election Held November 7, 1944* (Lincoln, 1944); Nevada Secretary of State, comp., *State of Nevada Official Returns of the Election of November, 1944* (Carson City, 1944); New Hampshire Department of State, "For Electors of President and Vice-President," *State of New Hampshire Manual for the General Court 1945* (Concord, 1945); New Jersey, "Votes Cast for President and Vice-President November 7, 1944," *Manual of the Legislature of New Jersey 1945* (Trenton, 1945); New Mexico State Canvassing Board, *Canvass of Returns of Election Held November 7, 1944, State of New Mexico* (Santa Fe, 1944); "Vote, New York State, by Counties, November 7, 1944, for Highest Elector for President and Vice President," *The New York Red Book 1945* (Albany, 1945); North Carolina Secretary of State, "Vote for President by Counties 1928–1948," *North Carolina Manual 1949* (Raleigh, 1945); North Dakota Secretary of State, comp., "Official Abstract of Votes Cast at the General Election Held November 7, 1944," *Compilation of Election Returns, National and State 1930-1944* (Bismarck, 1945); Ohio Secretary of State, *Ohio Election Statistics, the General Election Held on the Seventh Day of November 1944* (Cleveland, 1945); Oklahoma Department of Libraries, *Directory of Oklahoma State Almanac 1989-90* (Oklahoma City, 1990); Oregon Secretary of State, *Abstract of Votes Cast in the Several Counties in the State of Oregon at the Regular General Election Held on the Seventh Day of November, A.D. 1944, for Candidates for Presidential Electors . . .* (Salem, 1944); Pennsylvania Bureau of Publications, "Votes Cast for Presidential Electors of President and Vice-President on November 7, 1944," *The Pennsylvania Manual 1945* (Harrisburg, 1945); Rhode Island Board of Elections, "Vote by Counties for Presidential Electors," *Official Count of the Ballots Cast . . . at the Election Tuesday, November 7, 1944* (Providence, 1944); South Carolina Secretary of State, "Statement of the Whole Number of Votes Cast for Presidential and Vice-Presidential Electors at the General Election Held in South Carolina, on November 7th, 1944," *Supplemental Report of the Secretary of State to the General Assembly of South Carolina, Election, November 7, 1944* (Columbia, 1945); South Dakota Secretary of State, comp., "Presidential Electors," *Official Election Returns for South Dakota General Election, November 7, 1944* (Pierre, 1944); Tennessee Secretary of State, "Regular Election—November 7, 1944, Electors for President and Vice-President," *Tennessee Blue Book 1945-1946* (Nashville, 1946); Texas Secretary of State, Elections Division, *Presidential Election Results* (www.sos.state.tx.us/elections/index.shtml) (accessed February 1, 2002); Utah: Clerk of the House of Representatives, comp., *Statistics of the Presidential and Congressional Election of November 7, 1944* (Washington: U.S. Government Printing Office, 1949); Vermont Secretary of State, "Presidential Election, 1944," *Vermont Legislative Directory Biennial Session 1945* (Montpelier, 1945); Virginia: Clerk of the House of Representatives, comp., *Statistics of the Presidential and Congressional Election of November 7, 1944* (Washington: U.S. Government Printing Office, 1949); Washington Secretary of State, comp., "Presidential Candidates," *Abstract of Votes Polled in the State of Washington at General Election, Nov. 7, 1944* (Olympia, 1944); West Virginia Secretary of State, "Vote for President of the United States," *General Election Returns, 1944* (Charleston, 1944); Wisconsin Legislative Reference Library, comp., "Summary Vote for President by Counties, November 1944," *The Wisconsin Blue Book 1946* (Madison, 1946); Wyoming Secretary of State, comp., "Total Vote by Counties, General Election, November 14, 1944," *1945 Wyoming Official Directory and 1944 Election Returns* (Casper: Prairie Publishing Co., 1945)

1948

Alabama: Clerk of the House of Representatives, comp., *Statistics of the Presidential and Congressional Election of November 2, 1948* (Washington: U.S. Government Printing Office, 1949); Arizona Secretary of State, *Official Canvass General Election Returns,*

November 2, 1948 (Phoenix, 1949); Arkansas: Clerk of the House of Representatives, comp., *Statistics of the Presidential and Congressional Election of November 2, 1948* (Washington: U.S. Government Printing Office, 1949); California Secretary of State, comp., "Presidential Electors," *State of California Statement of Vote, General Election, November 2, 1948* (Sacramento, 1948); Colorado Secretary of State, comp., *State of Colorado Abstract of Votes Cast at the . . . General Election Held on the Second Day of November, A.D. 1948 . . .* (Denver, 1948); State of Connecticut, comp., "Vote for President of the United States, State Officers and U.S. Representative at Large—November 2, 1948," *State of Connecticut Public Document No. 26, Statement of Vote, General Election, November 2, 1948* (Hartford, 1949); Delaware Secretary of State, "Vote by Counties—Election of 1948," *Delaware State Manual 1949* (Dover, 1949); Florida Department of State, Division of Elections, comp., *Official Vote—State of Florida General Election—1948 Tabulated by Counties* (Tallahassee, 1948); Georgia Secretary of State, comp., "Returns of General Election, November 2, 1948, Presidential Electors," *Georgia's Official Register 1945–1950* (Atlanta, 1950); Idaho Secretary of State, Election Division, *State of Idaho Presidential Vote Cast at the General Election, November 2, 1948* (Boise, 1949); Illinois Office of the Secretary of State, "Vote for President—November 2, 1948," *Official Vote of the State of Illinois Cast at the General Election, November 2, 1948* (Springfield, 1948); Indiana Statistical Department State Board of Accounts, "General Election Returns—1948 President of the United States," *Year Book of the State of Indiana for the Year 1948* (Indianapolis, 1949); Iowa Secretary of State, "General Election Vote Cast at General Election, November 2, 1948, for President and Vice President of the United States," *Iowa Official Register 1949–1950* (Des Moines, 1949); Kansas Secretary of State, "General Election, November 2, 1948, for Electors of President and Vice President," *Thirty-sixth Biennial Report of the Secretary of State 1947–1948* (Topeka: Ferd Voiland Jr., State Printer, 1948); Kentucky: Clerk of the House of Representatives, comp., *Statistics of the Presidential and Congressional Election of November 2, 1948* (Washington: U.S. Government Printing Office, 1949); Louisiana Secretary of State, *Election Returns for Electors for President and Vice-President of the United States* (Baton Rouge, 1948); Maine Department of the Secretary of State, *State of Maine Presidential Election—-November 2, 1948* (Augusta, 1949); Maryland State Board of Elections, "For President of the United States and Vice President of the United States," *Maryland General Election Returns—November 2, 1948* (Annapolis, 1948); Massachusetts Secretary of State, "Presidential Electors of President and Vice President," *Public Document #43, Massachusetts Election Statistics 1948* (Boston, 1949); Michigan Department of State, "Official Canvass of Votes, Election November 2, 1948, President of the United States," *Michigan Official Directory and Legislative Manual 1949–1950* (Lansing, 1949); Minnesota Secretary of State, *The Legislative Manual of the State of Minnesota 1949* (St. Paul, 1949); Mississippi Secretary of State, *Mississippi Blue Book Statistical Register of State 1945–1949* (Jackson, 1949); Missouri Secretary of State, "General Election Returns, Vote for President, by Counties, at General Election, November 2, 1948," *State of Missouri Official Manual for the Years 1949–1950* (Jefferson City, 1949); Montana Secretary of State, *Official Montana General Election Returns, November 2, 1948* (Helena, 1949); Nebraska Secretary of State, comp., *Official Report of the Nebraska State Canvassing Board, General Election Held November 2, 1948* (Lincoln, 1948); Nevada Secretary of State, comp., *State of Nevada Official Returns of the Election of November, 1948* (Carson City, 1948); New Hampshire Department of State, "For Electors of President and Vice-President," *State of New Hampshire Manual for the General Court 1949* (Concord, 1949); New Jersey Secretary of State, "Votes Cast for President and Vice-President of the United States," *State of New Jersey Result of the General Election Held November 2nd, 1948* (Trenton, 1948); New Mexico State Canvassing Board, "Presidential Electors," *Report of the State Canvassing Board* (Santa Fe, 1948); "Vote, New York State, by Counties, November 2, 1948, for Highest Elector for President and Vice President," *The New York Red Book 1949* (Albany, 1949); North Carolina Secretary of State, "Vote for President by Counties 1948–1968," *North Carolina Manual 1969* (Raleigh, 1949); North Dakota Secretary of State, *Official Abstract of Votes Cast at the General Election Held November 2nd, 1948* (Bismarck, 1948); Ohio Secretary of State, *Ohio Election Statistics, the General Election Held on the Second Day of November 1948* (Cleveland, 1949); Oklahoma Department of Libraries, *Directory of Oklahoma State Almanac 1989-90* (Oklahoma City, 1990); Oregon Secretary of State, *Abstract of Votes Cast in the Several Counties in the State of Oregon at the Regular General Election Held on the Second Day of November, A.D. 1948, for Candidates for Presidential Electors . . .* (Salem, 1948); Pennsylvania Bureau of Publications, "Votes Cast for Presidential Electors of President and Vice-President on November 2, 1948," *The Pennsylvania Manual 1949–1950* (Harrisburg, 1949); Rhode Island Board of Elections, "Vote by Counties for Presidential Electors," *Official Count of the Ballots Cast . . . at the Election Tuesday, November 2, 1948* (Providence, 1948); South Carolina Secretary of State, "Statement of the Whole Number of Votes Cast for Presidential and Vice-Presidential Electors at the General Election Held in South Carolina on November 2, 1948," *Supplemental Report of the Secretary of State to the General Assembly of South Carolina, Election November 2, 1948* (Columbia, 1949); South Dakota Secretary of State, "Presidential Electors," *Official Election Returns for South Dakota General Election, November 2, 1948* (Pierre, 1948); Tennessee Secretary of State, "General Election—November 2, 1948, for Presidential Electors," *Tennessee Blue Book 1949–1950* (Nashville, 1950); Texas Secretary of State, Elections Division, *Presidential Election Results* (www.sos.state.tx.us/elections/index.shtml) (accessed February 1, 2002); Utah: Clerk of the House of Representatives, comp., *Statistics of the Presidential and Congressional Election of November 2, 1948* (Washington: U.S. Government Printing Office, 1949); Vermont Secretary of State, "Presidential Election, 1948," *Vermont Legislative Directory Biennial Session 1949* (Montpelier, 1949); Virginia: Clerk of the House of Representatives, comp., *Statistics of the Presidential and Congressional Election of November 2, 1948* (Washington: U.S. Government Printing Office, 1949); Washington Secretary of State, comp., "Presidential Candidates," *Abstract of Votes, State General Election, November 2, 1948* (Olympia, 1948); West Virginia Secretary of State, "Vote for President of the United States," *General Election Returns, 1948* (Charleston, 1948); Wisconsin Legislative Reference Library, comp., "Vote for President by Counties November 2, 1948," *The Wisconsin Blue Book 1950* (Madison, 1950); Wyoming Secretary of State, comp., "General Election—November 2, 1948," *1949 Wyoming Official Directory and 1948 Election Returns* (Sheridan: Mills Company, 1949)

1952

Alabama: Clerk of the House of Representatives, comp., *Statistics of the Presidential and Congressional Election of November 4, 1952* (Washington: U.S. Government Printing Office, 1953); Arizona Secretary of State, *Official Canvass General Election—November 4, 1952* (Phoenix, 1953); Arkansas: Clerk of the House of Representatives, comp., *Statistics of the Presidential and Congressional Election of November 4, 1952* (Washington: U.S. Government Printing Office, 1953); California Secretary of State, comp., "For Presidential Electors," *State of California Statement of Vote General Election November 4, 1952* (Sacramento, 1952); Colorado Secretary of State, comp., *State of Colorado Abstract of Votes Cast at the . . . General Election Held on the Fourth Day of November, A.D. 1952 . . .* (Denver, 1952); State of Connecticut, comp., "Vote for President of the United States, United States Senators, and U.S. Representative at Large—November 4, 1952," *State of Connecticut Public Document No. 26, Statement of Vote, General Election, November 4, 1952* (Hartford, 1953); Delaware Secretary of State, "Vote by Counties—Election of 1952," *Delaware State Manual 1954* (Dover, 1954); Florida Department of State, Division of Elections, comp., *Official Vote—State of Florida General Election—1952* (Tallahassee, 1952); Georgia Secretary of State, *Official State of Georgia Tabulation by Counties for Presidential Election Results . . . General Election, Nov. 4, 1952* (Atlanta, 1953); Idaho Secretary of State, Election Division, *State of Idaho Presidential Vote Cast at the General Election, November 4, 1952* (Boise, 1953); Illinois Office of the Secretary of State, "Vote for President—November 4, 1952," *Official Vote of the State of Illinois Cast at the General Election, November 4, 1952* (Springfield, 1952); Indiana Secretary of State, "General Election Returns, November 4, 1952, President," *Annual Election Report of the Secretary of State of the State of Indiana, 1952* (Indianapolis, 1953); Iowa Secretary of State, "General Election Vote Cast at General Election, November 4, 1952, by Counties for President and Vice President," *Iowa Official Register 1953–1954* (Des Moines, 1953); Kansas Secretary of State, "General Election, November 4, 1952, for Electors of President and Vice President," *Thirty-eighth Biennial Report of the Secretary of State 1951–52* (Topeka: Ferd Voiland Jr., State Printer, 1952); Kentucky: Clerk of the House of Representatives, comp., *Statistics of the Presidential and Congressional Election of November 4, 1952* (Washington: U.S. Government Printing Office, 1953); Louisiana Secretary of State, *Election Returns for Electors for President and Vice-President of the United States General Election, November, 1952* (Baton Rouge, 1953); Maine Department of the Secretary of State, *State of Maine Presidential Election—November 4, 1952* (Augusta, 1953); Maryland State Board of Elections, "For President and Vice President of the United States," *General Election Returns—November 4, 1952* (Annapolis, 1952); Massachusetts Secretary of State, "Presidential Electors of President and Vice President," *Public Document #43, Massachusetts Election Statistics 1952* (Boston, 1953); Michigan Department of State, "Official Canvass of Votes, General Election, November 4, 1952, President of the United States," *Official Directory and Legislative Manual 1953–1954* (Lansing, 1953); Minnesota Secretary of State, *Legislative Manual Compiled for the Minnesota Legislature 1953* (St. Paul, 1953); Mississippi Secretary of State, "General Election Held in the State of Mississippi Tuesday, November 4, 1952," *Biennial Report, Secretary of State, Mississippi, July 1, 1951, through June 30, 1953* (Jackson, 1953); Missouri Secretary of State, "General Election Returns, Vote for President, by Counties, at General Election, November 4, 1952," *State of Missouri Official Manual for the Years 1953–1954* (Jefferson City, 1957); Montana Secretary of State, *Official Montana General Election Returns, November 4, 1952* (Helena, 1953); Nebraska Secretary of State, comp., *Official Report of the Nebraska State Canvassing Board, General Election Held November 4, 1952* (Lincoln, 1952); Nevada Secretary of State, comp., *State of Nevada Official Returns of General Election of 1952 Election Held November 4, 1952* (Carson City, 1952); New Hampshire

Department of State, "General Election, November 4, 1952, for Electors of President and Vice-President," *State of New Hampshire Manual for the General Court 1953* (Concord, 1953); New Jersey Secretary of State, "Votes Cast for President and Vice-President of the United States," *State of New Jersey Result of the General Election Held November 4th, 1952* (Trenton, 1952); New Mexico State Canvassing Board, *General Election Summary for Presidential Electors* (Santa Fe, 1952); New York State Department of State, "Presidential Vote, New York State by Counties, November 4, 1952," *Manual for the Use of the Legislature of the State of New York 1953* (Albany, 1953); North Carolina Secretary of State, "Vote for President by Counties 1948–1968," *North Carolina Manual 1969* (Raleigh, 1953); North Dakota Secretary of State, *Official Abstract of Votes Cast at the General Election Held November 4, 1952* (Bismarck, 1952); Ohio Secretary of State, *Ohio Election Statistics Registration and Election Statistics General Election, 1952* (Cleveland, 1953); Oklahoma Department of Libraries, *Directory of Oklahoma State Almanac 1989-90* (Oklahoma City, 1990); Oregon Secretary of State, *Abstract of Votes Cast in the Several Counties in the State of Oregon at the Regular General Election Held on the Fourth Day of November, A.D. 1952, for Candidates for Presidential Electors . . .* (Salem, 1952); Pennsylvania Bureau of Publications, "Votes Cast for Presidential Electors of President and Vice-President on November 4, 1952," *The Pennsylvania Manual 1953–1954* (Harrisburg, 1953); Rhode Island Board of Elections, "Vote by Counties for Presidential Electors," *Official Count of the Ballots Cast . . . at the Election Tuesday, November 4, 1952* (Providence, 1952); South Carolina Secretary of State, "Statement of the Whole Number of Votes Cast for Presidential and Vice-Presidential Electors at the General Election Held in South Carolina on November 4, 1952," *Supplemental Report of the Secretary of State to the General Assembly of South Carolina, Election November 4, 1952* (Columbia, 1953); South Dakota Secretary of State, comp., "Presidential Electors," *Official Election Returns for South Dakota General Election, November 4, 1952* (Pierre, 1952); Tennessee Secretary of State, "General Election—November 4, 1952, for President of the United States," *Tennessee Blue Book, January First, 1954* (Nashville, 1954); Texas Secretary of State, Elections Division, *Presidential Election Results* (www.sos.state.tx.us/elections/index.shtml) (accessed February 1, 2002); Utah: Clerk of the House of Representatives, comp., *Statistics of the Presidential and Congressional Election of November 4, 1952* (Washington: U.S. Government Printing Office, 1953); Vermont Secretary of State, "Presidential Election, 1952," *Vermont Legislative Directory and State Manual Biennial Session 1953* (Montpelier, 1953); Virginia: Clerk of the House of Representatives, comp., *Statistics of the Presidential and Congressional Election of November 4, 1952* (Washington: U.S. Government Printing Office, 1953); Washington Secretary of State, comp., "Presidential Candidates," *Official Abstract of Votes, State General Election, November 4, 1952* (Olympia, 1952); West Virginia Secretary of State, "Vote for President of the United States," *General Election Returns, 1952* (Charleston, 1952); Wisconsin Legislative Reference Library, comp., "Vote for President and Vice President by Counties, November 4, 1952," *The Wisconsin Blue Book 1954* (Madison, 1954); Wyoming Secretary of State, comp., "General Election—November 4, 1952," *1953 Wyoming Official Directory and 1952 Election Returns* (Cheyenne, 1953)

1956

Alabama: Clerk of the House of Representatives, comp., *Statistics of the Presidential and Congressional Election of November 6, 1956* (Washington: U.S. Government Printing Office, 1958); Arizona Secretary of State, *Official Canvass General Election—November 6, 1956* (Phoenix, 1957); Arkansas: Clerk of the House of Representatives, comp., *Statistics of the Presidential and Congressional Election of November 6, 1956* (Washington: U.S. Government Printing Office, 1958); California Secretary of State, comp., "For Presidential Electors," *State of California Statement of Vote, General Election, November 5, 1956* (Sacramento, 1956); Colorado Secretary of State, comp., *State of Colorado Abstract of Votes Cast at the . . . General Election Held on the Sixth Day of November, A.D. 1956 . . .* (Denver, 1956); State of Connecticut, comp., "Vote for President of the United States, United States Senator, and U.S. Representative at Large—November 6, 1956," *State of Connecticut Public Document No. 26, Statement of Vote, General Election, November 6, 1956* (Hartford, 1957); Delaware Secretary of State, "Vote by Counties—Election of 1956," *Delaware State Manual 1960* (Dover, 1960); Florida Department of State, Division of Elections, comp., *Tabulation of Official Votes Cast in the General Election November 6, 1956* (Tallahassee, 1956); Georgia Secretary of State, *Official State of Georgia Tabulation by Counties for Presidential Electors . . . General Election, November 6, 1956* (Atlanta, 1957); Idaho Secretary of State, Election Division, *State of Idaho Presidential Vote Cast at the General Election, November 6, 1956* (Boise, 1957); Illinois Office of the Secretary of State, "Vote for President—November 6, 1956," *Official Vote of the State of Illinois Cast at the General Election, November 6, 1956* (Springfield, 1956); Indiana Secretary of State, "General Election Returns, November 6, 1956, President," *General Election Report of the Secretary of State of the State of Indiana, 1956* (Indianapolis, 1957); Iowa: Clerk of the House of Representatives, comp., *Statistics of the Presidential and Congressional Election of November 6,*

1956 (Washington: U.S. Government Printing Office, 1958); Kansas Secretary of State, "General Election, November 6, 1956, for Electors of President and Vice President," *Fortieth Biennial Report of the Secretary of State 1955–56* (Topeka: Ferd Voiland Jr., State Printer, 1956); Kentucky: Clerk of the House of Representatives, comp., *Statistics of the Presidential and Congressional Election of November 6, 1956* (Washington: U.S. Government Printing Office, 1958); Louisiana Secretary of State, *Election Returns for Electors for President and Vice-President of the United States General Election, November 6, 1956* (Baton Rouge, 1957); Maine Department of the Secretary of State, *State of Maine Presidential Election November 6, 1956* (Augusta, 1957); Maryland State Board of Elections, "For President of the United States," *General Election Returns—November 6, 1956* (Annapolis, 1956); Massachusetts Secretary of State, "Presidential Electors of President and Vice President," *Public Document #43, Massachusetts Election Statistics 1956* (Boston, 1957); Michigan Department of State, "Official Canvass of Votes, General Election, November 6, 1956, President of the United States," *Official Directory and Legislative Manual 1957–1958* (Lansing, 1957); Minnesota Secretary of State, *Report of the State Canvassing Board, General Election, November 6, 1956* (St. Paul, 1956); Mississippi Secretary of State, "Regular Election Held in the State of Mississippi Tuesday, November 6, 1956," *Mississippi Official and Statistical Register 1956–1960* (Jackson, 1957); Missouri Secretary of State, "General Election Returns, Vote for President, by Counties, at General Election, November 6, 1956," *State of Missouri Official Manual for the Years 1957–1958* (Jefferson City, 1957); Montana Secretary of State, *Official Montana General Election Returns, November 6, 1956* (Helena, 1957); Nebraska Secretary of State, comp., *Official Report of the Board of State Canvassers of the State of Nebraska General Election Held November 6, 1956* (Lincoln, 1956); Nevada Secretary of State, *Official Returns of General Election Held November 6, 1956* (Carson City, 1956); New Hampshire Department of State, "General Election, November 6, 1956, for Electors of President and Vice-President," *State of New Hampshire Manual for the General Court 1957* (Concord, 1957); New Jersey Secretary of State, "Votes Cast for President and Vice-President of the United States," *State of New Jersey, Result of the General Election Held November 6th, 1956* (Trenton, 1956); New Mexico State Canvassing Board, *Canvass of Returns of General Election Held November 6, 1956, State of New Mexico* (Santa Fe, 1957); New York State Department of State, "Presidential Vote, New York State by Counties, November 6, 1956," *Manual for the Use of the Legislature of the State of New York 1957* (Albany, 1957); North Carolina Secretary of State, "Vote for President by Counties 1948–1968," *North Carolina Manual 1969* (Raleigh, 1957); North Dakota Secretary of State, *Official Abstract of Votes Cast at the General Election Held November 6, 1956* (Bismarck, 1956); Ohio Secretary of State, *Ohio Election Statistics, Election and Registration Statistics, General Election, 1965* (Cleveland, 1967); Oklahoma Department of Libraries, *Directory of Oklahoma State Almanac, 1989-90* (Oklahoma City, 1990); Oregon Secretary of State, *Abstract of Votes Cast in the Several Counties in the State of Oregon at the Regular General Election Held on the Sixth Day of November, A.D. 1956, for Candidates for Presidential Electors . . .* (Salem, 1956); Pennsylvania Department of Property and Supplies, "Presidential and Vice-Presidential Electors, General Election, November 6, 1956," *The Pennsylvania Manual 1957–1958* (Harrisburg, 1957); Rhode Island Board of Elections, "Vote by Counties for Presidential Electors," *Official Count of the Ballots Cast . . . at the Election Tuesday, November 6, 1956* (Providence, 1956); South Carolina Secretary of State, "Statement of the Whole Number of Votes Cast for Presidential and Vice-Presidential Electors at the General Election Held in South Carolina on November 6, 1956," *Supplemental Report of the Secretary of State to the General Assembly of South Carolina, Election November 6, 1956* (Columbia, 1957); South Dakota Secretary of State, comp., "Presidential Electors," *Official Election Returns for South Dakota General Election, November 6, 1956* (Pierre, 1956); Tennessee: Clerk of the House of Representatives, comp., *Statistics of the Presidential and Congressional Election of November 6, 1956* (Washington: U.S. Government Printing Office, 1958); Texas Secretary of State, Elections Division, *Presidential Election Results* (www.sos.state.tx.us/elections/index.shtml) (accessed February 1, 2002); Utah: Clerk of the House of Representatives, comp., *Statistics of the Presidential and Congressional Election of November 6, 1956* (Washington: U.S. Government Printing Office, 1958); Vermont Secretary of State, "Votes for Federal Officers and Presidential Electors, General Election, Nov. 6, 1956," *Vermont Legislative Directory and State Manual Biennial Session 1957* (Montpelier, 1957); Virginia: Clerk of the House of Representatives, comp., *Statistics of the Presidential and Congressional Election of November 6, 1956* (Washington: U.S. Government Printing Office, 1958); Washington Secretary of State, comp., "Presidential Candidates," *Official Abstract of Votes, State General Election, November 6, 1956* (Olympia, 1956); West Virginia Secretary of State, "Vote for President of the United States," *General Election Returns, 1956* (Charleston, 1956); Wisconsin Legislative Reference Library, comp., "Vote for President and Vice President by Counties, November 6, 1956," *The Wisconsin Blue Book 1958* (Madison, 1958); Wyoming Secretary of State, comp., "Summary—Official Vote—General Election, November 6, 1956," *1957 Wyoming Official Directory and 1956 Election Returns* (Cheyenne, 1957)

1960

Alabama: Clerk of the House of Representatives, comp., *Statistics of the Presidential and Congressional Election of November 8, 1960* (Washington: U.S. Government Printing Office, 1961); Alaska Secretary of State, "United States President and United States Vice President," *State of Alaska Official Returns, General Election 11/8/60* (Juneau, 1961); Arizona Secretary of State, *Official Canvass General Election—November 8, 1960* (Phoenix, 1961); Arkansas: Clerk of the House of Representatives, comp., *Statistics of the Presidential and Congressional Election of November 8, 1960* (Washington: U.S. Government Printing Office, 1961); California Secretary of State, comp., "For Presidential Electors," *State of California Statement of Vote, General Election, November 8, 1960* (Sacramento, 1960); Colorado Secretary of State, comp., *State of Colorado Abstract of Votes Cast at the . . . General Election Held on the Eighth day of November, A.D. 1960 . . .* (Denver, 1960); State of Connecticut, comp., "Vote for President of the United States and U.S. Representative at Large—November 8, 1960," *State of Connecticut Public Document No. 26, Statement of Vote, General Election, November 8, 1960* (Hartford, 1961); Delaware Secretary of State, "Vote by Counties—Election of 1960," *Delaware State Manual 1963* (Dover, 1963); Florida Department of State, Division of Elections, *Official Vote—Florida General Election—November 8, 1960, President and Vice President of the United States* (Tallahassee, 1960); Georgia Secretary of State, *Official State of Georgia Tabulation by Counties for Presidential Electors . . . General Election, November 8, 1960* (Atlanta, 1961); Hawaii: Clerk of the House of Representatives, comp., *Statistics of the Presidential and Congressional Election of November 8, 1960* (Washington: U.S. Government Printing Office, 1961); Idaho Secretary of State, Election Division, *State of Idaho Presidential Vote Cast at the General Election, November 8, 1960* (Boise, 1961); Illinois Office of the Secretary of State, "Vote for President—November 8, 1960," *Official Vote of the State of Illinois Cast at the General Election, November 8, 1960* (Springfield, 1960); Indiana Secretary of State, "President and Vice President," *General Election Report of the Secretary of State of the State of Indiana, 1960* (Indianapolis, 1961); Iowa Secretary of State, *State of Iowa Canvass of the Vote, General Election, November 8, 1960* (Des Moines: State of Iowa, 1961); Kansas Secretary of State, "General Election, November 8, 1960 for Electors of President and Vice President," *Election Statistics, 1960* (Topeka, 1961); Kentucky: Clerk of the House of Representatives, comp., *Statistics of the Presidential and Congressional Election of November 8, 1960* (Washington: U.S. Government Printing Office, 1961); Louisiana Secretary of State, *Election Returns for Electors for President and Vice-President of the United States* (Baton Rouge, 1961); Maine Department of the Secretary of State, *State of Maine General Election, November 8, 1960* (Augusta, 1961); Maryland State Board of Elections, "For President of the United States," *General Election Returns—November 8, 1960* (Annapolis, 1960); Massachusetts Secretary of State, "Presidential Electors of President and Vice President," *Public Document #43, Massachusetts Election Statistics 1960* (Boston, 1961); Michigan Department of State, "Official Canvass of Votes, General Election, November 8, 1960, President and Vice President of the United States," *Michigan Manual 1961–1962* (Lansing, 1961); Minnesota Secretary of State, *Report of the State Canvassing Board, General Election, November 8, 1960* (St. Paul, 1960); Mississippi Secretary of State, "Official Vote Tabulation, State of Mississippi Regular Election, November 8, 1960," *Mississippi Official and Statistical Register 1960–1964* (Jackson, 1961); Missouri Secretary of State, "General Election Returns, Vote for President, by Counties, at General Election, November 8, 1960," *State of Missouri Official Manual for the Years 1961–1962* (Jefferson City, 1961); Montana Secretary of State, comp., *Official Montana General Election Returns, November 8, 1960* (Helena, 1961); Nebraska Secretary of State, comp., *Official Report of the Board of State Canvassers of the State of Nebraska, General Election Held November 8, 1960* (Lincoln, 1960); Nevada Secretary of State, *Official Returns of General Election Held November 8, 1960* (Carson City, 1960); New Hampshire Department of State, "General Election, November 8, 1960, for Electors of President and Vice-President," *State of New Hampshire Manual for the General Court 1961* (Concord, 1961); New Jersey Secretary of State, "Votes Cast for President and Vice-President of the United States," *State of New Jersey Result of the General Election Held November 8th, 1960* (Trenton, 1960); New Mexico State Canvassing Board, *Canvass of Returns of General Election Held November 8, 1960, State of New Mexico* (Santa Fe, 1961); New York State Department of State, "Presidential Vote, New York State by Counties, November 8, 1960," *Manual for the Use of the Legislature of the State of New York 1961–62* (Albany, 1961); North Carolina Secretary of State, "Vote for President by Counties 1948–1968," *North Carolina Manual 1969* (Raleigh, 1961); North Dakota Secretary of State, *Official Abstract of Votes Cast at the General Election Held November 8, 1960* (Bismarck, 1960); Ohio Secretary of State, *Ohio Election Statistics Election and Registration Statistics, General Election, 1965* (Cleveland, 1967); Oklahoma Department of Libraries, *Directory of Oklahoma State Almanac 1989-90* (Oklahoma City, 1990); Oregon Secretary of State, "President of the United States," *Official Abstract of Votes, General Election, November 8, 1960* (Salem, 1960); Pennsylvania Department of Property and Supplies, "Presidential Electors, General Election, November 8, 1960," *The Pennsylvania Manual 1961–1962* (Harrisburg, 1961); Rhode Island Board of Elections, "Vote by Counties for Presidential Electors," *Official Count of the Ballots Cast . . . at the Election Tuesday, November 8, 1960* (Providence, 1960); South Carolina Secretary of State, "Statement of the Whole Number of Votes Cast for Presidential and Vice-Presidential Electors at the General Election Held in South Carolina on November 8, 1960," *Supplemental Report of the Secretary of State to the General Assembly of South Carolina, Election November 8, 1960* (Columbia, 1961); South Dakota Secretary of State, comp., "Presidential Electors," *Official Election Returns by Counties for the State of South Dakota General Election, November 8, 1960* (Pierre, 1960); Tennessee Secretary of State, "General Election—November 8, 1960, for President and Vice-President of the United States," *Tennessee Blue Book 1961–62* (Nashville, 1961); Texas Secretary of State, Elections Division, *Presidential Election Results* (www.sos.state.tx.us/elections/index.shtml) (accessed February 1, 2002); Utah State Elections Office, *1960 General Election Abstract* (Salt Lake City, 1960); Vermont Secretary of State, *Canvass of Votes for Presidential Electors, General Election—November 8, 1960* (Rutland, 1960); Virginia State Board of Elections, comp., "Official Statement of the Whole Number of Votes Cast in the Commonwealth of Virginia for Electors of President and Vice-President, at the Election Held on November 8, 1960," *Statement of the Vote for President and Vice-President, United States Senator . . . General Election, Tuesday, November 8, 1960* (Richmond: Commonwealth of Virginia Division of Purchase and Printing, 1960); Washington Secretary of State, comp., "Presidential Candidates," *Official Abstract of Votes, State General Election, November 8, 1960* (Olympia, 1960); West Virginia Secretary of State, "Vote for President of the United States," *General Election Returns, 1960* (Charleston, 1960); Wisconsin Legislative Reference Library, comp., "Vote for President and Vice President by County, Wisconsin General Election, November 8, 1960," *The Wisconsin Blue Book 1962* (Madison, 1962); Wyoming Secretary of State, comp., "Summary—Official Vote—General Election, November 8, 1960," *1961 Wyoming Official Directory and 1960 Election Returns* (Cheyenne, 1961)

1964

Alabama: Clerk of the House of Representatives, comp., *Statistics of the Presidential and Congressional Election of November 3, 1964* (Washington: U.S. Government Printing Office, 1965); Alaska Secretary of State, "U.S. President and Vice President," *State of Alaska Official Returns by Election Precinct, General Election, November 3, 1964* (Juneau, 1965); Arizona Secretary of State, *State of Arizona Official Canvass, General Election—November 3, 1964* (Phoenix, 1964); Arkansas: Clerk of the House of Representatives, comp., *Statistics of the Presidential and Congressional Election of November 3, 1964* (Washington: U.S. Government Printing Office, 1965); California Secretary of State, comp., *California Statement of Vote General Election, November 3, 1964* (Sacramento, 1964); Colorado Secretary of State, comp., *State of Colorado Abstract of Votes Cast at the . . . General Election Held on the Third Day of November, A.D. 1964 . . .* (Denver, 1964); State of Connecticut, comp., "Vote for President of the United States and United States Senator—November 3, 1964," *State of Connecticut Public Document No. 26, Statement of Vote, General Election, November 3, 1964* (Hartford, 1965); Delaware Secretary of State, "Vote by Counties—Election 1964," *Delaware State Manual, 1965* (Dover, 1964); District of Columbia: Clerk of the House of Representatives, comp., *Statistics of the Presidential and Congressional Election of November 3, 1964* (Washington: U.S. Government Printing Office, 1965); Florida Department of State, Division of Elections, *Official Vote—Florida General Election—November 3, 1964, President and Vice President of the United States* (Tallahassee, 1964); Georgia Secretary of State, *Official State of Georgia Tabulation by Counties for Presidential Electors . . . General Election, November 3, 1964* (Atlanta, 1965); Hawaii: Clerk of the House of Representatives, comp., *Statistics of the Presidential and Congressional Election of November 3, 1964* (Washington: U.S. Government Printing Office, 1965); Idaho Secretary of State, Election Division, *State of Idaho Presidential Vote Cast at the General Election, November 3, 1964* (Boise, 1965); Illinois Office of the Secretary of State, comp., "Vote for President—November 3, 1964," *Official Vote of the State of Illinois Cast at the General Election, November 3, 1964* (Springfield, 1964); Indiana Secretary of State, "President and Vice President," *General Election Report of the Secretary of State of the State of Indiana, 1964* (Indianapolis, 1965); Iowa Secretary of State, *State of Iowa Canvass of the Vote, General Election, November 3, 1964* (Des Moines: State of Iowa, 1965); Kansas Secretary of State, "General Election, November 3, 1964, for Electors of President and Vice President," *Election Statistics* (Topeka, 1965); Kentucky: Clerk of the House of Representatives, comp., *Statistics of the Presidential and Congressional Election of November 3, 1964* (Washington: U.S. Government Printing Office, 1965); Louisiana Secretary of State, *Tabulation of Precinct Returns, Congressional Election, November 3, 1964* (Baton Rouge, 1965); Maine Department of the Secretary of State, Bureau of Corporations, Elections, and Commissions, *State of Maine General Election, November 3, 1964* (Augusta, 1965); Maryland State Board of Elections, "For President of the United States," *General Election Returns—November 3, 1964* (Annapolis, 1964); Massachusetts Secretary of State, "Presidential Electors of President and Vice President,"

Public Document #43, Massachusetts Election Statistics 1964 (Boston, 1965); Minnesota Secretary of State, "General Election Returns, November 3, 1964," *State of Minnesota Legislative Manual 1965–1966* (St. Paul, 1965); Mississippi Secretary of State, "General Election—November 3, 1964," *Mississippi Official and Statistical Register 1964–1968* (Jackson, 1965); Missouri Secretary of State, "General Election Returns, Vote for President, by Counties, at General Election, November 3, 1964," *State of Missouri Official Manual for the Years 1965–1966* (Jefferson City, 1965); Montana Secretary of State, comp., *Official Montana General Election Returns, November 3, 1964* (Helena, 1965); Nebraska Secretary of State, comp., *Official Report of the Board of State Canvassers of the State of Nebraska General Election Held November 3, 1964* (Lincoln, 1964); Nevada Secretary of State, *Official Returns of General Election Held November 3, 1964* (Carson City, 1964); New Hampshire Department of State, "General Election November 3, 1964, for Electors of President and Vice-President," *State of New Hampshire Manual for the General Court 1965* (Concord, 1965); New Jersey Secretary of State, "Votes Cast for President and Vice-President of the United States," *State of New Jersey, Result of the General Election Held November 3rd, 1964* (Trenton, 1964); New Mexico State Canvassing Board, *Canvass of Returns of General Election Held on November 3, 1964—State of New Mexico* (Santa Fe, 1965); New York State Department of State, "Presidential Vote, New York State by Counties, November 3, 1964," *Manual for the Use of the Legislature of the State of New York 1965–66* (Albany, 1965); North Carolina Secretary of State, "Vote for President by Counties 1948–1968," *North Carolina Manual 1969* (Raleigh, 1965); North Dakota Secretary of State, *Official Abstract of Votes Cast at the General Election Held November 3, 1964* (Bismarck, 1964); Ohio Secretary of State, *Ohio Election Statistics, Election and Registration Statistics, General Election, 1965* (Cleveland, 1967); Oklahoma State Election Board, comp., "Official Returns, General Election, November 3, 1964, Presidential Elector," *State of Oklahoma Election Results and Statistics 1964* (Oklahoma City, 1964); Oregon Secretary of State, Elections Division, comp., "President of the United States," *Official Abstract of Votes, General Election 1964* (Salem, 1964); Pennsylvania Department of Property and Supplies, "President of the United States General Election—November 3, 1964," *The 1965–1966 Pennsylvania Manual* (Harrisburg, 1966); Rhode Island Board of Elections, "Vote by Counties for Presidential Electors," *Official Count of the Ballots Cast . . . at the Election Tuesday, November 3, 1964* (Providence, 1964); South Carolina Secretary of State, "Statement of the Whole Number of Votes Cast for Presidential and Vice-Presidential Electors at the General Election Held in South Carolina on November 3, 1964," *Supplemental Report of the Secretary of State to the General Assembly of South Carolina, Election November 3, 1964* (Columbia, 1965); South Dakota Secretary of State, "Presidential Electors," *Official Election Returns by Counties for the State of South Dakota General Election, November 3, 1964* (Pierre, 1964); Tennessee Secretary of State, "November 3, 1964, General Election—State of Tennessee for President and Vice President of the United States" (Nashville, 1964); Texas Secretary of State, Elections Division, *Presidential Election Results*, Texas Secretary of State. Elections Division (www.sos.state.tx.us/elections/index.shtml) (accessed February 1, 2002); Utah State Elections Office, *1964 General Election Abstract* (Salt Lake City, 1964); Vermont Secretary of State, *Votes for Presidential Electors, General Election—November 3, 1964* (Rutland, 1965); Virginia State Board of Elections, comp., "Official Statement of the Whole Number of Votes Cast in the Commonwealth of Virginia for Electors of President and Vice-President, at the Election Held on November 3, 1964," *Statement of the Vote for President and Vice-President, United States Senator . . . General Election Tuesday, November 3, 1964* (Richmond: Commonwealth of Virginia Department of Purchases and Supply, 1964); Washington Secretary of State, comp., "Presidential Candidates," *Abstract of Votes Presidential and State, General Election Held on November 3, 1964* (Olympia, 1964); West Virginia Secretary of State, "Vote for President of the United States," *General Election Returns, 1964* (Charleston, 1964); Wisconsin Legislative Reference Bureau, comp., "General Election, November 3, 1964, Vote for President and Vice President by County," *The Wisconsin Blue Book 1966* (Madison, 1966); Wyoming Secretary of State, comp., "Official Vote—General Election, November 3, 1964," *Wyoming Official 1965 Directory and 1964 Election Returns* (Cheyenne, 1965)

1968

Alabama: Clerk of the House of Representatives, comp., *Statistics of the Presidential and Congressional Election of November 5, 1968* (Washington: U.S. Government Printing Office, 1969); Alaska Secretary of State, "General Election, November 5, 1968," *State of Alaska Official Returns by Election Precinct, General Election, November 5, 1968* (Juneau, 1969); Arizona Secretary of State, *State of Arizona Official Canvass, General Election—November 5, 1968* (Phoenix, 1968); Arkansas: Clerk of the House of Representatives, comp., *Statistics of the Presidential and Congressional Election of November 5, 1968* (Washington: U.S. Government Printing Office, 1969); California Secretary of State, comp., *Statement of Vote, State of California General Election, November 5, 1968* (Sacramento, 1968); Colorado Secretary of State, *Abstract of Votes Cast at the . . . General Election, Held November 5, 1968* (Denver, 1968); State of Connecticut, comp., "Vote for President of the United States and United States Senator—November 5, 1968," *State of Connecticut Public Document No. 26, Statement of Vote, General Election, November 5, 1968* (Hartford, 1969); State of Delaware Department of Elections, *State of Delaware Official Results of Presidential Election and Statewide Offices November 5, 1968* (Dover, 1968); District of Columbia: Clerk of the House of Representatives, comp., *Statistics of the Presidential and Congressional Election of November 5, 1968* (Washington: U.S. Government Printing Office, 1969); Florida Department of State, Division of Elections, *November 5, 1968, President and Vice President* (Tallahassee, 1968); Georgia Secretary of State, *Official State of Georgia Tabulation by Counties for Presidential Electors . . . General Election, November 5, 1968* (Atlanta, 1969); Hawaii: Clerk of the House of Representatives, comp., *Statistics of the Presidential and Congressional Election of November 5, 1968* (Washington: U.S. Government Printing Office, 1969); Idaho Secretary of State, Election Division, *State of Idaho Presidential Vote Cast at the General Election November 5, 1968* (Boise, 1969); Illinois Office of the Secretary of State, "Vote for President—November 5, 1968," *Official Vote of the State of Illinois Cast at the General Election November 5, 1968* (Springfield, 1968); Indiana Secretary of State, "President and Vice President," *General Election Report of the Secretary of State of the State of Indiana, 1968* (Indianapolis, 1969); Iowa Secretary of State, *State of Iowa Canvass of the Vote, General Election, November 5, 1968* (Des Moines: State of Iowa, 1969); Kansas Secretary of State, "General Election, November 5, 1968, for Electors of President and Vice President," *Election Statistics* (Topeka, 1969); Kentucky: Clerk of the House of Representatives, comp., *Statistics of the Presidential and Congressional Election of November 5, 1968* (Washington: U.S. Government Printing Office, 1969); Louisiana Secretary of State, comp., *State of Louisiana General Election Returns, November 5, 1968* (Baton Rouge, 1969); Maine Department of the Secretary of State, Bureau of Corporations, Elections, and Commissions, *State of Maine General Election, November 5, 1968, President and Vice President* (Augusta, 1969); Maryland State Board of Elections, "For President of the United States," *Maryland General Election Returns—November 5, 1968* (Annapolis, 1968); Massachusetts Secretary of State, "Presidential Electors of President and Vice President," *Public Document #43, Massachusetts Election Statistics 1968* (Boston, 1969); Michigan Department of Administration, "Official Canvass of Votes, General Election, November 5, 1968, President and Vice President of the United States," *Michigan Manual 1969–1970* (Lansing, 1969); Minnesota Secretary of State, "Returns of General Election in State of Minnesota, November 5, 1968, Official Canvass," *The Minnesota Legislative Manual 1969–1970* (St. Paul, 1969); Mississippi Secretary of State, "General Election, November 5, 1968," *Mississippi Official and Statistical Register 1968–1972* (Jackson, 1969); Missouri Secretary of State, "General Election Returns, Vote for President, by Counties, at General Election, November 5, 1968," *State of Missouri Official Manual for the Years 1969–1970* (Jefferson City, 1969); Montana Secretary of State, *Official Montana General Election Returns, November 5, 1968* (Helena, 1969); Nebraska Secretary of State, comp., *Official Report of the Board of State Canvassers of the State of Nebraska, General Election Held November 5, 1968* (Lincoln, 1968); Nevada Secretary of State, *Official Returns of General Election Held November 5, 1968* (Carson City, 1968); New Hampshire Department of State, "General Election November 5, 1968, for Electors of President and Vice-President," *State of New Hampshire Manual for the General Court 1969* (Concord, 1969); New Jersey Secretary of State, "Votes Cast for President and Vice-President of the United States," *State of New Jersey Result of the General Election Held November 5th, 1968* (Trenton, 1968); New Mexico State Canvassing Board, *Canvass of Returns of General Election Held on November 5, 1968—State of New Mexico* (Santa Fe, 1968); New York State Department of State, "Presidential Vote, New York State by Counties, November 5, 1968," *Manual for the Use of the Legislature of the State of New York 1969* (Albany, 1969); North Carolina Secretary of State, "Vote for President by Counties 1948–1968," *North Carolina Manual 1969* (Raleigh, 1969); North Dakota Secretary of State, *Official Abstract of Votes Cast at the General Election Held November 5, 1968* (Bismarck, 1968); Ohio Secretary of State, *Ohio Election Statistics, Election and Registration Statistics, General Election, 1968* (Cleveland, 1969); Oklahoma State Election Board, *Official Returns General Election, November 5, 1968, Presidential Electors* (Oklahoma City, 1968); Oregon Secretary of State, Elections Division, "President of the United States," *Official Abstract of Votes, General Election 1968* (Salem, 1968); Pennsylvania Department of Property and Supplies, "President & Vice-President of the United States, General Election—November 5, 1968," *The 1969 Pennsylvania Manual* (Harrisburg, 1969); Rhode Island Board of Elections, "Vote by Counties for Presidential Electors," *Official Count of the Ballots Cast . . . at the Election Tuesday, November 5, 1968* (Providence, 1972); South Carolina Secretary of State, "Statement of the Whole Number of Votes Cast for Presidential and Vice-Presidential Electors at the General Election Held in South Carolina on November 5, 1968," *Supplemental Report of the Secretary of State O. Frank Thornton to the General Assembly of South Carolina, Election November 5, 1968, and Primary of June 11, 1968* (Columbia, 1969); South Dakota Secretary of State, comp., "Presidential Electors," *Official Election Returns by Counties for the State of South Dakota General Election, November 5, 1968* (Pierre, 1968); Tennessee

Secretary of State, "General Election—November 5, 1968, President and Vice Presi-dent of the United States" (Nashville, 1968); Texas Secretary of State, Elections Division, *Presidential Election Results* (www.sos.state.tx.us/elections/index.shtml) (accessed February 1, 2002); Utah State Elections Office, *1968 General Election Abstract* (Salt Lake City, 1968); Vermont Secretary of State, *Canvass of Votes for Presidential Electors, General Election—November 5, 1968* (Rutland, 1969); Virginia State Board of Elections, comp., "Official Statement of the Whole Number of Votes Cast in the Commonwealth of Virginia for Electors of President and Vice-President, at the Election Held on November 5, 1968," *Statement of the Vote for President and Vice-President . . . General Election Tuesday, November 5, 1968* (Richmond: Commonwealth of Virginia Department of Purchases and Supply, 1968); Washington Secretary of State, comp., "Presidential Candidates," *Abstract of Votes Presidential and State General Election Held on November 5, 1968* (Olympia, 1968); West Virginia Secretary of State, "Vote for President of the United States," *General Election Returns, 1968* (Charleston, 1968); Wisconsin Legislative Reference Bureau, comp., "General Election, Novem-ber 5, 1968, Vote for President and Vice President by County," *State of Wisconsin Blue Book 1970* (Madison, 1970); Wyoming Secretary of State, comp., "Official Vote—General Election, November 5, 1968," *1969 Wyoming Official Directory and 1968 Elec-tion Returns* (Cheyenne, 1969)

1972

Alabama: Clerk of the House of Representatives, *Statistics of the Presidential and Con-gressional Election of November 7, 1972* (Washington: U.S. Government Printing Office, 1973); Alaska, "General Election, November 7, 1972," *State of Alaska Official Returns by Election Precinct, General Election, November 7, 1972* (Juneau, 1973); Arizona Secretary of State, *State of Arizona Official Canvass, General Election—November 7, 1972* (Phoenix, 1973); Arkansas: Clerk of the House of Representatives, *Statistics of the Presidential and Congressional Election of November 7, 1972* (Washington: U.S. Govern-ment Printing Office, 1973); California Secretary of State, comp., *Statement of Vote General Election November 7, 1972* (Sacramento, 1972); Colorado Secretary of State, *Abstract of Votes Cast at a General Election Held on Tuesday, November 7, A.D. 1972* (Denver, 1972); State of Connecticut, comp., "Vote for President of the United States, November 7, 1972," *State of Connecticut Public Document No. 26, Statement of Vote, General Election November 7, 1972* (Hartford, 1973); State of Delaware Depart-ment of Elections, *State of Delaware Official Results of Presidential Election and Statewide Offices, November 7, 1972* (Dover, 1972); Clerk of the House of Representatives, comp., *Statistics of the Presidential and Congressional Election of November 7, 1972* (Wash-ington: U.S. Government Printing Office, 1973); Florida Department of State, Division of Elections, *November 7, 1972, President and Vice President* (Tallahassee, 1972); Georgia Secretary of State, *Official State of Georgia Tabulation by Counties for Presidential Electors . . . General Election, November 7, 1972* (Atlanta, 1973); Hawaii: Clerk of the House of Representatives, *Statistics of the Presidential and Congressional Election of November 7, 1972* (Washington: U.S. Government Printing Office, 1973); Idaho Secretary of State, Election Division, *State of Idaho Presidential Vote Cast at the General Election November 7, 1972* (Boise, 1973); Illinois Office of the Secretary of State, "Vote for President and Vice-President of the United States—November 7, 1972," *State of Illinois Official Vote Cast at the General Election, November 7, 1972* (Springfield, 1972); Indiana Secretary of State, "President and Vice President," *1972 Election Report State of Indiana* (Indianapolis, 1973); Iowa Secretary of State, *State of Iowa Canvass of the Vote, General Election, November 7, 1972* (Des Moines: State of Iowa, 1973); Kansas Secretary of State, "General Election, November 7, 1972, for President and Vice President," *Election Statistics* (Topeka, 1973); Kentucky: Clerk of the House of Representatives, *Statistics of the Presidential and Congressional Election of November 7, 1972* (Washington: U.S. Government Printing Office, 1973); Louisiana Secretary of State, *Election Returns for Electors for President and Vice-President of the United States* (Baton Rouge, 1972); Maine Department of the Secretary of State, Bureau of Corporations, Elections, and Commissions, *State of Maine General Election, November 7, 1972, President and Vice President* (Augusta, 1973); Maryland State Board of Elec-tions, "For President of the United States," *Maryland General Election Returns—November 7, 1972* (Annapolis, 1972); Massachusetts Secretary of State, "Presidential Electors of President and Vice President," *Public Document #43, Massachusetts Election Statistics 1972* (Boston, 1973); Michigan Department of Administration, "Official Canvass of Votes, General Election President and Vice President of the United States," *Michigan Manual 1973–1974* (Lansing, 1973); Minnesota Secretary of State, "Returns of General Election in State of Minnesota, November 7, 1972," *The Min-nesota Legislative Manual 1973–1974* (St. Paul, 1973); Mississippi Secretary of State, "General Election November 7, 1972," *Mississippi Official and Statistical Register 1972–1976* (Jackson, 1973); Missouri Secretary of State, "General Election Returns, Vote for President, by Counties, at General Election, November 7, 1972," *Official Manual, State of Missouri, 1973–1974* (Jefferson City, 1973); Montana Secretary of State, *Report of the Official Canvass of the Vote Cast at the General Election Held in the State of*

Montana, November 7, 1972 (Helena, 1973); Nebraska Secretary of State, comp., *Offi-cial Report of the Board of State Canvassers of the State of Nebraska General Election Held November 7, 1972* (Lincoln, 1972); Nevada Secretary of State, *Official Returns of Gen-eral Election Held November 7, 1972* (Carson City, 1972); New Hampshire Depart-ment of State, "General Election, November 7, 1972, for Electors of President and Vice President," *State of New Hampshire Manual for the General Court 1973, No. 43* (Concord, 1973); New Jersey Secretary of State, "Votes Cast for President and Vice-President of the United States," *State of New Jersey, Result of the General Election Held November 7th, 1972* (Trenton, 1972); New Mexico State Canvassing Board, *Canvass of Returns of General Election Held on November 7, 1972—State of New Mexico* (Santa Fe, 1972); New York State Department of State, "Presidential Vote, New York State by Counties, November 7, 1972," *Manual for the Use of the Legislature of the State of New York 1973* (Albany, 1973); North Carolina Secretary of State, "Vote for President by Counties 1972," *North Carolina Manual 1973* (Raleigh, 1973); North Dakota Secre-tary of State, *Official Abstract of Votes Cast at the General Election Held November 7, 1972* (Bismarck, 1972); Ohio Secretary of State, *Ohio Election Statistics Election and Registra-tion Statistics, General Election, 1972* (Cleveland, 1973); Oklahoma State Election Board, *Official Returns, General Election, November 7, 1972, Presidential Electors* (Oklahoma City, 1972); Oregon Secretary of State, Elections Division, "President," *Official Abstract of Votes, General Election 1972* (Salem, 1972); Pennsylvania Depart-ment of State, Bureau of Commissions, Elections, and Legislation, *President & Vice President of the United States General Election, November 7, 1972* (Harrisburg, 1972); Rhode Island Board of Elections, "Vote by Counties for Presidential Electors," *Offi-cial Count of the Ballots Cast . . . at the Election Tuesday, November 7, 1972* (Providence, 1972); South Carolina State Election Commission, "South Carolina Votes Cast in General Election Held in South Carolina, November 7, 1972," *Report of the South Carolina State Election Commission for the Period Ending June 30, 1973* (Columbia, 1973); South Dakota Secretary of State, comp., "Presidential Electors," *Official Elec-tion Returns by Counties for the State of South Dakota, General Election, November 7, 1972* (Pierre, 1972); Tennessee Secretary of State, "General Election—November 7, 1972, President and Vice President—United States of America" (Nashville, 1972); Texas Secretary of State, Elections Division, *Presidential Election Results* (www.sos.state.tx.us/elections/index.shtml) (accessed February 1, 2002); Utah State Elections Office, *1972 General Election Abstract* (Salt Lake City, 1972); Vermont Sec-retary of State, *Canvass of Votes for Presidential Electors, General Election—November 7, 1972* (Rutland, 1973); Virginia State Board of Elections, comp., *Commonwealth of Virginia Official Election Results 1972 for President and Vice President . . . in the General Election, November 7, 1972 . . .* (Richmond, 1973); Washington Secretary of State, comp., "Presidential Candidates," *Abstract of Votes Presidential and State, General Elec-tion Held on November 7, 1972* (Olympia, 1972); West Virginia Secretary of State, "Vote for President of the United States," *General Election Returns, 1972* (Charleston, 1972); Wisconsin Legislative Reference Bureau, comp., "General Election, Novem-ber 7, 1972, Vote for President and Vice President by County," *State of Wisconsin 1973 Blue Book* (Madison, 1973); Wyoming Secretary of State, comp., "Official Vote—General Election, November 7, 1972," *1973 Wyoming Official Directory and 1972 Election Returns* (Cheyenne: Unicover Graphics Corporation, 1973)

1976

Office of the Secretary of State, State of Alabama, Elections Division, *Alabama Presi-dential General Election, 11/2/1976* (Montgomery, 1977); Alaska, "Alaska General Election Statement of Vote—Statewide Contests—Nov. 2, 1976," *State of Alaska Official Returns by Election Precinct, General Election, November 2, 1976* (Juneau, 1977); Arizona Secretary of State, *State of Arizona Official Canvass, General Election—Novem-ber 2, 1976* (Phoenix, 1977); Arkansas Secretary of State, comp., *1976 Arkansas Elec-tions, a Compilation of Primary, Run-Off, & General Election Results for State & District Offices* (Little Rock, 1977); California Secretary of State, comp., *Statement of Vote, General Election, November 2, 1976* (Sacramento, 1976); Colorado Secretary of State, *Abstract of Votes Cast at the General Election Held on Tuesday, November 2, 1976* (Denver, 1976); State of Connecticut, comp., "Vote for President of the United States, November 2, 1976," *State of Connecticut Public Document No. 26, Statement of Vote, General Election, November 2, 1976* (Hartford, 1977); State of Delaware Department of Elections, *State of Delaware Official Results of Presidential Election and Statewide Offices, November 2, 1976* (Dover, 1976); District of Columbia: Clerk of the House of Rep-resentatives, comp., *Statistics of the Presidential and Congressional Election of November 2, 1976* (Washington: U.S. Government Printing Office, 1977); Florida Department of State, Division of Elections, *November 2, 1976, President and Vice President* (Talla-hassee, 1976); Georgia Secretary of State, *Official State of Georgia Tabulation by Counties for Presidential Electors . . . General Election, November 2, 1976* (Atlanta, 1977); Hawaii: Clerk of the House of Representatives, comp., *Statistics of the Presidential and Congressional Election of November 2, 1976* (Washington: U.S. Government Printing Office, 1977); Idaho Secretary of State, Election Division, *State of Idaho Presidential*

Vote Cast at the General Election, November 2, 1976 (Boise, 1977); Illinois State Board of Elections, "Vote for President and Vice President of the United States—November 2, 1976," *State of Illinois Official Vote Cast at the General Election November 2, 1976* (Springfield, 1976); Indiana Secretary of State, "President of the United States, Vice President of the United States," *1976 Election Report State of Indiana* (Indianapolis, 1977); Iowa Secretary of State, *State of Iowa Canvass of the Vote, General Election, November 2, 1976* (Des Moines: State of Iowa, 1977); Kansas Secretary of State, "General Election, November 2, 1976, for President and Vice President," *Election Statistics* (Topeka, 1977); Kentucky State Board of Elections, *General Election, Nov. 2, 1976*, Kentucky State Board of Elections (www.kysos.com/index/main/elecdiv.asp) (accessed October 25, 1999); Secretary of State, *Election Returns for Electors for President and Vice-President of the United States* (Baton Rouge, 1977); Maine Department of the Secretary of State, Bureau of Corporations, Elections, and Commissions, *State of Maine, 1976 Enrolled and Registered Voters with Comparative Presidential, U.S. Senatorial, and Congressional Votes* (Augusta, 1977); Maryland State Board of Elections, "For President of the United States," *Maryland General Election Returns—November 2, 1976* (Annapolis, 1976); Massachusetts Secretary of State, "Votes for Electors of President and Vice President," *Public Document #43, Massachusetts Election Statistics 1976* (Boston, 1977); Michigan Department of Management and Budget, "Official Canvass of Votes, General Election President and Vice President of the United States," *Michigan Manual 1977–1978* (Lansing, 1977); Minnesota Secretary of State, "Vote for United States President, United States Senator, and Supreme Court by County," *The Minnesota Legislative Manual 1977–1978* (St. Paul, 1977); Mississippi Secretary of State, "General Election, November 2, 1976," *Mississippi Official and Statistical Register 1976–1980* (Jackson, 1977); Missouri Secretary of State, "General Election Returns, Vote for President, by Counties, at General Election, November 2, 1976," *Official Manual State of Missouri 1977–1978* (Jefferson City, 1977); Montana Secretary of State, *Report of the Official Canvass of the Vote Cast at the General Election Held in the State of Montana, November 2, 1976* (Helena, 1977); Nebraska Secretary of State, comp., *Official Report of the Board of State Canvassers of the State of Nebraska, Bicentennial General Election Held November 2, 1976* (Lincoln, 1976); Nevada Secretary of State, *Official Returns of General Election Held November 2, 1976* (Carson City, 1976); New Hampshire Department of State, "General Election November 2, 1976, for Electors of President and Vice President," *State of New Hampshire Manual for the General Court 1977, No. 45* (Concord, 1977); New Jersey Secretary of State, "Votes Cast for President and Vice-President of the United States," *State of New Jersey, Result of the General Election Held November 2, 1976* (Trenton, 1976); New Mexico State Canvassing Board, *Canvass of Returns of General Election Held on November 2, 1976—State of New Mexico* (Santa Fe, 1976); New York State Department of State, "Presidential Vote, New York State by Counties, November 2, 1976," *Manual for the Use of the Legislature of the State of New York 1977–79* (Albany, 1977); North Carolina Secretary of State, "County Tabulations for President November 2, 1976," *North Carolina Manual 1977* (Raleigh, 1977); North Dakota Secretary of State, *Official Abstract of Votes Cast at the General Election Held November 2, 1976* (Bismarck, 1976); Ohio Secretary of State, *Ohio Election Statistics Election and Registration Statistics, General Election, 1976* (Cleveland, 1977); Oklahoma State Election Board, *Official Returns, General Election, November 2, 1976, Presidential Electors* (Oklahoma City, 1976); Oregon Secretary of State, Elections Division, "President," *Official Abstract of Votes General Election 1976* (Salem, 1976); Pennsylvania Department of Property and Supplies, "President of the United States General Election, November 2, 1976," *The Pennsylvania Manual 1977* (Harrisburg, 1977); Rhode Island Board of Elections, "Vote by Counties for Presidential Electors," *Official Count of the Ballots Cast . . . at the Election Tuesday, November 2, 1976* (Providence, 1976); South Carolina State Election Commission, "South Carolina Votes Cast in General Election Held in South Carolina, November 2, 1976," *Report of the South Carolina State Election Commission for the Period Ending June 30, 1977* (Columbia, 1977); South Dakota Secretary of State, comp., "Presidential Electors," *Official Election Returns by Counties for the State of South Dakota, General Election, November 2, 1976* (Pierre, 1976); Tennessee Secretary of State, "President of the United States—Tennessee," *Certification of Election Returns for the General Election November 2, 1976* (Nashville, 1976); Texas Secretary of State, Elections Division. *Presidential Election Results* (www.sos.state.tx.us/elections/index.shtml) (accessed February 1, 2002); Utah State Elections Office, *1976 General Election Abstract* (Salt Lake City, 1976); Vermont Secretary of State, *Canvass of Votes for Presidential Electors General Election—November 2, 1976* (Rutland, 1977); Virginia State Board of Elections, comp., *Commonwealth of Virginia Official Election Results 1976 for President and Vice President . . . General Election, November 2, 1976 . . .* (Richmond, 1977); Washington Secretary of State, "President & Vice President," *Abstract of Votes Primary and General Elections Held on September 21, 1976, and November 2, 1976* (Olympia, 1976); West Virginia Secretary of State, "President and Vice President," *General Election Returns, 1976* (Charleston, 1976); Wisconsin Legislative Reference Bureau, comp., "General Election, November 2, 1976, Vote for President and Vice President by County," *State of Wisconsin 1977 Blue Book* (Madison, 1977); Wyoming Secretary

of State, comp., "Official Vote—General Election, November 2, 1976," *1977 Wyoming Official Directory and 1976 Election Returns* (Cheyenne, 1977)

1980

Office of the Secretary of State of Alabama, Elections Division, *1980 General Election, President and Vice President of the United States* (Montgomery, 1981); "State of Alaska—General Election November 4, 1980—State Wide Contests," *Official Returns by Election Precinct, General Election, November 4, 1980* (Juneau, 1981); Arizona Secretary of State, comp., *Official Canvass—General Election—November 4, 1980* (Phoenix, 1980); Arkansas Secretary of State, comp., *1980 Arkansas Elections, a Compilation of Primary, Run-Off, & General Election Results for State & District Offices* (Little Rock, 1981); California Secretary of State, comp., "President," *Statement of Vote, General Election, November 4, 1980* (Sacramento, 1980); Colorado Secretary of State, *Abstract of Votes Cast at the General Election Held on Tuesday, November 4, 1980* (Denver, 1980); State of Connecticut, comp., "Vote for President of the United States, November 4, 1980," *State of Connecticut Public Document No. 26, Statement of Vote, General Election, November 4, 1980* (Hartford, 1981); State of Delaware Department of Elections, *State of Delaware Official Results of Presidential Election and Statewide Offices, November 4, 1980* (Dover, 1980); District of Columbia: Clerk of the House of Representatives, *Statistics of the Presidential and Congressional Election of November 4, 1980* (Washington, DC: Government Printing Office, 1981); Florida Department of State, Division of Elections, *November 4, 1980, General Election Official Results, President of the United States* (http://election.dos.state.fl.us/online/index.shtml) (accessed March 31, 1999); Georgia Secretary of State, *Official State of Georgia Tabulation by Counties for Presidential Electors . . . General Election, November 4, 1980* (Atlanta, 1981); Hawaii: Clerk of the House of Representatives, *Statistics of the Presidential and Congressional Election of November 4, 1980* (Washington, DC: Government Printing Office, 1981); Idaho Secretary of State, "State of Idaho Abstract of Votes Cast at the General Election, November 4, 1980," *Idaho Blue Book 1981–1982* (Boise, 1981); Illinois State Board of Elections, "Vote for President and Vice President of the United States, November 4, 1980," *State of Illinois Official Vote Cast at the General Election, November 4, 1980* (Springfield, 1980); Indiana Secretary of State, "President of the United States, Vice President of the United States," *1980 Election Report, State of Indiana* (Indianapolis, 1981); Iowa Secretary of State, *State of Iowa Canvass of the Vote, General Election, November 4, 1980* (Des Moines: State of Iowa, 1981); Kansas Secretary of State, "Abstract of Votes Cast at the General Election, November 4, 1980," *Election Statistics* (Topeka, 1981); Kentucky State Board of Elections, *General Election, Nov. 4, 1980, U.S. President* (www.kysos.com/index/main/elecdiv.asp) (accessed October 25, 1999); Louisiana Secretary of State, *Election Proclamation, State of Louisiana Office of the Secretary of State, Electors for President and Vice-President of the United States* (Baton Rouge, 1980); Maine Department of the Secretary of State, Bureau of Corporations, Elections, and Commissions, *State of Maine, 1980 Enrolled and Registered Voters with Comparative Presidential and Congressional Votes* (Augusta, 1981); Maryland State Board of Elections, "For President of the United States," *Maryland General Election Returns—November 4, 1980* (Annapolis, 1980); Massachusetts Secretary of State, "Electors of President and Vice President," *Public Document #43, Massachusetts Election Statistics 1980* (Boston, 1981); Michigan Department of Management and Budget, "Official Canvass of Votes, State of Michigan General Election, November 4, 1980, President and Vice President," *Michigan Manual 1981–1982* (Lansing, 1981); Minnesota Secretary of State, "Vote for United States President by County, November 4, 1980, General Election," *The Minnesota Legislative Manual 1981–1982* (St. Paul, 1981); Mississippi Secretary of State, "General Election, November 4, 1980," *Mississippi Official and Statistical Register 1980–1984* (Jackson, 1981); Missouri Secretary of State, "General Election Returns, Vote for President, by Counties, at General Election, November 4, 1980," *Official Manual State of Missouri 1981–1982* (Jefferson City, 1981); Montana Secretary of State, comp., *Report of the Official Canvass by County of Votes Cast at the General Election Held in the State of Montana, November 4, 1980* (Helena, 1981); Nebraska Secretary of State, comp., *Official Report of the Board of State Canvassers of the State of Nebraska Bicentennial General Election Held November 4, 1980* (Lincoln, 1980); Nevada Secretary of State, comp., *1980 General Election Returns* (Carson City, 1980); New Hampshire Department of State, "General Election, 1980, for Electors of President and Vice-President," *State of New Hampshire Manual for the General Court 1981, No. 47* (Concord, 1981); New Jersey Secretary of State, "Votes Cast for President and Vice-President of the United States," *State of New Jersey, Results of the General Election Held November 4, 1980* (Trenton, 1980); New Mexico State Canvassing Board, *Canvass of Returns of General Election Held on November 4, 1980—State of New Mexico* (Santa Fe, 1980); New York State Department of State, "Presidential Vote, New York State by Counties, November 4, 1980," *Manual for the Use of the Legislature of the State of New York 1982–83* (Albany, 1982); North Carolina State Board of Elections, comp., *Certification of Votes Cast for President of the United States in the General Election Conducted on November 4, 1980* (Raleigh, 1981);

North Dakota Secretary of State, *Official Abstract of Votes Cast at the General Election Held November 4, 1980* (Bismarck, 1980); Ohio Secretary of State, *Ohio Election Statistics, Election and Registration Statistics, General Election, 1980* (Cleveland, 1981); Oklahoma State Election Board, *Official Returns, General Election, November 4, 1980, Presidential Electors* (Oklahoma City, 1980); Oregon Secretary of State, Elections Division, "President," *Official Abstract of Votes, General Election, November 4, 1980* (Salem, 1980); Pennsylvania Department of State, Bureau of Commissions, Elections, and Legislation, *President & Vice President of the United States General Election, November 4, 1980* (Harrisburg, 1980); Rhode Island Board of Elections, "Vote by Counties for Presidential Electors," *Official Count of the Ballots Cast . . . at the Election Tuesday, November 4, 1980* (Providence, 1980); South Carolina State Election Commission, "South Carolina Votes Cast in General Election Held in South Carolina, November 4, 1980," *Report of the South Carolina State Election Commission for the Period Ending June 30, 1981* (Columbia, 1981); South Dakota Secretary of State, "Presidential Electors," *Official Election Returns and Registration Figures for South Dakota General Election, November 4, 1980* (Pierre, 1980); Tennessee Secretary of State, "President of the United States—Tennessee," *Certification of Election Returns for the General Election, November 4, 1980* (Nashville, 1980); Texas Secretary of State, Elections Division, "President/Vice-President," *November 4, 1980, General Election Returns* (Austin, 1981); Utah State Elections Office, *1980 General Election Abstract* (Salt Lake City, 1980); Vermont Office of the Secretary of State, *Vermont General Election, November 4, 1980* (Rutland, 1981); Virginia State Board of Elections, comp., *Commonwealth of Virginia Official Election Results, 1980 General Election, November 4, 1980, President and Vice President . . .* (Richmond, 1981); Washington Secretary of State, "President and Vice President of the United States," *1980 General Election Returns for Legislative Races* (Olympia, 1980); West Virginia Secretary of State, comp., "President and Vice-President of the United States," *State of West Virginia General Election Returns, 1980* (Charleston, 1980); Wisconsin Legislative Reference Bureau, comp., "General Election, November 4, 1980, Vote for President and Vice President by County," *State of Wisconsin 1981–1982 Blue Book* (Madison, 1981); Wyoming Secretary of State, comp., "Official Vote—General Election, November 4, 1980," *Wyoming 1981 Official Directory and 1980 Election Returns* (Cheyenne, 1981)

1984

Office of the Secretary of State of Alabama, Elections Division, *1984 General Election, President and Vice President of the United States* (Montgomery, 1985); Alaska, "State of Alaska—General Election November 6, 1984—Nationwide and State Contests," *State of Alaska Official Returns by Election Precinct, General Election, November 6, 1984* (Juneau, 1985); Arizona Secretary of State, comp., *State of Arizona Official Canvass—General Election—November 6, 1984* (Phoenix, 1984); Arkansas Secretary of State, comp., "General Election Results—November 1984 U.S. Presidential Race," *Arkansas Election Results 1984* (Little Rock, 1985); California Secretary of State, comp., "President," *Statement of Vote, General Election, November 6, 1984* (Sacramento, 1984); Colorado Secretary of State, *Abstract of Votes Cast at the General Election Held on Tuesday, November 6, 1984* (Denver, 1984); State of Connecticut Secretary of State, comp., "Vote for President of the United States, November 6, 1984," *State of Connecticut Secretary of State, Statement of Vote, General Election, November 6, 1984* (Hartford, 1984); State of Delaware Department of Elections, *State of Delaware Official Results of General Election for Statewide Offices, November 6, 1984* (Dover, 1984); District of Columbia: Clerk of the House of Representatives, *Statistics of the Presidential and Congressional Election of November 6, 1984* (Washington: Government Printing Office, 1985); Florida Department of State, Division of Elections, *November 6, 1984, General Election Official Results, President of the United States* (http://election.dos.state.fl.us/online/index.shtml) (accessed March 31, 1999); Georgia Secretary of State, *Official State of Georgia Tabulation by Counties for Presidential Electors . . . General Election November 6, 1984* (Atlanta, 1985); Hawaii: Clerk of the House of Representatives, *Statistics of the Presidential and Congressional Election of November 6, 1984* (Washington, DC: Government Printing Office: 1985); Idaho Secretary of State, "State of Idaho Abstract of Votes Cast at the General Election, November 6, 1984," *Idaho Blue Book 1983–1986* (Boise, 1985); Illinois State Board of Elections, "Vote for President and Vice President of the United States, November 6, 1984," *State of Illinois Official Vote Cast at the General Election November 6, 1984* (Springfield, 1984); Indiana Secretary of State, "General Election President/Vice President," *1984 Election Report State of Indiana* (Indianapolis, 1985); Iowa Secretary of State, comp., *Summary of Official Canvass of Votes Cast in Iowa General Election, November 6, 1984* (Des Moines, 1985); Kansas Secretary of State, "President and Vice-President," *Election Statistics* (Topeka, 1985); Kentucky State Board of Elections, *General Election, Nov. 6, 1984, President and Vice President of the U.S.* (www.kysos.com/index/main/elecdiv.asp) (accessed April 11, 1999); Louisiana Secretary of State, *Election Proclamation, State of Louisiana Office of the Secretary of State, Electors for President and Vice-President of the United States* (Baton Rouge, 1984); Maine Department of the Secretary of State, Bureau of Corporations,

Elections, and Commissions, *State of Maine, 1984 Enrolled and Registered Voters with Comparative Presidential, U.S. Senatorial, and Congressional Votes* (Augusta, 1985); Maryland State Board of Elections, "For President of the United States," *Maryland General Election Returns—November 6, 1984* (Annapolis, 1984); Massachusetts Secretary of State, "Electors of President and Vice President," *Public Document #43, Massachusetts Election Statistics 1984* (Boston, 1985); Michigan Department of State, "President and Vice President," *Official Canvass of Votes General Election, November 6, 1984* (Lansing, 1984); Minnesota Office of the Secretary of State, "Voter Participation and Vote for President and Vice President . . . November 6, 1984 General Election," *The Minnesota Legislative Manual 1985–1986* (St. Paul, 1985); Mississippi Secretary of State, "General Election, November 6, 1984," *Mississippi Official and Statistical Register 1984–1988* (Jackson, 1985); Missouri Secretary of State, "General Election Returns, Vote for President, by Counties, at General Election November 6, 1984," *Official Manual State of Missouri 1985–1986* (Jefferson City, 1985); Montana Secretary of State, comp., *Report of the Official Canvass by County of Votes Cast at the General Election Held in the State of Montana, November 6, 1984* (Helena, 1985); Nebraska Secretary of State, comp., *Official Report of the Board of State Canvassers of the State of Nebraska Bicentennial General Election Held November 6, 1984* (Lincoln, 1984); Nevada Secretary of State, comp., *1984 General Election Returns* (Carson City, 1984); New Hampshire Department of State, "General Election, 1984, Electors of President and Vice President," *State of New Hampshire Manual for the General Court 1985, No. 49* (Concord, 1985); New Jersey Department of State, Election Division, "Votes Cast for President and Vice-President of the United States," *State of New Jersey Results of the General Election Held November 6, 1984* (Trenton, 1984); New Mexico State Canvassing Board, *Canvass of Returns of General Election Held on November 6, 1984—State of New Mexico* (Santa Fe, 1984); "Presidential Vote, New York State by Counties, November 6, 1984," *The New York Red Book 1985–1986* (Albany, 1985); North Carolina State Board of Elections, comp., *Certification of Votes Cast for President of the United States in the General Election Conducted on November 6, 1984* (Raleigh, 1985); North Dakota Secretary of State, *Official Abstract of Votes Cast at the General Election Held November 6, 1984* (Bismarck, 1984); Ohio Secretary of State, *Ohio Election Statistics, Election and Registration Statistics, General Election, 1984* (Cleveland, 1985); Oklahoma State Election Board, *Official Returns, General Election, November 6, 1984, Presidential Electors* (Oklahoma City, 1984); Oregon Secretary of State, Elections Division, "President," *Official Abstract of Votes, General Election, November 6, 1984* (Salem, 1984); Pennsylvania Department of General Services, "President of the United States General Election, November 6, 1984," *The Pennsylvania Manual Volume 107/1984–1985* (Harrisburg, 1985); Rhode Island Board of Elections, "Vote by Counties for Presidential Electors," *Official Count of the Ballots Cast . . . at the Election Tuesday, November 6, 1984* (Providence, 1984); South Carolina State Election Commission, "South Carolina Votes Cast in General Election Held in South Carolina, November 6, 1984," *Report of the South Carolina Election Commission for the Period Ending June 30, 1985* (Columbia, 1985); South Dakota Secretary of State, "Presidential," *Official Election Returns and Registration Figures for South Dakota General Election, November 6, 1984* (Pierre, 1984); Tennessee Secretary of State, "President of the United States—Tennessee," *Certification of Election Returns for the General Election, November 6, 1984* (Nashville, 1984); Texas Secretary of State, Elections Division, "President and Vice-President," *1984 General Election, Official Election Tabulation* (Austin, 1984); Utah State Elections Office, *1984 General Election Abstract* (Salt Lake City, 1984); Vermont Office of the Secretary of State, "1984 General Election Results, US President," *Primary and General Elections Vermont 1984* (Montpelier: Capital City Press, 1986); Virginia State Board of Elections, comp., *Commonwealth of Virginia Official Election Results, 1984, General & Special Elections, November 6, 1984, President and Vice President . . .* (Richmond, 1985); Washington Secretary of State, "President/Vice President of the United States," *Official Abstract of the Results of the November 6, 1984, Washington State General Election* (Olympia, 1984); West Virginia Secretary of State, "President and Vice-President of the United States," *State of West Virginia Office of the Secretary of State, General Election, November 6, 1984* (Charleston, 1984); Wisconsin Legislative Reference Bureau, comp., "General Election, November 6, 1984, Vote for President and Vice President, by County," *State of Wisconsin 1985–1986 Blue Book* (Madison, 1985); Wyoming Secretary of State, comp., "Official Vote—General Election, November 6, 1984," *Wyoming 1985 Official Directory and 1984 Election Returns* (Cheyenne, 1985)

1988

Office of the Secretary of State, State of Alabama, Elections Division, *Presidential Election, November 8, 1988* (Montgomery, 1989); State of Alaska Division of Elections, "1988 General Election Statement of Vote," *State of Alaska Official Returns, November 8, 1988, General Election* (Juneau, 1989); Arizona Secretary of State, *State of Arizona Official Canvass—General Election—November 8, 1988* (Phoenix, 1988); Arkansas Secretary of State, comp., "Arkansas Presidential Election Results, 1988

General Election," *Arkansas Election Results 1988* (Little Rock, 1989); California Secretary of State, comp., "President and Vice President," *Statement of Vote, November 8, 1988* (Sacramento, 1988); Colorado Secretary of State, *Abstract of Votes Cast at the General Election Held on November 8, 1988* (Denver, 1988); State of Connecticut Secretary of State, comp., "Vote for President of the United States, November 8, 1988," *State of Connecticut Secretary of State Statement of Vote, General Election, November 8, 1988* (Hartford, 1988); State of Delaware Department of Elections, *State of Delaware Official Results of General Election for Statewide Offices, November 8, 1988* (Dover, 1988); District of Columbia.: Clerk of the House of Representatives, *Statistics of the Presidential and Congressional Election of November 8, 1988* (Washington: Government Printing Office, 1989); Florida Department of State, Division of Elections, *November 8, 1988, General Election, President and Vice President* (Tallahassee, 1988); Georgia Secretary of State, *Official State of Georgia Tabulation by Counties for Presidential Electors . . . General Election, November 8, 1988* (Atlanta, 1989); Hawaii: Clerk of the House of Representatives, *Statistics of the Presidential and Congressional Election of November 8, 1988* (Washington, DC: Government Printing Office, 1989); Idaho Secretary of State, "Abstract of Votes Cast at the General Election, November 8, 1988," *Idaho Blue Book 1989–1990* (Boise, 1989); Illinois State Board of Elections, comp., "President and Vice President of the United States," *State of Illinois Official Vote Cast at the General Election of November 8, 1988* (Springfield, 1989); Indiana Secretary of State, "1988 Presidential Results," *1988 Election Report State of Indiana* (Indianapolis, 1989); Iowa Secretary of State, comp., "President and Vice President of the United States," *General Election, November 8, 1988, Official Canvass Summary* (Des Moines, 1989); Kansas Secretary of State, "U.S. President/Vice President," *1988 General Election Statistics* (Topeka, 1989); Kentucky State Board of Elections, *General Election, Nov. 8, 1988, United States President/Vice-President* (www.kysos.com/index/main/elecdiv.asp) (accessed April 11, 1999); Louisiana Secretary of State, *Election Proclamation, State of Louisiana Office of the Secretary of State, Electors for President and Vice-President of the United States* (Baton Rouge, 1988); Maine Department of the Secretary of State, Bureau of Corporations, Elections, and Commissions, *State of Maine General Election, November 8, 1988, Official Vote for United States President and Vice President* (Augusta, 1989); Maryland State Board of Elections, "For President of the United States," *Maryland General Election Returns—November 8, 1988* (Annapolis, 1988); Massachusetts Secretary of State, "Electors of President and Vice President," *Public Document #43, Massachusetts Election Statistics 1988* (Boston, 1989); Michigan Department of Management and Budget, "Official Canvass of Votes, General Election, November 8, 1988, President/Vice President," *Michigan Manual 1989–1990* (Lansing, 1990); Minnesota Office of the Secretary of State. Elections Division, "Voter Participation, Vote for President and Vice President, and United States Senator, November 8, 1988, General Election," *The Minnesota Legislative Manual 1989–1990* (St. Paul, 1989); Mississippi Secretary of State, "General Election, November 8, 1988," *Mississippi Official and Statistical Register 1988–1992* (Jackson, 1989); Missouri Secretary of State, "President/General Election: November 8, 1988," *Official Manual, State of Missouri, 1989–1990* (Jefferson City, 1989); Montana Secretary of State, *Report of the Official Canvass by County of Votes Cast at the General Election Held in the State of Montana, November 8, 1988* (Helena, 1989); Nebraska Secretary of State, comp., *Official Report of the Board of State Canvassers of the State of Nebraska Bicentennial General Election Held November 8, 1988* (Lincoln, 1988); Nevada Secretary of State, comp., *1988 General Election Returns* (Carson City, 1988); New Hampshire Department of State, "General Election—1988 President and Vice-President of the United States," *State of New Hampshire Manual for the General Court 1989, No. 51* (Concord, 1989); New Jersey Department of State, Election Division, "Votes Cast for President and Vice-President of the United States," *State of New Jersey Results of the General Election Held November 8, 1988* (Trenton, 1988); New Mexico State Canvassing Board, *Canvass of Returns of General Election Held on November 8, 1988—State of New Mexico* (Santa Fe, 1988); New York State Board of Elections, *State of New York—State Board of Elections Votes Cast November 8, 1988, for Electors Pledged to Support* (Albany, 1988); North Carolina State Board of Elections, *Abstract of Votes Cast for President at General Election Held on November 8, 1988* (Raleigh, 1989); North Dakota Secretary of State, *North Dakota Official Abstract of Votes Cast at the General Election Held November 8, 1988* (Bismarck, 1988); Ohio Secretary of State, *Ohio Election Statistics Election and Registration Statistics, General Election, 1988* (Cleveland, 1989); Oklahoma State Election Board, *Official Returns, General Election, November 8, 1988, Presidential Electors* (Oklahoma City, 1988); Oregon Secretary of State, Elections Division, "United States President," *Official Abstract of Votes, General Election, November 8, 1988* (Salem, 1988); Pennsylvania Department of State, Bureau of Commissions, Elections and Legislation, *Report A-424, President of the United States General Election, November 08, 1988* (Harrisburg, 1989); Rhode Island Board of Elections, "Vote by Counties for Presidential Electors," *Official Count of the Ballots Cast . . . at the Election Tuesday, November 8, 1988* (Providence, 1988); South Carolina State Election Commission, *South Carolina Votes Cast in General Election Held in South Carolina, November 8, 1988, Pres. and Vice Pres.* (Columbia, 1988); South Dakota Secretary of State, *1988 General Election, Statewide Officers* (www.state.sd.us/sos/sos.htm) (accessed March 30, 1999); Tennessee Secretary of State, *State of Tennessee Presidential Election, November 8, 1988* (Nashville, 1988); Texas Secretary of State, Elections Division, *General Election Returns by Race/County with Turnout Percentages, President/Vice President* (Austin, 1988); Utah State Elections Office, *1988 General Election Abstract* (Salt Lake City, 1988); Vermont Office of the Secretary of State, "State Totals, United States President, 1988 General Election," *Primary and General Elections, Vermont 1988* (Rutland: Sharp Offset Printing, 1989); Virginia State Board of Elections, comp., *Commonwealth of Virginia Official Election Results, 1988 General & Special Elections, November 8, 1988, President and Vice President . . .* (Richmond, 1989); Washington Secretary of State, "United States President/Vice President," *Official Returns of the State General Election Held on November 8, 1988, State of Washington* (Olympia, 1988); West Virginia Secretary of State, "President of the United States," *General Election Returns, 1988* (Charleston, 1989); Wisconsin Legislative Reference Bureau, comp., "General Election, November 8, 1988, Vote for President and Vice President, by County," *State of Wisconsin 1989–1990 Blue Book* (Madison, 1989); Wyoming Secretary of State, comp., "Official Vote—General Election, November 8, 1988," *1989 Wyoming Official Directory and 1988 Election Returns* (Cheyenne, 1989)

1992

Office of the Secretary of State of Alabama, Elections Division, *General Election Results November 3, 1992, for President of the United States* (Montgomery, 1993); State of Alaska Division of Elections, "1992 General Election Statement of Vote," *State of Alaska Official Returns, November 3, 1992, General Election* (Juneau, 1992); Arizona Secretary of State, comp., "Presidential Electors," *State of Arizona Official Canvass, General Election—November 3, 1992* (Phoenix, 1992); Arkansas Secretary of State, *1992 Arkansas General Election—U.S. President* (http://sos.state.ar.us/elect.html) (accessed March 7, 1999); California Secretary of State, "President and Vice President," *California Statement of Vote, General Election, November 3, 1992* (Sacramento, 1992); Colorado Secretary of State, *Abstract of Votes Cast at the General Election Held on November 3, 1992* (Denver, 1993); State of Connecticut Secretary of State, comp., "Vote for President of the United States, November 3, 1992," *State of Connecticut Secretary of State, Statement of Vote, General Election, November 3, 1992* (Hartford, 1992); State of Delaware Department of Elections, *State of Delaware Official Results of General Election for Statewide Offices, November 3, 1992* (Dover, 1993); District of Columbia Board of Elections and Ethics, comp., *Statistics of the Presidential and Congressional Election of November 3, 1992* (Washington, DC: U.S. Government Printing Office, 1993); Florida Department of State, *November 3, 1992, General Election Official Results, President of the United States* (http://election.dos.state.fl.us/online/index.shtml) (accessed April 17, 1999); Georgia Secretary of State, *Official State of Georgia Tabulation by Counties for Presidential Electors . . . General Election, November 3, 1992* (Atlanta, 1992); State of Hawaii Office of Elections, *1992 General Election Results, President/Vice President, County and Statewide Totals* (Honolulu, 1993); Idaho Secretary of State, "Abstract of Votes Cast at the General Election, November 3, 1992," *Idaho Blue Book 1993–1994* (Boise, 1993); Illinois State Board of Elections, comp., "President and Vice President of the United States," *State of Illinois Official Vote Cast at the General Election of November 3, 1992* (Springfield, 1993); Indiana Secretary of State, "President and Vice President of the United States," *1992 Election Report State of Indiana* (Indianapolis, 1993); Iowa Secretary of State, comp., "President," *General Election, November 3, 1992, Official Canvass Summary* (Des Moines, 1993); Kansas Secretary of State, "U.S. President," *1992 General Election Statistics* (Topeka, 1993); Kentucky State Board of Elections, "November 3, 1992, Presidential Election Official Results," *Official Primary and General Election Returns for 1992* (Frankfurt, 1993); Louisiana Secretary of State, *Election Proclamation, State of Louisiana Office of the Secretary of State, November 3, 1992* (Baton Rouge, 1992); Maine Department of the Secretary of State, Bureau of Corporations, Elections, and Commissions, *State of Maine General Election Tabulation for the Election of November 3, 1992, Official Vote for United States President* (Augusta, 1993); Maryland State Board of Elections, "For President and Vice President," *Maryland General Election Returns—November 3, 1992* (Annapolis, 1993); Massachusetts Secretary of State, "Electors of President and Vice President," *Public Document #43, Massachusetts Election Statistics 1992* (Boston, 1993); Michigan Legislative Service Bureau, comp., "Official Canvass of Votes, General Election November 3, 1992 President/Vice President," *Michigan Manual 1993–1994* (Lansing, 1993); Minnesota Office of the Secretary of State, Elections Division, "Vote for President and Vice President of the United States by County, November 3, 1992, General Election," *The Minnesota Legislative Manual 1993–1994* (St. Paul, 1993); Mississippi Secretary of State, "General Election, November 3, 1992, President/Vice President," *Mississippi Official and Statistical Register 1992–1996* (Jackson, 1993); Missouri Office of the Secretary of State, "President and Vice President General Election, November 3, 1992," *Official Manual, State of Missouri 1993–1994* (Jefferson City, 1993); Montana Secretary of State, comp., *Official 1992 General Election Canvass* (Helena, 1993); Nebraska Secretary of State, comp., *Official Report of the Board of State Canvassers of the*

State of Nebraska, General Election Held November 3, 1992 (Lincoln, 1992); Nevada Secretary of State, comp., *1992 General Election Returns, November 3, 1992* (Carson City, 1992); New Hampshire Department of State, "President and Vice President of the United States," *State of New Hampshire Manual for the General Court 1993, No. 53* (Concord, 1993); New Jersey Department of Law and Public Safety, Division of Elections, *Official New Jersey Presidential Election Returns by County* (Trenton, 1992); New Mexico State Canvassing Board, *Canvass of Returns, General Election Held on November 3, 1992, State of New Mexico* (Santa Fe, 1992); New York State Board of Elections, *NYS Board of Elections Presidential Election Returns, November 3, 1992* (Albany, 1993); North Carolina State Board of Elections, *Abstract of Votes Cast for President at General Election Held on November 3, 1992* (Raleigh, 1993); North Dakota Secretary of State, *North Dakota Official Abstract of Votes Cast at the General Election Held November 3, 1992* (Bismarck, 1992); Ohio Secretary of State, Election Services, *Report of Votes for U.S. President General Election, November 3, 1992* (Cleveland, 1993); Oklahoma State Election Board, "Official Returns, General Election, November 3, 1992, Presidential Electors," *State of Oklahoma Election Results and Statistics 1992* (Oklahoma City, 1992); Oregon Secretary of State, Elections Division, "U.S. President," *Official Abstract of Votes, General Election, November 3, 1992* (Salem, 1992); Pennsylvania Department of State, Bureau of Commissions, Elections, and Legislation, *Report ELC506, Official Election Results, General Election of November 3, 1992, President of the United States* (Harrisburg, 1992); Rhode Island Board of Elections, "Vote by Counties for Presidential Electors," *Official Count of the Ballots Cast . . . at the Election Tuesday, November 3, 1992* (Providence, 1992); South Carolina State Election Commission, *Official Results, State of South Carolina, November 3, 1992, General Election, President/Vice President* (Columbia, 1993); South Dakota Secretary of State, "General Election Presidential Electors, November 3, 1992," *Legislative Manual, South Dakota 1993* (Pierre, 1993); Tennessee Secretary of State, *State of Tennessee Electors for President of the United States, November 3, 1992, General Election* (Nashville, 1992); Texas Secretary of State, *1992 General Election, President and Vice President* (www.sos.state.tx.us/elections/index.shtml) (accessed March 7, 1999); Utah State Elections Office, *1992 Presidential Election* (Salt Lake City, 1993); Vermont Office of the Secretary of State, "1992 General Election Results, U.S. President," *Primary and General Elections, Vermont 1992* (Montpelier, 1992); Virginia State Board of Elections, comp., "General Elections, President and Vice President and Members of Congress," *Commonwealth of Virginia Official Election Results, 1992 General Elections, November 3, 1992* (Richmond, 1993); Washington Secretary of State, "President/Vice President," *Official Returns of the State General Election, November 3, 1992* (Olympia, 1992); West Virginia Secretary of State, "President," *General Election Returns, 1992* (Charleston, 1992); Wisconsin State Election Board, *State Canvass for the Office of President, Election Held on November 3rd, 1992* (Madison, 1993); Wyoming Secretary of State, comp., "Official Vote—General Election, November 3, 1992," *1993 Wyoming Official Directory and 1992 Election Returns* (Cheyenne, 1993)

1996

Office of the Secretary of State of Alabama, *Historic Election Results* (www.sos.state.al.us/election/index.cfm) (accessed February 28, 1999); State of Alaska, Division of Elections, *1996 General Election Statement of Vote* (www.gov.state.ak.us/ltgov/elections/homepage.html) (accessed April 11, 1999); Arizona Secretary of State, comp., "Presidential Electors," *State of Arizona Official Canvass—General Election—November 5, 1996* (Phoenix, 1996); Arkansas Secretary of State, *Summary of Election Results, November 5, 1996* (http://sos.state.ar.us/elect.html) (accessed Feb 28, 1999); California Secretary of State, "President and Vice President," *California Statement of Vote, General Election, November 5, 1996* (Sacramento, 1996); Colorado Secretary of State, *1996 General Election Results* (www.sos.state.co.us/pubs/elections/main.htm) (accessed February 28, 1999); State of Connecticut Secretary of State, comp., "Presidential Electors Summarized by County," *State of Connecticut Secretary of State, Statement of Vote, General Election, November 5, 1996* (Hartford, 1996); State of Delaware Department of Elections, *State of Delaware Official Results of General Election for Statewide Offices, November 5, 1996* (Dover, 1997); District of Columbia Board of Elections and Ethics, *Final and Complete Election Results for the November 5, 1996, General Election* (www.dcboee.org/) (accessed February 28, 1999); Florida Department of State, Division of Elections, *November 5, 1996, General Election, Official Results, President of the United States* (http://election.dos.state.fl.us/online/index.shtml) (accessed April 17, 1999); Georgia Secretary of State, *Official Results of the November 5, 1996, General Election, President of the United States* (www.sos.state.ga.us/elections/) (accessed March 2, 1999); State of Hawaii Office of Elections, *General Election—State of Hawaii, November 5, 1996, President/Vice President* (Honolulu, 1997); Idaho Secretary of State, *1996 Idaho General Election—November 5, 1996, Presidential Vote by County* (www.idsos.state.id.us/elect/eleindex.htm) (accessed March 2, 1999); Illinois State Board of Elections, comp., "President and Vice President of the United States," *State of Illinois Official Vote Cast at*

the General Election, November 5, 1996 (Springfield, 1997); Indiana Secretary of State, "President and Vice President of the United States," *1996 Election Report, State of Indiana* (Indianapolis, 1997); Iowa Secretary of State, *Iowa General Election—November 5, 1996, Canvass by Counties of the Votes Cast for President and Vice President* (www.sos.state.ia.us/) (accessed March 2, 1999); Kansas Secretary of State, Division of Elections and Legislative Matters, *President/Vice President* (www.kssos.org/election/elewelc.html) (accessed March 3, 1999); Kentucky State Board of Elections, *General Election, Nov. 5, 1996* (www.kysos.com/index/main/elecdiv.asp) (accessed March 3, 1999); Louisiana Secretary of State, *Election Proclamation, State of Louisiana, Office of the Secretary of State, November 5, 1996* (Baton Rouge, 1996); Maine Department of the Secretary of State, Bureau of Corporations, Elections, and Commissions, *State of Maine General Election Tabulation for the Election of November 5, 1996, Official Vote for President* (Augusta, 1996); Maryland State Board of Elections, *1996 Presidential General Election Results, President and Vice President of the United States* (www.elections.state.md.us/) (accessed March 3, 1999); Massachusetts Secretary of the Commonwealth, Elections Division, "Electors of President and Vice President," *Public Document #43, Massachusetts Election Statistics 1996* (Boston, 1997); Michigan Legislative Service Bureau, comp., "General Election, November 5, 1996, President/Vice President," *Michigan Manual 1997–1998* (Lansing, 1997); Minnesota Office of the Secretary of State, Elections Division, "Vote for President and Vice President, November 5, 1996, State General Election," *The Minnesota Legislative Manual 1997–1998* (St. Paul, 1997); Mississippi Secretary of State, "General Election, November 5, 1996, President," *Mississippi Official and Statistical Register 1996–2000* (Jackson, 1997); Missouri Office of the Secretary of State, "President and Vice President General Election: November 5, 1996," *Official Manual State of Missouri 1997–1998* (Jefferson City, 1997); Montana Secretary of State, comp., *1996 Statewide General Canvass—November 5, 1996* (Helena, 1997); Nebraska Secretary of State, comp., "President of the United States," *Official Report of the Board of State Canvassers of the State of Nebraska, General Election, November 5, 1996* (Lincoln, 1996); Nevada Secretary of State, comp., *1996 Official State of Nevada General Election Returns, November 5, 1996* (Carson City, 1996); New Hampshire Department of State, "President and Vice President of the United States," *State of New Hampshire Manual for the General Court 1997, No. 55* (Concord, 1997); New Jersey Department of Law and Public Safety, Division of Elections, *Official Results, Presidential Election, November 5, 1996* (Trenton, 1996); New Mexico State Canvassing Board, *Canvass of Returns of General Election Held on November 5, 1996, State of New Mexico* (Santa Fe, 1996); New York State Board of Elections, *NYS Board of Elections Presidential Election Returns, November 5, 1996* (www.elections.state.ny.us/) (accessed March 5, 1999); North Carolina State Board of Elections, *United States President Abstract of Votes Cast in the General Election Held on November 5, 1996* (www.sboe.state.nc.us/) (accessed March 5, 1999); North Dakota Secretary of State, *Official Abstract of Votes Cast at the General Election Held November 5, 1996* (Bismarck, 1996); Ohio Secretary of State, Election Services, *1996 General Election, Presidential Race Results* (www.state.oh./sos/) (accessed March 5, 1999); Oklahoma State Election Board, *1996 General Election Results by County, November 5, 1996, Race for President* (www.state.ok.us/~elections/) (accessed March 5, 1999); Oregon Secretary of State. Elections Division, *Official Results, U.S. President, November 5, 1996, General Election* (www.sos.state.or.us/elections/elechp.htm) (accessed March 5, 1999); Pennsylvania Department of State, Bureau of Commissions, Elections, and Legislation, *Report ELC506, Official Election Results, General Election of November 5, 1996, President of the United States* (Harrisburg, 1996); Rhode Island Board of Elections, "Vote by County for President," *Official Count of the Ballots Cast, General Election, November 5, 1996* (Providence, 1996); South Carolina State Election Commission, *November 5, 1996, South Carolina State Wide General Election—Official Results* (Columbia, 1997); South Dakota Secretary of State, "Presidential Electors—General Election, November 5, 1996," *Legislative Manual South Dakota 1997* (Pierre, 1997); Tennessee Secretary of State, *State of Tennessee Electors for President of the United States, November 5, 1996, General Election* (Nashville, 1996); Texas Secretary of State, Elections Division, *1996 General Election, 11/5/96, President/Vice President* (www.sos.state.tx.us/elections/index.shtml) (accessed May 21, 2000); Utah State Elections Office, *Official Results State of Utah General Election, November 5, 1996* (http://elections.utah.gov/) (accessed April 8, 1999); Vermont Office of the Secretary of State, "Summary Results by County for US President, 1996 General," *Primary and General Elections, Vermont, 1996* (Montpelier, 1997); Virginia State Board of Elections, *Election Results, November 5, 1996, General Election for Office of President/Vice President of the United States* (www.sbe.state.va.us/) (accessed March 5, 1999); Washington Secretary of State, "President/Vice President," *Official Returns of the State General Election, November 5, 1996* (Olympia, 1996); West Virginia Secretary of State, "President," *General Election Returns, 1996* (Charleston, 1996); Wisconsin State Election Board, *State Canvass for the Office of President Election Held on November 5th, 1996* (Madison, 1997); Wyoming Secretary of State, *1996 General Election Official Results, Statewide Issues Abstract* (http://soswy.state.wy.us/election/election.htm) (accessed March 24, 1999)

2000

Office of the Secretary of State of Alabama, Elections Division, *Historic Election Results* (www.sos.state.al.us/election/index.cfm) (accessed December 16, 2000); State of Alaska, Division of Elections, *Statement of Votes Cast, State of Alaska General Election 2000* (www.gov.state.ak.us/ltgov/elections/homepage.html) (accessed May 1, 2002); Arizona Secretary of State, comp., "Presidential Electors," *State of Arizona Official Canvass, 2000 General Election—November 7, 2000* (Phoenix, 2000); Arkansas Secretary of State, *State of Arkansas Certification Report, 2000 General* (http://sos.state.ar.us/elect.html) (accessed December 16, 2000); California Secretary of State, "County by County Vote Results for President," *Statement of Vote, November 7, 2000, General Election* (Sacramento, 2000); Colorado Secretary of State, *November 7, 2000, Colorado General Election Results, Final Certified Official* (www.sos.state.co.us/pubs/elections/main.htm) (accessed December 17, 2000); State of Connecticut Secretary of State, comp., "Presidential Electors Summarized by County," *State of Connecticut Secretary of State, Statement of Vote, General Election, November 7, 2000* (Hartford, 2000); State of Delaware, Department of Elections, *Election System Official Election Results, Statewide Results by Election District, 11/07/00, General* (www.state.de.us/election/index.htm) (accessed January 27, 2001); District of Columbia Board of Elections and Ethics, *Final and Complete Election Results for the November 7, 2000, General Election* (www.dcboe.org/) (accessed February 2, 2001); Florida Department of State, Division of Elections, *November 7, 2000, General Election Official Results, President of the United States* (http://election.dos.state.fl.us/online/index.shtml) (accessed January 27, 2001); Georgia Secretary of State, *Georgia Election Results, Official Results of the November 7, 2000, General Election* (www.sos.state.ga.us/elections/) (accessed March 17, 2001); State of Hawaii, Office of Elections, *2000 Election Results, General Election, November 7, 2000* (http://kumu.icsd.hawaii.gov/elections/) (accessed July 19, 2001); Idaho Secretary of State, *Official Abstract of Votes Cast at the General Election, November 7, 2000* (Boise, 2000); Illinois State Board of Elections, *Total Vote for President and Vice President in the 2000 General Election* (www.elections.state.il.us/) (accessed December 16, 2000); Indiana Secretary of State, "President of the United States," *State of Indiana 2000 Election Report* (Indianapolis, 2000); Iowa Secretary of State, November 7, 2000: *General Election, Iowa Official Results* (www.sos.state.ia.us/) (accessed December 16, 2000); Kansas Secretary of State, Division of Elections and Legislative Matters. *2000 Kansas Official General Election Results* (http://www.kssos.org/election/elewelc.html) (accessed December 16, 2000); Kentucky State Board of Elections, *Kentucky State Board of Elections Report of Official Election Night, Tally Results* (www.kysos.com/index/main/elecdiv.asp) (accessed March 21, 2001); Louisiana Secretary of State, Elections Division, *Election Results by Parish: Results for Election Data: 11/07/00 Presidential Electors* (www.sec.state.la.us/elections/elections-index.htm) (accessed December 16, 2000); Maine Department of the Secretary of State, Bureau of Corporations, Elections, and Commissions, *State of Maine General Election Tabulation for the Election of November 7, 2000, Official Vote for President of the United States by Municipality* (Augusta, 2000); Maryland State Board of Elections, *Official Results, Sorted by Office, Congressional District, and Party, for the November 7, 2000, Presidential General Election* (www.elections.state.md.us/) (accessed July 11, 2001); Massachusetts Secretary of the Commonwealth, Elections Division, *Official 2000 Massachusetts State Election Results,* (www.state.ma.us/sec/ele/eleidx.htm) (accessed December 16, 2000); Michigan Department of State, Bureau of Elections, *Election Results, General Election, November 7, 2000* (www.sos.state.mi.us/election/elect.html) (accessed March 26, 2001); Minnesota Office of the Secretary of State, Elections Division, "Vote for President and Vice President: November 7, 2000 General Election," *The Minnesota Legislative Manual 2001–2002* (St. Paul, 2001); Mississippi Secretary of State, "General Election, November 7, 2000, President," *Mississippi Official and Statistical Register 2000–2004* (Jackson, 2001); Missouri Office of the Secretary of State, "President and Vice President—General Election: November 7, 2000," *Official Manual, State of Missouri 2001–2002* (Jefferson City, 2001); Montana Secretary of State, comp., *2000 Statewide General Election Canvass—November 7, 2000* (Helena, 2000); Nebraska Secretary of State, Elections Administration, *Statewide General Election 2000 Results, President of the United States* (www.sos.state.ne.us/Elections/election.htm) (accessed December 16, 2000); Nevada Secretary of State, Elections Division, *Federal Government of United States, Election Results, State Summary* (http://sos.state.nv.us/nvelection/) (accessed December 16, 2000); New Hampshire Department of State, Elections Division, *State General Election, November 7, 2000, President and Vice President of the United States* (http://webster.state.nh.us/sos/electionsnew.htm) (accessed February 27, 2001); New Jersey Department of Law and Public Safety, Division of Elections, *Division of Elections, 2000 General Election Official Results* (www.state.nj.us/lps/elections/electionshome.html) (accessed December 16, 2000); New Mexico Office of the Secretary of State, Bureau of Elections, *Official 2000 General Election by County by Office* (www.sos.state.nm.us/elect.htm) (accessed December 18, 2000); New York State Board of Elections, *NYS Board of Elections President and Vice President Election Returns, November 7, 2000* (www.elections.state.ny.us/) (accessed December 16, 2000); North Carolina State Board of Elections, *Official Results by County for General Election of the State of North Carolina, Election Data, November 7, 2000, 2000 General, President and Vice President* (www.sboe.state.nc.us/) (accessed July 1, 2001); North Dakota Secretary of State, *North Dakota's Official Abstract of Votes Cast at the General Election Held on November 7, 2000* (Bismarck, 2000); Ohio Secretary of State, Election Services, *Election 2000 Official Results, Votes for President* (www.state.oh.us/sos/) (accessed February 26, 2002); Oklahoma State Election Board. *President and Vice President of the United States, General Election, November 7, 2000* (www.state.ok.us/~elections/) (accessed December 16, 2000); Oregon Secretary of State, Elections Division, *Official Results, November 7, 2000, General Election, United States President* (www.sos.state.or.us/elections/elechp.htm) (accessed December 16, 2000); Pennsylvania Department of State, Bureau of Commissions, Elections, and Legislation, *Official 2000 General Election Results, President of the United States* (www.dos.state.pa.us/bcel/bcel.html) (accessed December 16, 2000); Rhode Island Board of Elections, *November 7, 2000, Final Results, Presidential Electors for President and Vice President* (www.elections.state.ri.us/) (accessed August 16, 2001); South Carolina State Election Commission, *South Carolina Election Returns, November 7, 2000, SC Statewide General Election, Official Results, President and Vice President* (www.state.sc.us/scsec/) (accessed July 1, 2001); South Dakota Secretary of State, "Presidential Electors—General Election, November 7, 2000," *Legislative Manual, South Dakota 2001–2002* (Pierre, 2001); Tennessee Secretary of State, Division of Elections, *Official Results, November 7, 2000, General Election, United States President* (www.state.tn.us/sos/election.htm) (accessed December 16, 2000); Texas Secretary of State, Elections Division, *2000 General Election, 11/7/00, President/Vice President* (www.sos.state.tx.us/elections/index.shtml) (accessed December 16, 2000); Utah State Elections Office, *Official Results State of Utah, General Election, November 7, 2000* (http://elections.utah.gov/) (accessed December 16, 2000); Vermont Office of the Secretary of State, "For US President, Summary Results by County 2000 General," *Primary and General Elections, Vermont 2000* (Montpelier, 2001); Virginia State Board of Elections, *Official Election Results* (www.sbe.state.va.us/) (accessed December 16, 2000); Washington Secretary of State, *Washington State General Election—November 7, 2000, Final Report President/Vice President Results by County* (www.secstate.wa.gov/elections/) (accessed December 16, 2000); West Virginia Secretary of State, *State of West Virginia Certificate* (www.wvsos.com/) (accessed December 20, 2000); Wisconsin State Election Board, *Wisconsin State Elections Board Canvass—County Totals Fall General Election 11/07/2000* (http://elections.state.wi.us/) (August 5, 2001); Wyoming Secretary of State, Election Administration, *2000 General Election Results, United States President and Vice President* (http://soswy.state.wy.us/election/election.htm) (accessed December 16, 2000)

General Index

Biographical Index

WITHDRAWAL